# The Last Abolition

Seamlessly entwining archival research and sociological debates, *The Last Abolition* is a lively and engaging historical narrative that uncovers the broad history of Brazilian antislavery activists and the trajectory of their work, from earnest beginnings to eventual abolition. In detailing their principles, alliances, and conflicts, Angela Alonso offers a new interpretation of the Brazilian antislavery network which, combined, forged a national movement to challenge the entrenched pro-slavery status quo. While placing Brazil within the abolitionist political mobilization of the nineteenth century, the book explores the relationships between Brazilian and foreign abolitionists, demonstrating how ideas and strategies transcended borders. Available for the first time in an English-language edition, with a new introduction, this award-winning volume is a major contribution to the scholarship on abolition and abolitionists.

Angela Alonso is a Professor of Sociology at the University of São Paulo, Brazil and former Director of the Brazilian Center of Analysis and Planning (CEBRAP). *The Last Abolition* is a translation of *Flores, votos e balas: o movimento abolicionista brasileiro, 1868–1888* (2015).

# Afro-Latin America

## Series editors

George Reid Andrews, *University of Pittsburgh*
Alejandro de la Fuente, *Harvard University*

This series reflects the coming of age of the new, multidisciplinary field of Afro-Latin American Studies, which centers on the histories, cultures, and experiences of people of African descent in Latin America. The series aims to showcase scholarship produced by different disciplines, including history, political science, sociology, ethnomusicology, anthropology, religious studies, art, law, and cultural studies. It covers the full temporal span of the African Diaspora in Latin America, from the early colonial period to the present and includes continental Latin America, the Caribbean, and other key areas in the region where Africans and their descendants have made a significant impact.

*A full list of titles published in the series can be found at:* www.cambridge.org/afro-latin-america

# The Last Abolition

*The Brazilian Antislavery Movement, 1868–1888*

**ANGELA ALONSO**
*University of São Paulo*

# CAMBRIDGE
## UNIVERSITY PRESS

University Printing House, Cambridge CB2 8BS, United Kingdom

One Liberty Plaza, 20th Floor, New York, NY 10006, USA

477 Williamstown Road, Port Melbourne, VIC 3207, Australia

314–321, 3rd Floor, Plot 3, Splendor Forum, Jasola District Centre,
New Delhi – 110025, India

103 Penang Road, #05–06/07, Visioncrest Commercial, Singapore 238467

Cambridge University Press is part of the University of Cambridge.

It furthers the University's mission by disseminating knowledge in the pursuit of education, learning, and research at the highest international levels of excellence.

www.cambridge.org
Information on this title: www.cambridge.org/9781108421133
DOI: 10.1017/9781108367394

Originally published in Portuguese as *Flores, votos e balas: o movimento abolicionista brasileiro, 1868–1888* by Companhia das Letras and © Angela Alonso 2015

This publication is in copyright. Subject to statutory exception and to the provisions of relevant collective licensing agreements, no reproduction of any part may take place without the written permission of Cambridge University Press.

First published in English by Cambridge University Press in 2022 as *The Last Abolition: The Brazilian Antislavery Movement, 1868–1888*

English translation © Angela Alonso 2022

*A catalogue record for this publication is available from the British Library.*

*Library of Congress Cataloging-in-Publication Data*
NAMES: Alonso, Angela, author.
TITLE: The last abolition : the Brazilian antislavery movement, 1868–1888 / Angela Alonso, University of São Paulo.
OTHER TITLES: Flores, votos e balas. English
DESCRIPTION: Cambridge, United Kingdom ; New York, NY : Cambridge University Press, 2021. | Series: Afro-Latin America | Includes bibliographical references and index.
IDENTIFIERS: LCCN 2021029039 (print) | LCCN 2021029040 (ebook) | ISBN 9781108421133 (hardback) | ISBN 9781108431477 (paperback) | ISBN 9781108367394 (epub)
SUBJECTS: LCSH: Antislavery movements–Brazil. | Slavery–Brazil–History. | Slaves–Emancipation–Brazil–History–19th century. | Brazil–Politics and government–1822–1889. | Brazil–History–1822– | BISAC: HISTORY / Latin America / General | HISTORY / Latin America / General
CLASSIFICATION: LCC HT1128 .A4513 2021 (print) | LCC HT1128 (ebook) | DDC 306.3/620981–dc23
LC record available at https://lccn.loc.gov/2021029039
LC ebook record available at https://lccn.loc.gov/2021029040

ISBN 978-1-108-42113-3 Hardback
ISBN 978-1-108-43147-7 Paperback

Cambridge University Press has no responsibility for the persistence or accuracy of URLs for external or third-party internet websites referred to in this publication and does not guarantee that any content on such websites is, or will remain, accurate or appropriate.

• • • • • • • • • • • • • • • • • • • • • • • • • • • • • • • • • • • • • • • • • • • • • • • • • • • • • • • • • • • • • • • • • •

This translation was supported by the research project
FAPESP 2016/18790-6

*To Maria do Carmo Soler and Felix Alonso Garcia*
*in memoriam*

# Contents

| | | |
|---|---|---|
| *List of Figures* | *page* ix | |
| *List of Maps* | xi | |
| *List of Tables* | xiii | |
| *Acknowledgments* | xv | |
| *List of Abbreviations* | xix | |
| | Introduction | 1 |
| 1 | Elite Abolitionism | 24 |
| 2 | Pro-Slavery Rhetoric | 52 |
| 3 | The Moral Repertoire of Abolitionism | 85 |
| 4 | The Theatricalization of Politics | 109 |
| 5 | Expansion | 145 |
| 6 | Results-Based Abolitionism | 178 |
| 7 | Votes: A Movement/Government Alliance | 226 |
| 8 | Bullets: Movement and Countermovement | 271 |
| 9 | The March to Victory | 319 |
| 10 | Future of the Preterite | 344 |
| 11 | Abolitionism as a Social Movement | 352 |

viii           *Contents*

*Annex*                                                        363
   Tables                                       363
   Timeline                                     366
   List of Brazilian Abolitionist Associations (1850–1888)   378

*Bibliography*                                                 397
*Index*                                                        429

# Figures

0.1 José do Patrocínio delivers manumission letters to slaves during the staging of *Aida*, by Giuseppe Verdi, in the Teatro Lírico, on August 10, 1886.    *page* 3

1.1 André Pinto Rebouças (1838–1898), the abolitionist movement's national leader.    26

1.2 Abílio César Borges (1842–1891), the Baron of Macaúbas (Barão de Macaúbas), who inaugurated abolitionist civic ceremonies and networking with European abolitionists.    36

2.1 Official iconography celebrating the Free Womb Law. In the upper section, the Viscount of Rio Branco is above the Emperor and surrounded by his ministers. Below, slaves and allegorical figures that represent freedom, honor, and glory.    81

3.1 The abolitionist Luís Gonzaga Pinto da Gama (1830–1882).    88

4.1 The abolitionist José do Patrocínio (1854–1905).    110

4.2 At the bottom of the page, an artistic programming of a conference-concert, one of the means of diffusion of abolitionist ideas. *Gazeta da Tarde*, December 28, 1883.    128

5.1 The abolitionist Joaquim Aurélio Nabuco de Araújo (1849–1910).    147

5.2 Letter from the Spanish abolitionist Rafael María de Labra y Cadrana to Joaquim Nabuco, on October 8, 1881.    159

6.1 The Board of the Abolitionist Confederation, pictured on May 16, 1888. Standing from left to right: José do Patrocínio, Luís de Andrade, Inácio von Doellinger, Praxedes Medella, and Luiz Pereira. Sitting from left to right: André Rebouças, João Clapp, and José de Seixas Magalhães.    194

x List of Figures

7.1 The Liberal Prime Minister Manuel Pinto de Sousa Dantas (1831–1894) who came to power on June 6, 1884, on the eve of growing abolitionist mobilization. 230

7.2 Opponents attacking the progress of the Dantas Reform. 238

7.3 Abolitionist beer. During the elections in December 1884, abolitionists championed candidates and advertised them on cigarette packets and beer bottles. 260

7.4 One of the campaign meetings for the election of Joaquim Nabuco in Recife in 1885, supported by a national mobilization of abolitionists. 263

8.1 A disfigured Dantas Reform became the Saraiva/Cotegipe Law, approved on September 28, 1885, only conceding freedom to elderly slaves. 278

8.2 The lynching in February 1888 of police deputy Joaquim Firmino de Araújo Cunha by pro-slavery locals, in Penha do Rio do Peixe (Fish River Rock) (modern-day Itapira), accused of protecting abolitionists ("The barbaric murder of the police deputy in Penha do Rio do Peixe, SP"). 317

9.1 Senate session that approved the Golden Law (Lei Áurea), May 13, 1888. 336

9.2 Law 3353 promulgated on May 13, 1888 abolished slavery in Brazil, without compensation for the slave owners. 339

9.3 Abolitionists waiting outside the Senate for the end of the vote on the abolitionist project. 340

9.4 The outdoor Mass, promoted by the Crown on May 17, 1888 to celebrate the end of slavery in Brazil. 342

# Maps

| | | |
|---|---|---|
| **11.1** | National distribution of public abolitionist demonstrations. | 353 |
| **11.2** | Abolitionist civil associations. | 355 |
| **11.3** | The freedom soil campaign national distribution. | 357 |

# Tables

| | | |
|---|---|---|
| 2.1 | Free Womb Law votes in the Lower House and in the Senate, 1871 | *page* 80 |
| 7.1 | Anti-Dantas' Reform petitions sent to Parliament, 1884–1885 | 243 |
| 7.2 | Abolitionist candidates in 1884 elections by political party | 261 |
| A.1 | Abolitionist civil associations founded by political conjuncture, 1868–1888 | 363 |
| A.2 | Abolitionist public demonstrations by political conjuncture, 1878–1888 | 363 |
| A.3 | Repertoire of contention mobilized by Brazilian abolitionist movement, 1868–1888 | 364 |

# Acknowledgments

This book is a revised and expanded English edition of *Flores, votos e balas: o movimento abolicionista brasileiro (1868–1888)*, published by Companhia das Letras in 2015, and based on six years of research in primary sources at various archives (see Annex). I am grateful for comments on the Brazilian version from Angela de Castro Gomes, Antônio Sérgio Guimarães, Flávio Moura, José Murilo de Carvalho, Lilia Schwarcz, Luiz Werneck Vianna and, above all, Brasílio Sallum Jr.

The research was initiated at the University of São Paulo, but it took shape during a post-doctorate year at Yale University (2008–2009), when I benefited from conversations at the Gilder Lehrman Center (thanks in particular to David Blight, Edward Rugemer, Mariana Candido, and Amanda Bowie Moniz, and to the late and admirable professors Emília Viotti da Costa and David Brion Davis), the MacMillan Center for International and Area Studies (especially Stuart Schwartz and Kenneth David Jackson), and the Sociology Department (in particular Julia Adams). At Yale I first met Peter Stamatov and Richard Huzzey; they and Maartje Janse helped me to consider the Brazilian case in a comparative way.

In Brazil, I benefited from discussing my ideas with colleagues at Cebrap, especially José Arthur Giannotti, Miriam Dohlnikoff, and at the University of São Paulo, in particular with Leopoldo Waizbort and Samuel Titan Jr. I am very grateful for the long-term research assistance of Ana Carolina Andrada and Viviane Brito de Souza and timely help from Alexander Englander, Lilian Sendretti, Roger Cavalheiro, Daniel Waldwogel, Ricardo Caires, and Roberto Saba.

xvi *Acknowledgments*

Many thanks to all who discussed parts of what came to be this book at seminars along the way, especially at the Gilder Lehrman Center, Yale University (2010, 2017); the Federal University of Rio de Janeiro (2010, 2017), the National Association of Historians Meeting (2010); the Political Science Department Seminar series and the Sociology Department Seminar series, both at the University of São Paulo (2010, 2011, 2012); the Center for Latin American Studies, Yale University (2010); the Bildner Center for the Western Hemisphere (2010); Casa de Oswaldo Cruz (2011); the Program of Latin American Studies, Princeton University (2011); the Latin American Association Meeting (2012); Congreso Internacional de Americanistas (2012); the Social Science History Association Meetings (2013, 2015); the Comparative Sociology Seminar, Universidad Carlos III (2014); the Cebrap Seminar (2014); the Global Nineteenth Century Workshop, Pennsylvania University (2015); and the American Historical Association annual meetings (2017, 2018). In those occasions many contributed and I am grateful in particular to Arcádio Quiñones, Antônio Dimas, André Botelho, Christopher Schmidt-Nowara (in memoriam), Celso Castilho, Dain Borges, Daniel Domingues, Hendrik Kraay, Jeffrey Needell, João Reis, Leslie Bethell, Maria Alice Rezende de Carvalho, Maria Helena Machado, Mary Junqueira, Sérgio Miceli, Seymour Drescher for their thoughtful comments.

I thank the staff of all archives and libraries I consulted, in particular Cesar Rodriguez (Sterling Library, Yale University).

The research was possible thanks to support from the Guggenheim Foundation (fellowship, 2008–2009), Fundação de Amparo a Pesquisa (Fapesp) (fellowship, 2008–2009; research grant 2012–2015) and CNPq (fellowship, 2009–2015). As for this edition, it relied on the help of a Fapesp Translation Grant (2016/18790-6). I thank Anthony Doyle, for having translated all poems throughout the book; as for the final translation of the manuscript, the responsibility for the final text is mine alone.

I am deeply grateful to George Reid Andrews and Alejandro de la Fuente, who honored my work by including it in the Afro-Latin American Studies series, and for their kindness and insightful suggestions.

A special acknowledgment goes to Deborah Gershenowitz, who started this book's production as Senior Editor, U.S. and Latin American History, Cambridge University Press. This edition would have been impossible without her tireless work, generous suggestions, and thoughtfulness. Since the editorial process took a long time, in the final phase I also relied on the assistance of Cecilia Cancellaro, whose helpful hand and quick solutions in wrapping up this edition I really appreciate.

## Acknowledgments xvii

Lastly, it would have been impossible to finish this book without the love and company of Alice and Tomás Alonso Limongi, Daniel Limongi, and Fernando Limongi.

All Brazilians are, in one way or another, heirs to the way slavery ended in their country. The political decision in the wake of abolition to replace slave labor with immigrants, rather than fully incorporate former slaves into the social life, brought waves of people from Europe to Brazilian shores, including my grandparents Maria do Carmo Soler and Felix Alonso Garcia. If the outcome had been any different, all Brazilians would have been different too. They would not have come to Brazil and I would never have written this book.

# Abbreviations

| | |
|---|---|
| ACD | Anais da Câmara dos Srs. Deputados |
| ACE | Associação Central Emancipadora (The Central Emancipatory Association) |
| ACEI | Atas do Conselho de Estado do Império |
| AMI | Arquivo do Museu Imperial |
| AR | *A Redempção* |
| ASI | Anais do Senado do Império |
| BN | Biblioteca Nacional |
| CA | Confederação Abolicionista |
| CAI | Joaquim Nabuco: *Cartas a amigos*, Volume I, Nabuco, Carolina (ed.), São Paulo, Instituto Progresso Editorial, 1949 |
| CAII | Joaquim Nabuco: *Cartas a amigos*, Volume II, Nabuco, Carolina (ed.), São Paulo, Instituto Progresso Editorial, 1949 |
| CCE | Comissão Central Emancipadora |
| CIJN | Cartas inéditas de e para Joaquim Nabuco. Arquivo da Fundação Joaquim Nabuco – Fundaj, Recife |
| CIRB | Cartas inéditas de ou para Rui Barbosa. Acervo da Casa de Rui Barbosa, Rio de Janeiro |
| CIRD | Cartas inéditas de ou para Rodolfo Dantas. Acervo da Casa de Rui Barbosa, Rio de Janeiro |
| CPRB | *Cartas publicadas de Rui Barbosa*, Edição Casa de Rui Barbosa, Rio de Janeiro, 1962 |
| CR | *Cidade do Rio* |

xx                    *List of Abbreviations*

DIAR     Diários de André Rebouças, inéditos, Acervo IHGB, Rio
         de Janeiro
DJN      *Diários de Joaquim Nabuco*, 2005. Mello, E. C. (ed.).
         Recife: Bem Te Vi Produções Literárias, Editora Massangana,
         volumes I e II
DNAAR    Diários de André Rebouças, seleta publicada in
         Veríssimo, A. F. e J. (eds). *Diário e notas autobiográficas de
         André Rebouças*. J. Olympio, 1938
DRJ      *Diário do Rio de Janeiro*
EDEAR    Excerptos dos Diários do Engenheiro André Rebouças
         (manuscrito), Arquivo do Museu Imperial, Petrópolis
GN       *Gazeta de Notícias*
GT       *Gazeta da Tarde*
IHGB     Arquivo do Instituto Histórico e Geográfico Brasileiro,
         Rio de Janeiro
JC       *Jornal do Comércio*
OA       *O Abolicionista: órgão da sociedade brasileira contra a
         escravidão*
RCAR     André Rebouças. Registro da Correspondência.
         volume 1 – junho 1873 a janeiro de 1891, Fundaj, Recife
RI       *Revista Illustrada*
RN       *Rio News*
SBCE     Sociedade Brasileira Contra a Escravidão (Brazilian
         Antislavery Society)
SCL      Sociedade Cearense Libertadora (The Liberating Society
         of Ceará)
SCT      Sociedade Contra o Tráfico de Africanos e Promotora da
         Colonização e da Civilização dos Índios (Society against the
         African Slave Trade and for the Promotion of Colonization
         and Indigenous Civilization)

# Introduction

On one occasion, André Rebouças had such a hard time finding a theater that would agree to host an abolitionist conference that when he finally found one, he and José do Patrocínio had to sweep it out themselves, while the audience waited outside. Two black abolitionists were doing the work of slaves. The event on August 10, 1886, required no such effort, as there was little likelihood pro-slavery gangs would dare upset proceedings, because this time Rebouças had an opera star on his side.

Upon her arrival in Brazil that May, the Russian soprano Nadina Bulicioff could never have imagined the role she would be playing that August night at the Teatro Lírico in Rio de Janeiro. She had traveled as part of an Italian company – drawn by her passion for her profession and for the young Arturo Toscanini. During her Brazilian tour, she played *Tosca* and *Gioconda* and saw how widespread abolitionist mobilization was and how many artists were engaged in it. The soprano, whose homeland had only abolished serfdom itself a few years earlier, was so moved by the campaign that when admirers sought to lavish her with diamonds, she asked them to use the money to free slaves instead.

Rebouças' Abolitionist Confederation seized the opportunity, as it was wont to do. Since the start of the campaign, in 1868, the abolitionists had appealed to the arts, held civic ceremonies to sway public opinion, created associations and sought allies abroad, piecing together a support network that spanned France, Spain, the United States, and Great Britain. It had also wooed the Russian opera singer and made her an honorary member of the Confederation. And so the opera staged at Teatro Lírico became an antislavery demonstration.

## The Last Abolition

Rebouças' dream was to stage *O Escravo* (The Slave), a piece he had commissioned from Carlos Gomes in 1884 but which the maestro had yet to finish. So he had to look to the repertoire for an opera that expressed the event's political meaning, and there he came upon *Aida*, a strategic choice. Verdi's popular work was a proven crowd-puller and its theme was a snug enough fit: the homonymous protagonist, the daughter of the King of Ethiopia, had been captured and enslaved in Ancient Egypt.

When Bulicioff took to the stage before a full house, she found herself showered with flowers, the abolitionist movement's symbol of choice. The end of the first act was met with thunderous applause, and the rapture reached its height with the aria that closed the third act, when Aida flees captivity – her liberty represented by the switching-on of the very latest mod-con: electric lighting.

Cue José do Patrocínio, who arrived onstage with the Pauper Boys Band and six slave girls, or *enslaved* girls, as the abolitionists preferred to call them, since they were victims of an immoral, unjust, archaic institution. The girls wore white, matching Bulicioff's Pharaonic slave outfits. The band played the national anthem, and then the Russian broke her prop shackles as the audience rose to its feet, waving handkerchiefs in the air. She then hugged and kissed each of the girls and presented them with letters of manumission, transforming them into free women right before the eyes of a rapt audience, seven Aidas. The women wept; the audience wept, and delirium filled the house. Amid applause and cheering, flowers were hurled and doves released.

Patrocínio knelt at the diva's feet and kissed her hands. The now ecstatic audience chanted: "Viva Bulicioff!" "Viva the Liberator!" "Viva the abolition of slaves!" Next came a standing ovation for the leaders of the abolitionist movement, starting with Patrocínio, the orchestrator of many shows like this one, followed onstage by João Clapp, president of the Abolitionist Confederation, and by Joaquim Nabuco, leader of the campaign in Parliament. Last but not least, there was a round of applause for one final figure up in the boxes, the recently-ousted Prime Minister Manuel de Sousa Dantas, a Liberal Party ally of the movement. Patrocínio and Clapp, on one side, Nabuco and Dantas, on the other, personified the movement's main strategies thus far: propaganda in the public space and actions within the political institutions. On that evening, as throughout the campaign, Rebouças was the thread that bound them together, behind the scenes.

This kind of event was a main strategy to get to that point. In 1886, however, the abolitionists were changing tack. They were not staging

# Introduction

FIGURE 0.1 José do Patrocínio delivers manumission letters to slaves during the staging of *Aida*, by Giuseppe Verdi, in the Teatro Lírico on August 10, 1886.
Archive of the Fundação Biblioteca Nacional (National Library Foundation), Brazil.

# The Last Abolition

operas because they preferred theater to politics. They had lost at the polls and the new Conservative Party government had declared war against them as troublemakers who had dared to disrespect the laws and mores that had sustained the slave system in imperial Brazil for four centuries. Art was just one of many ways of doing antislavery politics. Another one was to confront the slavocratic order, inciting slaves to follow Aida's lead by running away. The movement was flirting with civil disobedience. Even Rebouças and Nabuco, pacifist aristocrats, were willing to take things to their ultimate consequences. Patrocínio wrote in his newspaper, "all true abolitionists are ready to die." At the Teatro Lírico, what seemed like a party was really a battle: abolitionist movement versus proslavery countermovement.

By rising to its feet for the Russian soprano, the audience was taking sides in this national struggle. It was the movement against slavery they were applauding. The abolitionists had been building this base of support for two decades, first through shows like Bulicioff's, with the same torrent of flowers, then by contesting elections and finally, as a last resort, threatening to take up arms. They had the backing to do it. Over the course of the abolitionist campaign they had gone from a handful of pioneers like Rebouças to a legion present in all twenty provinces of the Empire. In 1886, there were thousands, all of them like Bulicioff, willing to break the slaves.[1]

## A STRANGE ABSENCE

Brazil was one of the largest slaveholding countries in history and the last in the West to abolish slavery, in 1888. Despite its importance, the Brazilian abolitionist movement has not yet received the scholarly attention it deserves. The British and American cases are still central in the literature. More recently, other cases, such as Spain, Portugal, and France, have started to attract greater interest (for instance, Schmidt-Nowara, 1999; Marques and Salles, 2015), but Brazil remains in the shadows.

Even in the recent wave of comparative studies, the Brazilian case has barely been addressed. The overviews of David Brion Davis (2006) and Seymour Drescher (2009) have shown the vast geographic reach of abolitionism and its long duration, but Brazil is little explored.

---

[1] The information presented here is drawn from DNAAR, Apr. 17, 1881; letter from Carlos Gomes to Giulio Ricord, Jul. 16, 1884 in Vetro (1982); CR, Oct. 26, 1887; O País, Aug. 10, 11, 22, 23, 1886; GN, Aug. 23, 1886; GT, Aug. 9, 11, 1886; RI, Aug., 1886.

Introduction 5

The same is true for works with generalizing ambitions, such as Blackburn (2011) and Sinha (2017).

In the "global histories" of abolitionism, which have been bringing neglected cases to light, mention of the Brazilian abolitionist movement is also rare. The collection organized by Mulligan and Bric (2013), for example, brings analyses of abolition movements seldom addressed in the literature, such as Sierra Leone, Russia, and the Ottoman Empire, and the essays edited by Suzuki (2016) added Japan, China, and Iran to that list. Again, neither volume looks at Brazil.

Drescher is one of the few scholars to take Brazil into consideration, while distinguishing two abolitionist paths: one, the "continental," spread across much of Europe, elitist and grounded in lobbying and parliamentary action; the other, the "Anglo-American," based on social mobilization – with proselytism, public demonstrations, judicial processes, and boycotts, a de-centrally structured organization with socially diverse activists. Initially, he saw the Brazilian case as resembling the parliamentary approach (Drescher, 1980), though he later recognized a considerable public space mobilization and revised his opinion (Drescher, 2009), seeing Brazil as falling somewhere in between these two broad paths. However, his explanation is based on other scholars' research, without direct research on Brazilian primary sources.

As such, Brazil has been neglected by those interested in abolitionist comparisons and connections on the global scale. At least, one would expect Brazilian scholarship to fill the void, as research on slavery has done, but literature specifically dealing with Brazilian abolitionism retains a domestic focus, with little interest in comparing and linking the Brazilian case with its foreign counterparts.

## MEMORY AND HISTORY

"The abolitionists grew from one outrage to the next, as everyone knows," declared one of the newspapers sympathetic to the cause on Abolition day. They would suffer yet another outrage, oblivion. Much has been written about Brazilian abolition, but the movement's decisive role in ending slavery has never been fully recognized.

Part of the fault rests with the abolitionists themselves. Paradoxically, one of the foremost Brazilian abolitionist leaders, Joaquim Nabuco, did not even claim the laurels for the movement. Author of the most influential interpretation of abolition, Nabuco attributed the feat to the magnanimity of the Crown. In *Um estadista do império* (A Statesman of the

6                           *The Last Abolition*

Empire), published in the early days of the Republic (proclaimed eighteen months after abolition), when he was a monarchist militant, he identified a faction of the imperial elite and the Emperor himself as having been the driving forces behind the abolition process. In *Minha formação* (My Formative Years), Nabuco reiterated the point while playing down the role of the Republican abolitionists: "It means to claim for the Chamber of Deputies, for Parliament, the initiative that some have attempted to deny it on this issue, crediting to the grassroots, republican movement ..." (Nabuco, 1900, p. 138). Nabuco was disputing who would and who would not go down in the history books as the leaders of the movement, the abolitionists within the political institutions, like himself, or those operating within the public space.[2]

This version of events emphasizes the institutional political actors, such as Nabuco himself, a member of parliament; the Prime Minister who signed the Golden Law; and the Crown, which would have made a sacrificial gesture of eradicating slavery even if it meant losing the throne.

Not content with ordaining the protagonists in this drama, Nabuco, this time endorsed by another abolitionist leader, José do Patrocínio (*Cidade do Rio*, May 5, 1889),[3] also cropped the timeline. Both singled out 1879 as the start of the abolitionist campaign, for one simple reason: it was the year they got involved – Patrocínio as editor-in-chief of the *Gazeta da Tarde*, and Nabuco in Parliament.

This version became the canonic account for understanding Brazilian abolitionist mobilization. However, to follow it is to err threefold, as it is guilty of anachronism, partiality, and omission.

Ignoring everything that went before these activist-narrators' engagement is to become hostage to their selection of abolitionist events, emphases, and participants.[4] The fact that many abolitionists did not write about the part they played does not mean it never existed. Rather than follow this bias, I set as the beginning of the abolitionist movement

---

[2] Nabuco adds: "... the movement began at the Chamber in 1879, and not, as has been claimed in *Gazeta da Tarde* of Ferreira de Meneses, dating it to 1880, nor in the *Gazeta de Notícias*, where José do Patrocínio, writing the weekly political section, always supporting us, but still without having guessed his mission ..." (Nabuco, 1900, p. 137).

[3] This version was spread by younger activists in speeches in celebrations, retrospectives in the press, and memoirs, such as those by Duque Estrada (1918) and Evaristo de Moraes (1924), who joined the campaign much later on.

[4] Nabuco implicitly admits the movement's earlier origins when he says: "... for a long time it seemed that the emancipation movement, the abolitionist movement ..., had withdrawn ..." (ACD, Mar. 22, 1879). And, later (Nabuco 1897–1899, p. 849), he mentions in passing that it was in 1879 that "the abolitionist movement restarted."

## Introduction

the advent of the antislavery societies, that is, a timeline following actions rather than narratives. From this perspective, antislavery activism appears to be a lot older, with its pioneers taking up the gauntlet even before the abolition of the Atlantic slave trade, in 1850. However, one can only really speak of an abolitionist movement as such after the rise of a wave of association-building, which occurred during the debate in the late 1860s that would give rise to the Free Womb Law.

The second legacy of the old narrative is to overstate the importance of one sphere (the political institutions) and one actor (the monarchic elite) over and above the public mobilization. To do so is to overlook public space activism and leaders not belonging to the social elite, such as Luís Gama, and to ignore the fact that parliamentary initiatives were triggered by, or concomitant with, waves of public mobilization.

Another error is to downplay the importance of the political conjunctures and of the conflict between organized groups for and against slavery. To focus on one particular player, especially the political rulers, is to attribute to them what they always craved but could not obtain, namely control over the social forces in dispute and the power to decide the direction of history. This view confers upon abolition a coherence that a political process never had, as it results from contention between social groups and not from the skills, plans, or performances of any particular player.

In fairness, Nabuco (1900, pp. 245–6) did recognize his bias: "Who could write the history of his contemporaries impartially, fairly and completely, unaffected by political passion, sectarian bias, personal sympathy or friendship? No-one, of course, which means that various histories will be written in the future." Despite the warning, Nabuco became and remained a reference, whether for his emphasis on Parliament or for the richness of his own personal archive, for most interpretations of Brazilian abolitionism up to at least the late 1950s.

### INTERPRETATIONS OF BRAZILIAN ABOLITIONISM

The "various histories" came much later, starting in the 1960s, and, broadly speaking, they fall into distinct academic trends.[5]

The Marxist reading reacted to the emphasis on the Empire elite by underscoring the socioeconomic structures and processes. This view

---

[5] For an alternative classification of the bibliography, see Needell (2010). The analysis of the thinking of the intellectual and political elites on slavery and abolition, as in Azevedo (1987) and Carvalho (1988), can be seen as an additional line of argument.

8 *The Last Abolition*

painted abolition as part of the capitalist expansion in the country, which required a free labor market. The contradiction between capitalism and slavery would have pushed abolition, leaving little relevance to the political actors and institutions in the explanation. The abolitionist movement itself would be unworthy of specific investigation. This perspective, popular in the 1960s and 1970s, gave rise to Emília Viotti's 1966 classic *Da senzala à colônia* (From the Slave Quarters to the Colony).

A criticism of this perspective came during the centenary of abolition, in 1988, placing the spotlight on the agents. However, instead of the political and social elites, it underscored black leaders and the slaves themselves, adopting the perspective of the "enslaved" – a term the abolitionists themselves created as an alternative to slave – and supporting the black movement's struggle to replace the monarchist symbol of abolition, Princess Isabel, with Zumbi dos Palmares, the colonial black rebel. Drawing on E. P. Thompson, this perspective highlighted the agency of the lower social strata and mapped the varied forms of slave resistance to slavery, through rebellions, judicial activism, and in everyday life (for example, Chalhoub, 1990; Machado, 1994; Azevedo, 1999, 2010; Reis, 2003; Toplin, 1969, 1972). However, interest in the institutional dynamic was limited to the judiciary, with no regard for parliamentary or governmental actions.

The third trend underscored the relevance the political institutions had for abolition. Robert Conrad (1972, 1975)[6] produced the first and until now the only comprehensive work on Brazilian abolition, starting with the end of the slave trade and based on a wealth of documental research. Conrad mapped governmental, parliamentary, and street-level actions, but his focus was on the socioeconomic rifts and on conflicts between the regions, seeing abolitionism as a Northern phenomenon – where slavery's economy was on the wane. Carvalho (1988, 1980, 2007) and Needell (2006) also look to the political institutions, taking up Nabuco's argument that it was the Crown that steered the political process. They insisted on the incontrovertible fact that abolition came about by institutional means, a law, and not by a change in the productive system or through a slave revolt.

These interpretive lines divided the intellectual work: some focused on structural factors, others slave resistance, and a third group on the political institutions.

---

[6] Conrad's English original (1972) and its Portuguese translation (1975) diverge, as the Brazilian edition was revised to suit the Brazilian readership, with the inclusion of new subitems.

## Introduction

Works on abolitionist mobilizations in the public space are rare. Bergstresser (1973) mapped abolitionist associations and events in Rio de Janeiro in the 1880s, and Machado (1994) tracked grassroots mobilization and antislavery plots in the São Paulo countryside. Only in the last decade or so has research begun to emerge on Porto Alegre, Salvador, Recife, São Paulo, and Rio de Janeiro (Kittleson, 2005; Graden, 2006; Castilho, 2016; Albuquerque, 2009; Machado 2006, 2009; Silva, 2003), revealing a great number of public demonstrations by a varied demographic, including the lower strata and black groups themselves. Although very important, these studies remain local in scope and do not draw out any connections between social mobilization and the broader politico-institutional dynamics.

All these interpretations also follow an international trend to study abolitionism without any regard for its counterweight, the pro-slavery political reaction. When considered, social groups engaged in slavery-dependent activities are more often investigated as economic forces than as political agents, as if economic interest would convert automatically into political action. There is no systematic study on how these various pro-slavery economic actors came to produce a coordinated action targeting the same goal, a politically organized pro-slavery action.

Studying abolitionism as closed off from pro-slavery mobilization neglects the relational nature of politics. A social movement only exists vis-à-vis the State it contests and the groups who organize politically to preserve the status quo it seeks to dismantle. Dissecting the pro-slavery countermovement – an antagonist all but unexplored in the literature – is indispensable if we are to understand the actions of the protagonist. This book understands abolitionism as the apex of a triangle whose other vertices are the political institutions and the pro-slavery countermovement, narrating the conflicts between the two and the ways the State sought to mediate them.

Since Conrad (1972, 1975), there have been no panoramic visions of abolition. Scholars tend to compartmentalize the phenomenon. Broaching the "parliamentary" and "popular" movements as distinct "abolitionisms" has generated autonomous fields of investigation, with those studying one ignoring the other. Brazilian literature has been blind to the reciprocal impacts between mobilization in the public space and action within the political institutions. Just recently Needell (2010) proposed an integrated understanding of "Afro-Brazilian agency and the politics of the elite." In a book published five years after the Brazilian version of this one (Alonso, 2015), Needell (2020) converges with arguments raised here, regarding the necessity of a broad consideration of street mobilization and parliamentary struggles; the importance of a close study of the institutional political dynamics of the abolition process; and the uselessness of splitting abolitionists into moderates and radicals. We also coincide in acknowledging the central role played by the black abolitionist André Rebouças.

Nevertheless, my perspective is broader than Needell's, who focuses only on the post-1879 process in the Empire's capital. My analysis takes place on a national scale and on a longer timeline (starting in the late 1860s), and encompasses a greater number of activists and leaders. I also consider – which he does not – Brazilians' interaction with the transnational abolitionist network. Another major difference concerns the relevance of the Crown. Needell follows Nabuco's view of the monarch as a guide to abolitionist politics, leaving aside the massive republican participation and the crucial military adhesion in supporting for the abolitionist campaign – as I will show, both groups are very relevant. Although this book includes the Crown as one of the forces in the political contention, it does not consider it a decisive one, but, instead, as a force that shifts according to the balance of power between the two political parties, and between the political institutions and social mobilization. The final difference is methodological. While Needell does not define the "abolitionist movement" and relies on qualitative documents, I adopt a sociological concept of social movements that leads to the compilation of a dataset of civil associations and mobilizing events.

## A RELATIONAL APPROACH TO THE ABOLITIONIST MOVEMENT

Studying the abolitionist movement from a relational perspective means framing it as a case of contentious interaction with the State and countermovement that played out in three arenas: the political institutions, public space, and underground. It also means not considering abolitionism as a pre-defined agent. Social movements have tenuous frontiers and volatile participants who engage and disengage all the time. Movements are networks of social groups with no access to, or influence over, institutional politics (Tilly 2005, p. 308), that, during a conflict, built up interactions connecting each other, without erasing their differences and disputes among themselves around goals, strategies, and leaders (Diani, 2003). The movement shows itself as such through pressure campaigns directed at the authorities, and recalibrating strategies depending on how the balance of power shifts over the course of the political process.

## Introduction

This fluidity militates against rigid divisions (emancipationists/abolitionists, moderates/radicals, institutional/grassroots, gradualists/immediatists).[7] These categorizations ignore the constitutive heterogeneity of social movements. The abolitionist movement only existed as such in conflict with its polar opposite. So, rather than accentuate the rifts in the antislavery camp, this book will focus on the central polarity between abolitionists and the pro-slavery actors.

Since movements are fluid phenomena, the sociological literature developed an approach to capture it as empirical sequences of protest events. Here I rely on this scholarship to define the abolitionist movement as an extra-parliamentary political action, made visible through repeated public demonstrations, steered by the use of the same repertoire of contention (standardized forms of organization, expression, and action), and engaging a large number of people, which remained committed regardless of adversity, particularly repression (Tilly 2006, p. vii). Taking that conception as its guide and relying on the information found in thirty-five newspapers from nine of the twenty Brazilian provinces, I organized a dataset with 2,214 abolitionist events (institutional initiatives, direct and symbolic actions, acts of diffusion and confrontation, and the foundation of 367 civil associations). This material shows how the campaign spread to 206 cities throughout all the twenty provinces in the Empire between the years 1868 and 1888.[8]

---

[7] For example, Toplin (1972), and Célia Azevedo (2001). In Brazil, mobilization began after the end of the trans-Atlantic slave trade, so a distinction between trade abolitionists and emancipationists makes little sense here. The activists conflated the categories: "... abolitionist and emancipationist are synonymous, and no matter how relevant the differences between them may be in ideology, the discrete meanings of synonyms are of no significance whatsoever in politics" (Nabuco, *Jornal do Comércio*, Jun. 18, 1884). The terms became interchangeable: Nabuco's book O *abolicionismo* (Abolitionism) outlined an "emancipationist" proposal – gradual phasing out of slavery – while the self-proclaimed "emancipationist" Manuel de Sousa Dantas proposed the "radical" measure of coupling abolition with the introduction of smallholder agriculture. The distinction also alludes to the methods and the social extraction of the activists, with a prevailing supposition that the less privileged agents were more radical. That particular thesis has been widely criticized in the literature on social movements, which shows that the poor generally lack the means to organize and act politically (McCarthy and Zald, 1977), and, in Brazil, there was a counterexample, the wealthy "radical" abolitionist Antônio Bento.

[8] The campaign was more intense in the provinces of Rio de Janeiro, São Paulo, Rio Grande do Sul, Pernambuco, and Ceará, together accounting for 80 percent of all mobilization events. I have considered only civil associations that were *exclusively abolitionist*, that is, I have excluded societies founded around other causes, but which ended up engaging in the campaign.

12 *The Last Abolition*

The aim is twofold. On the one hand, the idea is to demonstrate that the campaign for the abolition of slavery in Brazil was more similar to the English and North-American cases than the literature tends to recognize: a large, structured, and lasting network of activists, associations, and public demonstrations that formed a national social movement – the first in the country. The goal, on the other hand, is to place Brazil in a global history of abolitionist movements, showing how local activists hooked into the global abolitionist network and appropriated the repertoire of contention put together by previous movements.[9]

## TRANSNATIONALISM AND REPERTOIRE OF CONTENTION

Approaching Brazilian abolitionism from a relational perspective also implies situating it within its international context, identifying its ties with similar movements abroad as opposed to studying it in isolation. The literature is very aware of the global nature of slavery, but most studies on antislavery tend to stick within the borders of nation states. However, in defining laws, strategies, rhetoric, and political performances geared towards the abolition of slavery, national states, abolitionist movements, and pro-slavery countermovements played an international game. Brazil needs to be seen as part of a long cycle of abolitions throughout the West, starting with Great Britain in the eighteenth century, and continuing into the latter half of the nineteenth in New Granada (Colombia, 1851); Hawaii (1852); Argentina (1853); Peru and Venezuela (1854); Moldavia (1855); India (1860); Russia (1861); Dutch Guiana (1862), Surinam and the Antilles (1863); Portuguese colonies (1869); Zanzibar and Madagascar (1873); the Gold Coast (1878) and the Ottoman Empire (1882) (Drescher, 2009, pp. 372 ff.).

New technologies – the steamship and the telegraph – facilitated and expanded transnational communications in the nineteenth century. Newspapers, mail, and travel made people and information circulate on

---

[9] The aim here is to draw a bigger picture of antislavery mobilization, working, as did Conrad (1972, 1975) and Needell (2010, p. 231, 2020), on intra and extra-parliamentary dynamics, albeit within another timeframe (I begin in 1868, while Conrad starts from 1850 and Needell, 1879), a broader spectrum (Conrad stresses regional differences and Needell, two specific moments in national politics), while I address four separate conjunctures (prior to the Free Womb Law, the rise of the Liberal Party to government, and the governments of Dantas and Cotegipe), and an alternative methodology (systematic research on abolitionist associations and events in newspapers). Furthermore, I stress the political organization of the countermovement as key to define abolitionist strategies.

## Introduction

an international scale,[10] enabling the formation of a worldwide antislavery network involving Europe, Africa, and the Americas (Stamatov 2010). Brazilian abolitionists engaged in that network. They saw the previous political experiences as a repertoire of contention (Tilly 2006, p. 35) to rely on: a tried-and-tested set of strategies, rhetoric, and political performances useful for guiding their actions in a new time and context.

For the political authorities, the core of this repertoire consisted of abolitionist processes from the United States and the Spanish colonies. When civil war broke out in the United States, Spain abolished the slave trade to Cuba (1862) and sped up abolition in Puerto Rico which was achieved in 1873. Abolition in Cuba would not come until 1886, but mitigating measures were already in place there, such as the Moret Law, passed in 1870, which freed slaves over the age of sixty and the children born to slave mothers from that year on. Besides Haiti-like slave uprisings, these cases pointed out two paths to end slavery: civil war and progressive abolition. To avoid the former, Brazilian governments opted for the latter. The Moret law would be taken as the model for the Free Womb Law (1871) and the Saraiva/Cotegipe Sexagenarian Law (1885). When the abolitionists generalized assisted slave runaways, the government's response was to pass repressive legislation modeled on the US Fugitive Slave Act.

The pro-slavery politicians also reached for the available repertoire. Wanting to be the sole slavery-based country among free nations, the Brazilian anti-abolitionists renounced bondage as a good social practice. Instead, the countermovement built up a "rhetoric of reaction" (Hirshman, 1991) that argued for the postponement of abolition in the face of unfavorable local "circumstances." This "circumstantial" pro-slavery rhetoric rested upon three schemata of interpretation:[11] the futility of abolition (demographics would eliminate slavery in due course); the perverse effects it would have on the economy (disrupting

---

[10] Anderson (2007), while presenting a network connecting anarchists from America, Europe and Asia in the nineteenth century, defines it as part of an "early globalization era."

[11] "Framework" or "schemata of interpretation" is a standardized form of perceiving the social reality that "... allows its user to locate, perceive, identify, and label a seemingly infinite number of concrete occurrences defined in its terms" (Goffman, 1974, p. 21) and providing cognitive guidance for agents through their interactions. The term, derived from Erving Goffman's "frame analysis," is used here as adapted by Snow and Benford (1992, p. 137) in their study of social movements, namely as schemata of interpretation that simplify the meaning of a given political situation by selectively highlighting certain traits over others, as in caricature, and so supplying swift guidance for political action.

14                          *The Last Abolition*

the workforce); and the threat it posed to the social and political order (anarchy and social upheaval).

The abolitionists, on their side, availed themselves of the foreign experience in two ways. They joined the transnational antislavery network, forming ties with British, American, French, and Spanish counterparts in search of support. This political solidarity enabled them to use, from the 1860s[12] onward, the "boomerang effect" (Keck and Sikkink, 1998): drawing upon alliances abroad to pressurize antireform-minded governments at home.

On the other hand, the strategies, rhetoric, and political performances of the British, North-American, and Spanish movements inspired Brazilian activism's choice of forms of organization (civil associations), forums of action (Parliament, the public space, the underground) and strategies (street demonstrations and rallies, institutional initiatives, direct confrontation). But the local political context and national political tradition – institutions, values, and practices legitimizing the status quo – forced adjustments on how the foreign antislavery repertoire was transposed and appropriated in Brazil.

This is quite clear in the strategies. While Anglo-American abolitionism hosted many events at Quaker meeting houses (Davis, 1984; Stamatov, 2010), the Brazilian movement could not rely upon organizational support from the Catholic Church. Catholicism was the official religion of the State, and it operated in favor of retaining slavery. This pushed the activists to go for the Spanish model instead, and look to the secular space of the theater. However, in so doing, Brazilian antislavery propaganda absorbed at a higher intensity the agents, resources, and language of art, which ended up theatricalizing its politics.

The same went for its rhetoric. The abolitionist moral repertoire, accumulated by previous movements, contained an arsenal of schemata, tropes, and patterns for morally delegitimizing slavery. Yet the Brazilians could only use those that resonated among the "feeling structures" (Williams, 1960) of the local society, capable of conversing with the national context and tradition.[13] They concentrated on three schemata

---

[12] Nabuco forged relationships with English, French, North-American, and Cuban abolitionists (Alonso, 2010). There was a marked foreign presence in the campaign, with such figures as the Portuguese Angelo Agostini.

[13] The notion of a "moral repertoire" refers to a limited set of schemata of thought, patterns of meaning, and moral evaluation (Halfmann and Young, 2010) of social reality available at any given time. It downgrades the rhetorical possibilities of justification, providing a "grammar of motives" and establishing the moral basis for claim-making. See also Steinberg (1995, pp. 60–1, 74).

# Introduction

of interpretation: rights, compassion, and progress. And they adapted each to the local reality. The first of these went way beyond individual freedom, with the addition of a sub-trope that posited abolition as a new Independence, a national liberation. The second, couched in religion abroad, was reconfigured in the artistic language of romanticism. And the third fed off the social sciences that were emerging in the last quarter of the nineteenth century, creating a trope of slavery as *social* backwardness, in this way going beyond the Enlightenment idea of human progress. With this, Brazilian abolitionism produced a *rhetoric of change* that was more secular and modern than its British and American counterparts. The appropriation of the foreign experience led to a reinvention, producing a unique style of Brazilian activism.

The transnational dimension therefore oriented all the players involved in the political conflict revolving around slavery in Brazil. The political transfer[14] exceeded the reproduction of stock models. The national context and tradition obliged abolitionists, pro-slavery agents, and governments to select, interpret, modify, adapt, and reinvent political strategies, rhetoric, and performances. Far from guiding their actions by abstract moral principles, they took contextual decisions, with each searching for the best weapons with which to confront the adversary over the course of the conflict.

## MOVEMENT, STATE, COUNTERMOVEMENT

As the abolitionist movement was part of a "contentious interaction," its stances depended on its relations with the State, the target of its demands, and with the pro-slavery countermovement, the political mobilization of the established social elites' members, whose beliefs and prerogatives the movement was threatening (Meyer and Staggenborg, 1996, p. 1635). The literature on abolitionist movements paid little heed to the relationship between movement and countermovement. Both vied for legitimacy in the public space and for control over the political institutions. It was a conflict mediated by governments, which were never neutral. In the Brazilian case, the balance of power between movement, countermovement, and

---

[14] Tilly (2005, pp. 223–4) identifies the balance of political opportunities and threats and rival performances as conditions upon transposing political repertoires. This process includes bargaining, brokerage and adaptation so that diffusion could be processed. However, he pays less attention to what is decisive in the Brazilian case, namely national tradition, which imposes conditions, choices, negotiations and the adaptation of what is transposed.

## The Last Abolition

government at each juncture conditioned the choice of strategy, performance, and rhetoric.

The collective options of the abolitionists at each phase of the political process depended on how permeable the political system was to the abolitionist agenda; the availability of allies within the political elite; the power of pro-slavery politicians and the State's disposition to co-opt, tolerate, or repress their actions. This movement/State/countermovement dynamic staked out the most fertile ground for abolitionists at each turn, leading them to focus their efforts successively on demonstrations in the public space, parliamentary politics, and underground activity.[15] Changes in this dynamic broke the political process around Brazilian abolition into phases.

### Genesis of Mobilization

There had always been antislavery statements in Brazil, but for a social movement to arise political opportunities propitious to the organization of public rallies and antislavery civil associations had to emerge. Movements tend to form during times of political crisis, when the coalition in command of the State divides, producing dissident elites that seek alliances within society. This intra-elite division reduces the State's capacity to repress protest, opening opportunities for politically underrepresented groups to express their claims in the public space (McAdam, Tarrow, and Tilly, 2001). Just such a conjuncture materialized in Brazil in 1868, when three processes triggered the onset of antislavery protest.

One of these was international. The end of the American Civil War and the acceleration of abolition in the Spanish colonies put the issue back on the Brazilian agenda. The imperial political elite – which had closed the political institutions' agenda for the subject since the end of the trans-Atlantic slave trade in 1850 – saw itself forced anew to discuss measures to mitigate slavery. In so doing, it looked abroad for models to follow. The theme divided the political parties into a modernizing wing and a change-resistant bloc.

The second process was the domestic political crisis partly caused by the difficulty in dealing with slavery and which, in 1868, led a Liberal Party

---

[15] McAdam, Tarrow, and Tilly (2001) argue that institutional politics (like party politics), non-institutional politics (such as social movements), and ruptures with the status quo (as revolts) form a continuum of modes of "contentious politics" that vary in degrees of violence and institutionalization, but not in nature. They are forms of action to which the discrete political actors can take recourse in different situations.

## Introduction

faction to contest the Conservative government in the public space and demand reforms, including gradual abolition. This protest, enacted outside the institutions, through conferences and newspapers, signaled that the themes the political system avoided could be raised in the public space.

The third structuring element in this conjuncture was the modernizing reform the Conservative Party flaunted as a response to the crisis. The Prime Minister, the Viscount of Rio Branco, fast-tracked the urbanization process already in-course, expanded access to tertiary education, and reduced printing costs, which made it cheaper to publish newspapers and books. These measures broadened the participants in the public debate in Brazil. The government proposed a Free Womb bill – inspired by the Spanish legislation – on the floor of the House. The Conservative Party was split down the middle, which reduced its ability to resist change.

This context provided the conditions for a first cycle of antislavery mobilization in the public space, led by dissident members of the imperial elite and their followers (Chapter 1). Twenty-four antislavery associations were formed between 1868 and 1871, some of which – such as the 7th of September Liberating Society – connected with foreign abolitionists. This initiated an onslaught of pro-abolition institutional actions (lobbying and freedom lawsuits) and proselytism (publications and demonstrations in the public space).

The pro-slavery backlash was quick in coming. Slavery had survived as long as it had in Brazil because it was all but unmentionable, out of the political deliberation sphere. When it entered into the parliamentary agenda, from the diffuse pro-slavery social groups (an entire social stratum had economic activities and a way of life based on slave labor) emerged a politically organized pro-slavery activism. This pro-slavery countermovement articulated around the whole country and made its voice loud in the public space and the political institutions. This pro-slavery political reaction diffused a pro-slavery rhetoric (a "circumstantial" defense of slavery), organized civil associations (Plantation Clubs) and formed a parliamentary bloc (the "Hardliners," see Chapter 2). The abolitionists responded with a rhetoric of change, presenting abolition as an act of compassion and in the interests of rights and progress (Chapter 3). The rhetoric for and against slavery clashed in the press, through pamphlets and from the pulpits.

Resistance did not prevent the Free Womb Law from being approved in 1871, liberating children born to slave mothers. It mitigated, however, the government's original bill and postponed its full enforcement until the newborns had reached the age of eight. After the promulgation of the law, abolition was dropped entirely from the institutional agenda.

18 *The Last Abolition*

The abolitionists continued their campaign in the public space. The government response to this small cycle of protest was tolerance, which allowed a pioneering generation of abolitionists to keep the activism alive and to transfer its rhetoric and strategies – lobbying, conferences, freedom suits, the boomerang effect – to the young.

### Nationalization

The nationalization of abolitionism came about when the problem came back to the institutional agenda in 1878, for two reasons. One was the impending full implementation of the Free Womb Law, and the other was the change of government. The Liberals were back in power, after a decade demanding reforms in the public space, abolition included, although not as a priority. The abolitionists seized the opportunity to step up their protest. A new generation, in part benefited by the educational reforms of the 1870s, joined the mobilization. Of these, Joaquim Nabuco and José do Patrocínio would emerge as leaders, the former in Parliament, and the latter in the public arena.

Liberal Party rule (1878–1884) was less conducive to abolition than the abolitionists had expected, but it did at least tolerate public demonstrations. Concert-conferences held in theaters were the preferred strategy of the period. Poetry and operas, like *Aida*, set the tone for their propaganda, with the events ending with the presentation of manumission certificates and a shower of flowers over the freed ones (Chapter 4).

During this cycle of flowers, the pacific style of mobilization conferred public legitimacy upon the campaign in the large cities, where over 1,000 demonstrations were held between 1878 and 1884 (Chapter 5). Numeric growth, geographic expansion, tactical variety, and the social diversity of the activists allowed the movement to make its campaign national.

In 1883, the abolitionists launched a strategy that followed the North-American example: creation of free soils. It consisted of buying up freedom certificates or persuading slaveowners to give them for free in a spatial sequence. The tactic was deployed in various cities and in one entire province, Ceará, selected as a pilot because it had small slave reserves, strong local abolitionist associations, and a provincial president willing to certify the movement. Abolitionists went house to house, city by city, and started a countdown to province-wide abolition (Chapter 6). In March 1884, abolitionists declared Ceará a "free soil." Patrocínio in Paris and Nabuco in London organized celebrations to showcase the

## Introduction

movement's international support and embarrass the national government, thus preventing repression.

This abolitionist strategy caused a crisis in the political institutions, culminating, in June 1884, in the appointment of a new Prime Minister, the Liberal Manuel de Sousa Dantas, the very man who would applaud Bulicioff's Aida from his box two years later. Dantas took office committed to putting in motion a moderate abolitionist reform.

### Institutionalization

The Abolitionist Confederation, founded in 1883 to coordinate abolitionists nationwide, endorsed the Dantas government and the movement helped draft a project for gradual emancipation, which was presented to Parliament in July 1884.

The project triggered a virulent pro-slavery political backlash, with the creation of new civil associations (Plantation Clubs) against the Dantas Reform, while the caucus worked to obstruct it in Parliament.

The Brazilian parliamentary system allowed Dantas to dissolve the Lower House and seek public endorsement at the ballot box. The movement/government alliance launched candidates in eleven of the twenty provinces of the Empire and in the capital, Rio de Janeiro. With a nationwide abolitionist electoral campaign, a time of searching for votes replaced the initial cycle of flowers (Chapter 7).

However, the pro-slavery political faction won the election and the gradual emancipation project was thwarted.

### Confrontation

In August 1885, the Conservative Party/pro-slavery countermovement took power. This strong political reaction closed the political agenda to abolition and it instilled a threatening atmosphere for abolitionists to act in the public space. The new Prime Minister, the Baron of Cotegipe, rolled out a repressive politics, using legal measures against abolitionists, and allowed the pro-slavery countermovement to rely on their own extra-legal methods. The frequency of harassing, persecuting, and arresting abolitionists increased. That is the reason why the movement opted at this point for "purely" cultural events, such as the staging of *Aida* starring Bulicioff.

It also pursued other lines of action, besides public demonstrations, investing in civil disobedience and direct confrontation. Based on the North-American underground railroad strategy, the movement set up

# 20 The Last Abolition

assisted collective runaway routes to get slaves to free soil in the North and South. It also declared in its newspapers the willingness to take up arms to defend its activists and liberate slaves. This radicalization made it impracticable to maintain slavery without the use of force.

This was a phase of confrontation, since the government relied on military repression and the pro-slavery countermovement organized militias to face the movement's new strategy. Then, the flowers and votes gave way to a time of bullets (Chapter 8).

## Certification

Being on the edge of a civil war, hitherto unengaged sectors of the social elite and civil organizations became involved in order to avert all-out conflict. The political process entered its final phase, one of certification, that is, of political and social authorities underwriting the main movement's demand before the government (McAdam, Tarrow, and Tilly, 2001, p. 121). The armed forces' decision to support abolition in October 1887 was decisive, depriving the State of its capacity to keep quashing the movement by force. Various segments of the social elite, the judiciary, the church, and the Liberal Party also came out in favor of abolition in the short term. In February 1888, the Crown and a dissident faction of the Conservative Party followed suit.

The new balance of power undid the confrontation between the pro-slavery countermovement and the abolitionists and produced a brokered compromise. Abolition came in May 1888, without indemnification to slave owners, as the abolitionists had wanted. However, the pro-slavery countermovement managed to block all their other demands, such as social protection and land for former slaves (Chapter 9).

As a whole, this book argues that the abolitionist movement chose rhetoric, strategies, and arenas to suit the shifting balance of power, taking decisions according to the levels of government tolerance or repression, the availability of allies and the pro-slavery countermovement's strength, in each conjuncture. The relational dynamics within the countermovement and State forced the movement to favor different arenas under each context. When the State was tolerant and the pro-slavery countermovement was concentrated in the political institutions, the abolitionists opted for demonstrations in the public space. When the pro-slavery countermovement was strong inside and outside political institutions, but the Prime Minister was favorable to an abolitionist law, the

*Introduction* 21

abolitionists allied with the government, and focused their efforts on avenues inside the political institutions. Finally, when the State and the countermovement turned the screw, allying in the use of repressive measures, the abolitionists responded with civil disobedience. First came the flowers (in public space), then the votes (in the politico-institutional sphere), and finally the bullets (in clandestinity).

### ACTIVISM NETWORKS, POLITICAL BROKERS, AND MODULAR STYLES OF ACTIVISM

Three mechanisms explain the geographical expansion and temporal continuity of Brazilian abolitionism: social networks, modular styles of activism, and political brokers.

The tessitura of the *activism networks* consolidated mobilization, facilitating the foundation of civil associations, the appropriation of social spaces (the press, theaters), and the dissemination of strategies and rhetoric. In the British and North-American cases, religious networks were key, but in Brazil, the main networks were all secular: personal (family ties, cronyism, friendship), professional (teacher/student, student/student, occupational), associative (belonging to same civil associations) and political (Liberal and Republican party members). These networks synchronically linked activists from different parts of the country and forged inter-generational bonds that allowed knowhow to be passed down from one generation to another. All of these networks came together under the umbrella of abolition, but, as is common among social movements, the members disagreed on the other reforms. The heterogeneity of the activists – in terms of social rank, status, region of origin, career, access to the political system – generated factions and rifts. However, the diversity also fostered alliance-building, recruitment of new members, and organization into activity niches, with *portable styles of activism*: those of André Rebouças (lobbying, brokerage between the public space and the political system), Abílio Borges (associativism, civic ceremonies, the boomerang method), Luís Gama (freedom suits), José do Patrocínio (concert-conferences, free soil campaign), Joaquim Nabuco (parliamentary actions, electoral campaigns) and Antônio Bento (assisted collective runaways).

The nationalization of the movement was possible because these portable styles of activism were "modular" (Tarrow 1998, pp. 37–41), stylized political performances, that were at the same time standardized and flexible, making them stock formulae that were easily reproducible.[16] Each abolitionist faction used them as templates and transposed and adapted them to suit their own contexts, creating local variations and nuances. Styles of activism ensured the diffusion of forms of organization, action strategies, and rhetoric, as well as a minimal homogeneity among the factions, which gave the campaign a national aspect.

"Brokers" (Diani, 2003) between the various factions and arenas of mobilization were key in disseminating this portable style of activism. There were many regional brokers, but only five on a national scale (three of them black): Abílio Borges, Luís Gama, José do Patrocínio, Joaquim Nabuco, and André Rebouças. As these factions were embroiled in constant negotiations, the brokers ensured that this polycentric activism network had minimum cohesion, allowing the abolitionists to present themselves in the public arena as a collective political actor, a single social movement.

These brokers, especially Rebouças, the key figure from the beginning to the end of the campaign, are the guiding threads that run through this book. These heroes would be incomprehensible without their villains, represented here by Paulino Soares de Souza and the Baron of Cotegipe, pro-slavery political leaders who served as brokers among the public space countermovement and the pro-slavery faction in the political institutions.

Bringing to light the people behind the conflict lends names and faces to the vast web of activism formed by the men and women, black and white, who rallied against (and for) slavery in Brazil, the book underscores the massive and continuous pressure the abolitionist movement put on the Imperial political institutions, over the course of two decades, and how decisive this mobilization was to the unfolding of the political process in 1888. Left to its own devices, slavery was always going to end someday, but in the latter half of the 1880s, there were proposals on the table that would have prolonged it into the 1930s. The abolitionist movement can be credited, at the very least, with shortening that timespan.

---

[16] Tarrow (1995) argues that diffusion usually operates from a national to a local arena. In this case, however, in addition to the vector of the political center (the Court, the national capital) emanating towards the outlying localities, regional hubs were also formed, as in Ceará, and these became epicenters of local-to-local diffusion.

# Introduction

Brazilian abolitionism existed at a time when social movements were only starting their long life as a kind of politics. However, its portable styles of activism, transnational network-building, and brokers speak to its modernity. It sounds contemporary also because the end of slavery was a watershed in Brazilian history, but its aftershocks are still felt in the country's current forms of inequality.

# I

# Elite Abolitionism

### ENGINEER OF MULTIPLE LEVÉES

André Rebouças was born in 1838, in the midst of the Sabinada political revolt[1]. For his father, a staunch supporter of the consolidation of the Second Reign, both his first-born son and the Brazilian Empire were barely delivered and already at risk. Yet the boy and the Second Reign would thrive, their fates entwined to the very last, which would come in the throes of another revolution.

With the Second Reign, André went from strength to strength. He grew up inseparable from his brother Antônio, in a family of six children raised by his mother, a merchant's daughter, and his father, Dr. Antônio Pereira Rebouças. Rebouças was a self-made man, granted the right to practice law in reward for political services rendered during Independence and the Sabinada Revolt, not to mention a knack for being in the right place at the right time. He became a member of the provincial and general parliaments, and a jurisconsult for the Council of State. He opened his law offices in Court[2] when André was only seven years of age, and crowned his new status by acquiring a batch of household slaves.

---

[1] Various separatist rebellions took place in Brazil in between the First (1822–1831) and Second (1840–1889) Reigns, such as the Balaiada in Maranhão and the Cabanagem in Pará, both in the North, and the Farroupilha, in Rio Grande do Sul. The Sabinada was one of this kind, in Bahia (1837–1838). Unlike the other revolts, the Sabinada claimed only for temporary provincial autonomy until the young prince Pedro II came of age. Like the others, it ended up crushed by the ones in favor of a centralized State.

[2] Court refers to the city of Rio de Janeiro not the court of the Emperor or the surrounding province.

## Elite Abolitionism

André inherited Dr. Rebouças' opportunism. In 1859, he and his brother enrolled at the Central School, a common path to a career in the Empire. The doctor sent his sons to study engineering, and during their undergraduate studies, the brothers took the classic trip to Europe, something of a rite of passage for young members of the imperial elite. André spent a while in Paris, as well as stints in Brest, Marseille, Arles, all civil-engineering hotspots.

He returned to Brazil to pursue an engineering career as well as a life as a political reformer. While he lacked a degree he nevertheless secured the post of inspector of fortresses (from Santos down to Santa Catarina) in 1863, proving to be a thoughtful and able lobbyist. With his father, he courted the upper strata of the ruling Liberal Party and received the go-ahead to test multiple levées, decorated by the Emperor for his work.

André's success was the result of a balance of complementary talents. In everything he did he employed trigonometry, and drew up plans and goals. He was systematic with meticulous work habits, buttressed by the relationships he cultivated, the authorities he courted, and his powers of soft persuasion to advance projects, careers, and salaries. His construction work took him to Maranhão, Minas Gerais, Pará, Ceará, and introduced him to the local heavyweights, provincial presidents and the manioc flour mills. Wherever he set foot, he suggested improvements. The backwardness of the backlands stirred his modernizing impulses. Rubbing shoulders with local elites and their slaves (his assistants on civil construction jobs), the latters' plight moved him, as he would record in his diary in 1863: "How I wish our forebears had not stained the Land of the Sacred Cross[3] with their abominable slave trade!"

Two unexpected turns of events took the spring out of André's step: the onset of the Brazil-Paraguay War, and the onslaught of the family's creditors, who prised away their diamonds and silverware. Not one to succumb to obstacles, when his construction projects and enterprises came to a halt, he sought favor from the Emperor and Conservative Party heavyweights, such as the future Viscount of Rio Branco, and managed to be appointed first-lieutenant with the engineering corps in Paraguay. Rebouças was a careful planner, and he plied the generals and the prince consort, whose side he seldom left, with a constant supply of plans for battles, the region, and indeed the nation.

---

[3] The second name the Portuguese had for Brazil was Terra da Santa Cruz, Land of the Sacred Cross. The first name given to the country was Vera Cruz (True Cross).

FIGURE 1.1 André Pinto Rebouças (1838–1898), the abolitionist movement's national leader.
Museu Afro-Brasileiro (Afro-Brazilian Museum)/Reproduction.

His wartime adventures were cut short, however, by his mother's death and a second bout of smallpox. On his return to Rio de Janeiro, he tried to secure a teaching post at his alma mater, the Central School, but there were many candidates for such posts, and the Empire had many patrons to whom it owed favors. He paid a visit to almost all of them, the Prime Minister included. He eventually landed a job as an inspector with the gas company and later as a construction foreman at the Customs Office, earning a salary that "exceeded my wildest expectations." At the age of twenty-nine, his pockets were full; he was well-connected politically and socially, and even had direct access to the princes' salons. He made the most of these stellar events to work his way into the circles of Brazil's power brokers, talking politics and business.

While reading J. S. Mill and working on a new model of diving helmet in 1867, he was asked by an engineer under his command for his help in manumitting a slave named Chico, who spent over a decade toiling away as a dam-builder. It was then, for the first time, that André really took stock of the issue of slavery. He had the slave freed and began to work on a law to tax slaveholders. Abolition, he felt, was indispensable to national progress. On April 10 of the following year, he decided to put his abolitionist ideas into writing, only to find himself accused of advocating the exact opposite of emancipation by his growing ranks of enemies who envied his success in securing coveted positions. In 1868, while presenting a project for a plowing school at the Central School, where he had secured tenure, he was shocked to hear himself branded "slaver" in the presence of the Emperor himself. In response, he freed his "house slave Guilhermina":

I am an abolitionist at heart and I avail of the present ceremony to declare as much out loud. My conscience bears the burden of not a single opportunity left untaken to campaign for the abolition of slavery, and I trust in God that I shall not die without having rendered to my nation the most exuberant proof of my dedication to the Holy Cause of Emancipation.[4]

So the engineer-cum-entrepreneur put his multiple levées to the service of abolition. Over the next twenty years, he would prove it time and time again.

### COMPARED PERSPECTIVES

Throughout 1868, abolition cast its pall over the political system. Talk of it had begun much earlier, with the founding of the nation, and by the late 1840s, the Minister of Justice, Eusébio de Queirós, and his colleagues in the Conservative Party were receiving considerable pressure from Britain to staunch the slave trade.

Like Brazil, many nations depended on slave labor through the eighteenth century, but during the first half of the nineteenth, the scene changed completely. A wave of abolitions began in São Domingos (Haiti), and the slave revolt led by Toussaint-Louverture in 1791, which secured abolition by decapitating white officers from three imperial armies. In 1807, the British Empire and the United States abolished the slave trade throughout the Anglo-American world. In 1815, the Congress of Vienna attended by Great Britain, France, Russia, Austria, Sweden, and Portugal outlawed the international slave trade. In the early 1800s, most of the colonies in Spanish America made a double whammy of independence and abolition, with chattel slavery ending in Peru, Chile, Costa Rica, Panama, Guatemala, Bolivia, and Mexico. In the latter half of the nineteenth century, British Honduras and Mauritius followed suit.

---

[4] On Rebouças, cf. Spitzer (1989, pp. 110, 115, 119 ff.) and Grinberg (2002, pp. 69 ff.). On Rebouças' life and ideas, cf. Spitzer (1989), Jucá (2001), Trindade (2011). The quotations from Rebouças are taken from his diary, respectively: DNAAR, Jan. 13, 1838, 1865, Oct. 7, 1863, Nov., 1864, Oct. 9, 1866, Jan. 26, 1868, Feb. 10, 1867, Jun. 15, 1868.

28 *The Last Abolition*

It is debatable whether the driving force behind this abolitionist domino effect was economic, with the expansion of capitalist forms of production that consumed free labor and required new consumer markets, or whether it was a consequence of a new humanistic morality that demanded the expansion of citizenship[5]. What is beyond question is that this series of abolitions created a new international political environment that did not bode well for slavery.

Ever since Independence, Brazil had suffered constant pressure from Great Britain to advance the cause of emancipation. The price for British recognition of the fledgling nation was a bilateral treaty in 1826, banning the slave trade three years after its ratification, which occurred the following year. On November 7, 1831, the Brazilian government actually enacted a national law prohibiting the transatlantic trade of Africans to the country, but there was a visible reluctance to honor it throughout the country[6]. The few attempts toward progressive emancipation, such as the bill José Bonifácio de Andrada put to the Constitutive Assembly in 1823, came to nothing. The same held for the Regency.[7] The slave trade, formally extinct, was back in full swing by 1835, with a further 600,000 slaves being shipped to Brazil by 1850, already under the Second Reign. Britain put its foot down: it boarded ships, seized hulls full of trafficked slaves, arrested their smugglers, and threatened national sovereignty by deploying warships along the Brazilian coast. Corralled into action, in 1850 the Conservative government had no choice but to bite the hand that fed it, plastering slave owners and traders with legislation – the Eusébio de Queirós Law – that put an end to the transatlantic slave trade once and for all. The British left their fleet patrolling Brazilian waters to make sure the sub-Equatorial upstart kept to the treaty.

The government compensated those affected as best it could: between the passing of the bill and the promulgation of the new law, it threw Brazil's ports wide open to a massive influx of trafficked Africans. After 1851, at least 9,309 Africans were illegally imported into the country. But it was not all plain sailing. In 1856, the smuggling of some 200 African

---

[5] The literature on abolition and abolitionist movements is vast. On the more influential positions in the debate, see Drescher (1977), Williams (1994) and Brown (2006). For overarching perspectives, see Davis (2006) and Drescher (2009).

[6] On the 1831 Law and its effects, see Mamigonian (2017).

[7] The Regency was the period between the abdication of the first Emperor of independent Brazil, D. Pedro I, in 1831, and the declaration of his son's majority and ascension to the throne as D. Pedro II, in 1840, starting the Second Reign. During the Regency, power was exercised by regent-ministers.

## Elite Abolitionism

slaves into Pernambuco earned the Prime Minister a final warning from the British. There would be no more trafficking. It was a violent, abrupt end to the most lucrative of trades, one that enriched the bowsprit families and filled state coffers. Pockets bled, businesses teetered, and a brow-beaten nation swore under its breath.

Yet no-one believed that this was indeed the end of slavery, the corner-stone of the economy, the mainstay of parties, and the cash-cow of the aristocracy since the very beginning. Over three centuries, Brazil imported more African slaves than any other nation on earth: 5,848,265 in all, and roughly a half a million of these during the Second Reign.[8] Landowners, the self-employed, the Emperor, the vast majority of social strata – in some cases even some former slaves – all owned captives, used them to staff businesses and ply trades, work in private and public domains, in the marketplace, in the streets, and in homes. Though it was the backbone of agricultural expansion, slave-owning was by no means the preserve of farmers. It was widespread; it pervaded the country's social life. It was good business in itself, and the lifeline of all others. The pillar of social hierarchy and of the lifestyle enjoyed at the top of the pyramid, slavery ran in the national veins. In politics, almost all of the voters and those they voted for owned slaves. Slavery structured their whole way of life, underpinned and underwrote the identities, possibilities, and destinies of members of imperial society. The whole country was built on slavery, which is why no-one was in any hurry to have abolition added to the public agenda.

With the abolition of the slave trade in 1850, the slave become an even more valuable asset, and slave stocks began to concentrate among the upper strata of society and in the agricultural commodity belts.[9] While this created a large contingent of slaveless families with no vested interest in preserving the institution of slavery, it also boosted the status of those

---

[8] After Brazil, the second-largest slave importer/exporter was Great Britain, followed by France, Spain, the Netherlands, the United States, and Denmark. Together, these seven nations received 12,521,336 African slaves between 1501 and 1866. This and previous data is from slavevoyages.org. For more on the end of slavery in Brazil, see Bethell (1970); on the economic and social dynamics of Brazilian slavery, see Costa (1966), Fernandes (1978), Cardoso (1977), Novais (1985), and Alencastro (2000); for an overview of this literature, see Marquese and Salles (2015).

[9] Slenes (2004) shows that the internal, inter-regional slave market prospered after the cessation of the Africa-Brazil slave trade, with stocks transferred from the cotton-growing regions of Rio Grande do Norte, Ceará, Paraíba, and Piauí to the sugarocracies of Bahia and Pernambuco, in the North of the country. Something similar happened in the South after the beef-jerky crisis, when slaves from Rio Grande were exported to Campinas, further north.

30    *The Last Abolition*

who owned captives. The more expensive the asset, the more prestige there is in possessing it.

From 1850 onward, pro-slavery politics focused on ensuring a line of interprovincial supply to the agricultural economy, and on keeping abolition on the political back burner. In 1852, when a Representative from the Lower House proposed a law that would make the offspring of slaves free from birth and therefore put a genuine end to the practice of slavery in Brazil, he heard in return that the institution would fizzle out of its own accord through the natural decline of a population that lived neither long nor well. The bill was not even sent to the floor, being dismissed by those present as mere Protestant sentimentalism: "We have another Quaker! (laughter)."[10]

Poking fun at the religious orientation of Anglo-American abolitionism did nothing to relieve the pressure of relentless British enforcement of the antislavery treaties Brazil had signed. In 1860, William Christie, British plenipotentiary minister to Brazil, denounced the enslavement of Africans whom he considered free, as they had been imported after Brazil's acceptance of the bilateral agreement of 1826 and the Brazilian law of 1831. He complained that the Brazilian government had turned a blind eye to the fact that 34,688 slaves had been shipped down the coast from the North to the South, in a clear breach of the Atlantic slave-trade ban. The quarrel deteriorated further after two episodes involving three Englishmen arrested by the Brazilian authorities at the turn of 1862/63. Christie demanded the payment of damages to his fellow countrymen, but the government refused. In retaliation, Christie ordered a six-day naval blockade of Rio de Janeiro and captured five Brazilian ships in national waters. Brazilian politicians and the Emperor himself spun their defense of the domestic slave trade as resistance against a British attack on national sovereignty. The port was reopened after fraught negotiations, and diplomatic relations between the two nations were severed for the next two years.[11] The end result of the Christie affair was a popularity

[10] Cf. Bastos (1863, p. 382); ACD, May 22, 1852. The joker in question was the future baron of Cotegipe. On the debate during the period 1840–1860, see Parron (2011).

[11] A Brazil-Britain Commission was established in 1858 to arbitrate on Brazilian demands for compensation for losses incurred during the British crackdown on the slave trade, all of which were rejected (Bethell, 1970, pp. 370 ff.). Yet the trade continued: in 1860 alone, 26,622 African slaves were sold and shipped from the North to Rio de Janeiro (Bethell, 1970, pp. 375 ff.). The usual explanations for the "Christie affair" ignored any link with the dispute over the slave trade, though Bethell (1970, pp. 382 ff.) and Christie himself (1865) were clear on the connection. The tension continued right up to the onset of the Paraguay War, when Brazil could not afford the luxury of being at loggerheads with the world's greatest military power.

## Elite Abolitionism

boost for the government and the Crown – after all, it was still a slave society – but the blockade left little doubt that even domestic trafficking in national waters would be difficult to maintain.

Brazil would never be able to trade its slaves in peace again. A new wave of international abolitionism eradicated bondage in Colombia (1851), Hawaii (1852), Argentina (1853), Jamaica and Venezuela (1854), Peru and Moldavia (1855), India (1860), and Russia (1861). In 1863, the emancipation process reached Surinam and the Antilles and in 1869, the Portuguese; Zanzibar and Madagascar, the Gold Coast, and the Ottoman Empire continued to bear the stain of slavery until 1876, 1878, and 1882, respectively.

The Brazilian elite knew all about the past and present successes of the abolitionist movement from books, visitors, foreign travel, and newspapers. This diversity of foreign experiences worked as a *repertoire of contention*[12] that informed pro and antislavery discourse and activism, as well as state decision-making and policy. It also served as a guide for dealing with the issue when it proved impossible to ignore.

This repertoire provided models to follow and examples to avoid. The dismantling of the slave system in Great Britain, France, Portugal, and the Netherlands hardly served as parameters, as in all these cases slavery was colonial and entirely overseas. In a similar position to Brazil were the United States and Cuba, both of which had received significant influxes of slave labor (although much less than Brazil), forming the continent's biggest slave economies. This, plus their geographic proximity, made the United States and Cuba Brazil's clearest mirrors. What happened to one tended to resonate among the others. In 1861, slavery was the core of a civil war in the United States, whose government signed an agreement with Britain the following year putting an end to the Atlantic slave trade. On the very first day of 1863, the United States issued its Emancipation Proclamation, freeing the nation's slaves. In the meantime, Cuba and Puerto Rico founded the Spanish Abolitionist Society and the government in Madrid opened debate on antislavery legislation.[13]

---

[12] "Repertoire of contention" refers to a "limited, familiar and historically constructed" set of political tools and claim-making strategies available at a given historical period (Tilly, 2006, p. vii). In this case, it included the body of foreign political experience concerning the end of slavery with which the Brazilians were familiar.

[13] Davis (1966, 1992, 2006); Drescher (1986, 2009, pp. 372 ff.); Jennings (2006); Bethell (1970, p. 385). Transnational circulation was constant. Brazilians corresponded or personally met with foreign abolitionists, and this contact furnished them with strategies and rhetoric, as Candler and Burgess attest (1854, p. 44), claiming to have seen

# The Last Abolition

This international conjuncture instilled in at least part of the imperial elite a sense of inevitability concerning abolition in Brazil, so that the country did not end up in the ignoble position of being the world's last slave-owning nation. On the one hand, there was the worst-case scenario, exemplified by the American Civil War. The specter of inter-regional conflict, a traumatic experience during the Regency, loomed large and dark, exacerbated by the geographically unequal distribution of slave stocks. The coffee-growing hub of Rio's Paraíba Valley and the Zona da Mata in Minas Gerais and the west of the São Paulo province were buying up the slaves from less profitable businesses in the North. On the other hand, the transition from slavery to abolition was relatively smooth in Spain, which had manumitted slave-born children at birth and adult slaves aged sixty or over. The *Libertad de Vientres* (Free Womb Law) had worked in various parts of Spanish America – Chile, Argentina, Venezuela, Peru, Colombia, Ecuador, Uruguay and Paraguay – and in the Portuguese colonies.

This past was adopted as a blueprint for a Brazilian future in various books, articles, and bills of law, of which there were many in the 1860s. Aurélio Cândido Tavares Bastos, a member of the Liberal Party and watchful observer of the international scene – he corresponded with the British and Foreign Antislavery Society[14] – saw slavery as the root of the nation's moral and material malaise. His suggestion was that it be phased out, starting with the application of a law passed in 1831 granting freedom to all slaves arriving in Brazil from that point on. Other measures were to concentrate slave stocks in the rural areas and tax the urban slave-owner, prohibit foreigners from owning slaves, and ease emancipation in by setting up a manumission fund and organizing annual, State-sponsored buy-outs, and setting a deadline for the end of the practice in provinces with smaller slave stocks. Abolition was part of a modernizing package that envisioned small rural properties, immigrant labor, and an expanded road network. In his book *A escravidão no Brasil: ensaio histórico, jurídico, social* (Slavery in Brazil: a historical, juridical and social essay), published in volumes between 1864 and 1867, the Conservative MP Agostinho Marques Perdigão Malheiros, who also

copies of *Antislavery Monthly* in newsrooms in Rio, Bahia, and Pernambuco. Cuba and the United States had been featuring in parliamentary debates since the 1850s (Bethell, 1970, pp. 327 ff.; Parron, 2011, pp. 274 ff.). On the Spanish case, see Corwin (1968) and Schmidt-Nowara (1999).

[14] The society formed in the 1830s, when the British expanded their abolitionist campaign worldwide. On the relationship between Brazilians and British abolitionists, see BFASS (1867) and Rocha Penalves (2008, pp. 397 ff.).

## Elite Abolitionism

maintained ties with the British and Foreign Antislavery Society, outlined the juridically-constructed character of slavery, as opposed to any natural emanation. As early as 1863, he could be heard at the Brazilian Bar Association arguing in favor of a free womb law similar to that adopted by the Spanish. The Viscount of Jequitinhonha, a senator, went a step further, declaring that abolition was a much more complex issue in the United States, Russia, and Brazil than it was for the French, Dutch, or Portuguese – all of whom had overseas colonies – because slavery was woven into the national fabric. To avoid a civil war like that in the United States, he suggested that Brazil opt for the Russian solution: abolition in fifteen years, with no compensation to the former owners. Proposals like these circulated with a certain frequency among the elite, and they all broached the same thorny question posed by Tavares Bastos: "How do we achieve abolition without revolution?"[15]

That was a hard question to answer. Despite the decline since the demise of the slave trade, the overall number of slaves in Brazil remained high. The census of 1872 revealed 1,510,806 slaves – 15.2 percent of the Brazilian population at the time. The highest concentrations were in Minas Gerais, São Paulo, Bahia, and Rio de Janeiro, together accounting for 61 percent of the nation's captives. In Rio, there were only 1.67 free men or women to every slave.[16]

If the demographics spoke in favor of slavery, the geopolitics argued against it. In addition to their domestic antislavery campaign, the British were taking the issue to the international forums. In 1864, as the American Civil War neared its end, the British and Foreign Antislavery Society sent a petition to Pedro II calling for an end to slavery. That same January, the Emperor wrote to the Prime Minister Zacarias de Góis e Vasconcelos, saying that events in the United States "urge that we reconsider the future of slavery in Brazil, lest we incur further problems such as those related to the trading of Africans," in other words, to avoid further foreign pressure. A member of the Progressive League,[17] a reform-minded

---

[15] Cf. Bastos (1863, pp. 123, 379, 383–4); ACD, Jun. 26, 1866; Needell (2006, p. 234); Jequitinhonha (1865, p. 12). Malheiros' book is the most complete overview of Brazilian slavery-related legislation and its impasses (sometimes slaves were considered people, other times chattel).

[16] Chalhoub (2012, pp. 41, 46) reached this tally based on the 1872 census. Reis (2000, p. 91) put the figure at 1,715,000 during the 1860s.

[17] The Progressive League was a splinter group of dissident Conservative Party members that formed in 1864. Though originally intended to become a new party, the group ended up joining the Liberals instead, in 1868.

# 34                                The Last Abolition

dissident group that had broken with the Conservative Party, Zacarias' résumé included membership of the Sete de Setembro – Sociedade Ypiranga (The 7th of September – Ypiranga Society), for which, as a lawyer, he had gone to court in 1863 to demand manumissions.[18] In 1864, at the head of the government, he continued to address the issue of slavery but had little time for any real measures as his government only lasted from January to August. When Zacarias was ousted, the issue of slavery was dropped from the political agenda.

Brazil was rowing against the international tide. In 1865, the abolitionist North won in the United States, with Lincoln's assassination as a parting shot from the pro-slavery South. In July 1866, Spain put an end to the slave trade in its colonies and fast-tracked discussions on the Free Womb and Sexagenarian Law.[19] In the meantime Brazil buried its head in the sand, in slave-owning solitude.

### BORGES-STYLE ACTIVISM

Anyone who has read Raul Pompeia's novel O *Ateneu* (The Atheneum) will have a grim view of Abílio César Borges, the inspiration for the fearsome Aristarco, principal of the boarding school from which the book takes its name, a fictional take on Colegio Abílio, where Pompeia studied as a youth. Other students had fonder memories of their headmaster, one of whom recalled him as being a sensitive, communicative, and enthusiastic man, who laughed and cried in constant communion with his pupils.[20]

Borges had a bushy beard and wore a top hat, aristocratic traits tempered with a modernizing bent. He was one of the few members of the imperial elite who was willing to discuss abolition in society at a time when it was all but stalled politically. Others like him convened, between 1850 and 1860, around three antislavery poles, each with one or two societies.[21]

---

[18] One of the members of the League, José Tomás Nabuco de Araújo, had undertaken studies for a Lei de Locação de Serviços (labor law) designed to regulate free labor (Holloway, 1984; Lamounier, 1988; Alencastro, 1989). The letter from Pedro II appears in Lyra (1977, p. 162). Chalhoub (1990, p. 110) tracked down the legal proceedings brought by Zacarias in 1863.

[19] Corwin (1968, pp. 182–3).

[20] The first description is Pompeia's and the second, by a former pupil named Macedo Soares (1885, in Alves, 1942, p. 99). On Borges, see Valdez (2006, pp. 33 ff.).

[21] Nabuco (1900, pp. 246–7), Patrocínio (*Cidade do Rio*, May 5, 1889). Duque-Estrada (1918), and Moraes (1924) date the beginning of the abolitionist movement to 1879, the year Nabuco first joined Parliament and Patrocínio took the helm at the *Gazeta da Tarde*.

In Rio de Janeiro, in addition to the 7th of September – Ypiranga Society, founded in 1857, the anniversary of Independence in 1850 saw the advent of the Sociedade contra o Tráfico de Africanos e Promotora da Colonização e da Civilização dos Índios – the SCT (Society against the African Slave Trade and for the Promotion of Colonization and Indian Civilization), with 215 members, all modernizers from the local elite, like Borges. The SCT sent a project to the government defending a free womb law with compensation to the former owners, and incentives for immigration and for smallholder agriculture.[22] The SCT forged links with the British and Foreign Antislavery Society and started promoting meetings modeled on British public assemblies.[23] Brazilian abolitionism was tied to international networks from that time on.

Another abolitionist nucleus appeared in Pernambuco, where two societies were formed late in the decade. A third center emerged in Bahia in 1850, the Sociedade Libertadora 2 de Julho (the 2nd of July Liberating Society), created by students at the Medical Faculty, but with some illustrious members in its ranks, including Senator Jequitinhonha. The 2nd of July Liberating Society held Brazil's first abolitionist rally, in Salvador in 1862. The "romaria cívica" (civic rally) associated the end

---

As I argued in the introduction, although accepted by many scholars, this departure point ignores the first cycle of activism by the previous decade's pioneers. To avoid this, rather than concentrate on memoirs, the focus here goes on the creation of antislavery societies as the dawn of the movement – dating it by actions rather than narratives. The first societies emerged from the debates on the Eusébio de Queirós Law, but one can only really speak in terms of a social movement once these societies had grown sufficiently in number to constitute a collective wave, as occurred in the late 1860s. A list of abolitionist societies and their founding dates is provided in the Annexes.

[22] The SCT manifesto also proposed a census and progressive tax on slaves, a ban on foreigners owning slaves, and compulsory sale in the event of cruelty. It also vouched for a Russian-style transition (a thirty-year maximum and restriction of ex-slaves to rural areas) and "the break-up of large landholdings and subsequent increase in the number of small rural landholders," a move it felt "would make it increasingly easier to eradicate slavery in Brazil" (SCT 1852, p. 13). A land law was passed concomitantly with the slave trade ban, but was never put into force. Most SCT members were also involved with the Sociedade Auxiliadora da Indústria Nacional – SAIN (National Association for Industrial Support), which discussed ways of substituting slave labor with free labor. Kodama (2008); Moreira de Azevedo (1885).

[23] On the relationship between SCT/BFASS, see the letter by Louis Alexis Chamerovzow to Manuel da Cunha Galvão, dated May 8, 1865; BN Manuscripts 1–03, 31, 47 A. In 1852, the SCT was visited by two abolitionists from the Religious Society of Friends of Great Britain and Ireland, who delivered an antislavery address to the Emperor, bishops, parliamentarians, and ministers. The SCT distributed some 300 copies of the pamphlet (Candler and Burgess, 1854, pp. 36–7 and 43) to farmers, merchants, parliamentarians, bishops, noblemen, and other courtiers.

of slavery with that date, July 2, when the province celebrated Independence. Another Bahian society had a greater impact, and brings us back to Raul Pompeia's headmaster, Abílio Borges. Originally trained as a doctor, Borges became a model educator and philanthropist, with many decorations and titles, and a member of various prestigious institutions, such as the Historical Institute. In order to promote his pedagogical principles, he launched the newsletter O Gymnasio, and established a college for orphans in Salvador. He was well-traveled, having visited Great Britain, Belgium, Germany, France, Italy, Switzerland, Argentina, and the United States, and his experiences in these countries helped form his punishment-free method of teaching by persuasion, which he implemented at his school, Ginásio Baiano. It was a progressive school attended by the children of the provincial aristocracy. At the ceremony at the beginning the 1866 school year, he declared that the student should not be the headmaster's slave, as all

Dr. Abilio Cezar Borges.
Barão de Macahubas.

FIGURE 1.2 Abílio César Borges (1842–1891), the Baron of Macaúbas (Barão de Macaúbas), who inaugurated abolitionist civic ceremonies and networking with European abolitionists.
The Archive of the Fundação Biblioteca Nacional (National Library Foundation), Brazil. Reproduction by Jaime Acioli.

*Elite Abolitionism* 37

slavery is against nature.[24] The same parallel was used in the anti-corporal punishment campaign he launched in the press, which also attacked the flogging of slaves. Borges did not keep slaves, either at home or at his schools, and prohibited his pupils from bringing theirs with them.

A cosmopolitan with connections to the transnational abolition network, in 1860 Borges became a member of the British and Foreign Antislavery Society in London and strengthened his relations with the French Society for the Abolition of Slavery, which was fighting against the practice in the French colonies. A member of the French society floated an idea by Borges, suggesting that they co-draft a petition to the Brazilian Emperor.[25] Borges belonged to the imperial aristocracy and had direct access to the imperial family, and saw outward shaming as the best means of forcing the agenda. Borges' European alliances resulted in an abolitionist petition signed by some eminent French politicians, much admired in certain Brazilian circles, and reached the Emperor in July 1866 through the French Foreign Affairs Ministry.

The document was an embarrassment to D. Pedro, condemning his Empire as a slave land. Both flattered and worried at having received such attention from European luminaries, his reply recognized that Brazilian opinion was shifting toward abolition, but admitted that it would be a difficult issue to resolve insofar as it largely depended on the advent of an "opportune moment and form." And so this inaugural cycle of abolitionist associativism in the 1860s proved efficacious in its use of the boomerang effect: Borges' strategy of forging alliances with abolitionists abroad

---

[24] Borges (1866, pp. 48–9). The Ginásio Baiano functioned in Salvador, Bahia, between 1858 and 1870. In 1871, Borges moved to the Court in Rio, where he opened Colégio Abílio (Gondra and Sampaio, 2010, pp. 78 ff.). On the first antislavery societies in Bahia, see Fonseca (1887, pp. 244 ff.) and Graden (2006, p. 13).

[25] For more on Borges' career, see Valdez (2006, pp. 34–6, 39). Cochin refers to the petition to the Emperor in a letter dated May 17, 1866, and mentions Borges' relationship with the English abolitionist Joseph Cooper in another dated July 13, 1870 (cf. Cochin, 1926, v.2). Borges' international networking is ignored by Nabuco (1897–1899, pp. 656–61), followed by later interpreters, who note that Pedro's response to the French petition triggered the debate on abolition like a "bolt of lightning in a cloudless sky." Following Nabuco, the literature has not noticed Borges' protagonism, having described the episode as a foreign action. Actually, Borges worked for this petition. He did not sign it, since he believed a petition by foreigners would have a stronger impact. French signatories of the petition were: Guizot, Laboulaye, Andaluz, Borsiet, the Duke and Prince of Broglie, Gaumant, Léon Lavedan, Henri Martin, the Count of Montalembert, Henri Moreau, Edmond de Pressensé, Wallon, and Eugene Yung.

38                                    *The Last Abolition*

took its toll on the Brazilian political system and dragged the issue back onto the institutional agenda.[26]

In 1866, the war with Paraguay also urged reconsideration of the slavery issue. The military alliance with Argentina and Uruguay made for a damning comparison between the South American nations, with Brazil leading with feet of clay, the only slave society among nations of free people. Criticism came from "the Paraguayan *Seminário* and the *Revue des Deux Mondes*, from Pan-American congresses, and from the *porteñas'* caricatures."[27] Besides this obvious blemish on the national reputation, the front line was chewing up cadets in droves, forcing the Council of State[28] to discuss replacing the war dead with freed-slave conscripts.

One of the councillors, the Conservative Viscount of São Vicente, thought the moment propitious for discussing the issue, particularly as Spain was in the process of studying emancipation measures for its colonies. "Among the slavers, only Brazil," he said: "Brazil alone!" São Vicente had been following antislavery legislation in the Americas and Europe very keenly, and drafted no fewer than five projects for gradual abolition, all based on the SCT free-birth program launched in 1852. At the same time, the oppositionist newspaper *Opinião Liberal* was also arguing for the substitution of slave labor with a free workforce.

Yet most of the Council of State, made up of dusty elders from the days of the slave-trade ban, rallied behind another Conservative, the Viscount of Itboraí, who, though mindful of the international pressure, was more concerned about the effects of emancipation the Free Womb Law would generate among the slaves, particularly the will to revolt.

Little by little, the slavery question seeped into the political system and it proved a thorny issue indeed. The Moderating Power[29] appointed a

[26] Keck and Sikkink (1998) argue that activists with some international mobility were able to rally foreign resources and alliances behind their cause on the home front. This "boomerang effect" began in Brazil's abolitionist campaign, strengthened and built abroad, and returned in the form of pressure upon the State.

[27] The quotation is from Nabuco 1897–1899 (p. 657), for whom the Paraguay War had put the abolition debate on hold. Schulz (1994), Salles (1990, 2009), and Doratioto (2002), however, show that the war actually forced the issue, given the wholesale enlistment of ex-slaves as "patriotic volunteers" released from the yoke of slavery to replace – and die instead of – their owners at the front.

[28] The Council of State was an advisory body of the Moderating Power; its lifetime members were usually senators, ex-prime ministers, and seasoned politicians from both parties.

[29] At the time, Brazil had a four-power system inspired by the ideas of Benjamin Constant. In addition to the Executive, Legislature, and Judiciary, there was a Moderating Power exercised by the Crown. The scope of this power was cause for debate throughout the

## Elite Abolitionism

party leader to assemble a cabinet and call elections for the Lower House. However, there were two considerable counterweights to the Emperor's will: the Senate and the Council of State. As appointments to these two organs were lifelong, their members tended to be more independent than the elected representatives, and they were usually seasoned politicians with the power to make or break policy. This power was clearly demonstrated in 1867, when, with abolition a reality in the United States and underway in the Spanish colonies, and with Brazil's image in tatters on the eve of Pedro's planned visit to Europe, Zacarias, Prime Minister once again, parried the slavery issue back into the Court of the Council of State. He forwarded the projects drafted by São Vicente to the Councillors along with three key questions: whether it was time to decide in favor of emancipation and, if so, how and when it should occur. These questions were debated at successive sessions between April 1 and 9, when the Liberal Nabuco de Araújo exclaimed: "Slavery has been abolished throughout Christendom, save Brazil and Spain," though it was well underway in the latter, with its free womb and sexagenarian laws.[30]

The council was unfazed by this approximation between the Conservative São Vicente and Zacarias' Liberal frontbenchers. However, the coalition did have some effect. A committee was formed on the subject and in the speech from the throne to Parliament in 1867, Pedro urged that the theme be addressed, albeit cautiously: "respecting present ownership, and without undermining our economic mainstay, agriculture." Zacarias pressed the commission to issue its report, which was discussed between April and May. At the epicenter of these talks was a free-birth approach.[31]

Men like Abílio Borges had set this wheel in motion, but modernizers like him invested in associativism and foreign support because their arguments

---

whole Second Reign, but it included the right to make appointments to certain key posts, chiefly the Prime Minister (President of the Council of Ministers).

[30] The quotations from the Council of State, mentioned earlier, are from ACE, Nov. 5, 1886; Apr. 2–9, 1867. In addition to the free-birth law, São Vicente's projects provided for provincial emancipations; a slave registry; immediate freedom for slaves owned by religious orders; and, over the course of five years, the release of all government-owned slaves. Together, these provisions would have phased out slavery by 1890 (*A Abolição no Parliamento*, v.1 pp. 243–57). Nabuco (1897–1899, pp. 656 ff.) and Needell (2006, p. 234) affirm that Pedro encouraged São Vicente to draft these projects, though this affirmation was never made in print. On *Opinião Liberal*, see Carvalho (2007, p. 20).

[31] Cf. ACD, May 22, 1867. Zacarias left São Vicente out of the commission, since he was from the opposition party, and appointed a group of men from his own circle to the task. Cf. letters from Zacarias to Nabuco de Araújo (Nabuco, 1897–1898, pp. 721 ff.).

40 *The Last Abolition*

had largely fallen on deaf ears in the Houses of Parliament, where abolition remained the most sensitive of sensitive issues. With the Paraguay War, slavery haunted the public order and was threatening the economy. Capital derived from the slave economy had underwritten the golden age of coffee in the Paraíba Valley, fueled the country's infrastructure, built roads, made urban improvements, and drove companies and businesses. If the nation was short on manual labor, abolition sounded like self-sabotage.

The Emperor found himself facing a vast majority of the political elite against abolition and only a handful of MPs in favor. At the beginning of his reign, he had strong Conservative Party leaders to deal with, the very people who were responsible for building the institutions of the Second Reign. However, as people like Eusébio left the stage, the Emperor started hard-balling the parties, benefiting one over the other, then turning the tables, so as not to create dependence on any one group. On slavery, he oscillated between backing and opposing reforms in order to maintain the delicate balance upon which his power and the monarchy rested. And so, while he supported the emancipation championed by the Liberal Zacarias in 1867, he did not hesitate to make a complete about-turn in the face of injunctions during the Paraguay War and throw his support behind the pro-slavery Conservative Viscount of Itaboraí, who took office in 1868.

Itaboraí brought from the coffee plantations of the Paraíba Valley a dark prophecy: abolition would cause murder, insurrection, and even civil war. His government was stocked with the staunchest anti-change Conservatives he could muster, nicknamed the "Emperrados" (the Hardliners). Among these was Paulino Soares de Sousa, his nephew and political heir, the Baron of Cotegipe, and the deputy and novelist José de Alencar. The Emperor's appointment of such an ultra-conservative government in 1868 was considered an affront to the largely Liberal Lower House and caused a political crisis that shunted abolition once again onto the back burner.[32]

The crisis had an unexpected effect. In-fighting among the elites threw up numerous opportunities for all sorts of criticism against the imperial institutions. In 1869, the Liberals were publicly protesting against their government being ousted. The Tavares Bastos faction, the self-styled "Radical Liberals," took to the newspapers, clubs, public conferences,

---

[32] ACEI, Apr. 2, 1867. The 1868 crisis is usually seen as having been caused by the Paraguay War (for example, by Holanda, 1972), and considered as a crisis of the representative system, since the majority party was overthrown by the appointment of a prime minister from the opposition. However, this explanation ignores the fact that slavery was a serious flashpoint here. On the Conservative Party during the 1860s, see Mattos (1987) and Needell (2006); on the Liberals, see Carvalho (2007).

and manifestos to demand political and economic modernization and an end to slavery. The more moderate Liberals, like Zacarias, created the "Liberal Center" and issued a manifesto calling for the immediate promulgation of free-birth legislation. These skirmishes, insofar as they attested to the existence of a reform-minded faction within the political system, legitimized the public debate on slavery and signaled possible abolitionist allies within the institutions. And so, against all expectations, pro-abolition associations grew in number and strength during the pro-slavery government of Itaboraí and on the spur of Liberal agitation, with new societies springing up in Amazonas, Bahia, Ceará, Espírito Santo, Maranhão, Minas Gerais, Pernambuco, Piauí, Rio de Janeiro, Rio Grande do Sul, and São Paulo.[33]

The result was an elite abolitionism, as the membership of these groups was mostly drawn from the upper strata of Brazilian society: viscounts, barons, high-ranking public functionaries and others with access to the political parties. Modernizers – including some women – offered a platform of reforms including gradual abolition, immigration, and support for the smallholder. The modernizers had one foot in institutional politics and the other outside it, and though they were averse to radicalism, they were nonetheless a worrying prospect for a political system that had thought it best to discuss the end of the slave trade at secret sessions in 1850.

The new societies started a propaganda campaign in favor of free birth, raising funds to manumit young slaves at public ceremonies that conflated abolition with Independence. An elaborate ritual of this kind was perfected by the 7th of September Liberating Society, founded in Salvador in 1869. At the head of the society's 512 members, including fifteen women, was none other than Abílio Borges. Libertadora started putting out a fortnightly newsletter called *O Abolicionista*, which covered the international history of the abolitionist movement, with special focus on Puerto Rico and Cuba.

---

[33] The emergence of social movements depends on interaction between groups both inside and outside the political institutions. Typically, these movements form when the ruling coalition is beset by crisis, giving rise to dissident elites who are open to alliance-building with groups outside the political system, while government instability reduces the State's repressive capacity. This usually results in windows of political opportunity for outsiders (McAdam, Tarrow, and Tilly, 2001). In Brazil, the domestic crisis, allied with the changing external scenario during the 1860s, paved the way for the advent of pro-abolition social mobilization in Brazil. Other balances of power would come and go up until 1888, and will be addressed in subsequent chapters, according to this theoretical approach, as political opportunities, when favorable to abolition, and as political threats, when favorable to the pro-slavery actors.

42    *The Last Abolition*

Borges was very familiar with the British antislavery mobilization repertoire, which blended lobbying and associativism with pamphleteering, manifestos, newspapers, and public demonstrations. But he could not simply replicate the British model, as abolition in the UK and in the United States had been largely driven by the Quakers, like those who visited the SCT in the 1850s. Protestant churches had laid the organizational ground for Anglo-American abolitionism, but things were very different in Brazil. There, the Catholic Church was the official religion of the Brazilian State. The overlap between the apparatuses of church and State gave rise to civil-servant priests who not only lacked the independence to criticize such state institutions as slavery, but were actually encumbered to legitimize them. This configuration meant that Brazilian abolitionists had to find a secular arena and liturgical model for grounding its propaganda.

Borges found that arena outside Parliament, in a public space the Radical Liberals were busy politicizing: trade guilds, schools, and town halls. Civic ceremonies were held at his Ginásio Baiano on key dates like July 2 and September 7 (Independence Day). At the head of a table draped in a green cloth with the words "trampling ignorance and vice underfoot" embroidered in gold, he exhorted patriotism. Teachers delivered speeches while the pupils, drawn from the Bahian elite, sang and recited verse. Borges brought the rite and its practitioners to the abolition movement. On September 7, 1869, the 7th of September Liberating Society held a bazaar at which it auctioned off donated objects to raise money to manumit slave women and their children. This was followed by a civic ceremony at which they delivered the letters of manumission. As they could not use the church, unlike their North-American counterparts, they used the theater instead. At the session on November 1, 1869, there was music and poetry:

> *Captive, do not despair!*
> *With untroubled head held high*
> *Arise and brighten the horizon*
> *of this your most unhappy fate!*
> *So you weep!...yet if in this here tear*
> *That swells and trickles down your face*
> *There any dishonor be, it is not yours...*
> *But belongs to our entire nation!*[34]

---

[34] The poem, entitled "O cativo" (The Captive), is by Antônio Augusto de Mendonça, in Fonseca (1887, pp. 314–15).

# Elite Abolitionism
43

Such romantic gestures, Borges intuited, had the power to rouse, and he put the staff and students of the Ginásio Baiano to precisely that task. Chief amongst these was Antônio de Castro Alves, whom Borges' *O Abolicionista* newspaper lauded as "Poet of Slaves." Alves, enrolled at the Faculty of Law in São Paulo, took the label seriously and at a Liberals' soirée of 1868, he recited his poetry of protest, his "Tragédia no lar" (Tragedy at Home), which was a piece of free-birth propaganda that gave voice to a slave mother:

> *– Slave mother, give me your child! . . .*
> *Said the planter, and smiled . . .*
> *– Forgive me, master! Forgive me, my infant sleeps. . .*
> *I put him down just now, the innocent thing,*
> *Who hasn't even an inkling*
> *of his fate. . .*
> *– Give him here, he's mine to sell! . . .*
> *– Master, no, mercy no . . .*
> *For mercy's sake, murder me! Oh, it cannot be*
> *That you would rob me of my life's only blessing . . .*
> *– Silence, heifer! Come, gentlemen,*
> *you may inspect the chattel. . .*
> *And the mother sobbing at the merchants' feet*
> *could but weep and entreat:*
> *– Oh masters, were it not hell enough*
> *to have neither homeland nor home . . .*
> *Leave to a mother her infant son,*
> *Some love to temper the dolor . . .*
> *But they yanked the babe from its cradle*
> *as it whimpered and clutched the air in vain!*
> *And in an instant all was changed. I have seen*
> *the jaguar roar in the jungle . . .*
> *and thus the slavemother growled and seethed,*
> *crouched and fearless sprang*
> *As the band of slavers*
> *shrank before her fury*
> *– Not another step, ye cowards!*
> *Not one more step, blackguards!*
> *Where others may steal purses,*
> *Thieves ye are of hearts!. . .*

The slave woman's appeals as she implores for her son are the poet's own entreaties to the audience:

*Reader, if you feel no disdain*
*To see the slaveshacks taken down . . .*
*Perhaps bleed a little pity,*
*Perhaps bleed a little remorse? . . .*

# 44                          *The Last Abolition*

Abolitionism found its stage in the public, lay space of the theater, and its propaganda came steeped in the arts, which took up the role religion had assumed in the Anglo-American cause. Abílio Borges' civic ceremonies were rituals that dramatized slavery and plucked at heartstrings, proclaiming emancipation the new Independence. One hundred and ninety-one manumission letters were delivered at these ceremonies between 1869 and 1871.[35] The result was a peculiar style of activism grounded in the dyad associativism/civic ceremonies.

This style was diffused through certain social networks – teacher/student, coworkers, friendship, kinship, *compadrio*. Borges may have been the most successful of the longstanding pioneers in the role of intergenerational broker, but he was not the only one. These men handed down their techniques to a new generation, ensuring that the campaign was carried forward and continued to expand in public space. For Borges, elite activism had to trickle down and spread out. *O Abolicionista* argued in favor of a switch from the philanthropic practice of buying slaves' freedom to a more broad-based mobilizing campaign: "... we have to work to ensure that the abolitionist movement circulates and deepens across the Empire, so that conviction and enthusiasm may take root in hearts and minds; that the whole nation may proclaim, loud and clear, the urgent need to abolish slavery."[36]

### REBOUÇAS-STYLE ACTIVISM

André Rebouças' diaries were packed with operas and blueprints: by day, building site and measuring tape; by night, quavers and falsettos. However, from 1868 onwards, a new issue began to bury all the others,

---

[35] The data for Bahia is from Caires (2009, p. 5). On the absence of the Catholic church in the abolitionist struggle, see Conrad (1975, p. xvi). In 1862, to underscore the lay character of the initiative, the medical students made a point of calling their street rallies "civic processions," so as not to be confused with religious processions. By "style of activism" I mean relatively stable arrangements of aesthetic codes (body marks, clothing, colors, etc.), political symbols (signs of belonging to movements, parties and groups), dominant political performances (marching, lobbying, etc.) and preferential organization techniques intertwined, which shape the self-presentation of protesters through a demonstration. They are loose bundles, but immediately recognizable and adaptable to different situations and local contexts.

[36] *O Abolicionista*, April 1871. Other intergenerational brokers were José Alves Branco Muniz Barreto and Nicolau Joaquim Moreira, from the SCT, who were in the Central Emancipatory Association in 1880, and Jerônimo Sodré, from the 2nd of July Liberating Society in Bahia, who relaunched the issue in the Lower House in 1879.

*Elite Abolitionism* 45

slavery. During Zacarias' third government, when the issue was making it onto the institutional agenda, Rebouças took up the abolitionist cause.

His construction work put him in close contact with the Society against the African Slave Trade and for the Promotion of Colonization and Indian Civilization (SCT) and Tavares Bastos, his partner in the Docks Company. This dual involvement landed him with a threefold agenda: small properties, immigration, and transport expansion.[37] Rebouças was handed the baton by older modernizers, but when he decided to commit to abolitionism, he figured that, besides Borges' style of activism, which favored association-building, rallying of international support (boomerang effect), and civic ceremonies, it would also be necessary to explore institutional networks. So he transferred into politics what had always been his modus operandi in business, lobbying.

If his experience with railroad contracts had shown him anything it was that crucial deliberations depend upon the government's hard core, which can be pressured, but never ignored. He saw two interconnected challenges ahead: persuading society, and cajoling the State. So he turned to his vast interpersonal network, a vital asset for court life, in order to bend the ear of the authorities and build bridges between abolitionist organizations and the government. For the geometrician, logic dictated taking a straight line to the center: to the Emperor, to the Prime Minister, and to the husband of the heiress to the throne, the Count D'Eu.

Count D'Eu took over the government of a devastated post-war Paraguay in 1869, and abolished slavery there. The British and Foreign Antislavery Society availed of the moment to send a new petition to D. Pedro, followed, a year later, by another, addressed to the Count. Rebouças, who had access to the imperial household, saw the effect this external conjuncture was having on the Emperor: in May 1869, he heard the monarch say that Brazil was now an exception among civilized nations and that "something had to be done" about emancipation.[38]

With his multiple levées, Rebouças had become something of a broker between the social elite, court society, and the political system. He had the skills and the connections, as he would later recall, saying "in 1870 and 1871, I was the number-one entrepreneur in Rio de Janeiro." To consolidate this bridge between high society's abolitionists and institutions, in April 1870 he drew up plans for an Associação Central Protetora dos

---

[37] Rebouças was introduced to the SCT by Nicolau Joaquim Moreira. DNAAR, May 8 and 31, 1871, 2 March 1868.

[38] DNAAR, May 9, 1869. The petition is transcribed in Rocha Penalves (2008, pp. 397 ff.).

Emancipados (the Central Association for the Protection of Freed Slaves). At a preparatory session, it was discussed whether or not the society should devote itself to freeing slaves through a manumissions fund. Rebouças took a bill of law along these very lines to the Prime Minister, the anti-abolitionist Itaboraí. Rebouças the engineer and businessman struck up a friendship with the viscount, a fellow math buff. Few men could have been more different, yet their mutual appreciation was sincere. Itaboraí referred to him as "my Englishman."[39]

Fondness between the two men, however, did not guarantee a smooth path to abolition. Itaboraí was a viscount in his seventies and he planned to see out his days without further political headaches. His "Englishman" was obsessed with abolition, his default mode for all his projects, and he reminded the viscount that, when it came to "serving Brazil and Liberty," he "had no qualms and boundless energy." As such he went to see the prince consort, and came away with a vague promise. Hounded from all sides, Itaboraí could forestall that headache no longer: he accepted the plan for the Central Association for the Protection of Freed Slaves, presided over by the Count D'Eu, and promised Rebouças that he would consult the ministry on the issue. Rebouças set about dismantling the Prime Minister's resistance in the same way he arranged his appointments, by knocking on doors. He spoke to deputies, circulated in the back rooms of Parliament, pitching his project to whoever would listen. This was Rebouças' style of activism: lobbying and brokerage. He wanted to lay the groundwork of minimal consensus between court society, the political institutions, and the social elite, and thus garner the support the abolitionists lacked.

His method was efficient in setting an agenda, but it failed to commute access into influence. Itaboraí left things as they stood. The Count D'Eu, criticized from all sides for having strong-armed abolition in Paraguay, was not the committed enthusiast Rebouças had supposed. He recognized that they were both good bills and institutional structures, but took matters no further. As the opposition was hardening, in June 1870 Rebouças reacted by practicing what he preached, freeing Roque, Júlia, and Emília, his last three house slaves.[40]

---

[39] Letter from André Rebouças to Joaquim Nabuco, June 7, 1891. DNAAR, April 11, 15 and 19, 1870; Aug. 11, 1868.

[40] Rebouças' liaising is noted in his diary (for example, DNAAR, May 15, Apr. 26, May 9, 1870), as are the manumissions (DNAAR, Jun. 24, 1870).

## FROM VISCOUNT TO VISCOUNT

Worse than Rebouças' constant agitation on the home front was the lambasting the Viscount of Itaboraí was receiving from abroad. In 1869, the International Abolitionist Association in Paris petitioned him and the *Antislavery Reporter* published a letter from Senator Nabuco de Araújo in defense of any emancipationist measure in Brazil. The North-American abolitionists had contacted the senator, perhaps encouraged by the imminent end to slavery in Alaska, which the United States purchased from Russia in 1867, and where abolition was passed in 1870.[41]

1870 also saw the end to litigation in Paraguay, hitherto a handy excuse for putting off tackling the slavery issue. But the Council of State and Parliament kept their silence on the matter. Nothing was happening, and, if Itaboraí and his right-hand man Paulino Soares de Sousa had anything to do with it, nothing would. The Emperor wrote to his Prime Minister saying that it would be a mistake for the throne to avoid an issue "foremost in everyone's minds save the government." That said, D. Pedro would not declare himself an abolitionist, rather, as he explained before a meeting of his government, he "would resist to the last that it should go beyond the free womb." The Baron of Cotegipe, then a minister himself, reminded the Sovereign that the Conservatives had only accepted their ministerial posts on condition that the issue not be raised at all, and, indeed, the speech from the throne opening the 1870 Parliament made no mention of abolition.[42]

In the Lower House, however, a Conservative dissidence demanded that the government take a stance on the free womb and create a Special Emancipation Commission to discuss the matter – the very group the Zacarias government had failed to get off the ground just years earlier. Rebouças was in the galleries: "I watched the proceedings with the greatest emotion." He listened as a deputy questioned the Viscount of Itaboraí and heard his reply, the tenor of which, he was happy to say, was precisely as they had agreed:[43] he would not obstruct the creation of the five-member commission. Rebouças sought these commissioners out directly. The episode had revealed a rift in the Conservative Party, with a

---

[41] Bethell and Carvalho (2008); Nabuco (1897–1899, p. 776).

[42] Letter from Pedro II to the Viscount of Itaboraí (May 1, 1870), and those of Cotegipe to his allies (May 5 and 6, 1870) are in Pinho (1933, pp. 133, 136–7).

[43] Cf. letter from Cotegipe to Paranhos, May 15, 1870 (Pinho, 1937, p. 151) and Monteiro (1982, pp. 17–18). The quote from Rebouças is from DNAAR, May 14, 1870.

48 *The Last Abolition*

modernizing faction supporting the projects of São Vicente against Itoboraí's Hardliners.

This split highlighted the Liberal position in favor of the Special Emancipation Commission when the project was submitted to Parliament in August. Zacarias and eight other Liberal Party stalwarts proposed a public manumissions fund to buy freedom certificates. One of the party leaders expressed his general dismay at the government's dithering in the face of abolitionist advances on the international and domestic fronts: "The gravest danger presented by the cause is propaganda ... Where little serves today, tomorrow a great deal will not suffice ... those who would rather not have to contend with the economic inconveniences experienced by the English and French Antilles risk having to endure the horrors of Santo Domingo."[44] It was a duel between political and economic *ratios*.

Various proposals were circulating among the institutions and in pamphlets, and many of those insisted on following the Spanish, who, in July 1870, approved the Moret Law, or *vientres libres* law, for Cuba and Puerto Rico. The measure freed all children born from slave mothers thereafter and any slaves over the age of sixty, with compensation paid to their owners.[45] The Spanish measure backed Brazil into a wall, though still the Conservative Hardliners refused to budge, with Paulino Soares de Sousa and José de Alencar taking to the tribune against the free womb idea. Faced with a divided party, Itoboraí preferred to throw in the towel rather than give ground, and stood down.

With the political system split down the middle, in late 1870 D. Pedro II appointed São Vicente, the author of the free womb bill discussed in the Lower House in 1866, his new Prime Minister. Rebouças, a reader of Benjamin Franklin, president of the Pennsylvanian Abolition Society, knew that "time is money," so he took himself off to see the new Prime Minister with a wad of projects under his arm. However, São Vicente was no Itoboraí, and no politician worth his salt agreed to join the government of such an irresolute leader.[46] Without party backing, and no support other than from the Moderating Power, his initiatives did nothing but deepen the schism among the Conservative Hardliners and reformers.

---

[44] Zacarias' group included Nabuco de Araújo, Paranaguá, Otaviano, Sinimbu, Chichorro da Gama, and Dias Carvalho, who submitted the project on September 19 as an addendum to the budget. The full document is in Nabuco (1897–1899, pp. 802–3). On the project's institutional processing, see Needell (2006, pp. 264–5 ff.). Nabuco de Araújo's comments are in ASI, Jul. 12, 1870.

[45] Corwin (1968).     [46] DNAAR, Oct. 2, 1870; Nabuco (1897–1899, pp. 821–2).

His government never found its way out of political limbo and barely made it to the end of the parliamentary recess.

## AT THE THEATER

Always well if soberly attired, Rebouças wore his tail coat on that December 2, 1870, a Friday. An opera buff, he, like the rest of the Empire's social elite, was excited to see Carlos Gomes, the new national prodigy, protégé of the Emperor and the toast of Milan, stage his grand opera *O Guarani* for the first time. The Teatro Lírico Provisório (Provisional Opera Theater) was bursting at the seams with aristocrats in full pomp, assembled at the gala performance to celebrate Pedro II's forty-fifth birthday, which was also the thirtieth anniversary of his reign and the end of the Paraguay War.[47] The Empire was in jubilant mood.

With the dynasty duly installed in the boxes, the orchestra hushed the murmur with the National Anthem. The curtain rose. Courtly dames, starched statesmen, and party leaders were introduced to the musical adaptation of the novel by José de Alencar, a former Minister of Justice and member of the Conservative Party. The orchestra shook the theater, with an Italian band and dancers dressed up as Aimoré Indians. The stage filled with the founding myth of the Second Reign, the love story of a girl of European origin and an Indian brave as noble as any aristocrat. There were Spanish and Portuguese adventurers, noblemen, tribal chiefs, Cecilia and Peri, but nobody with Rebouças' skin color.[48]

The opera was set at the beginning of colonization, before the nation was divided into masters and slaves, before the wholesale installation of the mother of all institutions, the cogs of the imperial machine – slavery, fundamental and tacit. Africans were absent from the opera's plot, while their descendants were the stagehands, the wardrobe women, the carriage drivers, the collar starchers, the shoe-shiners, the cooks and waiters of every morsel and sip that passed between the audience's lips, but *O Guarani* had nothing whatsoever to say about them.

The leaders of the two main parties, however, could avoid them no longer. After the Moret Law, which put an end to slavery in Cuba, Brazil oscillated between freeing its slaves or finding itself the last slaveholding society in the civilized world. For the tiny modernizing faction of the imperial elite, it was time to quicken the step toward emancipation. One

---

[47] EDEAR, Dec. 9, 1870.
[48] Letter from André Rebouças to Joaquim Nabuco, AMI, Nov. 21, 1896; Scalvini (1870).

## The Last Abolition

of those who subscribed to the abolitionist view was Manuel de Sousa Dantas, a former cabinet minister under Zacarias and then-president of the Libertadora, in Bahia, having succeeded Abílio Borges after the latter moved to Court.[49] But they were up against a whole slave-owning society, defended tooth and nail by the nephew and political heir of Itaboraí, Paulino Soares de Sousa, a Conservative every bit as refined as he was obstinate in his advocacy of slavery.

At the Teatro Lírico, Rebouças would certainly have heard the news that the Conservatives and Liberals were about to be joined by a third political party. Many Radical Liberals had abandoned the monarchy and were set to unveil, the very next day, their Republican manifesto. As a nod to the emancipatory measures in Cuba, and in order to placate the rebellious Liberals and contain the republican upswell, D. Pedro II decided to call upon a third viscount, Rio Branco, to lead the beleaguered government in tackling the emancipation issue. Loquacious and adroit, Rebouças would have spoken to them all as he worked the corridors, theater boxes, and anterooms of power. Never giving up on the prince consort, he enlisted followers to his emancipationist society.[50] He politicked and harnessed the power of spectacle.

The maestro received a standing ovation. From the boxes, ladies threw down flowers, while gentlemen bellowed "bravo" and "bravissimo." Carlos Gomes returned to the stage no fewer than eight times, and after the last bow was carried off into the gardens on a sea of shoulders. Rebouças applauded wildly,[51] right in the thick of it, both inside the theater and outside in the streets, the stage of choice for the movement of which he was to be the master engineer. How many times thereafter would he and José do Patrocínio organize concerts followed by street rallies? But instead of a Guarani Indian tale, they would stage an African tragedy.

In 1870, maestro, Emperor, parties, and courtiers celebrated the monarchy, the civilization it instilled, and the nation it imagined, but they would soon embark on a far more uncertain plot. United in applause for *O Guarani*, the Empire was on the brink of collapse. In the name of compassion, rights, and progress, those who stood with Rebouças demanded an end to slavery. Paulino and his cohorts would resist to the last, claiming that abolition would derail the imperial order, economy,

---

[49] Valdez (2006, p. 40).    [50] DNAAR, Apr. 11, 1870; EDEAR, Dec. 11, 1870.
[51] On the performance and Rebouças' reaction, see DRJ, Dec. 4, 1870, in Faria (1982, pp. 59–60) and Taunay (1916, p. 63).

*Elite Abolitionism* 51

political system, aristocratic society, and all the splendor so lavishly paraded on that gala night.

José de Alencar agreed. Freeing the slavewoman's womb as the Spanish had done in Cuba would be as bad as the librettist's tampering with his own *Guarani*: changing the plot of the opera would have spoiled his masterwork. The novel had a happy ending, with the villains shipwrecked and Ceci and Peri safe and sound to father a nation. In the theater, the technical impossibility of staging a storm called for an alternative denouement, with exploding barrels of gunpowder reducing the aristocrats' castle to a heap of rubble.[52] The blast was an omen for events offstage. That December would make way for 1871, the year when slavery, the imperial time-bomb, would emerge from backstage to take the play by storm.

---

[52] Alencar complained (in Faria, 1982, p. 60): "Gomes turned my *Guarani* into a nameless hotchpotch full of nonsense."

# 2

# Pro-Slavery Rhetoric

### IN THE NAME OF ORDER

Beard neatly trimmed, cashmere shirt snug on his tall, lithe frame, Paulino Soares de Sousa was ready for combat, a new experience in a life of steady ascent. Born on Tapacora farm in the Rio de Janeiro countryside and educated in the big-league schools, de Sousa graduated from Pedro II College with honors and a love of the classics. He left the São Paulo Law Faculty in 1855 with all the capacities one would expect of an imperial statesman's first-born son, schooled in setting up newspapers and composing speeches and political alliances. Politics was the air he breathed at home. His father was the Viscount of Uruguay, one of the Second Reign's champions of centralized political institutions. He was also a relative of another high-ranking Conservative, the Viscount of Itaboraí. This illustrious lineage paved the way to some top-tier posts in the Second Reign, starting in the diplomatic corps: Vienna, Paris, and London. Paulino became a knight of the Turkish Order of Medjidie, whose seven-pointed medallion bore a motto which he upheld: loyalty, zeal, and dedication. In 1856, in Rome, shortly after kneeling before the Pope, he received the news that he had just been elected, in absentia, to the post of Conservative Party MP for the third district of the province of Rio de Janeiro. He was only twenty-two.

Paulino Soares de Sousa followed in the footsteps of a father who was an exceptional political operator. "I learned from a young age to think on my feet and gauge the effects of my actions on public life," he would write to his electorate, courting and nurturing a support base that would earn him provincial party leadership. Running against the government in 1881, his was the largest haul of votes in the country. He was appointed minister and later Speaker of the Lower House, and in the future, he would become senator, State councillor and Speaker of the Senate. "In my chosen field, the Lord has given me everything one could possibly expect," he reflected, and all with pomp and ceremony. According to the Baron of Cotegipe, if his father could dance on a fully-laid table without breaking a single glass, his son could pull off the same feat blindfolded.

After his father's death, in 1866, Paulino became melancholic. His refuge was his wife Maria Amélia: "In my soul's greatest pains, my consolation, for which I thank the Lord, is your love, the sole tie that binds me to life." This marriage brought him wealth, five children, and the status of big landowner in Cantagalo, in the Paraíba River Valley.

Paulino straddled both halves of the Empire. From his father and uncle, Itaboraí, he inherited his political realism and an unwavering belief in the effectiveness of imperial institutions Paulino also married into the world of the major landowner and slaveholder. He moved effortlessly between both environments, Court and field, Parliament and plantation, welding his Conservative political inheritance with the slave-owning dowry of his wife, Maria Amélia, his bridge between civilization and the coffee fields.

Paulino enjoyed all the refinements of the imperial aristocratic lifestyle, which were all paid for off the backs of slaves. In uniform, manning the door, the bedrooms, darning and mending, running errands, cleaning latrines, house slaves were the invisible hands that held together the wealthy townhouses and rural estates, as they were on the plantations, plowing and picking; they were the Atlases on whose shoulders rested the world of the planters, middlemen, bankers, and traders. They were the cogs behind the luxury on Rua do Ouvidor (the most important street in Rio de Janeiro) and what drove the State machine. And the social cliques and circles, the literati, high society depended upon them one and all. Slaves were the base of the social pyramid that supported the propertied and the moneyed, rippling outwards in concentric circles like water disturbed by a dropped stone. In manner, actions, and thought, Paulino was the very embodiment of the elite slaveowner way of living and thinking. To the manor born, nothing about him spoke of brutality or greed, perversion or maliciousness. He was cultured beyond reproach, loved his wife and his Latin, believed in God, in the Empire, and in the right to own slaves.

Only a fool, he figured, could possibly buck against the natural order of things, an order that existed not on the whim of the few, but for the necessity of all. Without slavery there would be no coffee, no finances, no aristocracy or monarchy, no order and certainly no peace.

54                    *The Last Abolition*

On Wednesday, August 23, 1871, he headed to Parliament to oppose Rio Branco's bill to free Afro-descendants born from the wombs of slaves. The carriage driver who would take him to Parliament was one such fellow.[1]


## STATE ABOLITIONISM

José Maria Paranhos, from the Conservative Party, became Prime Minister on March 7, 1871. Paranhos was an inveterate smoker of no fewer than thirty Cuban cigars a day, which helped to defuse the many tensions that became his reality from that time on. From a decadent merchant family in Bahia, Paranhos graduated from the Military Academy, then became an MP for the Liberal Party. He defected to the Conservatives in the 1850s, with the blessing of the Marquis of Paranaguá, the most important political leader of the time, who launched his career by sending him to the Prata River Basin, where Brazil was embroiled in reams of litigation.

Thanks to his activities in the Prata, Paranhos became the Viscount of Rio Branco, handling numerous disputes with the southern border states as special envoy and minister of foreign affairs. He served during the Paraguay War and helped avoid a second war by negotiating a diplomatic resolution with Uruguay. The Liberal government opposed the settlement, but Paranhos stood his ground over the course of eight long hours at the Senate tribune, from which he emerged triumphant.[2] He organized the provisional government in Paraguay in 1869 and, upon his return to Court in 1870, received the title of viscount, which sat well with his character and prodigious sideburns.

Rio Branco was crystal clear on the issue of slavery. While in "Letters to an Absent Friend," his column in the *Jornal do Commercio*, he criticized English sanctions against Brazil during the slave traffic crisis of the 1850s and sided against the immediate measures taken by the Council of State in the 1860s, the time he spent on the River Prata changed his mind: contact with Brazil's southern neighbors impressed upon him that "the continuation of this odious regime in Brazil shames and humiliates us before the eyes of the world." With the end of the Paraguay War

---

[1] Sources on this are Soares de Sousa, in ACD, June 5, 1882; letters from Paulino S. de Sousa to Maria Amélia, Feb. 5, 1877, Nov. 2, 1866, in Soares de Souza (1923); the Baron of Cotegipe, in Soares de Souza (1923, p. 111). On Paulino's early career, see Needell (2006, pp. 225 ff.).

[2] On Rio Branco's personality and habits, see Besouchet (1985, pp. 28, 51 and 69). On his early career and activities in the Prata region, see Doratioto (2013, pp. 266 ff., 291).

approaching in 1869, he joined forces with the Count D'Eu to abolish slavery there. Justifying his actions before the Senate in 1870, he declared: "As the issue now stands [in Brazil], it certainly needs to be resolved."[3]

Rio Branco became Prime Minister a short time later, "at that point in one's political career when one can no longer be content to play a supporting role." With a love of mathematics, experience at the negotiating table, a modernizing streak, and the proverbial cold blood, Rio Branco became a captain capable of steering his ship across the rolling seas that had shipwrecked São Vicente. In the words of his admirer, Joaquim Nabuco: "All the rest were amateurs; he alone was a professional."

Rio Branco was a reformer who knew the kind of ground he was treading on, and his government, the most successful and longest-lasting of the Second Reign, made change its hallmark, with proposals for major alterations to the electoral system, the judiciary, the National Guard, and public education. Cognizant of an international scene predicated upon free labor and of a domestic front rife with abolitionist associativism, he wagered that the reform of this basilar institution was best undertaken by the Conservatives, as the suppression of the Atlantic slave trade had been.

The Baron of Cotegipe and Paulino Soares de Sousa, two other emerging Conservative Party leaders, disagreed, and pressed to prioritize electoral reform. However, as the pair were on bad terms, Rio Branco had room to maneuver, and he pressured Cotegipe for parliamentary support for the free womb bill, promising to ensure present slave holdings whilst bowing to "overwhelming public opinion" which saw the status quo as impossible to sustain. In exchange, Rio Branco offered a ministry, but Cotegipe had his sights on another position altogether, a plenipotentiary ministry in the Prata. Comfortably tucked away down South, he would neither support nor oppose the bill. With other pro-slavery stalwarts, Rio Branco adopted containment strategies.[4] He reduced vetoes, but could only stock his government with young and untested deputies, where the usual was to have more seasoned senators.

---

[3] ACD, Jul. 14, 1871; ASI, Jul. 6, 1870. Earlier, in 1867, Rio Branco had said to the Council of State: "As for the present state of Brazilian society, whether we look at it from the political and moral side, or we consider it from the perspective of economic interests, no precipitated action is incited on the social level, quite the contrary, it makes one shrink away in terror of it" (ACEI, Apr. 2, 1867).

[4] Letter from Rio Branco to the Baron of Cotegipe, Mar. 6, 1871, in Needell, 2006, p. 279. Rio Branco made an ambassador of Saião Lobato, whom Rebouças classified as a "slavocrat."

When Rio Branco's government was only two months old and the abolitionist project would start to be discussed in the Parliament, the Emperor took a year's leave in Europe. Conservative deputies Andrade Figueira and José de Alencar condemned the decision and one Liberal MP brayed that the Emperor had left the throne in the hands of an inexperienced Princess in the throes of the Empire's most fundamental reform, "throwing her into the storm without strong government to cling to. But the truth is, he [Pedro II] has no idea what he wants and is, when all is said and done, and despite his many personal qualities, very much the political fool."[5] This reaction made clear that the Prime Minister Rio Branco would weather the certain hell of resistance.

The abolitionist André Rebouças used his social and political connections to access and try to influence Rio Branco, a man he knew from the National Association for Industrial Support (SAIN) and from the Polytechnic School, and in whom he saw a cold-blooded fighter with permanently clenched fists, ready to deliver his punches.[6] This was a fitting posture under the circumstances, as the debate surrounding the first antislavery measure since the end of the Atlantic slave trade was brewing up a war.

Rio Branco sent the ten-article bill to the Lower House on May 12, 1871. Its backbone was the proposals São Vicente had submitted to the Council of State in 1866, with some modifications by the special commission of 1870. The Prime Minister outlined the main tenets before Parliament. In the molds of the Spanish Moret Law, the first and most important of the articles proposed a free womb arrangement with apprenticeship. Any children born to slave mothers after 1871 would remain under the master's tutelage for a period of eight years, after which he could hand the child over to the State in return for compensation, or keep the youth under compulsory service until the age of twenty-one. In addition, there would be three different routes to freedom. One was *peculio*, the slave's right to save up money for self-purchase – with or without the master's consent. Another was right of redemption, when a slave's freedom was bought by a third party – as the abolitionist societies had been doing. The third was an Emancipation Fund replenished with proceeds from lotteries and taxes on slave stocks, and which raffled a

---

[5] Alencar (1871). Letter from Francisco Otaviano to the Baron of Penedo, May 10, 1871. Nabuco de Araújo (in Nabuco, 1897–1899, p. 834) added: "It is deplorable to think that the Emperor would leave us under the present circumstances ... The young Princess's fledgling government will be the toughest test of the Second Reign."

[6] DNAAR, April 1865.

# Pro-Slavery Rhetoric

certain number of manumissions annually.[7] Of immediate effect would be slave registration and censusing, the release of State-owned slaves, and a ban on extreme forms of corporal punishment.

The project was the promise of gradual, long-term change, and Rio Branco expected objections from the abolitionists. "I never imagined there would be such apprehension and vitriol from those more inclined to maintain the status quo than change it," he remarked.[8]

## PRO-SLAVERY RHETORIC

In spearheading the backlash against Rio Branco's bill, Paulino Soares de Sousa was able to count on the best possible ally: common sense. Arguing in slavery's favor was its longevity as naturalized, sedimented inequality, a given in everyday life and on the national landscape. The master/slave hierarchy on which slavery rested was every bit as legitimate as that which put the elders in charge of the young, and the aristocrats in charge of the commoners.

David Brion Davis identified three main strains of justification for Western slavery. The first derived from Aristotle, who considered the master's supremacy over his slaves a matter of natural order. The second came from such Enlightenment thinkers as Voltaire, Kant, and Hume, for whom whites were simply superior to blacks. The third was rooted in religion and pitted sin versus virtue, focusing more specifically on God's decision to punish the fratricidal Cain by marking him and all his kin with a black complexion, the stain of his crime. These three lines of reasoning formed pro-slavery's moral repertoire in the Western world, a set of interpretive schemata that legitimized slaveholding in English, French, Portuguese, and Spanish colonies,[9] and which Paulino's cohort took recourse to in their opposition to the Free Womb Law.

This repertoire of ways of dealing with slavery had to be adapted to the local context. The mark of Cain made less of an impact on Brazilians

---

[7] ACD, May 14, 1871. Tutelage until the age of eight, extendable to twenty-one, is the main change in relation to the Special Commission project (Nabuco, 1897–1899, pp. 1227–49). ACD, May 14, 1871; Pereira da Silva (1895–1896, p. 423).

[8] ACD, Jul. 31, 1871.

[9] According to Temperley (1981, p. 29), "... slavery [up until the eighteenth century] was accepted with that fatalism which men commonly reserve for aspects of nature ... To argue against slavery was to argue against the facts of life." Davis (1992, pp. 68 ff.; 2006, pp. 54 ff.) mentions another biblical justification often brought into play, namely the conflict between Ham and Noah, which culminates in the latter cursing his grandson Canaan: "Let him be to his brothers as the lowliest of slaves!" The later overlap between the Canaanites and the tribes of sub-Saharan Africa tarred them with sin, blackness and slavery.

58                     *The Last Abolition*

than it did among the North-Americans and Hispanics. Catholics like Fr. Antônio Vieira justified bondage as a form of Christian charity, as a means of saving souls from damnation. The Conservative MP José de Alencar took the same approach, arguing that captivity was good for the slave, as it saved him from constant tribal warfare and African fetishism. Slavery as civilizing was corroborated as "the soundest doctrine of the Gospels." During a parliamentary debate on the Free Womb Law in 1871, Alencar quoted the Bible to support his arguments: "Slaves, obey your earthly masters."[10]

Racialization, a cornerstone of the US slave system, was mitigated in Brazil. In an aristocratic society, stratification based on social status is the very assurance of order, so no racial angle was really required in the Brazilian Empire, even if one was nonetheless ingrained. José de Alencar's novel *O tronco do ipê* (The Trunk of the Trumpet Tree), published during the free womb debate, featured an unflattering personification in the form of the old African father, Benedito, whom he describes as "a big black ape," a sorcerer in league with the Devil, who danced the "most infernal samba" beneath the trumpet tree to the sound of "demoniacal drums." Atavistic and satanical, racial damnation and cultural inferiority (witch-craft) were a cocktail that barbarized black people. Hence he was written out of another Alencar novel, *O Guarani*, which, like many other early Second-Reign novels, poems, and paintings, reduced the nation to an imaginary white community of aristocrats, Portuguese, and autochthons, without a hint of blackness.

Unlike in the United States, where pro-slavery rhetoric was explicit, in Brazil, the institution was rendered invisible, integrated, and natural. As in the Spanish rhetoric, the cliché of the exceptional nature of slavery in sub-Equatorial America also thrived, grounded in the myth of master-slave cordiality, a patriarchalism that not only buffered conflict, but was actually superior to the European social organization, at least to the mind of another character in *O tronco do ipê,* a councillor who bragged: "I wish … that the English philanthropists were here to witness this spectacle [the slaves' Christmas festivities] and the formal debunking of

---

[10] On Vieira, see Vainfas (2011); Alencastro (2000, p. 157). The citation is from Alencar, Jul. 20, 1867, p. 77. Another example of the use of the Bible to thematize slavery is found in the epic poem *Colombo* (1866), by Manuel Araújo de Porto Alegre: "When Abel's blood stained the ground/ At his brother's feet sprouted death/ And injustice spread across the earth/ Born from the race of Cam, the accursed race./ And with it came slavery; thence the slave […]." On the Spanish debate, see Corwin (1968, pp. 164 ff.).

their declamations, and to see that the London proletariat cannot boast the trimmings and entertainments of our slaves."[11]

In another work by Alencar, the trope of the benevolence of patriarchal slavery finds a counterweight in the figure of the ingrate slave. In the play *O demônio familiar* (The House Devil) the upstart Pedro takes the lead role in a comedy of errors. Taken in by his personable owners, Pedro turns out to be a "venomous reptile" intent on sowing the seeds of discord, although the patriarchal family ultimately prevails and the slave is given his just desserts. Much worse than a lashing, the boy's punishment is to be jettisoned from patriarchal protection. Liberty is meted out like chastisement: "I shall fix him well enough. I grant him majority and return him to society; though expelled henceforth from my family home, the doors to which shall be closed to him forevermore. (TO PEDRO) Take them: these are your manumission papers. Freedom shall be your punishment from this day on."

Alencar the Conservative Party member outlived Alencar the novelist. His *Cartas de Erasmo* (Letters of Erasmus) to the Emperor, written between 1867 and 1868, when the theme was heating up at the Council of State, painted slavery as a natural institution, typical of fledgling societies and crucial to Brazilian state-building, its colonization, and occupation: "Without African slavery and the Atlantic slave trade, America would still be a vast desert. ... the African race entered this continent and today composes much of its population ... That itself is one of the beneficial results of the slave trade."

This convoluted defense of slavery sufficed when attacks against it were still rare and tepid. During the free womb debates, Paulino recognized the strategic value of silence: "The slave issue! On this, Mr. Speaker, I find my hand somewhat forced by the present debate, for it is a subject on which I had not intended to opine."[12]

---

[11] The quotations from *O tronco do ipê* are from Alencar (1871, vol. I, p. 9, vol. II, p. 126). Other passages also attribute a wanton sensuality. For an analysis of representations of slavery in Brazilian literature, see Vainfas (1986, 1988), Azevedo (1987, 2003), Carvalho (2005), Haberly (1972), Schwarz (2000).

[12] The citations in the previous paragraphs are from Alencar (1856, pp. 37 and 94); Alencar, Jul. 15, 1867, pp. 65, 69–70, 74–5; and ACD, Jun. 5, 1882. Rizzo (2012, pp. 119–256) analyzes Alencar's novels along similar lines as I do here; for an opposing interpretation, see Faria (1987). On his political writings, see José Murilo de Carvalho (2005, p. 55), for whom Alencar was the figure "closest to the slavery theorists of the southern United States." See also Parron (2011).

60                      *The Last Abolition*

It was only faced with the concrete threat posed by the expanding number of abolitionist societies in the late 1860s and the free womb bill that slavery began to unfurl as a *rhetoric of reaction*.[13] Until then, however, Brazilian pro-slavery politicians were subtle in their defense of the institution. Instead of presenting an emphatic defense of slavery on principle as their North American counterparts did, the rhetoric of Brazil's pro-slavery politicians was *circumstantial*: they felt compelled to justify the "slavocratic situation" in which they lived, but did so without defending the institution of slavery as such, which, they recognized, was roundly condemned by both civilization and the prevailing morality. Slavery was a cancer eating treacherously away at the social fabric, the worst of all enemies because it was an enemy within, a House Devil. And yet, it had to be maintained, given the circumstances – the imperious needs of the economy. Or as the Emperor would respond to French abolitionists in 1866, freedom was a most noble principle, but "the dire circumstances in which the country finds itself" oblige it to postpone it a little longer – by about half a century, according to a member of the Lower House committee designated to draft a report on Rio Branco's project:[14]

"Save the principle, though society may perish" does not seem to me a sentence that befits those upon whom the people have conferred the sacred mandate of protecting their rights and upholding their security. It matters little that legislators of other nations have practiced [abolition]. *Ours are particularly special circumstances* ... I, too, Mr. Speaker, am an emancipator, but ... I do not want *emancipation to be a burden rather than a benefit.* ... That is why I oppose the idea. If the noble minister [Rio Branco] were to first pave the way over the next forty or fifty years, then come before the Houses and say: "We hereby decree the emancipation of the slaves," I would be the first to congratulate him and give him my vote.

That was the route taken at the Lower House and Senate in 1871: a defense not of the practice of slavery per se, but of slavery as a necessary foundation for maintaining the social order in Brazil. Decent men, Christian and civilized men, forced by economic and political imperatives,

---

[13] Hirschman (1991) used the term "rhetoric of reaction" to describe the set of pro-status quo arguments that arose in the face of reform projects and attempts at reform.

[14] Pedro II, in Nabuco (1897–1899, p. 661). Rui Barbosa (1884, p. 687) summed things up: "Amongst us slavery is clad in insidious veneers that make it even more dangerous than a frank apology for captivity because it dissembles as emancipatory." The MP in question was Rodrigo Silva, ACD, Aug. 15, 1870, who would later sign the law in 1888. My italics.

were *only* defending a postponement of abolition. "Nobody" – said Paulino – "is advocating the perpetuity of slavery. ... In this century of Enlightenment for all men who profess to uphold the law of the Gospels, the cause of slavery has been judged and condemned for all time!" However, principles must adapt to conditions:

The matter in-hand is, by nature, eminently practical and its solution *cannot be dictated by principles alone. ... the key points in this debate concern an appreciation of the national circumstances* ...: we have a duty not to run ahead of ourselves and plunge the country into a violent crisis, but must, first and foremost, consider and defend the structural interests of our nation. ... without assailing property, without disrupting the existing relations, without damaging the major interests that are, unfortunately and for the longest time, intrinsically tied to this institution. (Applause).[15]

Diffuse, sinuous, fragmented, circumstantial pro-slavery rhetoric abounded in parliamentary speeches from those opposing the free womb bill. At the Lower House, Paulino Soares de Sousa led the robust opposition, which included the likes of José de Alencar. Opponents to the bill were numerous and ardent, keen to legitimize the pro-slavery status quo with recourse to three typical schemata of interpretation for the rhetoric of reaction: that reform was perverse; that it was futile; and that it posed a threat to the social order.[16]

At the Lower House, the argument that abolition perverted the natural hierarchy resounded as a warning. As slavery was rooted in the economy and social habits, it was argued that gradual measures, rather than result in progress, would only cause social instability. From good intentions, warned Alencar, would come nefarious consequences: "Gentlemen, I am not here merely to defend the interests of the wealthy slaveowners, but first and foremost those of the infelicitous race about to be sent for sacrifice," for granting liberty to "brutish masses" unequipped to deal with it was tantamount to Prometheus handing the sacred fire to pyromaniacal mortals. The Free Womb Law would divide families among the free and unfree, kindling flames of revolt in the latter. What was intended as medicine would serve only as poison.

[15] ASI, Sept. 19, 1871, ACD, Aug. 23, 1871. My italics.
[16] The pro-slavery front line in 1871 was made up of the deputies Ferreira Viana, Antônio Prado, Pereira da Silva, Duque-Estrada Teixeira, Belisário and, last but not least, Perdigão Malheiros (Monteiro, 1913, pp. 20–1). Hirschman (1991, pp. 10 ff.) establishes the rhetoric-of-reaction triad based on debates on the French Revolution, the expansion of suffrage and the welfare state. He may well have listed the abolition of slavery too, because the rhetoric was the same.

## The Last Abolition

This tactic of aborting the reform without opposing it head-on, of calling it into question not on its principles, but in terms of the unintended and counterproductive consequences it would trigger, was also adopted at the Senate, where it was argued that there was no such thing as a pro-slavery politician in Brazil; what you had were men possessed of good sense and its inseparable companion, prudence. According to one senator, "nobody in Brazil is against emancipation ... However, we need to act in a rational, prudent, cautious manner, without sacrificing the owners' rights, tranquility, and security of the majority of Brazil's citizens to the rash triumph of an idea, no matter how noble." There were dire consequences to running ahead of oneself, as the American Civil War showed. In Spain, on the other hand, "progression was prudent." And prudence was something Brazil lacked. How, for example, was one to legislate on abolition without having a proper census of the slave population? Surely the ministry should conduct a survey first. And was it really the time to tamper with the status quo with elections looming? Should they not wait for the new parliament? And what of the results of abolition? Impossible to predict. "A single word that raises the specter of emancipation, however laudable, will kick open the doors onto a thousand disgraces... European publicists and statesmen don't take into account the circumstances that hold in slave-owning societies. Their ideas don't fit here."[17]

The Viscount of São Vicente, unsuccessful as Prime Minister the previous year, became a supporter of the Rio Branco project in 1871, claiming that, unless the free womb bill was passed, the slavery problem would linger. Paulino responded that demographics would do the job. All one had to do was wait.[18]

The second argument against the Free Womb Law was that legislation on the issue was a waste of time. For Alencar, the end of slavery had to "happen naturally, just as it had originated and evolved. No law can abolish what none decreed." Social laws prevented politics from meddling with the deeper structures of society, so any pretension toward governmental reform of slavery was an illusion. Paulino Soares de Sousa echoed this sentiment: the free womb bill, if passed into law, would be dead legislation at best, because it was an affront to society and its way of life.

---

[17] This quote from Alencar is in ACD, Jul. 13, 1871. The second quotation is from the Baron of São Lourenço (ASI, Jun. 8, 1868), and the one after that, from the Marquis of Olinda (in Nabuco, 1897–1899, p. 705). Other similar statements were heard in parliamentary debates throughout 1871.

[18] ACD, Aug. 13, 1871; ACEI, Nov. 5, 1866, Apr. 2, 1867.

## Pro-Slavery Rhetoric

Under this schema of interpretation any abolitionist law would be futile and only surface deep, incapable of effecting any genuine change.[19]

Words of this nature flowed freely at the Conservative Party meeting Paulino organized with fifty MPs at his home to orchestrate opposition to Rio Branco's bill. Andrade Figueira insisted, as he would also do in Parliament, on the "grave inadvisability of legislating without the concrete data that statistics alone can furnish, and which, on their own merits, might suffice to demonstrate the possibility of a slower, milder solution, with less impact upon public and private wealth and respecting the rights of one and all."[20] Besides, emancipation would create legions of ill-equipped individuals in need of discipline and guidance. God had created society with some on top and others at the bottom, the end of one hierarchy would just spawn the rise of another. The best policy in the case was *fare niente*.

Paulino subscribed to the very same view, accusing Rio Branco of being irresponsible, of clogging the parliamentary agenda with a matter Chronos alone could resolve. Rio Branco had not gone for emancipation in 1867; when loyal to the god of time, he had defended a twenty-year transition. However, he was now prepared to switch divinity, siding instead with Mars, the god of war, because abolition would certainly destroy his party.

In his campaign to demoralize Rio Branco, Paulino painted him as authoritarian: he was pandering to a minority at Parliament, was refusing to negotiate, and was showing blatant disregard for due process and political etiquette. With a straight face, he also accused him of being the Emperor's errand-boy. And, if that was indeed the case, he blustered, the whole bill was compromised from the very start, and therefore unconstitutional, as the Moderating Power was not entitled to start the legislative process. Paulino seldom spoke in Parliament, but he was devastating when he did, unbeatable in twisting his adversaries' reasoning, and industrious in trawling European abolitionists – Tocqueville, Grey, Broglie, the British and Foreign Antislavery Society – for cautionary tales against abolition by "half measures." Moral, economic, and political development, he argued, would be much more effective in eradicating slavery "than this unlawful, unjust, disturbing, incautious, inhumane and oppressive measure [the free womb

---

[19] Alencar, ACD, Jul. 20, 1867, p. 92. Alencar, ACD, Jul. 13, 1871; Soares de Sousa, ACD Aug. 23, 1871. []

[20] Pereira da Silva (1895–1896, p. 423). Figueira in Soares de Sousa, ACD Aug. 23, 1871.

64 *The Last Abolition*

bill] designed to secure freedom for the next generation to the detriment of the rule of law and vital interests."[21]

The third argument against the Free Womb Law, and a recurrent and compelling one at that, was that it posed a threat to public order. As had so often been said, the very raising of the issue was enough to send ripples of unrest through slaveholding groups. Andrade Figueira, always prone to hyperbole, described Rio Branco's bill as an air-raid on the plantations. It would destroy the economy, and destabilize the social order by freeing children but not their mothers. It would certainly sow the seeds of slave revolt, a theme that was omnipresent and even the subject of verse among the imperial elite:

> *So conspire the slaves, always irate*
> *against the ruling hand, and ever vengeful,*
> *crime they inject between the virginal lips*
> *of the suckling babe, who sours …,*
> *unbeknownst, unbelieving, harnessed to the yoke*
> *of the roaming cart of the master it hates …*[22]

Anti-abolitionists anticipated a perfect storm of economic upheaval and social and political disorder should the bill pass. Like their Cuban counterparts, Brazilian defenders of slavery were quick to recall histories of social mayhem. Abolition, they argued, was synonymous with convulsion, as in the American Civil War or the Slave Revolt in Haiti. One MP claimed the project would cause havoc among the workforce and the system of landownership, as each depended on the other.[23] Slave revolts, the fragmentation of the nation, the downfall of the monarchy, in short, the entire social order would crumble and the political order it had taken sweat and tears to achieve during the Second Reign would be shredded in an instant. The free womb was like Pandora's box; it would unleash a world of woe.

Though absent from the debates in 1871 (he was in the Prata region), the Baron of Cotegipe, while Itaboraí's minister in 1870, warned that abolition would trigger a war even worse than the one Brazil had waged against Paraguay. It was a boulder not to be disturbed lightly, he said, "lest it career downhill and crush us all." Alencar ran with the allusion:

---

[21] ACD, Aug. 23, 1871.    [22] Porto Alegre, *Colombo*, 1866.

[23] Alencar, ACD, Jul. 20, 1867, pp. 78, 86; Pinto Moreira, ACD, Aug. 7, 1871. The same arguments were used during the Spanish debate (Corwin, 1968, p. 164). On the political elite's thinking on slavery, see Azevedo (1987). and Carvalho (1988). "Haitianism," the fear of slave revolt, was a constant feature in the discourse of authorities and landowners.

the boulder "would roll to the abyss," "leaving civil war in its trail." Hence his promise: "I will do everything within my power" to forestall "the baleful notion that is free womb."[24]

In the clash between the government and the nation's major interests, there was no doubt on which side Alencar stood. Economy, Christianity, civilization, and the "cult of liberty" urged that slavery should be maintained. Only reckless imitators of all things foreign could disagree: "Ye, the propagandists, the entranced emancipators, are naught but emissaries of revolution, apostles of anarchy. The retrogrades are ye, who would have us brake the nation's progress, smiting it in its very heart, slaying first its industry, its plantations." In Rio Branco he saw a "fanatic emancipator," a revolutionary who dishonored the Conservative Party's tradition as the guardian of order. "It is said that the government would force emancipation upon us, by hook or by crook, in one fell swoop, because that is what the abolitionist society demands (*cries of yay and nay*)."

With his literary talent, Alencar produced the most polished version of the circumstantial pro-slavery defense against the bill, which he considered "a conjuration," "a pretext for revolution," which would bring about "public misery," "social disaster," and "the ruin of property." Thus he exhorted his colleagues to vote against the "iniquitous, barbarous" notion of free womb.

Neither Alencar nor Paulino expected slavery to last forever. They agreed with the Emperor: abolition was only a matter of how (orderly) and when (remote). Hurrying the social pace, the abolitionists would only sabotage their goals, because forced evolution, hasty change, breeds nothing but revolution. It would lead not just to the end of slavery, but the whole social order.[25]

This fervent opposition to the free womb motion came from hosts of Conservatives at the Lower House, but some Liberals were singing a very similar tune. The parliamentary stenographer registered a profusion of "yays" and "hear-hears" accompanying anti-free womb arguments during the debates. Slavery was a value shared across the spectrum of the imperial elite, embodied in its very way of life. It was the bone and the

---

[24] Cotegipe (1870), in Pinho (1937, pp. 137, 143); ACD, Aug. 10–13 Jul. 1871.

[25] The quotations from Alencar are from ACD, Jul. 13, 1871. In the Senate, the Baron of Três Barras spoke along similar lines and railed against the appropriation of the abolitionist repertoire, "false philanthropic notions imported from abroad," intended to "disturb the fundaments of society, attacking property, a right guaranteed by law and respected down through the centuries" (ASI, Jul. 31, 1871).

66 *The Last Abolition*

muscle of the Second Reign. Few railed against the bill with the virulence of Alencar or the brash straight-talk of the Liberal Martinho Campos, who claimed to be "a slaver through-and-through," but they were merely yelling what everyone else was whispering behind closed doors.

This mitigating pro-slavery rhetoric sustained a *pro-slavery political coalition* based on many forms of resistance: petitions, speeches, pamphlets, newspaper articles, serialized novels, poems, meetings, blockades, and the creation of a whole wave of Plantation Clubs (Clubes de Lavoura). Many in these groups used the word "revolution" to describe the government's proposal and the response it would surely incite. As one MP said:

Planters' protests could be heard from all corners of the Empire. ... In municipalities throughout the provinces of Rio de Janeiro, Minas and São Paulo plantation owners rallied, and they petitioned the Houses against the Ministry's proposal; they took up subscriptions to subsidize their position in the press and appointed commissioners to defend their interests. [26]

Resistance sprang up spontaneously, according to Paulino. This is inaccurate, as there was a deliberate political campaign to fan the flames of opposition, starting with Martinho Campos, who created the Plantation and Commerce Club in May 1871 to organize a front against free womb. Similar associations were set up between 1869 and 1871. High Street merchants in Rio de Janeiro held a protest meeting in the capital, and Paulino took petitions to Parliament compiled by traders and planters. There were thirty-three of these in all submitted to the Lower House and a further eleven to the Senate in 1871, with a combined total of 1,997 signatures. There was also a slew of anonymous, vitriolic, and incendiary articles and pamphlets.[27] Slave-owning society was not going to give up its privilege anytime soon, and certainly not without a fight.

Paulino commanded this resistance with the same impeccable care with which he polished his coat buttons. Further ahead, he would share the duty with the silky-smooth Cotegipe and the outspoken Andrade Figueira. The abolitionist threat galvanized this unlikely trinity of hardline Conservatives.

---

[26] Pereira da Silva (1895–1896, p. 426).
[27] ACD, Jul. 10, 1871; ASI, Sept. 4, 1871. On the plantation clubs, see Pang (1981, pp. 84, 96–8, 101–2).

## MOBILIZATION

Paulino accused Rio Branco of proposing the free womb bill out of personal conviction and without "any public clamor" that he should do so. This was not exactly true. While the Upper and Lower Houses were locked in vigorous debate on the issue, the press covered the institutional proceedings in minute detail and the House galleries continued packed throughout, with people for and against. Rio Branco continually evoked the "invisible, yet powerful force of public opinion" coming out of private societies. He reminded the Senate that abolitionist pamphlets, journals, and societies were proliferating. Various sessions at the National Association for Industrial Support (SAIN), of which Rebouças and Abílio Borges were both still members, discussed abolition and immigration in parallel with the parliamentary debate. On June 15, Rebouças addressed a session there to speak against a project to import cheap labor from China, which he claimed would be a new form of serfdom intended merely to replenish dwindling slave stocks in the wake of an approved Free Womb Law.[28]

Rebouças was never alone: twenty-four antislavery societies grew steadily during the free-womb debates between 1869 and early 1871 in eleven of the twenty provinces. Their geographical distribution is best explained politically rather than economically, as they arose in Liberal heartlands that were underrepresented in Parliament, and especially where the Radical Liberals were most active. This was the case in São Paulo, home to two societies, and Rio Grande do Sul and Pernambuco, home to three apiece. Liberals also established five antislavery groups in Bahia and two in Ceará. In Rio de Janeiro, the capital, there were two and one each in Amazonas, Espírito Santo, Maranhão, and Piauí. Many of these societies rallied behind free womb, and two of them – from Bahia and Pernambuco – petitioned Parliament in support of the bill.[29]

[28] ACD, Aug. 23, 1871. Pereira da Silva (1895–1896, p. 426); ACD, May 29, 1871. Francisco Otaviano, ASI, Sep. 12, 1871. *O auxiliador da indústria nacional*, v. xxxix, 1871. On proceedings at Parliament, see Nabuco (1897–1899), Duque-Estrada (1918), Moraes (1924), Conrad (1975), Carvalho (1980), Salles (1990) and Needell (2006). The general explanations underscore the relevance of the monarch's use of his moderating power in the approval of the Free Womb Law. Here I emphasize the pressure exercised by the abolitionists.

[29] The societies that sent petitions were the 13th of March Liberating Society (from Bahia) and the Emancipatory Society of Pernambuco (ACD, Jun. 12, Jul. 17–26, 1871). Conrad (1972, 1975) believed abolitionism was stronger in the north of the country because there were fewer slaves there, and weaker in the South, where slave stocks were large; however,

68 *The Last Abolition*

Abílio Borges, from the 7th of September Liberating Society, resurrected an approach that had worked for French abolitionists in 1866, the "boomerang effect." This time, he turned to the church for help, just as the British and Americans had done. He visited the Pope in 1870 and asked him to intervene in favor of abolition. Pius IX said that he could only intercede with the Lord. Borges sarcastically replied that he would have to shout unto the heavens with all his might if the Brazilian slaveholders were to hear him. However, the church remained silent on the issue of slavery.[30]

So Borges invested his energies in civic ceremonies. The April 1871 session of the 7th of September Liberating Society caused quite a stir in Bahia, thanks to the mise-en-scène laid on by one of Borges' former students, Antônio de Castro Alves. In a dramatic reading of a "Letter addressed to the Ladies of Bahia," he deplored the exclusion of women from party politics and called on womenfolk everywhere to join the abolitionist cause:

You have the duty, dear ladies, and indeed the right to protest on this matter and express your abhorrence. ... The clean-sweeping winds of this century have already vanquished slavery across the two Americas. The abolitionist flood has come to ferry the continents unto new generations. This Brazilian land stands alone, yet those waves now lap at the base of the final cornerstone of things that must but die.

In Rio de Janeiro, the 2nd of July Liberating Society (Bahia) organized a conference at the Teatro São Pedro. Rebouças was there, juggling his three great passions: construction projects (he was trying to create a Water Company), opera, and abolition. He also attended the session held at the Teatro Lírico on June 27, when the Fênix Theater Company freed a two-year-old slave girl on stage. It was a ceremony straight out of Borges' playbook, in which the lead actor made an emotional appeal to the Emperor (absent), saying "God has yet to disclose the color of his angels, but he has said that all men are equal: black, white, or any other color."[31]

---

the distribution of the societies was more or less balanced throughout the regions at the start of the campaign. Between 1868 and 1871 fifteen societies arose in the North and nine in the South, which shows that the North was not alone in mobilizing. The reasons for mobilization were more concerned with the political dynamic than the economic.

[30] Valdez (2006, p. 41).

[31] *O Abolicionista*, Jul. 31, Apr. 30, 1871. The letter from Castro Alves was also published as a pamphlet (Fonseca, 1887, p. 247). The actor was Ernesto Rossi, cf. DNAAR, Jun. 27, 1871.

## Pro-Slavery Rhetoric

Abolitionist mobilization was spreading its tendrils. Borges-style events were held in Rio Grande do Sul and, as if in response to Castro Alves' entreaty, support grew among the women of high-society. One of the pro-government indictments lampooning slavery was written by the first woman to study at the Medical Faculty in Rio de Janeiro, who, in 1871, published and sent to Parliament a piece entitled *Ideas to coordinate concerning emancipation*, in which she outlined the institutional mismatch between slavery, "a social cancer," and constitutional monarchy, and defended a gradual phasing-in of emancipation.

Rebouças, for his part, composed three draft bills for emancipation that would have put an end to slavery by 1890 and he took them to Rio Branco that June. It was the only issue in Rio de Janeiro at the time. Rebouças followed the US model, from which he took the proposal for the creation of Liberia, an African nation to which former slaves would be deported, but he preferred to keep his solutions domestic and centered on the slave-owning enclaves, as he made clear on another visit to the Prime Minister: "I argued for the creation of a large collective farm, a Liberia for freedmen and settlers, to serve the interests of propaganda in the Paraíba Valley, the heartland of slavery, in favor of free labor." He found a willing ear in Rio Branco, who railed at Parliament "against the pro-slavery camp's dirty tricks."[32] The truth was that ever since presenting his project Rio Branco had been caught up in a whirlwind. He had rallied a fleet, and would need it if he was to take the fight to Paulino and his battalion.

### THE LEGISLATIVE PROCESS

During the discussions at the Council of State in 1867, Rio Branco, Paulino recalled, seemed to have learned the virtues of inaction from observing the American Civil War. However, he had changed his mind. In the best spirit of Don Fabrizio, the main character in Giuseppe Tomasi

---

[32] The medical student in question was the Frenchwoman Maria Josephina Mathilde Durocher. The Rio Grande do Sul Society for the Promotion of the Emancipation of Slaves, based in Pelotas, had 160 members, of which six were women and many others foreigners (Xavier, 2010, p. 60). It was commanded by the engineer and businessman João Driesel Frick, who presided over Borges-style ceremonies at the Town Hall on September 7 1869, when, before "a throng of locals," he delivered four letters of manumission with some "words from the commission to the freed" "that moved the whole auditorium" (Frick, 1885, pp. 17–18, 23–4). The article against Rebouças was published in the *Diário do Rio* on February 19. DNAAR, Jun. 20, Jul. 10 and 13, 1871.

70 *The Last Abolition*

di Lampedusa's *The Leopard*, Rio Branco had begun to see that the best way to conserve the status quo was to bend it a little. For Paulino, on the other hand, the very semantics of the word conserve meant there was no room for change. This was the difference between Rio Branco's Moderate Conservatives and Paulino's Hardliners, who were willing to do whatever it took to contain the "emancipatory storm."

Rio Branco considered himself a centrist and sought the middle ground:[33] not as reformative as the abolitionists expected, nor as conservative as the stalwarts desired. His project involved compensation for the slaveholders, and that was a positive, but by no means an assurance. There was a Conservative majority in Parliament, which should have been a boon, but refused to fall in behind his bill.

Even before discussions got underway on the details of the free womb bill, objections were surfacing and proliferating, and continued to do so over the course of the three rounds of debate at the Lower House between Rio Branco's support base and the other, Paulino's. The Conservative Party was split in two.

Sixty-three deputies were needed to form a majority in the 125-member House. As was made clear from the special commission convened to formulate the project, that was always going to be a challenge. The government had its hardcore free wombers, who believed reform was inevitable in the face of the epilogue to slavery then playing out in the civilized world; and with them stood part of the Conservative majority and a smattering of the Liberal minority. Another bloc joined them under the whip of the minister Alfredo Correia de Oliveira. Leading the dissidents was Paulino, who stood in the name of Conservative Party unity and "in defense of the rights" of property against "exaggerated hopes," and demanded that the bill be withdrawn. He was betting on a hung parliament and success in the subsequent elections, when his minority would reincarnate as a majority. Rio Branco made the matter a cabinet issue and won the vote. But Paulino had thirty-five deputies under his control, which was roughly a third of the House.[34]

Heated debate and hard-fought battles continued throughout the latter half of May and the whole month of June, though the bill was only officially sent to the floor on July 10, when the dissidents tried to have it replaced with a draft bill drawn up by the special commission of

[33] This expression from Paulino is in ACD, Aug. 23, 1871, and from Rio Branco in ACD, Jul. 31, 1891.
[34] Nabuco, JC, Aug. 17, 1884, ACD, May 29, Jun. 1, 1871.

the Lower House, a subterfuge to postpone the debate. And it continued more or less in the same spirit, with all manner of obstruction, equivocation, filibustering, and ill-tempered exchanges. In the absence of a dazzling orator, Rio Branco did what he could, delivering twenty-six speeches in all, or forty-one, if one counts improvisations and rights to reply. "I will never be able to answer, as they keep interrupting me the whole time," he would say, claiming the floor for another attempt. His attacks seemed to work, to judge from the following quip: "The noble MP's ire is proof enough that the cause he defends is base and his argument, bogus."[35]

He left no contention unchecked, and returned fire on the spot and in the *Jornal do Commercio*. Though not an impassioned orator, at six foot four and firm in tone, he knew how to impose himself. He rebuffed the pro-slavery arguments point by point, claiming that far from hamstringing agricultural interests, abolition "was the best way to defend them," as it would indemnify the slaveholder when the freeborn turned eight, giving him plenty of time to prepare. He rejected the futility charge on the grounds that inaction, not reform, would lead to widespread unrest. Paulino's prudence, he said, was that of someone who "always arrives late for fear of taking a stand early." He confronted the pro-slavery rhetoric and its schemata of threat: "Does not maintaining the status quo itself present dangers and the gravest of disruptions? Stubbornly clinging to habit, to the way things are, is what provokes violent solutions."[36]

Rio Branco was a reformer, but he was far from being the "communist" he was labeled throughout the debates; and he prized order to such a degree that he supported a motion, approved by the Lower House and Senate during the free womb discussions, that condemned the "savage, bloody anarchy" of the Paris Commune. But he learned a great deal from the experiences of others. Slavery, he reminded the deputies, had been abolished in Sweden, Denmark, the Netherlands, the French, British, and Portuguese colonies and throughout most of the Americas. In the United States, "which might serve as some consolation and moral support for our tardiness," the delay in abolishing the practice had cost

---

[35] ACD, Jul. 10, May 31, Jul. 10, 1871. The twenty-six speeches are my own tally – ten in the Lower House (ACD, May 9, 29, and 31; Jul. 10, 14, and 31, Aug. 5, 7, 9, and 10) and sixteen at the Senate (ASI, May 10 and 15, Jun. 15, 22, and 27, Aug. 10, 11, 12, 14, and 29, Sept. 4 and 25); Nabuco counted forty-one (1897–1899, p. 839).

[36] Besouchet (1985, p. 51); ACD, May 23, 1871; ASI, May 29, Jul. 10 and 14, 1871.

72                    *The Last Abolition*

"rivers of blood," while Spain, spurred by "this influence," was taking large strides towards emancipation. As such, abolition had become "a near universal fact." The intensification of communications, said the man who would go on to introduce the telegraph to Brazil, meant such issues bled beyond the national frontiers and exposed the country to international opinion. The slave trade had ended under pressure from abroad. It was now impossible to say: "we do not care about foreign public opinion." Added to that was fervent public opinion at home, and the spread of antislavery associations all over the Empire, insisting, as Rio Branco was quick to point out, that abolition was a corollary of Independence and that it had always been on the horizon of such visionary statesmen as José Bonifácio de Andrada e Silva.[37] And taking a direct hit at Paulino, he recalled that the Viscount of Uruguay, his father, had endorsed the end of the slave trade with the same realpolitik with which he now opposed free womb.[38]

But no amount of argument was able to break the deadlock. The Speaker of the House held a meeting between the government and dissident sides at his house and tried to broker a resolution. Paulino refused to budge, and the government was intractable on the core of the project, free womb. With no alternative bill, the minority availed of every imaginable strategy to obstruct the motion: they emptied Parliament so a quorum would not be met, arranged meetings and functions to clash with the sessions, wound back deputies' watches, refused to register the presence of deputies arriving at the Lower House, and had the doctors among them summoned out of the session to treat imaginary patients. Faced with all manner of ruse and obstruction, it was a Herculean effort for the government to get its entire support base onsite. Minister João Alfredo went so far as to force into Parliament a feverish MP. As one government MP put it, if a session was declared open, there were "almost as many speakers as there were members of the illustrious dissidence." If lack of quorum could not be engineered, then the order was to delay proceedings in any way possible. This "stonewall opposition" had various sessions cancelled,

---

[37] José Bonifácio de Andrada e Silva (1763–1838) was a key politician during the process of Brazil's Independence from Portugal (1822) and throughout Pedro I's reign. After the first Emperor's abdication, in 1831, he became guardian to the heir to the throne, Pedro II. In the debates concerning the country's first constitution, in 1823, Bonifácio stood for gradual emancipation and, because of that, would later be celebrated by the abolitionist movement.

[38] ACD, Jul. 31, Jun. 26, May 29, Jul. 14, May 31 [1871].

# Pro-Slavery Rhetoric

including the one at which the rapporteur was to present the bill to the deputies.[39]

The entire process was an uphill battle. On August 2, pandemonium broke loose. Discussions on Article 4 descended into a dogfight, with deputies cutting in on each other the whole time. Paulino demanded a nominal vote. The government bloc had fallen to fifty-nine deputies, and the dissidents risen to thirty-nine. In speech after speech, the anti-free wombers were doing their best to prevent the next article from being put to the vote. Andrade Figueira managed to buy some time by talking for a whole hour about electoral reform. The Speaker of the House rebuked him for being off-topic, but it was no use, and others adopted the same tactic. The government camp reacted by demanding that the session be extended, which gave rise to some protracted bickering about the House rules. There were feisty exchanges and numerous volleys, but by the end of the day Rio Branco's men succeeded in pressing ahead with the debate, moving on to Article 5. The dissidents accused the Prime Minister of being subservient to the Emperor. Normally impassive, save for a single finger tapping on the table top as he listened to his adversaries, Rio Branco went flush with rage. He upbraided his attacker with virulence, addressing him as the Speaker of the House would an orator who was out of control: "The honorable minister is in no condition to deliberate!" The minority took to its feet, rowdily accusing the Prime Minister of breaking parliamentary decorum and disrespecting the Speaker. The majority rose in Rio Branco's defense. Bedlam broke out. The Speaker rebuked the Prime Minister: "The honorable minister cannot address a member of the house in such terms." Boisterous scenes ensued. Veins pounding in their temples, the deputies seemed on the verge of a pitched battle. The galleries invaded the floor. "Not even during the tensest days of the Majority debacle [when the 14-year-old Pedro II was declared Emperor before coming of age] did I see such scenes in the Lower House," said one of those present. Amidst "an infernal din of shouting and chanting," the Speaker of the House resigned from his post and the session was suspended. The throng spilled out into the streets. The Prime Minister, honoring the steely nerves Rebouças had seen in him, left with collected calm, and the crowd split down the middle to let him pass.[40]

---

[39] Needell (2006, pp. 290–1); Nabuco (1897–1899, pp. 858–9); ACD, Jul. 31, 1871. The Count of Baependi was Speaker of the House.

[40] Article 5 dealt with associations that had, "among other philanthropic ends, the manumission of slaves." ACD, Aug. 2, 1871; Monteiro (1913, pp. 22–3); JC, Aug. 2, 1871.

74 *The Last Abolition*

The following week, the wrangling was over the election of the new Speaker. False ballots were cast, which meant the vote had to be redone. The opposition floated a pamphlet inciting the public to invade the Lower House, which the government narrowly averted by calling in the police. Against the most acrimonious of backdrops, the government managed to elect one of its members to the post of Speaker of the Lower House, a step that would prove vital. The new Speaker pushed the articles through the House at a much swifter pace, drawing on two key sources of strength: the government majority, and liberal doses of courage. Chief whip João Alfredo Correa de Oliveira, the "ministerial lightning rod," provided the backing, dragging deputies out of their houses and posting minders to ensure they all stayed the course in Parliament. He stood firm, but keeping the debate open in the face of furious dissidence was a tough task. At each session, João Alfredo picked a MP to serve as the day's cannon-fodder whom he literally shoved right to the front line, where he drew fire from all sides. In the meantime, the whip provided the rear guard. This modus operandi ensured that the project made it through the two first rounds of debate in the Lower House.[41]

And all under vehement protest from the dissidents, as one of them would later say: "There was constant heckling that disturbed the speakers, and even threats of physical violence." The opposition's aim was to bar the bill without offering any alternative to it, but on the eve of certain defeat, as one last-gasp maneuver, the naysayers presented a substitute bill containing some articles from the government project, but with the notable exception of its cornerstone, free womb. The substitute was brought by the Conservative Perdigão Malheiros, who, though previously seen as an abolitionist, had become a congressional mouthpiece for the Plantation Club. When the substitute bill was rejected, cracks began to appear in Paulino's trademark cool, "because it pains my spirit to see my relatives, my friends, my fellows and so many Brazilians suffering under unbearable expectation, fraught with most justifiable unease and concerns, finding their lives, livelihoods and interests worthy of the greatest consideration so gravely threatened."[42]

---

[41] The new Speaker of the House was Jerônimo José Teixeira Jr., a MP who had questioned Itaboraí about abolition in 1870. ACD, Aug. 12, 1871; Nabuco (1897–1899, pp. 858–9); ASI, Aug. 10, 1871; Monteiro (1913, p. 22); ACD, Aug. 9–10, 1871.

[42] This description of the general atmosphere is from Pereira da Silva (1895–1896, p. 426). On the substitute bill, see ACD, Aug. 18, 1871. This quote from Paulino is in ACD, Aug. 23, 1871. Rio Branco sought in vain to obtain the support of Perdigão Malheiros, who had previously defended free womb at the Bar Association.

The Chief Impugner, as they called him, spent the next four hours inveighing against what he considered a government coup, the unconstitutionality of the bill, and the Emperor's meddling in the Legislature. It was intolerable – he said – that they should impose upon the nation a reform that changed the very state of things grounded upon an established legal bedrock and the right to property. The disastrous consequences that would surely come would be felt on all three fronts. Economically, it would drive great fortunes to ruin and throw production and labor into disarray; politically, it would discredit the institutions and invite revolution; and socially, it would uproot the aristocratic culture, along with its hierarchies and customs, "rupturing the many relations encoded into habit on which our way of life rests." In short, "slavery, gentlemen, is an institution ingrained in our society, it is intrinsically bound up with our social life, the bedrock of a social compact which cannot be torn out without invoking the chagrin of the whole and upsetting the order of things which, under different conditions, took hold within it." The danger of dangers, abolition would deracinate a "whole order of things on which our social faith rests."

Rio Branco, he continued, aped the foreign abolitionists in theory, but failed to follow their lead in practice, as the British, French, and Spanish governments had defended the owners' rights. Great Britain, he insisted, had resisted abolition for a quarter of a century out of respect for the overseas colonies, as had the French, who commissioned censuses and reports before taking concrete measures. A good example, he claimed, was that of the Russians, concerning whom he reached a conclusion contrary to the one that Jequitinhonha had drawn in the 1860s. Rather than see in the Russian approach an incentive to accelerate the process, he underscored the exact opposite. The Czar, he argued, had listened to the slaveholders, whose delegates, gathered at the national assembly, spent three and a half years discussing 331 different bills from provincial commissions. This was the example to be followed. However, the Brazilian government was backing the slave owners onto the edge of an abyss, with the help of the regime. Free womb would serve only "to divorce the merchants and planters from the monarchy, an institution they had hitherto unwaveringly supported. ... Does the Prime Minister really think that the constitutional monarchy of Brazil can dispense with the support of the most illustrious classes of society?" Normally serene, Paulino lost his temper: "What sort of bill is this that appeals to sentiment and pits it against the greater interest?

76                                    *The Last Abolition*

(Hear-hear)." Conclusion: "Simultaneous emancipation, whether immediate or deferred, is currently unacceptable in Brazil."[43]

Amid raised voices, threats of converting the Empire into a Republic and of insurrection by slaves and slavers alike, irate orators, handkerchiefs raised and waved, and barbs exchanged, the minority gnashed its teeth. The free womb bill dragged and crawled through Parliament for exactly what it was: the end of a world.[44] The minority haggled and whined down to the last article: "Objections overruled."

For Rio Branco, passing the bill was like a matter of life or death. He remained abreast of every development, monitored every move, ate his lunch in Parliament, and slept in his clothes so as to save time the next morning. According to one opponent, he had friends in both camps, having garnered a lot of respect over the course of his career, and because of his gentlemanly demeanor. He politicked, exploited divergences among the Conservatives, parlayed with opponents, bent the rulebook in his favor, availed of intimidation and even – according to one adversary – resorted to corruption. As he wielded the power to hire and fire, he kept the civil service deputies in-line. Iracundo, the former Speaker of the House, protested against the government bulldozer, saying: "At least have the decency to keep up appearances!"[45]

Government maneuvers, leadership ability, support from the modernizing Conservative faction which convinced the Prime Minister of the impossibility of postponing the inevitable all conspired in favor of the bill's approval, but not just that.

Over the course of the whole debacle, the government made some concessions that guaranteed slaveholder prerogatives. Article 1, which freed children born to slavewomen while placing them under their masters' tutelage until the age of eight, when these could choose either to hand them over to the State in return for an indemnity payment of 600 réis,[46] or avail of

---

[43] The quotations in this paragraph and the preceding one are from ACD, Aug. 23 and 24, 1871.

[44] The confrontation reveals a situation entirely different from that narrated by Nabuco (1897–1899, pp. 848, 661), for whom "Rio Branco is operating in such a way as to avoid senseless suffering" and is passing the Free Womb Law "without the least upheaval, with the backing of the slaveholders themselves – and in the Emperor's absence."

[45] Monteiro (1913, p. 23); Needell (2006, p. 289). The dissident was Pereira da Silva (1895–1896, pp. 423–4); Carvalho (2005, pp. 66 ff.); ACD, Jul. 28, 1871.

[46] The Brazilian currency was, through the Empire, the milréis (1$000). One conto de réis (1:000$000) was equivalent to one thousand milréis. According to Summerhill (2015, p. xiii): "The milréis was only rarely convertible to gold at a fixed rate of exchange; for most of the nineteenth century it floated freely against other currencies.

the child's services until the age of twenty-one, was slightly altered: in the revised bill, the master was only obliged to inform the State when opting not to retain the freeborn's services until he or she came of age. This meant the law would not come into immediate effect. Also, manumissions across the board now required the slaveowner's consent, and the paragraph emancipating slaves belonging to religious orders was dropped from the bill altogether. The revised text also contained checks against abolitionist meddling in private slave ownership. The original wording of Article 4 allowed "third-parties," which could be understood as the abolitionist societies, to buy the manumission of slaves without their owners being able to refuse the sale. This "third-party" interference was dropped, while another amendment restricted the Pecúlio – a saving the slave would be allowed to make to self-purchase freedom – to cases in which the owner gave consent. Paragraphs were elided from Article 7 that would have authorized public prosecutors to represent slaves and freedmen in freedom suits brought against the owners.[47]

These sweeteners secured the bill's passage through the Lower House on August 28, by sixty-one votes to thirty-five.[48] The following day, with the galleries chock-full, the problem was escalated to the Senate.

---

... In 1846 Brazilian legislation fixed 'parity' at 27 English pence per milréis. This parity was notional, representing an exchange rate target that was not supported on a continuing basis." This gives a rough idea of the contemporary value of the currency, that will be kept in milréis here.

[47] The text sent to the Senate did not contain Paragraph 3 of Article 7 from the original bill: "Public prosecutors may represent freedmen and slaves in civil lawsuits concerning their liberty." For a comparison between the draft bill and the amended bill, see ACD, Aug. 29, 1871.

[48] The result would have been 62 to 44 had the Speaker of the House voted and nine dissidents not failed to turn up. My numbers are different from those given by Conrad (1975, p. 362), who counts 65 for and 45 against. This is because Conrad bases his tally on the book *Discussão da reforma do estado servil*, vol. II, 1871 (pp. 128–50). However, the Lower House records register only 97 voters and a score of 61 for, 35 against and 1 abstention (numbers actually reproduced on pages 249–50 and 581–2 of *Discussão da reforma...*). I thank Jeffrey Needell for discussing this discrepancy with me. Needell confirmed the same results in his research on the *Jornal do Commercio*. Another reservation worth stating concerns any attempt to infer how deputies voted from the content of their speeches at Parliament. Silveira da Motta, for example, spoke against the bill, but voted for it. The same goes for regionalizing the votes (Carvalho, 1988, p. 66), as deputies could be elected to represent provinces they had not been born in. As there were 65 deputies representing the Northern provinces (Amazonas, Pará, Maranhão, Piauí, Ceará, Rio Grande do Norte, Paraíba, Pernambuco, Alagoas, Sergipe and Bahia) and 57 representing the Southern (Espírito Santo, Rio de Janeiro, São Paulo, Paraná, Santa Catarina, Rio Grande do Sul, Minas, Goiás, Mato Grosso), the north always had an eight-man majority. In other words, regional distribution does not express a specific stance on abolition, but rather the distortions of political representation under the imperial political system.

## The Last Abolition

Paulino lost the battle but never his head. He turned his energies toward whittling the little the bill had achieved down to nothing in the Upper House, where his uncle, Itaboraí, championed the planters' cause and parried every argument in favor of free womb in the minutiae. He complained against the government's steamrolling of Parliament, to which Rio Branco responded that never in the history of the Empire had any reform been so thoroughly debated – and would continue to be, as of August 30, when it was officially put to the Senate floor.

The debate in the Upper House was brief, largely because the legislative year was drawing to a close and because the discussions had already been underway in parallel with those in the Lower House. In comparison with the Lower House, the debate at the Senate was lukewarm, partly because the senators were a far more seasoned bunch whose lifelong tenure meant they would have to put up with each other long after the bill was passed. Even so, some of the earlier tactics were reprised, including time-wasting speeches, procrastinations, and absence of quorum. Once again, the government found itself having to contend with a riven party. It had stalwart support in people like São Vicente, the intellectual father of the project, and Torres Homem, the most eloquent pro-reform orator. But there were tough opponents too, such as the Baron of Três Barras, the author of most of the eleven petitions against the bill presented to the Senate, many of which demanded more generous compensation. This baron warned that the law would degenerate the "benevolent relationship between slaves and their masters" into one of "hangmen before their victims" – the victims being the slaveowners, of course.[49]

Where the Lower House had been almost all Conservative, the Senate was bipartisan, so resistance came from within and without. The Liberals protested. They were loath to see the Conservatives take the glory for the first main step toward abolition. Zacarias, the author of fifteen of the forty-seven speeches delivered on the subject at the Upper House, complained that this was a law it behooved his party to pass; after all, it had been his government that had first put the issue on the agenda in 1867. Silveira da Mota, author of an abolitionist project back in the 1850s, was Rio Branco's second most scathing bane from the Liberal camp, claiming that the bill was ragtag and devoid of any real guarantees.

---

[49] The quotations on the Senate debate are from ASI, Sept. 9, Aug. 10 and 14, Sept. 4 and 15, 1871. For a detailed analysis of this debate, see Needell (2006, p. 283).

Liberal opponents and Conservative dissidents combined to rail against the government's strong-arm approach and spoke at sleep-inducing length in a bid to run the clock down on the legislative year, which forced the government to extend it three times. The Prime Minister responded with some heated exchanges, insisting that the reform was in the nation's best interests and that to wait for other measures before implementing it would be "to procrastinate indefinitely and never graduate into action."[50]

Though subjected to every insult imaginable, on September 15, the government defeated the substitute bills to have its flagship Article 1 finally passed. Their strategy, Silveira da Mota bitterly complained, had been to let the opposition bluster without ever allowing it to shape the letter of the law. The government granted recess to the Lower House as soon as the bill was sent to the Senate and most of the deputies returned to their respective provinces. The Senate found itself caught between a rock (approving the bill without amendments) and a hard place (sending it back to the Lower House, which would only reconvene the following year). What proved key was that the majority of the Liberal senators, despite their grumbling, honored the Radical Liberal Manifesto of 1869 and voted in favor of the bill, which meant the government could ignore the dissident Conservatives. The project was approved exactly as it had arrived from the Lower House, freeing slave-born children from that date forward.[51]

Ultimately, freedom was only a future promise. The newborns would either stay under their mothers' care until the age of eight (in 1879), when they could be traded in for indemnification, or their owners could choose to waive indemnification and retain their services until 1892, when they turned twenty-one. In effect, the law protected slaveowners' rights into the third generation, because any offspring born to "freeborn" slaves before they reached the age of twenty-one also remained under the

---

[50] ASI, Sept. 12, May 23, 1871; Sept. 11, 1871. Nabuco (1897–1899, p. 837) relates Zacarias' speeches.

[51] For example, in the Lower House, the government defeated an amendment similar to that proposed by Perdigão Malheiros, that would have abolished slavery, without free womb, in 1899 (ASI, Sept. 6, 1871; Silveira da Motta, 1884; ASI, Sept. 25, 1871). In addition to the articles mentioned above, Article 6 freed slaves owned by the State, those used by the Crown, those belonging to unclaimed estates, able-bodied slaves abandoned by their owners, and those who had saved their owners' lives. Slaves freed under any of the above conditions remained under government supervision for a period of five years and were prohibited from vagrancy.

80 *The Last Abolition*

TABLE 2.1 *Free Womb Law votes in the Lower House and in the Senate, 1871*

| Province | For | | Against | |
| --- | --- | --- | --- | --- |
| | House | Senate | House | Senate |
| Alagoas | 4 | 1 | 0 | 0 |
| Amazonas | 1 | 0 | 0 | 0 |
| Bahia | 9 | 3 | 2 | 1 |
| Ceará | 6 | 2 | 0 | 0 |
| Espírito Santo | 0 | 1 | 2 | 0 |
| Goiás | 1 | 1 | 1 | 0 |
| Maranhão | 2 | 2 | 1 | 0 |
| Mato Grosso | 2 | 1 | 0 | 0 |
| Minas Gerais | 6 | 5 | 7 | 2 |
| Município Neutro | 0 | 0 | 3 | 0 |
| Pará | 3 | 1 | 0 | 0 |
| Paraíba | 3 | 1 | 0 | 0 |
| Paraná | 1 | 0 | 0 | 0 |
| Pernambuco | 8 | 4 | 2 | 0 |
| Piauí | 2 | 1 | 0 | 0 |
| Rio de Janeiro | 0 | 3 | 6 | 0 |
| Rio Grande do Norte | 2 | 1 | 0 | 0 |
| Rio Grande do Sul | 2 | 3 | 4 | 0 |
| Santa Catarina | 2 | 0 | 0 | 0 |
| São Paulo | 4 | 1 | 6 | 1 |
| Sergipe | 3 | 1 | 0 | 0 |
| not identified | 0 | 0 | 1 | 0 |
| Total | 61 | 32 | 35 | 4 |

*Source:* ACD, Aug. 28, 1871; ASI, Sept. 27, 1871

master's tutelage under the same terms. The bill's beneficiaries could still be inherited or transferred to new owners through the inheritance or sale of their mothers, and so remained commercially valuable assets.

The bill was passed into law on September 27 by thirty-two votes, thanks to the vote of eight Liberals, and besides the boycott of seventeen Conservatives. The ever-methodical Rebouças noted the exact time the free womb bill was approved: "Finally, the Senate votes in favor of emancipation amid a hail of flowers (at 55 minutes past 1)." Prohibited from manifesting their opinions in words, the abolitionists that packed the galleries celebrated with standing ovations, cheers, waved handkerchiefs and tossed bouquets: flowers rained from the galleries and carpeted the floor of the House, as the crowd cried "viva!",

# Pro-Slavery Rhetoric

FIGURE 2.1 Official iconography celebrating the Free Womb Law. In the upper section, the Viscount of Rio Branco is above the Emperor and surrounded by his ministers. Below, slaves and allegorical figures that represent freedom, honor, and glory.
Archive of the Fundação Biblioteca Nacional (National Library Foundation) Brazil. Reproduction by Jaime Acioli.

despite the Speaker's admonishments. The US minister in Brazil gathered some of these flowers from the floor, Rio Branco would later say, in order to send them back home as proof to his fellows that it was possible to achieve by peaceful means what had cost his nation rivers of blood to secure. And so – Senator Silveira da Mota observed, half in admiration, half in scorn – "over two rounds of voting, the Viscount of Rio Branco has succeeded in passing the law long considered a seven-headed hydra."[52]

[52] DNAAR, Sept. 27, 1871; ASI, Sept. 27, 1871. Silveira da Motta in Monteiro (1913, p. 23); ASI, Sept. 25, 1871. On the Senate vote, the same observations as made in footnote 48 also apply. The book *Discussão da Reforma do Estado Servil*, Vol. II, 1871 (p. 50) registers the presence of 40 senators, 33 in favor of the bill and 7 against. However, the House records (ASI, Sept. 27, 1871), transcribed in that same book (pp. 581–2), list 38 senators present, 32 voting for the bill (24 Conservatives and 8 Liberals), 4 against (including the Liberal Zacarias), and, supposedly, 2 abstentions. As there were 58 seats in the Senate and two of these were vacant, if all the absentees had

82 *The Last Abolition*

At one o'clock in the afternoon of September 28, at the Imperial Palace in Rio de Janeiro, the Princess Regent promulgated law 2040, the first of her "golden laws," though she had not been consulted at all throughout the deliberations. Nor was the Emperor, still in Europe, informed of the outcome by his Prime Minister. In the celebratory engravings and paintings, Rio Branco sits atop the Emperor, surrounded by his cabinet ministers and flanked by two goddesses: Glory and History.

### THE MARSHAL OF THE PAST

Arm-in-arm with Maria Amélia, Paulino opened the ball thrown to celebrate the end of this turbulent legislative session. His enormous house curdled with "vivid light that washed in waves across the artistically decorated rooms and the enchanted garden,"[53] packed with the cream of Rio society, figures from the press, party peers, political adversaries, and friends from the enemy camp. However, the atmosphere was more one of consternation than fraternization. Paulino was unhappy about the result of his battle with Rio Branco.

The Free Womb Law was passed with concessions and effective only as of a future date, but it still placed slavery in check, and everything that depended upon it. The fact that it put an end to slave-breeding meant that, for the first time in Brazil, the institution's days were truly numbered. The State had meddled deep within the social order of slavery by making excessive corporal punishment of captives grounds for liberation; obliging masters to register their slaves, under threat of liberation should they fail to do so within the period of one year, and with stiff penalties should they refuse; and by prohibiting the separation of slave families – if a husband or wife were sold, the spouse and children under the age of twelve had to be sold together. It maddened Paulino that a break-away faction of *his* party had teamed up with allies from the opposition to orchestrate one of the worst-ever offenses against the private life and economy of the Empire, a veritable coup d'état against his social group and its social bedrock, the right to own land and slaves.

---

voted against the bill it still would have passed by 32 votes to 22. The Liberals Silveira da Mota and Nabuco de Araújo voted with the government; the latter, painted as a key figure in his son's reconstruction of the debate (Nabuco, 1897–1899), delivered only one speech on the issue (ASI, Sept. 26, 1871). In terms of any regional determination of the vote, the same problems hold for the Senate as for the Lower House.

[53] DRJ, Sept. 14, 1874, in Soares de Souza, 1923, pp. 109 ff.

## Pro-Slavery Rhetoric

They feared knock-on effects too, deriving from the invention of an Emancipation Fund (Article 3), replenished with tax revenues on slave holdings, six different lotteries, fines, and the annual budget provisions from the different levels of government. Many provincial and municipal funds never made it off the drawing board, and the national fund received little by way of deposits, so many of the slavers' worst fears never materialized.

Of the unexpected consequences, one was the legal exploitation of loopholes the abolitionists would find in the new law. Another was the disintegration of the parties. While Rio Branco's faction had opted for reform over revolution, that was too much for Paulino and his men to bear. The Conservative Party's backbone had been broken, and with it the general coordinates the nation had been following since the start of the Second Reign. The Liberal Party had already splintered in 1870, with the foundation of the Republican Party. From 1871 on, there would be three factions as opposed to two parties: one modernizing group, largely consisting of Liberals; one moderate, composed by Liberals and Conservatives hesitant on reform; and the Hardliners, overwhelmingly Conservative with a few Liberal dissidents, and for whom change was anathema. This division weakened the political elite's ability to effect or block reform with any real efficiency, and the imperial political system became loose, diffuse, and rudderless. Political instability had reached chronic proportions.

Paulino assumed leadership of the resistance at this pivotal hour. His fellow planters from Cantagalo and other key areas were on the warpath. Reform of the slavery regime had dared to meddle with what they considered to be the natural order of things. Any change, as far as Paulino was concerned, was bound to lead to unrest and loss – an unwelcome visitor that came to his door not long afterwards, when his wife, "the flower of [his] soul," died while giving birth to their last child. After that, Paulino's eyes lost their luster, and his pale, balding visage was further darkened by a widower's gloom. Without his beloved Maria Amélia, life was "plunged into the pall of a grief so deep it would accompany [him] to the end." His powerlessness before this personal tragedy only fueled his public arrogance. From that time on, Paulino would not only represent his clique, he would embody, in the Lower House and Council of State, and in the Senate after 1876, the very politics of reaction: "resistance to all excess is a Conservative dogma; in this resistance I stand with my friends in the minority, and I will assist them to the extent of my powers."[54]

---

[54] Letter from Paulino Soares de Sousa to João A. Soares de Sousa, Sept. 25, 1877 (Soares de Souza, 1923); ACD, Aug. 23, 1871.

84 *The Last Abolition*

And so he did, for the next sixteen years. After the death of Itaboraí, Paulino, then aged thirty-seven, replaced his uncle as head of the Hardliners. As one who knew him would later say, "he ruled them with an iron will, solid as a rock, but beneath a velvety veneer. He was the sort of leader who asked rather than ordered, persuaded rather than threatened. Yet he embodied that apparatus so thoroughly, and with such gravity, that his followers accepted his leadership like that of some spiritual guide."[55] His light-handedness was the involucre of a fierce intransigence. Paulino was a slavocrat, member of an aristocracy whose whole way of life was grounded in slavery, and he owned it, becoming the leader of a pro-slavery coalition, the political faction committed to defending his social stratum and the status quo that favored it. The overlap between lifestyle and political activism was total. And so, in 1871, he took the bazooka of resistance into his slender hands. He may have lost a battle, but a good general never abandons the war.

With a nod to the bust of his father that adorned the entrance to his house, Paulino donned the uniform of the Hardliners. The Viscount of Uruguay had been one of the architects of the Second Reign. His son would be a staunch conservative, the guardian of the legacy of "higher souls" who, if they could "offer a word of inspiration to we who follow in their footsteps, they would certainly exhort us, now and forever: 'To defend this order; ... sustain the major interests of today, because they are the promise of lasting prosperity'." In defending that heritage, Paulino, as even his adversaries had to admit, demonstrated rare leadership:

invoking the principle of authority, the need for discipline, he enlarged his troop against the government, and held it together to the very end in complete thrall to his every order. No other politician in the Empire ... held sway for so long, come hail or shine, of such a numerous, disciplined party rank and file as Paulino de Sousa, ..., ever-loyal to the banner of resistance ... on the issue of slavery.

Watching him take the helm, one of his followers branded him as the "Marshal of the Future." He was wrong. Paulino was not there to herald the new. Before his father, tradition set in stone, he was a knight whose oath was to defend the order of slavery, the bedrock of the institutions and way of life of the Second Reign. A knight who would stand and be the last to fall, on May 13, 1888, a "Marshal of the Past."[56]

---

[55] Monteiro (1913, p. 21).

[56] ACD, Aug. 23, 1871; Nabuco (1897–1899, p. 859, note 24); Firmino Rodrigues Silva, in Soares de Souza (1923, p. 88).

# 3

# The Moral Repertoire of Abolitionism

### LUÍSA'S SON

Just as the Sabinada left its mark on Rebouças, it affected Luís Gonzaga Pinto da Gama, but in a very different way: his mother Luísa Mahin, an African freewoman who was a stall-worker and rebel in the Malê Revolt[1] in Bahia, went to Rio after a lover who, like herself, was mixed up in the slave uprising. The son stayed behind, nurturing the most incurable nostalgia. "My father, I won't go so far as to say he was white, . . . was a courtier; he came from one of the leading families in Bahia, of Portuguese origin"; "I was raised in his arms." Arms that dealt the cards on which he would gamble the fate of that very boy, lost to a friend who promptly cashed him in at the slave market. It was in this manner that in November 1840 ten-year-old Luís embarked in Salvador a freeman and disembarked in Rio de Janeiro a slave. His first owner was a candle salesman, followed by a slave trader, who failed to sell him to farmers, because the Bahian slaves reeked of revolt. So, the trader kept Gama as his own house and hire slave in São Paulo. There, "I learned to work as a scullion, as a shoemaker, how to wash and starch clothes, and how to sew." He met a law student, who taught him to read and write and told him that, under the legislation passed on November 7, 1831, which banned the Atlantic slave trade, African captives arriving after that date, and their Brazil-born children, were free in the eyes of the law. So, at the age of eighteen, he confronted his owner with the terms of this dead law: he had been born free, and free he would

---

[1] The Malê Revolt was a huge slave insurrection, led by Muslim slaves in Bahia province in 1835, cf. Reis, 1993.

86                            *The Last Abolition*

be. The trader, perhaps out of affection for him or out of ennui, or because the meddlesome law student hailed from an influential family, let him go without putting a slave catcher on his heels. Gama took one of the few safe routes open to an ex-slave and enlisted in the army, rising to the rank of corporal. He became a copyist, a scribe, joined the ordnance corps and became an amanuensis with the Police Department. These posts enabled him to hone his writing skills, but he always ended up being dismissed for insubordination.

He managed to land these jobs thanks to a series of recommendations, such as those from a professor at the São Paulo Faculty of Law who was also a member of the Liberal Party. These referrals got him into the press, a gateway into politics, where he was able to pen his *Primeiras troves burlescas de Getulino* (*Getulino's First Burlesque Quatrains*), in 1859, a collection of mono-stanza satires against the prevailing mores and institutions. The book was dedicated to this patron as a sign of his gratitude to his Liberal Party protectors.[2]

His social climbing seemed to know no bounds, and he aimed to bring it to completion beneath the Law Faculty arcades; a dream nourished by the porosity of public life and the social ascent of free blacks and mixed-race people ("mulattos") that enabled Gama to gain employment and a public voice in the press and at gentlemen's clubs, and tap into the social networks of political circles.[3] However, the leap from slavery to lawyer-dom took more than a formal education. Successful social mobility among what Pierre Bourdieu termed the *parvenus* required the assimilation of higher-class lifestyles, worldviews, and behaviors. Wont to rudeness and "off-color gags," Gama failed this particular test. Though accepted by São Paulo's Liberal circles, he failed to curry favor with the aristocratic gentry, which was paramount for a life in Court society. His penchant for ribaldry meant he would not fit in at the salons. Unlike Rebouças, he lacked the polish to lighten his color. Barred for his social ineptness, he never even made it into undergraduate school and was left bereft of a degree, the opening of the doors of Parliament. With no diploma and no refinement, his aspirations to the crème de la crème of

---

[2] The biographical information given here is based on Gama's own account (letter from Luís Gama to Lúcio de Mendonça, Jul. 25, 1880) and on the biographies by Menucci (1938), Azevedo (1999) and Ferreira (2001).

[3] The 1872 census registered sizeable contingents of blacks (919,674) and mixeds ("mulattos") (3,331,654), together accounting for 50.4 percent of the free population (Paiva et al., 2012, p. 20). As such, individual social ascension could not smile on many, lest the social pyramid should crumble.

## Moral Repertoire of Abolitionism

imperial society were reduced to dust. As he complained in his verses, no matter what he did, he would never be one of them:

> *Science and letters*
> *Those are not for you*
> *With your Slave Coast fetters*
> *You will never quite do.*

While Rebouças, André's father, used his title of attorney at law as a rung on the social ladder, and one which delivered him snugly into the aristocracy's favor, Gama wanted membership of this social stratum to thwart the tacit social norm that excluded him. His poem "Quem sou eu?" (Who am I?) ricochets the word "goat," which was used against him:

> *If I am black, or indeed a goat*
> *it matters not a blast.*
> *What's in it of any note?*
> *Goats there are in every caste*
> *As the species is so very vast...*
> *Billygoats black, and billygoats white*
> *Let us all be frank and forthright,*
> *Folks uncouth and folks refined*
> *One and all contains my kind.*

The closing verse pasteurizes the imperial elite – "It's all one tribe of goats" – and debunks the "natural" basis for white supremacy at the heart of the social hierarchy, highlighting the difficulty of taking skin color as a yardstick in Brazil. This ambiguity could be used in favor of assimilation by silencing color or it could be dispelled by being assumed outright. Gama opted for the latter, in both his public and private life (he married a black woman). The social identity that was tagged upon him from outside, he took upon himself as a defining factor. Rather than retreat to mixed-race camouflage, he identified as black.

The experience of enforced social subordination fed his political defiance. He started producing anti-monarchist and anti-clerical satire for the fringe press, joining forces with the Italian caricaturist Angelo Agostini on *Diabo Coxo* (The Lame Devil) (1864–1865) and with the Republican Américo de Campos on *O cabrião* (The Gadfly) (1866–1867). He wrote for the newspaper *Radical Paulistano* and joined the club of the same name, both Radical Liberal strongholds.[4]

---

[4] The description of Gama's habits is from Pompeia (1882, pp. 207–8, 210). See also Menucci (1938, p. 224). Gama's poetry is from Ferreira (ed. 2011, pp. 32, 61–5). On his relationship with Agostini and Campos, see Ferreira (2001, pp. 351–2) and Sodré (1966, p. 262).

FIGURE 3.1 The abolitionist Luís Gonzaga Pinto da Gama (1830–1882). Unknown photographer.

Gama belonged to a generation of young men outside the imperial aristocracy who were attracted to the Radical Liberal political faction and who flocked to their conferences after the political crisis of 1868. In protest against the government's ouster, the Liberals abstained from the ensuing legislative elections and instead opted for self-imposed parliamentary exile. They regrouped and redoubled their opposition by opening a public space for discussing politics in the press, pamphlets, and clubs. In 1869, the Zacarias wing opened the Clube da Reforma (Reform Club), while Tavares Bastos and Silveira da Mota set up the Clube Radical (Radical Club). The Radical Club lent political connotations until there were strictly cultural upper-strata conferences devoted to literature, arts, and entertainment. At these gatherings, "radical" was a buzzword and was invoked to defend their reformist platform, which included the gradual phasing-out of slavery. The literary conferences gave them a captive audience, namely the liberal professionals, scientists, literati, and ladies of the social elite, and attracted the beneficiaries of Rio Branco's modernization program, especially the students, who, like Gama, strove for social climbing through learning.

The viscount's government, which ended its term in 1875, followed up the Free Womb Law with a raft of judicial, electoral, and commercial

## Moral Repertoire of Abolitionism

reforms, which included expansion of the communications network, the installation of the telegraph, the standardization of weights and measures, the creation of a national census, the passing of the naturalization law, several attempts at secularizing the institutions, and a wide-reaching public land registration drive. Rio Branco's economic reforms included investment in urban infrastructure and increasing manufacturing by making machinery cheaper to acquire. He championed construction projects that required engineers like Rebouças, and fostered a banking system and trade environment that needed qualified professionals. This was the motivation for the higher-education reforms, which broadened access to the military and engineering faculties, allowing young outsiders, not part of the elite, to infiltrate the preserve of the landowning gentry, where they could acquire the educational capital to question their authority. Perhaps they would not have done so if a degree alone had afforded a better social standing, but with the reforms incomplete, many publicly complained of the same frustrated upward social mobility that had driven Luís Gama into politics. In fact, Gama himself delivered a speech at a "Radical Conference" in which he aimed all his firepower at the Moderating Power, the fourth constitutional power the Emperor himself represented.

The conferences were not alone in invigorating the public sphere. More affordable printing machinery had led to a proliferation of magazines and books and fueled the advent of new types of publication. During or soon after Rio Branco's government, a number of medium-sized newspapers emerged, including *A Gazeta de Notícias* (1874), *A Província de São Paulo* (1875), and *A Gazeta da Tarde* (1877), that were independent of the imperial parties. The *Província*, for one, was aligned with *A República* (1870), the official mouthpiece of the Republican Party. At least twenty smaller papers, such as *O Mequetrefe* (1975), appeared between 1870 and 1872. *Revista Illustrada* (1876), edited by Gama's friend Angelo Agostini, offered political criticism through cartoons. Modernization caused urban services and commerce to expand, along with tea rooms, cafés, bookstores, and theaters, which became hotspots for discussion of the arts and politics in Court and in smaller cities such as Recife and Salvador and even in the less culturally alive ones, such as São Paulo and Porto Alegre. In this expanding public space, Radical Liberals mixed with a new melting pot of social climbers facilitated by modernization: students, the beneficiaries of higher-education reform; journalists, typesetters, draughtsmen, writers, the staff of the new medium-sized press; musicians, singers, actresses, comedians, composers, all part of a fledgling entertainment theater industry; and young military officers with

## The Last Abolition

no clear post-Paraguay War career path. None of these had a voice at the political table, but they were all ignited by modern ideas and were critical of the Empire.[5]

As such, two processes set in motion by the political system paved the way for mobilization: the modernization of the Conservatives expanded the literati and opened up a new extra-parliamentary political arena, while the Radical Liberal conferences legitimized its use for political criticism. The result was new people using a new space. Talents from outside the social elite, like Luís Gama, soon organized their own conferences on the same themes during the Parliamentary debates on the Free Womb Law, especially the democratization of political institutions, the abolition of slavery, and, later on, the secularization of the State. Half on account of, and half in spite of, the Radical Liberals, new players outside of the land-and-slave-owning elite, joined the debate on the course Brazilian society ought to take. Gama proposed reform from top-down and bottom-up, "with neither kings nor slaves."[6]

This dilated public sphere provided new political spaces (theaters and the press) and social agents (educated individuals who had neither aristocratic origins nor access to Parliament) through which to generalize a Borges-style activism (associativism and civic ceremonies). Thus abolitionism was able to graduate from the elite activism it had been limited to in the 1870s to becoming a social movement.[7]

New borns were inadvertently engaged in a political war, since pro-slavery politicians, infuriated by attempts to meddle with the status quo in

---

[5] On the radical conferences, see Carvalho (2007); on the context of social modernization and political crisis at the end of the Second Reign and the rallying of the youths who joined the reformist movement led by the 1870s generation, see Alonso (2002); and on the expansion of the press, Sodré (1966, pp. 243–4). Student participation is a constant in social movements, given the "biographical availability" of the young, who, not yet enlisted into the workforce, have time on their hands and little to lose by actively engaging in protests (McAdam, 1986).

[6] Ferreira (2001, pp. 351–2).

[7] Far from suggesting an organic collective player that is unison in voice, a "social movement" is a type of extra-Parliamentary contentious politics, which tends to configure a network of interactions among a plurality of activists, associations, and events (Diani, 2003) constructed during a conflict. A high membership turnover and heterogeneity of social standing and beliefs is quite common to social movements, obliging activists to constantly negotiate and redefine their goals and identities and to replace their leaders. This format urges the reconstruction of the social movement out of its *practices of contention*: public campaigns, political performance repertoire (creation of associations, rallies, etc.), and public demonstrations of the worth, unity, number, and commitment of its members (Tilly, 2005, p. 308).

1871, began to use this public space as well, resorting to newspapers and Plantation Clubs to foment and expand their strategy. Ever since the free womb trauma, Paulino and his allies had been intent on thwarting Rebouças, Borges, and Gama at every turn.

### THE RHETORIC OF CHANGE

To grow from a handful of activists to untold legions of followers, abolitionism had to cross a symbolic Rubicon: it had to dismantle ways of thinking, feeling, and acting that ran deep in Brazilian society. It responded to pro-slavery rhetoric by delegitimizing it through a *rhetoric of change*.[8]

The Brazilian abolitionists did not have to start from scratch, though. Earlier movements in Europe, the United States, and throughout Spanish America had crafted antislavery arguments that remained available as a moral abolitionist repertoire. But it was one that needed adapting, hand-picking the elements that were compatible with the local tradition. In that sense, abolitionist rhetoric in Brazil was circumstantial pro-slavery rhetoric but through a looking glass, and was anchored in its own three schemata of interpretation: compassion, rights, and progress.

Compassion appealed to general sensibilities.[9] No abolitionist movement could possibly have existed if everyone subscribed to the same beliefs as Paulino and Alencar. The dismantling of slavery certainly involved changes to the economic structures, the logic of political conflicts, and the social hierarchy, but also to the prevalent ways of feeling and thinking. So long as the majority saw it as a natural state of things, slavery remained morally defensible and socially invisible. For the slave, seen as a mere *thing or domestic animal* that was simply part of the landscape, to be recast as an *enslaved person* worthy of political action and moral support was going to take a major shift in the schemata that underpinned the prevailing perception of the social world. In his *Sobrados e mucambos* (Mansions and Shanties), Gilberto Freyre described the long-term sociocultural change, already in motion, accelerated by late

---

[8] The term is Hirschman's (1991).
[9] In order to function efficiently, moral repertoires have to resonate among the society's "structures of feeling" (Williams, 1960), that is, they must converse with the morality and sensibilities of the man in the street. Agents deal with such repertoires much like jazz musicians: they select existing sheet music to suit their purposes and circumstances, considering the partnerships, audience, and antagonists involved, and improvise (Tilly, 2006, p. 35). As such, every interpretation is a singularization.

nineteenth-century urbanization and grounded upon two pillars. The first of these was technological progress. Steam trains and ships, typesetters and printers and, above all, the telegraph sent information, merchandise, people, social innovations, from scientific inventions to economic ventures, machines and ideas, swirling back and forth between the Americas and Europe. The second pillar was urbanization. The agricultural boom that followed the end of the Atlantic slave trade brought banking, commerce, services, businesses, and infrastructure projects (like those embraced by Rebouças) to the Court and other large cities, such as Recife. This process affected the social hierarchy through the rise of new professions, such as engineering, shifting the balance of social power from the fields into the city streets, from the landowning father to his urban, degree-holding sons and sons-in-law, from the symbolic power of the priest and his scriptures to the physician with his scientific tomes.

Modernization also concerned upending traditional mores and customs, as it undermined patriarchal authority. Men became more modern, more elaborately-dressed, like the dandy poet Castro Alves, and women moved from the domestic realm to public spheres such as the arts, education, and science. Brazilian society was still hierarchical and patriarchal, but, as novels from the 1860s onwards show, it now embraced a new, urban lifestyle that eschewed the rough behaviors of the ranch in favor of politeness, civility, and refinement. What ensued was a long, non-linear, but cumulative civilizing process that encouraged more contained, refined deportment over physical violence, opting instead for subtle, symbolic forms of imposing the hierarchy. Conduct that had once been considered normal, such as a father's use of force upon his children, a husband's upon his wife, a man upon his animals, was now seen as barbarous and repugnant.[10]

In the 1870s, these processes, which had been running more or less in parallel, converged: on the one hand, there was a new sensibility and modern lifestyle, and, on the other, the technical means for their dissemination via railroads, the printing press, and the telegraph. All of this enabled the assimilation of the abolitionist moral repertoire in Brazil.

A humanitarian sensibility that stressed social empathy laid the groundwork in Britain and the United States for an antislavery moral ethos.

---

[10] On the moral fundaments of abolitionism, see Temperley (1981) and Brown (2006). On the civilizing of behaviors, see Elias (1996). "New lifestyle" is an expression used by Freyre (2003, p. 952). Though politically conservative, Alencar captured this social change in his urban novels.

# Moral Repertoire of Abolitionism

For David Brion Davis, this antislavery sentiment spilled from four sources: the Enlightenment of Montesquieu and his theory of slavery as the bane of human happiness; Adam Smith's position between slavery and human progress; romanticism, which embraced primitivism in order to conflate the African with the noble savage; and, most important of all, Quakerism, which associated slavery and sin. These four conceptual cornerstones denaturalized the slave-owning way of life and redefined slavery – hitherto considered a natural and legitimate product of inequality – as an economically inefficient, morally reprehensible, and emotionally abject institution. This sea-change cleared the way for chattel to become individuals and for a political intervention to emerge in their favor,[11] drawing the lines of a battle that took on all the aspects of a moral imperative.

When Rebouças and Gama became interested in the subject, this repertoire had already spread in the Occident. Its assimilation was selective, in dialogue with local traditions. In Anglo-American abolitionism, antislavery rhetoric was buttressed by Protestant morality. In Brazil, Christianity translated into a hierarchical Catholicism whose rites, symbology, and language legitimized the imperial institutions as expressions of divine will, with slaves on the bottom rung of a ladder, the lowliest of God's human creatures, biblically exhorted to go forth and multiply. This local orientation of Catholicism left little room for a Christian questioning of slavery in Brazil.

During the free womb debate, Christianity reared its head in *A escravidão examinada à luz da Santa Bíblia* (Slavery examined in the light of the Holy Bible), an apocryphal representation to Parliament with an indefatigable list of episodes and passages from the Old and New Testaments painting the hardships of slavery as Christ-like sacrifice leading to redemption.[12] However, in Brazil, Catholicism oozed in drops what Protestantism had gushed in the Anglo-American world: pro-abolition sentiment.

---

[11] Haskell (1992, pp. 133 ff.) notes the expansion of "the conventional limits of moral responsibility" such that they now encompassed the evils of slavery. Most interpreters recognize the relevance of humanitarianism and its diffusion throughout the Quaker network to the genesis of Anglo-American abolitionism, though they diverge on the causal vector between humanitarianism and capitalism (Haskell, 1992; Davis, 1992, 2006; Drescher, 1986, 1997, 2009; Brown, 2006).

[12] Apocryphal (1871, p. 30). The manifesto of The Society Against the African Slave Trade and for the Promotion of Colonization and Indian Civilization affirmed that "our slaves are God's children, just like ourselves, and are our brothers before the Lord" (SCT, 1852, p. 21). See also Soares (1847, p. 24).

94 *The Last Abolition*

It must also be noted that Christian delegitimization of slavery rarely walked alone. Throughout the Second Reign, romanticism set the tone for the moral contestation of slavery. The major artistic movement of the nineteenth century, with its grandiloquent forms and emotional hyperboles – passion, compassion, devotion – flourished in novels, music, poetry, theater, romantic life, and in political rhetoric, the root and fruit of the new sensibility tailored to a public thirsty not for tragedy and its immutable pathos, but for the happy endings of drama. Brazilian romanticism, however, served two masters, one for and one against slavery. The primitivist justifications of Anglo-American antislavery were skewed on entry, with the African replaced by the Amerindian as the imperial tradition's embodiment of the noble savage. In literature, the African was painted as a wolf at the master's door – as seen in Alencar's *O demônio familiar* (The House Devil) – crystallized in the archetypes of the rebellious slave and the wily mulatta. Yet romanticism also depicted another type of bondsperson: the noble, faithful slave. The wet-nurse bound to the suckling babe; the girl ruined by her master's sexual proclivities; the pilloried elderly, women, and children; all of these figures endured the humiliation of a human being reduced to merchandise to be bought and sold. Through these characters, a panorama was drawn that spoke of the afflictions of captivity, a suffering that ennobled the African and fostered compassion in the nascent urban public opinion.

The 1859 novel *Ursula, romance original brasileiro*, in the mold of the international best-seller *Uncle Tom's Cabin*, took a moral pickaxe to the "odious chain of slavery." The lead character, Túlio, is a *man* of noble sentiment imprisoned in the *condition* of slavery, and – in reverse symmetry with Alencar's *House Devil* – he solves problems rather than causing them. Here, the good master/bad slave dichotomy of circumstantial pro-slavery rhetoric is turned on its head: the slave is ennobled, willing to sacrifice his life to save the hero, and his selfless decency relegates the master to the natural state of "barbarian," "indomitable beast," "tiger-hearted" brute. The novel demands our sympathy: "What a sorrowful thing is slavery!" For the slave, there is pain and resignation, for the master guilt and regret. The romantic framing serves to depict the slave as flagellated with trials and torments and unmasks the institution of slavery as morally inadmissible and emotionally harrowing, "an accursed chain" repugnant to all modern sensibilities.[13] The humanization of the slave dehumanized slavery.

---

[13] Cf. Sayers (1956, pp. 86 ff.); Reis (1859, pp. 13–4, 27–8, 136, 138, 146–7). Right from the first abolitionist associations, slavery is described as "the harshest of things, revolting

# Moral Repertoire of Abolitionism

The suffering slave became a leitmotif in romantic literature from the mid-1860s onward, just as the public debate on slavery was coming to a head. It was proliferated in novels and poems, particularly the verses of Castro Alves, the pupil of Abílio Borges, whose "Navio negreiro" (Slave Ship), published in 1868, took poetic liberties in its description of a slave galley, but hit the mark in terms of reader sympathies:

> ... What a harrowing picture!
> A funereal dirge...What rickety figures!...
> The clanking manacles...the scourging whip...
> These legions of men as black as pitch, ...
> Locked in the links of a single chain
> Comes stumbling on, the famished train, ...
>
> One rants delirious, another raves,
> another whom suffering depraves,
> ... And yet the driver orders with a quip, ...
> "Hearken sailors, make merry with the whip!" ...
>
> These are not even free enough to die.
> Bound in a chain they cannot break
> – an iron-clad, lugubrious snake –
> braced with the screws of slavery.
>
> There is a people that the flag befits
> to cover such infamy and cowardice...
> My God! my God! but what flag is this
> that impudent on the topsail flits?
>
> Arise now, heroes of the New World!
> Andrada! tear this flag down from the breeze!
> Columbus! close the gateways to your seas!

In framing slavery as a drama, romanticism shaped a new sensibility and stoked compassion for the slave.[14] Moreover, it made room for the ruination of slaveowners at the hands of their slaves. Instead of the emphasizing the damage the master could do to the slave – the perspective taken in *Ursula* – in *As vítimas e algozes: quadros da escravidão* (Victims

---

to the human heart" (Soares, 1847, pp. 20–1); however, compassion only spread as a formula in the mid-nineteenth century. On the dissemination of Beecher Stowe's book in the United States, see Surwillo (2005), and, in Brazil, Nabuco (1900). *Ursula* was written by the teacher Maria Firmina dos Reis (under the pseudonym Uma Maranhense).

[14] In poetry, the theme was even a frequent one in the "Burlesque Quatrains" of the bawdy Luís Gama: "Cry, slave, inside your cage/ ... The cage up on its perch/ where treacherous captivity/ grief and sobs provokes." In prose, a good example is Bernardo Guimarães' *Escrava Isaura* (Isaura, the slave). For an opposing view, on the "distance between romanticism and abolitionism," see Haberly (1972, p. 370).

96 *The Last Abolition*

and Their Tormenters: Scenes of Slavery), published in 1869 (before the Free Womb Law) by the Liberal Joaquim Manuel de Macedo, there are good examples of the unkindly end the owners could meet: the Creole Simeão kills his masters; the witchdoctor Pai-Raiol incites the salting of whole plantations, and the wet-nurse Lucinda corrupts the master's daughter. Danger brews on the home front. While in Alencar's *O demônio familiar* (The House Devil), the master maintains the social balance by wielding his power to manumit, in *As vítimas e algozes* the slave blows up the estate. The master finds himself at the mercy of a slave intent on spilling blood, as in Haiti. Slavery was a ticking time bomb, according to the introduction, one the politicians and slaveowners would do well to defuse while they still could. This loaded defense of abolition as a way of protecting slave owners from an even worse fate was all about rallying an "imaginary of fear"[15] like that employed in "Bandido negro" (Black Bandit), again by Castro Alves:

> *... throw, oh wind, oh grassland gust of death,*
> *this iron gauntlet at the master's feet, ...*
>
> *And the master ...*
> *He murmurs, and condemns himself in dream:*
> *"What demons are these that horrid team,*
> *that trudge on past, famished and nude? ...*
>
> *It is we, my master, but do not dismay*
> *our shackles we have cast away ...*
>
> *Let the howl of a life mowed down*
> *at the banquet of death resound ...*
>
> *Let the blood of slaves fall as dew*
> *a bloody dew upon the vexer's face,*
> *Grow fast, grow tall, crimson field,*
> *Grow tall, fierce vengeance.*[16]

The long-suffering slave was recast as the romantic rebel, particularly by Castro Alves, who masterfully combined the inversion of pro-slavery's

---

[15] However, Joaquim Manuel de Macedo (1869, p. 4) did not defend immediate abolition, which he described as an "insane jolt that would plunge the nation into convulsions, unprecedented disorder and a draining of public and private wealth, miring the people deeper into poverty and the State, into bankruptcy." On the "imaginary of fear" in political and literary writings, see Azevedo (2004) and Sussekind (1991).

[16] The poem is from the posthumous collection *Os escravos* (The Slaves) (1883), but it was written at around the same time as *Navio negreiro* (Slave Ship) (1868). A similar theme appears in *Tragédia no mar* (Tragedy at Sea) (1865).

rhetoric with an appeal to the slave's humanity, conjuring a poetic that exposed slavery's iniquity and called society to rally against it.

As a counterweight to the economic and political rationales of Paulino's circumstantial pro-slavery rhetoric, this line of combat pulled on heartstrings in order to stir up compassion and moral indignation. On an emotional level, this new poetic presented as unsustainable an institution that had hitherto been accepted as natural. In so doing, it triggered a chivalrous ethos (befitting the new mores of aristocratic society in a modernizing Brazil) that saw abolitionism as a just and noble cause in need of a champion.

While in the Anglo-Saxon world religion was the catalyst that turned the public tide against slavery, in Brazil, where the institution was protected by the official religion of the State, Catholicism, the job of generating antislavery sentiment fell mainly to the arts.

If this schema of compassion moved hearts and minds, another line of delegitimization was more concerned with busying arms and legs. In the eighteenth and the first half of the nineteenth century, when abolitionism was at its peak in Europe and the United States, progress was philosophically grounded, synonymous with liberty and civilizing mores. As abolitionism was a late arrival in Brazil, it was underscored by the new social sciences, especially the sociological tsunami caused in the latter half of the nineteenth century by positivism and its evolutionist peers, especially Spencerianism. All those kinds of evolutionism defined progress as the inexorable march of industrialization, urbanization, and secularization. The "march of civilization" would destroy the traditional institutions – Catholicism, agrarianism, monarchism, and slavery – and give birth to a modern, scientific, industrial, republican society based on free labor. Under this lens, slavery, adjusted for centuries to current social norms, became an anachronism to be eradicated by a "scientific politics." This schema of progress circulated in Brazil through books, the press, and graduate schools (like the Polytechnic where Rebouças lectured) and the new generation of students relied on those ideas to criticize the imperial status quo, slavery included.[17]

The moral cancer, as the compassion schemata would brand slavery, acquired a new meaning based on scientific metaphor: it was also a *social* cancer. At the time of the Free Womb Law, *A escravatura no Brasil precedida de um artigo sobre a agricultura e colonização no Maranhão* (1865) (Slavery in Brazil preceded by an article on agriculture and colonization in Maranhão), by Francisco Brandão Jr., resorted to Auguste

---

[17] On Brazil's scientific politics, cf. Alonso (2002, pp. 165 ff.); similar arguments can be seen in the Spanish debate (Corwin, 1968, p. 169).

98 *The Last Abolition*

Comte in order to classify slavery as an archaic institution that was holding back the "march of civilization" in Brazil. The State, the brain in the collective body, badly needed to prescribe some therapy against this social malaise. Similar theses appeared among the São Paulo Republicans in the mid-1870s. Raimundo Teixeira Mendes, whom Rebouças knew from the newsroom at the *Gazeta de Notícias*, persuaded a group of graduates from the Polytechnic and Military Academy in Rio de Janeiro to embrace the positivist idea of progress that took hold at the Faculties of Law in São Paulo and Recife, which turned out steady streams of abolitionists and republicans.[18]

If Catholicism was content to tolerate slavery, spiritism – the lay religion of science – condemned it outright. Adolfo Bezerra de Menezes, from the Liberal Party, a doctor and future spiritist icon, called his followers to rise up against this "social leprosy": "The cursed roots of slavery run deep in the heart of Brazilian society." His pro-free womb pamphlet, penned in 1869, entitled *A escravidão no Brasil e medidas que convém tomar para extingui-la sem dano para a nação* (Slavery in Brazil and the measures to be taken to eradicate it without harming the nation), proposed the introduction of a tax to cover the costs of settling and educating freed slaves and reversed the threat inherent in circumstantial pro-slavery rhetoric: postponing abolition would intensify social degeneration and increase manifold the likelihood of a Haiti-style revolt or Civil War like in the United States. The doctor's remedy was clear: "Faced with the eternal impassiveness of the government, let we, the citizens, march ahead of our representatives in forcing and promoting the major reforms so badly needed to civilize our century."[19] In short, the scientific brand of politics defined slavery as backward, fostered belief in the superiority of an industrial urban society based on free labor, and clamored for political intervention in order to eliminate the practice.

---

[18] The author of *A escravatura no Brasil*, Francisco Antônio Brandão Jr., was rebuked by his brother: "You could not have chosen a more detestable subject . . ., you'll be taken for a nutcase, a utopian!"; "reformer of Brazil" (in a letter from Francisco Antônio Brandão Jr. to Pierre Laffitte, July 4, 1865, in Lins (1964, p. 97)). However, in the 1870s and 1880s, the argument spread among the students of the faculties (cf. Alonso, 2002). The positivist character is in Nunes (1884, p. 29).

[19] Bezerra de Menezes (1869, pp. 31, 33–6, 50, 55–6). See also the Comte/Allan Kardec combination in *A Coroa e a emancipação do elemento servile, Estudos sobre a emancipação dos escravos em Brasil* (1866) and *Novos estudos sobre a emancipação dos escravos no Brasil* (1868), by the Bahian engineer Antônio da Silva Neto (Valle, 2010, pp. 30 ff.). Another spiritist who became a staunch abolitionist in the 1880s was MP Aristides Spínola.

## Moral Repertoire of Abolitionism

The spur of progress, like the schemata of compassion, was win-win: as slavery was a social relationship, in freeing their slaves the former masters would ascend the rungs of civilization. However, both approaches drew a stark border between the abolitionist and pro-slavery sides: according to romanticism, they were heroes versus villains; for scientific politics, they were modernizers versus reactionaries.

The third way of combating slavery was actually the oldest of the three. The Enlightenment schema of the natural right to freedom was common to all antislavery movements. In Brazil, it was a longstanding line of argument that stretched all the way back to José Bonifácio de Andrada e Silva and the manifesto issued by the society against the African Slave Trade and for the Promotion of Colonization and Indian Civilization (SCT), according to which slavery could "not be promoted on the grounds of slave utility" nor sustained by any natural law. One of the members of the SCT used Montesquieu to counter Aristotle: slavery was "not inherent to nature, much less a prerequisite for society." The law could not underwrite an institution born out of "brute force" that had robbed Africans of their natural prerogatives. The right to own slaves was incompatible with the natural right to freedom.[20]

Furthermore, the abolitionists had positivist legislation to brandish in the 1826 treaty with Great Britain and the Brazilian law of 1831, which freed all Africans imported into Brazil from that date on. A dead law, but a law nonetheless, it provided juridical grounds on which to question slave ownership – an approach that was Luís Gama's specialty.

One difference between Brazilian and foreign abolitionist rhetoric was the notion of incomplete citizenship. In the United States, the co-existence of liberalism and slavery never bothered the political elite, but in Brazil it caused immense discomfort. And the abolitionists used that to their advantage: freedom, like equality, was indispensable to complete the nation-building process,[21] hence the slogan, heard at abolitionist events since Abílio Borges' civic ceremonies, that abolition was a second Independence. Independence day, September 7, started to be used for events and in texts to suggest a synergy between the old Independence of the country and a new Independence of its people.

And so Brazilian abolitionism armed itself with the schemata of rights in three different keys: freedom as a natural right, borrowed from

---

[20] Carvalho (2005, p. 37); SCT (1852, p. 7); Soares (1847, pp. 8, 12, 15).
[21] Carvalho (2005, pp. 48 ff.).

philosophy; as a legal right, based on positive law and the courts; and, third, as a political right associated with citizenship-building.

## Castor and Pollux

Brazilian abolitionist rhetoric drew from foreign sources, but its adaptation to local circumstances generated a unique blend that was more lay than religious, more scientific than philosophical, and dramatic rather than circumspect. The trio of compassion, rights, and progress schemata were widely used, but tailored for diverse audiences: the dramatic appeal for compassion prevailed at public conferences and in the arts; progress, in pamphlets and speeches; and rights, in Parliament and in the courts. However, the three schemata were also combined into a single rhetoric of change, feeding a new sensibility, a new morality, and a new cognition regarding slavery, transforming slavery into an iniquity, an injustice, a retardation. Considered the product of social forces – neither the work of nature nor of divine will – it was alterable by political action. In this sense, the rhetoric of change provided the discursive bases for activism in favor of the slaves, and gave abolitionism antidotes to circumstantial pro-slavery rhetoric: against the futility of reform, it stressed the dangers of delay; against the perversion effect, it extolled the virtues of free labor and the economic, political, and moral progress of the nation; against the threat of rupture and mayhem, it warned of the catastrophe that would come from doing nothing.

This rhetoric of reaction and change arose from smoldering tensions, from modes of thinking that were relational and opposite. Like Castor and Pollux, they were twins with intertwined fates born to different fathers, and their fortunes tended to swing wildly, with Pollux on top one minute and Castor the next, depending on the conjuncture. In the 1850s, circumstantial pro-slavery rhetoric was the predominant thinking on the issue, and nascent abolitionism was its jarring underling. In the second half of the 1880s, the pro-slavery rhetoric was fast eroding, while the abolitionist moral repertoire ascended to the throne of common sense.

This was rhetoric that split the nation in two. On one hand, there were those who sympathized with the slaves' suffering, championed their right to freedom, and supported the march of progress. On the other, those who, armed with economic data, warned of the social and political disaster abolition would bring. It was Us – sensitive, civilized and modern – versus Them – obdurate, backward, barbarous. On one front, were the just, on the other, the purveyors of injustice. Two contrary political identities rallied around rival leaders: Rebouças and Paulino.

# Moral Repertoire of Abolitionism

## GAMA-STYLE ACTIVISM

All abolitionists used the rhetoric of change, but each tailored it to suit his particular style of activism. The schemata of interpretation of rights gelled with Luís Gama's strategy. In brandishing the 1831 law against his declared owner, Gama triggered his own conversion into a political activist. In an open letter to his partner on this and the republican cause,[22] he declared that he was ready and willing to use the same resource to help third parties. He had read a great deal in the library of his protector, a professor of law, at whose home he made contacts that would enable him to become an attorney and practice law in partnership with well-born Radical Liberals.

Gama's style of activism consisted in exploring ambiguities and loopholes in the legislation on slavery. Freedom suits were nothing new. The tactic had long been part of the international abolitionist toolkit: Spanish activists were already resurrecting similar dead treaties with Great Britain, while in Brazil, between 1847 and 1868, at least twenty-six lawyers, including Rebouças' father, had become adept at using slavery legislation against itself. However, Gama went further than any in stretching interpretations of the legal bases for slavery to their elastic limit. In the *Radical Paulistano*, in 1869, he wrote that:

the voices of abolitionists have brought to bear a highly criminal fact ... that most of the African slaves in Brazil *were imported* after the promulgation of the slave-trade ban in 1831. ... Should friends of humanity, the defenders of morality, simply cross their arms before such abominable crimes?[23]

This was certainly a rhetorical question. Gama was on a mission to save illegal slaves like himself by suing for their freedom.

His procedure was simple: establishing the date of entry established the legality or otherwise of the ownership of the slave. He used the 1826 treaty with Great Britain and the 1831 law to annul, through the courts, any deeds of ownership to free Africans and their descendants who made port in Brazil in or after that year. He also used the writ of habeas corpus and Article 179 of the Constitution of 1824, which outlawed the use of whipping, branding, and torture, as grounds on which to have ownership

---

[22] Letter from Luís Gama to Lúcio de Mendonça, Jul. 25, 1880. Other Republican friends were Lúcio's brother, Salvador de Mendonça, and Ferreira de Menezes. Gama served as apprentice typesetter at the brothers' newspaper, *O Ipiranga*.

[23] Corwin (1968, pp. 164–5); Grinberg (2002, pp. 202 ff., 244 ff., 258–9). Gama, *Radical Paulistano*, Sept. 30, 1869, Ferreira (2011, p. 117).

## The Last Abolition

declared void. On cases alleging mistreatment, he brought in abolitionists as witnesses and called to the stand evaluators who gave intentionally low estimates so as to facilitate manumission. Abolitionist doctors also testified to the ill-health or physical trauma of the plaintiffs. Gama even defended slaves accused of the most ignominious act of all: slaying a master, "Before the law, homicide perpetrated by a slave upon his owner is justified as self-defense."[24]

Gama started using these strategies during the Liberal Party radicalization, but it was only under Itaboraí's Conservative government that he began to devote himself exclusively to the cause. And he certainly had the time to spare, as his lawyering for slaves had cost him his post as a copyist with the Police Department. He responded with ads in the Radical Liberal press, offering his services "on freedom suits in favor of free people wrongfully enslaved" and promising to "provide any licit help, to the best of my abilities, towards securing slave manumissions." "My services of attorney at law are rendered free of charge out of sincere dedication to the cause of the downtrodden. I seek no profit and fear no violence."[25]

The Free Womb Law opened the floodgates on this kind of activism. Though shy on immediate manumission regulations, it was a watershed in terms of strengthening the State's hand against slavery within the private sphere. The effects were unexpected. Article 4 institutionalized the already usual Pecúlio, which allowed slaves to save for self-purchase. Under the new law, this came to be a legal right and slaves could now receive donations to help ransom themselves from slavery. As Sidney Chalhoub notes, this law carved out space for slaves to sue for their own freedom. Although self-purchase still technically depended on the owner's consent, if no agreement were reached as to the sum due, the matter would be arbitrated by the courts. This was a major boon to abolitionist lawyers like Gama, who used it to bring down the price of ransom and free more people for much less money. Another abolitionist favorite was Paragraph 3 of Article 4, which allowed the slave to hire out his or her services to third parties for up to seven years in exchange for the sum required for manumission. Though the law was clear on the fact that self-purchase required the consent of the master and the Orphan's Court,

---

[24] On Gama's strategies, see Azevedo (1999, pp. 255 ff.). Gama, in Menucci (1938, p. 154). One of the doctors who operated this way was Barata Ribeiro, also a member of an abolitionist society.

[25] Azevedo (1999, pp. 110 ff.). *Radical Paulistano*, May 31, 1869; *Correio Paulistano*, Nov. 20, 1869; Gama, Nov. 20, 1869, in Ferreira (2011, p. 126); letter from Luís Gama to Lúcio de Mendonça, Jul. 25, 1880.

## Moral Repertoire of Abolitionism

this approach became a short-cut to compulsory ransoming, as abolitionists interpreted the provision to mean that depositing the sum in court was enough to ensure liberty.[26] And that was how they proceeded.

The abolitionists also exploited legislation that banned cruel physical punishments, the separation of slave families, the sale of infants born after 1871, and a failure to register slaves. They sued for liberty in the event of breaches, claiming that ownership was rendered null and void under such conditions. After 1871, Gama started to make systematic use of habeas corpus, especially in relation to articles of the Free Womb Law. For example, in 1880, he filed with the court in Pirassununga in favor of the African João Carpinteiro, whom he claimed had been "criminally enslaved." He demanded the man's immediate liberation on the grounds that he had not been registered as per Decree 4835, which, per Article 8 of the Free Womb Law, made slave registration mandatory. This was just one of the many cases Gama won. All told, he freed about 500 slaves.[27]

Such uses of the legislation, especially the 1826 treaty, and the laws of 1831 and 1871, comprised a strategy for judicializing the fight against slavery, and rose to the level of judicial activism during the 1880s, triggering a deluge of freedom suits, appeals, and denunciations at court. Even cases that were lost served to put slavery on trial, resulting in a ritualization of the struggle that was effectively a variation on Abílio Borges' civic ceremonies.

Arguing so many freedom suits earned Gama notoriety, enemies, and emulators. To his bucolic home, with its lilies, jabuticabeira trees, and visiting birds, and his law offices on Rua da Imperatriz flocked a steady stream of followers and slaves of all sorts in search of his help. His was a social circle far removed from the aristocratic milieu of Abílio Borges and

---

[26] Chalhoub (1990, pp. 107–8, 155–61) states that, "up until the law of September 28, 1871, there had been no legal alternative for securing freedom without the master's consent" and that "the window of opportunity the law opened up facilitated collective freedom buy-outs, whether by the slaves themselves or, later on, by abolitionists and sympathizers" (Chalhoub, 2012, pp. 55, 75).

[27] Azevedo (1999, pp. 238, 251–2) documented Luís Gama's use of legislation and noted the change of strategy: "Within this new legal framework [the law of 1871], Luís Gama can lend new form to his abolitionist struggle in the courts." The habeas corpus mentioned above and the decree by the Orphan's Court judge, the Liberal Inglês de Sousa, are transcribed along with twelve cases brought before the courts in 1872, 1874, 1877, 1879, 1880, 1881, and 1882 in Câmara (2010, pp. 203–73). Menucci (1938, pp. 25 ff.) counted some 500 such freedom suits brought by Gama between 1868 and 1880. For more on freedom suits in the 1880s, see Mamigonian (2011) and Cota (2013).

Rebouças. As one observer recalls, he drew a social circle that included the partners in a hatmaker's and a tailor's, the manager of the municipal slaughterhouse, a solicitor, and a church painter known as Chico Dourador, a notary; in short, exception made to the last one, a whole lower stratum of imperial society composed of small merchants and the providers of downmarket services. And so abolitionism, which had begun among the social elite, began to percolate socially.

However, Gama's style of activism, which revolved around the courts, required lawyers, and these were part of the crème de la crème. Many of those who followed him were members of the São Paulo social elite, acquaintances from the Masonic lodge América, members of the Radical faction of the Liberals, or Republican Party colleagues such as the Campos brothers, Américo and Bernardino, nouveaux riches from the coffee plantations, educated in the schemata of interpretation of progress at schools abroad and unhappy with imperial politics, and their fellow abolitionists and republicans – always within easy reach, in the newspapers as in life.

Gama's mordant verve at the bench and in the press dazzled the students at the Faculty of Law. As the faculties were national hubs, in the early 1870s students from various provinces went back home with Gama-style activism in their luggage. Rui Barbosa, from Bahia, who knew Gama from the América lodge, and the Pernambucan Joaquim Nabuco, whose brother had worked alongside Gama at the *Diabo Coxo*, adopted his legal playbook for use back in their home provinces. The strategy proliferated thanks to the 1871 law, which, according to Eduardo Pena, facilitated freedom lawsuits by ensuring that manumission no longer hinged solely upon the owners' will, but now had a legal framework within which to work. The strategy's success from that point on would depend on the receptiveness of prosecutors and judges, but its adoption grew rampantly.[28]

Another institutional path explored was the Emancipation Fund, created under Article 3 of the Free Womb Law, which held on State-

---

[28] Though the exact number is uncertain, Grinberg (2002, pp. 258–9) identified 620 lawyers bringing manumission lawsuits, which would indicate a proliferation of the strategy. In another work, Grinberg (1994) sees the number of such suits dropping off after 1871, but this assertion is based on one batch of documents only. Pena (1996, p. 242) affirms the opposite, claiming that the 1871 law "triggered a slew of freedom suits (requesting the arbitration of demands for release from slavery)." On the use of the law passed on 7 September 1831 during court cases in the 1860s and 1870s, cf. Azevedo (2010), Mamigonian (2017).

sponsored manumissions. When the law was passed in 1871, there was some concern that it would spark an avalanche of slave freeing, but many provinces and most municipalities never allocated sufficient resources, and the national fund never functioned properly at all – governments generally dipped into these resources to plug budgetary holes. The abolitionists, however, put this to political use. As the law foresaw provincial and municipal manumission funds, they pestered all levels of government to make good on the obligation.

An additional effect came from the chapters of the law that recognized the abolitionist associations as such and so legitimized their practices in the public sphere. Article 2 addressed the formation of civil associations to look after slave children abandoned by their masters, set up trust funds in their names, and find new homes for them. Article 5 guaranteed these associations the right to buy manumissions. As such, the law encouraged the proliferation of abolitionist associations and manumission fundraisers.

The 1871 law therefore laid the groundwork for a diffusion of Borges and Gama-styles activism, and gave the abolitionists the means to attack slavery from inside the social order and legal framework. Added to this were initiatives that went against the grain of the law. Gama rolled out a style of activism that walked a fine line between these two approaches, pushing the legal envelope to the extreme. Sometimes he took the legislation at face value, but often he subjected it to tortuous and even reverse interpretations. "... I would advise and urge, not for 'insurrection', which is a crime, but for 'resistance', which is a civic virtue." He declared war "on courtly bandits, filthy contrabandists, prevaricating judges and false, wanton slavers." "This is the truth I proffer without the slightest qualm."[29]

This lack of qualms earned him death threats and saw him sued for slander in 1870, but he moved the jury with a recounting of his own life that made use of the schemata of interpretation of compassion, painting himself as a living example of the injustices of slavery. He left the courthouse on the shoulders of the people, a moment depicted by one of his many followers to mark the lawyer's feats in the cause of liberty.[30]

He was a legend inspired by others. While Abílio Borges walked arm-in-arm with the French abolitionists, Gama, who never set foot on foreign soil, sourced his own icons elsewhere in the abolitionist repertoire: "I want to be as mad as John Brown, as Spartacus, as Lincoln." Three different models of abolitionism, starting with the US President

---

[29] *Correio Paulistano*, 10 Nov. 10, 1871, Ferreira (2011, p. 143).
[30] Menucci (1938, p. 167); *Correio Paulistano*, Dec. 31, 1870.

responsible for the Emancipation Act, the man who put an end to slavery, initiated and won a civil war and ended up assassinated. Though an ardent Republican, Gama had no aspirations toward governing Brazil. On the other end of the spectrum was Spartacus, leader of the slave revolt in Ancient Rome, when slavery had no racial formwork. Somewhere in between fell the American John Brown, a free white man of no small wealth who ended his days swinging from a noose for instigating a slave revolt in the heartlands of southern slavery. Luís Gama, not so much interpreting as contorting the legislation, bending all the rules on evidence-gathering, and often putting up his slave plaintiffs under his own roof in the buildup to trial, skirted the fine line between the use of law in the courts and the crime of harboring fugitives; between Lincoln's institutional approach and the insubordination of Spartacus. In a portrait of Gama from the 1870s, his eyes gleam with the fervor of John Brown on the eve of revolt.[31]

### BLACK REBOUÇAS

The political outlook after 1871 confronted the Brazilian government with a series of complications that also served as windows of opportunity for abolitionist mobilization. An international sentiment that was increasingly hostile to slavery and the disintegration of the imperial parties heaped further woe on the collateral effects of the Conservative modernization championed by Rio Branco's administration, which introduced new players, new weapons, and new social spaces for abolitionist expansion. Under this scenario, the paths created by Borges (associativism and civic ceremonies) and Gama (legal action) were gradually replicated in various other provinces.

Yet the spread of this new sensibility and morality in relation to slavery, of the abolitionist moral repertoire, was slow. Like Rebouças himself, many people who were intellectually against slavery still owned slaves when they joined the abolitionist campaign. Intellectual subscription to abolition did not always convert into emotional adherence. In many cases, it took a *"moral shock"* in the face of concrete experience, a jolt that fanned the flames of a sense of injustice, for it to filter into action.[32]

---

[31] *Gazeta do Povo*, Dec. 28, 1880, in Azevedo (1999, p. 186).
[32] "Moral shock" refers to the situation in which some event, information, personal experience, or public act produces a sense of moral outrage that leads one or more individuals to rally behind a cause (Jasper, 1997, p. 106). Social movements use moral shock to denaturalize a situation and create motivation to change it (Halfmann and Young, 2010, p. 3).

## Moral Repertoire of Abolitionism

This was a bitter process for black activists outside the imperial elite, like Gama, who had experienced racial stigma in their own skin from a young age. The experience of Rebouças, on the other hand, who belonged to the social elite and the political circles of the Second Reign, was far less extreme.

For Rebouças, abolition had started out as just one of a raft of reforms proposed by an enterprising engineer. In the 1860s, he turned to political lobbying, building bridges between elite abolitionists and potential allies at the political institutions. An engineer of multiple levées, he put his networking skills to the service of the abolitionist cause. His was a cerebral abolitionism, one that distilled the schemata of interpretation of progress, avid to persuade his fellow glitterati of the economic advantages abolition would bring. He had none of Gama's passion, and it would only be in 1873 that his involvement in abolitionism became visceral.

Up until then he had seen himself as a member of the social aristocracy, an illustrious businessman. In fact, over the course of his successful career he had faced no obstacles beyond what was normal at a small court, where many vied for the same few posts and payouts. He did not win all his battles, because no-one ever did, but he won some important ones, resulting in lucrative contracts and administrative posts at the head of major construction projects. He had access to top government brass and to the imperial family itself. Rebouças achieved a social height that eclipsed his skin color. Between apparent indifference to his complexion among the upper social strata and his own self-camouflage, he was able to reach a mature age without ever referring to his color, not even in the confessional secrecy of his own private diary.

That was to change in New York. Rebouças had swanned through Europe, at operas and aristocratic receptions, such as those of the Brazilian chancellors in London, Venice, and Milan, all the while arms linked with Carlos Gomes. And it was the same in Vienna and in Paris. On his way back to Brazil, in June 1873, he dropped anchor in the United States. There, on Yankee soil, with its cult of progress, Rebouças experienced the same social subordination Gama had been subjected to in São Paulo. Among the nonpareil of Europe and Brazil, despite the odd jibe, obstacle, antipathy, and even a certain anonymous letter referring to his "condition of mulatto," he was, first and foremost, a member of the aristocracy who just happened not to be white.

In the bourgeois metropolis, averse to the etiquette of noblesse, color spoke loudest. Race was a social ceiling and a floor, and Rebouças found himself turned away from hotel after hotel: "After the first few attempts I realized that I was being refused hospitality on the grounds of my color."

108 *The Last Abolition*

In the end, after the intervention of the Brazilian consulate, Rebouças was given accommodation at the Washington Hotel on condition that he dine in his room and never appear in the restaurant. It was "a dirty room on the third floor ... The following morning I found myself forced to bathe at a barber's shop." He was even prevented from doing what he liked best: "The worst part was that I could not attend the performance at the Grand Opera House." On June 16, he went to bed hungry, thanks to the restaurant veto, and fled to Pennsylvania the next day. Rebouças thought Pennsylvania dirty, and Pennsylvania thought Rebouças black. "Once again the handicap of color had me dine in my room."

When friends managed to intervene and get Rebouças a room at French's Hotel, in New York, he tried to reassume his aristocratic airs, complaining of the "service far inferior to the attendance at the hotels of Europe." But his identity was now irremediably cracked. The United States had shattered his mirror, introducing him to an experience in which, shorn of the safety nets of aristocracy, color was a marker of place and rank, an indelible stigma. As someone who appreciated symmetries, precisely two years after freeing the last slaves from his own home, he was forced to realize that he was also a product of the African slave trade. He had been born into an unsheddable skin.

However, rather than intimidate him, humiliation made him fall upwards – aristocratic to a fault. He scanned American society for a role model: "The mulatto Douglass, an old friend of president Grant, very influential in his reelection, had, in similar fashion, been turned away from the hotels of Washington." Frederick Douglass, a former slave, was an autodidact who fled captivity and went north, where he became a leading antislavery activist, writing, lecturing, and weaving alliances within the political elite. Douglass was a living contradiction of the argument that posited the inferiority of the black people: he was active, intelligent, an efficient lobbyist and a first-rate propagandist.[33] Like Douglass, Rebouças was a captivating personality with passage in the antechambers of power, and he was also a victim of prejudice. All that remained was for Rebouças to become for Brazil what Douglass had been for the United States: the greatest black abolitionist of all.

---

[33] The quotations are all taken from Rebouças' diary: DNAAR, Sept. 20, 1871; May 29; Jun. 10 and 19, 1873; Jun. 21, 1873. Distinction, in Bourdieu's sense (1984), as a form of hierarchization, and stigma, as understood by Goffman (1963), as a form of social belittlement.

# 4

# The Theatricalization of Politics

### ZÉ WHO?

Some people are born with surnames that open doors for them, like Paulino Soares de Sousa. But what about those who do not have such luck? The illegitimate offspring of Justina do Espírito Santo, a freed slave, and João Carlos Monteiro, the Campos parish priest, did not have the right to a surname at all. Born in 1854, José Carlos do Patrocínio was called by a blend of his father's middle name and an interpretation of his mother's surname – "Espírito Santo" (Holy Spirit) changed to Patrocínio (Protection), also the saint of the day of his birth.

The priest had a legitimate son too, on whom he bestowed his surname and a diploma from Coimbra University, where part of the Brazilian elite studied. José do Patrocínio got much less, though it did take him into the family estate at Lagoa de Cima farm and the townhouse in Church Square, Campos, a backwater in the province of Rio de Janeiro. Amid a little schooling and a touch of politics – the priest was a provincial councilor and columnist in the press – his childhood was rife with mischief, and he was known for his very short fuse and "wild sincerity." One day, while out on horseback, Patrocínio lost his temper at an old slave's slowness in opening the gate for him and gave the man a bloody gash on the head with the silver handle of his whip. His father's rebuke and appeal to piety had such an effect on the boy that "the impression, he would say years later, seemed to transform his entire being as if overnight." Patrocínio attributed his transformation from slave tormentor to abolitionist to a romantic compassion. The transition he underwent became clear to him during another episode at Lagoa de Cima, when he tried to save a slave from the driver's whip. First, he shouted for the man to stop, but when that had no effect, he hurled himself from a flight of steps, bloodying his own forehead. Patrocínio would be precisely that kind of activist: dramatic, prone to theatrics.

Though he traced his profession of faith to childhood, his abolitionism dated from his youth. Furious about his father's lovers, who humiliated his mother, he raised his hand to one of them in 1868 and was sent off to the imperial capital as a result. First, though, he was put to work as a cashier, but that only lasted six days, partly because of the boy's temperament and partly because his boss realized that "customers didn't like seeing a boy of my color behind the till." So, at the age of fourteen, about the age when boys started making preparations for attending college, he left Campos with an allowance from the priest. The money did not last long, but his father's connections provided him with a safe social network like the one Luís Gama had had to create for himself, though not as extensive or powerful as Rebouças'. It got him free accommodation at boarding school, a job as a pharmaceutical apprentice, a post at the local hospital, and a place as a student in the medical faculty.

Patrocínio managed his poverty by developing an incredible knack of making friends and garnering influence. He struck up friendships with good families, where he was always guaranteed a comfortable bed and hot meals. One particular friend put him up for years before passing him

FIGURE 4.1 The abolitionist José do Patrocínio (1854–1905).
Iconographia (Iconography) Archive

# The Theatricalization of Politics

over to a former classmate at the boarding school, who gave him room and board and the job of tutor to his younger brothers. This second protector was the stepson of a well-heeled member of both the army and the Republican party with daughters of a marriageable age. Patrocínio fell in with the family rebel, Maria Henriqueta, also known as Bibi.[1] But his heart was of the roving sort. At the tea rooms, bookstores, theaters, or any corner of Rua do Ouvidor where there was room for politics and literature, Patrocínio was there. A friend of friends, a denizen of the night, and a seasoned tippler, he was a regular at Confeitaria Pascoal, where he rubbed shoulders with musicians, theater owners, penniless poets and, to Bibi's dismay, agentless actresses.

He was particularly close to the Liberals. Patrocínio in Rio, like Luís Gama in São Paulo, got involved in politics through the Radical Liberal rallies of the late 1860s and through the *A Reforma* newspaper, for which he worked as a proofreader. He also attended Teixeira Mendes' positivist reformist sermons and meetings of the Rio chapter of the Republican Party, in whose paper, *A República*, he married the twin causes of abolitionism and republicanism under a single figure, in a single poem, "À Memória de Tiradentes" (To the memory of Tiradentes):

> *Insufflate, genius of the Andes,*
> *the breast of each and every brave*
> *with hatred of the chains that make the slave*

And to his abolitionist and republicanist ideas he added the romantic form. In the college paper *O Lábaro*, in 1873, he wrote:

> *We shall break the shackles*
> *That oppress our brethren, . . .*
> *We shall cry to the four winds:*
> *"Slaves, ye are citizens!"*

However, as with Gama and Rebouças, the various insurrections against the Empire only really sunk in with Patrocínio after he, too, faced obstacles to his social ascent. He had previously experienced racism when prevented from working at the till in Campos, but the

---

[1] The information about Patrocínio's childhood and youth comes from his leading biographer, Magalhães Jr. (1969, pp. 38 ff.) and his brother-in-law, Sena (1909, pp. 299 ff.), who relates the episode of Patrocínio beating the slave. At the time, Patrocínio was accompanied by Luís Carlos de Lacerda, his friend and political ally in the 1880s. His future father-in-law was captain Emiliano Sena. See also Alencar (1906, p. 3) and Alves (2009, pp. 14, 20–1). Accounts from Patrocínio himself are in his conference from Sept. 8, 1884, in Alves (2009, p. 27) and Patrocínio, GT, May 29, 1884.

# The Last Abolition

real slight came at the Medical Faculty, when a professor failed him for unspecified reasons. Without referring to the student's skin color, social standing, or lack thereof, the only reason the professor in question – a friar – gave for failing Patrocínio was that he disliked him. Having his path to a career in medicine blocked, Patrocínio graduated in 1874 with a diploma in pharmacy.[2]

The experience of social exclusion stoked in Patrocínio's turbulent soul a criticism of all imperial institutions. In 1875, he and a faculty classmate founded *Os Ferrões* (The Barbs), a magazine devoted to berating and lampooning political parties, the church and the high-born. In exposing the barbarity of the slaveholders, he deployed the compassion schemata:

These wretches come to be sold like pigs or turkeys. It's only natural that they sell them, for they are mere *things*, or less than things – they are *captive negroes*. . . . It brings tears to one's eyes seeing these poor devils drubbed by disgrace, lined up on the footpath. . . . They look like the very statues of pain . . .

The paper also denounced the inefficacy of the Free Womb Law: "Almost four years on, and the government is still sitting on its hands." The charge was seconded in *O Mequetrefe*, where Patrocínio would meet young literati such as Aluísio Azevedo. At this small newspaper, Patrocínio wrote under the nickname Zé do Pato (Joe Duck).

Then, in 1875, a new, middle-sized, cheap, independent left-wing, vaguely antislavery paper called *Gazeta de Notícias* emerged, edited by José Ferreira de Araújo, a bohemian black man and medical school alumnus like Patrocínio. They became friends. Patrocínio started out proofreading columnists like Machado de Assis, then graduated to "Street news," crime and the "Metric Gazette," which delivered bite-sized news in verse:

> *A devotee of the mild martial arts*
> *only yesterday, the black Fabiano*
> *made sharp and pious pilgrimage*
> *into the guts of his mate Caetano.*
> *There was a great hullabaloo*
> *and cries of catch him! catch him you!*
> *But not an urban soul one jot would do.*[3]

---

[2] The poems are taken from Alves (2009, pp. 60–1) and Magalhães Jr. (1969, p. 27). The friar's declaration is in Alencar (1906, p. 2).

[3] *Os Ferrões*, Sept. 1, 1875, in Patrocínio (org. 2013, pp. 210–11). He wrote this monthly magazine with Demerval da Fonseca, a colleague from the medical faculty. Cf. Alves (2009, pp. 82, 91).

## The Theatricalization of Politics

113

With his talent and the friendship of Ferreira de Araújo, by 1877 Patrocínio was in charge of the Parliamentary column *Semana Política* (The Political Week), writing under the pseudonym *Prudhomme*, a play on Pierre-Joseph Proudhon's name. He also adapted the anarchist's maxim to the local context as "Slavery is theft!"

In 1878, promoted to reporter, he covered the discovery, in Macaé, that the last instance of capital punishment carried out in Brazil was on a wrongful conviction. A farmer and four of his slaves had been condemned to death in 1852 for the murder of a family living on his property. However, a deathbed confession by the real murderer proved the innocence of the five dead men. In addition to articles in *Gazeta de Notícias*, Patrocínio wrote a novel against capital punishment and the two pillars of rural life from which the episode had resulted, namely latifundias and slavery. He tempered the narrative with some personal experience, splicing into the story the romance between a white girl and a black boy, at the time when Bibi's parents were discovering the relationship between their daughter and Patrocínio.

The book caused a furor and consolidated Patrocínio's journalistic standing. In 1877, he was sent to cover another dramatic story: the prolonged drought in Ceará. The trip proved as eye-opening to the journalist Patrocínio as the dam-building projects in the hinterlands had to the engineer Rebouças: he got to know his country. He visited Pernambuco and Paraíba, witnessed the inequality, starvation, and desolation, all of which he registered for the *Gazeta de Notícias*: "Naked or half-naked little children, their cadaverous faces, ... bloated bellies, swollen feet, the toes and heels deformed by parasites." On this story, Patrocínio cemented a partnership with the cartoonist Rafael Bordalo Pinheiro, who transformed his photographs into drawings for the smaller outlet *O Besouro* (The Beetle). The experience gave rise to a second serialized work of fiction-cum-social critique entitled *Os retirantes* (The Migrants), which, in addition to decrying the decadence of the rural world of masters and slaves, was laced with anti-clerical sentiment and a touch of autobiography: the villain was a priest.

The trip also enabled Patrocínio to make new friends who he enlisted in the abolitionist campaign. But his bonhomie never canceled out his propensity for a good brawl. While wandering about the town one evening armed with a switchblade, Patrocínio ended up in jail.

Three key alliances helped transform Patrocínio's serial insubordinations against social injustice into a tenacious militancy against slavery. One such marriage was literal. In 1881, after some parental resistance, and with Ferreira de Araújo as his best man, Patrocínio wed Bibi. As his father-in-law owned real-estate and land, his dowry provided the capital he needed to buy the *Gazeta da Tarde* (GT) newspaper, for which he was writing at the time. He doubled circulation to 4,000 copies, almost a third that of the market leader, the *Jornal do Commercio*. The GT became a medium-sized outlet with influence that reached into other provinces. The publication's hard-hitting articles made them essential reading for the authorities, who often found themselves having to respond to the paper's allegations.[4]

The newspaper, headquartered at number 43 Uruguaiana Street, was the venue for another alliance much to Patrocínio's liking: bohemia and politics. Patrocínio staffed his paper with young writers and caricaturists who also joined him at his table at the Confeitaria Pascoal. One of these described the thrall in which "the master" held his drinking buddies. "He was the driving force behind the youngsters of my day, he coached my generation, . . . he was a force of nature, a firebrand. He was the genius: magnetic."[5] Patrocínio put these youthful poets and writers to work on the paper, and the paper to work on abolition.

The third alliance was political. In 1879, he joined forces with André Rebouças. The priest of Campos, who died in 1876, never got to see it: in the 1880s, his spurned progeny turned the GT into an abolitionist stalwart. Patrocínio, also known as Zeca, Zé do Pato, and Prudhomme, had become a leader, indeed a legend in the making. As his father had denied him a name, Patrocínio went ahead and made one for himself.

## LIBERAL ASCENSION, ABOLITIONIST ASCENSION

After all the fuss, one would think the Free Womb Law would have had immediate and earthshaking results, but it did not. In the words of one contemporary, the effects were "few and slow in coming." A decade after its promulgation, the law had been little enforced, and then only through

---

[4] The first novel was called *Mota Coqueiro ou a Pena de Morte* (Mota Coqueiro or The Death Penalty), after the name of the dead farmer, Manuel da Mota Coqueiro, GN, Jul. 23, 1878, in Alves (2009, p. 112). Patrocínio's arrest is related in GN, Jan. 30, 1878. It cost Patrocínio 15 contos to purchase the GT (GT, May 29, 1884) from a friend and fellow abolitionist, Ferreira de Menezes, who died in 1881. The circulation of the *Jornal do Commercio* at the time was 15, 000 (Ferreira, 1999, p. 83).

[5] Coelho Neto (1906, p. 2). The inner circle included Campos da Paz, Luis de Andrade, Júlio de Lemos, Luís Conzaga Duque-Estrada, João Ferreira Serpa Jr. (manager of the GT), and the brothers Aluísio and Artur Azevedo (Nabuco, 1929, p. 27).

Gama-style activism, with freedom suits in favor of slaves' right to have a Pecúlio. When not triggered by abolitionists, the Free Womb Law languished as the de facto dead-letter law Paulino always said it would. Throughout 1874, Rebouças wrote articles of protest in the press, railing against this "sad, flawed, lame law that takes ages to effect ... Today, three years since the law was passed, not even the bare minimum has been done to educate the freeborn and freed."[6]

The Conservative governments, still traumatized after the fight back in 1871, did little to push the law and, as they were the majority in Parliament, abolition slipped from the institutional agenda. Rio Branco made some other reforms, mainly in education and infrastructure, and courted controversy elsewhere by picking a fight with the church. When he left power in 1875, the mantle fell into hands even more Conservative than his, those of the Duke of Caxias and his Finance Minister the Baron of Cotegipe, whom Rebouças, like many others, considered the real head of government, and he was a man allergic to abolitionists.[7]

The Liberal opposition, which held a small number of seats, continued to use public venues to criticize the government, but the reformist agenda it had touted at the start of the decade wilted before the stability of the Conservative administrations and the deaths of the moderate reformer Zacarias de Góis e Vasconcelos and of key Radical Liberal leaders, as Tavares Bastos, a promoter of the discussion on slavery within the party ranks since the 1860s. The Radical Conferences bottomed out and the Liberal newspapers repeated calls for change that would generate "electoral truth." When Caxias decided to retire, D. Pedro summoned the opposition party to overhaul the electoral system.

The Conservative Party never gave critics much of a berth: when the Republican Party in Rio celebrated the fall of the Spanish monarchy in 1873, the government had A República's printers destroyed. This repressive politics explains why, during the Conservative establishment that followed the promulgation of the Free Womb Law, between 1872 and 1877, only six new abolitionist associations were formed, versus twenty-four during the Liberal radicalization that preceded the law, between 1868 and 1871. The Liberals' return to government in January

---

[6] On uses of the law at court in 1871, see Chalhoub (1990, pp. 155). The article by Rebouças (in Moraes, 1924, p. 23) would be republished, in 1883, in *Agricultura nacional: estudos econômicos: propaganda abolicionista e democrática*, Sept. 1874 to Sept. 1883.

[7] DNAAR, Mar. 24, 1877.

# The Last Abolition

1878 struck the abolitionists as a propitious moment in which to resume public demonstrations, as the Liberals had themselves taken to the streets during their long hiatus from power and so were likely to be more lenient to protesters.[8] The abolitionists believed that this would be a political opportunity to get the cause back on the parliamentary agenda, since the Liberal Party program included gradual emancipation, even if only last on the list.

Patrocínio, in Court (Rio de Janeiro), and Gama, in São Paulo, both of whom had entered politics through the Radical Liberals, set to work enlisting to the abolitionist cause young graduates who had earned degrees thanks to the Conservatives' modernizing reforms of higher education. As students, they were indoctrinated in the schemata of progress and compassion, and engaged in civic ceremony. The 7th of September Liberating Society had kept these ceremonies going in Bahia, and, from the eve of the Free Womb Law to 1878, they managed to award approximately 500 letters of manumission.[9]

D. Pedro curbed some of this enthusiasm when he overlooked the reformist wing of the Liberals while putting together the new cabinet, which was packed with Liberal traditionalists under Cansanção de Sinimbu, a landowner from Alagoas who had no traction with abolitionists. Under his government, more inclined toward the cause of the masters than that of the slaves, the issue of slavery came back to the political institutions.

Why? The core of the Free Womb Law was in suspension. The fate of children born to slaves' wombs after 1871 would only be decided eight years later: either they stayed in their mothers' owners' protection until the age of twenty-one or they would be placed under the tutelage of the State in return for compensation. The arithmetic was simple: 1871 plus eight makes 1879. Sinimbu came to power on the eve of what was the decisive year for making the Free Womb Law effective – or not.

As the British and Foreign Antislavery Society complained to the Viscount of Rio Branco and to the Empress herself, the government's

---

[8] Variations in political opportunities and threats, that is, depending on how indifferent, porous, or resistant the State remains to demands, drive the social movements to adopt distinct expressions. As Tilly argues (2005, pp. 105 ff.), the typical government responses are facilitation, tolerance, repression, and often the selective use of repressive strategies, for instance. In the Brazilian case, the rise of the Liberals to power signaled to politically unsatisfied groups the beginning of political opportunities to protest in the public space. In general, Liberal governments tended to be more tolerant of protests than the Conservatives.

[9] Caires (2009, pp. 5 ff.).

## The Theatricalization of Politics

handling of the problem was far from the stuff of abolitionist dreams. In 1878, landowners pre-empted the reforms they expected the Liberal Party governments to offer them and organized a Congress of Planters in Rio de Janeiro and another in Recife. Sinimbu gave them his backing. He saw slavery as a matter of hands in the fields, an economic question with nothing whatsoever to do with citizenship. He promised not to open any discussion about the Free Womb Law and kept the issue on the back burner by pointing toward an alternative source of proletarian immigrants: China. He sent a mission to Peking with a view to importing Chinese workers. Instead of coming good on the right of the "Rio Brancos" – as those freed in 1871 were known – he approved, in 1879, the Labor Leasing Act, which regulated free labor under a model that resembled serfdom.[10]

This new political configuration rekindled the debate on slavery and brought back into action the voices of both the pioneering abolitionists and a new generation of antislavery activists. The themes and strategies of the former were taken up by the latter and expanded into a new, more robust wave of mobilization. Two rising stars emerged on this new horizon. One was Joaquim Nabuco, at Parliament (subject of next chapter), and the other, in the public sphere, was José do Patrocínio.

### ALLIANCE

They were an odd pair. It is hard to imagine André Rebouças, swimming in the refinement and indeed the favors of the aristocracy, walking arm-in-arm with an inveterate bohemian like José do Patrocínio, Zé do Pato, a colorful bigmouth, André, all ceremony, profligate Patrocínio, unimpeachable Rebouças, one a man of public speeches, the other of public works. Despite their differences, they became *compadrios*: the childless Rebouças was godfather to José do Patrocínio Jr. Theirs was a lasting friendship and it is hard to imagine abolitionism without it. Patrocínio, with his cortège of artists, a man of the press from start to finish, never changed, while Rebouças's life turned upside-down.

On his return from the United States in 1873, Rebouças returned to his administrative post at the Pedro II Docks and resumed his lobbying

---

[10] BFASS petitions to Rio Branco and to the Empress are in Rocha Penalves (2008, pp. 397 ff.). The Liberal senator Nabuco de Araújo had been working on a Labor Leasing Act since the first debates on the free womb, and its final format contained numerous coercive measures, cf. Lamounier (1988).

activities. But his position on the local astral map had changed. In the grip of an international economic crisis, there was fierce competition for projects in a situation rife with political infighting and cronyism. Rebouças wanted tax exemption for his Docks Company and ended up locked in a battle of wills with the government, when it was still under Rio Branco: "I never met a minister as intractable or wont to cause such vexation!" He complained to the Emperor of the "Herculean effort it took to run a company in a Brazil," but it was all in vain. His prosperous business in partnership with the Viscount of Mauá was derailed. The death blow came when he lost the support of the major shareholder in the Docks Company, the usual fireman who had always put out the blazes Rebouças got himself into while burning his profits from one company in the losses of another. His ambition to expand his business multiplied his problems – and his debts. Having run out of operating capital, he used up his reserves. The Docks Company went under. So he ran to the prince consort and D. Pedro for a lifeline: "The Emperor went back on his word ... Ah! Kings! Kings!" Thus ended his bond with the imperial family, which had grown as tired of his requests as he had of their refusals. He did some business here, some more there, but never matched his earlier success. The slippery ladders of patronage proved another letdown, as the strings he pulled failed to conjure an even half-decent public post. His professorship at the Polytechnic School was a stopgap, and the symbolic distinction conferred upon him by Rio Branco – he was made a knight of the Order of the Rose – was cold consolation: "an honor I never used or even opened."

By the mid-1870s, Rebouças' once-rosy future turned to purgatorial gloom, and on the personal level too. He was now thirty-five and unmarried. An expert in the social network to be garnered from personal relationships, key to court society, he knew too well the value of a good marriage. In the margins of his notebook, a mixture of business agenda, political scrapbook, and personal wailing wall, the female presence dwindled. Sociable, prosperous, he may have wanted to find himself a white bride, like Patrocínio, but aristocrats only married within their own ranks. Solitude descended upon him once and for all, in 1873, when he lost his brother Antônio, his partner in business and travel, a lifelong companion: "One of the saddest days of my life! A sea-change in my life plan." Without a business, protectors, his brother, or a wife, the engineer of multiple levées found himself bereft. All that remained for him to lose, as he would, in 1880, was his career talisman and last emotional mainstay, his father.

So Rebouças turned to the press. From the end of 1874 to 1879, he wrote for *Novo Mundo*, a newspaper edited by José Carlos Rodrigues, the friend who had helped him out when he had fallen foul of racism in New York. In 1877, he joined *O Globo*, a medium-circulation newspaper, only to have his head called for by the Minister of Finance, the Baron of Cotegipe, unhappy about the articles he was writing in favor of free trade. On this moot point he wrote the pamphlet *A seca nas províncias do Norte* (Drought in the northern provinces), consonant with Patrocínio's articles on Ceará.

Like his father before him, in 1879 Rebouças tried his hand at party politics. He ran for provincial representative in Paraná, where he had directed numerous construction projects. He finished an underwhelming sixteenth. A veteran in construction works and business administration, that same year Rebouças found himself in the humiliating position of having to take exams in order to receive a diploma so that he could apply for the civil engineering position at the Polytechnic School. Albeit less vehemently than in the United States, he was reminded of the difference his "mulattodom" also made in Brazilian society.

By the time he was appointed to the chair in 1880, his skin had changed. After all his ill-starred multitasking on the business and electoral fronts, he threw himself into his newest venture: teaching the trigonometry of reform. He redirected his energy from small to broad politics – "I have begun working on abolitionist propaganda, something that has concerned me for quite some time"[11] – at Patrocínio's newspaper.

### ADAPTING A REPERTOIRE

Abolitionism had so far been confined to a small elite. With the Liberals in government, it encountered two conditions for expansion. On one hand, the Radical Liberals had been pushing associativism, the press, and conferences as platforms for criticism of the imperial institutions. On the other, the educational reforms ushered in by Rio Branco had thrown the colleges open to the talents of youths from outside the social aristocracy, broadening access to degrees, the keys to elite posts. However, keys need

---

[11] This biographical information on Rebouças comes from DNAAR, Aug. 28, 1873; Nov. 8, 1874; Mar. 24 and May 8, 1875; May 28, 1873; RCAR, Nov. 15, 1874; DNAAR, Mar. 24, 1877, May 21, 1880; Trindade (2011, p. 207). When he ran for provincial representative, Rebouças won a mere 126 votes (GN, Sept. 29, 1879). The shareholder in the Docks Company who had helped him out on various occasions was the Count of Estrela.

# The Last Abolition

doors, and these were few and far between. The result was a pooling of well-educated, but jobless youths concentrated in the cities. In this way, a cohort of young men prepared for public life, but marginalized by the aristocratic politics, were eager to engage with pro-change campaigns within the expanding public sphere. The republican movement would catch on much later. The abolitionist mobilization was ablaze.

Going from a handful of antislavery pioneers to a nationwide social movement was quite a leap. The international abolitionist repertoire of contention, which arrived in Brazil through newspapers, books, and travelers like Abílio Borges, contained at least three main ways of fighting for abolition. The English and North Americans had combined parliamentary strategies with major public campaigns, relying on newspapers, pamphlets, literature, associations, petitions, boycotts, and meetings. The French had preferred an elitist path based on lobbying and initiatives inside the political system, without expressive public demonstrations.[12] The third option was extreme action: Haiti-style slave revolts.

Of this repertoire of tried-and-tested experiences, two tactics were already applied in Brazil, and both were institutional: Gama-style judicial activism, with freedom suits, and Rebouças-style political lobbying targeting the Parliament and the governments. Patrocínio, who lacked Gama's technical knowledge and Rebouças' elite connections, needed a third way. Lacking the grassroots support for considering a revolution, he adopted Anglo-American-style public demonstrations.

In the *Gazeta da Tarde*, Patrocínio serialized the autobiography of Frederick Douglass, the North-American abolitionist movement leader who had so fascinated Rebouças. Douglass' writings, travels, and speeches, were effective ways of diffusing abolitionist rhetoric that coaxed moral and emotional reactions against slavery. They were key strategies for enlisting and rallying people in the public space and for putting pressure on the institutions. Patrocínio took that same course.

But admiring someone is one thing, emulating a model is quite another. Differences between the Brazilian and Anglo-American contexts made straightforward adoption impossible. One major difference was the target public. Making noise in books, manifestos, pamphlets, newspapers, and

---

[12] On the reformist movement of the 1870s generation, see Alonso (2002). Drescher (2009, p. 43) distinguishes two abolitionist paths: the "continental" path, which made Europe more elitist, with lobbying and Parliamentary actions; and the "Anglo-American" path, which was a grassroots movement. However, he overlooks the Hispanic case and the secular/religious divide. The Brazilian case received closer attention only in his more recent works (Drescher, 2015). On the French case, see Jennings (2006).

## The Theatricalization of Politics

petitions, which was so effective in Great Britain and the United States, would have only limited effect in Brazil. The fact, revealed by the 1872 census and lamented by Machado de Assis, was that the rate of literacy in Brazil was terribly low:

And speaking of that particular animal [the ass], just a few days ago the results of the imperial census came out, showing that 70% of our population does not know how to read. I like numbers, because they are not prone to half-measures or metaphors. They say it like it is; and how it is may not be pretty, but for the want of an alternative reality, they call a spade a spade. ... The nation can't read.

When the numbers were tallied, the extent of illiteracy was even larger: only 15.7 percent of the population of 9,930,478 was able to read and write.[13] If the delegitimization of slavery in the field of ideas would be confined to the written word, there would be a very low ceiling of support for abolition. This constraint pushed abolitionists to look for non-written forms of language to spread their message.

Another complicating factor was the religious roots of the Anglo-American campaign. Though inseminated by secular celebrations, the British and American abolitionists found their organizational base and liturgical source in the Quakers. They used churches, ministers, vigils, hymns, and the Protestant tradition to shape their antislavery arguments and demonstrations.[14] Religion served as motivational and legitimizing elements. Since the Brazilian political tradition was Catholic, Abílio Borges had diverged from the Anglo-American canon in starting his *civic* ceremonies, in 1869.[15] Catholicism, with its rites, masses, and processions, fitted into the Brazilian styles of life and sociability, and as part of the State, it regulated lives, births, marriages, and deaths. It helped ensure the social order and strengthen political control – the polling stations, for example, were all churches – and as a State religion, with its ecclesiastical structure, brotherhoods, and religious networks, it legitimized the Empire's institutional framework. From all of these angles, Catholicism

---

[13] Patrocínio began serializing Douglass' biography in the *Gazeta da Tarde* in April 1883. Machado's article is in *Ilustração Brasileira*, Jul. 15, 1876, just after the publication of the census results. After recalculating the figures, Paiva et al. (2012, p. 20) estimated 1,565,454 literate Brazilians versus 8,365,024 illiterate.

[14] Drescher (1988) attributes the institutional basis of abolitionist mobilization to religious associations. Rugemer (2008, pp. 224, 238) underscores the relevance of religious ritual in structuring public abolitionist expression. See also Davis (1984, pp. 122 ff.), Drescher (1980) and Stamatov (2010).

[15] By "tradition" I mean the set of beliefs, practices, and social institutions that legitimize and reproduce the status quo.

# The Last Abolition

always supported slavery. Antislavery brotherhoods and clergy were the exception among a largely slave-owning priesthood. Furthermore, as it bloomed late, Brazilian abolitionism was self-proclaimed reformist, a friend to science, an adept of progress for which the Catholic church was archaic and obscure.

All of this made it impossible to adopt the Anglo-American model of ceremony. Borges signaled as much by lending his ceremonies a civic character. Patrocínio followed the same line of reasoning and came to the conclusion that Catholicism would be far less efficient than Protestantism in combating slavery.[16] Abolitionist rituals would draw upon Christian imagery, episodes, and figures only parsimoniously. Even the trope of piety itself would come more from the vocabularies of literary romanticism and humanitarianism than of Catholicism. The Brazilian abolitionist campaign, based on the tripod of law, morality, and science, would be secular in character.

To recruit and rally new members beyond the social elite, Patrocínio sought secular spaces in which to work his propaganda. The Madrid-based abolitionists from colonies of Puerto Rico and Cuba were fresh examples, as they were dealing with a closed political system, an aristocratic society, and a Catholic tradition. Rather than working with the religious institutions, Hispanic abolitionists, like their Brazilian counterparts, clashed with them head-on. And while the English, North-American, and French emancipation movements were already history, the debate was still very much alive in Spain. Brazilian abolitionists who were circulating in Europe, such as Borges and Rebouças, had heard about the antislavery conferences held by the Spanish Abolitionist Society, founded in Madrid in 1865, and which had been staging secular events with recitals instead of prayer, directed at ladies and gentlemen, and accompanied with manifestos, pamphlets, petitions, exhibitions, processions, rallies, and marches[17], activities to which the activists credited the abolition of slavery in Puerto Rico in 1873. Patrocínio, already allied with Rebouças, focused on this approach, which was temporally and culturally closer to the local context than the Anglo-American experience.

---

[16] ACE, Dec. 28, 1880, pp. 30 and 31.

[17] Corwin (1968, pp. 166, 171) notes the anticlerical nature of the Spanish abolitionist movement. The first series of conferences in Madrid took place in 1865, and the second in 1872 (Vilar and Vilar, 1996, pp. 19 ff.; Castro, 1872). The leader of the Spanish Abolitionist Society was the Puerto-Rican Julio Vizcarrondo. All other information on Spanish abolitionism is from Schmidt-Nowara (1999, pp. 52 ff., 99, 118, 129 and 148 ff.).

# The Theatricalization of Politics

With the church gates closed to them, they pushed open the Hispanic, secular and public doors of the theater.

Abílio Borges' civic ceremonies had included recitals, but they were held in the closed and formal environment of schools and were attended only by the imperial elite. Rebouças had been to one such event himself, on the eve of the promulgation of the Free Womb Law. The Radical Liberal conferences of the 1860s had drawn large crowds, but they were not very appealing, featuring mainly political speeches which bored most of the public to tears. Patrocínio had attended some of these. Midway between Borges' events and those of the Radical Liberals were the Society for Public Instruction's "Popular Conferences" in Glória, a Rio de Janeiro neighborhood, which began in 1873. These events drew a more diverse public and followed a more varied agenda, from literature to mineral water, education to asphyxia, positivism to industrial expos.[18]

Combining homegrown and foreign examples, Patrocínio and Rebouças married political intent with cultural inclusion. Patrocínio moved among the artistic and theater crowd, while Rebouças had the attention of opera buffs. Together, they straddled the erudite and popular cultural milieus, a cocktail which they used to spice up Borges' civic ceremonies. They found in the arts a tool for the kind of political mobilization the Anglo-Americans had drawn from religion. Their conferences would be concerts.

## THE CONCERT-CONFERENCES

With the Empire rolling out its modernizing projects – railroads lined with smallholdings, central mills, and schools popping up all around the hinterlands – Rebouças gave up working within aristocratic political circles and decided it was time to pair up with Patrocínio, an agitator in need of logistics.

Together, they became a duo of black activists. Rebouças only recently discovered this occupation in the United States, while Patrocínio assumed his through the classic strategy of marrying into whiteness, opting – as had Douglass and indeed Machado de Assis – for social legitimization at the side of a white bride. But he had spent every penny of his wife's dowry reorganizing *A Gazeta da Tarde*, the biggest and best of all abolitionist newspapers. In terms of color, Patrocínio described himself as "burnt brick," and he had suffered

---

[18] On the conferences in Glória, see Bastos (2002, pp. 5, 8), who counted 465 in all, between 1873 and 1883.

successive acts of stigmatization, from the veiled sort at the medical school to the explicit, during the abolition campaign, when he was called a "half-caste" and a "monkey." At one conference in 1887, someone in the crowd started yelling "Shut up, nigger!" But Patrocínio was not to be cowed: "When the Lord gave me the color of Othello it was that I should be jealously protective of my race!"[19]

Rebouças and Patrocínio formed a triumvirate with Vicente Ferreira de Sousa. Also black, and married to a black wife, he was at peace with his color. In terms of studies, he had reached further than Patrocínio ever had: he was a fifth-year student at the medical school, which was where they had met. He went on to teach Latin and Philosophy at Pedro II College, where his students included the future abolitionist Raul Pompeia. It was a position of prestige that, in terms of social status, placed him midway between Rebouças and Patrocínio. However, in 1879, he was still teaching rhetoric at a boarding school and was an insubordinate student at the medical school – he signed a petition complaining about the exams.[20] Of the three, Sousa leaned furthest to the left. Later on, during the Republic, he would establish the Workers Federation and the Collectivist Socialist Party. In the past, while living in Salvador, he had attended the public ceremonies of another of Pompeia's teachers, Abílio Borges.

Of the three men, Rebouças was the most familiar with Borges. In 1879, he read *Desenho linear ou elementos de geometria prática popular* (Linear Design or Elements of Practical Popular Geometry), the school manual which Borges had launched the previous year and sent to him by post. Rebouças, a geometrical perfectionist, made some technical revisions, but expressed great enthusiasm at Borges' initiative in teaching the youth and modernizing the nation through "ideas that I have long espoused." He wrote a letter to the author full of praise and Borges, honored, had it published in the paper. The letter read: "We need to educate this nation for work. We're tired of empty speeches."[21]

The problem, however, was finding where to do that. Rebouças, Patrocínio, and Sousa set to work organizing events to swing public opinion. Instead of manumission in civic ceremonies, bankrolled with previously-raised donations, as Borges had done, they decided to turn

---

[19] Magalhães Jr. (1969, p. 98). Patrocínio, in Mariano (1927).
[20] GN, Jan. 6. 1878; Nov. 6, 1879.
[21] Valdez (2006, p. 40). The letter from Rebouças is dated Feb. 9, 1879 and was published in the *Correio Paulistano* on Apr. 2, 1879, with an introduction by Borges.

The Theatricalization of Politics 125

the events themselves into fundraisers. Patrocínio planted girls dressed in white and adorned with green and yellow sashes[22] at the theater's doors to draw in passers-by and collect donations.

The use of theaters for propaganda purposes was also inspired by Rio Branco's reforms, which, by promoting urban business, reinvigorated the sociability in the bigger towns. Theaters replaced churches as the grandstands of social life. Divas, actors, and plays were talk of the town and a constant feature in the newspapers during the 1870s and 1880s. Each provincial capital had its own theater, from Porto Alegre in the South to Manaus up North, such as the Lírico and Polytheama in Rio, and the Santa Isabel in Recife, which ran a busy weekly program.[23] Versatile spaces equipped to house everything from opera to vaudeville, cabaret to orchestras, popular fare to aristocratic refinement, theaters were at once worldly and family-oriented, accommodating everyone from the upper-social stratum to the demi-monde, the coquetry, and the politics.

Hosting these propaganda events at theaters provided the movement with artistic resources, already employed by Borges, but in small doses. Rebouças, a courtier, had a knack for the galas. In 1870, he hosted a serenade for the Emperor, with gardens decked with electric lights and lots of declamations, and, the following year, as a member of the National Association for Industrial Support – SAIN – put on a flower exhibition with ornamental pavilions and a medallion ceremony. The nephew of a violinist, he had a great appreciation for classical music and had served as Carlos Gomes' impresario, besides being godfather to the maestro's son. When he delved into the abolitionist cause he brought onboard his own expertise and that of his friend Gomes. At a staging of the opera O Guarani, on July 26, 1879, in Bahia, the maestro liberated two children – something he repeated in Rio de Janeiro, São Paulo, and Campinas.[24] Rebouças pushed the ceremonial meaning Borges had given to abolitionist events towards the world of concert music.

Patrocínio expanded it to the popular arts. He was an assiduous frequenter of the operettas and a fan of the coffee-concerts. He had a talent for improvisation that made him a natural at leading toasts, and his network of friends included theater owners and artists, such as the musician Chiquinha

---

[22] Duque-Estrada (1918, p. 83).    [23] Freyre (2003, p. 952); Holanda (2010, pp. 173 ff.).
[24] DNAAR, Apr. 20, 1870. SAIN session June 1, 1871 in O auxiliador da indústria nacional, v. xxix, 1871. Rebouças even helped Gomes with his librettos (DNAAR, Mar. 11, 1873) and the maestro's son was named Carlos André in Rebouças' honor. Letter from Rebouças to Sílio Bocanera Jr. 1897; EDEAR.

126                          *The Last Abolition*

Gonzaga. At the GT, he employed poets and actors, such as the popular comedian Francisco Correia Vasques – also black. Vicente de Sousa had theater connections of his own: he had published a play in 1875, and his wife was a singer.[25] It was an artistic strategy aimed at ordinary men and women, a counterweight to Rebouças' pomp and ceremony.

So they selected the theater as their social space for propaganda and set to work. The first to take to the stage as orator, at the Teatro São Luís on March 23, 1879, was Vicente de Sousa. The logistics were handled by the Fluminense Imperial Typographic Association and the Literary Essays Society. This was followed by sundry events until Rebouças' penchant for planning subsumed them all under a single descriptor: *Conferências Emancipadoras* (Emancipation Conferences). The first event to go by that name, held on July 25, 1880, was hosted by the Education School and held at Teatro São Luís. Vicente de Sousa was again the orator, and he manumitted a slave onstage. Rebouças took Carlos Gomes to watch, and at the next conference, in August, supported by the medical faculty's students union, the maestro joined him on stage to manumit a slave woman from his own household.[26]

Rebouças then convinced Sousa to revive his plan first devised in 1870 for a Central Association for the Protection of Emancipated Slaves. This time the idea took hold, and in August 1880 the Association's name was shortened to the Central Emancipatory Association (ACE). The Executive Board of the ACE began holding sessions at the same time every Sunday at the Teatro São Luís.

Rebouças had everything woven tightly together. He issued the invitations and covered the sessions the following day in the GT. He drew in politicians of known reformist leanings in order to maintain his strategy of keeping one foot in institutional politics. He brought onboard the Liberal senator Silveira da Mota, an emancipationist since the 1850s, and Nicolau Joaquim Moreira, from SAIN and a link between ACE and the pioneering Society against the African Slave Trade and for the Promotion of Colonization and Indian Civilization, which was evoked at the fifteenth conference. According to Patrocínio: "from the very beginning, the conferences were always presided over by men of

---

[25] Vicente de Sousa published *Horrores da Inquisição* (Horrors of the Inquisition), GN, Aug. 31, 1875.

[26] Souza, Mar. 23, 1879; ACE, Oct. 28, 1880, p. 3; EDEAR, Jul. 25, 1880. Conrad (1975, p. 169) says the first conference was held at the Normal School, but the ACE report (Oct. 28, 1880) says it was at the theater.

# The Theatricalization of Politics 127

enormous worth and prestige," such as those two gentlemen from the social elite, whose moral authority lent the events the respectability they needed to be tolerated by the government.[27]

The acts typically included one or two orators on stage speaking to an audience of both ladies and gentlemen. As the events proliferated with each new abolitionist association that was formed, they sometimes overlapped, so Patrocínio and Rebouças drew up a common timetable, deciding which association would host the Sunday event and so avoid spreading their audiences too thin. Rebouças, still depressed over his declining businesses, took care of the logistics, budget, and donations. Sousa brought medical students onboard and Patrocínio reached out to artists and booked theaters throughout Rio – besides the São Luís, there was the Recreio, the Dramático, and Polytheama – at low rates or free.

From 1880 to 1881, forty-four conferences were held, with Vicente de Sousa speaking at seventeen of these, and Patrocínio at eighteen. The agenda consisted of the inefficacy of the Free Womb Law, the mistreatment of slaves, attacks on State religion, and a demand for immediate and uncompensated abolition. Though Rebouças himself never took to the stage, Nicolau Moreira often repeated his ideals in rousing speeches against "barbarous feudalism," calling for "the subdivision of the soil and creation of a rural democracy," with legislation that offered incentives to the small and medium-sized landholder. These were all demands Rebouças had made in his articles for the *Jornal do Commercio* between 1874 and 1875.[28]

Another subject that spread by word of mouth was the dual affiliation of most activists. Patrocínio laid it out at the twenty-third conference, held on December 26, 1880: every abolitionist had the obligation to be republican as well, and vice-versa. In March 1879, Vicente de Sousa said the same thing loud and clear: ". . . both are born from the same origin, and both are sustained by the same means; and both aim toward the same end, for Empire and slavery are one and the same." The schemata

---

[27] On Rebouças' reporting on the Conferences: "The Seventh Emancipation Conference took place at the S. Luís Theater. I wrote up the event for the *Gazeta da Tarde*, as I did all the others" (DNAAR, Sept. 5, 1879). Cf. also DNAAR, Aug. 2, 1880. The most frequent orators were Patrocínio, Sousa, and Lopes Trovão (ACE, Oct. 28, 1880, p. 3). Other supporters who conferred respectability were Beaurepaire Rohan and Muniz Barreto who was blind. Cf. ACE, Nov. 28, 1880, p. 21. Patrocínio's comment is in CR, May 5, 1889.

[28] OA, Aug. 1, 1881; ACE, Jan. 28, 1881, p. 4. The first treasurer of the ACE was Francisco Castelões, the owner of a tea room of the same name and a regular haunt of Patrocínio's. One theater owner who was very helpful was Dias Braga (Duque-Estrada, 1918, p. 83). ACE, Sept. 28, 1880, pp. 15, 22. Rebouças' articles are in *Agricultura nacional: estudos econômicos: propaganda abolicionista e democrática*, 1883.

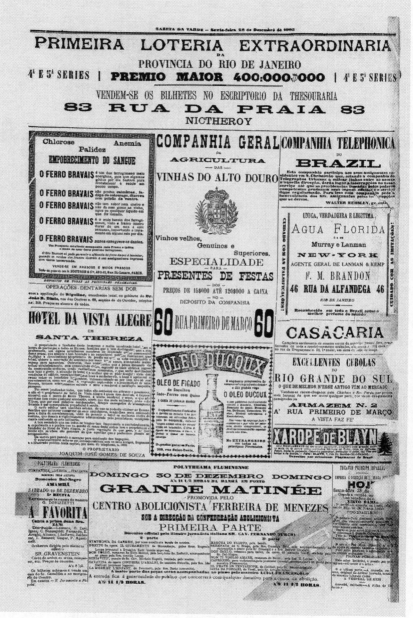

FIGURE 4.2 At the bottom of the page, an artistic programming of a conference-concert, one of the means of diffusion of abolitionist ideas. *Gazeta da Tarde*, December 28, 1883.
Archive of the Fundação Biblioteca Nacional (National Library Foundation), Brazil.
Reproduction by Jaime Acioli.

# The Theatricalization of Politics

of progress – "the light of the century" – demanded at once social and political reform, abolition, and a republic. Patrocínio thundered that "slavery is theft" and exhorted the audience to rally behind his "propaganda revolution" to honor "the martyrs of the revolution of 1789." Instead of religious symbols, like those used by the Anglo-American abolitionists, they lauded the French Revolution, with the speeches brought to a close to the sound of *La Marseillaise*.[29]

The abolitionist sound track was destined to expand. On September 5, 1880, something of a pattern emerged: from then on, all conferences were to have a musical part. At the twenty-fifth conference, on January 20, 1881, the arts took over, with a concert that included two pieces by Verdi, one by Donizetti, an aria from the opera *Martha*, by Friedrich von Flotow, and another by a local composer, Arthur Napoleão, performed by Cacilda de Sousa, Vicente Souza's wife. The concert came either before or after the speeches, performed by an illustrious list of artists. Those interludes swelled the conference audiences. On September 26, 1880, the theater was filled to capacity, with people listening in the street.[30]

Thus crystallized the main strategy in the abolitionist propaganda strategy employed throughout the first half of the 1880s: a blend of theater spectacle and political rally, a means of persuasion and fundraising, the concert-conferences. The venue ended up shaping the *propaganda style*. The setting of the theater spectacle provided the language for expression and ritualization of abolitionist proselytizing.

Conference preparations lasted the whole week. The GT announced the program, ornamentation, and artists for the coming Sunday. Instead of mixing abolitionism and religion like their counterparts in the United States, the ACE kept them as far apart as possible, scheduling the conferences for midday, after Mass, and after lunch. That way, the ladies could attend without interrupting any of their traditional duties. Some events were even preceded by a civic procession. Patrocínio would get the band playing – almost always for free – outside the *Gazeta da Tarde* headquarters on Uruguaiana Street. Passers-by would be invited to follow the marching band, the standard-bearer, and the abolitionists in a procession to one of the theaters downtown, already decorated, with a carpet of

---

[29] Souza, Mar. 23, 1879, pp. 10, 24–5, 30, 52–3, ACE, Jan. 28, 1881.

[30] ACE, Oct. 28, 1880, p. 5; Mar. 20, 1881, p.10; Oct. 28, 1880, p.13. Silva (2006) looks at the participation of artists in the campaign and traces the abolitionist conferences back to a show by Ernesto Rossi in 1870. However, Borges had already been staging events in this fashion since 1869.

leaves waiting for them on the sidewalk and the gardens aglow – electric lighting was the height of stagecraft and symbolized a beacon of liberty in the dark ages of slavery.

Those who entered the theater were swarmed by the sisters, daughters, and wives of abolitionists, a charming welcoming committee that squeezed the audience for donations. The decor – often provided by the Commercial Euterpean Society of the Devil's Lieutenants – was carnivalesque, with flowers, flags, coats of arms, curtains, flowing fabrics, laurels, scarves, lights, sequins, gilding, portraits of abolitionist heroes such as Victor Hugo, allegories, and GT insignia – often placed on a par with the Republican cap of liberty.[31]

With the theater packed to the rafters, the band poured in, followed by Sousa, Rebouças, Patrocínio, and usually six or seven others, all solemnly carrying the Brazilian flag – later replaced by standards of their own. As they marched up onto the stage, the curtains were raised.

The conferences lasted around three hours. During the political portion, the main orator was one of the directors of the fast-multiplying abolitionist societies. One frequent speaker was João Clapp, forty-three, the son of American parents, the manager of Brazil Bank, and the owner of a porcelain store. Patrocínio had met him at Republican Party meetings in São Cristovão. Clapp turned the Rebouças-Patrocínio-Sousa trio into a quartet, and by mid-decade, the role of greeter-in-chief and filer of the weekly activism report had fallen to him.

The political sessions were driven by the schemata of compassion, heavy on the romantic vocabulary and sentimental imagery, appealing to the audience's sensibility, nobility, and fraternity. The dramatics reached their height with Patrocínio, who highlighted the shared racial origin of the slaves and abolitionists like himself, Rebouças and Sousa:

... could there be anything more holy, more noble, than to have us, of African race, working day and night to free our brothers from the barbarous shackles of captivity?! (*Applause all round*). What would be vile, what would be shameful, ... was if we, out of fear, ... shrank from the vanguard, did not take our place at the front line, risking it all, to win or to die trying, for the most saintly cause of all; a cause that is entirely ours by our own blood, own minds, own hearts. (*Cheers and lengthy applause*).[32]

---

[31] GT, Dec. 16, 1883, Feb. 10, 1884, May 25 and Jun. 26, 1883, Dec. 10, 1883, Feb. 9, 1884.

[32] Patrocínio, Jan. 30, 1881, in ACE, Mar. 20, 1881, p. 17. A speech similar in tone was given on August 27, 1880 by Ubaldino do Amaral, a Republican-Abolitionist from the Luís Gama faction. On Clapp, see GT, Feb. 14, 1883.

The Theatricalization of Politics                131

Patrocínio cut an intense, theatrical figure who captivated his audience, as one witness would recall: "His speech was not melodic – it was hissed, or roared; his gestures were ungainly, and his gaze cast sparks all around. He would advance, then withdraw, hunker down, then spring and recoil, he was beside himself, on the tips of his toes, a spitfire . . . he was a tragic picture of a raging storm." With this ire and vim, he became the soul of the concert-conferences. When he took to the rostrum, the crowd cheered him on, applauded, and showered him with flowers – an ovation. It was said it was impossible to hear him speak without being moved to tears.[33]

In the speeches, the keystones of progress – freedom as a commandment of civilization – and rights – freedom as intrinsic to the human condition – flanked that of compassion. This was the way they found to combat the economic rationale behind pro-slavery rhetoric, as exemplified by one address at the Polytheama: "The slave has the same faculties as we do, the same heart, the same feelings and emotions, and very often far superior to those who call themselves his masters." Hence the affirmation that "slavery is theft; man cannot enslave man because they share the same nature and the same fate; we are all brothers, and our freedom can be neither bought nor sold, . . . we free the slave out of love for the dignity of man." At the end of his speech, like a performer in a show, the speaker received a bouquet.[34]

The sentimental indignation of these addresses perfectly complemented the concert portion of the event. A comic interlude by members of the Italian companies or by the proverbial Francisco Correia Vasques lightened things up ahead of the entrance of the four or five musicians. One day, a string quintet and two bands; the next, a singer, a quartet, a trio, some Italian waltzes, arias from Gounod's *Faust* or Bizet's *Carmen*. The opera singer Luísa Regadas was the "abolitionist nightingale." Opera companies, such as Del-Negro's – one of Rebouças' touches – rubbed shoulders with Patrocínio's purveyors of tango, zarzuela, lundu, or maxixe, an invention of Chiquinha Gonzaga. At the concert to mark the inauguration of the Commercial Abolitionist Center, Gonzaga conducted an orchestra and girls' choir. One of the crowd's favorites was the symphonic march "The Slave's Marseillaise," often played by the

---

[33] The witness in question is Coelho Neto, 1906. All the other descriptions are in ACE, Mar. 20, 1881, p. 17 and Oct. 28, 1880, p. 4.
[34] Speech by Antônio Pinto on Jun. 29, 1884; Pinto, 1884, pp. 9, 11–12; GT, Dec. 10, 1883.

132                          *The Last Abolition*

Invalid Boys Asylum band. Besides the oft-used *O Guarani*[35], nascent associations created their own songs, such as the Liberating Society of Ceará Anthem. The romantic tradition flourished in the poetry recitals, with the favorites being *Navio negreiro* (Slave Ship) and *Vozes d'África* (Voices of Africa), verses by Castro Alves, the former student of Abílio Borges, republished in 1880:

> Today America feeds on my blood
> A condor turned buzzard,
> the bird of slavery.

The arts conjured the sentimental atmosphere that set up the denouement. A slave, chosen by lots, would be brought up on stage to receive his manumission papers, purchased with audience donations – usually to the tune of 300,000 reis.[36] Vicente de Sousa conducted one of these emancipations: "Leading by the hand, he brought to the stage the African Juvêncio, handed him his letter of manumission, gave him the 'hug of equality and fraternity', and declared him a Brazilian citizen. The auditorium went wild with enthusiasm."[37]

On the stage, what pro-slavery rhetoric had defined as the basis of the political and economic order was lambasted as the bane and disgrace of the nation. The schemata of compassion dramatized the injustice of slavery and showed how it could be redressed: transform fungible chattel into living people, freed on stage. It packed a powerful punch. Having been primed with imagery, poetry, music, and sketches, the audience was taken to catharsis. In tears, on their feet, cheering loudly, the delirious crowd applauded, waved handkerchiefs, and showered liberator and

---

[35] The Italian comedians Stragni, Dominicci, Bonafous, Tanti, and Ferrari were frequent participants. GT, Jan. 16, 1883, Feb. 9, 1883 and May 25, 1883. Coelho Neto, 1899; CR, Mar. 20, 1888; GT, Mar. 17, 1883, May 25, 1883. The author of "Marselhesa dos escravos" (The Slave's Marseillaise) was Cardoso de Meneses; the Hino da Cearense (Anthem of The Liberating Society of Ceará) was by the Portuguese maestro Gomes Cardim. The presence of foreigners in the events is another evidence of Brazilian participation in an international abolitionist network.

[36] The first annual balance sheet for the concert-conferences lists a total of 2:573$840 reis (ACE, Dec. 28, 1880) and the second (Jul. 1880 to Jul. 1881), the sum of 5:912$540 reis (OA, Aug. 1, 1881). The funds were distributed, as in the following example: "Conference no. 10 collected the sum of 154$100. Dr. Vicente de Sousa set aside 77$ for the slave Justina, in whose name he promoted a concert and conference at the Club Mozart, and 77$ in additional funds for the self-purchase of Feliciano, taken from the current Emancipation Fund balance of 142:786$" (GT, Sept. 28, 1880).

[37] The description went on: "From the sad eyes of the venerable abolitionist Muniz Barreto streamed tears of the most ineffable joy." ACE, Mar. 20, 1881, p. 17.

## The Theatricalization of Politics

liberated with cut flowers. In June 1883, when Patrocínio presented not one but 115 letters of manumission, the emancipated slaves were met, each in turn, with a hail of flowers. And so the camellia became a symbol of the movement.[38]

The formula expanded and spread in Court and its environs. From 1878 to 1884, there were fifty-one abolitionist concert-conferences and a host of soirées, matinées, festivals, benefit concerts, parties, conferences, and public meetings, all with artistic elements of their own and totaling 161 public gatherings in closed spaces, mostly theaters. Though the names may have varied, the spirit was a constant, the melding of culture and politics. The format was adopted beyond Court, with events of this kind being held in eighteen different provinces by 1884, that means in every province in the nation save Piauí and Mato Grosso. In São Paulo, the method appeared in 1882, at the foundation of the Luís Gama Emancipation Fund, when a *festa da liberdade* (liberty party) was held at the São José Theater. The orator was Raul Pompeia and, as in Rio, there were women in the audience and a band played the Abolition Anthem. Later, further west in Goiânia, the rival Abolitionist Anthem appeared:

> *Hey-ha! Exult and clamor for liberty*
> *those who lately toiled with bended neck*
> *Break they shall, in lawful equality*
> *the shackles of a forsaken race.*[39]

The sessions did not always end in flowers. Patrocínio was afraid the police, which had attacked the Republican conferences in 1873, would crack down on three black men's attempt to take a pick-axe to a corner-stone of the Empire. He was right to be afraid. In a bulletin issued in November 1880, the ACE reported "persistent rumors that rancorous slavocrats were planning a raid on the São Luís Theater and an attack on the eminent orators José do Patrocínio and Vicente de Sousa." At the Senate, the Baron of Cotegipe called upon the government to put an end to the abolitionist party, but the conferences also had their defenders in Parliament. Minister Manuel de Sousa Dantas, a Liberal from Bahia and member of the 7th of September Liberating Society, refused to send in the police[40] and earned the lasting respect of the abolitionists for it, with key political consequences.

---

[38] GT, Jul. 27, 1880 and Jun. 26, 1883. Duque-Estrada (1918, p. 89).

[39] GT, Mar. 17, 1883. The words to the Goiás anthem are by the abolitionist Antônio Félix Bulhões, in Moraes (1974, p. 270).

[40] Santos (1942, pp. 125–8). ACE, Nov. 28, 1880, p. 24; Dec. 28, 1880, p. 3.

## ENGAGED ART

The arts were now a major part of the campaign. Whenever Carlos Gomes was in Brazil during the 1880s, Rebouças rolled him out on stage at some concert-conference or other in Rio. In 1883, he was the star of the show in Recife, promoted by the New Emancipatory Society. He was greeted by Tobias Barreto, another mixed-race person, professor at the Law Faculty, and the result was the foundation of the Carlos Gomes Club. The composer belonged to a vast troop who fought for abolition with chords and notes, verses, and feuilletons. Between 1880 and 1884, no fewer than sixty-three artistic events – concerts, plays, and even an opera – touted an explicitly abolitionist agenda. The artists used their shows as fundraisers for the campaign or as pretexts for the presentation of manumission letters. These beneficent events were palatable to the social elite as acts of philanthropy – and even the imperial family occasionally contributed to them. Halfway through the decade, however, their antislavery meaning became brazen when abolitionists like Patrocínio started to deliver the manumission papers themselves.

The comedian Vasques and the nightingale Luísa Regadas were ubiquitous. In addition to antislavery shows, they founded the Artists' Abolitionist Association, to which they enlisted some two dozen artists, including Coelho Neto. Nationwide, art became an important part of propaganda. Aluísio and Artur Azevedo, literati that relied on Patrocínio's friendship and purse strings, wrote abolitionist tirades in the Rio press, as well as poems and novels that were promoted in their home province, Maranhão. Others recited antislavery verses in Porto Alegre and rhyming acronyms circulated in São Paulo.[41]

Castro Alves' poetics of insurgency found a follower in Cruz e Sousa, the son of freed slaves from Desterro (Florianópolis). His "Escravocratas" (Slavocrats), published in 1882, transferred the animal sensualism Alencar had attributed to the African in his *O tronco do ipê* (The Trunk of the Trumpet Tree) to the master instead:

---

[41] In a roman à clef, Coelho Neto (1899, p. 163) mentioned various actors, actresses, and musicians. In Rio Grande do Sul, Kittleson (2005, p. 142) lists the poet Damaceno Vieira. *A Redempção*, in São Paulo, published verse by Valentim Magalhães and Amélio Braga.

## The Theatricalization of Politics

135

*Oh! deserters of the good, who 'neath the regal mantle squat*
*treacherous, hunkered down – like the vile crocodile,*
*basking sensual in the glow of privilege . . .*
*I, in rude and haughty verse, Adamastorian,*
*Red, colossal, thunderous, Gongorian,*
*Castrate ye like the bull – and hear ye squeal!*

In addition to the castration of the closing lines and the republicanism of the opening, the threat the imperial elite feared the most was voiced in another poem of his from the same year, "Da Senzala. . ." (From the Slave Quarters. . .), which clamored for slave revolt:

*Inside the slaveshack, dark and mud-caked*
*Where the despondent wretch,*
*In bilious tears, feeds on hate . . .*
*In feral impulsion;*
*No, he cannot leave,*
*A man of toil, a meaning, a reason. . .*
*and, yes, an assassin!*

The theme found its way into plays too. *Corja opulenta: drama aboli-cionista em 3 atos* (Opulent Mob: an Abolitionist Drama in 3 Acts), staged at theaters throughout the northern provinces and at the imperial capital in 1884, returned to the trope of the suffering slave already used in *Ursula*. It speaks of the disconsolate Alice, a free girl according to the Free Womb Law, but who was kept captive by her father-cum-master, a man who brags of impregnating eight slave women at the same time so that he could sell the offspring. The main character in the plot was the abolitionist Jorge, poor, fair and positivist, who expounded the three mainstays of abolitionist rhetoric – rights, compassion, and progress. He is a "combatant in the march of civilization" who protests against the "swine who would crush the proletariat with the miserable power of money!" The conflict acquires social density and overflows the subjective plane. Guerra, the slave owner, and Tibúrcio, the slave trader, represent their respective social groups, "lousy contrabandists of human flesh," the key elements in the "opulent mob" of the title. Villains selected as the targets of a rhetoric of threat: "Well, look ye how the Brazilian people sits. In every part one hears: I am an abolitionist! Death to the slavers! Long live abolition!" Engaged art, however, like the concert-conferences, strove for a solution that fell within the bounds of law. When Jorge saves Alice, it is through Gama-style, the enforcement of rights guaranteed by the Free Womb Law.[42]

---

[42] Nunes (1884, pp. 18–19, 22, 32, 35, 58).

136 *The Last Abolition*

*O escravocrata* (The Slavocrat) (1882), by Urbano Duarte and Artur Azevedo, both members of Patrocínio's circle, also broached the theme. Gabriela, her beloved Lourenço, a slave, her daughter, and the girl's boyfriend are the protagonists versus the evil master Serafim (Gabriela's husband and Lourenço's owner). Between the opposing camps flits Gustavo, whose paternity is revealed at the end: he is the son of Lourenço, not Serafim. The novelty here is that it is a black slave man, unlike the white girl in *Escrava Isaura*, who is worthy of an aristocrat's love. The novel does not have a happy ending: Gabriela goes mad, Lourenço commits suicide, and Gustavo redeems himself and the reader by disowning his reputed father in order to die by his biological father's side. A second novelty is that the tragedy triggers a revolt against Serafim (a name that breaks down into *será o fim* – "it will be the end"). Yet the end is reconciliatory: the victims forgive the slave owner and he repents, his eyes opened by the abolitionist sentiments of his future son-in-law:

... slavery is the greatest of our social iniquities, absolutely incompatible with the principles upon which all modern societies rest. It and it alone is the true cause of our material, moral and intellectual backwardness, given that, as it is the sole basis of our economic constitution, it exercises its fell influence on all other branches of social activity ... Oh! No! Each day longer this state of affairs abides is a spit in the eye of civilization and all humanity.[43]

Here, as in *Corja opulenta*, the dramatic tension shifts from the slave to the slaveowner, and slavery is exposed as a *relationship of domination*. More oblique is Machado de Assis' 1882 short story *O espelho* (The Mirror), in which Jacobina loses his identity when a farm's slaves run away. There can be no master if there are no slaves.

Pro-slavery politics reacted to these literary broadsides through censorship. The Brazilian Dramatic Conservatory banned Duarte and Azevedo's play on the grounds that it was morally offensive. Unable to stage their piece, the playwrights decided to publish it instead.[44] Poetry and plays were swift ways of diffusing the abolitionist moral repertoire across to the urban population, a strategy of playing to sensibilities in order to mobilize more people, hence the numerous stagings of Harriet

---

[43] Azevedo and Duarte (1884, pp. 24, 15).

[44] The title was more explicit than the piece itself, *A família Salazar* (The Salazars) (Azevedo and Duarte, 1884, p. 2). Another work, *Cora, a filha de Agar: drama abolicionista em 4 atos* (Cora, daughter of Agar: an abolitionist drama in 4 acts), by José Cavalcanti Ribeiro da Silva, was staged in Pernambuco in 1884. Many other performances of the same genre would follow.

# The Theatricalization of Politics

Beecher Stowe's international abolitionist classic *Uncle Tom's Cabin*, beginning in 1879. Nabuco proposed to translate the book in 1884, and it was published in Brazil in serialized form in 1888, in the abolitionist newspaper *A Redempção* (The Redemption).

The abolitionists tried to avoid the already established romantic feuilleton, perhaps because, inextricably associated with Alencar, it required a counterplot. The other Azevedo, Aluísio, turned his hand to the naturalist thesis-novel. The theme, which Rebouças had been mulling over since his trauma in New York, was color prejudice and post-abolition backlash. How was white society, in which upward mobility was a rare occurrence, to assimilate so many blacks? The 1881 novel *O mulatto* resurrected the old trope of the black as a corruptor of social mores, but subverted it. Rather than being diabolical, as in *O demônio familiar* (House Devil), Raimundo is a cultured and irresistible mestizo hero. The son of a Portuguese father and a former slave, Raimundo, with a European education behind him, was something of an alter-ego of the author, who used the schemata of progress to criticize the barbarity of slavery. A case in point is his description of the genital burns Raimundo's father's wife has inflicted upon his mother. Another character carries her cruelty in her name: Maria Bárbara (Barbarous Mary).[45]

The scientific lens picked out a subject dear to Rebouças, who argued for a land tax and agrarian reform in *Novo Mundo* in 1877, in the *Jornal do Commercio* in 1884, and in the *Gazeta da Tarde* in 1887. The novel *Os latifúndios* (The Latifundia) versified and dedicated to Luís Gama, was published in serialized form in *A Redempção* starting on October 13, 1887, and it was scathing on monopoly landowning.[46] If slavery, monoculture, and latifundia formed an unholy trinity, then, as Rebouças liked to say, the solution was equally triangular: they had to be taken down together.

Caricature was another tool of abolitionists, and the golden pencil belonged to Angelo Agostini, a friend of Gama and Patrocínio. Novels hit the higher-brow segments of society, but the caricature or cartoon, like the plays and recitals, spoke to the lower strata. In *Minha formação* (My Formative Years), Nabuco defined the *Revista*

---

[45] Magalhães Jr. (1969, p. 78). Examples of abolitionist novels: *Os herdeiros de Caramuru* (Caramuru's heirs), by Domingos Jaguaribe Filho, 1880, and *Quilombo dos Palmares* (The Palmares Quilombo), by Tristão de Alencar Arrive Jr., 1882. See Sayers (1956), Haberly (1972), Brookshaw (1983), Proença Filho (2004), Treece (2008).

[46] On Rebouças' activities in the press, see Trindade (2011, pp. 268–9). The novella is by Hipólito da Silva.

138 *The Last Abolition*

*Illustrada* as the non-reader's abolitionist Bible, and in it Agostini rendered his own inimitable depiction of the whole campaign. Where theater pulled heart strings and the novel appealed to reason, cartoons attacked slavery with the wrecking ball of laughter.

The use of the arts delegitimized slavery by diffusing a moral repertoire, branding slavery illegal, immoral, and archaic. The political use of familiar artistic formulae rattled the social conventions by calling the natural order of things into question. Ownership of slaves, once a sign of social distinction, became a badge of shame, while emancipating the enslaved became a testament to a nobleness of soul. The slave owner was no longer seen as the paternal master, but was upbraided as vile and backward, a drag on the onward march of civilization in which the African, the erstwhile savage, was a victim of social injustice on whose side the decent had to take a stand.

The discourse was critical, not revolutionary. The schemata that ran through antislavery output – compassion, rights, and progress – funneled into a rhetoric of change and redemption: by extinguishing once and for all the master-slave dichotomy, abolition could save both.

The concert-conferences and the various forms of engaged art that gravitated towards them infused the campaign with a language and set of artistic formulae that dramatized slavery. Together, they sensitized urban public opinion to the slave's plight, roused collective emotions against slavery, and converted a swath of the audience into activists. With no religion to fall back on, Brazilian abolition ran a secular propaganda campaign that was artistically grounded. In theater, it found its prosody: drama. Thus was shaped the peculiar Brazilian brand of activism, a theatricalization of politics.[47]

### AN AUDIENCE FOR ABOLITIONISM

The concert-conferences became a fixture in Court in the first half of the 1880s. João Clapp celebrated them as "a safe way of getting the people to identify with our ideas."[48] The Polytheama sat 2,000, and, according to the newspapers, there was a full house at each session, and more people waiting outside. So who were these people?

---

[47] "Theatricalization" because the events were solemn, dramatic stagings in the molds of opera and tailored to the theater space. As such, their effects were very different from "Carnivalization" (Conrad, 1975; Drescher, 1980).
[48] CA, 1884, p. 8.

The Spanish abolitionist mobilization had grown out of middle-class associativism. In aristocratic Brazilian society, the situation was different. Economic dynamism produced diversified strata, yet these were muffled by a patrimonial logic that never allowed a market society – and the classes deriving therefrom – to bloom. In this society, transitioning from traditional to modern, abolitionist activists and supporters came not from one, but from various social layers. Throughout the 1880s, the original sliver of modernizing aristocrats, such as Borges, continued to be engaged while the concert-conferences trawled the middle and lower tiers.[49]

An expressive contingent of the abolitionist support base had little direct relationship with slavery. As the interprovincial slave trade pooled slave stocks on export farmlands and in the mansions of the wealthy, in the 1880s large contingents of the population could not afford many or indeed any slaves. The abolitionist campaign spread among this demographic. The conferences drew droves of civil servants, liberal professionals – lawyers, engineers, scientists, chemists, dentists, journalists, and writers – public schoolteachers, musicians, lower-ranking military, small retailers like Clapp, a storeowner, and, to a lesser degree, businessmen and even a landowner. They also attracted the new students benefiting from the reform of the undergraduate schools of the 1870s, those with more ambition than lineage. Tasked with persuading these audiences were two men, and two schools: Rebouças, a professor at the Polytechnic, and Sousa, a student in the medical faculty. Both brought students from these institutions to the concert-conferences, along with the cadets from the Military Academy and those in the high schools (preparatórios). Patrocínio counted a good number of positivists and teachers among the attendees.[50]

Patrocínio also dragged along writers, artists, and theater professionals, the various moths drawn to the flame of his *Gazeta da Tarde*, and journalists from the medium-sized vehicles of the new press, such as the

---

[49] On Spanish abolitionism, see Schmidt-Nowara (1999, p. 74). An example of a modernizing aristocrat engaged with the movement was the MP Macedo Soares, an adept of Gama-style activism (he wrote *A campanha jurídica pela libertação dos escravos 1867–1888* (The Juridical Campaign for the Liberation of Slaves, 1867–1888)). On the social profile of the activists, see ACE, Mar. 20, 1881; CR, May 5, 1889.

[50] Bergstresser (1973, pp. 51 ff.) identified abolitionists belonging to 254 professions, but she did not include low- and high-ranking military, such as Benjamin Constant, who met Rebouças in the Paraguay War and had sat on the board of the Collective Workers Union along with Vicente de Sousa since 1880 (Mattos, 2009, p. 58). Among the professors of the Polytechnic was Enes de Souza. Patrocínio, CR, May 5, 1889.

140          *The Last Abolition*

*Gazeta de Notícias, Globo, Revista Illustrada* and, later on, *O País*. All those newspapers gathered men interested in becoming politicians, but with no chance at all, given the ongoing rules, of being elected to Parliament. Quintino Bocaiúva was one of these. He kept one foot in the Republican campaign, but he also gave Rebouças a helping hand. Many others who, like him, subscribed to the schemata of progress were demanding the whole suite: declaration of abolition, the secularization of the State, and the proclamation of a republic. These were separate campaigns but sometimes overlapped. Students and artists rallied behind abolitionism in the same numbers and with the same fervor as they had for republicanism.

Though this portion of the public enjoyed limited career options in imperial society, they were cultured and educated, and so part and parcel of "good" society. The profile of the members of twenty-two of the forty-four associations formed in Rio de Janeiro between 1880 and 1885, registered in the *Gazeta da Tarde*, reveals the presence of less illustrious individuals from less prestigious professions, including cashiers, typesetters, craftsmen, solicitors, newsagents, and cooks – there was the Abolitionist Club of Confederated Cooks and Caterers, later the Culinary Confederation Abolitionist Club. Vicente de Sousa hailed the group at one of his events, lauding them as "sons of the people, of the hardworking poor."[51]

As it was a complex web, abolitionism was hard to pigeon-hole either as an elite movement, or a grassroots activism. The movement swelled because it spread beyond a single social stratum.

The same holds for gender. There was considerable female involvement, despite the fact that women had not yet obtained the vote. However, they did not participate as a single bloc, but were scattered across the various levels of the imperial hierarchy and largely became involved via one of three main doors. The flagship was philanthropy: slave society spared upper-stratum ladies from the drudgery of domestic chores, but never gave them much by way of career opportunities. This meant they had plenty of free time to devote to beneficent causes and the creation of societies to free children and slave women, such as the Slave Child Redemption Society, founded in São Paulo by a lady from the Andrada clan, and the Ave Libertas (Hail Liberty), a group established in Recife by high-society women. A second way in was on the arm of

[51] CR, Mar. 26, 1888; ACE, Dec. 28, 1880, p. 45.

# The Theatricalization of Politics

abolitionist fathers, husbands, or brothers. An example was the José do Patrocínio Club, led by his wife Bibi, who immersed herself in her husband's public life upon realizing that it was where he spent most of his time. These women, initially occupied with decorating the halls, collecting donations, and selling raffle and show tickets, soon started playing the piano, singing, and reciting poetry – like Clapp's wife and daughters.[52] Rebouças and Clapp referred to this bourgeois audience as "the abolitionist family." These respectable ladies, however, had less time on their hands than the women artists, singers, writers, actresses, and musicians, who, single, separated, or married within the liberal artistic milieu, had none of the impediments of the patriarchal family. Through theater, many women followed in the footsteps of Chiquinha Gonzaga and Luísa Regadas.

The men clamored for their participation. At the GT, in January 1884, Patrocínio created a column provocatively called "Are the Brazilian ladies pro-slavery?" in which Aluísio Azevedo exhorted the ladies to join the fray, much as Castro Alves did in Bahia. On February 6, 1881, Clapp created a musical matinée tailored to this audience, featuring galas, poetry, and lots and lots of flowers.[53] The abolitionists wanted women on site to swell the audience numbers and protect the campaign from the threat of invasion by pro-slavery retainers. But they served other purposes besides that of the human shield. Attending the concert-conferences as one would an opera, they went from being politically invisible to active participants in street politics. One of the few female students at the medical faculty, Josefa Mercedes de Oliveira, addressed a conference in January 1884. Though her voice was shaky, she spoke as someone on an equal footing with the men, causing great frisson among the female audience, who responded by waving their handkerchiefs. This was in Rio, the capital, where tolerance was to be expected, but the same was also happening in over half the provinces of the Empire. At least thirty-six abolitionist associations were exclusively female or had significant numbers of women and were scattered throughout the country in Amazonas, Bahia, Ceará, Pará, Paraíba, Paraná, Pernambuco, Rio de Janeiro, Rio Grande do Sul, Rio Grande do Norte and São Paulo.[54]

Mothers brought their children to concert-conferences. The cast of *A corja opulenta* included a ten-year-old southern actress. Various young

---

[52] Sister-in-law and former student of Patrocínio, Rosália Sena, the wife of Vicente de Sousa and Honorina Ferreira all gave declamations (GT, May 25, 1883).
[53] Azevedo, GT, Jan. 29, 1884; ACE, Mar. 20, 1881, p. 19.   [54] GT, Jan. 28, 1884.

142                                  *The Last Abolition*

girls gave recitals and a boy even addressed the audience.[55] The aim was to contrast childhood innocence with the sordidness of slavery.

Of course, participation is not the same as equality, and abolitionism was not feminism. Gender hierarchy, a very pronounced trait of imperial society, broke through from time to time, with some activists expressing moralistic value judgments. However, by involving women and children, the movement attacked slavery where it was strongest as well as where it was most silent: in the household. It politicized private life.

The greatest transgression of all was bringing the slave into politics. Rebouças dreamed of setting up schools for freed slaves nationwide, but it was Clapp who created the Niterói Freedmen's Club, a model that was widely replicated, and the GT called upon the abolitionist associations to found schools of their own. Abílio Borges, now the Baron of Macaúbas and still living in Court, taught at the Portuguese Literary Lyceum, a free night school for the poor, that taught soldiers, sailors, and slaves how to read and write. Literacy schools under abolitionist teachers took in illiterate slaves and turned out freedmen and activists. One of those manumitted at a concert-conference became an orator at later conferences and vice-chairman of the José do Patrocínio Emancipation Fund.[56]

The conferences were absorbing "all the nation's unbridled talent, knowledge and character," not to mention its mandateless politicians, the middle and lower strata, Portuguese immigrants who still had not found their feet on Brazilian soil, free mestizos and blacks, freed slaves, women, and children. Abolitionism was expanding its base to encompass what Patrocínio called "citizens of all classes."[57]

By broadening the spectrum of the politically-involved, the movement challenged Brazilian tradition and proved more inclusive than its Spanish counterpart, which spoke to slaves from across the Atlantic. Brazilians, however, like the rare abolitionists of the US confederacy, went about

---

[55] GT, Feb. 12, 1883 and Feb. 9, 1884.

[56] Other examples are the Free Night School at 97 Rua das Flores, founded by the Gutenberg Abolitionist Club with materials donated by local merchants, and the Cancella Night School, which opened in 1881. GT, Feb. 10, Apr. 9 and 17, 1883; Valdez (2006, p. 36); GT, Jun. 26, 1883. The Emancipatory Savings, born out of the Rio Branco Law Emancipation Fund, collected subscriptions and held raffles to stock a common reserve for the purchase of letters of manumission. The abolitionists registered a group of slaves as members and, as the money came in, raffled among the enlisted the ones to be freed. These Emancipatory Savings were named after leaders, such as the José do Patrocínio and Luís Gama funds. The freed slave who became an orator was Abel Trindade.

[57] GT, May 5, 1889. Cf. Table A.2 of the Appendix; GT, Feb. 18, 1884.

## The Theatricalization of Politics 143

their daily lives in the company of slaves, and even for them the leap from slave owner to abolitionist proved daunting and difficult. Rebouças was not the first to join the movement with slaves under his own roof, and he would not be the last.[58]

The more varied membership did not change the movement's core demands. As per its SCT pamphlet in 1852, abolition was the linchpin of a modernization program whose other two pillars were immigration and small land property. There were variations between factions, as there always are in social movements, but the eradication of slavery remained the core. And so, rather than between radicals and moderates, the root antagonism was and would remain between an abolitionist movement and a pro-slavery countermovement.

### FLOWER POLITICS

The concert-conferences inaugurated a new type of politics in Brazil, conducted not in Parliament, but in the public space, and operated by relatively marginal social groups vis-à-vis the aristocratic political institutions. Abolitionism positioned itself as street-level politics, geared towards rallying the urban masses, just like its Anglo-American counterpart.

Abolitionist propaganda was devised to persuade. Just as Luís Gama used the letter of the law against the lawmakers, exploiting loopholes within the legal framework of slavery itself, Rebouças, Patrocínio, Sousa, and Clapp turned against the politicians the weapons they – the Radical Liberals – had themselves fashioned: propaganda in the public space. This mobilization strategy dominated the first phase of the campaign, a cycle of peaceful protest, a phase of flowers: "Decidedly, flowers," said Patrocínio, "are destined to play a pivotal role in emancipation."[59]

But these roses had their thorns. Abolitionist noise galvanized the pro-slavery activists. Paulino Soares de Sousa, ever-vigilant, called for measures to "deflate impatient and potentially dangerous agitators." And even in the public space, the same 1870s generation that had produced so many abolitionists fielded some opponents too. In the late 1880s, Sílvio

---

[58] On the social extraction of Hispanic abolitionists, see Schmidt-Nowara (1999, p. 87); Joaquin Serra was one abolitionist to emancipate slaves at a concert-conference (ACE, Jan. 18, 1881, p. 32).

[59] ACE, Dec. 28, 1880, p. 6. Cycle of protest is a mobilization peak, when collective public demonstrations occupy public space with high frequency and intensity, spreading to different sectors of society and public spaces, using new demonstration and organizational techniques and disrupting social routines (Tarrow, 1983, 1995).

144 *The Last Abolition*

Romero, an orator invited to speak at a concert-conference, failed to show up, alleging ill health. The following February he published a text titled "The question of the day – the emancipation of slaves," in *Revista Brasileira,* in which he trotted out all of José de Alencar's arguments against the Free Womb Law: abolition should be brought about slowly and by society's own will, without the intervention of the State. And he branded the ACE's front line – Patrocínio, Rebouças, Sousa, Clapp – as obdurate. Patrocínio replied in the GT, saying that what Romero was proposing was a very good way to never get anywhere at all. The result was a lasting spat between the incensed Rebouças and the "slavocrat" Sílvio Romero.[60]

He and Patrocínio – friends with complementary talents – would remain fighting until 1888. For Rebouças, a respected businessman and son of a member of the political elite, it would be hard to fight the Empire at this stage. His method was to bait and attract, finance, manage, develop, put the abolitionist apparatus to work. Patrocínio, on the other hand, was bored to death by the ten-to-four working hours of the 1880s. His stomping ground was the night, and that was where he raised his own army. Rebouças was rational, Patrocínio explosive. He mixed abolitionism with other subversions. In January 1880, he backed the Vintém (20 cent) Revolt against the proposed taxation of tram fares. Rousing speeches by himself and the Republican Lopes Trovão led to a tram boycott, the vandalization of tram tracks and skirmishes with riot police.

Patrocínio and Rebouças, like Frederick Douglass before them, bet on mobilization in the public space as the best way to pressure Parliament and the government. If cerebral Rebouças was the organizer, the impulsive and somewhat reckless Patrocínio was the agitator without whom no social movement can prosper. He became the leader of abolitionism in public space thanks to his complementary methods: flowers in-hand, and a pocketful of rocks.[61]

[60] GT, Sept. 25, 1880; ACE, Oct. 28, 1880, p.17. Romero (1881, p. xvii) lists various others, such as Nicolau Moreira. The fight reverberated nationally. See *Libertador,* Mar. 17, 1881, DNAAR, Jun. 3, 1881.

[61] On the Vintém Revolt against the fare increase, see Graham (1980). On Douglass, for example: "Douglass is one of those great, heroic organizations. Born a slave …, he is today considered a writer of merit, a vehement orator and the most ardent defender of his race" (GT, Apr. 25, 1883).

# 5

# Expansion

### THE LIBERAL HEIR

A prince, that was what the US ambassador to Brazil thought when, in the late 1870s, he met the handsome, charming youth. "In the whole course of my life I had met no one whose future seemed brighter. . . . He glittered in the firmament of his country like a morning star, and his subsequent career has fulfilled the promise of his youth." To understand this brilliance, one has to first grasp the social configuration in which Joaquim Nabuco emerged, and which helped him rise into the political sky. Far from being a self-made man, he was, to use Bourdieu's term, an heir, a member of the social aristocracy and political elite. His father was the Liberal leader, senator, and statesman José Tomás Nabuco de Araújo, whom we met in Chapter 1 during the debates on the Free Womb Law. Nabuco de Araújo left young Joaquim with his godparents at Massangano mill, near Recife, soon after his birth in 1849. Growing up at the mill, he was intimately exposed to slave life and economy, which, he later recollected, was one of the roots of his eventual conversion to abolitionism.

On afternoon, I was sitting on the landing of the outside stairs to the house, when a young black man, about eighteen years old, previously unknown to me, hurled himself upon me, clutching my feet and begging me, for the love of God, to have my godmother purchase him to serve me. He had come from the vicinity, desperate to change master, because his owner, as he told me, punished him mercilessly, and he fled at the risk of his life. This unexpected turn of events unveiled to me the nature of the institution that I had always taken for granted, never suspecting the pain it concealed.[1]

---

[1] Hilliard (1892, p. 381); Nabuco (1900, p. 128). This chapter revisits the material and ideas in Alonso (2007). See also Vianna Filho (1969) and Nabuco (1949).

146    *The Last Abolition*

As with Patrocínio, the dramatic encounter that made Nabuco balk at what had previously seemed so natural came during childhood and was narrated from the perspective of compassion, that romantic sensibility that inspires clemency. However, the two men had very different emotional upbringings. Patrocínio, the son of a priest and a freed slave woman and therefore untethered to genteel society, had been able to vent his feelings with virulence and violence from a young age. The statesman's son, on the other hand, was raised as an aristocrat, trained to keep a stiff upper lip and his emotions in check, taking recourse to words, not force. The difference can be seen in their very distinct reactions to similar episodes. While the young Patrocínio got himself hurt stopping a slave from being whipped, Nabuco managed to convince his godmother to intervene in the captive's favor. Patrocínio, rash and passionate, trusted in his own initiatives; Nabuco, persuasive, believed in authority's power to change fates. Two origins, two different upbringings, two styles of activism.

Nabuco etched his own style young. Taken to Court at the age of eight, he continued his aristocratic education at Colégio Pedro II and at the Law Faculties in São Paulo and Recife, as was par for the course. Stirred by the lively debates on the Free Womb Law in the Parliament, of which his father was a member, he advocated the use of Gama-style juridical activism, as was popular among the students. In 1870, he argued against the circumstantial pro-slavery rhetoric in his defense of a slave charged with two counts of murder: the slave was not the barbarian here; barbarous was the institution that reduced a man to the situation of a cornered animal with no other means of defense than attack. He set to work on a book entitled *A escravidão* (Slavery), in which he unleashed the whole arsenal of abolitionist rhetoric: the schemata of compassion – based on the moral condemnation of slavery; the progress prong, with its metaphor of slavery as a social disease, a "wound in the nation's side"; and the schemata of rights, slaveholding as based upon a crime – slave-trafficking – and liberty as a natural right.[2]

At that point, however, he neither published the book nor pursued the subject itself. Instead, like Rebouças, he set off on the European grand tour that was the ritual of the Brazilian elite, and there he refined his aristocratic manners. Elegant and gallant, he honed his charisma and trained himself in the arts of seduction and making a good impression. He found a fiancée of equal caliber, Eufrásia Teixeira Leite, a strong

---

[2] Nabuco (1870, pp. 3, 8, 2).

FIGURE 5.1 The abolitionist Joaquim Aurélio Nabuco de Araújo (1849–1910). Archive of the Fundação Joaquim Nabuco (Joaquim Nabuco Foundation) – Ministério de Educação (Ministry of Education).

woman with whom he had a long and tempestuous romance,[3] with slavery as something of a backdrop: her family were landowners in Vassouras, Paulino Soares de Sousa's heartland.

In 1875, he returned to Brazil, and to the topic of slavery. He published a collection of poetry and articles on literature, in one of which he criticized José de Alencar's *O demônio familiar* (The House Devil), which was being restaged. Nabuco noted that the country's leading author was having a hard time drawing the crowds, a clear indication that the end was nigh for his Indianist literature. Alencar was enraged, and the pair traded barbs in the *O Globo* newspaper. The spat was given a political spin when Nabuco, the son of a Liberal, mentioned that the Conservative Party (to which Alencar belonged) had "fought intrepidly for slavery" during the debate on the Free Womb Law. Alencar shot back, saying: "Politics is something I'm more used to discussing with the father," not with his "pup."[4]

Alencar was alluding to the fact that Nabuco's fate was in his father's hands. As the Conservatives were in government at the time, there was

---

[3] On Eufrásia Teixeira Leite, see Falci and Melo (2012).
[4] Nabuco, *O Globo*, Nov. 21, 1875; Alencar, Nov. 20, 1875, in Coutinho (ed. 1978).

not much chance of Nabuco, a Liberal debutant, being elected to Parliament. Nabuco de Araújo, calling in favors from his relationship network in Court, had his son established on the feeder road of diplomacy. He took the post of attaché at the Brazilian diplomatic office in the United States in 1876 and when the Liberals returned to power in 1878, transferred to London. Whilst abroad, Nabuco consolidated himself as a modern man, conversant in political ideas, fascinated with European civilization, and aghast at the bumpkin ways of his provincial homeland. His time in Washington and London showed him changing worlds. As an aristocrat, he disliked the bourgeois brashness of US society and the violence of its politics, much preferring the gradual reforms carried through, with public support, in Britain. Not only had the British abolished slavery in the colonies – a tense affair, if ultimately peaceful – but they were also democratizing the monarchy at home. At the age of thirty, when his father's death brought him back to Brazil, he took this political model of reformism with him in his baggage.

In 1879, like many sons of Liberal leaders, he joined Parliament, embracing the political legacy of his father and the Radical Liberal agenda, recently orphaned by Tavares Bastos. Nabuco was a worthy substitute, and staunch defender of the package of gradual abolition of slavery and promotion of rural smallholdings – just like Rebouças.

Charming and captivating, intelligent and audacious, that was how the young aristocrat was described by his contemporaries; a polished example of his social group. As the American diplomat had foreseen, here was a man destined for great things.

### IN PARLIAMENT

Paulino Soares de Sousa suffered some significant losses in the 1870s. In addition to Maria Amélia, he also lost his party colleague and comrade in resistance, José de Alencar. The Grim Reaper, however, would even the score somewhat by also claiming his arch-rival, the Conservative Party stalwart and reformer Rio Branco, and his fellow party member São Vicente. On the Liberal side, death took Zacarias, Tavares Bastos, and Nabuco's father. Another casualty was his uncle Itaboraí, whose absence deprived him of a pillar of support, without a doubt, but also cleared the way for his own uncontested rise: he became a State Councilor in 1876, provincial leader of his party in Rio de Janeiro, and a leading light of the Conservatives, respected throughout the nation. But he was still in opposition to the government and its own party.

## Expansion 149

The Conservatives had controlled the national executive from 1868 to 1878, but the Liberals held sway from then right up to 1885. With his adversaries in government, Paulino was afraid that the old sore of emancipation, which had grown a scab since the Free Womb Law, would be reopened. The international scene was pulling in that direction: a new Spanish law had set 1880 as the date for the end of apprenticeship in Cuba – the transition to free, paid labor. On the national level, antislavery associations and the concert-conferences were growing in number and force. In squaring up to Patrocínio, Sousa, and Rebouças, Paulino had allies of his own.

The government of Cansanção de Sinimbu, the first prime minister of the seven-year Liberal rule (1878–1885), was full of them. Sinimbu's Chinese-immigrant project was more pleasing to Paulino than it was to many Liberals. This issue, like another pillar of the reformist agenda, the electoral system, had split the Liberals into two camps: reformists and recalcitrants. Faced with this impasse, a reformist faction from Bahia took a public stance in Parliament in March 1879, through its spokesman Jerônimo Sodré Pereira, who, in addition to being a professor at the medical faculty and the son-in-law of Senator Manuel de Sousa Dantas, was a member of the 2nd of July Liberating Society, whose banner he unfurled at the House, declaring: "Brazilian society sits upon a volcano. ... I hereby appeal for the swift and total extinction of slavery."[5]

Sinimbu, a mill owner, gave the lava wide berth. He stated that he would not advance on the issue a single step beyond the 1871 law. He avoided even the precautionary project of banning the inter-provincial slave trade so as to avoid slave stocks being concentrated in the southern region of the nation, the state of affairs that had given rise to the American Civil War. Afraid of a similar outcome, the provincial assemblies of Rio de Janeiro, in December 1880, and São Paulo, the following January, pushed legislation by themselves, approving local restrictions to the trade.[6] But law is one thing, enforcement quite another.

This was the state of play when Nabuco arrived at Parliament. Having observed his father at work, he knew that politics was all about standing for a cause, so he needed one to brandish. Of the most important ones, electoral reform was already taken, while abolition, before Sodré's speech at least, lay dormant. Stowed in the imperial cloakroom,

---

[5] His speech (ACD, Mar. 22, 1879) represented this faction that had come from Bahia (Nabuco, 1900, p. 137).

[6] Moraes (1924, pp. 35–6).

150 The Last Abolition

it was a political hat as fine as it was hard to wear. It could sink a career more easily than it could make one. When Nabuco reached for that hat, it was as if they had been made for each other.

Nabuco burst into Parliament with all the dramatic flair Patrocínio displayed at his concert-conference. His name ensured access to the lectern, but Nabuco owned it, managing the romantic sensibility, studied mannerisms, and an incendiary discourse. Guided by an inspired sense of timing, he took the baton from Sodré on March 22, 1879, the eve of Patrocínio, Sousa, and Rebouças' first concert-conference. Armed with the schemata of progress, he framed his subject within the international conjuncture: "The whole world's opinion on the matter is more than formed. Forced labor has to end." He upended the rhetoric of threat: the murder of masters by their slaves in Brazil pointed to the North-American path, a bloody one. It was a model to be avoided. The path to follow should be the progressive reforms of the British: "Gentlemen, I am not one of those clamoring for immediate emancipation."[7] Egged on by hear hears and cheers, he galvanized the debate for the very first time – and would never stop.

His program was the same as that of Tavares Bastos and Rebouças: use fiscal policy to create a land market, with the State selling off or granting railroad lands to immigrant settlers, like the United States. Hence, its core consisted of introducing land tax, offering incentives to small properties, and attracting European immigrant labor. Abolition was just the beginning.

His next line of attack came from Patrocínio, who, in 1879, wrote an exposé for the *Gazeta de Notícias* about an English mining company based in São João del-Rei that was illegally holding 200 Africans. Nabuco demanded explanations from the government. The story caused a furor: *Rio News*, an English-language paper, ran an editorial on it, and it was covered in the prestigious Paris-based *Revue des Deux Mondes*.[8] The British and Foreign Antislavery Society sent him documents, thus beginning a relationship that would last throughout the campaign. Nabuco adopted the boomerang method pioneered by Abílio Borges in 1866: fight internal resistance by garnering support abroad.

---

[7] In Parliament, he read a letter which the North-American abolitionist senator Charles Sumner had sent to his father just before the promulgation of the Free Womb Law (ACD, Mar. 22, 1879).

[8] Magalhães Jr. (1969, p. 77); Childs (1998); Campbell (2010, p. 55); Bérenger (1880, p. 440).

*Expansion* 151

It was an attack wasted on Sinimbu, who fell anyway, due to Liberal Party in-fighting. He was replaced by José Antônio Saraiva, who like his predecessor had absolutely no interest in the subject. Nabuco broke protocol and grilled the incumbent prime minister. He spoke a total of thirteen times, always on slavery and riffing on all three schemata of interpretation – compassion, rights, and progress – of abolitionist rhetoric, holding Brazil up to the world for comparison and finding its closest resemblance with Turkey, the last of the slaveholding nations. He demanded commitment to abolition, and the word stuck to him like a badge. The more fuss he caused, the more the already tall Nabuco seemed to grow: "... let me remind you of the gaping inequality that exists in our society ... you must surely see that on our sun there sits a garish stain; the blemish of the fact that, as the 19th century draws to a close, there are still slaves in this land."[9] He also revived Abílio Borges' tropes, abolition as a complement to political Independence. He systematically cited the pro-emancipatory declarations of deceased statesmen and began to build a national pro-emancipation tradition that straddled the Liberal and Conservative parties, incremented with some illustrious abolitionists from abroad.

Martinho Campos, leader of the House majority and a friend of Paulino's, did not delay in counter-attacking. He urged the government to backtrack: "... whilst we fail to find the right means by which to abolish slavery, do not disrupt, do not imperil, I'll not say merely the ownership of, but indeed the very existence of the most important parcel of our population."[10] Saraiva agreed: the Free Womb Law had been as broad a step as could have been taken, and all the concert-conferences and pamphlets in the world could not dent his resolve. Saraiva dug his heels in, afraid to meddle with the nation's workforce, economy, politics, in short, the established order, the supreme value for the circumstantial pro-slavery politics.

Then, in August 1880, Nabuco created something out of nothing: he sifted through the ideas expounded by Tavares Bastos before him and arranged them into a gradual, compensation-based abolition bill that would phase slavery out by January 1, 1890. Straight off, the plan would ban the inter-provincial slave trade, corporal punishment, and the separation of slave children from their mothers, curtail urban slavery (abolishing state ownership and the hiring-out system), and prohibit slaves'

[9] ACD, Apr. 22, 1880.     [10] Ibid.

geographical mobility. It also proposed a slave-education program, respect for the integrity of slave families, and welfare safeguards for the elderly and infirm. This policy was to be funded by taxes on convents, government contracts, unclaimed inheritances, the sale of government debt bonds and a land tax in the molds Tavares Bastos and Rebouças had long been calling for. Nabuco's plan also nodded to the public space abolitionists by proposing state funding for emancipatory associations and extending legal guarantees to compulsory emancipation financed by third parties (in other words, by the abolitionists), so long as a market price was paid. Some of these measures were already in the Free Womb Law, but had gone unenforced. Nabuco also wanted to beef up the Emancipation Fund provided for under the law by introducing provincial committees in charge of administrating the saved money and to conduct the annual manumissions raffles. The symbolic dimension of the project was to create, in an aristocratic fashion, honorific titles for emancipators and ban slave-sale ads in newspapers. It was nothing drastic – it even prescribed punishments for runaway slaves – but it was more than the government and the pro-slavery political coalition could take.

On August 24, the government dropped the ball, with a low turnout and key leaders absent. Nabuco seized the opportunity and requested the introduction of the bill, which, considered harmless, was admitted with thirty-eight votes out of the possible one hundred and twenty-two. The prime minister responded at the next session, saying that pretty ideas make for opposition discourse, and that "the minister in charge of imperial politics does not have the right to enunciate a line of thought in such obvious disharmony with that of the nation," a slave-owning nation. Saraiva's cabinet tore the bill to shreds, and it never even reached the floor. However, on August 30, 1880, eighteen MPs from nine provinces voted in favor of its urgent discussion on the House floor. An abolitionist bloc was emerging in Parliament.[11]

Nabuco needed to singularize his own style and set himself apart from Rebouças, Gama, and Patrocínio, whose role model was the black activist Frederick Douglass, a self-made man and former slave, who campaigned against slavery in public space, at conferences and in the press. In choosing his own activist role model, Nabuco, too, looked in the abolitionist repertoire for someone like himself, and settled on William Wilberforce, the parliamentarian leader of British abolitionism in the late eighteenth

---

[11] ACD, Sept. 2, 1880.

# Expansion

153

century. Wilberforce had fought for the abolition of the slave trade and slavery throughout British domains. His action was mainly inside institutions, with a modus operandi revolving around delivering speeches and introducing and obstructing bills of law – many of which were rejected. Since his death, in the 1830s, he had since become the icon of a style of abolitionism that focused on political institutions. His legend reverberated in Spain, where abolitionists emulated his parliamentary techniques. Nabuco wanted to be the Brazilian Wilberforce, and there were similarities between them. Both were Liberals, from aristocratic families, who had chosen Parliament as their main sphere of action. Nabuco's style of activism would be a replication of Wilberforce's: he would draft bills, address the floor, form coalitions, and drum up support for an abolitionist law, as he wrote to the British and Foreign Antislavery Society:

This bill will not be converted this year into a law, but introduced every Session, in a Liberal House by myself or some of my friends, in a Conservative house by some prominent Conservative Abolitionist ... increasing every time in votes, it will triumph at last.[12]

Nabuco adopted a bold tone in re-presenting his eight-part bill on September 4, 1880, saying: "The State does not dare to step inside the farm's gates." Martinho Campos replied that, were the State to do so, the reaction would come on horseback and from the barrel of a gun.[13]

Nabuco's bill did not pass, but he had garnered authority for the next one. He had become the abolitionist spokesman in Parliament, with a bloc of eighteen members behind him, seven of whom would stay the course through to 1888. They were all cut from much the same cloth as he: the sons or godsons of Liberal Party leaders, reform-minded men with modernizing ideas for politics and society.

Just as he was realizing how harsh resistance would be in Parliament, Nabuco received a visit from the son of councilor Rebouças, who had died blind on June 19. (Nabuco's congressman father died a year and a half earlier.) They will have recalled their respective progenitors, who were both defenders of a centralized Empire against the Sabinada (Antônio Rebouças) and Praieira (Nabuco de Araújo), two autonomist revolts. Their sons, on the other hand, were scathing critics of the imperial order. Rebouças mentioned the concert-conferences, an alternative stage

---

[12] Letter from Joaquim Nabuco to Charles Allen, Apr. 8, 1880, Bethell and Carvalho (eds., 2008). On Wilberforce (1759–1833), who was also an example to the Spanish abolitionists, see Fradera and Schmidt-Nowara (2013), and other British abolitionists, see Hochschild (2005).
[13] ACD, Sept. 4, 1880.

154 *The Last Abolition*

for Nabuco, where he could rally forces for future investment in Parliament. As was his wont, he left a copy of his project "Land Tax applied to Slave Emancipation," along with clippings of his articles in *Jornal do Commercio* and *Gazeta da Tarde*, which Nabuco would take to the rest of the fledgling bloc.[14]

Nabuco and Rebouças were both Liberal and aristocrats. The former, however, possessed something the latter lacked, namely eloquence, a public vocation, and a white complexion. Rebouças, Patrocínio, and Sousa needed a voice in Parliament, just as Nabuco needed a support base outside it. They complemented each other, and that was why the bridge-building engineer went to see the representative in July 1880: "I have formed an alliance with MP Joaquim Nabuco for the promotion of the abolitionist propaganda."[15]

Rebouças converted all his allies into friends, and it was no different in this case. However, Patrocínio and Nabuco would never be close. They shared no common ground socially, no overlap in background, and they both had strong personalities that demanded the limelight. Each wanted to be center-stage and neither would ever be content to play second fiddle. They were competitive, and Rebouças spent the best part of the decade snuffing out the sparks that flew whenever these two egos came too close.

They would never be friends, but allies, yes; that they could manage. Nabuco took to Parliament many of the themes that emerged out of the concert-conferences and the abolitionist press, and Patrocínio endorsed him in his articles, such as when Nabuco challenged Saraiva: if the government and Parliament think the issue has been put to bed, he wrote, public opinion would demand its right to "agitate and insist" in the name of Rebouças' "rural democracy," which the trio so staunchly defended. "The Law, in the name of society, must intervene to create rural small-holdings, establish a colony in the heartland of the current workforce," and so shift the focus from the rancher to the nation.[16]

Out of favor with the two Prime Ministers, stripped of his diplomatic post in London (he was until then just on leave), and finding all his moves in Parliament ruined, Nabuco declared, in November 1880:

---

[14] The most dedicated members of the bloc were Joaquim Serra, Jerônimo Sodré, Sancho de Barros Pimentel, José Mariano Carneiro da Cunha, Marcolino de Moura, Francisco Correia Ferreira Rabelo, José da Costa Azevedo (Nabuco, 1884, p. 81). They called themselves the "new Liberals" in order to set themselves apart from the previous generation (Alonso, 2002). It was with this group that Rebouças first made contact (DNAAR, Sept. 4 and Jul. 9, 1880).

[15] DNAAR, Jul. 9, 1880.     [16] Patrocínio, GN, Sept. 6, 1880.

# Expansion 155

"As an abolitionist, in the light of recent events, I must address public opinion and draw therefrom the power to make the House reconsider its vote."[17] So he invested in this new alliance with public space abolitionism in order to amplify his voice in Parliament.

## ELITE ASSOCIATIVISM REBOOTED

Society meant something very different to Nabuco and Patrocínio. When Nabuco ventured beyond Parliament, rather than join the triumvirate's ACE, then barely a month old, he formed his own Brazilian Antislavery Society (SBCE). He invited Rebouças, who never demanded fidelity, and was a member of as many reformist societies as people could found. So he joined Patrocínio in one, and Nabuco in another, becoming the hinge without which the door would never have opened.

The SBCE was similar to Abílio Borges' 7th of September Liberating Society. It was aristocratic and encompassed most of the abolitionist parliamentary bloc that supported Nabuco's bill. Rebouças brought on board respected politicians with abolitionist sympathies whom he had previously tried to lure into the ACE. In a symbolic measure, they appointed the Viscount of Rio Branco an honorary member, though the champion of the Free Womb Law, then on his deathbed, probably never knew.

The SBCE manifesto repeated the interpretive schemata of abolition as a second Independence in its choice of founding date while the title of its periodical, *O Abolicionista* (The Abolitionist) – was inspired by the paper of Abílio Borges and the Madrid abolitionists, *El Abolicionista Español*. It carried over the cosmopolitanism of the previous generation's elite abolitionism, with a portrait of Lincoln on the wall, and adapted its name from the British and Foreign Antislavery Society (BFASS), which was delighted with the initiative. The SBCE manifesto was published in English and French translations,[18] steeped in the rhetoric of change – compassion, rights, progress – and blasting slavery as a nefarious colonial legacy.

On the articles of association there were fifteen members, but, in practice, only Rebouças, the treasurer, and Nabuco, the president and secretary, were hands-on. They soon received reinforcements in the form of two MP journalists, the Liberal Joaquim Serra, and the Conservative

---

[17] ACD, Nov. 15, 1880.
[18] Corwin (1968). *Rio News* and *Le Messager du Brésil* published the manifesto. Nabuco mentions a Spanish version (letter from Joaquim Nabuco to the British Museum, Jul. 11, 1882, CIJN), but I was unable to find it.

156                    *The Last Abolition*

Gusmão Lobo, who started writing for *A Reforma* and *Gazeta da Tarde*, respectively. With Lobo, the SBCE, which already had Liberals and Republicans, became truly cross-partisan. The quartet set up offices for *O Abolicionista: Órgão da Sociedade Brasileira contra a Escravidão* (The Abolitionist: Organ of The Brazilian Antislavery Society), which, between November 1880 and December the following year, pursued three master themes: the history of emancipation in Parliament, subsuming all the politicians sympathetic to the cause under one single tradition; examples, citations, remits, and transcriptions of the foreign antislavery repertoire; and news of newly-founded abolitionist associations and their activities nationwide. Nabuco had a proselytizing plan: publish abolitionist works; translations, like that of *Uncle Tom's Cabin*; biographies of foreign abolitionist leaders; poetry, as in the case of Castro Alves; and a history of the slave trade.[19]

In addition to serving as a bridge between parties, the SBCE also mediated between aristocratic politics and the public space, lending continuity to Borges-style activism, hence the use of that quintessential manifestation of the aristocratic world – the banquet. Unlike the concert-conferences, these were all-male affairs at swanky restaurants, by invitation only, and full of solemnity and high-society etiquette. The concert-conferences stoked public opinion, while the banquets cemented the support of aristocratic networks and consolidated international allies. A case in point was Nabuco's wooing of the US diplomat in Petrópolis, whose glowing praise was cited at the opening of this chapter.[20]

The diplomat was Henry Hilliard, a confederate during the American Civil War and, later an abolitionist convert. Nabuco wanted to promote him among Brazilian slavocrats as an example of a change of heart. In October 1880, by prior arrangement, he published an open letter to Hilliard asking his views on the effects the immediate substitution of slave labor for free labor had had in the southern United States. In his reply,

---

[19] Letter from Joaquim Nabuco to Domingos Jaguaribe, Nov. 16, 1882, CAI. Lobo published abolitionist articles in GT in November 1880. The Republican Saldanha Marinho, a supporter of Nabuco's bill in Parliament, became a president of honor of the SBCE, and the Liberals Marcolino Moura and Adolfo de Barros (recently ousted from the presidency of Pernambuco), both vice-presidents. Rebouças brought Beaurepaire Rohan and Muniz Barreto over from the ACE as honorary presidents. Nicolau Moreira assumed the post of honorary secretary; Senator Jaguaribe, that of honorary partner; and Rebouças' journalist friends José Carlos de Carvalho and José Américo dos Santos, that of secretaries (OA, Nov. 1, 1880).
[20] Hilliard (1892, p. 381).

*Expansion* 157

Hilliard lamented the Civil War, praised Lincoln for his leadership and for the economic prosperity that had followed the war, and recommended peaceful abolition in Brazil. Hilliard's receptiveness encouraged Nabuco to try his hand at the boomerang method Borges had employed, rallying abroad the support he lacked at home. So he and Rebouças organized a banquet at the Hotel dos Estrangeiros (The Foreigners' Hotel) at which Hilliard would be made an honorary member of the SBCE and garner as much attention as possible for his reply in the local press. The event drew journalists, politicians, and thirty-two abolitionists, including the pioneer Borges himself. However, Nabuco took the Borges model a step further by launching himself as an articulator between the social mobilization of the ACE and the abolitionist caucus.[21]

The cosmopolitan abolitionist repertoire was evident from the toasts to the menu – *mayonnaise de homards à la Wilberforce. Jambon d'York à la Garrison*. Nabuco had the speeches translated and distributed to the international press. The local papers gave ample coverage, with special mention of the fury of the Speaker of the Lower House at the intromission of a foreign authority in Brazil's domestic affairs – Hilliard quickly returned home, but Nabuco commemorated the effect of his visit: "No other manifestation ever caused such chagrin in the pro-slavery camp."[22]

The success, however, was relative. Not all of the fifty guests turned up. Some, from the political system, were afraid attending might blemish their careers. Others, from the press, chiefly Patrocínio, hesitated in ratifying Nabuco's leadership. Nabuco, for his part, offered a bridge to the ACE: he was a speaker at the ninth Emancipatory Conference and, in 1881, put together the board of the SBCE to represent all three main activist lines: his own, the parliamentary; the public space – Patrocínio and Vicente de Sousa were given honorary posts – and the judicial, led by Luís Gama. He also attracted some positivist abolitionists, who published a manifesto

---

[21] Hilliard (1892, pp. 391 and 395); SBCE (1880b). Attending the banquet were Vicente de Sousa, Ubaldino do Amaral, Nicolau Moreira, Rebouças and Clapp, from the ACE, and M. E. Campos Porto (The Abolitionist Club of Riachuelo). From the press were Angelo Agostini and Ferreira de Menezes, with ties to Patrocínio, and A. J. Lamoreaux, owner of *Rio News*, a paper with abolitionist sympathies. From the Liberal Party: Jerônimo Sodré Pereira (from the 2nd of July Liberating Society in Bahia), Adolfo de Barros, Marcolino Moura, Antônio Pedro de Alencastro, and Joaquim Serra, and, from the Republican Party, Joaquim Saldanha Marinho. Gusmão Lobo, Rodolfo Dantas, Barros Pimentel, Costa Azevedo (all from Liberal Party), and Ferreira Araújo wrote to say that they would be absent (SBCE, 1880c).

[22] Durham and Pruitt Jr. (2008); Hilliard (1892, pp. 396 ff.); OA, Jan. 1, 1882. Presiding over the House was the anti-abolitionist Moreira de Barros.

158 *The Last Abolition*

against the government bill for "trafficking" a Chinese workforce in *O Abolicionista*.[23] With this, Nabuco took a decisive step towards a truly *national* abolitionist coalition.

It was an alliance of very different factions in which each maintained its autonomy so as to avoid conflicts between Liberals and Republicans inside the abolitionist movement. Rebouças was behind the architecture, headquartering the SBCE on Rua do Ouvidor, near Uruguaiana,[24] home to Patrocínio's GT, near, but not too near.

### THE BOOMERANG METHOD

The Hilliard banquet was a first step towards wider employment of the boomerang method: "external pressure against internal resistance."[25] Toward the end of 1880, Nabuco went on a quest for the moral authority of European reformers. In Portugal, he made a splash in the Lower House of Parliament, where, in his honor, a bill was passed banning corporal punishment in the army. The local press published a lot about Nabuco and his cause, and Rebouças made sure to reproduce their articles in the Brazilian newspapers.

The Portuguese abolitionist movement was concluded many years previously. In the Spanish Empire, in its final throes, the antislavery movement had ended in Puerto Rico, but was still operative in Cuba. In Madrid, Nabuco visited his Spanish counterpart, Rafael María de Labra y Cadrana, president of the Spanish Abolitionist Society and editor-in-chief

---

[23] The SBCE board was as follows: President: Nabuco; Vice-president: Adolfo de Barros; Editor-in-Chief of *O Abolicionista*: Joaquim Serra; Secretary: José Américo dos Santos; Honorary Secretary: Nicolau Moreira. Rebouças continued as Treasurer. Clapp, who, in 1882, would form the Niterói Freedmen's Club, joined the board, as did Luís Gama, as an honorary member and columnist with *O Abolicionista*, and his disciple Ubaldino do Amaral, as a lawyer (OA, Apr. 1, May 1, Jul. 1, and Aug. 1, 1881; RI, n. 301, 1882). The positivists were represented by Teixeira Mendes, from Rio, and Aníbal Falcão, from Pernambuco.

[24] DNAAR, Jan. 12, 1881.

[25] SBCE, 1889a; OA, Mar. 1, 1881. In the nineteenth century, there was a transnational antislavery network of abolitionists, linking activists from Great Britain and the United States (Keck and Sikkink, 1998, p. 41), and Africa (Stamatov, 2010), and circulating ideas and strategies. Abílio Borges had explored it, but it was Nabuco who became the first truly Brazilian "cosmopolitan activist" (Tarrow, 2005) or "activist without borders" (Keck and Sikkink, 1998), the mediator between the local movement and the trans-national network and a propagandist. The way the Brazilian situation resonated abroad and the support the abolitionists garnered prevented the supporters of the circumstantial pro-slavery rhetoric from building defences. On Nabuco's transnational activity, see Alonso (2010).

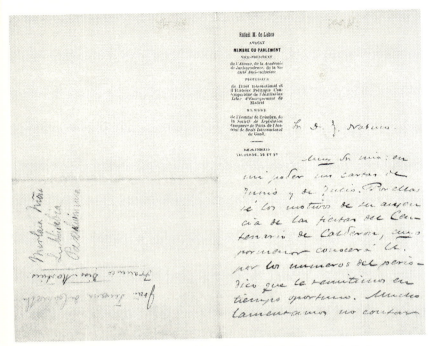

FIGURE 5.2 Letter from the Spanish abolitionist Rafael María de Labra y Cadrana to Joaquim Nabuco, on October 8, 1881.
Archive of the Fundação Joaquim Nabuco (Joaquim Nabuco Foundation), Ministério de Educação (Ministry of Education).

of *El Abolicionista Español*, who had been battling against slavery since 1872 and was an expert in straddling the line between Parliament and the public space, just as Nabuco was doing now.

*El Abolicionista Español* received him in the salon of the Academia Madrileña de Legislación y Jurisprudencia, and published his address there, which appraised Brazil's place in the world history of abolition: "The emancipation cause does not belong to any one people, but to all peoples." He was wined and dined at the Lhardy Restaurant, made an honorary member of the Spanish Abolitionist Society, and was asked to convey the very best Spanish wishes to the Brazilian movement. Nabuco had sealed an antislavery alliance with Spain.[26]

---

[26] Letters from Rafael de Labra to Joaquim Nabuco, Jan. 18, 22, 24, and Mar. 10, 1881, CIJN. In his speech, the Cuban MP Bernardo Portuondo Barceló mentioned the presence of "Hispano-Americans" (OA, May 1, 1881).

160     *The Last Abolition*

In Madrid, he earned his passport to an international network. Labra recommended him to the Cuban, Philippine, Puerto-Rican, and French abolitionists, as well as to the British and Foreign Antislavery Society, and invited him to pro-abolition events in Cuba and to an international antislavery conference. Nabuco could not attend, since he already left Spain, but followed up on all of these contacts.[27]

This warm reception fitted well with Labra's expansionist plans. Eager to make connections in all the main slavocratic capitals in America, he asked Nabuco to give him the names of people in Brazil who could represent the Spanish association there. Nabuco sent him five potential contacts, all from the SBCE. This way he could keep this Spanish connection under his control. He recommended Rebouças, but excluded Patrocínio. Rebouças saw in this a potential souring of relations between leaders who were only beginning to consolidate, one in the public space and the other in Parliament. So he smoothed things over. He wrote to Nabuco saying that the *Gazeta da Tarde*, larger and more powerful than *O Abolicionista*, ought to be the movement's national mouthpiece, becoming "the vehicle of this society [SBCE], and thus compensating Patrocínio for his exclusion from the Committee." The price was killing the SBCE's own journal. Nabuco reluctantly agreed. He could only effectively mediate between the international and Brazilian abolitionists if the latter were a genuine network rather than a cluster of separate factions. He informed Labra that the *Gazeta da Tarde* would now be the SBCE's official vehicle.[28]

The next step was France, where the process was confined to the political institutions and spearheaded by moderate leaders, many of whom were already deceased. However, Nabuco believed that those who remained would have unparalleled symbolic value in Brazil, where the culture and politics owed a huge debt to all things French. He trained his sights on Victor Schoelcher, an acquaintance of his, and now president

---

[27] Letters from Rafael de Labra to Joaquim Nabuco, Jan. 24, Feb. 25, Mar. 10, 1881, CIJN. Labra gave Nabuco letters of introduction for Antonio Regidor y Jurado, the Philippine rebel "representing our society in England," and for the doctor Ramon Emérito Betances, "an important abolitionist from Puerto Rico," then living in Paris. Nabuco lost Jurado's address, but sent him the letter via Charles Allen, in 1881.

[28] Letters from Rafael de Labra to Joaquim Nabuco, Oct. 8, 1881, CIJN. Nabuco recommended Rebouças, Nicolau Moreira, Joaquim Serra, Marcolino Moura, and Alencastro Jr. (letter from Rafael de Labra to Joaquim Nabuco, Mar. 2, 1882, CIJN). Letter from André Rebouças to Joaquim Nabuco, Apr. 16, 1882, CIJN; letter from Joaquim Nabuco to Rafael de Labra, Apr. 16, 1882, CIJN.

*Expansion* 161

of the Commission for the Abolition of Slavery in the French Colonies, where emancipation arrived in 1848. Schoelcher was a shadow of his former self, but a seasoned senator and still at war with West African slavery. The effect of the visit would be felt at the 1882 commemorations of the end of slavery in the colonies, held in Paris, at which Schoelcher embarrassed D. Pedro and lauded the Brazilian abolitionists:

> The Emperor of Brazil, who claims to be a liberal man, must certainly feel the cruel humiliation of being the only sovereign in the civilized world who reigns over slaves. Luckily, there is the abolition society founded in Rio de Janeiro, and its president Mr. Nabuco, recently here in Paris on a visit, but who unfortunately could not be here with us today. He tells me that the movement is full of steam and belief and very much decided not to rest until it has slain this monster. With them lies our hope.[29]

Schoelcher claimed that the Spanish and Brazilian campaigns were the heirs to the French and declared abolition to be a global movement: "War on slavery! Freedom! Freedom to slaves all around the world!" The organizer of this declaration exhorted fraternity among abolitionists everywhere.[30]

Finally, Nabuco turned to Great Britain. He loved the local aristocratic lifestyle and, to boot, his surrogate father the Baron of Penedo was there, ensconced among the high society and the upper-social strata of political power. His relationship with the Baron made it easy for him to approach the already legendary British and Foreign Antislavery Society. The organization's public demonstrations and representatives in Parliament had been decisive in the suppression of slavery in the British colonies at the start of the century. Like Schoelcher, the BFASS was working against colonial slavery in Africa and Asia and pressuring pro-slavery countries in the Americas. Nabuco had maintained correspondence with the BFASS secretary, who introduced him to the whole group at a banquet held in his honor at the Charing Cross Hotel in London, with 150 guests, including fifteen members of Parliament and a Filipino abolitionist, a friend of Labra's. In his speech, Nabuco celebrated abolitionism as an international movement: "... we need foreign support to compensate for our nation's lack of bedrock ... In Brazil today, we are fighting what SHARPE and

---

[29] Schoelcher (1882, p. 273). On the meeting between the two men, see the letter from Victor Schoelcher to Joaquim Nabuco, 1874, CIJN. On French Abolitionism, see Jennings (2006).

[30] Schoelcher (1882, pp. 274, 276); letter from G. Gerville-Réache to Joaquim Nabuco, May 6, 1881, CIJN.

CLARKSON, WILBERFORCE and BUXTON fought in England." The grandson of one of these English abolitionists responded to this mention of the Anglo-American icons by comparing Nabuco to William Garrison, one of the leaders of the campaign in the United States. The BFASS held a special session to hear Nabuco's report on Brazil and appointed him a corresponding member. Once again, he included his SBCE companions. Everything was covered with British sobriety in the *Antislavery Reporter*, the association's journal, and gushingly by Rebouças in O *Abolicionista*.[31]

The Nabuco mission – as Rebouças called it – yielded returns in double. The Brazilian movement emerged from it as part of a transnational abolitionist network spanning France, Great Britain, Spain, Cuba, Puerto Rico, and the Philippines. That, plus their connections in Portugal and the United States, meant Nabuco had curried sympathies in eight different nations and truly internationalized the Brazilian antislavery struggle. The practical effects on the Brazilian authorities were more modest than those inflicted in 1866, when Abílio Borges pioneered the boomerang method, but they did embarrass the national parties and reinforce the image of Brazilian slavery as an aberration among civilized nations.

Another result of the trip was the consolidation of Nabuco's leadership. According to *The Times*, despite his youth, Nabuco had cemented a reputation at home and abroad as a "parliamentary leader of the Brazilian Antislavery Party."[32]

The Brazilian abolitionists, miles away from configuring a political party as such, were buoyed by the attention, and Nabuco was hailed upon his arrival home. Rebouças had a banquet thrown for him at the Hotel dos Estrangeiros, and an ACE concert-conference at São Pedro Theater, where Vicente de Sousa welcomed him to the sound of the march "Saudação abolicionista" (The Abolitionist Salute).[33] The foreign alliances solidified the sputtering coalition between Parliament and public space abolitionists. Much to Rebouças' liking, a triangulation was in course. Differences remained, but they were now subsumed under a common identity: they were all Brazilians before the foreigners, and abolitionists before the pro-slavery countermovement. They became a

---

[31] The Secretary of the BFASS was Charles H. Allen. The conference was held on March 23, 1881 (OA, May 1, Jun. 1, 1881). Nabuco suggested Rebouças and Gusmão Lobo as BFASS members (letter from Charles H. Allen to Joaquim Nabuco, Feb. 14, 1881, Bethell and Carvalho, 2008).
[32] *The Times*, Feb. 24, 1881.
[33] DNAAR, Nov. 5, 1881; DJN, Feb. 6 and May 21, 1881.

## Expansion

single movement. Nabuco had the capacity to think and believe big, hold those around him in thrall to those ideas and, ultimately, bring those ideas to bear.

### TOWARD A NATIONAL MOVEMENT

In 1878, Patrocínio traveled to the North part of the country in charge of covering the drought in Ceará for a newspaper. He and a friend from the State toured the beleaguered region, felt its misery, and met those attempting to alleviate it. Patrocínio was impressed by a little charity that was aiding the people there, and he made contact. The man leading the campaign was João Cordeiro, president of the Fortaleza Trade Association and a businessman who seemed to run on the same batteries as Rebouças, traveling the whole of northern Brazil and half of Europe, setting up factories and plants to produce oils and soaps and seeded cotton. He also shared many of Patrocínio's interests – he was a guitar-playing poet and artist and a rabble-rousing Republican who had been proclaiming the new regime in the little town of Mossoró two decades ahead of time. And he was just as fervent an abolitionist: "I say what I think without any mind for those who may not agree."[34]

Cordeiro teamed up with José Correia do Amaral, his partner in a hardware store, and together, on the anniversary of the Free Womb Law in 1879, they created the embryo of the group called the Perseverance and the Future Emancipation Association, with twenty men and sixteen women. The idea behind the organization was to host Borges-style manumission ceremonies. Cordeiro was president and Amaral deputy president, and, toward the end of 1880, they converted the outfit into the Liberating Society of Ceará (SCL), the first of its kind outside of Court to garner nationwide visibility.

The SCL was big: 227 members (including women), mostly liberal professionals and, above all, small merchants, mostly Portuguese by birth or descent. One of the members, Frederico Borges, though no relation to Abílio Borges, had been his pupil at the Ginásio Baiano. Starting in April 1881, the SCL organized "freedom parties" similar to the concert-conferences in Court, with a reading of Castro Alves' "Carta às Senhoras" (Letter to the Ladies), the presentation of manumission papers,

---

[34] Patrocínio, GN, Jun. 16, 1878, in Magalhães Jr. (1969, p. 66); Nobre (1943, pp. 48–9); Cordeiro, in Nobre (1943, pp. 69, 70, 120, 121). The friend who put Patrocínio in touch with the group from Ceará was Francisco de Paula Nei.

164                    *The Last Abolition*

recitals of poetry, a brass band, and speeches loaded with the rhetoric of compassion, rights, and progress – "freedom, the beneficent sun of all societies and all nations, shines forth from those horizons on which progress and civilization take their place." As in Court, slaves were gaining space. At one SCL party, a freed slave went down on bended knee in thanks for his manumission papers, but Cordeiro, like Vicente de Sousa, raised the man to his feet and replaced the gesture of subservience with an "embrace of fraternity."[35]

Like the ACE, which drew politicians to its conferences, the SCL lured in all the local institutions and authorities. One of its secretaries was a public prosecutor from Fortaleza. The connection with the local elite was evident in the association's inaugural event, held at the Provincial House and attended by the president of the province, who exhorted the society to follow the English example of buying letters of manumission.[36]

In addition to the concert-conferences, the SCL formed a panel of lawyers to employ Gama-style judicial activism. However, it did not take the SCL long to reveal itself as by far the most drastic of the abolitionist associations. At its first assembly, held on January 30, 1881, the partners sat at a table draped in a black cloth with oil lamps at either end. According to one of the group, João Cordeiro, seated at the head of the table, jumped to his feet, drew a dagger, and stabbed it into the tabletop before solemnly exclaiming: "Friends, I demand of each of you your oath, upon this blade, that you will kill or die, if need be, for the cause of abolition." That said, of the twenty present, nine swore allegiance and the articles of association were penned in accordance with their knightly ideal: "Article 1: One for all and all for one. § – The society shall free slaves by whatever means within its reach."[37] This included illicit means, referred to in code.

Like the Rio groups, they created a proselytizing paper, *Libertador* (Liberator), borrowing the watchword from the French Revolution. The group's first rally borrowed from the political repertoire of the European workers. Members of the SCL incited – and, just to be sure, paid – dockers from the port of Fortaleza to go on strike, preventing the departure, on January 27, 1881, of a ship of slaves to be sold outside the

---

[35] Studart (1980); *Libertador*, Apr. 24, 1881; Antônio Martins (1879, in Girão, 1988, pp. 96, 115).

[36] Girão (1988, p. 95); Studart (1980); Girão (1988, p. 86); Antônio Martins (1879, in Girão, 1988, p. 95).

[37] Bezerra, in Nobre (1943, pp. 62–3); Bezerra, in Girão (1988, pp. 97, 100).

## Expansion

province. They marched again on the thirtieth and thirty-first of the same month. The *Libertador* estimated the turnout as 1,000 demonstrators, but this is likely to be an exaggeration. The "liberators" even launched a late-night raid in which they released from confinement nine slaves awaiting shipment and set fire to the depot where they were being held.[38]

This confrontational strategy was praised in Court. Rebouças organized a concert-conference in the SCL's honor at Teatro Pedro II on March 6. Apprised of the event's tone and topic, the São Luís theater, the ACE's usual venue, refused to host it, and proved reluctant to host later events too. For the thirty-sixth concert-conference, the group managed to secure the Ginásio Theater at the last minute, and the finishing touches were still being made as the audience filed through the doors. The SCL returned the favor with an ACE-style concert-conference in Fortaleza, on March 25, complete with a march, poems, handkerchief-waving, flowers, fireworks and the Liberator's Anthem. Between the Decembers of 1880 and 1881, the SCL notched up 379 manumissions in concert-conference emancipations, with 109 being delivered on the anniversary of the Free Womb Law alone.[39]

The SCL managed to combine the orderly and disorderly because they had friends in high places. Frederico Borges' brother was an army doctor linked to the commander of the fifteenth Battalion, who publicly toasted the SCL board and promised his troops would not shoot the "freedom-givers." Quite the opposite, they formed the Military Abolitionist Club in Fortaleza. On the downside, the SCL lost the leader of the port workers in the very first strike, but they managed to replace him to their advantage with Francisco José do Nascimento, known also as Chico da Matilde, a tugboat worker described as dusky, strong, lively, and hard-working: he persuaded his colleagues to strike again, in August 1881. With allies in the army and among the lower social strata, the SCL drew some 6,000 protestors to the docks, chanting "No more slaves will ship from the port of Ceará."[40]

The provincial president, who had kept a low profile thus far, saw himself forced to dispatch the chief of police to the port. In the ensuing mêlée, the liberators made away with a pair of slaves. When the army was

---

[38] Girão (1988, pp. 106, 107).
[39] DNAAR, Apr. 17, 1881; GT, Feb. 3, 1883; *Libertador*, Dec. 8, 1881.
[40] Colonel Lima e Silva, in Girão (1988, p. 124). Frederico's brother, Pedro Borges, had been a student under Abílio Borges (cf. Studart, 1980). On Francisco do Nascimento and the closure of the port, see Girão (1988, pp. 108 ff.).

166 *The Last Abolition*

called in to restore order, they soon showed whose side they were on, arriving at four in the afternoon to quash a skirmish that had taken place early that morning. But the police went ahead and launched an investigation. Many members of the SCL were civil servants and they were punished with transfers or dismissal. Chico da Matilde was dismissed from his post.[41]

The repression put the brakes on conflict-based abolitionism and encouraged underground actions. Various small farms belonging to abolitionists or sympathizers, such as Chácara Benfica, Porangabuçu, São Francisco, and Ipioca, were transformed into safe houses. Communication was by code: *baldear* (bail) meant to hide slaves from the capital in the countryside and vice-versa, while *libambo* (neck shackles) meant to steal them. The slave owners sued the SCL, which was defended by SCL lawyers, while other members disrupted proceedings at court by protesting from the gallery and hounding the plaintiff into dropping the suit.[42]

Though far removed from his normal aristocratic habitat, Nabuco, like Rebouças and Patrocínio, forged a connection with the SCL through José Correia do Amaral, who wrote to him from the heat of the fray: "The abolitionists of Ceará take great heart every time your lordship is mentioned, always with enthusiasm for the cause we share and of which your lordship is patron." He also asked Nabuco to publish the SCL manifesto in Court, and had his wish doubly fulfilled as copies ran in both O *Abolicionista* and *Gazeta da Tarde*, with write-ups on the movement in Ceará.[43] Nabuco also sent a letter of encouragement to the SCL members who had lost their jobs, though he considered it prudent to do so in code:

When I heard about the dismissal of Dr. Frederico Borges, I sent him a telegram congratulating him on his stance ... I know that the word established for our communications is "trenches." ... The raftsmen's movement, the cooperation of all social classes that is the glory of the Ceará Liberators, all of this has gone into history. Imagine the gusto with which we read, some days back, a telegraph ... informing us of the emancipation headway achieved in Ceará .... You, gentlemen, are at the vanguard .... Do not be disheartened by the fact that our environment

---

[41] Almino Affonso lost his job as a tax inspector, Frederico Borges was fired as public prosecutor, and Pedro Borges was transferred.

[42] Sued were Antônio Bezerra, Isaac Amaral, and Chico Matilde, defended against the accusations by Alminio Affonso and Pedro Borges (Girão, 1988, pp. 129–30).

[43] Letter from José Correia do Amaral to Joaquim Nabuco, Aug. 30, 1881, CIJN. Letter from Joaquim Nabuco to José Correia do Amaral, Sept. 29, 1882, CIJN.

## Expansion 167

here in Court prevents us from following your example. The imperial capital is, and shall remain for God knows how long, a vile slave market ...[44]

A technical change facilitated this solidarity between abolitionists in Court and in Ceará. Though the telegraph had been installed during the Rio Branco government, it was slow in expanding. When it arrived in Ceará in 1881, the SCL sent a telegram saluting the *Gazeta da Tarde*. Patrocínio promptly replied, and the contact remained constant from that point on. The telegraph also served as a conduit to the SCL for news of foreign abolitionists. Kept abreast of events, they celebrated the advances toward abolition in Cuba with a literary festival held on the Fortaleza Public Promenade and covered Nabuco's every move during his European tour.[45]

In 1881, there were strong ties between Brazilian and foreign abolitionists, the Court and Ceará, and between these two flashpoints and other provinces in the North. For example, on August 9, 1881, the *Libertador* announced the preparatory meeting for the creation of an abolitionist association in Manaus, Amazonas. Abolitionism was expanding.[46]

### THE ABOLITIONIST CANDIDATE

His European tour and relationships with militant abolitionists soured the Liberal Party's openness for Nabuco. He just managed to arrange his candidacy for the 1881 elections, counting on almost no support. Abolitionist-leaning Liberals had been quiet in Parliament, and Rebouças was trying in vain to extract a statement from the Justice Minister, Manuel de Sousa Dantas, a member of the 7th of September Liberating Society, regarding a report he had sent him denouncing indigenous enslavement in Amazonas.[47]

Nabuco ran for the Lower House as a candidate for the First Constituency of Rio de Janeiro thanks to the Liberal senator Silveira da

---

[44] Letter from Joaquim Nabuco to José Correia do Amaral, Sept. 29, 1882, CIJN. The Nabuco/Amaral connection (Amaral would send further news on Aug. 31, Sept. 9 and 10, 1881, CIJN) shows that, contrary to what the bibliography on Brazilian abolitionism tends to claim, there was no real separation between the "moderates" active in parliament and the "radicals" engaging in illicit protest, but one broader nationwide activist network.

[45] *Libertador*, Mar. 3 and 17, 1881.

[46] The *Libertador* (Feb. 23, Aug. 8, 1881) republished articles from the *Gazeta da Tarde* and publicized the activities of Rio-based groups, such as the Abolitionist Club of Riachuelo's bulletin.

[47] He was accompanied by Joaquim Serra (DNAAR, Mar. 28 and Apr. 14, 1881).

Mota, an emancipation defender during the free womb debates and one of the concert-conference goers. His candidacy was endorsed by the public space abolitionists, but opposed by the government. The Conservatives exploited his keenness on enlisting foreign help as unpatriotic. Nabuco defended himself against the charge: "... Name one abolitionist, whether in the United States, France, Spain, England or Brazil, who never appealed for the intervention of some foreign government?" His platform was heavy on the abolitionist rhetoric, particularly the trope of abolition as a second Independence.[48] He touted the British example, eschewed the dangers of the American, and drove home the point he had pressed during his trip to Europe, that slavery was a nefarious colonial legacy that the nation urgently needed to shed.

The election was held under a direct-vote regimen, passed in 1881, that disenfranchised all illiterate people and introduced strict proof of income as a requirement to register to vote. These requirements suppressed the poorest voters – whom the law-makers considered corruptible – and drastically reduced the electoral college. For the Liberals, who defended the change, it meant switching from voter patronage to voter persuasion. Especially in the imperial capital, some abolitionists agreed with this view and felt confident they could muster votes among the liberal professionals, urban traders, and all other literate individuals with no direct ties to the slave-based economy. Rebouças, with an eye on the concert-conference goer, devoted the whole thirteenth issue of O Abolicionista to Nabuco's candidacy. But Nabuco himself was not at all happy about door-to-door canvassing: "... I will not run an electoral campaign that involves importuning the voter even more than it does the candidate."[49]

The events in Ceará in August – when abolitionists forced slaves out of captivity – were still fresh in the national press when the elections arrived in October. To assuage political concerns, Nabuco offered his guarantee that the abolitionists would respect the limits of the law, restricting their remit to legitimate concert-conferences and civil lawsuits. But that kind of activism needed tentacles in Parliament: "A group of Abolitionists in the Lower House would not resolve the issue, but it would prevent the majority from taking it off the agenda altogether. It is in Parliament that

---

[48] OA, Oct. 28, 1881. Another Liberal leader in Court, Francisco Otaviano, supported Nabuco (DNAAR, Oct. 28, 1881).

[49] The Saraiva Law has been interpreted as both a means of limiting the electorate (Carvalho, 2003; Graham, 1997) and of expanding it (Buescu, 1981). Letter from Sancho de Barros Pimentel to Joaquim Nabuco, Oct. 4, 1880, DJN, Jul. 9, 1880.

# Expansion 169

the slavery debate must be decided, not on the streets." He sent his propaganda to members of the SCL and ACE, reminding them that recourse to institutional channels was "a concession to the unignorable fact that any emancipation law that may arise will have to be passed through a Parliament mostly composed of slave owners."[50]

His commitment to legality was an attempt to enlist support for his candidacy inside the political system. However, his earlier attacks against two former MPS over the abolition issue had left him vulnerable. And there was fresh competition in Court. In a letter to the SCL, he wrote: "My candidacy is fraught with difficulties, and it is very possible that I will not make it into Parliament. It matters not. We have already succeeded in transforming emancipation, a subject to which no one was giving a single thought, back into a factor of weight in our politics – and each concession will leverage others." His imperiled candidacy was the flagship of the small abolitionist electoral ticket, which was largely a re-fielding of the bloc that had carried his 1880 bill.[51] They suffered a stunning defeat at the polls.

The electoral results belied the idealism of Liberals like Rui Barbosa, who had seen the electoral reform as putting an end to cronyism. Instead, Conservative realism won the day, earning them a considerable minority: 38.5 percent of the seats. João Alfredo Correira de Oliveira, who had been Rio Branco's minister, returned as leader of the moderate Conservatives, while Paulino Soares de Sousa, sleeves rolled up and ready to go at the abolitionist riffraff, was back at the helm of the Hardliners. As Nabuco put it, "the fiercest defenders of slavery have prevailed at the ballot." So, between then and 1884, when the government ran its course, there were two parties in Parliament. If the direct election regimen delivered electoral truth, as its defenders claimed, that truth ended up being pro-slavery.[52]

---

[50] Nabuco, OA, Oct. 28, 1880; Aug. 1, 1881.

[51] Letter from Joaquim Nabuco to José Correia do Amaral, Sept. 29, 1881, CIJN; OA, Dec. 1, 1881; letter from Joaquim Serra to Joaquim Nabuco, Feb. 3, 1882, CIJN; letter from Hilário de Gouveia to Joaquim Nabuco, Apr. 30, 1882, CIJN.

[52] Nabuco, OA, Dec. 1, 1881. Of the original abolitionist bloc, two members (Beltrão and Costa Azevedo) did not run for election. Bezerra de Menezes was elected in Court, and José Mariano Carneiro da Cunha for Pernambuco. Joaquim Serra, Correia Rebelo, Artur Silveira da Mota, Saldanha Marinho and Jerônimo Sodré failed to get elected; Marcolino Moura, Sancho de Barros Pimentel, and Martins Filho were elected, but not ratified. All "out of hatred for abolitionism" (letter from Joaquim Serra to Joaquim Nabuco, Feb. 3, 1882, CIJN). Contrary to the oft-propagated thesis that politics during the Second Reign displayed little in the way of partisan distinction, Summerhill (2012, p. 18) demonstrates that intra-partisan cohesion was high in the parliament convened in 1881.

170 *The Last Abolition*

The ground had collapsed under Nabuco's feet, and further misery was heaped upon him on the home front. His engagement to Eufrásia Teixeira Leite had never been smooth, but it became even rockier as he came to the fore as an abolitionist ringleader in Parliament. Eufrásia was a modern woman who managed her own finances and businesses on the Stock Exchange, and if the marriage had gone ahead Nabuco would have ensured the capital he needed to set up an abolitionist newspaper and further his campaign. This may have been precisely the reason why his fiancée's family, coffee growers from Vassouras with ties to Paulino's family and friends, objected to the union. Nabuco saw out the year of 1881 with no mandate, no fiancée, and no job – he refused to accept a public post so as not to appear to have sold out to a pro-slavery government.

The Baron of Penedo, head of the Brazilian legation in London, arranged a job for Nabuco as foreign correspondent for the *Jornal do Commercio* in Great Britain. As he prepared to leave, he explained his decision in an open letter to the abolitionists, saying: "I feel I cannot serve the cause of emancipation in any other way than by rejecting out of hand everything that slavery currently offers to those who refuse to abandon it: political positions, social esteem, public respect."[53] In Great Britain, he resorted to the boomerang method, strengthening relations with foreign abolitionists. His other function, as articulator between Parliament and public space activism, was left vacant, and this earned him sustained accusations of having abandoned the cause.

The tide turned against abolition once and for all when Saraiva left the government. The Emperor announced Martinho Campos, a Liberal who was every bit as conservative as his friend Paulino, as his replacement.[54]

### NEW ASSOCIATIVISM

Every story has its antagonists, and this one has the elegant Conservative villains Cotegipe and Paulino, and others not so refined, such as the Liberal Martinho Álvares da Silva Campos. Martinho das Cebolas (Onion Marty), so named after the crop he grew, wore his heart on his sleeve when it came to circumstantial pro-slavery rhetorics: "... he is genuinely of the opinion that slavery is proof of Christian charity; that the master does a great service to his slaves." It was none other than Patrocínio who said that[55], and he was not exaggerating: Martinho was a

[53] OA, Dec. 1, 1881.   [54] Ibid.   [55] GT, Dec. 27, 1886; GN, Feb. 21, 1881.

## Expansion

self-confessed "slavocrat through and through." Born at the beginning of the century, he gave the sentimentalisms of its denouement a very wide berth. Living in Minas Gerais and Vassouras, he saw slavery as the bedrock of Imperial prosperity and defended it tooth and nail during the free womb debate, as chairman of the Plantation Clubs.

He had a venomous tongue. Angelo Agostini, whose abolitionism was waged in ink, drew his face on a snake's body in *Revista Illustrada*. But Martinho was used to being the butt of opposition ire, and was not above poking fun at himself either: he referred to his ministerial cabinet as "my college," due to the number of young Liberals he employed. Two of these were former students of Abílio Borges and the political progeny of Senator Manuel de Sousa Dantas: his godson, Rui Barbosa, and his son Rodolfo, a friend of Nabuco's. They were abolitionists, but they were also career-minded and wise to imperial ways. Rodolfo accepted the position of Minister of Internal Affairs with an untroubled conscience, with Rui as his aide and defender at the Lower House. "Slavery's firebrand",[56] as Patrocínio called him, Martinho Campos sang from Paulino's hymn book and closed all political chances of abolitionist influence on the ministry or in Parliament.

His rude pro-slavery rhetoric, Nabuco would observe, forced many a fence-sitting politician to take sides: "... his permanence as minister has had one positive effect, that of obliging all Liberals who have expressed opposition leanings to make a profession of their abolitionist faith."[57] While Nabuco was away in London, the movement produced other voices within the political system. During the Legislature of 1881 to 1884, fourteen MPs expressed their sympathies for the cause, though not necessarily at the same time or even all the time. Three of these were Conservatives from outside Paulino's sphere of influence. On the Liberal side, one would stand out as an earnest abolitionist, José Mariano Carneiro da Cunha, an emerging leader from Pernambuco.[58] None of

---

[56] ACD, Mar. 6, 1882; GT, Feb. 23, 1883.

[57] Letter from Hilário Gouveia to Joaquim Nabuco, Apr. 30, 1882, CIJN. Dissidence was accumulating in Parliament: "... in opposition are Martins Francisco and his son, Carlos Affonso, Prado Pimentel, Ignácio Martins, and five MPs from Rio Grande do Sul. ..." (letter from Joaquim Serra to Joaquim Nabuco, May 13, 1882, CIJN).

[58] The abolitionist caucus was able to count on the following MPs: the Conservatives Antônio Pinto de Mendonça (Ceará), Severino Ribeiro Carneiro Monteiro (Rio Grande do Sul), and Rebouças' friend Alfredo Escragnolle Taunay (Santa Catarina); the Liberals Adolfo Bezerra de Menezes (Rio de Janeiro), Adriano Xavier de Oliveira Pimentel (Amazonas), Afonso Celso de Assis Figueiredo Jr. (Minas Gerais), Aristides César Spinola Zama (Bahia, one of the founders of the 2nd of July Liberating Society, in 1852), Franklin Américo de Menezes

172    *The Last Abolition*

them, however, could rival Nabuco for rhetorical prowess. An intractable government and only a few abolitionists in the political institutions made 1883 a disappointing year for abolition at Parliament.

Unlike their allies in government, the public space abolitionists continued to agitate for their cause under the steadfast leadership of Rebouças and Patrocínio and following the triangular strategy of visibility in the press, associativism, and public demonstrations. In order to grow, the movement needed organizational power – and that was precisely what the ACE and SBCE provided. However, Nabuco's self-imposed exile had left his association drained and anemic. In vain, he urged its members, Rebouças especially, to revive it. In his absence, the mantle of leadership had fallen to the Liberal Joaquim Serra, a journalist who had cut his teeth on a much larger vehicle, *A Reforma*, and had "become a veritable Proteus" of abolitionism, shape-shifting across columns in *Globo* and the *Gazetinha*.[59]

Rebouças tried to persuade the ACE people to join the SBCE, but what happened was the reverse. Patrocínio's orbit was thickening. Regional groups formed at the Court's colleges crowded his favorite table at the Pascoal coffee shop. Every now and then he stopped by the Positivist Church, which turned out pamphlets and sermons laced with the rhetoric of progress, and he would come away from there with a following of students and lecturers from the military academy and school of engineering eager to write for him in *Gazeta da Tarde*,[60] one of his most powerful weapons. The *Gazeta* was, by now, a medium-sized outlet, which Nabuco had accepted as the SBCE's mouthpiece, to the lasting detriment of *O Abolicionista*.

---

Doria (Piauí), José Leopoldo de Bulhões Jardim (Goiás), José Mariano Carneiro da Cunha (Pernambuco), José Viana Vaz (Maranhão), Rodolfo Epifânio de Sousa Dantas (Bahia), Rui Barbosa (Bahia) and Tomás Pompeu de Sousa Brazil (Ceará). ACD, 1882–1884; GT, Feb. 14, 1883; Pinto (1884, p. 16); Fonseca (1887, p. 244).

[59] Letter from Joaquim Serra to Joaquim Nabuco, May 13, 1882, CIJN; letter from Joaquim Nabuco to Gusmão Lobo, Nov. 12, 1882, CAI; letter from Silveira da Mota to Joaquim Nabuco, Jul. 22, 1882, CIJN. The growth in abolitionist associativism during Liberal rule did not signify alignment. There is clear proximity between Nabuco, Serra, and Patrocínio, in Court, Gama, in São Paulo, Cordeiro and Amaral in Ceará and the Liberal Party. However, there were also members of the Conservative Party involved in the movement and most abolitionists were Republicans. So as not to break apart, the movement tried to present itself as supra-partisan and independent, supporting both the Liberal (1884–1885) and the Conservative (1888) governments, when they fell behind abolitionist measures, as the forthcoming chapters will show.

[60] Magalhães Jr. (1969, p. 91). The positivists engaged with various reform campaigns (Alonso, 1996; Carvalho, 1998; Ribeiro, 2012).

# Expansion 173

Patrocínio himself went on captivating the crowds live on stage while Nabuco's charm took most of three weeks to arrive by steamship. Patrocínio dealt the SBCE its death blow by poaching Serra, whom he had known from the newsroom at *A Reforma*, as editor-in-chief of *Gazeta da Tarde*. Serra came aboard all guns blazing: "At the *Gazeta da Tarde*, as you will have seen, I do my utmost to further our ideas, delving headlong into all its issues, in which I am fortunate enough to have Patrocínio for company."[61] Though nominally alive, the SBCE was de facto defunct. Nabuco tried to hold things together from afar, sending friends to the *Gazeta de Notícias* and preserving his ties with the SCL in Ceará. However, Patrocínio's thrall was strong and, in 1882, transformed the *Gazeta da Tarde* into the abolitionist bunker from which all abolitionist propaganda and government lobbying were planned.

At the GT, Patrocínio and Rebouças wove a nationwide network out of the new regional groups that were cropping up – as in São Paulo, where Luís Gama's mobilization resulted, in 1882, in the creation of the São Paulo Abolitionist Center, the *Ça-Ira* newspaper and the Luís Gama Emancipation Fund, all frequented by law students, such as Raul Pompeia. In the North, abolitionists in Pernambuco, led by the MP José Mariano, were forming ties with Teixeira Mendes, with whom they shared positivist affinities, and with the SCL in Ceará. The SCL, for its part, expanded into Rio Grande do Norte. Rebouças served as the Court-Maranhão link, sending to the North important pamphlets and instructions about the abolitionist movement. Associations were popping up all over the provinces considered second-tier in imperial geopolitics, such as Goiás, the electoral home turf of Silveira da Mota.[62] Connections were growing between the pioneering groups, and neophytes were multiplying. During Liberal Party rule (1878–1885), associativism exploded. Like the concert-conferences, the societies took off in the cultural and political capital of the Empire, home to forty-four of them during the Liberal tenure. But they were sprouting up outside Court too, as mobilization gathered momentum, with the formation of 279 associations, at an

---

[61] Letters from Joaquim Serra to Joaquim Nabuco, Feb. 3 and Apr. 20, 1882, CIJN.
[62] The São Paulo Abolitionist Center was founded on July 23, 1882, with twenty-two members, Luís Gama as honorary chairman and Alcides Lima as chairman (*Correio Paulistano*, Jul. 24, 1882). In Pernambuco, the positivists Aníbal Falcão and Martins Jr. were at the front line of abolitionism. In Maranhão, Rebouças' contact was Temístocles Aranha (DNAAR, Nov. 12, 1880). Goiás, where the Emancipatory Society of Goyana was founded in 1879, was the back yard of the Liberal Leopoldo Bulhões, a member of Nabuco's bloc in Parliament.

174 *The Last Abolition*

average of 34.9 a year, nationwide. The movement had hit the national arteries and was proliferating fast, especially in Pernambuco, Rio de Janeiro, and Ceará.[63]

In both the North and the South, activism followed a political rather than an economic logic. The associativist boom occurred during the Liberal rule for three political reasons: first, the expectation that surrounded the Liberal Party, for which abolition was on the agenda, second, the existence of allies within the political institutions, given the formation of the abolitionist caucus in the House, and, third, the tolerance of the Liberal governments, which took a far more lenient approach to the concert-conferences in the public space. All of this combined favored the growth of abolitionist protest and associations.

The associations were heterogeneous, ranging from micro-organizations with half a dozen members to heavyweights with over 200. They were everywhere from State capitals to rustic hamlets, some of them were long-lived and others ephemeral. In variety and volume, they revealed just how widespread antislavery activism had become in Brazil in the mid-1880s, both in regions with large slave populations – the South – and in those with sparse slave stocks – the North. It was also growing inside and beyond the elites. Added to that were the pro-abolition declarations of societies founded for other ends, such as SAIN, the Bar Association, and press associations. Abolitionism was spreading beyond its political and geographical origins and assuming national contours.

### AN ICON

Always enthusiastic about progress, Rebouças kept Nabuco abreast of the campaign. At the fifty-second concert-conference, Patrocínio was the keynote, as always, and the pro-slavery-besotted government of

---

[63] The associations that arose in the North fitted nicely with Conrad's regional economic argument (1975, p. 83), according to which abolitionism grew in force in the region because slave stock was thinning out there. However, Slenes (2004) relativizes Conrad's thesis by showing that the slave trade continued in the region, as it did in the South – for example, between Rio Grande do Sul (seller) and Campinas (buyer). If it were the case that associativism grew in regions with low slave stock, there would have been none in São Paulo, where slave holdings were large due to the coffee plantations. What we see, however, is that between 1878 and 1885, thirteen new associations were formed in São Paulo. During the same period, 159 associations were created in the North (Amazonas, Bahia, Ceará, Maranhão, Pará, Pernambuco, Piauí, Rio Grande do Norte, Sergipe) and, 120 appeared in the South (Espírito Santo, Goiás, Mato Grosso, Minas Gerais, Paraná, Rio de Janeiro, Rio Grande do Sul, São Paulo).

## Expansion

Martinho Campos was its prime target. The government, however, was teetering, and Rebouças was celebrating:

It seems that the Paulino [Soares de Sousa]/Martinho [Campos] pro-slavery company has broken up ... Everyone is now considering the government a lame duck, and what's killing it is the irresistible force of abolitionism. The horror it has caused among Martinho's slavemongering abominations is proof that it is no longer possible for a government to ground itself upon hideous slavery.[64]

In fact, this intractably anti-abolition government did not last very long. A doctor specializing in tetanus, Martinho Campos found no remedy to save his ailing cabinet. Having entertained Parliament with his comic vein between January and July 1882, and finding himself blocked in his attempt to change electoral law, he withdrew from office with a joke: "Oh well, there goes my job!"

A sad note rained on the abolitionist parade at Martinho's downfall. According to a stricken Raul Pompeia, on the morning of August 24, 1882, a bright sunny day, Luís Gama lost his voice. By nightfall he was dead from diabetes. His body was laid out on a pair of joined tables in the sitting room of his house, "covered to the waist in a sackcloth sheet." Colleagues and ex-slaves he had helped free came to pay their respects, and the wake extended to three o'clock the following afternoon, when his cortège set out for Consolação cemetery. Black-iron carriages, a huge turnout, were joined in the Brás neighborhood by a brass band and, at the Carmo rise, by the Nossa Senhora dos Remedios brotherhood, with its blue and white banners and tall candles. Six of his charges from the São Paulo Abolitionist Center carried his coffin, followed by members of the Luís Gama Emancipation Savings and various Republican groups. Wreaths were sent by the *Gazeta do Povo*, the Portuguese Gym Club, the Faculty of Law, and the Provincial Vice-president. Luís Gama had come far, from ex-slave to an illustrious public figure whose funeral drew "representatives of every social class." Shops closed, the flag flew at half-mast, speeches were given, and from the balconies of buildings banners were draped, like those unfurled for Holy Week processions.[65]

The cortège arrived at the little chapel at seven in the evening. The moon was already shining, and the priest sprinkled holy water upon the casket of the deceased anticleric, and when it was all over, someone was

---

[64] Letter from André Rebouças to Joaquim Nabuco, Mar. 5, 1882, CIJN.

[65] Pompeia (1882, pp. 211 ff.). Also in attendance were two Masonic lodges, the July 14 Society, the Girondine Club, both Republican-oriented. Menucci (1938, p. 206), Azevedo (1999), and Ferreira (2001, 2007, 2011). See also Alonso (2016).

176                    *The Last Abolition*

rumored to exclaim between sobs: "Wait!" "He said a few words, with no rhetoric . . ., and the crowd wept. Then . . . he exhorted the gathering to swear on Gama's dead body that they would never let die the idea for which that giant had fought . . . And the crowd swore its oath."[66] Those words, recorded nowhere in print, are said to have been ascribed to Antônio Bento de Sousa e Castro, the only disciple of Gama's said to possess "leadership qualities" at a time when abolition in São Paulo was left leaderless. As Serra would lament to Nabuco, "the death of Luís Gama was a dismantlement" there. Unlike Gama in so many ways, Antônio Bento – white, Catholic, a Conservative, a former judge – shared his devotion to abolition and his sheer audacity, and he stood up to be counted. He picked up where Gama had left off, at the crossroads between judicial activism and the rough-and-ready disorder of the SCL.[67]

However, death did not wipe Gama from the campaign. His fate would be similar to that of the Viscount of Rio Branco, who, only two years earlier, had received a state funeral. Rebouças had seen in the free womb cabinet chief a Brazilian Wilberforce, the ideal figure with which to open the pantheon of abolitionist heroes. Writing in the *Gazeta da Tarde*, Patrocínio remarked that in Rio Branco the nation had lost a leader capable of "mining citizens from the black deposits of slavery." An editorial in *O Abolicionista* praised the Free Womb Law, "the prologue to a much anticipated epilogue." Nabuco, Rebouças, and other abolitionists with access to the political system attended the Viscount's funeral, despite the reproachful glares of the deceased's closest followers and those of Paulino and his ilk, united in their objection to any attempt to transform a member of their party into an abolitionist icon. Not to be deterred, the abolitionists vied to be pallbearers with Conservative Party members. The Baron of Cotegipe would have none of it: no one was going to wrest from him any of the eighteen glowering candlesticks.[68]

The movement incorporated Rio Branco into the fledgling abolitionist tradition, alongside Castro Alves, its poet laureate crowned with the romantic halo of a brief life. The nascent pantheon was swollen with dead reformists, presented as the icons of abolitionism. The greater the figure's visibility in life, the more frequent and more laudatory was the

---

[66] Pompeia (1882, pp. 220–1).

[67] Letter from Joaquim Serra to Joaquim Nabuco, Sept. 19, 1882, CIJN. Pompeia (1882, p. 221) attributes the oath to another abolitionist, Clímaco Barbosa, and Andrada (1918, p. 214), to Antônio Bento.

[68] GT, Mar. 8, 1880; OA, Dec. 1, 1880; ACE, Oct. 28, 1880.

mention made of him in books and articles: José Bonifácio incarnated the abolition/Independence juxtaposition, with reprints of his *Representação à constituinte*. And so the abolitionists inflated the status of its dead statesmen, raising the bar for measuring the living.

Patrocínio knew the value of a dead Luís Gama. He and Quintino Bocaiúva made a dash from Rio to São Paulo for the funeral, one representing the abolitionists and the other the republicans. In his dead colleague he saw the stuff of heroes: a freeman enslaved who, at great pains, had broken through the bars of slavery to pursue, not personal success, but the collective track of protest. Dying now, as the campaign was growing, he would not have to face the dilemmas of activism, make none of the concessions to politics which Rebouças, Patrocínio, and Nabuco eventually would. His image would go unstained in its immaculate radicalism. In this, he would be irreplaceable. Patrocínio did not make it in time for the funeral, but he paid an even more powerful tribute. In the death of "the general who all wished could lead them into battle for the national honor," he saw a symbol. Luís Gama would remain very much alive among the abolitionists as the crystallization of an "inimitable heroism";[69] a key piece in the consolidation of a social movement: the leader who went down fighting.

[69] GT, Aug. 28, 1882.

# 6

# Results-Based Abolitionism

## POLITICAL OPPORTUNITY

João Lustosa da Cunha, first Viscount, then Marquis of Paranaguá, presided over three provinces before becoming Prime Minister on July 3, 1882. He had the misfortune of a blind daughter and the habit of walking to the ministry, in white pants, burgundy coat, and top hat. Initially Conservative and known for his courtly demeanor, the Marquis eventually became a pro-reform Liberal, so long as the reforms were moderate. When he came to power after Martinho Campos' fall, he put abolition back on the agenda, for two reasons: the progress made in Cuba, stating "... every other State has abolished slavery, and Brazil is now the only Christian nation to preserve it, seeing as it will be but a matter of days before Spain resolves the issue once and for all," and propaganda on the home front, which had "been stirring up opinion that [could] not be left unanswered."[1]

The propaganda to which he referred denounced corruption and ineptitude in the handling of the Emancipation Fund set down in the Free Womb Law. According to the American diplomat in Brazil, falsifications were rife: owners were registering a larger number than demographics would allow of slaves born in 1870, as if no children had been born to slave mothers ever since the passing of the law on September 28, 1871. Fiddling with the birth dates turned the freeborn back into slaves. By the law's eleventh anniversary, it had freed only 11,000 people, a paltry 0.7 percent of the slave population. Without meddling in property

[1] GT, Apr. 23, 1883.

rights or the direct interests of the slaveholders, Paranaguá intended to fix the situation by raising the deposits in the Emancipation Fund, with a tax on the purchase and sale of captives and banning the interprovincial slave trade.[2]

The Conservative minority in the Lower House, more robust since the 1881 elections, and with Paulino as its ever-effective spokesman, warned against it: "... do not instill illusory expectations that will only yield bitter disappointments; do not fuel interests mounting on the murky fringes of the law; do not spark fears and moral reactions it will be beyond our ability to control (*rapturous applause*)." Paranaguá replied, combining the schemata of rights and compassion: "Whose fears? Those of the landowners? ... whose interests surely cannot run counter to the better sentiment of humanity, the laws of a great state, one that must take its place among the civilized Christian nations." He spoke of the fast-growing abolitionist movement, which was already outstripping the State's own efforts, and threw in even the pro-slavery schemata of threat: "There are certain aspirations that cannot be supplanted and which threaten catastrophe when stifled. It is therefore essential that the government bring them under rein; that the public authorities harness their charge."[3]

The abolitionists welcomed this discourse with joy. Three Liberal governments had come and gone since 1878 with few results. Antislavery writings, associations, and rallies had flourished without government repression, but without its endorsement either. In Paranaguá they saw the political opportunity for a new antislavery law, as Serra would declare to Nabuco: "... his program may be limited, but it's still a great deal better than the silence of its predecessors. The slavocrats in Parliament are furious ..., I don't know how Paranaguá stands it ... We, in the abolitionist press, wait with sympathetic bated breath."[4]

### INTERNATIONAL NETWORK

With the tide high, Rebouças departed from Brazil. In September 1882, disgruntled with his partners and with the imperial family, he went to London to take care of business with some local investors in his company, the Conde D'Eu R W. He stayed at the Charing Cross Hotel.

---

[2] US Legation, May 21, 1884, JC in Moraes (1924, p. 25), Paranaguá, ACD, Jul. 5, 1882.
[3] ACD, Jul. 5 and Aug. 10, 1882.
[4] Letter from Joaquim Serra to Joaquim Nabuco, Jul. 15, 1882, CIJN.

180                          *The Last Abolition*

He had none of the problems he had experienced in the United States on aristocratic soil. He also met with Nabuco, who was buttressing the international support network for Brazilian abolitionism, having cemented ties with the antislavery movement in France; with the Spanish abolitionists, to whom he sent honorary titles through the moribund SBCE; and with the women's abolitionist associations the Alliance and Temperance Mission. He had also been trying to make contact with Rebouças' American hero, Frederick Douglass. Nabuco had further deepened his connections with the British and Foreign Antislavery Society, writing for its newsletter and speaking at meetings and conferences. He had even represented the BFASS at the eleventh International Juridical Association Congress in Milan, in 1883, which approved his project for an international treaty that would define the slave trade as piracy. So the Nabuco that Rebouças met there was a man entirely plugged into a complex transnational activism network. Nabuco used his European connections to foster those in Brazil and exert some influence on domestic policy. He sent back articles, news clippings, and speeches and ran updates on the Brazilian movement in the *Antislavery Reporter*. Rebouças' London stay was a whirlwind of activity, and he urged Nabuco to secure a favorable declaration from the British Prime Minister. They celebrated together the anniversary of the Free Womb Law at the Brighton headquarters of the English abolitionists and at a function in London hosted by the British and Foreign Antislavery Society, at which Nabuco spoke and Rebouças mingled, expanding his own network and cultivating his contact with the society's secretary-general, whom he would later furnish with documents.[5]

During his years in London, Nabuco became more familiar with the diversity of tactics of the European political repertoire, but he was still a follower of Wilberforce's Parliamentary strategy. In June 1882, he wrote a petition to be sent to the Lower House and to the Provincial Assemblies. Rebouças promised to implement it, but, as the petition crossed the

---

[5] DNAAR, Sept. 24 and 25, Oct. 30, 1882; letters from Victor Schoelcher to Joaquim Nabuco, May 26, 1882 and Oct. 27, 1883, CIJN; OA, Jun. 1 and Jul. 1, 1881; letter from Joaquim Nabuco to Adolfo de Barros, Nov. 17, 1882, CIJN; letter from Rafael de Labra to Joaquim Nabuco, Dec. 3, 1883, CIJN. There is no record of any letters to or from Douglass. On Nabuco's international connections at the time, see Bethell and Carvalho (2008). Alonso (2009); letter from Joaquim Nabuco to Adolfo de Barros, Nov. 17, 1882, CIJN; letter from Rafael de Labra to Joaquim Nabuco, Dec. 3, 1883, CIJN; letter from André Rebouças to Joaquim Nabuco, Apr. 16, 1882, CIJN; DNAAR, Sept. 28 and Nov.15, 1882; DNAAR, Jan. 16 and 20, Mar. 15, 1883; DNAAR, Oct. 14, 1882. The third Brazilian abolitionist in England was the journalist José Carlos Rodrigues, a friend of both Rebouças and Nabuco, who was scouting for space in the British press.

Atlantic, the abolitionists back in Brazil realized that Paranaguá's overtures had gone cold and that it would be a bad idea to send the motion to Parliament. So they avoided signing it, as Serra would inform Nabuco by letter: "What would be the point in Rebouças or I signing the motion if the objections of others are as futile as they are persistent? . . . [Someone] claimed that he would be crazy to sign a petition coming from London if he didn't draft one of his own here in Brazil."[6]

In the end, the motion was sent to the floor by one of the three Conservative abolitionists in the Lower House. It was stonewalled and consigned to review-committee limbo. Nabuco took a leaf out of Rebouças' book – the lobby – and appealed to Saraiva: "Your lordship can achieve, this very day, and in favor of the nation's slaves, what none ever could, and that burdens your lordship with a great duty before history should the wrong decision be reached." At this point, in Brazil, the MP Paranaguá included the gradual abolition of slavery in the Emperor's discourse at the opening of the 1883 parliamentary year. In the interests of visibility, Nabuco sent the government an open letter denouncing the sale of "ingênuos," the children liberated by the Free Womb Law, but Paranaguá deflated the bid by replying through private channels. The press, for its part, ignored the tactic. Nabuco still saw abolitionism through the same political institution lens as his father: his propaganda was focused on pushing the issue inside the Parliament. The SBCE was a stepping stone toward an abolitionist party.[7] However, where Nabuco de Araújo had been a member of a large faction able to reach the national government, his son had the disadvantage of living abroad after a failed attempt at re-election.

To be sure, abolitionism was growing *outside* the party system. In the public space, political articulation was required. The Nabuco and Patrocínio cliques never did fully merge, despite Rebouças' best efforts, because they belonged to different social circles. Nabuco's group

---

[6] Letter from Joaquim Nabuco to André Rebouças, Jun. 6, 1882, CIJN; letter from André Rebouças to Joaquim Nabuco, Jul. 7, 1882, CIJN. Serra added that: "The petition to be sent to lower house is great and most welcome. It has been forwarded as arrived, signed only by yourself and José Costa [Azevedo, the Baron of Ladário, a former MP then resident in London]." Letter from Joaquim Serra to Joaquim Nabuco, Jul. 15, 1882, CIJN.

[7] Motion submitted by Antônio Pinto. Letter from Joaquim Serra to Joaquim Nabuco, Sept. 19, 1882, CIJN; letter from Joaquim Nabuco to Antônio Saraiva, Nov. 28, 1882, CAI. "I am greatly incensed by the non-publication of your letter to Paranaguá," letter from Joaquim Serra to Joaquim Nabuco, Feb. 15, 1883, CIJN; letter from Joaquim Nabuco to Domingos Jaguaribe, Nov. 16, 1882, CAI.

182                              *The Last Abolition*

consisted of the aristocratic heirs of Liberal Party stalwarts, waiting in line for their own day in the Parliamentary sun. Patrocínio was the Pied Piper followed by young upstarts with no names to trade on, dependent on patrons and the press, and their futures were as uncertain as their refinement was relative. Nabuco had his peers from the salons, while Patrocínio had hangers-on from the bars of Rio de Janeiro. With none of Nabuco's finesse, Patrocínio never acquired the stiff upper lip essential to be accepted in the upper social circles. His gift lay in stirring love and bile in those around him.

Polished like Nabuco and black like Patrocínio, Rebouças could move smoothly between both circles, deploying Nabuco's aristocratic, party-political approach and Patrocínio's popular assaults from the stage and page. They were parallel tracks, but they were also interlinked – the abolitionist steam engine needed them both in order to run.

With Rebouças and Nabuco in London, Patrocínio filled the vacuum. Abolitionists inside the political system were hamstrung by alliances and track records: Artur Silveira da Mota did not want to rock the boat for his father, a senator, while Rodolfo Dantas and Rui Barbosa bore the stigma of having served in Martinho Campos' pro-slavery government. The most active Parliamentary abolitionist, Joaquim Serra, joined the *Gazeta da Tarde* (GT). From all the way across the ocean in London, Nabuco's influence was pale and weak. On the local scene, Patrocínio shone.

Fellow abolitionists, seeing Nabuco's parliamentary approach come to little, were drawn to Patrocínio's public space propaganda strategy. Paranaguá was all talk and no action. The path ahead lay outside of the political system and would require coordinated, concerted action on a national scale and a new strategy capable of delivering immediate, deep impact.[8]

### THE FREE SOIL CAMPAIGN

Luís Gama was dead and Nabuco and Rebouças absent. The planets were aligned for Patrocínio to shine in the abolitionist campaign. He spearheaded the ACE strategy of continuing with the concert-conferences and creating the Central Emancipation Commission (CCE) early in 1883, always with Vicente de Sousa and the team veteran Nicolau Moreira.

---

[8] Letter from Joaquim Serra to Joaquim Nabuco, Jul. 15, 1882, CIJN.

The CCE was a bold twist on Rebouças-style lobbying. On February 8, 1883, armed with cut flowers, the members invaded the City Council of Rio de Janeiro to demand an end to slave auctions. The Speaker of the House saw in the protest his own personal burden and promised action, though he neglected to say how or when it would come. Five days later, the CCE visited the Trade Association, three MPs, and the manager of Brazil's Bank, pure theatrics, in this case, as the manager in question was João Clapp, a commission member. They also called in on the bishop and the Prime Minister, though those two refused to commit to anything. Another CCE strategy, the boycott, was borrowed from the British abolitionist repertoire. In Great Britain, the target had been slave-produced sugar. In Brazil, the abolitionists did not dare challenge the coffee business, still the economic mainstay, so they shifted their strategy onto the symbolic plane instead. The GT called on the press to ban all classified ads for the purchase or sale of slaves and created a special section called "Scenes of Slavery," devoted to reporting on the barbarities masters perpetrated against their slaves. The CCE waged a moral crusade that traded in the hard currency of aristocratic society – prestige. The commission went a step beyond the benefactor's award customarily conferred by Rebouças to create a Golden Book, in which it named and honored, week-in, week-out, all those who made donations towards the purchase of manumissions. The tactic spread to other cities and was even inverted in the form of the *Gazeta da Tarde*'s Black Book, which named and shamed bad masters, complete with addresses, in a format similar to the "reward" posters for runaway slaves. For example, the caption below an illustration showing a slave with a truncheon in one hand and a stick-and-bindle in the other: "Citizen Egydio, thirty years deprived of his liberty, offers a generous reward for the capture of the slavemonger Leocádio Gomes Franklin, resident at Abundância Farm." To the ally, abolitionists provided glory, to the enemy shame.[9]

But the main objective behind the founding of the CCE was to create a strategy as efficient as the concert-conferences, using the public space in an even bolder fashion. Tired of governmental ineptitude, the members were adamant: "Gone are the days of sentimentalism. It's time for a phase

---

[9] Nicolau Moreira led the invasion of the city council. The MPs sympathetic to the cause were Bezerra de Menezes, Fernandes de Oliveira, and Duque-Estrada Teixeira (GT, Feb. 8, 14, 20, 1883; GT, Feb. 20, Mar. 6 and Feb. 22, 1883). The idea of compiling a Golden Book came from Tristão de Alencar Jr., a MP for Ceará and a member of Patrocínio's circle. The strategy of playing on a prestige/anathema dichotomy, praising allies and excoriating adversaries, is common among social movements (Tilly, 2008).

# The Last Abolition

of action."[10] The foreign abolitionist repertoire was taken as the guiding light here. This time, the movement looked toward the United States for a tactic: the underground railroad, a network of escape routes, and safe houses to get runaway slaves to free soil up north or into Canada, where slavery was illegal. The most famous runaway was Rebouças' idol, Frederick Douglass. In Brazil, there had been *quilombos* (runaway slave communities) since colonial days, and new ones began to appear throughout the abolitionist campaign, but they were clandestine enclaves. Brazil had nowhere resembling the free states of the American North, where runaways could live and breathe freely. The CCE decided to create its own slavery-free zone, a place that could challenge slavery's institutional validity and serve as a refuge for runaways (whether aided and abetted by abolitionists or not), making feasible the underground railroad strategy in the near future. It would also be proof that a free civil order was achievable in Brazil, debunking the pro-slavery schemata of threat, the claim that abolition would lead to anarchy. Thus began the free soil campaign.

Planned in 1882, the strategy was rolled out in January 1883, with the capital Rio de Janeiro as its target.[11] Instead of raising money to buy manumissions, as at the concert-conferences, abolitionists asked the owners to grant their slaves freedom – all of them – voluntarily and foregoing all monetary compensation. It was a shoe-leather campaign, following a space sequence, pursued door to door, block by block. The aim was to free whole neighborhoods, towns, cities, provinces and, if all went to plan, the nation itself.

The same social strata that had helped out in the theaters rallied behind this new strategy: small-business owners, civil servants, journalists, artists, teachers, all owners of small slave stocks who could adhere, converting slaves into household staff, keeping them in the same functions, but with a small wage. During the campaign, commissions were set up to obtain letters of manumission without compensation and some of them celebrated with parties[12]. Of course, the success depended on the economic dispensability of the slaves to the owners in question. Because of that, the free soil places that began to open up were tiny enclaves in commercial areas or in the vicinity of colleges, local press vehicles, such as the *Gazeta da Tarde*, and the residences of abolitionists.

---

[10] GT, May 18, 1883.    [11] GT, Jan. 16, 1883.

[12] The news about the commissions is in CA (1884, p. 9). There was no correspondence between social position and political radicalism inside the movement.

It was a liberal-spirited mobilization, demonstrating that private initiatives could solve the problem if the political institutions keep failing to pass a law.

### BEACON LAND

The free soil strategy in Court stalled after a promising start. The capital was the seat of government and the imperial household and was never going to abdicate its authority that easily. The CCE, in alliance with abolitionists from the provinces, started scouting for somewhere else they could operate on a large scale. Factors to be considered were the number of slaves in a particular region and how central they were to the provincial mainstays and markets. São Paulo, Minas Gerais, and Rio de Janeiro were all taken off the table straightaway, as abundant slave stocks lay at the heart of their economies, so resistance was bound to be fierce. Demographics and economics were necessary factors, but they were not sufficient in themselves. Pará, Santa Catarina, Piauí, and Goiás all had small slave stocks engaged in fringe economical activities, but that did not make them prime targets. The real swing factor was political. The abolitionists kicked off their free soil campaign with energy and consequence in a province where it could obtain maximum effect, that is, where there was a good chance of the political and social authorities certifying and recognizing the movement's legitimacy, and lower likelihood of facing police repression.[13]

In the centralized system of the Second Reign, the national government appointed the provincial presidents. That meant that the appointees stayed in the post only as long as the national government lasted. During the Liberal governments of 1878 to 1885, this usual instability reached its pinnacle. The seven Liberal governments that briefly held power during that interval saw a string of provincial presidential appointments: Amazonas, Maranhão, Piauí, Rio Grande do Norte, Sergipe, Bahia, Rio de Janeiro, Minas Gerais, Goiás, and Paraná all had seven; Ceará, Rio Grande do Sul, Pernambuco, and Espírito Santo had eight apiece; Paraíba and Santa Catarina, nine; and Alagoas, ten during the period – not counting interims. These flash-in-the-pan governments conferred a certain

---

[13] Conrad (1972, p. 121) argues in the opposite direction here, stressing the relevance of the economy to abolitionism. Social certification is the endorsement of a social movement's actions by political or social authorities. Social de-certification is the opposite (McAdam, Tarrow, and Tilly, 2001, p. 121).

186                    *The Last Abolition*

independence upon the provincial presidents vis-à-vis the local elites. As presidents who were just passing through, they could implement policies without having to face the consequences themselves.[14] That was the case in Ceará.

When the mobilization grew, the incumbent in Ceará was Sancho de Barros Pimentel, a former MP who had sat in the same Legislature as Nabuco, a member of the SBCE and part of the 1880 caucus. The leader of the SCL, José Correia do Amaral, celebrated his appointment: "... I believe our hopes have been given a boost." Pimentel ordered a census of the slaves under his constituency. The 31,975 slaves counted in 1874, roughly 5 percent of the population of 721,600, had fallen during the 1877–1878 drought, when they had been sold South by the wagonload[15] and there was a major depreciation in price of the remainder. No other president had made much of a fuss about this, but Pimentel did, implementing what Paranaguá had proposed but not enforced: he slapped fiscal fines on the interprovincial slave trade. A state representative floored the bill at the Provincial Assembly, and peppered his address with names of SCL abolitionists. The opposition claimed it was unconstitutional and the bill was amended, and passed nonetheless in July 1882.

In addition to having a facilitating local government, the SCL also had the sympathies of those who would have been called upon to quash its activities: the Fifteenth Infantry, the very battalion that had lent a helping hand during the port blockade in Fortaleza in 1881. Repression troops would have had to be deployed from some neighboring province or from Court, which was conveniently distant. These conditions encouraged the SCL, which, betting on its strong rallying power, decided to try the free soil strategy on a province-wide scale. To this end, in 1882, Patrocínio traveled to Fortaleza.

Once again, he was heading North at a propitious hour. On his first journey to Ceará he had been fleeing Bibi's father. This time, he was running from Bibi herself: a jealous woman whose explosiveness matched

---

[14] According to Sérgio Buarque de Holanda (2010, p. 171), "an estimate for all provinces, for the entire period of the monarchy, puts the average duration of each provincial presidency at seven months." Javary (1962, pp. 431–53) identifies particular instability in São Paulo, which had six presidents, and in Mato Grosso, which had five. Though they were crucial, the literature did not factor the provincial presidents into its explanation of why Ceará and Amazonas came to declare themselves liberated from slavery.

[15] Letter from José Correia do Amaral to Joaquim Nabuco, Oct. 10, 1882, CIJN. Pimentel was still a partner in the law firm of Rui Barbosa and Rodolfo Dantas. The data on slavery in Ceará are from Reis (2000, p. 91).

her husband's own outbursts. Patrocínio arrived on November 30, and faced a conference and honorary membership of the SCL. He did the rounds of the newspapers, and attended banquets with music provided by the Fifteenth Battalion's band. In a parade of rafts, Zé do Pato met Chico de Matilde, the raftsman who had furthered the abolitionist cause by orchestrating a blockade at the port of Fortaleza the previous year. Welcomed as a national leader, Patrocínio was given a new nickname – one fitting for the battles he would enjoin with Paulino, the Marshal of the Past: Zé do Pato was now the "Black Marshal."[16]

During the two months he spent in the province, Patrocínio consolidated a lasting connection with the local abolitionists, fostered the concert-conferences, and championed the creation of new societies, such as the women's branch of the SCL, The Ceará Women Liberators, formed by the wives, daughters, and sisters of the abolitionists.

The transfer of the free soil strategy to Ceará began at Acarape, a town with few slaves joined to Fortaleza by a railroad. An SCL caravan, with Patrocínio aboard, combined with its concert-conference, a fundraising strategy to buy manumissions and urge voluntary emancipations. The honor of proclaiming Acarape the first free town in the Empire fell to Patrocínio on New Year's Day 1883.[17]

Among confetti and fanfares, the caravan trundled on to the neighboring towns, with the women always leading the way and Patrocínio arm-in-arm with them. The process won over the wife of João Cordeiro, endowed with a personality every bit as strong as her husband's. During one of the concert-conferences, she stood up in the middle of the audience and, in a dramatic gesture, started pulling off her rings and bracelets, earrings, and necklaces, which she declared she was donating to the cause. The other ladies in the auditorium followed suit.[18]

Wherever it stopped, the caravan founded a brace of abolitionist societies – one male and one female – and announced the date of the municipality's "liberation." Over 1,000 were freed in February 1883, according to the *Gazeta da Tarde,* with sequential emancipations in Pacatuba, São Francisco, Icó, and Baturité, the province's agricultural hub and home to Antônio Pinto, one of the Conservatives of the

---

[16] This was a nephew's opinion of Bibi (in Magalhães Jr., 1969, p. 131); GT, Feb. 14, 1883; Morel (1967, pp. 141–2).

[17] Girão (1988, p. 136). Patrocínio's concert-conferences alone raised 260 thousand reis (GT, Feb. 21, 1883).

[18] This was Carolina Cordeiro, who would pass away in the middle of the campaign (*Libertador,* Apr. 14, 1884).

188 The Last Abolition

abolitionist bloc in Parliament, who rushed back to commemorate the emancipation of 880 slaves in under a fortnight.[19]

Twenty "liberation committees" were set up as well as a press commission in charge of propagating the movement's feats throughout the Empire. The ladies scoured Fortaleza, door to door, eager to meet their May 24 deadline to declare the city free. And they achieved a huge success: at long last, a provincial capital was declared free of slavery, and three days ahead of schedule. From then on, the towns fell like ninepins: Maranguape, Soure, Mecejana, Aquiraz, Pedra Branca, Pentecoste, Príncipe Imperial, Quixadá, Granja, eighteen of them in all, at a rate of two a month. In all cases, the movement gained the adherence of local prosecutors, MPs, and members of the social elite. Having begun with the goodwill of the provincial president, the process of certification eventually arrived at the Catholic church. More antislavery than anticlerical, Patrocínio welcomed the unexpected presence of priests at abolitionist gatherings. The national political institutions were forced to be aware of those facts, since the GT ran an updated timeline of liberations called "chart of light." Insolent as ever, Patrocínio sent a telegram to the Emperor: "Your Highness's name does not yet figure on the membership rolls of the Liberating Society of Ceará."[20]

With Ceará pushing full-steam ahead, Patrocínio spent another two months campaigning in the North. On his return to Court, he was greeted at the port by an abolitionist crowd, a brass band, fireworks, bouquets, the manumission of seven slaves, and speeches from João Clapp, the president of the Abolitionist Confederation, and the secretary of the Court branch of the Liberating Society of Ceará – a group created by Cearenses based in Rio as a tribute to the movement back in their home province. When he arrived at the offices of the GT, festooned with flags and bunting, he was met by typesetters and youths carrying broken shackles in their hands. That night, the Court branch of the Liberating Society of Ceará held a concert-conference at the Recreio Dramático theater, inaugurating Ceará's Golden Book. In May, the society itself was honored at a similar function at the São Luís Theater, decorated with banners, coats of arms, and garlands bearing the names of leading

---

[19] GT, Mar. 5, Feb. 13, Mar. 15, Feb. 12, 1883; Filho, Albano (1883, p. 12); Pinto (1884, p. 14).
[20] GT, Jan. 1, Feb. 2, Mar. 15, Apr. 17, May 20, 21, 23, Jun. 3, Jul. 8, Sept. 27 and 29, Oct. 4, Nov. 3, 1883. Patrocínio, accompanied by the SCL board, met with the parish priest of Cachoeira (*Libertador*, Feb. 28, 1883). Cf. telegram from Patrocínio, in Morel (1967, p. 143).

abolitionists. Over 1,000 people turned out for the tribute, over half of them women. Those events consolidated the political inclusion of women in the movement. Also, the free soil campaign popularized the use of electric lights as a symbol of freedom. Abolitionists contrasted the "Beacon Land" of Ceará to the darkness of slavery in other parts of the country.[21]

Overseas, Nabuco was trying to keep a foothold in Patrocínio's fast-moving juggernaut. He sent letters of congratulation to each of the newly-founded municipal organizations by name. If Patrocínio was giving a national political meaning to Ceará's achievements, Nabuco tried the same on an international scale. He celebrated the advances in the *Antislavery Reporter* and at a banquet held at Queen Anne's Mansions on June 9, with a Chilean diplomat in attendance and the plenipotentiary ministers of Argentina and the United States. French and Spanish abolitionists forwarded addresses to be read on their behalf. A member of the SCL spoke of the participation of raftsmen and typesetters, civil servants, and the armed forces in the Ceará campaign, and paid homage to Nabuco that he, being overseas and out of sight, so badly needed: he called him the leader of Brazilian abolitionism.[22]

ACTION, REACTION

Rebouças arrived back in Rio de Janeiro amid enormous enthusiasm about what the GT was calling the "Ceará Revolution." Students and professors from the Polytechnic School and members of the Niterói Freedmen's Club packed the ferryboat in the early hours, complete with marching band, to greet the returning abolitionist, who described his reception as worthy of a Prime Minister: "... I have arrived at an opportune time. I was given a welcome comparable only to that of Rio Branco."[23]

The moment was indeed opportune because the mobilization was in danger of turning sour. Ceará had elevated Patrocínio to the status of national leader, but if his feisty temperament made him a great crowd-

---

[21] GT, Feb. 22, Mar. 10 and 12, May 23 and 25, 1883.

[22] "Please transmit my warmest congratulations on the resounding success of the arduous initiative undertaken ... and to any other abolitionist association operating in the province," letter from Joaquim Nabuco to José Correia do Amaral, Mar. 7, 1883, CIJN. GT, May 16, 1883; letter from Joaquim Nabuco to José Correia do Amaral, May 31, 1883, CIJN; Filho, Albano (1883, p. 10).

[23] GT, Mar. 3, 1883; letter from André Rebouças to Joaquim Nabuco, Mar. 10, 1883, CIJN.

rouser, it also rubbed up his peers the wrong way. Serra complained to Nabuco: "I'm leaving the *Gazeta* [*da Tarde*] because of my absolute incompatibility with Patrocínio, who is putting the whole cause in jeopardy..."[24] Rebouças soothed frayed tempers and placated Patrocínio, who, together with the SCL (which complained to Nabuco that the institutional abolitionists were lagging behind), could have burned the whole house down. Towards the end of 1882, with only a handful of municipalities left to liberate, the SCL pressured Pimentel to legitimize abolition province-wide. The national government was equally insistent, but contrariwise. Pimentel, a man with a foot in either camp, with his twin capacities as activist and politician, loyal to the movement, but mindful of his career, was caught between a rock and a hard place. In the impasse between maintaining the social order and losing the respect of his fellow abolitionists, or of decreeing abolition in Ceará and being censured by the central government, he chose to stand down, though his resignation was not readily accepted, despite his repeated attempts.[25]

The problem was, with Ceará having become something of a hot seat, the government had nobody to appoint in his stead. The abolitionist onslaught had even depressed the slave market. In 1881, the mortgages market calculated an adult slave's property paper as good for the next twenty-nine years; that meant there was an expectation slavery would rest for this time. By 1883, the same papers were good for just six years. Hence, the market's outlook for the demise of slavery was now 1889. As one MP observed, slave prices, which ought to have been rising due to short supply, were "slumping wholly because of abolitionist agitation." This deflation, of course, boosted the CA's strategy of buying manumissions.[26]

In the Upper and Lower Houses, pro-slavery politicians cited the liberation of Fortaleza as the touchstone for a regional revolt in the mold of the ones experienced during the early days of the Second Reign. And there was a chance it might spread. Slave revolts, some of them supported by the abolitionists, were beginning to proliferate, as were skirmishes

---

[24] Letter from Joaquim Serra to Joaquim Nabuco, Sept. 19, 1882, CIJN; other abolitionists connected to the political system, such as Gusmão Lobo, had similar experiences (letter from Artur Silveira da Mota to Joaquim Nabuco, Jul. 22 1882, CIJN).

[25] Letter from José Correia do Amaral to Joaquim Nabuco, Oct. 10, 1882, CIJN; letter from Sancho de Barros Pimentel to Joaquim Nabuco, Dec. 7, 1882, CIJN.

[26] Asset market data is from Pedro Carvalho de Mello, in Slenes (2004, p. 357); ACD, Aug. 4, 1884. Rebouças also commented on the lower costs of manumissions: "In Rio, the liberations only cost us 300,000 (letter from André Rebouças to Joaquim Nabuco, Sept. 24, CIJN).

between pro-slavery advocates and abolitionists in various parts of the land, such as Vassouras and Campinas.[27]

Caught between abolitionist advances and a pro-slavery backlash, the Emperor and government tried to keep both camps happy. Paranaguá spread a rumor that he was planning on taking an emancipation bill to the Council of State, while D. Pedro responded to Patrocínio's telegram with a donation to the SCL – though, it was made by the imperial butler. In so doing, the Moderating Power not only legitimized the free soil strategy, but did so through the only abolitionist society that was taking an openly confrontational stance. On the other hand, as Patrocínio made his way back to Court, the government ordered the SCL-friendly Fifteenth Battalion to relocate from Fortaleza to Belém, in the distant Amazonian state of Pará. The Seventh Battalion was sent to replace it and restore order in Ceará. Under this new military force's view, the SCL responded with a 15,000-strong street demonstration in defense of the redeployed battalion, but without attempting to block its departure: "In this way [a pacific demonstration] we refute the government who sent the army to repress us."[28]

To avoid being tarred as slavocratic, the Prime Minister and the Emperor, through his close friend the Countess of Barral, arranged a manumission ceremony in the style of the 1860s, at which Paranaguá attacked Patrocínio's impetuousness and exhorted the nation's freedmen to become "scribblers" of a more serious ilk than he. Retaliation was swift and scathing: the very next day, the *Gazeta da Tarde* opened its pages to freedmen to "scribble" to their hearts' content and accused Paranaguá of betraying his origins: "This vehicle can only lament having to deal with mulattos of the caliber of your Excellency and his son-in-law Doria, both absolute abnegations of the qualities of the mixed race."[29] Patrocínio made ample use of the difficulty of pinpointing someone's color in Brazil by accusing almost all the pro-slavery activists – except the pearly white Paulino – of being "mulattos" in denial.

Faced with abolitionist mobilization, a strong Conservative minority in the Lower House and a rift-ridden Liberal Party, Paranaguá had to decide where he stood, and that was on the outside of government. Instead of

---

[27] GT, Feb. 20 and 26, 1883. Machado (1994) identified the organization of slave revolts in the hinterlands of São Paulo.

[28] GT, Feb. 12, 14, 15, and 17, 1883; telegram from the SCL, GT, Mar. 1883.

[29] GT, Apr. 1883.

192 *The Last Abolition*

grabbing the bull of abolition by the horns, he chose to go down in history as the man who installed Brazil's first telephone line.[30]

### NEITHER YES NOR NO

The Moderating Power swayed this way and that throughout the abolitionist campaign. It never threw all its weight behind the abolitionists or facilitated the pro-slavery reaction. However, had D. Pedro wanted to further the cause, the man to appoint as Paranaguá's successor in May 1883 would have been Manuel de Sousa Dantas, who the *Gazeta da Tarde*, in a fit of wishful thinking, had gone so far as to announce as the new incumbent. Paranaguá, however, recommended Saraiva, the Emperor's favorite fireman, but he fled from these flames and from the political etiquette, declining to suggest another member of his party instead. So D. Pedro went back to Paranaguá and told him to pick a new name. The next in line was Manuel de Sousa Dantas, but Paranaguá suggested José Bonifácio, also known as the Lad. Nephew to the founding father of the Empire, Bonifácio broke the boycott and recommended Dantas, who, finding himself as a last best option, declared that no minister could obtain success with a Liberal Party split into moderate and reformist factions. A Conservative MP joked: "The power's been dropped in the middle of the road."[31]

Someone would have to go fetch it. Sancho Pimentel lamented that the ten-day crisis that had left the Liberal Party without a leader ended up conveying Lafaiete Rodrigues Pereira into power. An adversary summarized the new Prime Minister's career with the following withering comment: "He has never directed party policy, nor that of his own province, not even that of his own town." Worse still, he had betrayed the Liberals by defecting to the Republican Party in 1870, only to betray them too, by returning to the Liberals. Pereira considered himself "a new man, without the prestige and authority to appoint a cabinet."[32] And yet, it was he whom D. Pedro found to dig his Empire out of the abolitionist hole.

---

[30] Castro (2009, p. 76).

[31] GT, May 16, 1883; letter from Sancho de Barros Pimentel to Joaquim Nabuco, May 30, 1883, CIJN; Paranaguá, ASI, May 26, 1883; Dantas, ASI, May 26, 1883. The Conservative was Ferreira Viana (in Pujol, 1919, p. 224).

[32] Letter from Sancho de Barros Pimentel to Joaquim Nabuco, May 30, 1883, CIJN; Ferreira de Araújo in Pujol (1919, p. 224); Lafaiete, ACD, May 26, 1883.

## Results-Based Abolitionism

At Parliament, the Conservative minority ignored the new government, which could not even command the respect of its own party. One Liberal leader described the new Prime Minister as a man who "reduces life to comedy, promising the world and delivering less than nothing." Lafaiete ventured only to request that the House ratify the agenda he had inherited from Paranaguá: to curb the interprovincial slave trade and buttress the Emancipation Fund. On the one hand, he made overtures to the abolitionists; on the other, he offered a gift to the pro-slavery coalition: the appointment of a sworn enemy of the SCL as Minister of War. Pandering to all without committing to anyone, Lafaiete's political motto was an anodyne: "Maybe yes, maybe no."[33]

### THE CONFEDERATION'S BATTALION

There are eight men in the photo. Five standing at the back, three sitting at the front: Clapp, with a half-smile on his face with the hand of a tall and grey-haired Rebouças on his back; Patrocínio stands slightly apart on the back row when he should have been in the center.

The invitation from the ACE, signed by Vicente de Sousa, was issued in July 1882, but the meeting, of nine abolitionist societies and new adherents, would only convene the following May, at an abolitionist congress in Rio de Janeiro.[34] The plan: congregate the abolitionists under a single, national civil association – not a political party, as Nabuco had wanted. The idea was to badger the government with symbolic but impactful deeds like the liberation of Fortaleza.

But what was it to be called? Patrocínio suggested *Centro Abolicionista* (Abolitionist Center), but that inadvertently underscored, as had the Central Emancipatory Association and the Central Emancipation Commission (CCE) before it, the political centralization of the Second Reign. As most abolitionists were federalists and republicans – including Aristides Lobo, who chaired the meeting – another name won the day: *Confederação Abolicionista* (CA). The Abolitionist Confederation came into being on May 9, 1883, at six in the afternoon, in a meeting room at

---

[33] Letter from Sancho de Barros Pimentel to Joaquim Nabuco, May 30, 1883, CIJN; letter from Francisco Otaviano to the Baron of Penedo, May 20, 1884. Lafaiete, ACD, May 26, 1883. "Maybe yes, maybe no" began to appear systematically at Parliament and in newspapers (Celso Jr., 1901, pp. 39 ff.).

[34] The photo of the CA board was taken on May 16, 1888 (DNAAR, May 16, 1888). Brício de Abreu Archive, reproduced in Magalhães Jr. (1969, p. 434); Jul. 25, 1882, Feb. 14, May 3 and 10, 1883.

FIGURE 6.1 The Board of the Abolitionist Confederation, pictured on May 16, 1888. Standing from left to right: José do Patrocínio, Luís de Andrade, Inácio von Doellinger, Praxedes Medella, and Luiz Pereira. Sitting from left to right: André Rebouças, João Clapp, and José de Seixas Magalhães.
Unknown photographer.

the *Gazeta da Tarde*, according to the "birth certificate" signed by Rebouças, one of the proud fathers.[35]

There were fifteen founding member associations, most of them based in Rio. Four of them were formed by students from the provinces of Espírito Santo, Pernambuco, Ceará and Rio Grande do Sul inside their colleges in Court. However, the CA also attracted societies encompassing quite diverse social groups, such as a typesetters' association, a commercial employees' association, and even one formed by freed slaves. Other societies would join later. The GT became the headquarters and official mouthpiece of the Confederation, churning out its pamphlets and hosting its meetings. Rebouças was designated treasurer, in charge of fundraising and management; Patrocínio was responsible for proselytism; and Clapp, with his commercial respectability, was elected chairman. These three

[35] DNAAR, May 9, 1883.

comprised the core of the CA, while a trio formed by Rebouças, Patrocínio, and Aristides Lobo was tasked with penning its manifesto. However, Lobo, a fervent republican, was dropped from this duty in order not to scare away the monarchists. The handwritten document, approved at a general assembly and published on August 11, 1883, ended up being signed only by Rebouças and Patrocínio.[36]

### A BOOK, A MANIFESTO

The CA Manifesto systematized the movement's ideas in Court. Nabuco was doing the same, but in the form of a book: *O abolicionismo* (Abolitionism). Both book and manifesto were convergent productions molding a tradition of Brazilian abolitionism, listing politicians from the past who were sympathetic to the cause, rolling out the three abolitionist schemata – compassion, rights, and progress – and employing the interpretive schemata of abolition as a national re-founding. In this they were in mutual agreement and in unison with other abolitionist writings.[37]

However, there were differences between *O abolicionismo* and the manifesto, born from the circumstances in which each text was written. Writing in London, Nabuco penned a dense and analytical pamphlet that explained the logic of Brazilian slavery and presented moderate proposals for its extinction. Back in Brazil, in the thick of public space campaigning, Rebouças and Patrocínio produced a manifesto that was

---

[36] The founders were: the Abolitionist Society of Espírito Santo, the Liberating Society of Pernambuco in Court, the Liberating Society of Ceará in Court, the Sul-Rio-Grandense Abolitionist Society, the Joaquim Nabuco Abolitionist Fund, the José do Patrocínio Emancipation Fund, the Ferreira de Menezes Abolitionist Center, the Gutenberg Abolitionist Club, the Niterói Freedmen's Club, the Abolitionist Club of Commercial Sector Workers, Clube Tiradentes, *Gazeta da Tarde*, the Medical School Liberating Society, the Abolitionist Club of Military Academy Cadets, and the Brazilian Antislavery Society (CA, 1883). The Brazilian Orient Masonic Lodge attended the first meetings, but did not sign the manifesto (GT, Jun. 19, 1882). Other groups, such as the Bittencourt Sampaio, the Carlos Gomes Club, and the 7th of November Club joined later on. The internal structure of the CA included an organizing committee (Rebouças, Patrocínio, Clapp, Aristides Lobo, and João Paulo Gomes de Matos (then president of the Liberating Society of Ceará in Court)) and an executive committee (Rebouças, Clapp, Matos, Bittencourt Sampaio, Julião de Lemos, Alberto Victor, Manoel Joaquim Pereira, Eduardo Nogueira, Pau Brasil, José dos Santos Loiveira, Domingos Gomes dos Santos, and Jarbas F. das Chagas). The manifesto was approved at a CA assembly held on July 27 (GT, May 10 and 14, 1883; DNAAR, Jul. 27, 1883; CA, 1884, pp. 10–11).

[37] For example, Lemos (1884).

less robust in its fundamentals, but far more aggressive in its proposed measures.

*O abolicionismo* was the most sophisticated intellectual piece of Brazilian abolitionist propaganda ever, rich in both analysis and style and combining mentions of the foreign moral repertoire with the local Radical Liberal tradition. It burnished the tripod of abolitionist rhetoric: with the schemata of rights it stressed the illegality and illegitimacy of slavery in the face of natural and positivist rights. Relying on the schemata of compassion, it painted the slave as a Pietà and slavery as barbarity; and supported by the schemata of progress conducted a genetic analysis of Brazil's social building process and its nefarious colonial legacy of latifundia, monoculture, and slavery. Slavery was presented in terms similar to what sociologist Erving Goffman called a "total institution": "the blood running through the social organism," irrigating the economy, society, culture, and State. As the cornerstone of the nation's export-agriculture, it concentrated land and social power among a clique of major landowners and their clientele networks, that encompassed all the professions and trades, preventing the development of an urban economy, a working class, and a middle class. Deeply rooted in the national lifestyle, it contaminated family and religion and stifled the emergence of a work ethic. It also undermined politics, as the right to vote based on the ownership of land and slaves occluded the consolidation of autonomous public opinion and of independent political parties. As a relational phenomenon grounded in interdependence, slavery as an institution imprisoned masters and slaves within its perverse logic. Abolition would therefore be a question of collective benefit, to be completed with small land holdings and European immigration.

The CA Manifesto also deployed the schemata of rights, in the very best Gama-style, proclaiming liberty as a natural and juridically inalienable right – arguing that "present-day slavery does not have a genuinely legal origin," as no provision was made for it in the Constitution. Accordingly, it demanded the full enforcement of the 1831 and 1871 laws. The schemata of compassion decried "the sweat and blood of fellow men and women oppressed by a parricidal law" over the course of "three centuries of pain." As in *O abolicionismo,* the manifesto manipulated the schemata of progress by cobbling slavery, latifundia, and monoculture into a heinous trinomial that blamed economic inefficiency and social subordination on the landowners, the two major obstacles to modernization. Slavery was killing the city and thwarting the development of the markets and a work ethic. The State, it claimed, needed to free itself of "a policy with no horizons beyond the farm fence."[38]

Both texts were similar in many ways, but the manifesto went further than O abolicionismo. Although not directly stated in the text, it was read as a demand for a collective scale for unindemnified abolition, that is because "Abolition without compensation" was the title of a series of articles Rebouças published in the GT, starting in May that year, putting the economic onus on the landowner. Rebouças proposed to create a market for rural smallholdings by taxation, in a bid to promote rural democracy: "Abolition will bring land redistribution in São Paulo province; the landowners will no longer be able to sustain their territorial monopoly." The State should intervene by creating taxes on larger land properties and introducing credit for the small producer, two incentives for a new type of economy and society. This was a liberal project, but against the landowners, Rebouças proclaimed: "Abolition is virtually sealed ... Now it's time to eliminate the latifundia."[39]

The content was radical, but its procedures were moderate. The manifesto, like O abolicionismo, addressed the political institutions – "Legitimate offspring of the law, abolitionist propaganda has the right to cross the threshold of Parliament ... August, most excellent lordships, representatives of the Brazilian nation: pass it into law." They called for a law while keeping on the not exactly legal free soil strategy in Ceará.[40]

The book outlined the fundaments of the cause, the reasons behind the movement, while the manifesto painted a political path, a line of action. O abolicionismo called for "a mandate in the name of the black race" so as to make a pact, gathering together public opinion, the political parties, the Emperor and the slave owners. That only could mean a gradual, compensation-based abolition. The manifesto demanded immediate emancipation, and not a cent in exchange for it.

This disconnect within the movement had less to do with difference of principle than it did with timing. The manifesto was riding on the wave of the free soil campaign in Ceará that had offered *no indemnity* to the slave

---

[38] CA, 1883, pp. 7, 9, 10, 14, 17, 18, 20.

[39] In June 1883, he began a series "calling for immediate, unindemnified abolition" (DNAAR, May 31, 1883), compiled as "Abolitionist Propaganda. National Agriculture" (GT, Nov. 6, 1883). Letter from Rebouças to Nabuco, Sept. 24, 1883, CIJN.

[40] CA, 1883, pp. 3, 21. It proposed the enforcement of the 1831 law in the southern part of the country, since "the majority of actual slaves" in this region would have resulted from the "unpunished piracy." For the North, it would be enough just to expand the successful strategy applied in Ceará (CA, 1883, pp. 9, 8).

198         *The Last Abolition*

owners. The majority of the abolitionist press argued that the slave owners deserved no compensation anyway, as a matter of principle, but it was the *fact* that Fortaleza had been liberated without it that consolidated this slogan nationwide. So Rebouças published fourteen articles calling for immediate unindemnified abolition.[41]

*O abolicionismo* was the ace up Nabuco's sleeve in staking his claim to the movement's leadership, and he asked his allies to promote it. Pimentel advised him to dissociate himself from Patrocínio's aggressive approach, so that it would not imperil his future candidacy for the House, and warned him against having the *Gazeta da Tarde* lead the field in promoting the book. However, with *O Abolicionista* a dead duck, the GT was the movement's official vehicle and it was there that Rebouças published a summary and the preface to *O abolicionismo*, and Serra, who had managed to unruffle some feathers, his review (another came out in the *Jornal do Commercio*). Nabuco encouraged the abolitionist caucus to publish a string of pamphlets to be called National Reforms, of which *O abolicionismo* would be the opening volume.[42]

[41] Letter from Joaquim Nabuco to José Correia do Amaral, May 31, 1883, CIJN; letter from Joaquim Nabuco to the Baron of Penedo, Aug. 14, 1883, CIJN; DNAAR, Aug. 24, 1883; GT, Mar. 12, 1883. Here it is necessary to make an observation about the terms "abolitionist" and "emancipationist." Where, in the English-speaking world, the former designated those fighting for the abolition of the slave trade, and the latter those calling for the emancipation of slaves, in Brazil, where the movement only gained momentum after the end of the trans-Atlantic slave trade, the distinction was never really pertinent. Some analysts (Toplin, 1972; Azevedo, 2001) use the terms to distinguish between degrees of radicalism, but the fact that certain activists started out moderate and later became radical, and vice-versa, blurs this somewhat. The main Brazilian campaigners used the terms interchangeably. According to Nabuco (JC, Jun. 18, 1884): "... Abolitionist and emancipator are synonyms, and the difference between synonyms is less than insignificant in politics, no matter how much weight it may carry in ideology." When I define abolitionism as a social movement I am supposing the existence of factions and unstable alignments – as opposed to very cohesive groups – that change with the shifting balance of power throughout the political process. I believe that highlighting intra-abolitionist rifts obscures the crucial polarization, namely that between abolitionists and pro-slavery activists.

[42] The advertisement for the book ran the following title: "National Reforms – Abolitionism." Nabuco asked Sancho Pimentel to write about "administrative decentralization" or the "reform of the representative system," Rui Barbosa about religious freedom, and Rodolfo Dantas about education. He kept the topic "financial reconstruction and foreign relations" for himself (letter from Joaquim Nabuco to Sancho de Barros Pimentel, Aug. 31, 1883, CAI). See also letter from Sancho de Barros Pimentel to Joaquim Nabuco, Aug. 6, 1883, CIJN; GT, Aug. 31, Sept. 25, Oct. 6, 1883; letter from Joaquim Nabuco to Jaguaribe, Dec. 21, 1883.

## Results-Based Abolitionism

The CA put the same plan into action first. The manifesto inaugurated the Abolitionist Confederation's Collection, a complimentary series featuring speeches and addresses given at its acts. In so doing, it pipped Nabuco to the post, just as the *Gazeta da Tarde* had slain *O Abolicionista*. Patrocínio seemed to be always one step ahead of Nabuco.

Rebouças reconciled them. He appointed Nabuco the CA delegate in Europe and made the *Gazeta da Tarde* serialize his speech in Milan, when he represented the British and Foreign Antislavery Society. He also put the CA to work promoting *O abolicionismo*: "The Abolitionist Confederation will buy a hundred copies and distribute them to key figures, recommended by Serra, so they can spread the word in the provincial papers. Have you sent, at least, five-hundred to Ceará?" To get around the book's moderate solution, Rebouças commissioned a summary from a trusted abolitionist. That done, 5,000 copies were sent out to the provinces.[43]

A lot? The manifesto circulated far more widely than that, among authorities, newspapers, associations, and every illustrious figure imaginable. The CA changed the abolitionist logic with mass propaganda. It drew upon its extensive membership in the typesetting profession to bash out some 18,000 copies of the manifesto just in Court. It was something to rub the deceased pro-slavery deputy Alencar's nose in: *O Guarani*, his biggest success, had an initial print run of 1,000 copies.[44]

### PORTABLE ACTIVISM

In Enrique Vila-Matas' *Historia abreviada de la literatura portátil* (A Brief History of Portable Literature), the type of literary production stipulated in the title requires "that one's work mustn't weigh very much and should easily fit in a suitcase."[45] The Abolitionist Confederation adopted a similar method, a portable activism, that furthered the movement's expansion by being easy to reproduce.

The CA took charge of coordinating activism in Court, hosting public sessions, conferences, and abolitionist association festivals.[46] It also worked

---

[43] GT, May 14 and 18, Aug. 31, 1883; Jan. 8, 10, 11, 16, 18, 22, and 26, 1884; letter from André Rebouças to Joaquim Nabuco, Sept. 24, 1883, CIJN. Rebouças encumbered "Miguel Antônio Dias – the best of mulattos" and "tireless abolitionist leader" to write the summary (letter from Miguel Antônio Dias to Joaquim Nabuco, Oct. 8, 1883, CIJN; GT, Oct. 3, 1883). The pamphlet was written and distributed, but I was unable to find it.
[44] GT, Aug. 29, 1883; Alencar (1893, Chapter VII).     [45] Vila-Matas (2015, p. 4).
[46] GT, Nov. 26, 1883.

200 *The Last Abolition*

to promote a range of written genres, encouraging small newspapers and making use of the ones already available, as well as publishing and circulating articles, pamphlets, essays, translations, manifestos, and literary fare. The aim was to subsume a whole gamut of disparate initiatives under a national umbrella network. Hence the unwavering search for connections and incessant dispatch of envoys throughout the provinces.

By word of mouth, school, family, and friendship networks and GT advertising, the CA would recruit young men from outside Court to attend weekly meetings or founding ceremonies for new associations (or indeed the re-foundation of old ones). These drew in large numbers of students, many of them pupils of Rebouças and Vicente de Sousa in the colleges, or hangers-on already indoctrinated in abolitionism from frequenting Patrocínio's bohemian circles. The faculties provided a bountiful source of youths from different regions, so all it took was to persuade one of them to create an association, club, or emancipation fund representing his home province. There was already a name template, as a tribute to the Liberating Society of Ceará, which was basically Libertadora plus the name of the province in question. The next step was to send the neo-abolitionist back to his home turf with a portable activism kit.[47]

Propaganda tours were part of international abolitionism repertoire: Thomas Clarkson had done them in Great Britain, and Frederick Douglass in the United States. In Brazil, Patrocínio was the abolitionism-on-tour pioneer. His trip to Ceará in late 1882 ramified into concert-conferences in Bahia, Maceió, and Recife. He would deliver a speech while another activist collected donations and sold GT subscriptions. Many others replicated the method. The report of activities for 1883, compiled by the ever-systematic Rebouças, registered the dispatch of delegates to the capitals of Ceará, Pará, and Pernambuco, as well as to Pelotas, in Rio Grande do Sul. One of these set out in December 1883, after a departure meeting, and toured various northern provinces. The following January, more CA representatives were dispersed to Alagoas, Bahia, and Rio Grande do Sul.[48]

---

[47] In 1883, Rebouças re-founded the Polytechnic School Emancipatory Society and the SBCE. Letter from André Rebouças to Joaquim Nabuco, Apr. 7, 1883, CIJN. An example of a student activist was Dunshee de Abranches (1941, pp. 170 ff.), from Maranhão, GT, May 14, 1883.

[48] Accompanying Patrocínio on his trip was the fundraiser Alípio Teixeira (Magalhães Jr., 1969, pp. 126–7). The departure meeting was for the Paraense José Agostinho dos Reis, a black professor from the Polytechnic School with ties to Rebouças. Rebouças' report is in CA, 1884. Aquino da Fonseca and F. Almeida went to Alagoas; Arlindo Fragosa, from

## Results-Based Abolitionism

Having arrived in the provinces, they started recruiting from their relationship networks, bringing aboard people with abolitionist sympathies and getting them to diffuse Court-style activism: concert-conferences to cobble together new local associations or reinvigorate existing ones from which to launch new free soil campaigns. Ideally, the provincial groups would repeat this approach on a municipal level.

Portable activism was viable because the strategy was modular: its simple syntax facilitated its transposition. While traveling to the provinces, the style of activism in use in Rio de Janeiro went through a tactical adaptation, reduced to a stylized form easy to suit new contexts.[49] The *minimum minimorum* in each new city or town was a stage, preferably in a theater, but association assembly halls would also do, as would town halls or the living room of a local abolitionist, if there was one, and, if not, of a politician, student, or benefactor (often in the loosest possible sense) converted to the cause at the eleventh hour with the embrace of liberty and fraternity after emancipating slaves (his own or someone else's) during a concert-conference. The icing on the cake would be provided by a local artist or poet, but, in the event that neither would be found, one of the town's ladies could be roped in to display her talents at the piano.

Though not everything can be attributed to the CA, the year of its founding saw the creation of 116 associations – against twenty the previous year – throughout seventeen provinces. There was noticeable concentration in the two main hubs, Ceará and Rio de Janeiro, where thirty-one and twenty-nine new groups were founded, respectively, but there was also considerable expansion in the two Rio Grandes, five down South and eight up North, besides eight in Pernambuco and six in Pará. This diversification went beyond the provincial capitals of Rio Grande do Sul, Rio de Janeiro, and Pará. With Ceará still leading the field, the free soil campaign spread through thirteen provinces, including ten provincial capitals besides Fortaleza, namely: Curitiba, São Luís, Maceió, Ouro Preto, Belém, Recife, Rio de Janeiro, Porto Alegre, Desterro, and Aracaju.

---

the Polytechnic School Emancipatory Society, traveled to Bahia (GT, Dec. 30, 1883, Jan. 15, 28, 1884) and Bruno Gonçalves Chaves, to Rio Grande do Sul (Monti, 1985, p. 124).

[49] Tarrow (1995, p. 110; 1998, pp. 37–41) argues that innovations in the forms of political mobilization are transposable to new contexts if they are modular, that is, if they serve as a formula which the new agents can endow with new specific meanings, as with marches, rallies, and strikes. What actually circulates is a stylized strategy, the syntax rather than semantics, as the transfer is never a passive operation, but one that demands "tactical adaptation" to the new context, agents, and local meanings (Tilly, 2008).

202                          *The Last Abolition*

The CA's modular style of activism spread across the hinterlands. By the latter half of the 1880s, it reached where local abolitionism had barely left a mark or had been absent, through a vertical diffusion from Court to the provincial capitals. However, the decision to call itself a confederation as opposed to a center showed coordination rather than subordination of provincial groups to the CA. From the beginning of Liberal rule, abolitionist flashpoints had been proliferating in both halves of the Empire. In 1883, the abolitionist campaign was functioning, with varying degrees of vigor, in seventeen of the twenty provinces. Patrocínio's travels caused the list of local allies to swell fast, and he made good use of Rebouças' little black book, which, in 1882, was packed with solid links to abolitionists in Ceará, Rio Grande do Sul, Amazonas, and São Paulo.[50] Where there was well-established provincial abolitionism, the CA sought alliances. Combined, the strategies of sowing the seeds of abolitionism and collaborating where buds had already sprouted nationalized the campaign once and for all.

### A DISCIPLE OF ABÍLIO BORGES

The free soil campaign was successful where the appointment of an abolitionist to the provincial presidency recognized ("certified") the local activism. The liberation of Ceará was only possible because it was presided over by two abolitionists, with back-to-back mandates. When Sancho Pimentel left office he was replaced by Sátiro de Oliveira Dias, who answered the call of the CA manifesto, according to which: "... a sincere and impartial legislator could summarily decree the abolition of slavery in the North." Dias was another man from Abílio Borges' circle, and had worked as his assistant at the Bahian Gymnasium. He had also participated in Borges' civic ceremonies and was converted to the cause at one of these in 1869, when he made the profession of faith.[51] Borges had introduced him to abolitionism and the Liberal Party had ushered him into the provincial presidencies of Amazonas, Rio Grande do Norte, and,

---

[50] "In Ceará we've got João Cordeiro, president of the Perseverance and the Future Emancipation Association. In Rio Grande do Sul, Maciel recommended Bernardo Taveira [Jr.], director of the Municipal School of Pelotas. In Amazonas, the MP Adriano Pimentel, president of the province's Abolitionist Association, recommended one Dr. Aprígio Martim de Menezes, with a practice in Manaus. ... [And there's Domingos] Jaguaribe at the São Paulo Assembly ..." (letter from André Rebouças to Joaquim Nabuco, Jul. 7, 1882, CIJN).

[51] CA, 1883, p. 8; Blake (1970, pp. 200–1); Dias (1911, p. 199).

in August 1883, upon Manuel de Sousa Dantas' recommendation, that of Ceará.

Lafaiete, still Prime Minister, accepted his nomination as if it were a needle plucked from a haystack. Nobody wanted to take over a province in upheaval. Dias told the Prime Minister that he would only assume the presidency of Ceará if given free rein to grapple once and for all with the slavery issue. "I have waited for an answer, which has not come. Another evasive move which I have interpreted as 'maybe yes, maybe no' ..."[52]

Arriving in Fortaleza midway through 1883, he soon earned the trust of the abolitionists. That was easy enough to do, as he was a former college classmate of two SCL members. The coalition between the provincial government and the local abolitionist movement enabled Dias to enforce the use of the emancipation fund provided by the 1871 law. This he did on August 28. Later, on October 1, he declared before the Provincial Assembly, in an address characterized by abolitionist rhetoric – peppered with mentions of law, rights and reason – that, with society's initiatives having gathered such momentum, "the extinction of slavery was a foregone conclusion" and that it would "not be long before Ceará [became] the first among its sisters, amid glorious hymns of victory, to emblazon its borders with the words FREE PROVINCE." And if it were up to him, it really would not be long at all. He negotiated a high tax on the sale of slaves, and the bill was passed in the Provincial Assembly on October 3. The law was the death blow for what remained of the slave trade inside the province, forced to hold a half-price fire-sale before the law could come into effect. As such, the impact was more symbolic than practical, as there were only somewhere between 3,000 and 5,000 slaves left in the whole province anyway. Politically, though, it made a major splash: here was a provincial government certifying the abolitionist movement against the national imperial institutions. Dias knew he was pushing the boat out: "the law was borderline unconstitutional." "But I 'burned all my bridges' and passed it anyway."[53]

However, he would not be left to stand alone. Between the sanctioning of Law 2034, on October 19, and its enactment four months later, the national government could have intervened in the province's affairs as it had in 1881, so the CA went ahead and commemorated province-wide

---

[52] Dias (1911, p. 199).

[53] Dias (1911, pp. 200, 201). Projects submitted by the provincial representatives Justiniano Serpa and Martinho Rodrigues. The GT noted that slave prices in Ceará "had slumped to 50$," GT, Nov. 10, 1883. Dias (1911, pp. 202, 203).

204 *The Last Abolition*

emancipation as presumed, though not a consummated fact. The GT ran a daily countdown and asked for contributions to the celebrations scheduled for June and promptly brought them forward to March 25, 1884, which became something of a decisive day for slavery in Ceará and for the abolitionist movement.

The euphoria – "after three years of work and abolitionist propaganda Ceará has achieved abolition!" – met with a fierce pro-slavery counter-attack: "The provinces" – wrote one of the Ceará abolitionists to his colleagues – "have waged upon us outright war. . . . and are even calling upon the central government to outlaw us."[54]

## FROM PROVINCE TO PROVINCE

"It's a pity that Ceará cannot inundate the rest of Brazil, invade the strongholds of slavery, where it is truly powerful . . ." This impossibility, which Nabuco lamented early in 1883, would crumble over the course of that year.[55] Ceará had become an example to be followed. The campaign progressed nationwide, albeit with varying results. The virtuous equation took place where three factors combined: a local structured movement with ties to Court, weak political organization of the local pro-slavery politicians, and a facilitating provincial executive. All three boxes were ticked in Amazonas and Rio Grande do Sul.

In Amazonas, the process was swift to unfold, for reasons not unlike those which had prevailed in Ceará. In fact, the mobilization there grew following the SCL's initiative, which sent Almino Affonso there as its envoy. Having been dismissed from his public post in 1883 for hailing the Fifteenth Battalion, and having taken an active role in the liberations of Acarape, where he had accompanied Patrocínio, and Fortaleza, Affonso arrived in Manaus in April 1884, ready to unpack the portable activism. He made an alliance with the 25th of March Liberating Society, founded only a month earlier and named for the date of Ceará's "liberation." Soon other societies were popping up throughout the hinterlands, in Manicoré, Codajás, Manacapuru, Coari, and Itacoatiara.[56] Fast-expanding activism found much reduced slave stock in Amazonas – roughly 1,500 individuals. However, neither demographics nor activism was sufficient in itself

---

[54] GT, Nov. 10, 1883; letter from José Correia do Amaral to Joaquim Nabuco, Jul. 30, 1883, CIJN.

[55] Letter from Joaquim Nabuco to José Correia do Amaral, Mar. 7, 1883, CIJN.

[56] Affonso (1998, pp. 33–5, 44–5).

to bring about emancipation. The decisive factor, as in Ceará, was the existence of a certifying provincial president. Teodureto Carlos de Faria Souto took office on March 11, 1884, two weeks before the date set for the complete liberation of Ceará. He was from Ceará himself, and decided to follow Sátiro Dias' lead, adopting collaboration between the provincial executive and the local abolitionist movement. Souto sent a bill to the Provincial Assembly, like Dias, prohibiting the entry or exit of slaves across the province's borders and designating a budget for the emancipation fund that would be sufficient to buy up the whole slave stock.[57] As there were not many slaves or pro-slavery activists, opposition was minimal. On April 24, the project was approved and the abolitionists celebrated in courtly style, with flowers and music.

As in Ceará, the heaviest investment was in the provincial capital, which, on May 11, was decorated with lanterns and flags. The 25th of March Liberating Society held a concert-conference at the presidential palace, to Souto's delight, and, as had happened in Ceará, the borders were declared closed to the slave trade. That night, a marching band did the rounds of the four pro-abolition newsrooms. At least a dozen new abolitionist societies were formed during this cycle of mobilization, with the support of state representatives and city councils and members of the two Masonic lodges, and they all converged in the Manaus Abolitionist Congress. From May onwards, the local government and abolitionist movement co-orchestrated the free soil campaign, to which end they formed a women's association, the Ladies of the Amazon Liberating Society. As with Fortaleza, Manaus was divided into six committees staffed with excited students from the lyceum and normal school, and all under the benign gaze of the local elite, which stood to gain a lot more in prestige than they would lose in money, as the newspaper O Abolicionista do Amazonas opened a Golden Book of its own and a Black Book to boot, like Court. The free soil campaign spread to neighboring towns. In May 1884, the provincial president distributed freedom certificates to the last remaining slaves in Manaus. A second provincial capital in the Empire declared itself slavery-free.[58]

---

[57] Cf. distribution of the slave population per province, available at https://ia601506.us. archive.org/4/items/recenseamento1872bras/ImperioDoBrazil1872_text.pdf. Affonso (1998, p. 44). In 1869, Amazonas created a local emancipation fund and, in 1882, a tax on slave imports. Saldanha Marinho, an honorary member of the SBCE in 1880 and Republican leader, supported the movement in Amazonas.

[58] Conrad (1975, p. 244). Note the modularity of the names given to the newspapers, which, like the associations, repeated near-identical titles: after the very first

206 *The Last Abolition*

Abolitionism also grew at a steady pace throughout the decade in Rio Grande do Sul, where activism was longstanding, with elite associativism dating back to 1869. Fresh life was breathed into this tradition by the young heirs of ranchers, politically marginalized by the Empire's centralized institutions, yet socialized in positivism, federalism, and abolitionist rhetoric at the law faculty in São Paulo. This group, led by Júlio de Castilhos, joined the São Paulo Republican Party and, back in Rio Grande in 1882, founded its local branch and the republican and abolitionist September 20 Club. Castilhos, an astute political operator, attracted new membership and, in 1884, took over as director of the *A Federação* newspaper, the soapbox for the group's ideas. Two other antislavery factions also grew in Rio Grande do Sul at the time, one Liberal and the other Conservative. Despite never quite erasing their party distinctions, these three factions came together under the Abolitionist Center of Porto Alegre, founded on the anniversary of the Free Womb Law in 1883. The style of activism employed was the same as that propagated by the CA: concert-conferences, the participation of women, and a free soil campaign. However, though the slave population itself was small in Rio Grande, the free soil strategy failed to take off there at first. The province was lacking the magic ingredient enjoyed in Ceará and Amazonas: a provincial president eager to enforce abolitionism.[59]

The mobilization grew in various other provinces, but without the virtuous equation that had prospered in Ceará and Amazonas. Where the problem was weak local mobilization, the CA and SCL in Ceará sent emissaries to shake the local abolitionism movement up. The expanding telegraph system in the North helped spread portable activism farther and faster afield. For example the SCL made direct contact with the Abolitionist Society of Maranhão, founded in 1883, which, in turn, established connections with the Liberating Society of Aracaju. Besides, SCL mobilization hypertrophied: the success of its free soil strategy

---

O *Abolicionista*, the newspaper created by Abílio Borges and his group, namesakes arose in Rio de Janeiro, Maranhão, Bahia, Pará, and Amazonas. Similarly, there were *Libertadores* in Ceará, Sergipe, and Pernambuco.

[59] The Liberal faction was commanded by Senator Silveira Martins, and the Conservative, by MP Severino Ribeiro, who had supported the Nabuco project in 1880 (Kittleson, 2005, pp. 129 ff.; Monti, 1985, pp. 70 ff.). The Rio Grande do Sul group included Francisco de Assis Brasil, Ramiro Barcelos, Argemiro Galvão, Ângelo Pinheiro Machado, Alcides Lima, Homero Batista, Pereira da Costa, and Barros Cassal, all either relatives or friends (Franco, 1967; Alonso, 2002). At much the same time, associations were founded in two other provinces in the south of the country, Santa Catarina and in Paraná, but the campaigns there were gentle.

worked as a demonstration-effect for the neighboring provinces. Rebouças was delighted, fully assured that Rio Grande do Norte, Paraíba, and Pernambuco would follow in Ceará's steps. Indeed, following Ceará's lead, in November, the Provincial Assembly of Paraíba approved a tenfold hike in the annual slave tax. The SCL kept Rebouças abreast of developments in Piauí, Maranhão, Paraíba, and Rio Grande do Norte. In the latter province, proximity to Ceará injected extra impetus, with one campaign feeding off the other. Once again, the SCL's Almino Affonso was a key activist. Born and raised in Rio Grande do Norte, he arrived in Mossoró, on the border with Ceará, to rouse the local campaign based on portable activism, as he had done in Amazonas. He founded societies, held conferences, delivered ten speeches in a single day, and launched a free soil campaign. Amid streets decorated with carnauba palm leaves, it was Affonso who, on September 30, 1883, declared Mossoró the first free town in Rio Grande do Norte.[60]

Mobilization in Amazonas, as in Ceará, rippled outwards. In Pará, the Amazon Club, created on May 1 and related to the associations in Amazonas, published a manifesto in which it called for "the restitution of natural property long usurped" in the Amazon and set up municipal and parochial liberation commissions to promote unindemnified emancipation in a free soil campaign. They also used Gama-style judicial activism, with freedom suits, and created their own version of a Golden Book, a book of honor.[61] The campaigns in Amazonas and Pará grew interconnected, given the geographic proximity among themselves and their distance from the country's capital.

The Ceará and Amazonas campaigns led to regional offshoots in provinces where the abolitionist movement was still weak, but where the pro-slavery resistance was also feeble, given the low relevance of slave labor to the local societies and economies. Even so, and once again in the absence of a local facilitating government, new free provinces were not viable.

Things were rather different in Pernambuco, Bahia, São Paulo, and Rio de Janeiro, all provinces in which abolitionism was already rooted. In

---

[60] *Libertador*, Aug. 15, 1883; Jul. 22, Aug. 12, Sept. 1884; GT, Nov. 10, 1883; letter from André Rebouças to Joaquim Nabuco, Sept. 24, 1883, CIJN; letter from José Correia do Amaral to Joaquim Nabuco, Feb. 11, 1884, CIJN; Affonso (1998, pp. 33–8) founded the Liberating Society of Mossoró and the Spartacus Club.

[61] Many of the concerts were held at the Riachuelo Dramatic Theater (GT, May 22, 1883). The Amazonian Club, May 1, 1884, pp. 6, 18, 19. In Belém, the Viscount of Rio Branco Liberating Society was founded in the mold of the CA.

208 *The Last Abolition*

Pernambuco, the free soil strategy prospered in the capital, Recife, where there was a longstanding activist tradition, with four groups already up and running, such as the New Emancipatory Society; José Mariano, a brash MP, from the 1880 abolitionist caucus; and organizational support from the local law faculty, where students and some lecturers had been engaged in the concert-conferences since 1881. Leaving the movement in Ceará on its set course toward emancipation, Patrocínio visited Recife in 1883, where shortly thereafter eleven new societies were formed, all cast in the molds of the CA and named after the students' home provinces – for example, the Emancipation Savings of Piauí. Recife was the main hub for shipping routes that covered the northern coast, and this led to fruitful interprovincial exchanges between abolitionists. João Cordeiro called there to participate in an event hosted by the New Liberation Society of Pernambuco. This pooling of energies in Recife, as in Court, favored the creation of a local confederation of associations, and this time Patrocínio had his way in naming it; it would be the Emancipatory *Central* of the City of Recife. The Central commanded the free soil campaign and organizing committees. Patrocínio kickstarted this effort, which, were it to prove successful, would free the Empire's third provincial capital.[62]

Likewise in Bahia, home to the 7th of September Liberating Society Abílio Borges, abolitionism was now entrenched, a tradition nurtured by *Gazeta da Tarde*, which emulated the name and methods of Rio, and by *O Alabama*. In 1881, Eduardo Carigé came to the fore as a leader, founding the Liberating Society of Bahia, disseminating Gama-style judicial activism, with freedom suits, and replicating the SCL in blockading the port against shipments of slaves. The blockade took place in the provincial capital, Salvador, in May 1883, and the victim was handpicked: the Baron of Cotegipe, chosen as a symbol of the social slaverism, by being a landowner and slaveowner, and of the pro-slavery politics, by being a high-ranking leader inside the Conservative Party. The Liberating Society of Bahia stopped a slave from disembarking from a ship en route for the Baron's plantations. Notified of the blockade, the first thing the Baron did was change wharf. The steamship in question was flying the British flag, so the Liberating Society of Bahia sent a committee on board to appeal to the captain in the name of British antislavery pioneerism and the anti-slave-trade treaties celebrated between the two nations. The captain would not be persuaded. On the way back to port, the boat

[62] GT, Feb. 15, 1883; Castilho (2008, pp. 55 ff., 77 ff., 85, 155); GT, Mar. 1, 1883.

## Results-Based Abolitionism

ferrying the abolitionists intercepted the dinghy bringing the slave to the wharf and they yelled at the man to jump overboard. Without hesitation, the slave jumped into the water, where he was rescued by the abolitionists and taken to the headquarters of the *Gazeta da Tarde*. The police arrived soon afterwards and took the slave into custody, but the damage had already been done: his escape had become national front-page news. Patrocínio's GT praised the initiative in an editorial and blasted the captain of the English steamship: as British law did not recognize slavery, British ships were prohibited from carrying slaves. All the vessels involved in transporting the slave had therefore broken the law. Cotegipe distilled his rage by suing one of the abolitionists for sedition, and, from the stand at the Senate, demanded repression: either something be done about the unrest, or public order would be undermined.[63]

The third province with strong local abolitionism was São Paulo. In 1882, Antônio Bento de Sousa e Castro – the man who was said to have sworn at Luís Gama's funeral to keep the mobilization alive in the province – took over as leader of the São Paulo Abolitionist Center. A member of the Conservative Party, a white Catholic born into the elite and trained in law, he was, nevertheless, a clumsy man with no love of grammar. He had also been ruffling feathers as far back as 1872, when, as judge and police commissioner in Atibaia, he had championed philanthropic subscription lists to help measles sufferers and ruled in favor of abolitionist lawyers in Gama-style freedom suits, raking up a lot of enemies and death threats in the process. It cannot all have been down to him, but from 1882 onward, Gama-style activism flourished and abolitionism grew in São Paulo. The police commissioner said as much in a report to the provincial president in 1883:

The liberation and abolitionist societies are growing by the minute and have become more demanding and disrespectful of the legitimate right to own slaves. In the capital alone there are over a hundred slaves with manumission fees (Pecúlios) in judicial deposit currently suing for their freedom.

São Paulo was a political hub, with strong Liberal and Republican parties and a law faculty, which plied the movement with new members. In May 1884, these students created the Academic Liberating

---

[63] Also active in Bahia were Jerônimo Sodré and Luís Anselmo Fonseca, both from the 2nd of July Liberating Society. *O Alabama* dropped out of circulation for a while, but returned in 1887 (Graden, 2006, p. 79). See Caires Silva (2007, pp. 250 ff.) on the Cotegipe episode. The abolitionist Panfilo de Santa Cruz ended up being sued (GT, May 2, 1883).

## The Last Abolition

Commission, with ties to the CA. The commission took the free soil campaign to the faculty's environs.[64]

In addition to the provincial capital, activism in São Paulo was concentrating forces in another large city, Santos, a commercial entrepôt and seaport. Without abandoning the law-abiding element (conferences at theaters and freedom suits in the courts), activists in Santos began to flirt with illicit methods: Bento beseeched Clapp and the CA to harbor a runaway slave. Rebouças recognized it: "The slave-strong provinces are few in number and so delivered into the hands of our more hardline comrades." From 1883 onwards, São Paulo abolitionism immersed itself in clandestine activities, creating *quilombos,* and encouraging collective runaways and slave revolts on the plantations.[65]

In 1883, the free soil campaign was advancing in various provinces. However, the feat achieved in Ceará would not be repeated in all of them. The strategy's success had less to do with the demographic and economic relevance of slavery per se than with two key political factors. One was the blessing of the provincial authorities, willing to certify the abolitionist effort, as was the case in Ceará and Amazonas. The second was the ability of the slaveowners to politically organize themselves to resist the abolitionist onslaught, something already active in both provinces with growing slave stocks, such as São Paulo and Rio de Janeiro, and those where slave numbers were dwindling, as in Pernambuco and Bahia. In these four cases, the public campaign grew, but was met with resistance.

Sátiro Dias credited the success achieved in Ceará to the combined efforts of the abolitionists and the provincial government.[66] Indeed, the propitious political configuration for the success of the free soil campaign would involve an organized local movement, with its ties to Court, and a facilitator provincial executive. However, there was another key factor that Dias had ignored: the local degree of pro-slavery political organization. The campaigns in Pernambuco, São Paulo, Bahia, and Rio de Janeiro stalled because of this third ingredient: the pro-slavery political backlash came swift and strong.

---

[64] Brief from Antônio Bento to João Clapp (GT, Feb. 4, 1884). *Correio Paulistano,* May 30, Dec. 24, 1874, Sept. 12, 1884. Though often mentioned, Antônio Bento is seldom studied (Fontes, 1976; Azevedo, 2003, 2007; Alonso 2016). Machado (2009, p. 378) located this document from the police commissioner and mapped other evidence of collective runaways' plots in São Paulo. See also Conrad (1975, p. 239).

[65] Letter from Antônio Bento to João Clapp, Jan. 5, 1883 (in *Revista Illustrada,* May 19, 1888); GT, May 2, 1883; Machado, 2006, p. 378.

[66] Dias (1911, p. 15).

## Results-Based Abolitionism

This was what thwarted the attempt to put in motion the free soil strategy in the imperial capital in July 1883, after a promising start on Rua da Lagoinha, decorated and festooned for a civic procession with cut flowers and the playing of "The People's Marseillaise." In the municipality of Paraíba do Sul (the rural parts of the province of Rio de Janeiro), there were 600 liberations that year. However, in Paulino's heartland, pro-slavery political organization had deep roots, and it mustered its political clout in the form of Plantation Clubs, whose protests echoed through Parliament and in anonymous pamphlets, one of which accused Teodureto Souto of having done in Amazonas "what only a monkey let loose in a china shop would do, or perhaps a runaway from a madhouse."[67]

The movement was growing and bearing out Rebouças' summing up that "From Manaus to Rio Grande do Sul the abolitionist machine is up and running" – a machine whose cogs turned at different speeds across the nation, depending on the balance of power between the spread of the abolitionist movement and pushback of the pro-slavery countermovement. The provincial governments were the tie-breaker, while the central government languished in Lafaiete's "maybe yes, maybe no" limbo. Just in response to complaints from pro-slavery politicians, the national government removed Sátiro Dias from the provincial presidency in Ceará. It was a late show of force in the face of consummated fact. When he left the post, he was a household name and the Abolitionist Club of Recife gave him a hero's welcome at port.[68]

In the light of the government's dithering, the abolitionist campaign cemented activism in rallying public opinion through the concert-conferences, and walked to direct action via the free soil strategy, and to the illegality, encouraging slaves to collectively run away. In 1884, a pamphlet by the Positivist Center at Court, dedicated to Ceará and to the memory of Toussaint-Louverture, the leader of the slave revolt in Haiti, sent the authorities a message from the movement: "Prevarication is no longer acceptable and any government that sits idly by, shirking from leading the movement as it should, or – worse – endeavors to stand in its way, shall be swept up by the wave and barreled under."[69]

---

[67] GT, Feb. 12, 1884. Early in 1884, the president of the municipal assembly agreed to forward a bill that would use a percentage of the town's taxes toward its "liberation" (GT, Feb. 22, 1884, Jul. 2, 1883). The anonymous pamphlet was signed by Um Lavrador (a planter) (1884, pp. 54–5).

[68] GT, May 2, 1883; *Libertador*, Jul. 28, 1884.

[69] Lemos (1884, p. 3). On free soils, cf. Map 11.3.

## 212 *The Last Abolition*

Lafaiete's government was a shipwreck waiting to happen. The optimum conditions for mass mobilization occur when activism acquires efficiency while the government loses credibility.[70] That was the lie of the land in Brazil at the beginning of 1884. Abolitionism was becoming national, expanding its strategies, gaining strength and visibility, with two provinces already liberated. The noise of abolition in Ceará and Amazonas, challenging the central government authority, woke the pro-slavery countermovement from the hibernation they had been in since 1871. Even the somnolent government of Lafaiete woke with a fright, but without the consolation of seeing the nightmare dissipate with the daylight.

### BACK TO THE INSTITUTIONS

While it set about promoting the free soil campaign (or anarchy, as the pro-slavery countermovement at the Lower House preferred to call it), the CA was also pressuring the government with a stepped-up brand of Gama-style judicial activism, filing freedom suits, lodging appeals, bringing denunciations before the courts and the police. To further these ends, it founded the Forensic Abolitionist Center in 1883, transformed the following year into the Lawyers Against Slavery Club, whose manifesto affirmed that slavery, in the absence of a law that had created it, with natural law against it, and no provision for it in the Constitution, had no legal substance whatsoever. The schemata of rights simmered in the GT's "free Africans" section, which denounced illegal enslavements – that is, of Africans imported into Brazil after the 1826 agreement with Britain and the 1831 November 7 law (supposed to have banned the slave trade). On the anniversary of Luís Gama's death and the twelfth anniversary of the Free Womb Law, the issue took center stage when the CA hosted a protest banquet against the law's ineffectiveness at the newsroom of the *O Globo* newspaper, owned by Quintino Bocaiúva, who was president of the Republican Party.[71] Of course, the intertwining of abolitionism and

---

[70] Cf. Gamson (1968). Gamson and Meyer (1996, p. 283) argue that the balance of power varied over the course of the political process, and that the social movements changed their strategies accordingly, adopting whichever was viable under their circumstances as opposed to following abstract principles.

[71] GT, May 18 and Jun. 19, 1883. Leading the Lawyers Against Slavery Club, whose manifesto was published on April 14, 1884, were Araripe Jr., from the CA, Ubaldino do Amaral, from Gama's group, and Sizenando, Nabuco's brother (GT, Dec. 15, 1886). GT, Apr. 19, 1883; DNAAR, Sept. 28, 1883.

# Results-Based Abolitionism 213

republicanism, the dual causes of Luís Gama, was not lost on the political environment.

Gama's style of activism had even seeped into the political institutions. In the Lower House, abolitionism had few MPs, but it was a bit stronger in the Senate. With lifetime tenure elderly senators were more concerned with what that venerable old lady, the angel of history, would have to say about them when they were gone. Social mobilization had pressed some to declare themselves in favor of legal measures in the short term. Senator Silveira da Mota remained the movement's main backer in political institutions. He presided over an abolitionist festival at the Niterói Freedmen's Club and took up the theme of "free Africans" with the Prime Minister. The abolitionists packed the galleries to hear him grill Lafaiete. The Liberal Cristiano Otoni seconded Mota's move, which was couched in Gama's arguments: "... most of the existing slavery consists of individuals imported between 1831 and 1850 and their descendants, to all of whom the law passed on November 7, 1831 now applies." Both men called on the government to produce new statistics on the slave population in order to ascertain how many of them had entered the country between 1831 and 1850 and free them. As such a large percentage of active slaves fell into this category, or were descended from someone who did enter the country between 1831 and 1850, applying the 1831 law would have been tantamount to liberation en masse. With the streets and now the Senate on his back, Lafaiete deferred to the judiciary and took a brief break from his "maybe yes/maybe no" default mode and sent a revised bill of law to the Lower House on August 2, 1883, that would require fixed abodes for slaves and increase the emancipation fund.[72]

The CA gave no respite. At Rebouças' and Patrocínio's request, Silveira da Mota read the CA manifesto from the speaker's stand at the Senate and sent a copy to the Legislation Commission for publication in the *Official Gazette*. Pro-slavery political coalition leaders such as Cotegipe and Martinho Campos (a senator since 1882) could accept the reading, but publication was too much, so they blocked it. In retaliation, the CA exhorted people to flood the galleries, while two MPs, veterans from Nabuco's 1880 bloc, affronted the government from the House stand: one of them read the manifesto anew, in the name of the Abolitionist Center of Porto Alegre, and demanded, as Mota had done, its publication in the *Official Gazette;* the other crowned this institutional

---

[72] ASI, Jun. 27, 1883; GT, Apr. 24 and Jun. 26, 1883; ASI, Jun. 26 and 30, 1883.

## The Last Abolition

attack with a bill requiring the immediate emancipation of elderly slaves – the other flank of the Spanish Moret Law.[73]

In the latter half of 1883, the movement was established in most of the provinces, with public and institutional support (two provincial presidents, some senators, and various MPs), and the government was on the ropes. There would be legislative elections the following year. The movement needed candidates who could be a strong voice in Parliament. Rebouças and numerous comrades were convinced that Nabuco would be the best candidate. The son of Senator Silveira da Mota wrote to him: "The next general election has to be dominated by the abolition issue ... It is, therefore, time you returned in order to prepare your election for the province of Ceará."[74] Nabuco, however, was not in good spirits and broke. In his private life, his on-and-off relationship with Eufrásia was taking its toll, while, on the professional level, he was about to lose his job as foreign correspondent with the *Jornal do Commercio* because he had taken up a similar post with *La Razón*, from Montevideo, without clearing it first with the *Jornal*. He decided to return and wrote to the SCL, saying, for Fortaleza, the only electoral district without slaves, the candidate should be "the best man in the country to promote emancipation at Parliament." For Nabuco, that man was himself: the honor would be "the greatest recompense [he] could be given."[75]

However, the electoral process had incited party-political rivalries within the movement. And Patrocínio and Rebouças, having made their abolitionist quilt with Liberal and republican patches with Conservative stripes running in between, got caught in the crossfire. Owing to these difficulties and some local political injunctions, the SCL informed Nabuco that it would not be launching his candidacy in Ceará.[76] Nabuco insisted and in order to persuade the locals, he resorted to some international figures, and planned an antislavery congress featuring a heavyweight lineup of European and American abolitionists. Rebouças guaranteed the

---

[73] The first MP was the Conservative Severino Ribeiro, and the second was the Liberal from Goiás, Leopoldo de Bulhões, who submitted his bill on September 3, GT, Aug. 29, 1883; ACD, Aug. 30, 1883; DNAAR, Sept. 3, 1883.

[74] Letter from Artur Silveira da Mota to Joaquim Nabuco, Jun. 10, 1883, CIJN.

[75] Letter from Joaquim Nabuco to José Correia do Amaral, May 31, 1883, CIJN.

[76] "... upon consultation, some sub-leaders of the parties in action voiced many objections. During election time, 'The Liberating Society of Ceará' becomes somewhat divided; many of its members, beholden to their bosses, be they Liberal or Conservative, will not be working for emancipation; hence the difficulty in electing a MP who is solely an abolitionist." Letter from José Correia do Amaral to Joaquim Nabuco, Jul. 30, 1883, CIJN.

## Results-Based Abolitionism

funding, date, venue, and list of celebrities. But here the boomerang method failed to work, as the local abolitionists thought it best to focus on the domestic arena. Neither the congress nor Nabuco's candidacy for Ceará ever got off the ground. Another possibility was to run for election at Court. At a concert-conference in Niterói, the night's orator defended Nabuco against the accusations lodged by other abolitionists that implied he had been living the high life in Europe while the public space activists were slogging it out on the ground. Ubaldino do Amaral, from the Luís Gama faction, pulled on the hangman's mask: an acclaimed leader, he said, must honor his responsibilities, not slink away to sulk over a lost election or job – Nabuco's justifications for his European sojourn. Out of sight, out of mind, by absenting himself, he "had erased his very memory from the minds of his friends, to say nothing of those who once feared him."[77]

Factionalism, typical of social movements, gathered momentum in the abolitionist movement. A visible schism was running through the CA on preferential strategies and on whether or not to include doubtful defenders of abolition in its Golden Book. The purists wanted to keep it a very select group while focusing on practical actions: inciting slave revolts, promoting collective runaways, and tormenting landowners. These voices had been there from the start, and included the likes of Ubaldino and João Cordeiro, but they were a minority. However, the success in Ceará, initiated with insubordination and answered with inertia by the political system, had swelled their ranks. On the other side, Rebouças' faction wanted to broaden the movement's base, even if that meant accepting reticent emancipationists and repentant slavocrats. This group believed that slavery would only disappear once and for all with its social delegitimization and legal embargo, without which there would be no citizenship for the former slaves, who would remain ensconced in clandestine *quilombos*.

Patrocínio had a foot in both camps, incendiary on one hand, aggregating on the other. But once the viscera began to spill, he soon realized what they stood to lose – the movement itself. And so, despite his leadership dispute with Nabuco, he stood up in the audience and defended him before Ubaldino do Amaral's attacks. He made a long and emphatic defense of the absent Nabuco, saying that his residence in

---

[77] The Congress was scheduled for August 10 to 17, 1884, at the Grand Hotel d'Orleans in Petrópolis. Rebouças wanted to bring Frederick Douglass as a guest of honor (letter from André Rebouças to Joaquim Nabuco, Mar. 22, 1884, CIJN), but that never happened. At the event in Niterói, the speaker was Campos Porto, from the GT, and the confusion caused the "concert part" to be cancelled (GT, Apr. 23, 1883). Raul Pompeia seconded Ubaldino and debated with Nabuco in the press over subsequent days.

216 *The Last Abolition*

Europe was proof of his political acumen, as it was internationalizing the campaign. Clapp also voiced his concerns, saying that a fractured movement would get them nowhere, and stood down as CA president in protest. This cooled tempers, as the membership called on him to stay. Nabuco, for his part, placated Ubaldino, sending him a letter enveloped in the same silkiness with which he opened doors.[78]

Abolitionism needed unity if it was to face politically organized proslavery countermovement. A CA assembly held in November 1883 healed the rifts and defined the movement's electoral strategy. First, they decided to support as candidates people who agreed with financing manumissions. Later, they considered that it would be even better to have abolitionist candidates. If the CA were to distribute 18,000 copies of its manifesto and convert 10 percent of those into votes, they could elect a MP. And so, according to Clapp, it was decided that the CA would launch three or four tickets in Rio de Janeiro city representing its main factions: Patrocínio and Ferreira Araújo, from the public space, and Nabuco and Serra, from the political system. They planned major candidate coalitions in various provinces. Rebouças booked Nabuco onto a transatlantic liner so that he could launch all candidacies on March 25.[79]

As Nabuco observed in 1884, the movement's cohesion was not born from any substantial consensus, but was rather a consequence of the enemy's consolidation: "... We are now seeing a certain pro-slavery backlash, but rather than damage the movement, it has done us good. As I always say, nothing does propaganda more harm than the silence of the adversary."[80] Divisions, factions, and abolitionist infighting never compromised the movement's unity because it was imperative in the face of the pro-slavery countermovement.

### THE NATIONAL CELEBRATION

It was a Sunday morning, and a band was playing outside the offices of the GT. Liberal professionals, students, journalists, artists, former slaves, ladies, and children had gathered in the streets outside. And off they all

---

[78] GT, Mar. 3, 1883; letter from Joaquim Nabuco to Ubaldino do Amaral, May 31, 1883, CIJN.

[79] Initially, "a group of abolitionist voters agreed to proceed as follows: each vote would cost the candidate two letters of manumission," GT, Nov. 9, 1884. The decision to launch in-house candidates was reached in 1884 (CA, 1884, p. 8). Letter from André Rebouças to Joaquim Nabuco, Mar. 4, 1884, CIJN.

[80] Letter from Joaquim Nabuco to José Correia do Amaral, May 23, 1884, CIJN.

went on a march through the city, complete with music, flags, and banners, to the Polytheama theater, garlanded with flowers and electric lights. The theater, adorned with the whole abolitionist pantheon (portraits of Rio Branco and Luís Gama), was packed to the rafters, with curious onlookers piling up in the gardens. The directors of the Abolitionist Confederation entered to a standing ovation and marched down the aisles before standard bearers carrying the flags of the various abolitionist associations and of the Ceará movement's representatives in Court. Once up on the stage, they sat on high-backed gilded thrones before flower-laden trellises. An emotional João Clapp addressed the crowd. He was speaking for Patrocínio and Nabuco, as the former was leading a similar event in Paris, and the latter one in London, while up North, in Fortaleza, the SCL was also celebrating. The orchestra played the national anthem.

That March 25, 1884, was the first of three days of festivities celebrating the movement's greatest achievement, the liberation of a whole province. Over the last five months, the CA had worked hard to hype the date, ratcheting the rhetoric of five years' worth of concert-conferences and months of free soil campaigning. It was an effort that had focused on liberating blocks of Rio's streets in the vicinity of Rua do Ouvidor. Preparatory parties were held at the Recreio Dramático theater, with portraits of the leaders from Ceará and events held on the promenade (passeio público). The GT had run a countdown, and called for and listed donations: a chambray scarf, mother-of-pearl items, gemstones, satin pillows, a crystal parrot, a feather duster, and an iconic signed portrait of the French celebrity abolitionist Victor Hugo. These would be distributed through raffles, lotteries, bazaars, festivals, that earned the CA, according to Rebouças' ever-careful accounts, the tidy sum of 15:065$560 reis (roughly equivalent to 1.7 bars of gold at the time or 17,733.50 dollars nowadays).[81]

Unsure about how the government would react before the announcement of what was, after all, an act of civil disobedience on the part of a province, the CA invited numerous authorities for the big day, including the Prime Minister and the Emperor. The movement tried to coax public endorsements from key figures, as the pro-slavery countermovement, piling on circumstantial pro-slavery rhetoric, attempted to have the act repressed for being an attack on political, social, and economic order. Lafaiete was

---

[81] GT, Dec. 7, 1883, Feb. 13 and 22, 1884. Between May 1883 and May 1884, the total raised was 24:926$340 reis, the equivalent of a little over two bars of gold (Rebouças, CA, 1884, p. 13).

218 *The Last Abolition*

laconic, and this time the "maybe yes, maybe no" came from D. Pedro, who replied to the CA's invitation as follows: "If I do not attend the liberty festivities it will be because my doing so could be misinterpreted by certain people."[82] The abolitionists interpreted it as a refusal to endorse abolition.

Pro-movement MPs and Senators, ladies and gentlemen, all concert-conference regulars, packed the commemorations. There were declamations, theater sketches, comic interludes, orchestral music, and opera arias. Rebouças commissioned a piece from Carlos Gomes featuring two liberator rafts. The maestro sent over from Italy a composition entitled "Popular March for Free Ceará." The orchestra also played O *Guarani*, some tangoes, and the "Slave Marseillaise."[83]

The nationwide celebrations spread beyond the theaters. The Commercial Euterpean Society of the Devil's Lieutenants carnival block produced the pavilions and gas nozzles were installed free of charge throughout the gardens for a three-day festival.[84] Festivals and bazaars continued for nearly a fortnight. There was a street march and a regatta, prepared by the Liberating Society of Ceará in Botafogo Bay, with Francisco José do Nascimento, the man behind the port blockade in Fortaleza, as a special guest. It was then that he was given his symbolic nickname: Dragão do Mar (Sea Dragon). Roughly 10,000 people turned out for the event, testifying to the strong and voluminous support abolition could muster in the imperial capital.

Such overwhelming support was not confined to Rio. In Salvador, the Liberating Society of Bahia marched from the São João Theater to the Polytheama and ended the day with a concert-conference. In Ceará, from January to March, the SCL liberated the thirty-eight remaining towns, and, on the decisive day, the abolitionists in Fortaleza gathered in Castro Carreira Square to play the Liberation Hymn. A letter from Nabuco was read, and Sátiro Dias announced the magic words: there were no more slaves in the province of Ceará.[85] An apotheosis followed.

---

[82] CA, 1884, pp. 4, 5, 8, 9; GT, Feb. 25, 1884.

[83] Letter from Carlos Gomes to Giulio Ricordi, Jul. 16, 1884, in Vetro (1982); letter from André Rebouças to Joaquim Nabuco, Nov. 21, 1896, AMI.

[84] The person responsible for the festival was the CA's João Ferreira Serpa Jr. (CA, 1884, pp. 6, 7), who would organize the Leblon Quilombo.

[85] *Libertador*, Mar. 20, 1884. The leader in Salvador was Eduardo Carigé, who used the freedom suits, and Teodoro Sampaio, engineer and friend of Rebouças, who had been in campaign for a long time (Albuquerque, 2009, p. 82). Amaral (letter from José Correia do Amaral to Joaquim Nabuco, Mar. 22, 1884, CIJN) informed Nabuco about the reading of his letter. Dias (1911, p. 203).

Nabuco presided over a banquet in London with the Antislavery Society, authorities, and the press, with accounts of the event in *The Times* and *New York Times*. However, it was Patrocínio who repeated, in 1884, the propaganda flourishes that had marked Nabuco's trip in 1880. After Sátiro Dias' decree, all that was missing was for the imperial government to recognize the liberation of Ceará. Patrocínio sought that certification abroad. He visited Portugal, was received by the Spanish Parliament, and obtained high political dividends in Paris, all thanks to the cosmopolitan bonds Nabuco had forged: "One can easily imagine the emotion that filled me. Right there before me was one of the greatest colossi of contemporary history." Patrocínio was referring to the veteran abolitionist Victor Schoelcher, who welcomed him with the same enthusiasm he had Nabuco. They discussed the movement's progress, and Patrocínio nudged the Brazilian presence in the international network some notches to the left, with the help of a French newspaper, which called him Brazil's Rochefort, after the local socialist. He also met with another socialist, the Puerto-Rican Ramón Betances, whose biography of Toussaint-Louverture he admired, and they soon struck up an affinity of ideas. Patrocínio mobilized this transnational network to garner visibility abroad ahead of the March 25 declaration of the liberation of Ceará. Betances helped him muster abolitionists at a banquet in Paris. Thirty guests filled Le Brébant restaurant, among them journalists, MPs, republicans, socialists, and Schoelcher, at the head of the table. Victor Hugo was ill and sent a message instead. At the banquet, Patrocínio outlined the movement's development and said that abolition, blocked by Parliament, was being achieved nonetheless on the strength of "the deep masses of the people."[86]

Schoelcher closed the ceremony with his endorsement of Patrocínio and, as he had done on Nabuco's visit, a criticism of the Emperor:

Do not cease to stoke opinion until you have dragged the entire Empire of Brazil to its feet, following the noble example of the province of Ceará. Rebuke your Emperor, who is said to be a liberal fellow, with the humiliation of being the sole sovereign in all the civilized world to reign over slaves. ... a toast to the full and total abolition of slavery in Brazil and the world.[87]

---

[86] Letter from Joaquim Nabuco to José Correia do Amaral, Apr. 7, 1884, CIJN; *New York Times*, Apr. 27, 1884; GT, Jan. 22, Feb. 27, 1884; letter from José Patrocínio, Mar. 29, 1884 (GT, Apr. 19, 1884). For the celebration in Paris, Patrocínio (1884) wrote *L'Affranchissement des esclaves de la province du Ceará au Brésil*.

[87] Schoelcher (1884), in Magalhães Jr. (1969, p. 150).

## The Last Abolition

220

The boomerang method, invented by Borges back in the 1860s, honed by Nabuco in the early 1880s, and adopted by Patrocínio in 1884, fostered moral opprobrium toward the Brazilian government among the Western powers. And it all resonated in the international and domestic press. The US diplomat in Rio de Janeiro raved about the celebrations in Ceará and Rio, during which he was assured that the campaign would not stop until the entire Empire was awash with liberty.[88]

Simultaneous celebrations in Rio de Janeiro and Fortaleza, London, and Paris denoted the intricate weft of local, national, and international networks that underpinned the movement at that stage, with one level shoring up the others. From theater to theater, port to port, from Acarape to Paris, abolitionists like Rebouças were crowned with the halo of the unwavering and omnipresent. As Clapp proudly put it, they were civilizing heroes who were winning the symbolic battle:

The slavocrats sneered at our conferences, our flowers, our verses and our music [bravos]. They thought that verse and music could build nothing at all; and yet, there they are today, witnessing that words and music can achieve great things.[89]

### BEYOND THE THEATER

From 1878 to 1885, the cycle of abolitionist protests hinged around proselytizing. There were 597 demonstrations in the public space targeted to persuade public opinion and attract new activists. The orderly, law-abiding nature of these events was expressed in a symbol: flowers. Gradually, however, the repertoire of protest techniques expanded. The concert-conferences spilled out of the theater doors. In Court, the gatherings in public squares and gardens that often preceded the concert-conferences turned into festivals, fairs, dawn gatherings, sing-alongs, and street marches en route to the theaters, listed in CA reports as walks, parades, cortèges, civic processions, *marches aux flambeaux* (torchlit marches). Outdoor meetings also proliferated: night and day, and often accompanied by a marching band, street gatherings and demonstrations became routine.[90] Abolitionism became visible in the public space.

In addition to these protest modalities, already used by abolitionist movements elsewhere, the Brazilians invented new and expressive ones

[88] Legation of the United States, May 21, 1884.    [89] CA, pamphlet no. 7, 1884, p. 14.
[90] On the origins of the contemporary repertoire of protest, see Tilly (2004).

# Results-Based Abolitionism

compatible with the local conditions. North-South travel and transport was maritime-based and quays were a crossroads of business, sociability, and politics. Ever since that first blockade of the port of Fortaleza and the enforced redeployment of the Fifteenth Battalion, regattas and a parade of rafts had become one of the symbols of resistance to the pro-slavery countermovement. Abolitionists would march to the docks to see their leaders off or home, and these processions maintained the theater's flamboyant style. They rented and decorated boats to sail during ships' departures or arrivals, when abolitionists were on board. On the way, there would be fireworks, a band playing, speeches, and a hailstorm of flowers. This was how Rebouças was met on his way back from London, and Patrocínio, when he set sail for Ceará. It was also the send-off and welcome home Nabuco received on his various jaunts across the Atlantic. These embarking/disembarking meeting parties proliferated, no matter how short the journey. On March 8, 1884, for example, at the end of a party at the Niterói Freedmen's Club, the activists marched from the theater to catch their ship back to Court, despite the fact that the two cities were very close. From the central port, Rio de Janeiro, this style of activism spread to other port towns, such as Santos, Fortaleza, Recife, Maceió, and even to the train stations, such as in São Paulo.[91]

Adapting foreign models to national contingencies or inventing new forms, the movement was advancing spatially, by appropriating the urban territory, shifting from the theaters into that public space par excellence, the streets. There, support for abolition was amply evident, with buildings adorned with flags, fairy lights, and other decorations during the free soil campaign. Even beer bottle labels and cigarette packs bore the pictures of abolitionist leaders – Nabuco, José Mariano, Antônio Bento. The use of written symbols (Golden and Black Books) and visual markers (camellias in buttonholes, a CA membership sign) figured an abolitionist collective identity that left its mark on the major cities it permeated.

And this identity was substantiated with shared practices. Just like the Borges, Gama, and Rebouças styles of activism, public events in closed (assemblies, conferences, concert-conferences, artistic events, parties, banquets) and open (meetings, street marches, rallies) spaces and the

---

[91] This was the case with the embarkation of José Mariano Carneiro da Cunha, José Agostinho dos Reis, Arlindo Fragoso, Aquino da Fonseca and F. Almeida (GT, Mar. 10, 1884). There were 108 open-air protests until 1884, and 289 other acts of diffusion, intended to enlist new members and garner visibility for the movement.

222                    *The Last Abolition*

free soil campaign functioned as modular strategies replicable for different activists and transposable from one context to another, from the capital to the provinces, between provincial capitals and from these to smaller cities and towns. This modularity afforded the movement both scale and homogeneity to consolidate itself as *national*. This diversity of antislavery techniques turned a hitherto invisible institution into an unavoidable subject and made the abolitionists an ubiquitous presence in the public space. From an elite associativism, in the 1860s, the activism had turned, by the mid-1880s, into a street-level abolitionism. It was now impossible to ignore.

### WITH A WHACK OF THE CANE

Paulino Soares de Sousa and his pro-slavery coalition repeated the same circumstantial pro-slavery rhetoric mantra in Parliament and complained that the abolitionists were causing unrest in the streets and had even provoked the insubordination of a whole province. Martinho Campos summed up in one word what the group thought of the stunt Sátiro Dias had pulled in Ceará, crackpottery.[92]

Abolitionism was getting under their skin. In 1883, the Liberal Afonso Celso Jr., who would convert to abolitionism the following year, slammed the GT, calling it gutter press. Patrocínio hit back in articles, and the response he received was literally slapstick. On June 13, at the end of the second act of *Juanita* at Teatro Pedro II, Celso Jr. struck Patrocínio with his cane as the abolitionist made his way into the foyer from the boxes. Zé do Pato, never one to take a gripe home with him, flew at his assailant, and they brawled in the lobby until being pulled apart by onlookers. Early in the campaign, anti-abolitionist feelings were often expressed in this manner. After the free soil campaign in Ceará, violence began to creep into proceedings. The president of Pernambuco called upon the national government to help to control the abolitionists in his province, while others were attacked outright, as in Vassouras, or received death threats, such as in Recife and Salvador. In São Paulo, the police started surrounding or raiding residences suspected of serving as safe houses for runaway slaves. On St. Stephen's Day 1883, the CA petitioned the Ministry of Justice, in the best Rebouças style: "The government cannot permit São Paulo landlords to go rushing from borough to borough harassing abolitionists." The response: the board of the *Gazeta da Tarde* was

[92] Dias (1911, p. 197).

summonsed before the court to answer charges of slander. Open letters to the Emperor by an anonymous pro-slavery activist and published in the *Brasil* newspaper, loyal to Paulino, complained about Lafaiete's cautious handling of the situation: he had only dismissed the provincial president of Ceará after the damage had been done, and he had taken no steps at all to prevent Amazonas from following the very same path. The Plantation Congress of Recife also petitioned Parliament: they would take up arms unless the government did something to control the abolitionists.[93]

Under a week after Sátiro Dias decreed Ceará a slave-free province, a storm brewed in Court. At the heart of the debacle was the mixed-race Apulco de Castro, whose paper, *O Corsário*, had been stress-testing freedom of the press in Rio de Janeiro from its inception in 1880 to October 1883, when it was shut down. Castro's paper had gone to town on the imperial elite, the government, the Emperor, the army, and pretty much every public figure of note and he was detested for it. The backlash was so fierce he had to go to the police station to request an escort. He and the officer in charge of his protection had barely set foot in Lavradio street when twenty plainclothes soldiers in fake beards murdered him with a single gunshot and ten stab wounds.

Castro had a long list of enemies – even Patrocínio, whom he had called the "Zulu king of the abolitionists" – but he had political allies too. Not only was he a republican, but he was a member of the CA-affiliated Luso-Brazilian Abolitionist Society directed by Vicente de Sousa. *O Corsário* had supported Nabuco's campaign in 1881, and had already declared: "We stand with the people, and abolition is a popular aspiration." On the night of his murder, and three nights thereafter, Castro was avenged by an angry mob that flooded downtown Rio de Janeiro, tearing down lampposts and burning barrels on Rua do Ouvidor. Despite attempts by the mounted police to contain the disorder, the crowd succeeded in laying siege to the ministry building, where an emergency cabinet meeting had been called, obliging the ministers to beat an ashamed retreat through the back door.[94]

---

[93] GT, Jun. 11 and 21, 1883. Other abolitionists were threatened, including João Ramos, in Recife, Antônio Henrique da Fonseca, in Araraquara, and Francisco da Rocha Martins, in Jacareí (GT, Feb. 20, 22, 26; May 1; Nov. 7, 26; Dec. 1, 26, 1883; Feb. 6, 1884). The complaint against Lafaiete is in *Um Lavrador* (1884, pp. 54–5). The petition was sent on August 9, 1883 (Saba, 2008).

[94] Magalhães Jr. (1969, p. 129). Cf. *O Corsário*, Dec. 31, 1881; Dec. 11, 1880, in Holloway (2009, pp. 4, 11). The details about Apulco de Castro's death are taken from Holloway (2007, 2009).

# The Last Abolition

According to the German Carl von Koseritz, who was unlucky enough to be passing through the city on those days, the police prohibited a public funeral in order to avoid further unrest. The government spilled fuel on the flames by arranging an imperial visit to the cavalry regiment heavily suspected of having furnished Castro's murderers. In the days that followed, "large numbers of *capoeiras* (black street fighters) and other 'rabble-rousers'" tried to burn down the Fluminense Casino and cut supply to the gas nozzles on Rua do Ouvidor amid cries of "Long live the Revolution." Though a colleague of Rebouças and Vicente de Sousa in the Central Immigration Society and, like them, an advocate of smallholdings and an end to the latifundia, Koseritz disapproved of the "abolitionists' revolutionary propaganda, inciting colored folks into revolt over the murder of the negro Apulco."[95]

A seven-day Mass was held for Castro at the church of the Third Order of St. Francis, commissioned by the Luso-Brazilian Abolitionist Society, and it was transformed into an abolitionist rally attended by over 1,000 people. Religion, usually part of the enemy's repertoire, in this case provided a more fitting context than the festive concert-conferences. The police, worried about further rioting, forced the local shops to close for the day just in case.[96]

Castro was not murdered because of some slavocratic vendetta, but because he had offended the military. However, an act of force against an abolitionist at a time when so many others were receiving death threats signaled potential repressive waves that could come both within and outside of the institutions. In an editorial, the GT warned that the flowers would start to bear thorns if the government sanctioned the use of violence by the pro-slavery countermovement:

... we will not, then, have any scruples about calling abolitionists everywhere to arms! No qualms whatsoever in sending them out to exact retaliations, because we, acting within the law, were attacked nonetheless ..., history will say that it was not we who took the first step down this dangerous road, and that, if we did carry guns in the streets, it was only after dire provocation, ... and in legitimate self-defense ...

The pro-slavery blockage was undermining the movement's belief in the institutions, and thus in the British model of Parliamentary activism, and pushing it to cogitate insurrection: "If they deprive us of light, we

---

[95] Koseritz (1883, p. 239); Pereira da Silva (1895–1896, p. 526); Koseritz (1883, p. 243).
[96] Holloway (2007, p. 4).

shall conspire in the shadows ..., Wilberforce's quill shares the same sheath as Brutus' dagger. ..." In early 1884, having grown in numbers, geographical expansion, and in political clout, the movement felt strong enough to challenge the status quo. At the same time, the pro-slavery countermovement rearmed itself and reacted. What the country saw then was one pro-slavery and an abolitionist bloc on the verge of contention, pointing to the possibility of a bloody solution such as in the United States. The title of an article Patrocínio then published proclaimed "Civil War" in block capitals. In 1884, therefore, the question raised by Sancho Pimentel two years earlier was more urgent than ever: who would be the new Rio Branco? Who could put the genie back into the political institutions bottle?[97]

[97] GT, Dec. 7, 1883; letter from Joaquim Serra to Joaquim Nabuco, Jul. 15, 1882, CIJN.

# 7

# Votes: A Movement/Government Alliance

### CANDIDACIES

Despite spasmodic attacks from within the movement, Nabuco was its best candidate: he had devoted his whole first mandate to the cause, possessed unrivaled oratory skills, and was the son of a Liberal leader at a time when the party was in power. Then again, the simultaneous publication of O *abolicionismo* and the Abolitionist Confederation's manifesto showed that the movement's proposals had progressed in Brazil while Nabuco, across the water in Great Britain, had remained true to the campaign's original message. If he was to build a platform upon his return, he would have to modulate his discourse.

He planned his arrival to coincide with the publication, in January 1884, of his *Henry George. Nacionalização do solo, apreciação da propaganda para abolição do monopolio territorial na Inglaterra* (Henry George. Nationalization of the Land, Appreciation of Land Monopoly Abolition Propaganda in England). The pamphlet was a commentary on *Progress and Poverty* (1877), a book by the US activist Henry George, which had sold 100,000 copies in Great Britain, and was a good measure of the expansion of socialist ideas in Europe. George identified land concentration as the cause of poverty and proposed abolishing private property through unindemnified state expropriation. While Nabuco opposed an end to private ownership, he was sympathetic toward the creation of a special tax incentive for rural smallholdings in the mold of that introduced in Ireland by the British Prime Minister W. E. Gladstone in the Irish Land Act (1881). Nabuco considered land expropriations, so long as acquired rights were respected, something he felt would be easy and useful to achieve

# Votes: A Movement/Government Alliance 227

in a new country like Brazil, with vast swathes of virgin land. A package including a land tax, the creation of rural smallholdings, the immigration of European peasant families and a taxation policy to accompany abolition complemented Rebouças' rural democracy, and as such, Nabuco's piece was published as part of the CA's series of linked pieces, in print runs of 3,000. This propaganda piece earned Nabuco the epithets of nihilist (anarchist) and "petroleiro" (incendiary) – synonymous in nineteenth-century Brazilian political vocabulary. Of course, this did little to enhance his chances at the ballot box. The SCL launched one of its own members in Ceará, so when he arrived in Rio in May 1884, Nabuco found himself on a ticket he did not want: running for the CA in Court.[1]

Rebouças planned to receive Nabuco with a triumphal march to celebrate the success of the free soil campaign achieved in the Ouvidor and Uruguaiana streets, home to the GT, and in the streets around the Polytechnic School – mostly the work of Rebouças' students. There were to be firecrackers, bands, and fairy lights marking liberated houses and stores. However, the Chief of Police, still traumatized after Apulco de Castro's funeral, banned the event.[2]

With abolitionist growth, on the one hand and pro-slavery bristling on the other, the pro-slavery troop, forged during the Free Womb Law debates, grew with a fury in 1884 ready to fight the abolitionists. Disembarking at port, the gentleman Nabuco had to trade in his silk gloves for boxing gloves.

### THE HUGGER

The Emperor's speech at the inauguration of the 1884 Parliament on May 5 ignored the abolitionist success in Ceará: he only mentioned the revitalization of the flagging Emancipation Fund of 1871. In the meantime, in the

---

[1] Nabuco (1884, pp. 5, 6, 9, 10, 12); letters from André Rebouças to Joaquim Nabuco, Mar. 4 and 22, 1884, CIJN. The *Rio News* supported the movement both in its coverage and with the use of its typography to print pro-abolition pamphlets. Nabuco was still insisting on running for Ceará and was gathering endorsements from "various Cearenses," such as the CA's Araripe Júnior, and Antônio Pinto, a Conservative MP, both of whom were resident in Court, and Jaguaribe, in São Paulo – none of these men had any contact with the daily reality of the province and were unable to define the electoral ticket composition. In the end, the candidate chosen to represent abolitionism in Ceará was Frederico Borges (letter from José Correia do Amaral to Joaquim Nabuco, May 9, 1884, CIJN; letter from Joaquim Nabuco to José Correia do Amaral, May 23, 1884, CIJN).
[2] Letter from André Rebouças to Joaquim Nabuco, May 2, 1884, CIJN; DNAAR, May 13, 1884.

228                    *The Last Abolition*

assessment of the US representative to Brazil, the country was on fire, with slaves murdering their masters and overseers and vice-versa, pointing toward "a civil insurrection." Ignored by the institutions, abolition was fighting its own war. Carlos de Lacerda, a childhood friend of Patrocínio who had stayed behind in Campos, was taking to the stage every Sunday to instigate the scorching of cane fields. *O Brasil,* the mouthpiece for Paulino's pro-slavery coalition, accused the abolitionists of inciting breakouts, strikes, and the murder of rural landowners. It grumbled loudly against Lafaiete's government and called for the immediate removal of Teodureto Souto from the presidency of Amazonas, claiming that "we cannot condone that any province tear up the laws and violate the Imperial Constitution in the act of expropriating slave property."[3]

Lafaiete's long-teetering "maybe yes, maybe no" government finally fell in May 1884 because it lacked political capacity to handle the crisis produced by Ceará's abolition. The Emperor called upon the Liberal Antônio Saraiva, the crisis-controller man, to form a new cabinet. Having purged the opposition of his own party through less dramatic electoral reform in 1881, Saraiva stated the obvious: he could see no way of assembling a cabinet capable of providing "a satisfactory solution to the grave problems raging in Parliament *and beyond,* the slavery issue." The badgering to have the subject reinstated matched the pressure to keep it off the agenda. Saraiva declined the invitation. Nabuco and Rebouças, who had optimistically taken projects to Saraiva, were left breathing sighs of disappointment. The Emperor received two more noes in sequence, prompting Silveira da Mota to quip: "... With a ministerial crisis in full swing, we see the Crown out searching, crook in-hand (laughter), for someone willing to stick his neck out and say: 'I want something done about the emancipation of slaves!'" Mota went on to celebrate the fact that, in the throes of crisis, the time for an emancipator had come, "someone with his mind made up on the matter (hear-hears), with his heart set on a good cause," a man willing to assume "the great responsibility that all others [had] so far declined, namely to form the government that will finally put the issue to rest."[4] That man was Manuel de Sousa Dantas, who, on June 6, 1884, accepted the job no one else wanted.

---

[3] Legation of the United States, report, May 21, 1884. *Brasil,* Jun. 1, 1884. Strikes were a recently invented form of political action, another element of the European repertoire which the abolitionists adapted to the Brazilian reality.

[4] Saraiva, ASI, Jun. 9, 1884, my italics; DNAAR, Jun. 4, 1884; Nabuco (JC, Jun. 12, 1884). Others who declined the invitation were Sinimbu and Afonso Celso (Silveira da Mota, 1884, pp. 12–13).

# Votes: A Movement/Government Alliance

Dantas was fifty-three, wore round spectacles beneath his broad forehead and a vast goatee. He was the outgoing sort, known for being fond of hugging. As an assiduous frequenter of funerals, he spent a good deal of his time in a black overcoat: "I had the slight discomfort this past 22nd of having rather imprudently attended two funerals: one in the morning and the other in the afternoon."[5] As Prime Minister, he made good use of these inclinations towards affability and fatality.

Born and raised in Salvador, Bahia, Dantas was a senator and councilor of state, but he had also been a prosecutor, judge, chief of police, representative in four legislatures, president of three provinces, and minister in three cabinets. He had the credentials to vie for the top spot, but in that he had competition. What made him unique was that he kept a foot in both of the country's main political arenas: the institutions and the public space. A reformist across the board (pro-federalism, pro-immigration, and pro-civil marriage), and a member of Abílio Borges' 7th of September Liberating Society, he had agendas converging on the abolitionist movement's one. He had been a member of Zacarias' cabinet back in 1867, which had introduced the slavery problem into the political system, and he put Sátiro Dias' name forward for the presidency of Ceará. Dantas was identified, and self-identified, with change. His acceptance of the Emperor's invitation to govern was conditional but clear, and he would do so only: "should your majesty deign to assent to *the terms under which I see myself as being able to undertake the organization of a ministerial cabinet,*" adding that "the government urgently needs to intervene more seriously in proffering a progressive solution to this problem [slavery], addressing it frankly in Parliament, which should command its solution (*hear-hears and cheers*). On this issue, we cannot backtrack, stop or rush."[6]

Rooted in the schemata of compassion ("generous sentiments") and progress (slavery as an "anomalous institution") and with the promise not to sacrifice property rights, his speech brought abolition in from the public space through the institutional arena:

It is the imperious duty of government, and in this aided by the Legislature, to draw the line no further than prudence will allow and the civilization must

---

[5] Monteiro (1913, p. 39). Letter from Manuel de Sousa Dantas to Rui Barbosa, Jun. 27, 1876, CIRB.

[6] Letter from Manuel de Sousa Dantas to Rui Barbosa, Jun. 27, 1876, CPRB (ACD, Jun. 9, 1876), my italics.

FIGURE 7.1 The Liberal Prime Minister Manuel Pinto de Sousa Dantas (1831–1894) who came to power on June 6, 1884, on the eve of growing abolitionist mobilization.
**Archive of the Fundação Biblioteca Nacional (National Library Foundation), Brazil. Reproduction by Jaime Acioli.**

impose; only thus can we curb the excesses and unruliness that would hinder rather than furnish a solution to the problem.[7]

Excesses could be read in two ways: those of the movement, or of the pro-slavery political coalition, with their endlessly long finger. Dantas represented the midway point between the movement's demands (immediate, unindemnified abolition) and what the political institutions were willing to negotiate (a phasing out).

"I am the cabinet," Dantas might have said. He was the minister of Finances and Foreign Trade. Justice was in the hands of a brother of his son-in-law Jerônimo Sodré, who had brought the subject to Parliament in 1879. His son Rodolfo was his leader in the House and his godson, Rui Barbosa, the director of his *Diário da Bahia* and a government spokesman. The latter two were brought in from the Martinho Campos

---

[7] Dantas (ACD, Jun. 9, 1884).

administration. To honor his new public position, Rui manumitted Lia, his last remaining slave.[8]

### THE DANTAS REFORM

In rising to power in 1884, Dantas had proved able and adroit, but once installed, one contemporary recalls, he assumed "an ardor nobody had suspected him to possess." He "fell out with friends and won over others, breathed fire into the meek and placated the febrile ire of the impatient, and, throughout a whole year of giving and taking, day after day, hour after hour, he had surrounded himself with the mild yet penetrating perfume of a conviction as strong as it was sweet."[9] He arrived at the government with the steady decision to table a progressive abolition law, although he was aware that he had to negotiate his reform, since it would face strong opposition.

Off the table, however, was the ban on the interprovincial slave trade, something on the agenda of the last few governments, but never passed. Taxes raised on slave exports were a windfall for provinces in financial difficulty: between 1850 and 1881, 222,500 slaves – 7,200 a year – were transferred to the plantations of Rio de Janeiro, Zona da Mata in Minas Gerais, and São Paulo. Slave stocks were concentrated in the fields and wearing thin in the towns, with urban household slaves sold to the plantations in large numbers. Between 1872 and 1887, Court lost 79 percent of its slaves, and Recife, in the province of Pernambuco, 88 percent. Dantas wanted to stem the sales flow at its source, the urban centers. He met with immediate resistance: D. Pedro disagreed, since it would be tantamount to banning the slave market altogether. Rodolfo confided in Rui Barbosa that, without the Emperor's backing, his father was experiencing difficulties in negotiating amendments. He believed he would have to give up trying to ban the inter-municipal slave trade and focus on banning only the interprovincial trade.[10] Dantas conceded on this point, but his "Project 48" hit the slavery system hard on three other fronts.

---

[8] Dantas treated Rui, whose father "at the last hour, entrusted him to me" (letter from Manuel de Sousa Dantas to Nabuco de Araújo, May 24, 1876, in Dantas, 1962), as a son. Manumission letter, Jun. 1, 1884, CIRB.

[9] Letter from "Fr.co" to Rodolfo Dantas, Jun. 1, 1994, CIRB.

[10] Slave market data is from Slenes (2004, pp. 331, 337, 338–9, 344, 346, 350, 351), who says the shortage of workers caused a male exodus to the fields, while the towns and cities retained women slaves as wet nurses. Letters from Rodolfo Dantas to Rui Barbosa, Jul. n.d., Jul. 1, 1884, CPRB.

232    *The Last Abolition*

One was a return to the Spanish Moret law. The Free Womb Law had been emulated at one end of the biological limits model (free womb), and Dantas now demanded the other: the emancipation of slaves aged sixty or over. This group accounted for more or less 10 percent of the slave population, some 110,000 people, plus a further 95,000 who would come of age between then and 1894. By these calculations, slavery would only fizzle out on September 27, 1931, when the younger children of those born the year before the promulgation of the Free Womb Law would reach the age of sixty. The trick was there were plenty of fake sexagenarians out there. The slave registration, prescribed in the 1871 law, was undertaken the next year, but with an abundance of age falsifications. In the opinion of Rui Barbosa, there had been a "general conspiracy on the part of the slave owners, who had tacitly agreed to pile twenty to thirty years onto the ages of their younger slaves so as to evade the November 7 [1831] law," which freed slaves imported into the country after that date. Afraid of registering the actual ages of illegally imported slaves, they had increased them. For example, a slave who had arrived in Brazil in 1845 at the age of fifteen would have been fifty-four in 1884, but as his date of entry had been changed to, say, 1830, that slave was now sixty-nine. In their attempt to dodge the 1872 slave register, many slave owners had transformed large numbers of middle-aged slaves into legal elderly slaves, and, as such, eligible for freedom under the law Dantas was proposing. The falsifiers themselves admitted that half of the country's slave stocks were now legally registered as being sixty years old or more. That was, as Rui Barbosa pointed out, a juridical reality, although demographically impossible. The Dantas Project proposed a new registration of slave stocks, giving the owners two choices: they could either stick to the dates they had registered back in 1872 and grant a major percentage of their working-age slaves their liberty, or they could declare the correct ages of the slaves who were actually imported in or after 1831 and thereby admit their prior ruse, which would lead to a legal challenge to their property rights.[11] So Dantas' age-based project would have released seniors and false-seniors alike, immediately and with no indemnity.

---

[11] Barbosa (1884, pp. 765, 786). The far more accurate slave registration of 1887, without the Damocles sword of no indemnity, found the following: slaves aged thirty to forty, 336,174, forty-one to fifty, 112,097, fifty-one to fifty-five, 40,600, fifty-six to sixty, 28,822 (Conrad, 1975, p. 348). Barbosa (1884, pp. 731–86).

# Votes: A Movement/Government Alliance

Another attack on slavery was fiscal in nature. The project promised to reinvigorate the Emancipation Fund, which was to be financed by two taxes, a 6 percent cut of all national receipts, and an extra tax on slave stocks: 5 percent in large cities, a more moderate 3 percent in towns, and a lowly 1 percent in villages and farms. The idea was to encourage the demographic process already in-course, namely the concentration of slave stocks in the rural zone. In order to prevent Emancipation Fund buyouts from fueling inflation, slave prices were frozen, with caps established for different age brackets.[12] This moderate state intervention in the slave economy, injecting resources into the Emancipation Fund, reinforced the initial abolitionist strategy of freeing slaves by buying manumissions.

The third controversial point concerned the rights of freed slaves. The Dantas Project retook the Labor Leasing Act (1879) agenda of controlling the free labor force. The new reform stated that those benefiting from the Emancipation Fund would remain under Cuban-style tutelage for a period of five years, during which they were prohibited from vagrancy and from moving to other towns. This was a nod to the landowners and a wink to the abolitionists, but with a twist over and above what had been done in former abolition processes elsewhere, the creation of "an administrative, tutelary entity encumbered with fixing *a minimum wage,* obligatory to the employer, *to be paid to the freed worker,* when the former, working for himself or for others, cannot find better rates of pay."[13]

In addition to a minimum wage, the sensitive Article 15 also made provisions for agricultural colonies for freed slaves. Similar to the plans put forward by Tavares Bastos in the 1860s, by Rebouças since the 1870s, and even Nabuco's pamphlet on land nationalization, Dantas' plan aimed to expropriate tracts of land along the railroads and navigable rivers, which would then be "divided into lots etc., for immigrants looking to settle in our nation." The target beneficiary of this land redistribution would be the European immigrant, invited to build America along the edges of the latifundia. However, the project also set land

---

[12] Project 48 set prices according to slave ages, considering their productivity would go down with the years: under thirty years-old, 800 mil-réis; thirty to forty, 700 mil-réis; forty to forty-nine, 600 mil-réis; fifty to fifty-nine, 400 mil-réis. The project banned slave trading houses and set a fine for such operations at 5 mil-réis, and twice that for reoffenders (cf. Project 48, Article 13).

[13] Cf. Project 48, Article 6, item IV. The passage is in Barbosa (1884, p. 770; my italics), which clarifies (p. 773): "During the five-year transition period, the project denies the freed slave the right to work for free or for a merely symbolic wage for the benefit of employers who would exploit the freedman's inexperience, credulity or weakness."

aside for former slaves: "The regulations for freedman colonies will prescribe rules for the gradual conversion of leaseholders of State-owned lands into *owners of said lands* under a tenant-farmer regime."[14]

The Dantas Reform, which came to be known afterwards as the Sexagenarian reform, presented the nineteenth-century citizenry with a bundle of wider and more controversial measures than the emancipation of elderly slaves: the project cancelled ownership titles of middle-aged slaves registered as being older; regulated the market by fixing the prices for interprovincial slave sales; rolled out a pilot plan for rural smallhold-ings and a minimum wage for former slaves and set the date for total abolition, without indemnity, sixteen years from that date.[15] Project 48 was taken up with the model of a new post-slavery society based on wage-earning former slaves, immigrant labor, and the proliferation of rural smallholdings. It therefore expressed many of the abolitionist move-ment's ideas as a passport to Rebouças' rural democracy. And for that, it would face resistance far worse than the Purgatory through which Rio Branco had had to drag his Free Womb Law. Dantas would have to descend into Hell.

DON'T STOP

In order to push through his reform Dantas would need to distribute a lot more than hugs. He needed MPs' votes. His motto was "don't stop, don't rush, don't backtrack," but he was at risk of never getting started at all. Without a solid parliamentary base, he wavered between persuading Parliament and dissolving it.[16] The makeup of the Lower House explained much of the instability of previous Liberal governments. As it had been elected in 1881, under the law that had restricted enfranchise-ment in order to combat fraud and ensure representation for the oppos-ition party, the opposition was indeed strong, with forty-seven Conservatives. The Liberal majority ran to seventy-five MPs, but this advantage was relative only, as the reforms on the agenda since 1878 had split the party down the middle. The Conservative minority was therefore what swung the vote. Between 1878 and 1885, the power

---

[14] Dantas (ACD, Jun. 9, 1884); Project 48, Article 2, item 15.
[15] Barbosa (1884, p. 747). The project also released slaves over the age of sixty who were listed in wills (Barbosa, 1884, p. 774).
[16] Letter from Manuel de Sousa Dantas to Rui Barbosa, Jul. 24, 1884, CPRB.

## Votes: A Movement/Government Alliance

to make, break, or resurrect cabinets depended on which coalitions emerged from the struggles among the three factions. The Conservative minority alliance with the moderate Liberals had sustained the Saraiva and Martinho Campos governments and sunk both Paranaguá and Lafaiete. Would it be any different with Dantas?

Not if it depended on the Conservatives. After the schism over the Free Womb Law, the party had reunited in 1884, and, as Dantas had to recognize, it was a pretty galvanized bloc. In the South, Paulino Soares de Sousa led the party with an iron hand, with his sidekick Andrade Figueira, an explosive speaker, while João Alfredo Correia de Oliveira and the Baron of Cotegipe ran the show in the North. They were united on the slavery issue and, as Nabuco observed, in support of the "black pennant of the pro-slavery reaction."[17]

From this Conservative stonewall, the cabinet stole three bricks. Only one immediately escaped Paulino's whip to join the twenty-eight Liberals who endorsed Project 48. These supporters hailed from thirteen provinces: Dantas had his fellow Bahians on board, but also Pernambuco. Between dribs and drabs, the Prime Minister controlled a third of the Lower House. In spite of not achieving a majority, Dantas trusted himself. An adversary defined his personality in this way: he was "like those Homeric giants pleased when fighting battles with a great number of enemies. ... Nobody relied as much as him on luck!"[18]

Dantas also had ample backing from outside the political institutions. The task of enlisting this support fell to his son Rodolfo, a man of gentility and finesse capable of weaving together fast-knit alliances. Mild-mannered like his father, he curried favor among the newsrooms and had a knack for defusing enemies, such as Martinho Campos, who, having fallen ill, was thankfully far less virulent in 1884 than he had been in 1871. Rodolfo sealed an alliance between the cabinet and the

---

[17] Dantas (ACD, Jul. 9, 1884); Nabuco (CIJN, Jul. 19, 1884).

[18] The Conservative abolitionists were Severino Ribeiro, Antônio Pinto, and Alfredo Taunay. The last one was a friend of Rebouças and the two joined in forming another association, the Central Immigration Society (letter from André Rebouças to Joaquim Nabuco, Mar. 4, 1884, CIJN). In Pernambuco, Dantas could count on the leadership of José Mariano, and, in Rio de Janeiro, brought aboard the Liberals Adolfo Bezerra de Menezes, author of an emancipationist pamphlet in the 1860s, and the recently-converted Afonso Celso Jr., the man who had struck Patrocínio with his cane the previous year. The description of Dantas' behavior is from the Conservative Ferreira Viana (ACD, Jul. 31, 1884).

236    *The Last Abolition*

abolitionist movement. At the beginning of the decade, he had withheld support for the Nabuco Project, but with his father as Prime Minister, he made up with his old friend and encouraged him to turn out for the government in the coming elections. He was the ideal name, the son of an emancipationist Liberal statesman, known for his eloquence and pivotal position between the political system and social mobilization. Nabuco was glad to have another pillar on which to prop his candidacy. "On not a single point in its program will the new government find itself bereft of abolitionist support," promised Nabuco in his column in the *Jornal do Commercio*.[19]

Dantas senior and junior urged Rui Barbosa to include suggestions from the movement in the wording of the project. Rodolfo worked his charm on abolitionist friends and acquaintances from Teixeira Mendes' positivist lectures and came away with an open letter in support of the new government, describing Dantas as the leader who would place the government at the helm of social movement. This government/movement alliance was cemented by Patrocínio, to whom they looked for suggestions while writing the project. Patrocínio provided books and documents and sent them to Barbosa with whole passages underlined so that he could find them easily. He put himself at the government's disposal: "If I have omitted anything important on the matter discussed with MP Rui, just let me know ... and I'll send it to you straight away." Patrocínio also dedicated the GT's 12,000-copy circulation to praising Dantas and pillorying Paulino.[20] The movement and the government were teaming up.

Rebouças ran articles in the GT with such titles as "Resistance to abolition" and tried to eke out some space in the nation's most respected

---

[19] Letter from Rodolfo Dantas to Rui Barbosa, Apr. 12, 1878, CPRB; letter from Rodolfo Dantas to Rui Barbosa, Jul. 3, 1884, CPRB; letter from Rodolfo Dantas to Joaquim Nabuco, n.d., Apr. 1884, CIJN, JC, Jul. 13, 1884. Rodolfo ran a legal practice with his brother-in-law Jerônimo Sodré Pereira, unelected, and was a personal friend of Silveira da Mota Jr. and Gusmão Lobo.

[20] Letters from Rodolfo Dantas to Rui Barbosa, Jul. n.d., 1884 and Aug. 2, 1884, CPRB. Patrocínio wrote to Rui: "I will send the discussions from [18]27 underlined, as for the complaints from 1830 and 31 ... Eusébio [de Queirós]'s speech is of immense value, as it proves that there was intent to evade the law"; letter from José Patrocínio to Rodolfo Dantas, Jul. 26, 1884, in Magalhães Jr. (1969, p. 169). The pro-Dantas positivist declaration is in Lemos (1884, p. 62). There was disagreement. Raul Pompeia considered the support to Dantas a "lowering of arms": "Abolitionism has become this trivial thing: a government prop" (CIRD, Aug. 24, 1884).

## Votes: A Movement/Government Alliance

broadsheet, the *Jornal do Commercio*, in which, since March 1884, he had been touting his project of land nationalization through progressive taxation. But he wanted more, specifically a column for the movement, and he had a plan B: if the *Jornal do Commercio* refused, they would go to the *Gazeta de Notícias*, a medium-circulation paper, instead. Gusmão Lobo, who worked for the *Jornal*, offered a counter proposal that would enable them to dribble their way around the paper's moderate editorial line. The abolitionists could have the "A Pedidos" (Readers section).[21] Starting in June, they were allowed to use this space as long as they wrote under pseudonyms.

They looked to the foreign antislavery repertoire for fitting pen-names. Rui, who also wrote for the *Diário da Bahia*, adopted the moniker Count Grey, after one of the authors of the law that abolished slavery throughout the British Empire. Gusmão Lobo took the name of the greatest English propagandist of them all, [Thomas] Clarkson. Others, such as Rodolfo Dantas, borrowed the names of William Wilberforce, the Earl of Chatham, Thomas Buxton, Abraham Lincoln, and John Bull, in this case, the codename for Sancho Pimentel, whom Dantas appointed to the presidency of Pernambuco. These references earned the section the nickname "Mr. Dantas' Englishmen."

Nabuco adopted an American name already used by Lobo, which reflected his changed role in the campaign. At the start of the decade, as a MP, he had emulated the parliamentary strategy of Wilberforce. In 1884, with no mandate, he needed to associate himself with a less aristocratic figure. Frederick Douglass was off the table, having been commandeered by Patrocínio and Rebouças, so Nabuco opted for William Lloyd Garrison (1805–1879), the bold propagandist who had edited the high-impact newspaper *The Liberator*, founded antislavery societies, and had been one of the first white Americans to call for immediate abolition. Signing as Garrison indicated his willingness to engage outside of the political institutions, swapping the speaker's stand in Parliament for the town square, and going deep into the everyday task of canvassing door to door, as in the freedom soil campaigning. He was prepared to work with street-level abolitionists, just as Garrison had with Douglass.

---

[21] DNAAR, Mar. 11 and 25, 1884; letter from André Rebouças to Joaquim Nabuco, Apr. 7, 1883, CIJN. Nabuco called him the "great unknown behind the abolitionist idea" (ACD, May 11, 1885).

FIGURE 7.2 Opponents attacking the progress of the Dantas Reform.
Archive of the Fundação Biblioteca Nacional (National Library Foundation), Brazil.

In his newspaper column, between June and October, Nabuco, under the pen name Garrison, commented on the parliamentary debate, urged swing voters to join the government, called for the re-founding of the Liberal Party, and the modernization of the Conservatives, and goaded

## Votes: A Movement/Government Alliance

the Emperor to stand up and be a true statesman. Picking apart the "slave-based feudalism" of Paulino and his cronies, Nabuco took the parallels with the Americans to heart and began to display some Patrocínio-style verve: "...Brazil finds itself embroiled in a fierce political combat, which would be civil war were the pro-slavery defenders amongst us nearly as brave as those in the southern United States ... it is no longer possible to stop, or backtrack, but we can hurry, especially if the resistance proves blind." Of the abolitionists without mandates, Nabuco was one of the most assiduous frequenters of Parliament, where the galleries were packed with supporters eager to watch the skirmishes between "two phalanxes: one, championing a national aspiration, the other, the misconceived interests of a class."[22]

The side fighting for this national aspiration, the alliance between the government and the movement, revealed itself on July 10, 1884. With certifying authorities of all types in attendance, civilian, military, and even ecclesiastical, the provincial president, Teodureto Souto, amid effusive enthusiasm from the movement and with the approval of the national government, declared Amazonas a free soil territory. As massive celebrations filled the streets of Manaus, Souto addressed the crowd in the name of civilization and the nation, relying on abolitionist rhetoric. He was received with confetti, flowers, concert-conferences, a gun salute, a march to the Liberty Pavilion in Pedro II Square, and a procession of twenty freedmen in white suits and straw hats. Amazonas had become the second liberated province in the Empire. Celebrations proliferated throughout the country. Wherever he went on his triumphant journey to Court, Teodoreto Souto was given a hero's welcome.[23]

With the backing of the central government, the abolitionists wanted to repeat the action in other provinces. Clapp, the eternal president of the CA, summed up just how fully the movement felt represented by the new government: "Dantas' cabinet had the courage to retrieve abolitionist propaganda from the squares and streets and make it echo throughout the halls of Parliament." The movement was characterized by indefensible cooperation, lamented the pro-slavery political coalition, with one of its members referring to the abolitionist clubs, acts, and articles in the press as "encouraged, sponsored and directed by the Prime Minister." Paulino was there to create obstacles, and that he did. He blocked a motion in the Lower House that would have congratulated Teodureto Souto on the

---

[22] JC, Jun. 18, Jul. 16, 27, and 30, 1884.
[23] Affonso (1998, pp. 28–9, 45); *Libertador*, Jun. 10, 1884.

240                    *The Last Abolition*

liberation of Amazonas, arguing that it was forbidden for Parliament to endorse "illegalities and acts of violence."[24]

## DON'T RUSH

The US diplomat in Brazil, Charles Trial, did the arithmetic: according to the official figures from 1882, there were 1,346,648 slaves in the Empire; 1.7 million if one counted the ones released into tutelage by the Free Womb law. With the overall population standing at 10.1 million, that meant one in every six Brazilians was a slave. The magnitude of interests involved explained why slave owners were so set against any changes in the prevailing legislation. The project in itself, and the alliance between the government and the abolitionist movement, sent chills down the spines of Paulino and his fellow Conservatives, both inside and beyond the political system. A member of one of the Plantation Clubs called upon the police to do something about the abolitionists' conferences and their involvement in slave runaways, which he believed the CA was behind: "... these plans can be traced back to Rua de Uruguayana [where the CA kept its headquarters], just like those for the manumission of slaves over sixty, and that's when they are not the reveries of that illustrious lunatic [Rebouças], such as the geometric land tax." Patrocínio and Rebouças were accused of being the masterminds behind the Dantas Reform.

For these reasons and others, whenever Dantas had to wrangle with the slave owners, he came back empty handed. Out of Paulino's ranks came the sardonic Ferreira Viana, a straight-shooter whose tongue knew no protocol: on one occasion he had called the Emperor a cartoon Caesar. It was Viana who came out in 1884 plying the pro-slavery rhetoric born on the eve of the Free Womb Law debates in 1870. Freeing the slaves, a Christian act, would have been a moral imperative were it not for the fact that the financial recoil would trigger chaos like that experienced in the United States: "On this matter we cannot get ahead of ourselves. The issue permits only one of two solutions: due process of law, or revolution. Either one of the parties seizes the revolutionary bull by the horns and pulls off a coup d'état, or we must obey the existing law, progressively honing it until the evil [of slavery] is finally extinguished." If Dantas fully sponsored slave reform it would bring the twin evils of civil war and bankruptcy to Brazil. Or, in the words of a shocked English

---

[24] CA, Jun. 7, 1885; Pereira da Silva (1895–1896, p. 532); *Brasil*, Jul. 24, 1884. Severino Ribeiro proposed the congratulatory motion.

# Votes: A Movement/Government Alliance 241

visitor, "These Abolitionists, as far as I can see, are Brazil's Nihilists and Socialists, and they exercise great influence among the slave population."[25]

The rhetoric of reaction deployed in 1871, with its triptych of perversity, futility, and jeopardy arguments, provided the template again in 1884. The old naysayers of the Free Womb Law were now dressing themselves up as its Paladins. Slavery had been over since 1871, said Paulino, Martinho Campos, Andrade Figueira, just as they had said in 1871 that slavery had in fact ended with the ban on the transatlantic slave trade in 1850. Chronos was still the god they prayed to. Dantas' Reform would fly "the flag of danger," trigger a "hecatomb," which would, Ferreira Viana was quick to add, push the Conservatives to republicanism.

The Dantas Project suffered opposition on two fronts, one inside and the other outside of Parliament. It sent high-voltage shockwaves of uncertainty sizzling through the economy. Were it to pass into law it would affect the rural producers, their brokers, and middlemen, who controlled two-thirds of all mortgages as a collateral. The market reacted skittishly, with the banks cutting credit and slave prices plummeting and dragging the price of acreage down with them, despite the booming international coffee market. The abolitionist play *A Corja opulenta* (The Opulent Horde) summed it up: a slave trader persuades a landowner to sell off his slave stocks before they became worthless. Many flesh-and-bone traders were doing the very same. The market raised the alarm: banks started refusing slaves as collateral on loans.[26] The feeling among those whose business depended on slaves was that the government had abandoned them.

Patrocínio summarized: "the agricultural oligarchy" hated the Dantas Reform. Groups forged and nourished by slavery protested against it, claiming that it threatened the very fundamentals of the economy, and the hierarchies of social prestige and political power, in short, their way of life. Like the abolitionists, they appealed to the institutions: associations and town councils petitioned the Lower House. Dantas responded to the three main formal denouncements against abolitionist propaganda, which all demanded some guarantee of public peace. In 1884, twenty-four petitions were lodged against Project 48. Complaints were neither

---

[25] Legation of the United States, May 21, 1884. The complaints against Rebouças are in *Um Lavrador* (1884, pp. 55, 62); ACD, Jun. 9, 1884. The Englishman was Dent (1886, p. 287).

[26] Pang (1981, pp. 358, 363, note 78). The piece was by Nunes (1884). On the mortgages, see Mello, in Slenes (2004, p. 357).

242 *The Last Abolition*

restricted to the old coffee region of the Paraíba Valley, nor to the new and modern coffee-producers from São Paulo's hinterlands. Many petitions arrived from Minas Gerais – Martinho Campos' stronghold – and from six other provinces. They were voluminous in signatures and intense in their wording, as seen from the following, dated July 8, from Salvador and Recôncavo:

More than a patrimonial asset, more than an element in private fortunes, the slave is a social institution, an integral part of labor, a force of production, an aspect of national wealth ... the growers and traders of this province cannot but express their just fears at the abolitionist propaganda leveled against them ...[27]

Dantas had a hard time having these petitions dropped.

The shoe was now on the other foot. It was the pro-slavery political coalition's turn to be cut adrift by government. With their faith in the institutions undermined, they decided, like the abolitionists had before them, to vent their frustrations in the public space. Since 1871 there had been a diffuse social resistance from the slavocrats, whose way of life was based on the slavery economy. In 1884, with slavery being threatened by the government, this opposition took the form of organized political action, as a social countermovement that fought to preserve slavery, backing the political coalition inside the political institutions, with mobilization within the public space – in short, a *political pro-slavery activism*. This pushback loomed large, but it was actually twofold, with a social support network out in the open and a shadow network pieced together underground, which Nabuco called "Slavocratic Masonry." The civil associations' resistance to abolition emerged with a new surge of Plantation Clubs. The first wave had appeared during the free womb debate, followed by another batch when the Liberals came to power in 1878, with the organization of a Planters Congress in Rio and another in Recife. The growing of the abolitionist mobilization in 1883 triggered a

---

[27] GT, Jul. 19, 1884; ASI, Jul. 1884, in Fonseca (1887, pp. 285, 286). Dantas replied to the complaints of Rio Novo, Barbacena, and Sarandi. See also Pang (1981, p. 349). Mobilization is always mobilization against someone else's beliefs and interests. When a social movement threatens the interests of social elites that have the power to respond, a countermovement emerges (Meyer and Staggenborg, 1996, p. 1635). The relationship between the two is dialogic: they vie for social legitimation and the State's power of implementation and play this political game in two arenas: the political institutions and public space. Studies on Brazilian abolitionism tend to overlook the relationship between the movement and the countermovement. Bethell (1970) pointed this out, saying that the first social movement in Brazil concerning slavery was in favor of preserving the African slave trade.

## Votes: A Movement/Government Alliance 243

TABLE 7.1 *Anti-Dantas' Reform petitions sent to Parliament, 1884–1885*

| Province | Petitions |
|---|---|
| Minas Gerais | 12 |
| Rio de Janeiro | 4 |
| São Paulo | 4 |
| Espírito Santo | 2 |
| Bahia | 1 |
| Pernambuco | 1 |
| Total | 24 |

*Sources:* Conrad (1975), Pang (1981), Saba (2008), Fonseca (1887), ASI (1884).

third pro-slavery onslaught, with a new Planters Congress in Recife and the creation of associations in almost every municipality in the Zona da Mata region, in Pernambuco. In 1884, Plantation Clubs multiplied fast, with forty-nine robust and raging units hatched that year.

Emulating the CA, the Plantation Club in Court set up provincial and municipal chapters and subsumed like-minded organizations. The club in Vassouras set the mold for a national anti-abolitionist associations wave. In São Paulo, these associations had an immigrant twist, with one eye on the future. Paulino's Paraíba Valley and the Zona da Mata region of Minas, where the dominant tense was past, were home to thirty-nine of the forty-nine clubs, formed by plantation owners, coffee middlemen, brokers, and financiers of slave-driven businesses, all eager to freeze the clock with palliative measures and injections into the Emancipation Fund, or to control the countdown to an indemnity-based abolition; some were talking in terms of seven years down the road.[28]

The Rio de Janeiro City Trade Association issued a manifesto and the president of the Santo Antão Plantation Club, a member of the Recife Planter Congress, spoke for his fellows when he said: "Immediate abolition presents a terrible danger: I am against it, in the interests of the nation, the masters, and slavocrats, upon whom it would be a most mournful imposition." Unabashed pro-slavery citizens took to the pages of papers like *O Brasil*, run by Rio's Conservatives, to attack the CA and the government.

Again, like the abolitionists, the pro-slavery clubs created a national Plantation Congress in July 1884, when Dantas was presenting his project

---

[28] JC, Sept. 3, 1884; ACD, Jun. 9, 1884; Hoffnagel (1988, p. 197). On the Plantation Clubs and their actions, see Pang (1981, pp. 337–40, 350, 353–4, 356, 362).

244                           *The Last Abolition*

in Parliament. They called for Chinese servitude to replace African slavery. If abolitionism was transnational, so was its adversary: the Congress' main interlocutor was a Portuguese coffee broker. However, this public backlash had clandestine tentacles: the civil militias. Nabuco denounced collusion between the parliamentary pro-slavery coalition and the underground one, which created a "system of terror and persecution the Plantation Clubs ha[d] been waging nationwide with the express approval at the Senate of a former Prime Minister, Mr. Martinho Campos," restored to good health and back at Paulino's side.[29]

Following the abolitionist example, the pro-slavery countermovement coopted strategies from the foreign repertoire, especially that of the American Confederacy. Cristiano Otoni, who had stuck with the abolitionists, took to the Senate to decry that armed gangs expulsed lawyers arguing freedom suits and even of judges who had ruled in their favor. He also reported gruesome cases of jailed slaves breaking out of prison only to be hacked to pieces in the town square. Brazil, in his opinion, was beginning to have US-style lynchings.

Where, hitherto, the reaction had been more in the style of an occasional whack of a cane than the mob murder of Apulco de Castro, things took a violent turn in 1884. There was mudslinging and slander (Nabuco was accused of owning slaves) and police repression, for instance in Sergipe, where the president of the Liberating Society of Aracaju was jailed for inciting slave runaways. Andrade Figueira demanded the dismissal of abolitionist civil servants and action against Rebouças, the "Polytechnic [College] agitator." In this he obtained some success, as Rebouças himself registered: "Under pressure from the Senate, the imperial ministry has barred the Abolitionist Centre [The Polytechnic School Emancipatory Society] from functioning out of the Polytechnic and that I associate the institution's name with my abolitionist writings." On a local level, pro-slavery bully boys were out in force. The *Gazeta da Tarde* in Bahia denounced contracts being taken out on the lives of Patrocínio and other abolitionists. Nabuco protested: "What sort of country condones the creation of associations intent on generating a system of complete intolerance and persecution against a parcel of the population ..., what else could such a threat be than the declaration of civil war ...?" If the pro-slavery revolver was being cocked, the abolitionist sword was being drawn

---

[29] JC, Jun. 22, 1884. The President of the Santo Antão Plantation Club was Beltrão (1884, p. 8). Nabuco, JC, Jun. 13, 1884. The mentioned Portuguese was Ramalho Ortigão (Pang, 1981, p. 348).

from its sheath: "... the bucket of slavery's crimes is already so full that a single drop of abolitionist blood will make it overflow."[30]

## DON'T BACKTRACK

On July 15, minister Rodolfo Dantas read out his father's project in Parliament. He was barely finished when the world came crashing down around his ears. The government found itself stonewalled by the forty-seven Conservative MPs and a dissident splinter group of nine of the seventy-five Liberals. Together, they made up almost half the House and they denied Dantas everything, including, the Prime Minister complained, the most run-of-the-mill administrative measures. Worst of all, they refused to put the budget to a vote. In order to block the emancipation bill, the Speaker of the House, Antônio Moreira de Barros, from São Paulo, a man whom Patrocínio had dubbed a member of the "Unholy Alliance," sparked an institutional crisis. He created a problem for the government of his own party by resigning from his post. The government had to regroup in the face of a three-faction Parliament – pro-government Liberals, dissident Liberals, and the Conservative minority. Dantas, however, managed to twist the arms of half the Parliament because the same political realism that had led so many MPs to vote for the Free Womb Law in 1871 drove as many again to shore up the government. MPs from seventeen provinces, for whom the liberation of Ceará had sounded alarm bells – the fear of seeing facts outstrip the parliamentary vote – stood with the government against the Speaker of the House. It was enough to win the first round, barely, and on points. Dantas had survived the first charge fifty-five to fifty-two, with swing votes poached from under Paulino's nose.[31]

Having weathered one storm, Dantas scheduled another for August 1: the opening of the debates on his project. The opposition, however, was not content to wait, and went straight for the jugular on July 28, bringing two motions to the floor. The first of these, which did not make explicit reference to the project, Dantas was able to bury. The second, brought by

---

[30] Otoni, ASI, Jul. 9, 1884; JC, Oct. 30, 1884; letter from José Correia do Amaral to Joaquim Nabuco, May 9, 1884, CIJN; DNAAR, Jun. 21, 1884; Nabuco (1884, p. 10). Nabuco, JC, Jun. 18, 1884; GT (Bahia), in Magalhães Jr. (1969, p. 161).

[31] ACEI, Jul. 29, 1884. Decree 3227, Jun. 27, 1884; Patrocínio, GT, Jul. 19, 1884; ACD, Jul. 15, 1884. Dantas' greatest support came from Rio Grande do Sul, which voted as a bloc, and from Bahia, his home province, which gave him eight votes. He also asked for the votes of two Conservative abolitionists, Antônio Pinto and Severino Ribeiro (letter from Manuel de Sousa Dantas to Rui Barbosa, Jul. 24, 1884, in Dantas, 1973).

246                                  *The Last Abolition*

a Liberal dissident, rejected the reform and called for the government's collapse. This motion led to vicious debate, replete with protests, flaring tempers, shout-downs and posturing.

So who was to come to the government's defense? A statesman's son with stature, charm, and verve, the situation screamed for the unelected Nabuco. But in his absence, the gauntlet fell to Rui Barbosa.

Barbosa was the opposite of Nabuco in physique and temperament: he was slight, spoke in a monotone, and was capable of staying almost still for hours on end while speaking, but what he lacked in charm he made up for in juridical precision and fearlessness. During the clashes at this stormy session, Barbosa emerged from the shadow of both Dantases to occupy the light. He delivered long, detailed, yet incisive rebuttals of the pro-slavery arguments and heaped opprobrium on the guerrilla tactics being employed against the project. He challenged the Conservatives to reaffirm the pro-slavery rhetoric that obstructed the Free Womb Law in 1871. Andrade Figueira took the bait and declared that yes, his party's position had not changed. Barbosa shot back with accusations of subterfuge against Paulino, leader of the Conservative dissidents back then. Paulino de Sousa said little. Unlike the last time, when he had to cause a rift in his own party, he could now afford to sit back and let the Liberals tear each other apart, with the dissidents defending the status quo and branding the abolitionists revolutionaries. Moreira de Barros obliged on this score, accusing Dantas' supporters of "waving the Red flag of the Commune."[32]

Rui Barbosa loved a monologue, but on this day he was interrupted thirty times between addenda, hear-hears, ripostes, clarifications, and secondings. He attacked the fanaticism of those who had chained themselves to an institution that was "accursed to every conscience, and which nobody of sound mind could see lasting more than another twenty years." Among cheers from the galleries, packed with abolitionists, he threw down the gauntlet: "The pro-emancipation parliamentary movement will not concede on a single line (*hear-hears from the galleries*). There is no majority capable of blocking it (*hear-hears*)."

There was, however, a majority. Treading on the government's hot coals, the unshakeable Paulino rose to the challenge. A "twangy-voiced

---

[32] Dantas (ACEI, Jul. 29, 1884). The motion of no confidence was brought by the MP for Minas Gerais João Pereira da Silva (1895–1896, p. 530); ACD, Jul. 28, 1884. According to one contemporary, Barbosa's addresses were "brimming with facts, dates, laws, names," "with flourishes of classicism and rare terms," and they "were wearisome for their monotonous perfection" (Celso Jr, 1901, pp. 81, 82). Moreira da Silva, ACD, Jul. 28, 1884.

Machiavelli" in Patrocínio's view, Paulino was, Nabuco had to admit, a polished articulator. Nothing short of a master politicker could have pulled the Conservative Party back together and turned it into "a force to be reckoned with."[33] And he had done it all without raising his voice or crumpling his suit.

Pro-slavery interests and pro-abolition passions clashed during the voting of a new no-confidence motion brought by the same MP as the first. The House split down the middle. Even the coffee-growing provinces were divided: São Paulo produced three votes for and three against. The opposition coalition, as Dantas called it, had the last word, with fifty-nine votes – all forty-two Conservatives and seventeen Liberal dissidents – to fifty-two.[34] Paulino had called Barbosa's bluff, and Dantas was floored.

While the Lower House was at war, the Senate, under the presidency of the Baron of Cotegipe, was sharpening its knives. Denunciations of illicit, violent acts perpetrated by the Plantation Clubs brought by Silveira da Mota and Cristiano Otoni coaxed a declaration from Saraiva, the most respected Liberal leader, in favor of imposing some limit on slavery. The majority of the senators, however, stood with João Alfredo Correia de Oliveira, who, having worked for the Free Womb Law, believed it was a solution unto itself and that there was something poetically appropriate about ending slavery on the centenary of the nation, in 1922.

The Council of State, formed by the Senate elite, subscribed to this same view. Having been knocked down in the Lower House, Dantas asked the Emperor to dissolve it, as the Constitution allowed. D. Pedro followed protocol and, at eight o'clock on the evening of July 29, convened the Council of State to discuss the matter. The upbeat Dantas arrived looking glum, with his cabinet in tow. He recapped both sides of the argument and

---

[33] Barbosa, ACD, Jul. 28, 1884; Patrocínio, GT, Jun. 19, 1882; Nabuco, JC, Aug. 19, 1884.

[34] At the vote, the cabinet counted on four Conservatives, but also had to subtract six Liberals from the tally: one was absent, four were unelected ministers, and therefore not entitled to vote, and the new Speaker of the House, who, Dantas reasoned, "does not vote, but obviously represents a vote, on the Government's side" (ACEI, Jul. 29, 1884). Conrad (1972, pp. 217–18) argued that Dantas' support came from the North, while the southern provinces, with their coffee-dependent economies, blocked him. However, the South was heterogeneous, with some economic powerhouse provinces, such as São Paulo, and others far weaker, such as Espírito Santo. Moreover, if economic power converted so readily into political power, the Dantas Reform would never have been conceived, since Dantas himself would never have risen to power. On the other hand, attributing the political struggle in the institutions to tension between the State and landowners (Holanda, 1972) obscures the existence of two political groups, with different projects, rooted in the same social strata, disputing control of the national State.

248                    *The Last Abolition*

lamented that the majority in Parliament had "refused to tackle the problem." He went on: "Exacerbating the nature of this issue is the fact that, now that it has been brought before Parliament for deliberation, we can no longer shrink from a resolution, one that will assuage frayed tempers and express the nation's thinking on the matter, as manifested in free elections."[35] Grave he entered; grim he left.

The councilors read their votes. Dantas received three; one from a Liberal with abolitionist sympathies, and two from former Prime Ministers. One of those was Paranaguá, impressed by Dantas' display of courage which he, himself, had lacked in 1882, and also in the interests of keeping the peace, which had been rattled by the abolitionists. Not only did they have Ceará and Amazonas, but the campaign was plowing towards a similar outcome in Rio Grande do Sul. In the meantime, "in the other provinces, the emancipatory movement gathers support and speed by the day; in Court, opinion is almost unanimously in their favor; the entire press, with very few exceptions, supports it and fosters it; numerous associations have formed around it." Lafaiete, as always, came with his "maybe yes, maybe no." He believed that voting against dissolution would mean supporting a government that had "abandoned the interests of the very class that gave it actual support" in order to side with abolitionists on a reform that, to his mind, amounted not to gradual emancipation, but proposed abolition. That said, and not seeing any other resolution of the crisis, he gave Dantas his vote.

Seven other councilors were on Paulino's team. Teixeira Jr., who had fought for the Free Womb Law in 1871, felt that Project 48 was a step too far. It was an attack on pre-existing rights and so was bound to cause conflict. The others, who followed suit, resorted to the pro-slavery rhetoric and its schemata of threat: preserving the government would be "unnecessary, inconvenient and dangerous." Liberal dissidents like Sinimbu seconded the Conservatives: "Only a coarse, ignorant, clueless populace with lax habits could tolerate having a solution of this nature foisted upon them by a government that had bedded down with the

---

[35] Correia de Oliveira (ASI, Sept. 23, 1885). Dantas' speech at the Council of State, like those of the councilors cited in what follows, are in ACEI, Jul. 29, 1884. The Emperor asked the council how the Prime Minister would have the budget approved if Parliament were dissolved. As this second question implied the government's survival, the councilors repeated their positions on the main issue. On D. Pedro's position in the conflict, I agree with Conrad (1972, p. 212), for whom, caught between opposing forces, the Emperor did little to support the abolition.

movement" and "endorsed the dangerous demands of an impatient, radical abolitionism," provoking the fury of the social strata responsible for keeping the economy working.

Paulino crowned this ebullient opposition with his trademark sang-froid. He presented his holy book, the Constitution, which, he said, prohibited Dantas' attempts to jump the gun. To grant dissolution would endorse his urgency for a reform based on nothing but "the irresponsible tantrums of unthinking abolitionist propagandists," while the legitimate Parliament, without party-political distinction, had condemned it. On this "incandescent issue," Paulino, in the name of the growers and traders of rural produce, called upon the Council of State to shoulder the responsibility. Without defending slavery as such, but rather enumerating the damaging effects its eradication would bring, he bent moral principle to economic conjuncture. Paulino was the very embodiment of pro-slavery rhetoric. He declared that the majorities of the Lower House, Senate, and Council of State were all against Project 48, as were the social bases they represented, of which the various petitions from landowners and businessmen were ample proof. Possessing none of that moral support, Dantas would be incapable of governing and thus had the duty to stand down: "Or is the Prime Minister to understand that abolitionist propaganda represents sufficient and adequately stable interests in our society on which to ground a successful government?" If Dantas was not honorable enough to resign, the Moderating Power would have to remove him as unworthy of the confidence of Parliament and the nation.

The result was three for Dantas and his reform, and nine against – with one abstention, the Viscount of Bom Retiro (Good Retreat), who was no friend of abolition. The Council of State echoed the division in the Lower House, with Liberal stalwarts thwarted by a coalition of Conservatives and Liberal dissidents.

The clash at the institutions and within society threw open the possibility of arbitration by the Moderating Power. D. Pedro usually preferred to hover above the debate rather than take a clear stance on it. This particular conjuncture, however, forced him to deliberate. If he granted Dantas a stay of execution he would ruffle pro-slavery feathers both within and outside the institutions. If he fired him, abolitionist civil disobedience of the sort carried through in Ceará and Amazonas would escalate. The session wore on late into the night. Paulino, the last to speak, did not have the last word. D. Pedro, normally one to waffle, kept it uncharacteristically brief. Over breakfast the following morning, Dantas celebrated victory.

## COMMUNISTS

On July 30, Dantas marched to Parliament intent on putting an end to the crisis. With all the MPs present and the galleries packed, he dissolved the Lower House and called elections. Flowers, "vivas," applause. The abolitionists were beside themselves with joy. However, the story was far from over. D. Pedro had granted conditional dissolution. First, Dantas would have to pass his budget because the entire Council of State had been adamant on this.

Although dissolved, the House went about its business as usual. Paulino spoke against the "dictatorship" that had tried to run roughshod over the opposition and tear up the Constitution. The Conservative Ferreira Viana expressed his astonishment at what he called the abolitionist "mob," branded D. Pedro a conspirator, and exhorted the Conservative Party to reject the budget. The Lower House pussyfooted, prolonging its existence and the government's misery, and sending ripples of distress through the Senate in the process.

Among the abolitionists, there was a rush to revive support for public opinion in Court. Rebouças' friend and fellow SBCE member José Carlos Rodrigues took care of things on the foreign front, informing *The Times* (London) that the antislavery movement had made fresh headway in Brazil, and that the Dantas Reform was the bill that would put an end to slavery for good.[36]

Rui Barbosa was in charge of drafting an assessment of Project 48 for the Ways and Means and Civil Justice Joint Committees, and in this, despite the time constraints, he produced his tour de force. In just nineteen days he wrote a fifty-page document in which he appropriated from the international antislavery repertoire examples of post-abolition peace and prosperity around the world, and armor-plated his contentions with statistics from economists and demographers, and arguments from sociologists, anthropologists, philosophers, jurists, and statesmen from France, Great Britain, and the United States. He drew up a history of the issue in Brazil since the end of the transatlantic slave trade and padded it out with reports, bills, and speeches from the Council of State and Parliament. Patrocínio had provided him with part of this material. The document itself was structured around the rhetoric of compassion, rights, and progress, and included a painstaking comparative analysis of the

---

[36] Nabuco, JC, Jul. 31, 1884; ACD, Jul. 30, 1884; *The Times*, Aug. 1, 1884.

## Votes: A Movement/Government Alliance 251

arguments posited against Dantas vis-à-vis those lodged against Rio Branco: they were identical. The irony was that many of Rio Branco's critics back in 1871 were now ardent supporters of the Free Womb Law, which they claimed was a more than definitive solution. This free womb "emancipationism" was the mask pro-slavery rhetoric had chosen to don in 1884. Even the speakers were the same: though Alencar had passed away, Paulino, Andrade Figueira, and Martinho Campos were still prophesying the same post-slavery ruin.[37]

Rui Barbosa defended Project 48 against the accusation that it was communist, a charge that was grounded in a disseminated prejudice against Proudhon, Marx, Saint-Simon, and a special one against the rural democracy of Rebouças and Nabuco's book on Henry George. Instead of dousing the flames, Barbosa kicked a can of gasoline over them by comparing the Dantas Project with the 1881 reform the British Prime Minister W. E. Gladstone had implemented in Ireland. Both projects sought to limit the power of the landed gentry: Gladstone, by fixing land prices; Dantas, by establishing a minimum wage for the freed slave and taking measures to prevent the continuation of slavery under another name, as had occurred in the British, French, and Spanish colonies. According to Barbosa, the project not only prohibited freed slaves from continuing to work for free or for "illusory pay," "for the benefit of employers who would exploit their inexperience, credulity or weakness." He went on:

Liberty (ye shall object) and the right to property conjointly oppose any official fixing of fees for provided services. ... In absolute agreement, say we. Except for when dealing with whole classes that have been disenfranchised and condemned since immemorial times to abject misery and civil slavery.[38]

Moving against the social strata benefiting from slavery in this way, Project 48 would never have met with the approval of all the slaveowners, or all the Liberals, much less Paulino and his battalion. Rui Barbosa recognized as much in his report, signed by twenty-seven pro-Dantas MPs and received with scathing criticism from the Ways and Means and Civil Justice Joint Committees, which had to ratify it. Two MPs did so with reservations, while one Liberal dissident voted against it, invoking Chronos for support: "The time remaining before slavery comes to a natural end, and thus dispenses with any further law ..., is insignificant for an institution that has stood for so many centuries." The elderly

---

[37] Barbosa (1884, pp. 687, 703, 789).     [38] Barbosa (1884, pp. 712, 714, 770–1, 773).

252                         *The Last Abolition*

would be liberated out of sentimentalism alone because what they required "more than liberty was support, protection, and tutelage": "a revolting iniquity" exacerbated by the "spoliation of slave owners" according to some "communist principle [no indemnisation] that would later be extended to slaves of all ages." The Dantas Project was seen as "emancipation en masse forced upon the land which would, according to the public registries, slash slave stocks to under half their present size." It was governmental despotism heaped on "abolitionist furor" that would culminate in revolution and "national suicide."[39] With its large-scale emancipation, lack of indemnification, and redistribution of the land, the Dantas Reform sailed much closer to Rebouças' rural democracy than to Paulino's pro-slavery prudence.

Besides the inclement opposition to the bill, everything else seemed to be turned on its head, with the atypical situation of a dissolved Lower House still working and a government going ahead without an approved budget to follow. Weighing up the two ills, and finding budgetary approval preferable to chaos, Paulino ordered his troops to pass the budget and be done with it to avoid institutional disorder. And so, a month after its dissolution, the debilitated House finally dissolved and elections were called for December, for inauguration of a new parliament on March 1.

There was small relief for Dantas, however, as the battle merely switched arena, as Ferreira Viana had threatened it would, shifting from the closed House to "the tempestuous arena of violence," where all the embraces in the world would do him no good. Otoni recommended that he call on reinforcements from "upstairs": "May God help you."[40]

### FROM NORTH TO SOUTH

While the cabinet languished, the movement orchestrated an avalanche of events across the nation. One Liberal dissident who was infuriated by all this described how abolitionist rallies occupied public buildings and faculties, such as the Polytechnic, where Rebouças was still a professor, and even – he was shocked to behold – the Military Academy. He was stunned by the sheer number of propaganda events, especially the "incendiary

---

[39] Visconde de Sousa Carvalho (ACD, Aug. 4, 1884).
[40] Paulino, ACD, Aug. 2, 1884. The dissolution decree is number 9270, Sept. 3, 1884. ACD, Jul. 31, 1884; ASI, Jul. 1, 1884.

## Votes: A Movement/Government Alliance

marches" under the banner of the Abolitionist Confederation, which he called a "communist organization."[41]

The CA was plowing full-steam ahead, and when the electoral campaign hit the streets, the government/movement alliance bared its teeth. Pro-Dantas parliamentarians attended the concert-conferences and the CA published pro-cabinet speeches, such as that delivered by Antônio Pinto on June 29, at the Polytheama theater, in which he echoed Patrocínio's "Slavery is theft" slogan, adding: "Liberty can be neither purchased nor sold." Gone were the days of buying manumissions, he said; it was time to demand them. Hence, the abolitionists and Dantas parliamentarians took to the streets to do just that. When critics sneered that the government was stooping to the people, Pinto shot back, saying: "No, the government is rising to the people, because the people are the true sovereign." He also accepted the accusations of being a communist: "Yes, gentlemen, we are the anarchists of big ideas, we are the socialists of love." He concluded with a question: "Could it be, gentlemen, as one senator of the French Revolution so eloquently put it, that the tree of liberty only bears good fruit when sprinkled with blood?"[42]

At a CA event the previous week, the third in June, the keynote speaker was Nabuco. Arresting and elegant, he silenced the crowd with his presence. He spoke to and of the crisis, summarizing *O abolicionismo*: slavery was a structural system because it "had a monopoly over the land, prevented industrialization, and kept commerce beholden to its produce." As the "sole industry, it is also the monopoly of a single class" upon which all other professions depend for their livelihoods. The result of this, he said, was visible in the country's social stratification, with "a tiny, opulent landowner class on top, attended upon by a small clientele and all that sat atop a nation of proletariats." Reigning above it all was D. Pedro, "slavery's most trusted bastion." He went on: "... slavery must be awfully grateful to the sovereign, who does his best to serve it as his favorite feudalist, appointing magistrates who will do its bidding and granting it the assistance of the armed forces should it ever require such a last resort." For all that, he was quick to underscore, the movement's alliance was with Dantas, not with the Emperor: "we have no such

---

[41] Related by Visconde de Sousa Carvalho (ACD, Aug. 4, 1884).

[42] Pinto (1884, pp. 6, 10–11, 17–19). The CA published the speeches given by Rui Barbosa, Cristiano Otoni, and Silveira da Mota, and republished *Os escravos* (The Slaves), by Castro Alves, and translations of foreign abolitionist propaganda.

254 *The Last Abolition*

general. If we had, we would not now, forty-three years into his reign, be struggling to secure emancipation of sixty-year-old slaves!"

Nabuco mapped the three main phases of the conflict: abolitionist mobilization, culminating in the liberation of Ceará; the pro-slavery backlash, strengthened by the proliferation of Plantation Clubs; and the Dantas Project, a transaction, a reform that was doable. Under applause from the audience, Nabuco hailed André Rebouças as the scaffold on which the movement in the streets and in the backrooms obtained its shape and sustenance, "the abolitionist whose name expresses unwavering dedication to our common cause; whose selflessness knows no sacrifice, whose heart has become that of a whole race." They were the three sides of a triangle: the industrious Rebouças, the provocative Patrocínio, and the charismatic Nabuco. Complementary and tireless, they coordinated amongst themselves and with activists from the provinces and the government. Never had abolitionism stood so united, both within the institutions and beyond them, without fragmenting into factions, but speaking as one voice and one movement. "We are an idea, a cause, an epoch. ... We are those with nothing to lose," said Nabuco. "In order to defeat us in this combat, slavery will have to repeat Joshua's miracle and make the sun stand still! (*Applause*)."[43]

The abolitionist sun continued apace. The CA held a banquet at Hotel do Globo on August 19, Nabuco's birthday, but the guest of honor was the president of Amazonas, Teodureto Souto. It was an event of abolitionist ecumenism, with activists from the institutions and the public space. Invited to attend, journalists from four broadsheets, including the *Jornal do Commercio*, spoke of the alliance between the institutions and the movement, which could be read off the menu: Bisque à l'Amazone; Consommé à la Confederation Abolitioniste; Cimier de dain [*sic*] à la Ceará; filet de boeuf à la conselheiro Dantas; Gibier piqué à la Theodureto Souto; Jambon d'York à la Luís Gama.

The pro-slavery countermovement said that Amazonas had not really abolished anything, because there were so few slaves there to start with.

---

[43] Nabuco (1884, pp. 17, 23, 45–6). Nabuco also rejected Chinese immigration, which was resurfacing in some quarters: "Brazil is not up for auction, and it belongs to those who already dwell here. ... It belongs to its 11 million inhabitants and to their descendants, not to a privileged class of landowners, or any other people they may choose to import" (Nabuco, 1884, pp. 5, 38). This anti-immigration argument was common among the positivist abolitionists in Court (Lemos, 1884). The phases Nabuco distinguished are inspired by an old pamphlet by Justiniano José da Rocha, entitled *Ação, reação, transação* (Action, Reaction, Transaction). Nabuco (1884, p. 11).

# Votes: A Movement/Government Alliance

Yet, as Silveira da Mota, who chaired the banquet, pointed out, what really mattered was the political symbolism of there being a second freed province. It was a spice the CA was eager to sprinkle on at least six more, Rio Grande do Sul, Goiás, Paraná, Santa Catarina, Pernambuco and Rio Grande do Norte. All declared new foci. The freedom soil campaign was nationalizing, and appropriately, the dessert was named *Pudding à la Rio Grandense*.[44]

The Rio Grande do Sul bloc in the House had voted with Dantas, and, in April 1884, the Abolitionist Center of Porto Alegre launched its offensive with a series of pro-reform events. In August, the manifesto of the Sul-Rio-Grandense Abolitionist Society, formed in the molds of the CA by Rio Grande do Sul's activists living in Court, was read in the House. Other societies sprang up in quick succession. On August 6, the first streets and blocks in Porto Alegre were declared free soil by a drive led by Júlio de Castilhos and the provincial MP Assis Brasil. The modus operandi was pure CA: a Golden Book was opened to honor the liberators, and the city was divided into three areas, each with its own committee entrusted with convincing slave owners to manumit. The campaign also spread into the backlands of the province.[45]

Rio Grande do Sul not only had a structured movement, but also the decisive ingredient that had freed Ceará and Amazonas, a certifying provincial president in José Júlio de Albuquerque Barros, appointed by Dantas. Barros worked in harmony with the local abolitionists, who reported back to him on their progress. On the symbolic date of September 7, a solemn session of the city council was held to celebrate both the national Independence anniversary and abolition, as Barros had declared slavery extinct throughout Porto Alegre, the province's capital. His reasoning was clear: "Ceará made 20,000 new citizens; Amazonas

---

[44] In attendance at the tribute to the abolitionists from Amazonas and to "those MPs who so boisterously applauded and sanctioned the government project for the servile element" were the MPs Rodolfo Dantas, Rui Barbosa, José Mariano, Antônio Pinto, Adriano Pimentel, Leopoldo de Bulhões, and Aristides Spínola Zama, the provincial MP for Amazonas Rocha dos Santos, Sátiro Dias, and Senator Silveira da Mota, and Patrocínio, Rebouças, Clapp, and other members of the CA, a total of fifty guests, with forty-five of them paying 15$000 each (CA, pamphlet no. 7, 1884, p. 4). The priority provinces are listed in CA, pamphlet no. 7, 1884, pp. 8, 12.

[45] The Sul-Rio-Grandense Abolitionist Society used Gama-style activism, with freedom suits demanding the execution of the 1831 Law and of a provincial law on slaves confined to the cities where they already were living (which would make it impossible to sell them to other cities or provinces). Cf. Laytano (1985, p. 106); Perussatto (2009); Monti (1985, pp. 85 ff.).

256 *The Last Abolition*

made 1,600; ye [Rio Grande's people] are making 60,000." What followed were celebrations in the best CA style, with flowers, flags, speeches, a festival in Pedro II square, buildings illuminated, bands playing, and stalls named after abolitionists selling their wares: the José Patrocínio sold flowers, the Luís Gama champagne. There was a procession of carriages with ladies waving, music, and a parade. In those events abolitionists from the three parties collaborated: Liberals, Republicans, and even some Conservatives.

In September, more cities and towns declared themselves slave-free and threw parties of their own. On October 17, the provincial president, who had been following events via telegraph, declared Pelotas free soil. And many other municipalities followed suit: thirty-five more were liberated throughout Rio Grande over the course of that year.[46]

The campaign also made progress in the North. Abolitionism was strong in Recife, and, like Rio Grande do Sul, it involved Liberals and Republicans, as well as lecturers and students from the law faculty. Many of these gathered at the *Journal do Recife*. Concert-conferences and theater events with manumission ceremonies became more and more frequent. The abolitionist positivists Aníbal Falcão and Martins Junior formed the front line of the Central Emancipation Commission of Recife, which deployed the freedom soil campaign strategies, going door to door around town. Something similar was underway in Goiás and Mato Grosso, in the midlands, in the Amazonian province of Pará, and down south in Santa Catarina and Paraná.[47] With less intensity, free soil campaigns were afoot in São Paulo, Espírito Santo, Bahia, Piauí, and Rio Grande do Norte. All told, in 1884, the strategy liberated seventy-three towns and cities and was at work in all twenty provinces. Three of these freed cities had the added bonus of being provincial capitals: Fortaleza, Manaus, and Porto Alegre.

However, not all campaigns were glorious successes. Conservatives protested against this abolitionism in open spaces, seeing the marches through capitals and big cities as "underclass bands," roaming around asking for manumissions or donations, and threatening to take them by force if necessary.[48] This sort of opposition was an obstacle in the

---

[46] Barros, in Monti (1985, p. 106); Perussatto (2009, p. 214); Barros, in Monti (1985, p. 132).

[47] Castilho (2008, pp. 93, 106 ff., 153, 164); Falcão (1885, p. xi). Nabuco, JC, Aug. 19, 1884.

[48] Pereira da Silva (1895–1896, p. 532).

## Votes: A Movement/Government Alliance

campaign's way, and progress stalled where it was vociferous. Even in places where slave stocks were small, if the local authorities were not sympathetic to the movement, as they had been in Ceará and Amazonas and, more recently, in Rio Grande do Sul, the strategy would be blocked by the pro-slavery countermovement. In São Paulo and Minas Gerais, it was not the economic clout of slave-driven cash crops that curbed abolitionist expansion, but the conversion of a social group that depended on them into a politically organized pro-slavery political group, which presented itself in the public space in the form of Plantation Clubs acting with the tacit approval of the local judicial and law enforcement authorities. The countermovement had grown.

This was the case in Campos, in the countryside of Rio de Janeiro, where Lacerda, Patrocínio's friend, had created the periodical *Vinte e Cinco de Março*, after the date of the liberation of Ceará, and a local Carlos de Lacerda Abolitionist Club with aspirations toward the free soil campaign. Yet such weapons were useless in Paulino's heartland where slavery was entrenched and intractable, and the pushback was too strong.[49]

Paulino, circumspect as ever, was not one to waste much breath on abolitionists, although his sidekick Andrade Figueira, to his displeasure, seldom shut his mouth. His response to Dantas' Reform and to the mischief-making of street-level abolitionism came with the Senate elections held fifteen days after the dissolution of the government. The abolitionists had launched thirteen candidates, with the most significant being Rebouças, Clapp, and Nicolau Moreira who knew that they stood no real chance. Two and a half decades of career politics, total command over the Conservatives within the institutions and deep roots in society, patiently cultivated with periodic letters to his electorate, all converged to hand Paulino a resounding victory that August, with an expressive vote even in the Court. For Nabuco, the discipline of Rio's Conservatives inspired awe: "in the last Senatorial elections they voted as one, single man, in absolute obedience to Paulino."[50]

This election, on the eve of the second round of Project 48, held a political and symbolical meaning. The Senatorial election was an indirect

---

[49] Conrad (1975, p. 239).

[50] Paulino, who only ever failed to get elected in 1863 and 1876, won 2,137 out of a possible 4,000 votes in 1884 (JC, Aug. 19, 1884; Nabuco, JC, Sept. 3, 1884). The abolitionist candidates were announced as a single ticket in the *Diário de Notícias*, Oct. 14; *Diário do Brasil*, Jun. 20, 24, Aug., 1884; *Gazeta de Notícias*, Jul. 31, Nov. 23, 1884; and *Folha Nova*, Jun. 20, 1884.

258                                    *The Last Abolition*

vote, which meant the final selection fell to D. Pedro. He could appoint
the candidate with the fewest votes, as he had done before, to punish José
de Alencar, and this would have signaled support for Dantas. In 1884,
however, he decided to even the score. As he had authorized the dissolution of the House in favor of an abolitionist cabinet, he conveyed the
Marshal of the Past's pro-slavery political coalition leader to the Senate.

## THE ELECTORAL COALITION BETWEEN THE GOVERNMENT AND THE MOVEMENT

In his column, Machado de Assis announced the 1884 elections as a
referendum on the big issue of the day, the Dantas Project, and gave
advice to a pro-cabinet candidate, a friend of Rebouças and himself: "At
this solemn moment ... a man needs electoral suspenders to hold up his
legislative pants." As candidates in the odd position of being in government, yet stripped of the full arsenal of the party in power, the abolitionist
candidates needed suspenders all round. The three districts in Court were
strategic. The CA had its support base there and the pro-government
Liberals greater force in the coffee belt. The best solution was to launch
a trio of candidates that reflected this spread: Patrocínio, representing the
CA, Bocaiúva, the Republicans, and Nabuco, the pro-Dantas Liberals.[51]

The Liberating Society of Ceará came out with a liberation ticket
featuring a candidate for each of the eight districts of Ceará. In Rio
Grande do Sul, the movement ran a ticket for the Lower House and
launched Júlio de Castilhos for the provincial chamber. The Rio Grande
do Sul group had ties with São Paulo and, in 1884, they aligned their
actions. Castilhos penned various testy articles against slavery and in
favor of unindemnified abolition. In São Paulo, an agricultural district,
launching pro-Dantas candidates had a symbolic value, but success would
be hard to achieve. Republicanism was strong there, and priorities were
stacked: "Our objective is to found a Republic, which is a political end;
not to free slaves, a social one." Many believed that the monarchy, which

---

[51] The mentioned friend of Rebouças and Machado was Taunay (Machado de Assis, "Balas
de estalo," Aug. 4, Oct. 29, 1884). Patrocínio ran for the third district of Rio de Janeiro,
in alliance with the Central Immigration Society, and launched his electoral platform on
November 24 (Magalhães Jr., 1969, pp. 179, 181). During the Dantas government,
Bocaiúva (Dec. 10, 1885, p. 594) put the abolitionist campaign ahead of the republican
one: "I am an abolitionist at heart ... I believe that the solution to all the serious problems
plaguing our domestic politics, and social, economic and administrative order largely
depend on the extinction of slavery in Brazil and the organization of the free workforce."

# Votes: A Movement/Government Alliance

had planted the poisoned fruit of slavery, ought to be the one to choke on it, but Bernardino de Campos, from the Luís Gama faction, managed to extract a commitment from the party in 1884. Seeing some "common ground"[52] with Dantas on certain issues, Prudente de Morais, one of the parliamentary candidates, promised that the São Paulo Republicans would support him in their electoral platform and conferences.

However, most abolitionists were on the fringes of party politics, for social status, economic or generational reasons: many were born outside the imperial aristocracy, earned less than the minimum income threshold to be a candidate, or were not yet twenty-five years old, the minimum age for elected office. The movement therefore had a great deal riding on the candidacies of Nabuco, Rui Barbosa, and Rodolfo Dantas, all of whom hailed from the political elite and stood a real chance at the ballot box. Dantas personally arranged the ticket in Bahia, telegraphing the local leaders to call in support for Rodolfo and Rui Barbosa. Nabuco had his eye on various constituencies, but after the territories were carved up and allotted to local candidates, he was left with the first district of Recife, alongside José Mariano, who ran for the second. Both men were friends of the provincial president of Pernambuco, Sancho Pimentel, who ensured the dissident Liberals did not get a look-in. As he prepared to travel north to Recife, Nabuco received the movement's blessing at an embarkation meeting and the support of the Prime Minister.[53]

---

[52] The Ceará ticket was as follows, per district: First District: Frederico Augusto Uorgo; Second, Antônio Pinto de Mendonça; Third, Paulino Nogueira Borges da Fonseca; Fourth, Teodureto Carlos de Faria Souto; Fifth, Miguel Joaquim de Almeida; Sixth, Joaquim Bento de Sousa Andrade; Seventh, Tomas Pompeu de Sousa Brazil; Eighth, Álvaro Caminha Tavares da Silva (*Libertador*, Oct. 16, 1884). In Rio Grande do Sul, the candidates were Ramiro Barcelos and Assis Brasil (*A Federação*, Nov. 22, 1884); Castilhos supported Dantas in various articles in the press (collected in Castilhos, 1981) throughout 1884. Alberto Sales did the same in *A Província de São Paulo* between 1884 and 1885 (Schwarcz, 1987, pp. 80 ff.). In São Paulo, two Republicans from Gama's group both ran: Américo de Campos for the Provincial Assembly and Ubaldino Amaral for town council (*A Federação*, Oct. 6, 1884). Letter from Francisco Glicério to Bernardino de Campos, Jun. 10, 1884 (in Santos, 1942, p. 152, note 1). Prudente de Morais, in Boehrer (1954, p. 105). See also Santos (1942, pp. 215–16) and Boehrer (1954, pp. 101 ff.).

[53] Telegrams from Manuel de Sousa Dantas to Diocleciano Pires Teixeira and Tobias Coutinho, 1884, in Dantas, 1962. Nabuco insisted: "My candidature has gained a lot from the dissolution. I shall run for the Court, Pernambuco, and perhaps for Ceará. We are organizing a major campaign for the year and I must be in Parliament" (letter from Joaquim Nabuco to the Baron of Penedo, Jul. 31, 1884, CA). "If I am not elected this time it will be for lack of electoral vision, because the Prime Minister is identified with me"

FIGURE 7.3 Abolitionist beer. During the elections in December 1884, abolitionists championed candidates and advertised them on cigarette packets and beer bottles.
Príncipes da Liberdade (Princes of Freedom) beer label. Britto Alves Collection. Lithograph, 9.2 × 17.8 cm. Nineteenth century. Archive of the Fundação Joaquim Nabuco (Joaquim Nabuco Foundation), Ministério da Educação (Ministry of Education).

His candidacy was emblematic of the coalition between the movement and the government, which was up and running in various provinces, with no fewer than fifty-one abolitionist candidates for the Lower House from fourteen provinces (Amazonas, Bahia, Ceará, Goiás, Maranhão, Minas Gerais, Pará, Pernambuco, Rio de Janeiro, Rio Grande do Norte, Rio Grande do Sul, Santa Catarina, São Paulo and Sergipe), including the liberator presidents of Ceará and Amazonas, Sátiro Dias and Teodureto Souto. The vast majority belonged to the Liberal Party. The positivist abolitionists in Court, usually averse to parliamentary politics, launched a manifesto demanding indemnity for former slaves in the form of social rights and calling for "citizens to use their direct or indirect influence to canvass for votes for abolitionist candidates who deserve the government's trust." It was a national campaign, with candidates for one electoral zone attending the events of others. Nabuco, for example, attended a

(DJN, Sept. 24, 1884). See also letters from Joaquim Nabuco to the Baron of Penedo, Sept. 26, 1884, CIJN; Sept. 14, 1884, CAI.

## Votes: A Movement/Government Alliance

TABLE 7.2 *Abolitionist candidates in 1884 elections by political party*[54]

| Party | Number of candidates |
| --- | --- |
| Liberal Party | 29 |
| Conservative Party | 9 |
| Republican Party | 5 |
| No party | 8 |
| Total | 51 |

concert-conference in São Paulo. The editorial pages of various reform-minded newspapers endorsed abolitionist candidates.

The campaign was spreading domestically and abroad, with *The Times* (London) covering the progress of the Dantas Project. On the jubilee of the abolition of slavery in the British colonies in August 1884, at Nabuco's behest, the British and Foreign Antislavery Society secured a declaration from the Minister of Foreign Affairs, and the Prince of Wales, a BFASS patron, which stated: "Brazil still retains the curse it inherited from its Portuguese rulers. At the present time, it possesses nearly a million and a half slaves, whose lot in life is worse than the beasts of burden." He congratulated the abolitionists on the liberation of Ceará and Amazonas and positioned Brazil within the geopolitics of slavery on a par with Morocco.[55]

The electoral reform passed in 1881, on which Rui Barbosa had been rapporteur, had disenfranchised the illiterate and introduced far more restrictive requirements for voter registration. The result was an electorate whittled down to roughly 100,000 people. The abolitionists were counting on part of the urban population sympathetic to the campaign

---

[54] The identification of the Liberals, Republicans, Conservatives, and independent candidates (which were allowed under electoral law at the time) were based on the candidates propaganda circulated in *A Província de São Paulo*, in São Paulo; *A Federação*, in Porto Alegre; *Libertador*, the Liberating Society of Ceará; *Órgão de Propaganda Abolicionista*, from Maceió; *Abolicionista*, Amazonas; *O Abolicionista*, Teresina; *Abolicionista: Órgão Literáro e Noticioso dos Typographos da Regeneração*, in Desterro; *A Vela do Jangadeiro: Periódico Abolicionista*, in Ouro Preto; *O Diário da Bahia*, Dantas' paper in Salvador; *Gazeta da Tarde*, both Patrocínio's and its namesake in Bahia; and *O País*, run by Bocaiúva.

[55] The references to the paragraphs above are in Lemos (Nov. 19, 1884, p. 3); DJN, Sept. 15 and 16, 1884; Fonseca, 1887, p. 289; *The Times*, Jun. 6, Aug. 1, Dec. 20, 1884. Nabuco, JC, Aug. 26, 1884. The Prince of Wales' declaration is in "The Jubilee of Freedom," *South Australian Register, Adelaide,* September 22, 1884: 4, and also mentioned in Davis (1984, p. 299).

262    *The Last Abolition*

and less susceptible to the pressures of the landowners, to vote for its candidates. So they took their campaign to the streets. Given the strong pro-slavery reaction, fewer theaters were willing to host concert-conferences, afraid of violent conflicts. Because of that, the abolitionists had to improvise their speeches in town squares, markets, ports, and even from newsroom balconies and the windows of houses. The concert-conferences became rallies that spilled over into huge pro-Dantas marches. In 1884, the abolitionists flooded the streets, with campaigns making a big splash in fifteen provincial capitals – Belém, Cuiabá, Desterro, Fortaleza, Maceió, Manaus, Ouro Preto (then capital of Minas Gerais), Paraíba, Porto Alegre, Recife, Rio de Janeiro, Salvador, São Luís, São Paulo and Vitória, orchestrating no fewer than 587 propaganda events.[56]

The meetings in open, public spaces, originated during the eighteenth-century British electoral campaigns were emulated in Brazil and reached their height with the rousing propaganda of Nabuco and José Mariano in Recife. Abolitionists of every sort canvassed for the duo. The Central Emancipation Commission of Recife held conferences at the Santa Isabel and Santo Antônio theaters, and the feminist group the Hail Liberty Abolitionist Society held a women-only concert as well. At these and many other events, Nabuco addressed women, teachers, students, journalists, civil servants, traders, clerks, typesetters, artists, and workers, the same audience that attended the concert-conferences in Court. If Patrocínio and Rebouças were expanding the social base from the closed theater to the public space of the streets, Nabuco was doing the same with parliamentary politics. He went after votes in Recife the same way the CA sought manumissions, canvassing door to door. In all, he delivered twenty-three speeches, at marches and rallies, with average turnouts of 4,000 enthusiastic supporters.[57]

---

[56] Pereira da Silva (1895–1896, p. 490) estimates 150,000 voters, and Carvalho (2003, p. 39), 100,000.

[57] "In conjunction with the recently organized Liberal Party board in Recife, the Central Emancipation Commission, presided over by a Conservative and largely composed of Republicans, was the largest center of supporters of Nabuco's candidacy" (Falcão, 1885, p. xi). On the Hail Liberty Abolitionist Society, cf. letter from Odila Pompílio to Joaquim Nabuco, Mar. 26, 1885, DJN. Nabuco held meetings in Peres, São José de Ribamar, Afogados, Passagem da Madalena, Pátio de Santa Cruz, Boa Vista Square, Corpo Santo Square, Patio da Princesa (DJN, Oct. 28; Nov. 2, 5, 9, 10, 13, 16, 20, 23, 28, 29, 30, 1884). On the audience, cf. letter from Joaquim Nabuco to Rodolfo Dantas, Nov. 2, 1884, CAI. On the British meetings, see Tilly (1993–1994).

FIGURE 7.4 One of the campaign meetings for the election of Joaquim Nabuco in Recife in 1885, supported by a national mobilization of abolitionists.
Archive of the Fundação Joaquim Nabuco (Joaquim Nabuco Foundation). Ministry of Education.

Though he was unique in every way, when speaking at public rallies, before crowds of ordinary folk, Nabuco simplified his arguments and adopted a more Patrocínio-like tone, rousing the crowd with emotional appeals couched in the rhetoric of compassion. He would evoke the schemata of progress too, attacking the slavery-latifundia-monoculture trinomial as the root of the nation's backwardness and proposing "an agrarian law, which by means of land taxation and expropriations, would give back to the State all those vast tracts of land which the slavery-based monopoly do not plant in or let others do so." He envisioned the Rebouças' rural smallholdings nation: "... I will no longer separate these two key topics, the emancipation of the slaves and the democratization of the land." He wanted a "reform so thorough, so broad, so deep that one could even call it a Revolution."[58]

Many abolitionists wanted to redistribute the land in 1884, but not all. Positivists like Aníbal Falcão, who was canvassing for Nabuco that year,

---

[58] Conferences on Nov. 1, 5, 16, 30, 1884, in Nabuco (1885).

figured that in a modern, urban, industrial society, a decent wage and social rights would be far more beneficial to the freed slave than a patch of rural land. The abolitionists were in agreement one way or the other, so long as it meant giving the freedman a safety position rather than to indemnize the former owner. That was the reason why a local Conservative newspaper run by one of Paulino's peers, João Alfredo Correia de Oliveira, accused Nabuco of preaching against the landowners and promising land to those without it. The local Trade Association also refused to receive Nabuco, while the Liberal dissidents pegged him with every radical epithet that was going round in the late 1800s: anarchist, nihilist, communist. Nabuco retaliated: "Well, if anything resembles communism around here, would you not agree it is slavery? The worst possible breed of communism is because it is communism for the benefit of a single class."

The audience lapped up these rhetorical flourishes. A powerful orator in Parliament, Nabuco in 1884 was quickly mastering how to pull on the heart-strings of the wider public with what contemporaries described as organized and impassioned speeches that were simple yet imaginative, and always packed with quotations, allegories, and metaphors that seared the movement into the listener's mind. An example of this was when he compared himself to Odysseus facing the Cyclops: "Gentlemen, it is neither you nor I that shall slay slavery, but the spirit of our age, which is why the name of the true abolitionist is 'No one'; and I want no other name for myself than that."[59]

This was the general atmosphere that hung over the elections of December 1884. Dantas had promised never to interfere in the elections, "because to do so would go against my conduct and my character, and ill befit the post I occupy." But when it came to the crunch, like all imperial Prime Ministers, he proved otherwise and he had his cabinet put the provincial presidents, chiefs of police, and administrative officials to work assisting his candidates and obstructing their adversaries, using posts and titles as bargaining chips.[60] Dantas may well have been less insidious in this than his adversaries made out, and they were certainly just as guilty of tampering themselves, minus the plum

---

[59] The position of the positivist abolitionists is outlined in Falcão (1885, p. xviii) and Lemos (1884). The Conservative attack on Nabuco is in O Tempo, Nov. 7, 1884. The description of Nabuco's effect on the audience is in Falcão (1885, p. x). Nabuco's speeches at the conference held on Nov. 16, 1884 are in Nabuco (1885).

[60] ACD, Jun. 9, 1884. The Conservative is Pereira da Silva (1895–1896, p. 534).

# Votes: A Movement/Government Alliance 265

government jobs to hand out. The fact is both sides resorted to playing fast and furious electoral hardball.

The sides disputed each vote like the Montagues and Capulets, and there were widespread reports of voter fraud, intimidation, and violence. In Recife, where pro-slavery Liberal dissidents were running against abolitionists, a clash broke out at the close of voting. In response to Conservative provocations that Nabuco had been defeated, the abolitionists, led by José Mariano Carneiro da Cunha, burst into the parish church, where the last votes were being cast. The Termites Club (Clube do Cupim), of which Carneiro da Cunha was a member, bragged about the robust reaction of the abolitionists, "willing to sacrifice their lives so that 1 million enslaved men might have as their defender Dr. J. Nabuco, the most eminent figure in all of Brazil." The Conservatives were just as vigorous and seized the ballots. Punches were thrown, kicks swung, and Carneiro da Cunha was struck by a passing bullet. The Liberals took all their fury out on a pair of enemy canvassers, killing both. It was, Nabuco lamented, their St. Bartholomew's Day. Accused of having blood on their hands, Nabuco and Carneiro joined the pallbearers at the funeral of one of the dead men. It was a way of showing that they did not want war, but that they were not afraid of it either.[61]

Sancho Pimentel, still president of Pernambuco, informed Dantas of the fracas. The electoral committee voided the election. The movement responded, early in 1885, with disembarkation meetings in Court for Nabuco (in January) and Carneiro (in February); both meetings attracted thousands of supporters. While the nation careened between abolitionist celebrations and pro-slavery bickering, the heiress to the throne attended Mass in São Paulo, with Paulino's son also in the congregation. At the city hall, she presided over the presentation of fourteen letters of manumission paid for by the Emancipation Fund. Out of touch with the conflicts raging throughout her reign, the Princess noted that: "The masters seemed almost happier about it than the freedmen themselves."[62]

---

[61] Clube do Cupim, Dec. 5, 1884. Conference, Jan. 6, 1885, in Nabuco (1885), Alonso (2007).

[62] There were ovations at newspaper newsrooms and receptions at the Hotel Ravot and the Polytechnic School Emancipatory Society (DIJN, Jun. 28, 1885). Isabel's diary, Nov. 3 and 8, 1884, in Daunt (1957).

## SERIAL SETBACKS

One hundred and twenty-one thousand, two-hundred and twenty-six votes were cast on December 1, 1884. The count was as hard-fought as the vote itself. On the first tally, the result was a close-run forty-eight Liberals to forty Conservatives. Most of the results were met with protests and accusations of fraud, with many duplicate votes having been cast for and against.[63]

The GT said that the election was in favor of the government. The abolitionists were certain they could not possibly have lost at the ballot box. But election is one thing; being sworn in is another, and what had been tough on one level proved impossible on the other. Gusmão Lobo lamented to Rodolfo Dantas: "Fate is conspiring against our noble cause! Not a single pleasant surprise among a slew of disappointments!" The Cabinet, Lobo continued, might still save itself by negotiating with the dissident Liberals, granting an additional year or two of service as compensation to the landowners who stood to lose slaves under Project 48. In his estimation, the Conservatives had won fifty seats, which meant Dantas would have to negotiate. "We could only win, and then only just, if the majority [of Liberals] were fervent abolitionists of our mettle." They were not. Even so, Dantas kept the glimmer of hope alight, to Lobo's surprise: "... I found him with strength, belief, and serenity nothing short of admirable under the adverse and disheartening circumstances to which he has been exposed." When, on February 10, 1885, Parliament held preparatory sessions to ratify the mandates of the elected members, all hope was snuffed out and hell broke loose. As Nabuco described events to the Brazilian head of the diplomatic office in London:

Brazil has never seen anything like the new Parliament. Indeed there are two parliaments and if the Emperor chooses to dissolve the aberration there will be three, and the anarchy that will come with them. I cannot see how the Conservatives can possibly take power. I am not exaggerating when I say that it would be the eve of revolution, and that the cane fields and coffee plantations would soon start to burn. ... veritable civil war.[64]

Abolitionists and pro-slavery sides, both with their documents proving it, claimed victory, and each impugned the success of the other. At least

---

[63] Pereira da Silva (1895–1896, p. 534). Cf. list of those elected in Javary (1962, p. 388).
[64] Nabuco, JC, Aug. 14, 1884; letters from Gusmão Lobo to Rodolfo Dantas, Jan. 14 and 15, 1885, CIRD; letter from Gusmão Lobo to Rodolfo Dantas, Jan. 22, 1885, CIRD; letter from Joaquim Nabuco to the Baron of Penedo, Jan. 7, 1885, CAI.

twenty-eight parliamentarians-elect had their mandates contested. Eleven of these were in the Dantas camp, and two of them on the front line of abolitionism: Nabuco and Teodureto Souto. In this fight to have mandates ratified, the control of the certification committee was crucial. With a wily interpretation of the House Standing Orders, Paulino's followers demanded that the longest-serving MP among all those whose election was not in doubt be appointed Speaker of the House. The gentleman in question just happened to be a Conservative, who took office under energetic protest. Three sessions later, the Dantas bloc managed to approve an election for choosing the Speaker, restraining the right to vote to the seventy MPs now sworn in. Conservatives and dissident Liberals teamed up again and won the vote. The definitive Speaker was to be none other than Moreira de Barros, the pivot of the original crisis, with a dissident Liberal as his deputy. The government also lost control of the certification committee, formed by two Conservatives, two dissidents, and one pro-government MP. With a four to one majority, the committee certified the pro-slavery mandates and rejected the credentials of many of the impugned abolitionists.

And so the new Lower House was convened around the same fault lines as the old, though with some significant losses for Dantas: Rodolfo, Rui Barbosa, and two ministers all failed in their bids for reelection. Nabuco was declared winner after a second round in Recife on January 9, 1885, after a concerted effort by the abolitionists. It was a victory celebrated in Recife and in Court, with parades, a welcoming committee formed by the cadets at the Military Academy, a hailstorm of flowers, and roughly 5,000 well-wishers. Their celebrations, however, proved premature: Nabuco's mandate was axed.[65]

Nabuco tried to create a new paper, O Século (The Century), and convert it into the government/movement alliance mouthpiece, with financial support from the Dantas family. Rebouças, Clapp, and the Dantas electoral casualties all would contribute, but the idea was put on ice when the beleaguered government slipped into a coma. When all the shouting was over, the 125 seats in Parliament were distributed as

---

[65] *Correio Paulistano*, Feb. 17, 1885. Moreira de Barros' vice-president at the House was the pro-slavery Lourenço de Albuquerque. The Foreign Trade Minister was not elected and the Justice Minister only got through on the second vote (the elections had two rounds). Of the Republicans, Prudente de Morais and Campos Sales both got elected, but Bocaiúva did not, nor did Marcolino Moura, Aristides Spínola, or Antônio Pinto, all from Dantas' parliamentary base. See letters from Joaquim Nabuco to the Baron of Penedo, Jan. 29, 1885, CAI, and to Rodolfo Dantas, Apr. 1, 1885, CAI.

268 *The Last Abolition*

follows: fifty-five seats for the Conservatives, sixty-seven for the Liberals, of which fifteen belonged to dissidents, and three Republicans, whose loyalty was still uncertain. "It's been crushing," wrote Lobo to Rodolfo, after a tête-à-tête with Rebouças and Nabuco at the Ministry of Foreign Affairs.[66]

On the streets, however, blood was boiling. Anti-Dantas MPs were booed and threatened wherever they went, and things got so bad that even the hot-tempered Patrocínio found himself calling for people to cool off. A CA manifesto published on February 17 urged for calm, instructing abolitionists to keep their heads and not give in to pro-slavery activists' provocations. When the House opened on March 9, the CA orchestrated a standing ovation for Dantas from the packed galleries. Instead of a grand finale there came a reprise. On April 13, Moreira de Barros brought another no-confidence motion against Dantas: "Rejecting the hypothesis of any solution to the servile problem that withholds indemnity, the Lower House withdraws its support for the government." On the same crux came the usual stalemate: fifty-fifty. The cabinet was floored. Shaken by the whole crisis, Dantas fainted.[67]

Having lost in the institutional arena, the movement took to the streets. According to one damning report from a friend of Paulino, right from the very day the no-confidence motion was brought, there was bedlam in and around the Lower House. Abolitionists laid siege to the vicinity and harangued and insulted as many dissident Liberals as they could, and the Speaker of the House to boot. Moreira de Barros called in the police and brought another no-confidence motion, accusing the government of being incapable of keeping the public order. Nabuco proposed to Clapp that the CA should organize a massive concert-conference: "Get to work on this with Rodolfo straight away. I'll address the audience ... We have no time to waste. The meeting has to be on Tuesday or Wednesday night, and then we'll march by torchlight to Dantas, who is hanging by a thread." Clapp started rounding up the cavalry, but the government was dead in the water before much could be done, sunk by fifty-two votes to fifty. So off went Dantas, bereft of his trademark smile, to request the

---

[66] Letter from Joaquim Nabuco to Rodolfo Dantas, Jan. 29, 1885, CAI; letter from Rodolfo Dantas to Joaquim Nabuco, Jan. 31, 1885, CIJN; Pereira da Silva (1895–1896, p. 537); letter from Gusmão Lobo to Rodolfo Dantas, Feb. 14, 1885, Cird; DNAAR, Feb. 10, 1885. João Penido, author of the no-confidence motion that triggered the whole crisis, was elected.

[67] DNAAR, Feb. 17, 1885; ACD, Apr. 13, 1884; DNAAR, Apr. 13, 1885.

## Votes: A Movement/Government Alliance

dissolution of yet another Lower House to the Moderating Power. This time, D. Pedro refused, preferring to honor the promise he had made when Dantas was first appointed: "If you run, I shall pull you back by the coat-tails."[68]

### TO THE STREETS

The CA harbored the ousted government. The concert-conference Nabuco had wanted to use to save it was held to avenge it instead. Nabuco's first-choice venue, the Pedro II theater, an elite stomping ground, closed its doors to the abolitionists. The "Tribute to the Patriotic Dantas Cabinet" was held on June 7 at the ever-loyal Polytheama, decorated with association flags, and it featured every member of the CA, all sixteen defeated candidates from Dantas' coalition and the man's three sons. Dantas himself, afraid of triggering unrest (he was a reformer, not a revolutionary), retreated to his country home in Friburgo and sent a telegram, which an emotional Patrocínio read with a cracked voice. In his message, Dantas thanked the CA for supporting his project "to free the nation's slaves, a cause that has emerged victorious in public opinion." Rodolfo Dantas oversaw proceedings, which Clapp initiated and Rui Barbosa, in the name of the deceased government, took off from there as the night's keynote speaker. He railed long and hard against the Conservatives, D. Pedro, and the pro-slavery political coalition. But the crowd wanted Nabuco and Patrocínio, who delivered impromptu speeches. Nabuco whipped up such a frenzy that the stenographer gave up trying to keep track of his tirade and the equally furious approval it evoked from the crowd.[69]

Fury was also the mood in Recife, where abolitionists livid at the invalidation of Nabuco's mandate stoned the façade of the Conservative

---

[68] Pereira da Silva (1895–1896, pp. 540–1). The undated letter from Joaquim Nabuco to João Clapp is in Nabuco (1949), who dated it to May 8, though May 4 or 5 would appear far more likely. D. Pedro, in Monteiro (1913, p. 41).

[69] Present at the event in Dantas' support were: Frederico Borges, Sátiro Dias, Marcolino Moura, César Zama, Aristides Spínola, Moreira Brandão, Adriano Pimentel, Ratisbona, Galdino das Neves, Sancho de Barros Pimentel, Carneiro da Rocha, Silva Mafra, Artur Silveira da Mota, Nabuco, Rodolfo, José and João Dantas. Lobo did not attend, as he was afraid of reprisals from the *Jornal do Commercio*: "Were I to attend the banquet I would violate the anonymity that I have made my citadel, and would, then, the *Jornal* continue to publish my column?" (letter from Gusmão Lobo to Rodolfo Dantas, Jul. 16, 1885, confidential, CIRD). Dantas in CA (1885, p. 6). The CA published Rui Barbosa's speech as its pamphlet number 10 (CA, 1885, pp. 11, 52–3).

newspaper *O Tempo*. The BFASS saw to it that the news appeared in *The Times* (London). When all seemed lost, fate struck a blow: the death of an MP-elect meant there would have to be a new vote in Pernambuco, to be held on June 7, 1885. Out of solidarity, the Liberal candidates withdrew in favor of Nabuco, an act which Rebouças recognized in a letter of thanks in the name of the CA. And so Nabuco found himself running for the same seat for the third time. The abolitionists campaigned like never before, and Nabuco's picture was to be seen on fabrics, scarves, hats, beer bottles, and cigar wrappers. The Hail Liberty – Abolitionist Society produced cigarette packets with his picture and name on them. This support and the blessing of the provincial president Sancho Pimentel saw Nabuco elected by a large margin, a victory that resonated nation-wide and indeed abroad. *The Antislavery Reporter* described a massive parade, with a marching band and flags, fairy-lit streets, and triumphal arches all the way to the Santa Isabel Theater, where a grand gala was held. The city came to a halt, with shops being shut as if it were a bank holiday. The victorious Nabuco could be carried through the city on the people's shoulders.[70]

All across the country, conferences, civic processions, torches, garlands, flags, and flowers melded into a loud and colorful celebration of a hard-won victory. On July 3, under a blizzard of petals, Nabuco was sworn in. Overcoming all the hurdles of three elections in a row had endowed him with a heroic aura: he was the Dantas Reform in person, the embodiment of abolitionism and of the abolitionists who had seen their mandates cancelled. Now, he could say his name, like Odysseus, loud and clear: "I am no one." He was the movement and he would need to be as quick-witted and crafty as the Greek hero, because the countermovement had donned the Cyclops' cowl and was stomping out of its cave.

---

[70] *The Times*, Aug. 6, 1885; letter from Joaquim Nabuco to the Baron of Penedo, May 17, 1885, CAI. Ermine César Coutinho and Joaquim Francisco de Melo Cavalcante were the candidates who stood down (DNAAR, Jun. 8, 1885). The local Liberal leader Luís Felipe de Sousa Brandão supported Nabuco (DJN, May 14, 1885). *The Antislavery Reporter*, Oct., 1885.

# 8

# Bullets: Movement and Countermovement

Born into a family of mill owners and endowed with a handsome dowry from his Bahian in-laws, João Maurício Wanderley, the Baron of Cotegipe, may have had a drop or two of African blood in him, something he neither admitted nor denied, despite the pressing relevance of the issue. He was a pristine aristocrat, dapper in appearance and home, a man who lived among silks, perfumes, and Havana cigars. Fashionable without affectation, he had a taste for card games and literature and could just as easily put together a soirée – attended by the beautiful and the talented, including Machado de Assis – as chair a committee or assemble a cabinet.[1]

All this refinement never robbed the Baron of his practical good sense. He was a politician of indomitable realism which no idealism could corrupt. When he became Prime Minister in 1885, the abolitionist campaign had already succeeded in stripping slavery of all social legitimacy. An institution hitherto couched in tradition was now dependent on legal sureties for its continued existence. For as long as society had been uniformly pro-slavery, the State could afford to let the odd abolitionist roam free, but once public opinion split between abolitionist disorder and slavery-based order, it had to make concerted efforts to preserve the status quo. The imperial family had donned its kid gloves, ashamed to admit just how deeply its Empire was mired in slavery; but if the crown was wavering, the Conservatives were hard at work armor-plating their social order. Paulino and Cotegipe were prepared to get their hands dirty if it

[1] The adversary was Nabuco (1897–1899, p. 828); Pereira da Silva (1895–1896, pp. 88–9).

272 *The Last Abolition*

meant saving the world as they knew it, and it mattered little whether they did so by means of the institutions, speeches, or force.

### THE TIME-BUYER

During the interim between the fall of Dantas and the ascension of Cotegipe, D. Pedro summoned his super-sub statesman, the Liberal Antônio Saraiva, to take charge as he was considered the only man who could stem the flow of discord from brimming over. His government was the exact inversion of Dantas', supported by dissident Liberals and the Conservative minority, and the Dantas group in opposition.

The Dantas Liberals were furious, hence the outburst at the inauguration. Machado de Assis (GT, May 10, 1885) prefigured it:

... tomorrow morning smacks of strife, ill-tempered debate, vehemence, torrents of asides and profanities, raised voices and turmoil. ... the cabinet is announced, making its harried way through a sea of onlookers. ... Saraiva takes to the stand to present his program ... and war breaks out – insults fly, tempers boil; another speaker addresses the floor, then another – heavy crossfire, fists are waved, ires bay, enthusiasms tinkle ... the issue is graver still. ... How joyous we were, how sad we have become.

How happily the abolitionists had gone to the polling station, and how crestfallen they had returned, watching the Conservatives win. The new Prime Minister declared that it was impossible to refuse "the gradual liberation of slaves," but the similarities to Dantas' Reform ended there. Circumstantial pro-slavery rhetoric was once more the order of the day: concede the least possible ground over the longest possible term. Agriculture would need time to reorganize so that it could make the transition, and the government was willing to grant it in abundance.[2] Formally, the project was maintained, but in real terms, it was a pitcher of water thrown on the Dantas bonfire.

Freedman rights had gone. Five-year apprenticeships were retained, but they were now designed to protect the owner, not the slave. A low wage was set for the transition period, which took the form of a compulsory service lease, breached under penalty of fines or imprisonment. The freedman colonies promised by Dantas were repackaged as "agricultural colonies, ruled according military discipline" for "jobless freedmen."

[2] ACD, Aug. 3, 1885.

## Bullets: Movement and Countermovement

The minimum age for release was kept at sixty, plus three years of additional service in lieu of compensation to the master. For slaves aged sixty-three, the age of release could be extended to sixty-five. The whole age controversy went up in a puff of smoke with the elimination of the need to declare a slave's place of birth. Slaves still had to be registered, as under the Dantas Reform, but instead of stating where they came from, the registration required only their filiation, "if known." This change legalized the ownership of slaves smuggled into the country between 1831 and 1850, and so also their stock, which could be registered under "unknown filiation" – under which they did not need to declare their provenance. This was a way of getting out of the legal snooker: while Dantas would have released slaves registered as older than they were in order to evade the 1831 law, Saraiva allowed owners to register real ages without leaving themselves open to freedom suits under that law (which the abolitionists continued to bring to court nationwide), since the unknown filiation option meant it would be impossible to attest the slave had been imported from Africa. As a result, the sexagenarian law ended up emancipating far fewer slaves than it would have done under Dantas, as, according to Otoni, it now applied only to 107,331 genuinely elderly slaves, under 10 percent of the total stock, then estimated at 1,186,272.[3]

The third crucial alteration concerned indemnification. The liberation of elderly slaves, which would have been indemnity-free under Dantas, was compensated under Saraiva, and handsomely too. The new plan offered 50 percent of sales price and drafted a table of progressively depreciating prices that was capped high. This, the opposition argued, fueled slave-market inflation. As expressed by Otoni: "Prices have ballooned because they had fallen too sharply, to facilitate manumissions." With the Saraiva project, the government tilted things back in the slave owners' favor, as it would now "take five years for a 20 percent drop and even then [slave prices] would still be higher than they are now." The Dantas Reform would have had an immediate impact on slavery and all but stifled the market, with progressive depreciation over sixteen years. While at first glance, Saraiva's project purported to quicken the pace of depreciation, which now took twelve years to bottom out, it actually fired up the market by hiking prices and promising to keep them high. The tax that was supposed

---

[3] Project 1B, 1885, Articles 1, 4, 8, and 13; Barbosa (Jun. 7, 1885, CA, 1885, p. 150); ASI, Sept. 23, 1886. The slave registration would only be completed in 1887 (RN, May 4, 1887). It was also said that the registration was "a ruse to have the ingénus [freed under the Free Womb Law] registered in the name of deceased slaves" (A.P de A., 1885, p. 62).

274                                    *The Last Abolition*

to replenish the Emancipation Fund was partially rerouted into subsidizing immigration.[4] And all of this would only come into force the following year, after the completion of the new slave registration.

With these distortions, Saraiva turned the government/movement relationship on its head, reinforcing the slave-economy Dantas had sought to undermine. The focus now shifted from the freedman to the former owner. Rui Barbosa defined the Dantas and the Saraiva projects as thesis and antithesis. He had the patience to compare them point-for-point at the CA's conference-tribute to the deposed Prime Minister: "The July 15 Project [Dantas] was an abolitionist compromise; the May 12 Project [Saraiva] is a capitulation to the slave owner." "A minor reform" to eclipse the "sweeping reform the nation desires," added Nabuco, who reported to the British and Foreign Antislavery Society that slave owners and pro-slavery parliamentarians would vote for Saraiva's project out of fear of a more progressive cabinet. "The political oligarchy which governs this country cannot resist the cry for abolition, but they contrived to replace the abolition bill by one ... for helping the planters to get rid of their slaves at a *minimum* of loss ..."[5]

To try to counter all this, in August that year Nabuco founded the Abolitionist Parliamentary Group (GPA), a caucus of fourteen MPs who had made it through the post-Dantas cull. Together, this group orchestrated a blitz of requisitions, interpellations, amendments, all manner of procedural checks and blocks, attempted to have the bill divided into separate smaller bills or otherwise disfigured, and bombarded the House with alternative proposals. They delivered speeches appealing to the Prime Minister's patriotism, liberalism, and compassion, and demanding an end to the slave market. They drew on foreign examples and made ample use of their international megaphone, the *Antislavery Reporter*.[6]

---

[4] ASI, Sept. 21, 23, 1885. Various denunciations were also made at the House, for example ACD, May 11, 1885. The price table is in Law 3270, Article 1, paragraph 3. According to the *Rio News* (Mar. 15, 1887), only 7,522 slaves had been freed by the Emancipation Fund since 1883, and, probably, most of them by abolitionist associations.

[5] Barbosa (Jun. 7, 1885, CA, 1885, p. 41); ACD, Aug. 3, 1885; letter from Joaquim Nabuco to Charles Allen, Aug. 6, 1885; Bethell and Carvalho (2008).

[6] The parliamentary bloc consisted of Nabuco, Aristides Zama, Francisco Sodré, José Viana Vaz, Ulisses Viana, Antônio Bezerra, Silva Maria, Amaro Bezerra, Bernardo M. Sobrinho, Carneiro da Rocha, Aristides Spínola, Frederico Borges, José Mariano Carneiro da Cunha, Álvaro Caminha, and Leopoldo Bulhões (DJN, Jul. 8, 1885). The last five of these signed a project that would have extended equal treatment to former slaves and immigrant workers. Carlos Afonso proposed another project containing clauses from the Dantas Bill, and various other MPs presented amendments intended to disfigure Saraiva's project, such as the substitute clause 1C, dated July 9, proposing immediate abolition followed by five years of additional services rendered for slaves aged fifty and under (Senado Federal,

## Bullets: Movement and Countermovement

Saraiva headed off the charge. Before presenting his bill to the House on August 6, he manumitted his own slaves. However, his real view on the servile institution was clear from his address to the House, which played straight from the circumstantial pro-slavery rhetoric tablature. As slavery is a cancer, he said, "its removal involves grave risk"; the national interests meant this "saddest evil" had to be tolerated, though anathema to morality and civilization.[7] Paulino savored each word.

If, under Dantas, the battle had been between the government/movement alliance and the pro-slavery countermovement, under Saraiva, the government/pro-slavery countermovement alliance faced the abolitionist opposition. This new balance of power also materialized in a repressive strategy, which was evident in the choice of Afonso Pena (a future President of the Republic) for Justice Minister. Pena had been part of the anti-Dantas Liberal dissidence in 1884, and was, Nabuco complained, biased in the eyes of the abolitionists. Dantas' embraces were out. In came the truncheons.

The former opposition was now in power and full of plaudits for the new administration. Paulino sang its praises in the Senate, as did Antônio Prado, São Paulo's leading coffee planter, in the House. Prado declared that "it was time to soothe the tempers stoked by belligerent propaganda" and that the government, having accepted the Conservatives' modifications to its project, would have their full support.[8]

Hammering out the finer points had been hard-going. Andrade Figueira, a pro-slavery politician as longstanding as he was unflinching, still saw the bill as the death-knell of the nation. The problem was Saraiva had made a concession, putting an end to the interprovincial slave trade. This proved a bone of contention among abolitionists as well. Nabuco and José Carneiro da Cunha were against it, but three members of the abolitionist bloc, figuring something was better than nothing, decided to vote in favor of Saraiva's bill. The Republicans abstained. Calls for amendments rained in from all sides, but Saraiva ignored them and sent his bill to the floor. On August 13 the Conservative/Dissident Liberal

---

1988, v. ii, pp. 836–55; ACD, 3, 9, 13, 14, 18, 20, 24, 25 Jul.; 4, 8, 24 Aug. 1885). An example of the notes run about Brazil in the *Antislavery Reporter* (Jun. 4, 1885): "A letter just received by us from SENHOR JOAQUIM NABUCO ... He states: ... We will fight the indemnity principle ... Publicity given to the movement in the columns of *The Times* always does much to assist the efforts of the abolitionists, the planters being peculiarly sensitive to the criticisms of the English people."

[7] Toplin (1972, p.105); ACD, Jul. 3, 1885.

[8] Nabuco (ACD, Aug. 3, 1885); Prado (ACD, May 18, Aug. 6, 1885).

276                     *The Last Abolition*

coalition voted in favor of it, seventy-three to seventeen. Saraiva, considering his mission accomplished, left the government and entrusted the rest of the fight to the Senate.[9]

### VELVET REACTIONARY

D. Pedro could have called up another dissident Liberal to keep things moving along as they were, but, as he had done in 1871, he decided to hand the Reform to the Party of Order, the Conservatives. First in line for the top spot was, of course, Paulino – *El Supremo*, as Nabuco dubbed him – but as the very personification of pro-slavery political coalition, appointing him would have been as good as a declaration of war.[10] So the Emperor went for Cotegipe instead, the velvet reactionary.

The defeat of the Liberals in 1885 seemed like a repeat of 1868, when Zacarias' reformist government was succeeded by that of the reactionary Itaboraí. This time, there had been the three-month Saraiva interlude that had reversed the wheel's spin, from Dantas' abolitionism to Cotegipe's pro-slavery intransigency. The movement responded to D. Pedro II's choice of Prime Minister with a pamphlet penned in the tone of dismay: "How can His Highness appoint a slave owner to oversee the dismantlement of slavery ...?" The Emperor's choice in 1885 was far more difficult to explain than it had been in 1868. Back then, the nation was at war and D. Pedro had to share power with the politicians who had conveyed him to the throne, so he enjoyed neither autonomy nor authority. In 1885, he was a mature sovereign and the generation of politicians to whom he had been beholden was now dead and gone. He held sway over many of the politicians, especially those younger than himself and dependent on his favors. In 1885 D. Pedro could have attempted structural reforms, but he chose not to. Perhaps, as one of his biographers suggests, he allowed himself to get bogged down in the details he so adored and ended up missing the bigger picture.[11] Then again, perhaps the years had taught him that his reign depended on Conservative forces and institutions – of which slavery was second to none – that were impossible to reform without bringing down the monarchy itself.

[9] Saraiva (ASI, Aug. 24, 1885). The abolitionists Aristides Zama, Viana Vaz, and Ulisses Viana voted with Saraiva.

[10] JC, Sept. 3, 1884.

[11] The pamphlet was anonymous (A. P. de A., 1885, p. 10). Barman (2000).

Cotegipe aligned his Bahian conservatism with the São Paulo brand of Antônio Prado and the Pernambucan variety of João Alfredo Correia de Oliveira.[12] They formed a brotherhood of four with Paulino, united in their intent to sustain slavery. The quartet represented the most important economic regions in the country, North and South.

The story of Brazilian abolition can be divided into BC (before Cotegipe) when the movement was growing and AC (after Cotegipe) when the government and countermovement allied.

First of all, Cotegipe fulfilled his gentlemanly duty and approved the Saraiva Reform that the Emperor had left in his care. Otoni was livid, and claimed that the government was maneuvering to squeeze another thirteen years out of slavery, which they knew could never last so long without it. Two other Liberal senators weighed in against it: Bonifácio, the Lad, moved for an addendum, and the abolitionist veteran Silveira da Mota, for a replacement clause, measures that would have put an end to slavery in 1893 and 1892, respectively. João Alfredo Correia de Oliveira responded on the government's behalf: as "the evil of slavery must not be cured by causing further ills," the Saraiva/Cotegipe Reform was the best of all possible worlds, fruit of an agreement among the parties and vastly superior to that obtained in 1871, and it was Rio Branco's former right-hand-man who was saying so. Dantas shot back: "Does His Excellency really believe the bill under discussion is definitive?" João Correia de Oliveira rejoined: "God alone knows what the future holds!" Little did he know that that future would end up in his very hands.

With an overwhelming majority, Cotegipe had the reform sail through the Senate and handed it over for the Emperor's approval on a symbolic day, September 28, the anniversary of the inoperable Free Womb Law. The new law, like the old one, was all talk and no action. The state of affairs in 1885 differed little from that of 1850, because those born since the 1871 law continued under their masters' "protection," and were to remain so until 1892, when the youngest of them turned twenty-one. As for the sexagenarians, the new law kept them under slavery for three additional years, and as servants thereafter because they were forbidden to leave their places of work without authorization from the Orphans Court. The Saraiva/Cotegipe Law, as Otoni put it, was an aberration that delayed abolition while appearing to further it.[13]

---

[12] ASI, May 12, 1888, May 6, 1885.

[13] Otoni (ASI, Sept. 23, 1886); Correia de Oliveira (ASI, Sept. 23, 1885). Law 3270, Article 3, paragraphs 10 and 13.

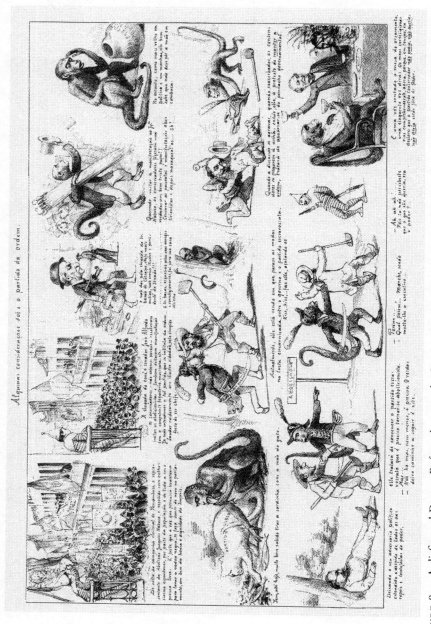

FIGURE 8.1 A disfigured Dantas Reform became the Saraiva/Cotegipe Law, approved on September 28, 1885, only conceding freedom to elderly slaves. Drawing by Angelo Agostini. Archive of the Fundação Biblioteca Nacional (National Library Foundation), Brazil. Reproduction by Jaime Acioli.

## TRUNCHEON POLITICS

Cotegipe had cut his political teeth under Eusébio de Queirós, the Conservative leader from the dying days of the transatlantic slave trade. From him he learned how to overcome adversaries in a manner that "honors us greatly": that of "*crushing* the opposition."[14] In 1885, with the blessing of government, he took that approach to the abolitionists: combat by all means and at all costs, across the board.

He began his new policy in July. A surviving pro-Dantas MP took to the stand in Parliament to denounce conflict between the police and abolitionists in Campos, during which Lacerda, Patrocínio's friend, was dealt a blow on the head. No investigation was opened into the episode. A Conservative MP replied that a cracked skull was an occupational hazard for abolitionists, drawing accusations from the pro-Dantas bloc that the statement was an apology for the murder of abolitionists. The session descended into chaos, with Conservatives railing against the orator, Nabuco claiming that the rule of law did not seem to apply in the hinterlands, and José Mariano Carneiro da Cunha branding the new administration a "truncheon regime."[15]

This truncheon politics had three modalities: electoral fraud, evasion of the law, and repression of opponents.

The first of these reared its head almost immediately. Just as he had sustained Dantas, D. Pedro backed Cotegipe, authorizing him to dissolve the House. Elections were called. Despite no real chance of winning, with the whole State apparatus working against it, the CA launched a unified ticket, with candidates in Ceará, Bahia, São Paulo, Pernambuco (Nabuco), and in Court, with Patrocínio running for the city council.[16] Patrocínio was elected with 201 votes, having led the field in almost every district. His victory was celebrated with parades and conferences. In Rio, where the movement was strong, there were sufficient pro-movement voters to elect councilors, but not enough to send anyone to the House. At the election held on January 15, 1886, the benefits of the electoral reform of 1881, which was supposed to guarantee representation to the

---

[14] Cotegipe, in Pinho (1937, p. 181).
[15] The pro-Dantas MP was Bezerra de Menezes (ACD, Jun. 8; Jul. 20, 1885).
[16] Frederico Borges (Ceará) and Frederico Lisbon (Bahia) ran for the House, and Sizenando Nabuco (Joaquim Nabuco's brother) and João Brasil Silvado, from Gama's group, ran for the municipal council in Court. The CA sent out flyers canvassing for votes for all these candidates. GT, Dec. 16, 1886; Fonseca (1887, p. 311); DNAAR, Aug. 9, 1886.

# The Last Abolition

minority party, turned sour. It had worked for the Conservatives when the Liberals were in power, but no reciprocity was forthcoming. Cotegipe did not want any of the electoral surprises that had undermined Dantas, so he did not get any. He rigged the ballot and ensured himself a steam-rolling 103 Conservative seats to twenty-two Liberal ones (most of those were anti-Dantas dissidents). Carneiro da Cunha took Nabuco's place as the only abolitionist leader to hold a mandate in the House, having been elected for the second district of Pernambuco (after his election was voided in the first district). It was quite an achievement: Carneiro had managed to triumph against a Conservative candidate who had done everything he could to bribe and pressurize the civil service. The result was received with celebration, as Nabuco had won in the former election, but it also met with the same fate: Carneiro's credentials were rejected.[17] The movement defended Carneiro da Cunha as they had Nabuco in Recife, with a public rally attended by 3,000 people and another at the Polytheama in Rio, where the audience of 2,000 heard the protests of Nabuco, Patrocínio, and Clapp. This time, however, there would be no happy ending.

With a tame House at his feet, Cotegipe set about pursuing his second anti-abolitionist measure: fudging the law. The actual perpetrator was the Minister for Agriculture, Commerce, and Public Works, Antônio da Silva Prado, who, two weeks after the promulgation of the Saraiva/Cotegipe Law, turned little into nothing by issuing a decree that scheduled the slave registration for the year starting March 1886. As the new law would only come into effect after the registration was supposed to be completed, in March 1887, the decree postponed its enforcement for another year and a half, hence the formally freed elderly slaves were kept as actual slaves. The decree also reiterated that the registration was not to ask where the slaves came from, thereby legitimizing the spurious ownership of contraband slaves who could be chalked up under "unknown filiation." The minister found a dastardly way around the interprovincial slave-trade ban as well, alleging that it applied only to trade between *provinces*, which meant that the Court, as a *municipality*, could continue to buy or sell its slaves in the hinterland.

---

[17] DNAAR, Jul. 1, 1886; Carvalho (1886); GT, Jul. 13, 1886. Nabuco (letter to Charles Allen, Jan. 23, 1886, Bethell and Carvalho, 2008, p. 268) made the following accusation: "The majority of the Conservative candidate [Pereira da Silva] over me was wholly due to the pressure of the government on the public *employees*, who form a large portion of the small electorate of this town, and to the promises of employment profusely distributed among the poor classes of our people." Cf. election results in Javary (1962, p. 398).

## Bullets: Movement and Countermovement

Patrocínio called the move the "Black Regulation," "an ominous law that maligns for all posterity the names of Saraiva, Cotegipe, and D. Pedro II, fruit of a consortium between the oligarchy and the throne, ... an injurious law, the regurgitation of happy wine that has soured for all time the date of September 28 [Free Womb Law anniversary]." An abolitionist from Bahia had this to add: "[this law] could only be passed in a second-rate Empire like this, with legislators lifted from the cane fields and coffee plantations." It was an ignoble measure "that nobody had the right to pass and none the obligation to obey."[18]

The abolitionists came out fighting in the GT and in the movement's newer gazettes, such as *A Redempção* in São Paulo. Though these abolitionist newspapers were local and small, they were abundant in number and added up to quite a bombardment and grabbed nationwide attention. Hence Rebouças advised Nabuco not to open another vehicle, saying that it would be cheaper and more effective to concentrate their energies on the GT. However, the GT was mired in debt, which Patrocínio decided to flee by starting another paper, *Cidade do Rio*, to which the whole abolitionist troop migrated. Rebouças began to use this new paper to publish articles similar in tone to the CA pamphlets, such as his "abolitionist decalogue": propaganda for a land tax and agrarian distribution.[19]

Despite their united public front, Nabuco and Patrocínio continued to compete for the leadership of the movement. The latter had the edge, as not only did he have a newspaper behind him, but he was also now a councilor. So Nabuco went looking for a soapbox of his own, and, in April 1886, joined the largest reform-minded broadsheet of the moment, the abolitionist and republican *O País*, directed by Quintino Bocaiúva. In his parliamentary column he proffered the speeches against Cotegipe which his lack of mandate prevented him from delivering in the House. He accused the Emperor of betrayal, saying that he had signaled his support for the Dantas Reform only to throw it to the pro-slavery wolves. D. Pedro, he claimed, had missed an opportunity to go down in history as a reforming despot, like the Roman dictators. Nabuco shared the positivist abolitionist yearning for a strong and modernizing executive, so, for him, as the title of one of his 1885 pamphlets read, "The Emperor's error"

---

[18] Decree 9517, Nov. 14, 1885. The registration is covered in Article 1, paragraph 1. Prado's interpretation refers to Article 2, paragraph 1. Patrocínio (GT, Jun. 21, 1886); the other abolitionist is Anselmo Fonseca (1887, pp. 343, 345).

[19] Letter from André Rebouças to Joaquim Nabuco, Feb. 9, 1886, CIJN; DNAAR, Jun. 14 and 15, 1885.

282                              *The Last Abolition*

had been to abandon the movement at its height. As he explained to the
British abolitionists: "... the Emperor encouraged our movement to the
point of forming an abolitionist government, and then gave way to a pro-
slavery coalition. ..."[20] The pro-slavery countermovement responded
with yet another anonymous pamphlet: "Joaquim Nabuco's error: the
eclipse of patriotism."

The abolitionists might as well have been talking to the parliamentary
wall. Nothing could derail the Black Regulation. Attempts in the Senate
by Bonifácio, the Lad, were all thwarted with the Emperor's approval.
The press decried the gaps in slave registration and accused the government of dallying in order to postpone the roll-out of the Saraiva/Cotegipe
Law, as they had done before with the Free Womb Law. The registration
was muddied beyond recognition, and when it was finally completed in
March 1887 it offered a slave tally short of the estimates on which the
Saraiva/Cotegipe Law had been based, a mere 723,419 slaves.[21] So few,
the government reasoned. Let death liberate them.

Cotegipe crowned his anti-abolitionist strategy with the third prong of
his trident: repression. And in this he took a leaf out of the foreign
repertoire, emulating the US Fugitive Slave Act of 1850, which penalized
any person aiding, abetting, or sheltering runaway slaves. The government followed this model: penalties included fines and even criminal
proceedings resulting in up to two years' imprisonment.[22]

Paulino, now a senator, followed the lead of the pro-slavery MPs and
helped twist the garotte. In the name of the slave-owning societies of
Minas, Pernambuco, and Rio de Janeiro, he called upon the government
to charge the abolitionists. A member of the Plantation Club even sent
open letters to the Emperor, defending the slave-owning strata by

---

[20] He went on, saying that the emperor ought "to assume the rôle of a civilizing despot
instead of ruling without any heartrending for more than forty-five years over a large
slave market and a nation's paralytic bed" (letter from Joaquim Nabuco to Charles Allen,
Jan. 23, 1886; Bethell and Carvalho, 2008, pp. 274; 276). A similar argument is made in
positivist writings, cf. Lemos 918–84. Nabuco's pamphlets *O error do imperador*,
*O eclipse do abolicionismo*, "Eleições Liberais e eleições Conservadoras," and *Escravos*
(verse) were all published under the title "Propaganda Liberal."

[21] Letter from D. Pedro II to the Baron of Cotegipe, Sept. 18, 1886 in D. Pedro II (1933,
p. 271); RN, Mar. 24, Jun. 26 and 29, Sept. 25, 1887; *A Redempção*, Apr. 21 and Aug. 1,
1887. Of the total number of slaves, 238,000 were in Rio, and 107,329 in São Paulo
(Rodrigues Alves, 1887, p. 16).

[22] The Saraiva/Cotegipe law (3270, Article 4, paragraph 3) punished "the sheltering of
slaves" as per Article 260 of the Criminal Code: one month to two years' imprisonment
or a fine of 5% to 20% of the "artcle's value."

## Bullets: Movement and Countermovement 283

describing them as "by far the most threatened by the revolutionary propaganda convulsing the nation," disrespecting the law, and endangering the rights and even the lives of slave owners. He blamed the CA: "The abolitionist conferences are veritable incitements to murder, threatening the lives of mill owners and their families. I was present at one ... and I HEARD these very words: 'let's go to the woods and to the mills, don't waste more time or saliva; send guns and bullets to the slaves.'"[23]

Just as the abolitionists established international support networks, the pro-slavery political coalition also attracted foreign solidarity. An Englishman writing in *The Times* claimed that the Brazilian abolitionists were troublemaking communists. Another, on a visit to Brazil, witnessed three slaves, jailed for the murder of their master, break out of prison and lynched in the streets by an angry mob. Rather than condemn the lynch mob, the European traveler saw fit to blame the movement for having incited disorder: "at socialist meetings of the abolitionist underclass, war is routinely declared upon all slave owners, advocating their murder and the dishonoring of their wives and daughters. ... No house or property is safe."[24]

The same schemata of threat, the pain of a bloody revolt, used in 1871 returned. For better or for worse, since the beginning of the movement's mobilization, the governments had all been Liberal, and so, in theory at least, defenders of freedom of thought, and they had, to differing degrees, refrained from reacting to peaceful protest with acts of violence. Cotegipe had no such qualms. He was a Hardliner from the start, using mounted police to hunt down runaway slaves, shut down abolitionist conferences, and disperse public rallies, while having such rallies banned altogether in various parts of the Empire. In this he had the backing of the police, accused of sabotaging Carlos Lacerda's *Vinte e Cinco de Março* newspaper in Campos.[25]

The Brazilian pro-slavery political coalition absorbed the foreign repertoire, starting with Cuba, from which it took what suited it of the Moret Law, first the Free Womb, then the Sexagenarian act. Then, from 1884 onwards, it borrowed from US slavery tactics, setting up Plantation Clubs as a counterweight to the abolitionist associations and sending out armed

---

[23] Three letters were published in the *Jornal do Commercio* and nine in *O Brasil*, under the pseudonym Um Lavrador (A Farmer) (1884, pp. 11, 50–1).

[24] The assertion of communism was made by Goldwin Smith. Nabuco replied in a letter to the editor of *The Times*, to no avail. The letter ended up being published in the *Antislavery Reporter* (Aug./Sept. 1886). Dent (1886, pp. 285–6).

[25] Fonseca (1887, pp. 569–70).

# 284 The Last Abolition

militias to track down fugitive slaves, as Rui Barbosa was quick to denounce. In areas where abolitionism was growing, Cotegipe also followed the repressive US strategy and sent the police after runaways and the abolitionists accused of harboring them. In Court, he entrusted the task to the chief of police, the judge João Coelho Bastos, who was more than suited to the requirements. The abolitionist Angelo Agostini drew him for the *Revista Illustrada*, gun in-hand, pointed hat on his head, policeman's cape aflutter and a long, shaggy beard. "The Hairy Slaver," in the words of another abolitionist, was obsessed with the hair on other people's heads. His favorite way of humiliating captured runaways – and, given half the chance, abolitionists too – was to shave their heads, earning himself the near-instantaneous hatred of the movement, and another nickname: "the Noggin Shearer." Coelho ("rabbit," in Portuguese) resembled a fox: he hunted by stealth, patrolling the streets, cafés, and newsrooms. He also raided homes, harassed suspects, and put plain-clothes officers on abolitionist tails such as Nabuco's. He showed zero tolerance, especially for the CA, whose members he tried to catch red-handed as slave-liberators.[26]

In bringing the Conservatives to power in 1885, D. Pedro II had perhaps thought he would have the government under his control. Cotegipe, however, kept a firm rein on the legislature and on a repressive police. The Emperor would occasionally ask him to ease off: "May I recommend the observance of the law and the avoidance of such measures as might seem unnecessarily violent, in case they are not necessary."[27] As the Baron considered them very necessary indeed, he continued with his crackdown for the next three years, without D. Pedro dismissing him for his excesses.

### FROM FESTIVITIES TO DRAMA

The abolitionists tried to keep their rhythm under Cotegipe, diffusing their portable activism package throughout the provinces: freedom suits, concert-conferences, free soil campaign, association founding. On this last activity, *A Redempção*, run by followers of Luís Gama, published its

---

[26] Barbosa, Jun. 7, 1885; *Revista Illustrada*, no. 422, 1885; CR, Oct. 18, 1887; Duque-Estrada (1918, p. 88).
[27] Letters from D. Pedro to the Baron of Cotegipe, Jan. 31 and Apr. 7, 1886; D. Pedro II (1933, p. 271). On D. Pedro's relationship with the governments, see Schwarcz (1998), Barman (2000), Carvalho (2007), Needell (2006).

## Bullets: Movement and Countermovement

"Plan for an emancipation society," a step-by-step instruction manual for how to set up an abolitionist association. Thanks to efforts like this, new associations continued to appear nationwide, and some of them were quite robust, such as the 400-member Abolitionist and Federal Union of Pernambuco, founded by Nabuco. But the reality was that these societies were appearing at a much slower rate than before, only fifty during the Cotegipe government versus 279 during Liberal rule. In terms of annual averages, it was down from 34.9 a year to 16.7, less than half.[28]

Gama-style activism also had to change tack under the Cotegipe administration. In response to the "Black Regulation" swindle of registering slaves under "unknown filiation," abolitionist lawyers began freedom suits against slave owners on the grounds that omission of origins was an admission that the slaves had been born to free mothers. The CA picked its targets for maximum judicial effect, either because of a long record of cruelty or symbolic exemplarity of the whole social group, as was the case of the campaign Patrocínio's *Cidade do Rio* ran against a slave-owning priest, a clear contravention of all Christian teachings.[29]

Many provincial abolitionist associations used judicial activism, but it did not always work. Key to its success was having a certifying judge willing to rule in their favor. This was the case in Bahia, where the Liberating Society of Bahia won various cases thanks to sympathetic judges. Sometimes the abolitionists went to the judge with the slave they planned to liberate and made a judicial deposit of the market price. A foreign visitor was thoroughly scandalized by this: "... one of the main leaders of the Abolitionist Party in Rio [Clapp] abuses the 1831 law. ... he sent a message to a slave owner saying that his charge wanted his freedom and that he had set the price at 200 mil-réis, which the owner could withdraw from the Treasury."[30]

As public generosity failed to accompany the hike in slave prices under the Saraiva/Cotegipe Law, the number of manumissions at concert-conferences began to decrease. Letters of Manumission had become too expensive to buy and donate. Nabuco took to the foreign press to expose the law for having as much as tripled slave prices in some parts of the Empire, and that the government made use of it to favor the slave owners

---

[28] *A Redempção*, Jan. 27 and Feb. 6, 1887; letter from Joaquim Nabuco to Charles Allen, Jan. 23, 1886; Bethell and Carvalho (2008).

[29] CR, Dec. 11, 1887.

[30] Eduardo Carigé and Abdon de Morais Vieira were the main abolitionists to use this tactic in Bahia (Caires Silva, 2009, pp. 19 ff.); Dent (1886, p. 287).

286         *The Last Abolition*

and prevent the abolitionists from repeating in new provinces the success they had enjoyed in Ceará and Amazonas.[31] With slaves now a more considerable asset, it became increasingly difficult to convince owners to concede voluntary freedom. The prestige that came with titles and having one's name written in a Golden Book did not justify the financial loss. And, with even Cotegipe passing as an emancipationist, the glory to be had by releasing slaves was no longer so clear-cut.

The conferences, the abolitionist flagship, continued, and in 1885, a wave of these events called for civil disobedience against the Black Regulation. The government reacted by pressuring the theater owners not to host them, and deploying plain clothes police to break up any they did. The movement responded by dropping the "conference" part from the name and putting on propaganda-rich concerts instead. That was the backdrop, in August 1886, to the staging of *Aida* starring the Russian soprano Nadina Bulicioff, described at the beginning of this book. It was an abolitionist conference masquerading as opera and attended by the two abolitionist national leaders, Patrocínio and Nabuco, and also by their allies in political institutions, including Manuel de Sousa Dantas. That same year, a banquet was held at Hotel Glória, ostensibly as a literary tribute, and it too was converted into an antislavery act, as was another, presided over by Machado de Assis and attended by Serra.[32]

The closing of the public space to abolitionism under Cotegipe changed the activism pattern. A pupil of Patrocínio's noted that "nobody attended the conferences without a revolver and a knife in their waistcoat." Speakers were often interrupted mid-flow by "gangs proffering threats." They got as good as they gave, "driven from the theater with canes, rocks, and even bullets, as they fled the furious crowd." All of this forced a change in strategy and tone. At the beginning of the campaign, the theater offered a combination of drama and festivity, even comedy. But during the Cotegipe years, the constant threat of violence turned the gatherings into more saturnine affairs. In 1885, the abolitionist Cruz e Sousa, from Bahia, penned some verses that wrapped slavery and the Emperor in one and the same burial shroud, under a title that declared the movement's new approach – *War Cry:*[33]

---

[31] *The Times*, Oct. 2, 1885. According to Conrad (1972, p. 226), in the coffee-lands of São Paulo, a young, able-bodied youth could fetch 900 mil-réis.

[32] DJN, Jun. 29, 1885; Barbosa, Jun. 7, 1885; CA, 1885; Barbosa, Aug. 2, 1885, CA, 1885b; *O País*, Aug. 11, 1886; Serra (1986, p. 54).

[33] The pupil was Coelho Neto (1899, p. 387), who described the role Patrocínio's circle played in the campaign. Another poem by Cruz e Sousa was named for the date of the

## Bullets: Movement and Countermovement

> *... No more the slave, the pleading supplicant,*
> *Rising above the ethereal gauzes*
> *of ideas bright and resplendent as the sun,*
> *shall burn, burn away those rutilant wings.*
>
> *... It is time to tear from the faces*
> *the bloody veils of fatal disgraces*
> *and fill with light from the vast horizon*
> *the saddened hearts of the races.*
>
> *... That the evil may agonize in its den,*
> *Before the thoughts of blood that frighten,*
> *To rise up – essential – first needs must*
> *Dark night descend upon the slave-pen [senzala].*

Verses and flowers were of little effect under a government intent on putting an end to the occupation of public space for the purposes of protest, starting with the GT, which was vandalized in 1885. Rather than preach piety at concert-conferences held in luxurious theaters, the movement took to the streets to incite moral shock.[34] Lugubrious processions depicting all the horrors of slavery impressed on the slaves' bodies slouched through the streets like a protracted Day of the Dead. In Court in February 1886, the CA paraded the fifteen-year-old slave girl Eduarda, baring for all to see her bruised and bloodied skin, her eyes swollen shut, the bruising on her flesh, all the handiwork of a well-born lady, Francisca da Silva Castro. The CA sued for the girl's freedom and filed for the immediate release of a second victim, Joana, aged seventeen, face deformed by beatings, raging with fever, her body pocked with oozing sores. Patrocínio and Clapp walked arm-in-arm with the two girls at the head of a civic procession of scores of abolitionists, exhibiting slavery sadism. They confronted the government, marching straight to the front door of the Conservative Ferreira Viana, a fierce opponent of the Dantas Reform who was moved to tears by what he saw. The following day, the two tortured slave girls were in all the newspapers, though they would never get to see themselves. Eduarda was blinded and Joana dead.

The CA held a meeting-cum-funeral for Joana, with a procession to the cemetery, where speeches were delivered at her graveside. Relying on freedom suits in Gama's style, the CA sued the girls' owner for torture and murder and had Joana's body exhumed for evidence. The police

---

liberation of Ceará: "25 de março" (in *O livro derradeiro*, 1885). It reads: "The insect of terror, the pall of the shroud/ the tears of the king and the dastardly bravos/ the same old sterile slavery succumbs."

[34] Jasper (1997, p. 106), Halfmann and Young (2010, p. 3).

report stated that the girls had suffered three years of torture and imprisonment, during which they were stripped and whipped with abandon every single day, which would finish with them left "with their arms bound behind their backs for long periods of time, without any nourishment. When food did finally come, it was placed onto the floor, where they had to lap it up with their mouths." With every gory detail of Joana's treatment described in the press, the owner was charged with murder and arrested pending trial.

Castro's defense lawyers delayed the judicial process, resorting to every trick in the book to have her freed, claiming she suffered from drowsiness, illness, and even dementia. When the case came to trial in October 1886, it became a national drama. Fearing tumult, the defense requested a closed court, but the *Cidade do Rio* got around this by running a blow-by-blow coverage of the entire trial anyway. The pro-slavery counter-movement came to Francisca's rescue. She feigned madness and was absolved, despite all the evidence against her. The movement may have lost the case, but it won urban opinion. The exhaustive coverage in the press (the *Cidade do Rio* dedicated a whole section to the case entitled *Barbarity*), and the way in which it so graphically underscored the abolitionist rhetoric, produced widespread indignation.[35]

The moral shock strategy took the suffering slave trope used in literature and at the concert-conferences and made it savagely concrete. The movement also resorted to Christian symbolism. Rui Barbosa compared the abolitionist setbacks with those experienced by Jesus, and *O País* ran an emancipation fundraising campaign under the heading "In the Name of Christ." Antônio Bento renamed the group inherited from Luís Gama the Caiaphases, after the prophet who foresaw the second coming of the Son of God to redeem the people. Bento was a member of the Remédios Brotherhood and he came up with the idea of installing a museum of horrors in the church nave, exhibiting all the paraphernalia of torture, including a huge meat hook from which to hang slaves. Similar exhibits were set up in Campos and Recife. Bento turned the Mass liturgy into a propaganda strategy. In 1887, he took a slave, also called Antônio, on a torchlit march displaying "the instruments of torture dangling from long

---

[35] Sizenando Nabuco was the slave girls' lawyer (GT, Dec. 15, 1886). The quotation is from the report submitted by chief inspector João Manuel Carlos de Gusmão on March 11, transcribed in full in GT, March 13, 1886. Coverage of the case is in GT, Oct. 19, 24, May, and Oct. 25, 1886. CR, Oct. 25, 1887, and subsequent editions.

# Bullets: Movement and Countermovement

poles: iron chokers, leg irons, wooden stocks, whips."[36] In this Christian civic procession, the slave, rather than hanging from the rafters, walked behind the cross, holding out scourged hands for all to see, staggering through the eerie torchlight, a battered Christ.

Ratcheting up the Christian metaphors, the abolitionists turned the slavery requiem into an endless Good Friday Passion. In addition to the poems, plays, novels, musical compositions, and drawings they had been using since the start of the campaign, they began to delegitimize slavery with public performances that enacted its many injustices.[37]

They used traditional rituals too. Their sporadic political appropriation of high-profile funerals – those of Rio Branco, Luís Gama, Apulco de Castro – soon became systematic. Besides the symbology, which was hard-hitting in itself, repressing this kind of abolitionist event would have meant loss of face for the government. When Patrocínio's mother died of cancer in August 1885, her funeral was turned into a public event, with the mourners including various members of the CA, representatives from the antislavery newspapers, members of the Dantas Cabinet (father, son, and Rui Barbosa), the Republicans Prudente de Moraes and Campos Sales and numerous students. Abolitionists and Republicans carried the casket to a hearse draped in black and followed by a cortège of 100 carriages. Waiting to receive the procession at the São Francisco Xavier Cemetery were Nabuco, Carneiro da Cunha, Rebouças, and Clapp. The image of the former slavewoman's coffin surrounded by the banners of abolitionist associations was transmuted into speeches mixing the schematas of compassion and of law, justice for Justina.[38]

After showcasing the myriad torments of slavery, the abolitionists turned to the abusive practice of lashing. Nabuco had taken the issue to

---

[36] GT, Dec. 14, 1886; AR, May 15 and Jun. 5, 1887; CR, Feb. 17, 1888; Andrada (1918, p. 218). The campaign in *O País* was successful; however the *Rio News* (May 4, 1887) pointed out the Catholic tone and suggested a lay alternative: "in the name of abolition." On the museums: in Campos, *Vinte e Cinco de Março* ran photos of tortured slaves and the Carlos de Lacerda Abolitionist Club planned a "wax museum" of torture (Monnerat, 2012, pp. 92–3). In Recife, the Termites Club came up with the idea for a monument consisting of "articles of torture," intended to "make our descendants blush with shame and indignation at the errors and evils of slavery!" (Clube do Cupim, session Sept. 3, 1885).

[37] For the use of the Goffmanian notion of performance in political analysis, see Tilly (2008).

[38] Magalhães Jr. (1969, p. 195). The use of slaves' funeral cortèges as a means of abolitionist protest was also seen in the provinces, as in Cachoeiro do Itapemirim in Espírito Santo, in October 1887 (Novaes, 2010, p. 107).

290 *The Last Abolition*

the House in Cotegipe's first Cabinet and wrote about it in his newspaper column in 1886, denouncing the increasingly frequent and severe punishments owners were meting out in the face of simmering slave unrest. He brought to light the case of five slaves in Paraíba do Sul convicted of murdering their overseer. One of them was sentenced to perpetual hard labor and the rest to 300 lashes each – six times the legal limit of fifty, and further multiplied by being administered with a cat-o-five-tails. After the whipping was done, they were strapped and sent straight back to the fields, on foot. Two of the men died on the way. Nabuco called the Crown to account: "... this case will enable the future Empress to understand the conditions under which our slaves live and to comprehend the mission of the abolitionists under her father's reign."[39]

Cotegipe had the House in the palm of his hand, but in the Senate, where his majority was less robust, he met with stiff resistance. Dantas was leading the Liberal caucus in the fight against the government's pro-slavery policy, first in relation to the "unknown affiliation" question – Antônio Prado's interpretation for the Saraiva/Cotegipe Law – and later on the issue of lashing. Dantas dragged the subject onto the Senate agenda with a string of compelling speeches. As the owner of the dead slaves in Paraíba do Sul had purchased a fraudulent coroner's report that found no evidence for the whipping being the cause of death, Dantas called for exhumations. He demanded action on the part of the Justice Minister, but not only in this particular case: "I invite Your Excellency, who wields great power, to assist me in this concerted effort to rid Brazil of slavery without delay." Another Liberal Senator brought a bill of law to ban corporal punishment, and Bonifácio the Lad, spoke about the Paraíba do Sul case in an address to the House. Cotegipe was feeling in the Senate all the heat he was insulated against in the House, as he would himself admit some time later: "If the abolitionist movement made swift progress, it owes much of it to the noble Liberal senators."[40]

Pinned to the ropes in the Upper House, the government was also suffering added pressure from a changing international conjuncture. On October 7, 1886, Cuba put an end to its forced apprenticeships. In practice, this was abolition. Just as the Spanish law of 1870 (Free Womb and Sexagenarian Law) had led, a year later, to the Brazilian Free Womb Law and, in 1885, to its own Sexagenarian Law, the final abolition of slavery by Brazil's Caribbean neighbor urged for its own

[39] *O País*, Jul. 29, 1886.
[40] ASI, Jul. 30, 1886; Ignácio Martins, ASI, Aug. 2, 1886; Cotegipe, ASI, May 12, 1888.

equivalents. Brazil had finally become what many abolitionists had feared it would since the 1860s: the last slave-owning society in the Americas and one of the few remaining anywhere in the world. Cotegipe realized that he would have to send some signals to the international community, but he did so in the usual pro-slavery style: instead of abolishing the institution, he banned whipping. The Justice Minister himself proposed the injunction and it was sanctioned on October 15.[41] Once again, it was all for show, as the law made no provisions for how it would be enforced. Banning extreme corporal punishment spared the government from embarrassment in the national and international press, but in reality the slaves were still very much at their owners' mercy. In a sense, the move also inadvertently pushed the conflict to the private sphere, seeing as the abolitionists now took to pestering the slave owners directly to ensure that they were complying with the new law.

That October, José Bonifácio (the Lad), from the anti-whipping bloc in the Senate, died. A meeting was held at the newsroom of O País, and the decision was taken to schedule abolitionist demonstrations during the funeral. Nabuco and Artur Silveira da Mota traveled down to São Paulo in order to prepare a funeral meeting there. They arrived at already packed streets, thanks to Antônio Bento, who had mustered a crowd of 4,000, with a band playing and flowers thrown from the windows. Nabuco gave a speech, followed by Bocaiúva, the leader of the Republican Party, lending the event an anti-monarchist flavor. The Emperor responded with a breach of protocol, refusing to send a representative to a senator's funeral.

That same October, Patrocínio attended a ceremony in Santos and, in November, a civic session was held in José Bonifácio's honor at the São José Theater in São Paulo, with various Liberals in attendance and representatives from São Paulo's many abolitionist associations. This event proved that the alliance between public space abolitionists and the parliamentary Dantas bloc remained strong, as the attendees included Clapp, president of the CA, Rui Barbosa, as Speaker, and Dantas presiding. Antônio Bento made a tribute to the illustrious visitors in the name of freedom for Brazilian slaves. It was apparent from their speeches that these figures were there less to mourn Bonifácio than to fight Cotegipe. That night, at a session packed with men in black and ladies in evening

---

[41] Law 3310. The only article on slave whipping is by Needell (2012). However, he argues in the opposite direction, saying that the Prime Minister had hoped to assuage abolitionist opposition by making this concession.

## 292 · The Last Abolition

hats, Bonifácio, the Lad, never a great combatant in life, it must be said, was inducted into the pantheon of the movement's icons. Up on the stage, he was represented in an allegory that showed him mounted "on a cloud of smoke resting resplendent upon Luís Gama and Rio Branco."[42]

### A NEW WAVE OF FREE SOIL CAMPAIGN

Under Cotegipe, the free soil campaign strategy, hitherto supported by local authorities, encountered fresh resistance. In order to continue in its attempt to liberate provinces, the movement responded with a *shift in scale*: they handpicked cities and towns where their presence was strong, but which were also central to the pro-slavery countermovement. The port town of Santos, where slave stocks were tiny – according to the 1886 registration, there were only fifty-eight slaves in the whole town – became their main priority. The movement had failed there in 1883, but the 27th of February Emancipatory Society, named after its foundation date in 1886, decided to have another shot at it, this time using the new dramatic-style based on Christian symbolism. On Good Friday that year, the society called upon the town's slave owners to manumit their charges in the name of their religious values. The choice of Santos was also strategic. The town was a transport hub where the coast-bound inland railroads met the North-South shipping routes, which, in addition to proximity to the Jabaquara quilombo in the Sea Mountains, made Santos the ideal place to receive assisted runaway slaves for shipment north to Ceará's free soil. Santos came to be the heart of the contention. In November, Cotegipe informed the Emperor of how he planned to deal with the abolitionists:

We have a law, which the government is obliged to enforce, that recognizes the ownership of slaves, and so long as that law abides, the ownership it protects must be guaranteed ... I see no advantage, if advantage there be in disobeying the law, in allowing places where slavery is no more to become inviolable asylums for fugitive slaves, something more dangerous than the harboring already penalized under the Law of September 28, 1885.

If the authorities fail to assist the slave owners, not only will they be remiss in their duty, but will become accomplices to the disorder that shall inexorably

---

[42] DNAAR, Oct. 26, 1886; DJN, Oct. 26, 1886; Duque-Estrada (1918, p. 163). The Liberal MPs were the Baron Homem de Melo and Afonso Celso Jr.; among the São Paulo abolitionists were Francisco Rangel Pestana, Francisco Glicério, Ciro Azevedo, Clímaco Barbosa, and Fernandes Coelho. Tributes turned into abolitionist demonstrations in other towns too, such as Caçapava (GT, Dec. 6, 8, 10, 22, 1886).

## Bullets: Movement and Countermovement

derive from the owners' direct efforts to take back what is rightfully theirs. .... As such, it is my understanding that these lawless acts be repressed prudently, yet vigorously.[43]

So with the Crown's approval or omission, Cotegipe set about fulfilling his duty of repressing abolitionists and runaways. In November 1886, the very month the above letter was written, the Minister for Agriculture Antônio Prado sent the provincial chief of police to teach the abolitionists a lesson by recapturing four slaves who had fled to Santos. The movement, however, was a step ahead, and the police were assailed by an angry crush that prevented the captives from being loaded aboard a waiting train. Bedlam ensued, with gunfire and casualties, and in the middle of the chaos, the abolitionists managed to get the slaves onto a boat and safely out to sea.[44] Soon after the ruckus, Santos was declared free soil and was turned into a new asylum for fugitive slaves.

This was the impulse needed to spark a new wave of the free soil campaign. The CA captained commissions to free more street blocks in Court, liberating 7,484 slaves. In the capital of Minas Gerais, the movement for the liberation of Ouro Preto used the same method, mounting two commissions to raise funds for manumissions. Carlos de Lacerda took the strategy into the environs of Campos, where he orchestrated a civic session to promote mass manumissions at the Simão Farm on New Year's Eve 1887, with the CA invited to attend. Clapp was unable to go, as he was touring various other locations, but at a meeting in Goiás he explained that the CA had considered all abolitionist associations part of its confederation and would support them in any way possible.[45]

Antônio Bento's group launched a free soil campaign in São Paulo in June 1887, during which it used *A Redempção* to call on all three parties to fall in behind the cause. In August, the same strategy was put in motion in Salvador. Between August 1887 and February 1888, a further fourteen cities were declared free soils, scattered throughout Alagoas, Maranhão, Minas Gerais, Paraná, Rio de Janeiro, Rio Grande do Norte, Santa

---

[43] RN, Jun. 9, 1886; AR, Mar. 6 and Aug. 23, 1887; Machado (2006); letter from the Baron of Cotegipe to D. Pedro II, Nov. 22, 1886; D. Pedro II (1933, p. 286). "Scale shift" is the mechanism by which social movements, when faced with stiff opposition on a given level of action – local, national, global – move their efforts to another level (McAdam, Tarrow, and Tilly, 2001).

[44] AR, Mar. 27, 1887; Conrad (1975, p. 292).

[45] The CA veteran Nicolau Moreira led the campaign in Court – the province still had 238,631 slaves (RN, Feb. 17, 1887, Jun. 30, 1886). GT, Dec. 15 and 29, 1886; AR, Apr. 29, 1887; Cota (2013).

294 *The Last Abolition*

Catarina, and São Paulo. In January 1888, two provincial capitals were also declared liberated, namely Natal and Curitiba, as was the capital of the Empire itself, Rio de Janeiro.[46] In addition to the free provinces of Ceará and Amazonas, with Rio Grande do Sul on the cusp of joining them, the movement managed to challenge the slavery system over half of the Empire.

And yet the public celebrations were discreet. The central government's repressive turn made them dangerous for the participants. The abolitionists found other ways to mark their achievements. In Paquetá, they decorated one of the local abolitionist's houses and threw a party there, complete with fireworks, band, *marche aux flambeaux*, flowers, and speeches by Carneiro de Cunha and Dantas. There was nothing Cotegipe could do about it: though no mention was made of a newborn, the gathering was officially a baptism party.[47]

### CIVIL DISOBEDIENCE

Cotegipe's policy forced the abolitionists to diversify their arenas. Concert-conferences, freedom suits, association-forming, and free soil campaigns continued, but another tactic that had previously only been secondary now came to the fore, civil disobedience. The movement embraced an open battle.

In March, Patrocínio went to Campos, where he was welcomed with flowers, fireworks, and civic parades. But he was there on a dual mission: he had come to throw a lighted match into a haystack. His friend Lacerda, leader of the Campos' Liberating Society, had been fighting pro-slavery countermovement by hook and by crook, in his newspaper *Vinte e Cinco de Março*, and by promoting assisted collective runaways, burning plantations and raiding farms. Patrocínio's visit signaled a change of tack for the movement, turning away from the institutions, where their best attempts under Dantas had come to little, toward a more incendiary and self-directed approach. In this, he had Nabuco's blessing. After all, if Parliament was deaf to the issue, the nation must take matters into its own hands. Swept from the institutions, the abolitionists turned against them.[48]

---

[46] AR, Jun. 9, Aug. 14; CR, Oct. 23; AR, Nov. 24, 1887; CR, Jan. 21, Feb. 8 and 27; Feb. 14, 15, 16, 28; Mar. 7 and 15, Apr. 2 and 19, 1888; AR, Feb. 1, 5, and 12; Mar. 22 and 25; Apr. 19, 26, 29, 1888.

[47] CR, Feb. 6, 1888.

[48] Magalhães Jr. (1969, p. 192); Lima (1981, pp. 139 ff.); Monnerat (2012, pp. 95–6). Letter from Joaquim Nabuco to José do Patrocínio, May 3, 1886, CAI. The form of expression a social movement opts for largely depends on its interpretation of the balance between opportunities for action (such as the existence of allies inside the institutions) and

## Bullets: Movement and Countermovement

Collective slave runaways, quilombos, slave revolts, the murder of masters and slave overseers, and the torching of plantations had always existed. During the Second Reign there had been maroon colonies and rebellions in at least half of the Empire, in Pernambuco, Mato Grosso, Maranhão, Rio Grande do Sul, Pará, Espírito Santo, São Paulo, Minas Gerais, and in the countryside of Rio de Janeiro. In the Campos region, resistance was endemic. Hence, the fight against slavery was not exclusive to the abolitionists; there were autonomous slave resistances too. However, as Flávio Gomes, João Reis, and Maria Helena Machado point out, there was some overlap and collaboration between these fronts. During the Cotegipe government, two social processes overlapped: expelled from the public space, abolitionists adopted extra-institutional modes of action, and the slaves, realizing that they now had a support network, felt encouraged to escape. This convergence led to a new strategy, the assisted collective runaways.

This was not a Brazilian invention. Once again, the abolitionists dipped into the international abolitionist repertoire. The underground railroad in the United States provided a tried-and-tested model. In 1883, Patrocínio published an article in the GT under the title "Caminho de ferro subterrâneo emancipador" (Emancipating underground railroad), which didactically explained the secret system of slave escape routes and marked with codes safe houses that led – with or without abolitionist help – thousands of runaways out of the Confederacy and to safety in the slavery-free North. To avoid being hunted down by posses of slave catchers, some of these escape routes went all the way into Canada, which, as part of the British Empire, prohibited slavery. Brazilian abolitionists adopted and adapted the strategy, with the free soils of Ceará, Amazonas, and Santos serving as a sort of internal Canada. Unlike in the United States, those runaways in Brazil were, as Eduardo Silva points out, more break-ins than break-outs. They were attempts to implode rather than explode the slavery system.[49]

---

the threats, especially chances of coercion. Under repressive governments, activists tend to switch from public demonstrations, which leave them exposed, to less visible or even clandestine forms of action. Where they are violently repressed, they may react violently themselves (Tarrow, 2005).

[49] Gomes (2006, pp. 49–107, 209–303); Reis (1995–1996, pp. 18, 19, 31, 33); Machado (1994). The strategy of "mass escapes" intensified in the 1880s, "with or without the assistance of abolitionists" (Reis, 1995–1996, pp. 29–30). See also the collection by Reis and Gomes (1996), Silva (2009, p. 72). I am only mentioning runaway events in which

Assisted collective runaways grew in number and frequency after the promulgation of the Black Regulation, a local version of the Fugitive Slave Act, which backfired in Brazil as it had in the United States: rather than prevent, it encouraged clandestine actions. And it was not just one group or other that adopted the strategy; the whole abolitionist movement turned to civil disobedience as a last resort: "Why flowers, why music . . .? It's a waste of time! . . . Abolitionists need to go underground, as they have in the capital [Court], and work together. . . ."[50] This was the orientation given in Antônio Bento's newspaper in São Paulo. This was also what the CA was doing in Court, assisting runaways. In partnership with provincial associations, the CA generalized this strategy that had previously been only secondary. According to Patrocínio, the CA had already been working with Antônio Bento, and with Luís Gama before him, on the "getaway of woebegone slaves."[51]

With a nationwide abolitionist activism network in place by that stage, the assisted collective runaways also spread across the nation. In 1887, an abolitionist from Bahia declared that it was the duty of all defenders of liberty to participate in forming an underground railroad in Brazil. In 1885, Rebouças said that "Rui Barbosa, Joaquim Nabuco, José Mariano [Carneiro da Cunha], and José do Patrocínio were ready to harbor runaways." He planned an escape route along the Upper São Francisco river into free soil Ceará, with Luís Gama's tomb in downtown São Paulo as its symbolic starting point.[52]

The strategy, like those before it, was a modular, portable activism. It required a secret society, a system of codes, a network of safe houses, and the collusion of transport system workers, which was why the routes had to be set up near tramways or railroads in the South and the ports of call of steamships in the North. It also took a great deal of audacity on the part of the abolitionists and negligence on the side of the authorities. This strategy depended on something the other tactics had not, namely the active participation of the slaves. Rather than going door-to-door appealing to slave owners' pockets or better natures, as under the free soil campaign, abolitionists started to go from farm to farm, house to house, in the dead of night, pursuing a modus operandi described in *A Redempção*:

---

I have been able to identify the direct participation of the abolitionist movement. Patrocínio's article on the underground railroad is in GT, May 21, 1883.

[50] AR, Jul. 21, 1887.    [51] CR, Apr. 30, 1888.

[52] Fonseca (1887, pp. 341–2, 344–5, 350); DNAAR, Sept. 18, 1885.

# Bullets: Movement and Countermovement 297

Incite slave workers to strike, make them realize that they are being worked to death, make them abandon the farms, obliging the owners of these Bastilles to start employing paid labor instead; this should be the mission of all abolitionists.[53]

The system was installed in various provinces, with adjustments tailored to local conditions. The CA tried to coordinate the sundry initiatives under a national system, which Rebouças rather wordily called the Patriotic League for the Harboring of Escapees from Slavery. These assisted collective runaways were channeled through a network of local associations cultivated throughout the campaign. Without the centralization Rebouças was hoping for,[54] the system ended up being federal, like the CA. The modular strategy gave room to local adaptations, with each group customizing the format to suit its own local reality.

### The Northern Liberation Network: the Dead and Termites

The network of assisted collective runaways in the North began to form straight after the liberation of Ceará. Far away from Cotegipe's bayonets and the furiously pro-slavery Paraíba Valley, in Rio de Janeiro, where Paulino reigned supreme, it functioned rather smoothly. The brainchild of abolitionists from Ceará, Amazonas, Rio Grande do Norte, Paraíba, and Maranhão, it operated at ports where steamships joined the dots of the region's provincial capitals, with Recife as the epicenter. Recife was home to the law faculty, a steady source of abolitionist recruits, and also of Carneiro da Cunha's group, which had been collaborating with the Termites Club since the Dantas government's crisis.

The initiative came from an accountant from Maranhão called João Ramos, a member of the Abolitionist Club of Recife, and a founder, in 1884, of *Relâmpago* (Lightning strike), dedicated to help slaves to flee as fast as the speed of light from bondage. Ramos was joined by a dozen or so law students from the faculty, and each of them adopted a codename referring to one of the provinces. Ramos was Ceará and Carneiro da Cunha, the last to join, ended up as Espírito Santo. Since the Relâmpago's secret was soon disclosed, the group renamed itself as the Termites Club, an allusion to the silent chipping away at the foundations of slavery.

---

[53] Silva (2009, pp. 19 ff.); AR, July 21, 1887.

[54] Rebouças (1889), in Silva (2003). Conrad (1972, pp. 189–90) speaks of a system originating in São Paulo, Minas Gerais, and Rio de Janeiro with Ceará as its destination, but he does not go into detail.

298                    *The Last Abolition*

According to its articles of association, the Termites Club members were there to "rescue the highest possible number of citizens from the hands of the catchers." They had codes for everything: slaves were "Englishmen" (an allusion to the 1831 law) and the password for boarding trains and other forms of transport was "love and patria." The euphemism for escape was "citizen switch" and the meeting points were given enigmatic names like "pau de pinho" (pine staff).[55]

The Termites Club members' daily routine consisted of rescuing and hiding fugitive slaves. The member who went by the name of Acarape, after the first free soil town in the nation, freed seventy-odd slaves from a local mill without leaving a single trace. Amazonas transported thirty-four slaves to Ceará aboard a sailing ship. It was all done under the cover of darkness, and it was a thoroughly risky business. On one occasion, Carneiro de Cunha and João Ramos managed to make a slave climb from balcony to balcony until she reached the house of one of the Termite Club members. Then, on Carnival Sunday, the three of them dressed up as dominoes, Ramos and another Termites Club member snuck the slave woman to the port, where she boarded a boat for Aracati in Ceará. As the ruse had ended in confetti and streamers, they repeated the strategy with a sweet seller. They whitened the girl with face powder and dressed her in a fancy gown. Out in the streets, they ran into the slave's owner. With some quick thinking, the Termites Club member bowed to the gentleman, who raised his hat to the lady and went on his way.[56]

Women were key to the success of the escapes because by opening their homes to meetings or fugitives they gave law-breaking an air of respectability. D. Olegarinha, Carneiro da Cunha's wife, put her farmhouse, Poço da Panela (Pot Well), at the club's disposal. The house served as an overflow for assisted runaways that had to be evacuated from other safe houses during raids, like the one that took place in September 1885, when she received the express order: "Get them to relocate all the existing Englishmen from said place, without delay."[57]

---

[55] The Termites Club was started in October 1884 (Clube do Cupim, minutes, Dec. 5, 1884). The original members were João Ramos (also known as Ceará), Numa Pompílio (Mato Grosso), Alfredo Vieira de Melo (Minas Gerais), Antônio Farias (Rio Grande do Sul), Gaspar da Costa (Rio de Janeiro), Guilherme Pinto (Goiás), Nuno Alves da Fonseca (Alagoas), J. Lages (Amazonas), Luís Amaral (Pernambuco), Joaquim Pessoa (Rio Grande do Norte), Fernando Castro (Maranhão), Alfredo Pinto (Bahia). Cf. Clube do Cupim, minutes, session Oct. 8, 1884, Aug. 30, 1885, Nov. 21, 1884 and Aug. 22, 1885.
[56] Clube do Cupim, Nov. 21, 1884; Aug. 22, 1885; May 13, 1905, in Silva (1988, pp. 31–2).
[57] Clube do Cupim, Sept., 1885.

## Bullets: Movement and Countermovement

A lot of people took part in these operations, including abolitionists from the political institutions. For example, while Nabuco was doing the rounds of Pernambuco with Carneiro da Cunha to denounce the illegal use of whipping, he harbored a fugitive slave and defended the Termites Club strategy in the local press. He said that, wherever the pair went:

[S]laves came up to us, and in many places I learned that they escaped soon after our departure. This will be inevitable from now on. Abolitionism will spread throughout the province. The underground railroad will become just as strong as the submarine [escapes through Santos], and ... the so-called Termites Club will set to work the length and breadth of the province .... We are moving into a new phase. ... The abolitionists of this province are slave-harborers one and all. ... It's the only way to enforce what the law abolished.[58]

The Pernambuco/Ceará itinerary was viable because of their geographical proximity and the longstanding relationship between two Joãos, Romão, in Recife, and Cordeiro, in Fortaleza. They arranged transportation for fugitives by letter, enabling the Termites to extend their tunnels into the neighboring provinces. They sent "Englishmen" to Mossoró, a free town in Rio Grande do Norte, and had ties with fellow abolitionists in Belém and Manaus, Goiás and Paraíba. The member codenamed Alagoas wanted to start a quilombo in Amazonas to settle fugitives coming from Recife. The Termites also dug a new route South, from Rio de Janeiro to Rio Grande do Sul and from there to Montevideo, and they sent a delegation to request the collaboration of Rio's abolitionist societies.

The Termites Club's members mainly operated behind the scenes, but they also had a public face and occasionally even appealed to the authorities, calling for slave-trading operations to be shut down, and denouncing the continued use of lashing. In 1885, horrified by the Saraiva bill, they drafted an open letter of disgust toward the government and published it in the *Jornal do Recife*: "The Termites Club has no political color and pledges to continue with its assistance to free slaves." Though they remained active until April 1888, and were hounded here and there, they abandoned the register of their illegal activities and went underground for good.[59]

---

[58] Various others also participated, such as Martins Jr. and Aníbal and Júlio Falcão (Castilho, 2008, p. 225). DJN, Nov. 1, 1886; Nabuco, *O País*, Apr. 19, 1887.

[59] Gaspar (2009, p. 1); Castilho (2008, p. 77); Vilela, May 13, 1905, in Silva (1988, p. 33); Medeiros (1925), in Leonardo Dantas Silva (1988, p. 44); Gaspar (2009, p. 1). Word began to appear in October 1885 about the formation of "an English colony in Amazonas" (Clube do Cupim, Oct. 15, 1885). Clube do Cupim, Sept. 3, 1885; Nov. 27, 1884, Aug. 22, 1885; Castilho (2008, p. 202).

300    *The Last Abolition*

In the North, there were other secret organizations at work, and as they were less bombastic than the Termites, they were harder to trace and track. The Diretório dos Cinco (Board of Five), otherwise known as the Club of the Dead, was a youthful organization in São Luís, in the province of Maranhão, with roughly sixty members, most of them college students like Aluísio and Artur Azevedo, versed in the methods of Patrocínio. Like their master, they ran their operations from a local bar. These well-heeled students provided the group with financial backing, but the actual foot soldiers came from the lower-strata – for example, one of them was a barber. The name of the outfit – the Club of the Dead – was an allusion to the phantom-like stealth it took to sneak fugitive slaves into Ceará, but it was also a reference to a member's family farm they changed to quilombo. The abolitionists simulated strange noises and spread rumors that the property was overrun with ghosts. Making the place seem haunted kept wanderers away and allowed the fugitives to stay in peace and even continue subsistence farming.[60]

The Club of the Dead mixed concert-conference style propaganda with clandestine activity. They formed an activist network between Ceará and Belém, and though more modest in size and results than the Termites, their members were just as daring, with some escapes pulled off during the daylight hours. For these operations they relied on "the rough-and-ready, as the local tough guys were called, ... a group of intelligent, idealistic colored men who always turned up at our freedom rallies." These free black men were the founders of the Maranhão Abolitionist Arts Center, set up to work in conjunction with the Club of the Dead.[61]

The success of the assisted runaways depended on a cooperation network in the towns, the help of transport workers, and a blind-eye from the local authorities. For example, when a slave owner telegraphed the police in Mossoró asking them to intercept a fugitive named Matias at the station there (he was one of twenty "Englishmen" of one Termites Club's relocations), the telegraph operator contacted João Ramos, who passed himself off as the owner and sent a follow-up telegraph saying, "Matias just turned up."

This call to clandestine action left the House in a rage. An MP from the pro-slavery caucus denounced the SCL as a subversive organization because it had received, in Fortaleza, slaves the Cupins had smuggled out of Recife. One dumbstruck slaveowner recounted how "an

[60] The farm belonged to the family of Dunshee de Abranches (1941, pp. 169, 170, 179–80).
[61] Abranches (1941, pp. 182–3, 185).

## Bullets: Movement and Countermovement

abolitionist propagandist turned up on his farm preaching to his slaves," "urging them to *emigrate to the beacon land [Ceará]."* Another grumbled in a pamphlet that "everyone knows that that province [Ceará] has become an asylum for slaves from all over the Empire, including many shipped out of here [Court]."[62]

Interprovincial connections and widespread social support solidified the assisted runaways, generating unrest among slaveowners everywhere.[63] If Cotegipe had sought to prolong slavery by law, the abolitionists were striving to put an end to this institution by direct action.

### The Southern Liberation Network: Caiaphases and Camellias

In the South, the strategy faced additional difficulties: it was far away from the free provinces, and it was dangerously close to the Paraíba Valley and the west of São Paulo, where the country's largest slave population was held and the political pro-slavery movement was strongest. The importance of slave labor to the local economy meant the people were less sympathetic to abolition and the authorities far less lenient. Operating in such inhospitable territory required redoubled daring.

From the beginning of the campaign, São Paulo abolitionists had provided cover for fleeing slaves, but it was Antônio Bento de Sousa e Castro who made this assistance systematic. John Brown had been Luís Gama's idol, but it was Bento who resembled the American more closely. They were from the same social position, a wealthy background, both white, and chose the same method, the use of violence in the fight against slavery. Having been hanged in 1859, by the 1880s Brown had become a global abolitionist icon, famous for a heterodoxy of methods that ran from assisting on the underground railroad to inciting slave revolution.

Bento followed in his footsteps. "Thin, straight as an arrow from ankle to ear, tubelike in his greatcoat and tall hat," he wore a "wire-taut goatee and kept his glare concealed behind blue-tinted glasses like a blade in its sheath." He was a "man of contrasts, gentle, but violent," who "gives orders like a general yet obeys like a foot soldier." When the Dantas government collapsed, he turned the São Paulo Abolitionist Center into a

---

[62] The telegraph operator was the abolitionist Júlio Falcão; Vilela, May 13, 1905, in Silva (1988, pp. 31–2). The pro-slavery MP was Rodrigues Jr. (GT, May 11, 1885); Um Lavrador (1884, p. 22).

[63] Rebouças also mentions the connection with the Termites Club, which was sending fugitives to Rio Grande do Norte as well (DNAAR, Feb. 4, 1889).

302    *The Last Abolition*

fortress behind an escape and safe house network. Raul Pompeia, who followed him with the same bravery as had Gama, spoke of how the Caiaphases operated in the shadows, "without name, residence, or profession, always disciplined, resolute, elusive, impalpable." Disguised as peddlers or workmen, they infiltrated the slave pens so they could win their trust and put to work their "revolutionary plot." As in the North, collaboration was key: a rural smallholder would offer to harbor fugitives at his property after their escape, and they would then be collected there at an arranged time. It was a risky mission, and one of these collaborators was murdered at the gate of a farm in Belém do Descalvado. In the obituary of another Caiaphas, *A Redempção* laid the procedure bare: the activist, "leaving his home late at night, would come to us to arrange how best to snatch the unhappy slaves from the catchers' claws."[64]

Bento orchestrated escapes even against his own brother-in-law, who, like Jacobina in Machado de Assis' short story "The Mirror," ended up alone on a deserted farm. In town, on feast days, he would go knocking on mansion doors asking for letters of manumission in honor of the occasion, while Caiaphases helped slaves escape out the back door. To cover his tracks, he drew upon his position with the Remédios Brotherhood.

If the escape was successful, the slaves would find a network of helpers and be delivered to a provisory safe house, which could have been the home of anyone from a pharmacist to a wealthy trader. Bento kept a house for precisely this purpose, marked by a white flag. The most critical part was transportation, which fell to the law students, who persuaded or bribed the coach drivers and train-station inspectors. Sometimes abolitionists counted on the collaboration of the authorities, even policemen, to coordinate the escapers' helpers in São Paulo with handlers in Santos and Court.[65]

One possible haven was the Jabaquara quilombo, built along the road to Santos in 1882. It was commanded by a Portuguese and a former slave who had worked as a cook for a Republican party family. The quilombo grew to the point that it held an incredible 20,000 inhabitants at its zenith. Usually, after lying low for a time, the fugitive slaves were given fake certificates of manumission and had jobs arranged for them loading

---

[64] Pompeia, GN, Aug. 27, 1888. The following were all mentioned as being Caiaphases: José Mariano Garcia, Antônio Paciência, and João Antônio Ribeiro de Lima (AR, May. 5, 1887; CR, Feb. 17, 1888; Duque-Estrada, 1918, p. 82, note 23; GN, Aug. 27, 1888; Andrada, 1918, pp. 213, 216, 219). The only study about the group is by Fontes (1976) who draws a distinction between a legal phase (1882–1887) and a clandestine one (1887–1888).

[65] Andrada (1918, pp. 217, 219, 221); Conrad (1975, p. 296); Fontes (1976, p. 76).

## Bullets: Movement and Countermovement

coffee at the docks or as paid farm hands. Bento would negotiate collective contracts: "He made agreements with farmers whose lands he had already emptied of labor so that they would hire slaves from other owners."[66]

Like the Termites, the Caiaphases communicated in code: slaves were "loads," "turkeys," or "piglets",[67] and the abolitionists recognized each other from the camellias they wore on their left lapels. Raul Pompeia, for example, stole a slave in São Paulo and sent him to Rio de Janeiro, where, at the Central Station, he was met by a member of the CA. The communication was conducted by telegram: "Sending baggage train." The fugitive was then taken to an abolitionist's house while transport could be arranged to Ceará.[68]

Camellias also marked the quilombos that were forming in Court. The largest of these, in Leblon, with gardens of camellias, was run by a member of the CA. This quilombo harbored many for a long time, and under relative normality. In 1887, for example, a birthday party was held there by roughly fifty quilombolas, one of whom saluted the abolitionists. The compliment was returned by Nabuco, who, like most CA activists, maintained connections with the harboring network, from North to South.[69]

Rebouças recorded seven other CA-run quilombos in or around Court. One of these, under Patrocínio's command, and bearing his name, functioned out of his own home and his newspaper's newsroom. Clapp's was practically institutional. It was based at the CA headquarters and at Clapp's own house. His whole family was involved in running it, and one of his sons was arrested on charges of slave-springing. Advertisements in the GT described Clapp's porcelain shop as an office at which fugitive slaves could seek help day or night.[70]

---

[66] Andrada (1918, p. 217); Silva (2009, pp. 12, 72).
[67] Schmidt (1981); Sampaio Azevedo (1890, p. 9).
[68] Andrada (1918, p. 217); Duque-Estrada (1918, pp. 86–7).
[69] The birthday boy was the quilombo's leader, the Portuguese José de Seixas Magalhães, from the CA, who organized a festival commemorating the liberation of Ceará (Brício Filho, 1928, p. 106). Nabuco, who is often portrayed as having remained aloof from the "radicals," was there for the party, and so was clearly involved with the clandestine networks in the North and South.
[70] GT, Dec. 11, 1883. Other quilombos were the Senna, in São Cristovão, run by Patrocínio's mother-in-law, the Miguel Dias in Catumbi, run by a member of the CA, the Camorim in Serra, the Raymundo in Engenho Novo, the Padre Ricardo and the Tipografia Central de Evaristo da Costa, which was not a quilombo, but operated as one (Rebouças, 1889, in Silva, 2003, pp. 98–101).

304 *The Last Abolition*

The Patriotic League, as Rebouças called it, offered a wide-ranging informal asylum network:

At the houses of abolitionist families, commercial offices, newspaper newsrooms, hotels, bakeries, large factories, army barracks, print shops, everywhere there was an abolitionist soul safe haven could be found.[71]

The assisted collective runaway subsystem in the South had three main poles (farm/house, transport, safe haven) and two destinations, local quilombos or the free soils of Santos and Ceará. This circuit, which had already existed, was honed in the latter months of 1887, channeling escapes from various towns throughout the São Paulo hinterland. In Piracicaba, a plantation owner woke up one morning to find himself 100 slaves short.[72]

In the province of Rio de Janeiro, the focus was Campos. Towards the end of 1887, Lacerda and his people were both harboring slaves from elsewhere and springing slaves from local properties. As the pro-slavery countermovement was strong in the region, the conflict was tough. Local hooligans spoiled newspapers going to print and broke up conferences. The abolitionists retaliated by burning plantations and inciting slave revolts. In Ouro Preto, then capital of Minas Gerais, the chief of police recorded countless slave breaks. In Paraná, in June 1887, a secret group was formed under the apt title of Ultimatum, which was willing to use force to get what it wanted.[73]

As well as in the North, the network in the South had society support. Rather than discouraging the sheltering of runaway slaves, Cotegipe's Black Regulation rallied people to the cause who would not have otherwise engaged, and this allowed the abolitionist network to expand beyond the big cities and the urban middle strata, conquered by concert-conferences. The movement gained capillarity, with its tendrils reaching into the lower social strata, the transport workers (engine drivers, coachmen, dockers,

---

[71] Rebouças (1889), in Silva (2003, p. 96).

[72] There was news of escapes in Belém do Descalvado, Pirassununga, Rio Claro, Santa Rita do Passo Quatro, Campinas, Amparo, Casa Branca, Taubaté, São José dos Campos, Moji das Cruzes, Guaratinguetá, Caçapava, Santa Isabel, Pindamonhangaba, Jundiaí, Itatiba, Tatuí, Itu, Atibaia, Serra Negra, Penha do Rio do Peixe, Mogi-Mirim, Botucatu, Limeira, Araras, Jacareí, Capivari (Machado, 2009, pp. 376–7; Andrada, 1918, p. 216; Fontes, 1976; Sampaio Azevedo, 1890, pp. 9 ff., and Fonseca, 1887, p. 602).

[73] Fonseca (1887, p. 602); Toplin (1972, pp. 182 ff.); Ianni (1988, pp. 228–9). Abolitionists had been fired from newspapers, such as Joaquim Serra, who was forced out of the *Folha Nova* "under pressure from slavocrats" (DNAAR, Aug. 5, 1884). The fearless abolitionist in Minas was Américo Luz (Cota, 2013, p. 232).

## Bullets: Movement and Countermovement

and seamen), and local apothecaries and peddlers, who roamed the backlands. This solidarity network hid and covered for assisted runaways, threw predators and police off their trail, and enabled escapes on a scale that activists alone could never have achieved. One example is that of a slave dressed as a priest who spent a whole train ride pretending to be engrossed in his Bible. As he was illiterate, he did not notice that the book was upside down.[74]

Thus, Cotegipe's truncheon politics backfired, fostering a strategy of civil disobedience. Thanks to the assisted collective runaways the abolitionists went deep down in the society. The movement's public face shrank before repression, but its clandestine operations grew longer and broader. They were halves of the same moon, and it waxed to fullness in the second half of 1887. The movement, already a nationwide and coordinated activism network in the main urban centers, had now seeped into the backlands, with enormous social support. It was chewing away at slavocrat social order like termites in an old wooden house.

### BACK TO PARLIAMENT

In the Senate, Dantas, Otoni, and Silveira da Mota, now joined by others balking at Cotegipe's hardline methods, continued to torment the government. A pair of snap elections provided perfect opportunities. The first of these was the by-election to replace the deceased Bonifácio (the Lad). There was no victory in this one. The vote went to the Dantas government's arch-enemy Moreira de Barros. The second was called when Cotegipe replaced one of his ministers in July 1887. The new minister was Nabuco's adversary in the 1884 elections, and his appointment had to be ratified by the electoral college of the first district of Recife. In an attempt to block it, the movement relaunched Nabuco's candidacy.[75]

This time, however, under Cotegipe's truculent administration, the campaign of concert-conferences and street rallies from the 1884 elections could not be re-implemented on the same scale. The president of Pernambuco banned marching bands and threatened to fire civil servants

---

[74] Toplin (1972, p. 185) registers popular support for the slave escapes sprung by abolitionists in 1887–1888 as pushback against the Black Regulation. The Bible episode is in Schmidt (1981).

[75] In other snap elections that same year, the abolitionists launched Artur Silveira da Mota and supported Homem de Melo in Court (AR, Feb. 3, Mar. 4, 1887). The same occurred in São Paulo, where Antônio Bento ran for the Conservatives (CP, Jul. 7, 1887). The praise for Nabuco's candidacy is in *A Redempção*.

306 *The Last Abolition*

who participated in abolitionist events. The Cabinet went so far as to call in the navy to disperse street demonstrations, but to its dismay and the movement's delight, the warship sank en route.

When the abolitionists pressed ahead with their plans to hold a rally at Afogados, Recife, they were met by battalions of riot and mounted police. In the ensuing mêlée, a supporter of Nabuco's opponent was killed and, once again, Nabuco and Carneiro da Cunha turned up to carry the dead man's coffin, despite the large presence of pro-slavery locals and the police.

The election was held amid an explosive atmosphere. Cotegipe used all the dark arts the apparatus of power could deploy; however the abolitionists canvassed vote to vote and they won the day: 1,407 votes for Nabuco versus 1,270 for his opponent. It was a miraculous victory: ". . . the city is delirious with joy. We've made history today!" Students at the law faculty defied Cotegipe with a march in Recife, with the shops all closed and the streets decorated with lights. Nabuco was given a hero's welcome everywhere he stopped on his way to Rio de Janeiro. Though a local election, the victory was national, with celebrations in Fortaleza, Ouro Preto, São Paulo, and in Court, as abolitionists everywhere united against Cotegipe.[76]

Instead of dismounting, as one would expect after having a minister's appointment rejected at the ballot box, Cotegipe decided to flog the dead horse. Cadets at the Military Academy, many of whom were Republicans and members of the Abolitionist Society of Privates and Cadets, were charged with insubordination and sentenced to twenty days in jail for having greeted Nabuco upon his arrival at the quays. It was one of many spats he would have with the armed forces throughout 1887, a bad time to be at loggerheads with the people in charge of the firepower, since he needed them to keep the slave-owning social order. Nabuco, Patrocínio, and Rui Barbosa were astute enough to pander to the bruised egos of the imprisoned cadets and the military top brass, when they said "Cotegipe treated us like slaves." The army returned the abolitionist compliment in August, when Lieutenant-Colonel Sena Madureira allowed an abolitionist rally to go ahead outside the headquarters of *O País*, against "Noggin Shearer" Coelho Bastos' orders. Bocaiúva delivered a speech calling for abolition and the proclamation of a republic and celebrated the fact that

---

[76] Letter from Joaquim Nabuco to the Baron of Penedo, Sept. 15, 1887, CAI; DJN, Sept. 15, 26, 29, 1887; AR, Sept. 18, 1887. On the military issue, see Schulz (1994) and Castro (1995).

# Bullets: Movement and Countermovement

"freedom of assembly, denied by the police, [was] being exercised in the middle of the street nonetheless, in the presence of the mounted troops and the humiliated authorities who purport to wield them ... Hail to the army!"[77]

The army/government conflict gave a window of opportunity to the movement to find new allies inside the institutions. Nabuco decided to act: "I'm going to Rio just to get the army not to capture fugitive slaves." On his triumphant return to Parliament, on September 1887, this was precisely the speech he delivered from the stand.[78] Cotegipe had opted for force, so the abolitionists would do their utmost to deprive him of weapons.

## THE REGENT'S POLITICS

Revolutions are rare phenomena. However, revolutionary situations, when the pot threatens to boil over, are more frequent. According to Charles Tilly, a revolution produces a government overthrow and a replacement of the ruling elites, whereas in a revolutionary situation there is multiple sovereignty, with different groups competing for the state power, without any succeeding in establishing a monopoly or control, even by force.[79] This was the situation in Brazil in late 1887, when abolitionist civil disobedience, slave revolts, pro-slavery militias, Republican rallies, and insubordination among the armed forces conspired to put in check the government's capacity to rule. What was a government crisis escalated into a political regime crisis, when the question of dynastic succession emerged, causing the seemingly ceaseless uncertainty to reach its pinnacle.

The inheritance of the Crown, long expected given D. Pedro's advanced age and deteriorating health, had come to the fore at the turn of the year. In February 1887, the Emperor, drowsy with diabetes, fell ill in public. It was to be, Rebouças described, "that fatal malady that would lead him to Águas Claras, S. Cristovão, Tijuca, Europe." However, between sickness and departure there was a protracted wait. D. Pedro was afraid to leave the throne vacant, as Princess Isabel was out of the

---

[77] AR, Apr. 24 and Aug. 11, 1887.  [78] DJN, Sept. 24, 1887; ACD, Oct. 7, 1887.

[79] "A revolutionary situation begins when a government previously under the control of a single, sovereign polity becomes the object of effective, competing, mutually exclusive claims on the part of two or more distinct polities. It ends when a single sovereign polity regains control over the government" (Tilly, 1978, p. 191). See also Bennani-Chraïbi and Fillieule (2012).

308            *The Last Abolition*

country, and would only return four months later. During her absence, the moderating power was all but relinquished. While rumor had it that the Emperor, stricken with illness, moroseness, and ennui, had left the regime in Cotegipe's hands, he was still, up to that point, the moral authority behind the government. His transatlantic withdrawal with the nation in turmoil stripped him of that role. Moreover, Isabel had none of her father's appreciation of the subtleties of politics and no authority whatsoever over the party leaders, much less a political program of her own to offer. The future of the monarchy was now the main topic in the press. The Republicans saw D. Pedro's impending death as a golden opportunity for regime-change. Bocaiúva titled an article on the ship taking the Emperor to Europe "the monarchy's coffin." In the *Cidade do Rio*, Patrocínio started a new section under the self-explanatory title *O rei phantasma* (The Ghost King).[80]

The vacant throne cast a troubling shadow across the imperial elite. At a time that called for unity in the face of abolitionist and republican pressures, the political elite was divided on the prospect of a Third Reign. Few politicians were enthusiastic about Isabel, who was too Catholic even for the clericalists and was married to a Frenchman who had not hit it off at all well with the party leaders. So they came up with a Plan B (the Princess's firstborn son) and a Plan C (her nephew, Pedro Augusto).[81] The Princess was arriving on a weak footing for her first rehearsal as queen.

Some of the abolitionists found this rather auspicious. At the end of the Brazil-Paraguay War, in 1869, the Count d'Eu had released Paraguay's slaves and his wife Isabel now needed a symbol to mark her reign. Rebouças, used to princely company back in the 1860s, decided it was time to polish his courtly skills and win Isabel's ear, something he had failed to do with her father.

Cotegipe was also eager to step into the void. And he did. Overwhelmed by filial and maternal concerns, her nephew's rivalry, her duties to the court and the church, it was all Isabel could do just to keep the Second Reign alive long enough for a third to begin. The Prime Minister, now in his seventies, had been a politician long before Isabel

---

[80] DNAAR, Feb. 27, 1887; Coelho Neto (CR, Dec. 7, 1887). Barman (2000) describes the elderly D. Pedro as becoming mired in the details and so blind to the bigger political picture. His stubborn and overly cautious approach led to a political standstill. See also Schwarcz (1998) and Carvalho (2007).

[81] Del Priore (2007).

## Bullets: Movement and Countermovement 309

was born, and he told her that reform would signal the end of the monarchy. He clinched the deal with an appeal to their Catholic affinities, as the Princess noted in her diary: "The Prime Minister offered me his resignation, which I refused. The Baron of Cotegipe strikes me as a man who can steady the [Conservative] rule, and I see in him a firm tendency towards support on the religious front as well. Sadly, rare attributes both."

It was a delegation born of a muddied perception of the conjuncture. The military and slavery issues were blowing up in imperial faces before they had even registered as potential threats. In a letter dated July 1887, the Count d'Eu wrote that "despite what they say, the political situation is not so bad ... the Parliamentary year is half-way through and I believe we shall be able to end it without troubles." On July 14, when the Republicans celebrated Bastille Day in Rio de Janeiro, with Silva Jardim promising something similar in Brazil the coming year, the Princess wrote to her preceptor: "As for the ministers, so far they have been no trouble at all. Our meetings with them are few and brief: naturally, in the Emperor's absence, politics has slumbered."[82] Or was it she who was slumbering?

Without the Crown's yoke, Cotegipe could run amok. He cleared more space in which to pursue, out in the open, the politics he was already spinning in the shadows. Landowners and the market were spooked by the spiraling disorder and plummeting prices. In 1887, the slave market was predicting abolition the following year. It was then that Cotegipe's "rare attributes," and those of his fellows in the Senate (Paulino and Martinho Campos), began to bloom. The illustrator Agostini denounced the Prime Minister's African origins with a stereotype: he painted him as a monkey in a crown. Cotegipe ruled. It was a rule of violence.

Under the Dantas government, the struggle in the streets and in Parliament had been between the government/movement alliance and the pro-slavery countermovement. Under Cotegipe, the equation was reversed. The movement was being persecuted and driven out of the public space, while the government and countermovement became indistinguishable from each other. Nabuco put it in a nutshell: the pro-slavery movement could well say "I am the State."[83]

---

[82] Isabel, memorandum dated December 1888, in Barman (2002, p. 243); letter from the Count d'Eu to the Marchese D'Oraison, Jul. 11, 1887 (in Rangel, 1935, p. 360); letter from Isabel to the Countess of Barral, Jul. 14, 1887 (in Barman, 2002, p. 243).

[83] On the mood of the market, see Pedro Mello, in Slenes (2004, p. 359). Nabuco, *O País*, Oct. 16, 1887.

## The Last Abolition

In August 1887, gatherings in the streets and, in the evenings, in public buildings were prohibited and abolitionists were purged from the civil service. The CA reacted by holding a conference on August 6 at the Polytheama and were met by a gang of Noggin Shearer's boot boys, who were sent by the chief of police. The event degenerated into a battle between abolitionists and the police. After a veiled threat was made on Patrocínio's life by a plainclothes policeman, the activist came out to say that militias working under police orders would disrupt their meetings as the "slavery government ha[d] now resorted to making threats."[84] With no way of guaranteeing the physical safety of those congregating in the theaters and streets, Patrocínio, now a councilor, requested the use of the Town Hall for the CA's conferences. His request was denied.

As they hunted fugitive slaves and their harborers, Noggin Shearer and his gang combed the streets and houses, giving rise to a series of incidents involving threats or violence against abolitionists. Clapp, the CA's eternal president, had his work cut out for him, sheltering, escorting to safety, or rescuing his fellow members. The persecution was such that it won the abolitionists the sympathy of the population of Rio de Janeiro, outraged by this near-martial law.

Nationwide, abolitionists were being chased, with many being jailed in Bahia and São Paulo and in Caçapava, seven at once, all charged with stealing slaves. In Jacareí, two abolitionists were chased out of town. In Recife, the chief of police prohibited "colored folks from disembarking without the appropriate pass" in a bid to stem the flow of fugitives into Ceará. In Cachoeira, Bahia, police attacked an eighty-year-old abolitionist, the editor-in-chief of O Asteroide. Fellow activists came to his aid and the fracas ended with various people injured. Death threats became widespread, and Antônio Bento was lucky to survive an attempt on his life. The would-be assassin was caught and given the full Noggin Shearer treatment: hair, mustache, and eyebrows all shaved off.

Abolitionist retaliation against the government was violent. At Court, an abolitionist meeting scheduled for August 8, outside the Campo da Aclamação barracks, never even got started, as a police inspector ordered its cancellation. Resulting from this, the chief of police and police inspector were pelted with stones, as was the war minister, who was in the wrong place at the wrong time.[85]

---

[84] CR, Oct. 18, 1887; Duque-Estrada (1918, pp. 168–99).
[85] AR, Aug. 1 and 3; Sept. 4, Aug. 7, 1887; Vilela, May 13, 1905, in Silva (1988, p. 34); O País, Oct. 16, 1887; AR, Aug. 25, 1887; Fontes (1976, p. 66); AR, Aug. 11, 1887.

## Bullets: Movement and Countermovement

In Campos, a string of incidents marred the month of October: after a rally went ahead despite an express ban, the police broke down the door of printers of the *Vinte e Cinco de Março* and raided the place, guns blazing. Retaliation came swift in the form of gunfire and dynamite, leaving four police officers injured and one dead. Some abolitionists were captured in the mayhem. Lacerda, now a marked man by the police, fled to Court. The *Cidade do Rio* dedicated its October and November headlines to the conflict in Campos. The CA mounted a habeas corpus petition to release the prisoners. Nabuco and Carneiro da Cunha (Pernambuco), Antônio Pinto (Ceará), and Clapp and Patrocínio (CA) signed it to show that the national movement as a whole supported their fellow members in Campos.

As at the start of the campaign, the movement invested in the boomerang strategy, looking for foreign support to pressurize the national government. They promoted some of their events in French and sought the moral sanction of foreign authorities as a way of embarrassing the State into easing off. In 1886, working through the British and Foreign Antislavery Society, Nabuco finally managed to obtain the long-awaited statement from the British Prime Minister W. E. Gladstone. While this may have caused D. Pedro a few blushes, it did nothing to frustrate Cotegipe, who went straight ahead and banned the *Cidade do Rio* in prisons, depriving the jailed Campos activists of information.[86]

In the Senate, Dantas demanded assurances of the abolitionists' safety from the Justice Ministry and called upon the CA to mount a commission to appeal to the Princess. In receiving the delegates, Isabel displayed all her political naivety saying: "I pray that slavery will end soon." The Campos abolitionists remained in jail and the pitched battle continued, with more gunfights and an attempted raid on another abolitionist newspaper, *O Gazeta do Povo*. Amid the pandemonium, a by-election was called in Campos, and despite it, the abolitionists managed to elect one of Lacerda's brothers, right in the middle of Paulino's heartland. The MP-elect organized a celebratory conference at the Empyreo theater, but the police set up a blockade at the entrance, so he led his followers to his own house instead. He was speaking from the balcony when the mounted police attacked the crowd, first using whips, and then guns. Shutters went down all around the town. The abolitionists, three of them injured, retaliated with rocks and stones. At a fresh attempt at organizing a

---

[86] Monnerat (2012, p. 145); CR, Oct. 26, 27, 30, Nov. 2, 1887.

312 *The Last Abolition*

meeting, freed blacks launched an armed attack on the police. Chaos reigned for the next few days, leaving one dead and many injured. In Bahia, an abolitionist noted the historical irony at play: "ha[d] the government not stopped to consider the possible consequences? ... Ha[d] it not reflected upon the effects triggered by the *legal* murder of John Brown?" Brown, the revolutionary who took to arms, inciting America's slaves to revolt, the man whom Luís Gama had so admired, had become a collective idol for the Brazilian movement. The mood was tense, and rather than discouraging adherence to the abolitionist cause, it invited droves of young students to join, and they, like Brown, were passionate and hell-bent on making history.

Yet none of this put abolition back on the government agenda. The abolitionists were left disappointed when the Princess Regent's closing address to the legislature of 1887 made no mention whatsoever of the "servile question." Under the headline "The blood-spattered Regency," printed in large capital letters, Patrocínio's newspaper accused her of connivance with pro-slavery violence. Rebouças' hopes of an alliance with the Princess were dashed, because "in a bid to assert her regal authority and shore up the throne that is soon to be hers, her Highness sanctions whatever crimes the government chooses to commit."[87]

Slave revolts broke out simultaneously on plantations in the Campinas region in December 1887, and the chief of police in São Paulo was forced to admit that his troops were unable to get the situation under control because the slaves, working under the "malignant" guidance of abolitionists, had made for Santos en masse, killing plantation owners in various towns. "Individual and patrimonial security cannot be satisfactorily guaranteed in this province, nor indeed anywhere in the Empire." Francisco de Paula Rodrigues Alves, president of São Paulo and, later, of the Republic, informed the Provincial Assembly of mass slave escapes from numerous farms and plantations province-wide, posing, in his opinion, a major threat to public order. Unable to meet the "more than just" demands for reinforcements from police divisions across São Paulo, he requested military backup from the central government. Cotegipe was more than eager to put the house in order, because "the widespread abandonment of plantations and the increased slave vagrancy it spawned, doubtless

---

[87] On events in Campos, see CR, Oct. 28, Nov. 7, 16, 21, 22, 23, 1887. The Bahian abolitionist was Anselmo Fonseca (1887, p. 604); Fonseca (1887, pp. 569–70). Patrocínio's article came out in CR, Nov. 21, 1887.

## Bullets: Movement and Countermovement

orchestrated by anarchists, constituted a grave threat." So the Baron redeployed cavalry from Curitiba to Santos, the nerve center of the underground railroad, but he had to admit that "we do not have the manpower to contain or quash the disorder and the disasters it prefigures." The fact that this national government could not respond with force because it was still at loggerheads with the military meant that "the pro-slavery part of society would have to defend" themselves by militarization. The president of São Paulo supported the coffee planters by authorizing their use of slave hunters to "inspect" black and mixed-race travelers on trains at Jundiaí.[88]

If the abolitionists were a nationwide network, the anti-Dantas bloc was still very much nationally alive. The countermovement endorsed the State's repressive measures in Parliament, in public spaces, and with its own guns. Pro-slavery associations, such as Coffee Center, Plantation Center, Plantation Club, and anti-abolition newspapers began to multiply. In the province of São Paulo, the pro-slavery countermovement organized themselves in Limeira, Lorena, Brotas, and Pinhal. Back in 1884, a member of the Plantation Club in Recife wrote to the president of Pernambuco to say that the farmers would be grateful for a repressive line from Olinda to Boa Viagem, as they could take care of the other ports themselves, using their own private militias. These were the same henchmen who sabotaged newspapers, broke up conferences, and harassed abolitionists and sympathetic judges hearing freedom suits. In São Paulo province, in the cities of Araraquara, Belém do Descalvado, Capivari, Paraíso, and Penha do Rio do Peixe, where there had been Plantation Clubs since 1884, all hell broke loose.

Nabuco protested against the wheels of repression being greased by the Prime Minister and members of the Plantation and Trade Club, "all the bane of slaves," with their centuries-old methods, seeing that the ban on whipping was just another addition to a growing heap of dead-letter laws. It was, Nabuco said, a calamity to see slaves being slaughtered by their masters while the government looked on and the Princess kept her silence. Atrocities continued to occur, like those at Santa Maria Madalena, in October 1887, where there was a repeat of the cruelty seen in Paraíba do

---

[88] Machado (2009, p. 394) documented the planning of escapes in the Campinas region on Christmas Eve. Report by Salvador Antônio Moniz Barreto de Aragão, Dec. 31, 1887, pp. 4, 10; Rodrigues Alves (1887, pp. 22–3); letter from the Baron of Cotegipe to Rodrigues Alves, Dec. 12, 1887, IHGB; AR, Jun. 14, 1887.

314                    *The Last Abolition*

Sul the previous year. Dantas called the government out on the case in the Senate.[89]

That same October, a remarkable episode occurred in the São Paulo countryside. It began in Capivari and spread to Itu, where the dumfounded locals stood and watched 150 fugitive slaves march through town en route to Santos. With the press covering every move, a stunned society accompanied the black march as it crossed the province in what was a dress rehearsal for a slave uprising. The leader of the exodus, a man named Pio, marched with his fellow slaves through hunger and the wild woods, leading their elderly and young, up to the Mar mountains. The government banned telegrams on the subject in an attempt to cut off lines of encoded abolitionist communication, and called in the army to halt the march. Patrocínio defended the fugitives: "These slaves are not the tools of anarchy; they are the victims of law. They call not for blood, but for justice." And he warned: "The abolitionists of Santos are on stand-by." Nabuco tried to reach out to the military, entreating them to hold their fire and avoid a bloodbath. He begged them to take the right side in the matter, because "the sympathies, hopes, and heart of the whole nation will be with the slaves and against the law!"[90]

Patrocínio and Nabuco were in Court, the Caiaphases in Jabaquara. Abolitionists were waiting at Santos, and yet none of them witnessed the Mar mountains massacre. Near Cubatão, the army and runways met. The cavalry opened fire. The slaves, armed and ready, responded in kind, "fighting bravely against the powers of the State, amid cries of 'freedom or death'," in the words of São Paulo's chief of police, who could only recognize their valor. Pio, who had survived slavery, exhaustion, and starvation, died a warrior's death. Of his comrades, fifteen were recaptured and thirty or so managed to flee into the thickets. When they reached the Jabaquara quilombo, moribund from battle and fatigue, they were met with a banquet honoring the dead, personified in the figure of Pio, who now joined the pantheon of abolitionist heroes as a martyr.[91]

Though the Brazilians never came close to anything like the butchery that occurred in the United States, violence was a feature of the closing

---

[89] Um Lavrador (1884, pp. 50–1); Pang (1981, pp. 338 ff.); Nabuco, *O País*, Oct. 16, 1887.

[90] Schmidt (1981), in the roman à clef *A marcha, romance da abolição*, narrates these events. Fonseca (1887, p. 603) also documents them. CR, Oct. 22, 24, 1887. *O País*, Oct. 21, 1887.

[91] Report by Salvador Antônio Moniz Barreto de Aragão, 1887, p. 8, original emphasis; CR, Oct. 24 and 26, 1887.

## Bullets: Movement and Countermovement 315

phase of abolitionist mobilization. Patrocínio declared an end to the time of flowers and votes:

The government does not want abolitionist propaganda to continue treading upon a carpet of flowers to the sound of bands and blessings for the converted. Such propaganda of persuasion has been outlawed and branded revolutionary. ... So what must abolitionism do? Go like a lamb to the slaughter, or react?

The time had come for bullets, declared the abolitionists from São Paulo. If abolition could not be achieved "by a path strewn with flowers, then let it be won on a path spattered with blood, through revolution."[92]

The CA built up an armed force of its own in Court, with gangs of capoeira martial artists providing security cordons against the militias and the police. The capoeirists went by colorful names that alluded to their methods: Cá Te Espero (I'll wait for you here), Boca Queimada (Burned mouth). In São Paulo's coffee lands, violence was escalating. During that endless October of 1887, a group of free blacks raided the São Francisco church fête and sparked a running battle that lasted through to the following day. In November, another mob prevented the arrest of a slave in Santos. In Piracicaba, in January 1888, a mob invaded a train looking for a farmer who had recaptured a fugitive. A week later, in Campinas, the townsfolk booed some slave catchers who were transporting captured runaways. The police arrested one of the protesters. "In the evening, the folks surrounded the jail and started pelting the troopers with stones, then answered their bayonets with revolvers. The shooting went on until after eleven o'clock that night."[93] All this was from the abolitionist side.

The pro-slavery side wanted nothing more than to crush abolitionist activism. In Campos, in 1888, an acolyte informed Paulino that: "arrangements had been made with the police commissioner and local chief inspector to raid the offices of the *Vinte e Cinco de Março* newspaper on the night of March 7 and the early morning of March 8, where around thirty fugitive slaves were harbored, whose return to their owners would put an end to abolitionism in Campos." This disposition toward extralegal coercion came to fruition in February 1888. Earlier that month, planters had put together a posse to round up abolitionists in the area of Muzambinho, Minas Gerais. One activist managed to get away, but he

---

[92] Toplin (1972) and Machado (2009) documented this use of violence in the final years of slavery. Patrocínio, CR, Oct. 31, 1887; AR, Jul. 14, 1887.

[93] Duque-Estrada (1918, p. 89); CR, Jan. 13, 24, 1888.

316                          *The Last Abolition*

was hunted down by four militiamen who tried to kill him and those who were sheltering him in São Paulo. Two weeks later, the US repertoire was once again employed by the Brazilian pro-slavery countermovement. Just as the government had adopted the Fugitive Slave Act, the pro-slavery citizens were resorting to lynch law. In the Confederate States, the planters had set up tight-knit, territorial militias to (as Robert Brent Toplin puts it) geographically contain abolitionist activities. The Ku Klux Klan was formed in 1865. This privatization of repression was not adopted in Brazil at the same level; however two former Confederate soldiers from the American Civil War brought with them their homeland techniques. They roused members of the Plantation Club in Penha do Rio do Peixe (present day Itapira) to action, saying that they were "lily-livered and [that] there would have been a revolution by now if half of what was going on here had happened in another country." Their goading worked. At four in the morning on February 21, the pair marched a mob of 200 to 300 men, including the deputies of a marshal and a municipal judge, to the home of police deputy Joaquim Firmino de Araújo Cunha, accused of protecting abolitionists. They beat down his door and stormed in. His wife tried to plead for her husband's life, but she was beaten back. Their nine-year-old daughter fell to her knees before the intruders, pleading for them not to hurt her father, and she was kicked out of the way. Mother and daughter were forced to take cover in an oven, where they were jabbed with stick-ends. They lived to see the rabid mob beat Joaquim Firmino to a pulp, his arms broken, face and body torn from being kicked to a deliberately slow and agonizing death with spurs.[94]

The abolitionists protested as loud and hard as they could, and called for exemplary punishment. Firmino was another addition to the hall of martyrs to the cause. His murderers, however, were defended as upstanding citizens and, like the slave-torturer Francisca da Silva Castro before them, were absolved on all counts – this time, for lack of evidence. What

---

[94] Notes of Councilor Paulino José Soares de Sousa on the organization of the cabinet, Mar. 10, 1888, IHGB, Wanderley Pinho Archive, DL 1593-02. Many thanks to Felipe Nicoletti for giving me a copy of this document. Toplin (1972, p. 206); Pang (1981, p. 338). The Penha do Rio do Peixe episode is recounted in CR, Feb. 21, 1888. The words of the confederate soldiers James Ox Warne and John Jackson Clink are in JC, Feb. 21, 1888. According to Machado (2009, pp. 389–90), Firmino was "harboring two slaves at his home, both of whom were suing for their freedom, and he was also taking part in abolitionist events." There are no reliable figures for those killed or injured in the conflict between the abolitionist movement and the pro-slavery countermovement, but Toplin (1972) and Machado (2009) indicated the numbers were high. Conrad (1972, p. 257) underestimates the violence, which he describes as "exceptional."

FIGURE 8.2 The lynching in February 1888 of police deputy Joaquim Firmino de Araújo Cunha by pro-slavery locals, in Penha do Rio do Peixe (Fish River Rock) (modern-day Itapira), accused of protecting abolitionists ("The barbaric murder of the police deputy in Penha do Rio do Peixe, SP").
**Drawing by Angelo Agostini. Archive of the Fundação Biblioteca Nacional (National Library Foundation), Brazil. Reproduction by Jaime Acioli.**

was the point in talking to the executive, or the judiciary, or the Princess, or of talking at all? "What will history say of the Regent when it comes ..., that she tolerated in her government those who colluded with murderers who killed women in Campos, mowed down citizens in Rio do Peixe, and plunged to such frenzied depths as to dig their spurs into a cadaver and kick a child?" "The government revels in an orgy of blood," wrote Patrocínio. "The Baron of Cotegipe's call to arms – 'in war as in war' – has been taken literally by his chiefs and agents. Slaughter has become a necessary complement of slavery." If there was no authority left to appeal to, then all that remained, as Patrocínio was quick to point out, was an eye for an eye: "These murderers must be brought to justice, whether by the courts of law or the people's revenge."[95]

---

[95] CR, Feb. 21, 27, 29, 1888. Brasílio Machado, an abolitionist, defended those accused of murdering Firmino, during the trial, for which he earned the movement's lasting ire (CR, Mar. 2, 1888).

318                    *The Last Abolition*

This was the fuel the activists were now running on. In 1885, in Mato Grosso, "a greatly impassioned abolitionist proffered these mighty words: 'If I were a slave, I would do all I could to get past my master's guards and escape. And if I couldn't do that, I would murder him myself.'" As 1887 became 1888, it was that very spirit that had been breathed into the *collective* mindset. The whole movement, declared Patrocínio, was ready for the last resort:

> Abolitionism does not need a government to decree abolition. Rather it has one of its own, gathered now on the battlefield, and in its Cabinet sit João Cordeiro, Antônio Bento, João Clapp, Carlos de Lacerda . . . It matters naught to us what the Baron of Cotegipe . . . wants. . . . Slavery's end date is this: 1889. Not a day more, even if that means going further than we ever thought we would.

The drama had climbed down from the stage, where the abolitionists had sung and performed at the start of the campaign, and slipped out of Parliament's door to turn its back on the ballot box, through which it had squeezed itself in 1884. If the pro-slavery countermovement was resorting to US-style lynching to save its status quo, the abolitionists would dip into the foreign repertoire for radical models that led to a tragic end. Where before their idols were propagandists (Garrison, Douglass, and Clarkson) and parliamentarians (Wilberforce), they would now turn to the revolutionary side of the mirror. Nabuco had likened Antônio Bento to John Brown, whom Luís Gama had so admired. And what had Brown done in Kansas? Seeing slavery as a war between masters and slaves, he raised an army and started an uprising. Though he ultimately failed to rouse the slaves to insurrection, there were five dead slavery defenders to show for his attempt. Violence begat violence. As 1888 loomed, Brown became the role-model for Brazilian abolitionism. Patrocínio, usually a festive man, turned up in a tragic spirit and he spoke for all his fellows when he stood up for any destiny: "True abolitionists are all ready to die."[96]

---

[96] On the event in Mato Grosso, see Frick (1885, p. 15). The quotations from Patrocínio are in CR, Feb. 16, 1888, Oct. 26, 1887. On Brown, see Reynolds (2006).

# 9

# The March to Victory

On February 12, 1888, Rebouças left suite 72 at Hotel Bragança, Petrópolis, where he lived, to catch the train. He was a busy man, dividing his time between teaching at the Polytechnic, pursuing his business dealings, and mainly working on the campaign: producing reports for the CA, articles for the *Cidade do Rio*, and pieces of abolitionist and democratic propaganda such as his plans for distribution of public land for settlements in Piauí. As he traveled into town, he read with satisfaction the news he had been battling for during the last two decades; the Princess Regent had pronounced herself in favor of abolition.[1]

## CERTIFIERS

During major political crises, contentious movements on the rise tend to encounter governments on the wane. The ruling political coalition falls apart and the State's repressive capacity declines, while factions of the political elite and previously unengaged social elites defect to the challengers. Mobilization spreads out across various sectors, disrupting everyday life. Political fluidity increases, distinctions become blurred, and adversaries become allies and vice-versa.[2] The result can go either way. The swing factor relies on the successful wooing of the part of society that has so far stayed out of the conflict to jump in. In extreme cases, if all or most of them side with the challengers, the result is revolution; if it balances out, it

---

[1] DNAAR, Aug. 28 and Dec. 11, 1887; Jan. 1, 1888.
[2] Charles Tilly and Sidney Tarrow list the characteristics of political crises. For a systematic look at this debate, see Bennani-Chraïbi and Fillieule (2012).

320                           *The Last Abolition*

is civil war. A reformist outcome is one in which the movement tips the balance of power in its favor, but cannot quite vanquish the adversary. That was the state of play in Brazil at the turn of 1888.

The final months of slavery in Brazil bear some resemblance to the eve of the political elite's visions of apocalypse: the American Civil War and the slave revolt in Haiti. But the similarities ended there on the eve of emancipation. The same part of the foreign repertoire, the Spanish example of a negotiated solution, that had furnished the templates for the 1871 and 1885 laws, pointed the way again in 1888. The social authorities, traditional institutions, and the armed forces, mere spectators while the struggle was limited to the public space and Parliament, decided to step in when clandestine and violent actions increased. They entered to achieve a compromise. The pro-slavery countermovement should stop trying to resuscitate a dead system, and the abolitionists should go back to staging concerts and throwing flowers.[3]

In 1887, slavery found itself deprived of two of its pillars, faith and force. Army officers, cadets at the military academy, even whole battalions, as in Ceará in 1883, had long been on the abolitionists' side, but as a corporation, the armed forces only came on board in the wake of the Sea Mountain massacre. The army was through with doing the dirty work for a government that was deaf to its demands for space, promotions, and better pay. Spurred on by articles from Nabuco, Rui Barbosa, Bocaiúva, and Silva Jardim, and with the impact of the Sea Mountain massacre still sinking in, on October 25, 1887, the president of the Military Club, Manuel Deodoro da Fonseca, delivered a petition to the Regent in the name of the Brazilian armed forces. Insubordination came wrapped in the schemata of compassion and progress, as the army stated its refusal to go on:

capturing poor black folks fleeing slavery, or running because they have had enough of suffering, or because the flame of liberty has been kindled in their hearts ..., who flee calmly, ... avoiding both enslavement and confrontation, setting an enormous moral example as they pass through our cities and towns.

With these words, the army withdrew from its commitment to defend the slavocrat order.

---

[3] In late 1887 Brazil saw the simultaneous "certification" of abolition, with the adherence of political and social authorities who legitimized the movement's demands, and the "decertification" of the government, with loss of support among allies and the populace in general and impaired capacity to command the apparatus of the State (McAdam, Tarrow, and Tilly, 2001, p. 121).

# The March to Victory

This crisis would have sent the government into a tailspin had not a regency staffer taken the decision to not pass it on to the Princess. In the end, it did little to dampen the impact, as the Deodoro manifesto appeared in all the newspapers. After that, the military, fed up with Cotegipe, felt free to disobey the government at will, refusing to enforce the Baron's smash-and-grab approach to free assembly and slave escapes. While the ban on whipping put a *formal* end to private repression, the army's refusal to arrest runaways was an *effective* derailment of the State's coercive power. Slavery had lost its teeth.[4]

It also lost the support of the church. Nabuco had a hand in that. He had been sent to Europe by *O País* to cover the Emperor's impending death, and he used the visit to do some boomerang-style activism. He enlisted the help of Wendell Garrison, the son of his pseudonym during the Dantas years and editor of *The Nation*, who agreed to collect signatures from US Congressmen on his behalf for a pro-abolition petition. He also called a new motion for the venerable abolitionist Victor Schoelcher, to embarrass D. Pedro, who was still in Europe. Nabuco also repeated Abílio Borges' strategy in 1870 and appealed to Pope Leo XIII, who was in his jubilee year, so all eyes were on Rome. Nabuco knew that a declaration from him would have a huge impact on Princess Isabel, a fervent Catholic. With some help from the British and Foreign Antislavery Society, on February 10, 1888, Nabuco was given an audience with the Pontiff, who promised to address an antislavery encyclical to the Brazilian episcopacy.

Accusing the abolitionists of "pestering the Papacy for a missive on emancipation," Cotegipe ordered the Brazilian diplomatic office in Rome to ask the Pope to kindly keep out of Brazilian affairs. The encyclical *On the Abolition of Slavery – A Letter to the Brazilian Bishops* was put on hold,[5] but the news that the supreme leader of the church had condemned slavery weighed upon the local clergy.

---

[4] Fonseca, Oct. 25, 1887; CR, Oct. 30, 1887.

[5] DJN, Dec. 27, 1887; letter from Wendell Phillips Garrison to Joaquim Nabuco, Jan. 9, 1888; CIJN, letter from Joaquim Nabuco to Victor Schoelcher, Feb. 15, 1888; letters from Victor Schoelcher to Joaquim Nabuco, Apr. 11, Nov. 29, 1887, CIJN. There was a precedent: in 1839, the Protestant Thomas Buxton asked the Pope for an encyclical against the slave trade (Davis, 1984, p. 304). Nabuco had the help of a diplomat friend in Italy, to whom he wrote: "It would be an immense help to abolition if the Pope ... were to recommend the complete extinction of slavery to the Catholic flock" (letter from Joaquim Nabuco to Sousa Correia, Dec. 14, 1887, CIJN). He recounted his audience with the Pope in *O País*, and it was amply covered in other newspapers too (letter from the Baron of Cotegipe to Artur de Sousa Correia, Mar. 23, 1888 – Oliveira Lima Library, II, 18).

# The Last Abolition

Throughout 1887, the movement's religious language and adoption of the Christ-the-slave cult spread, first among the priests and followed by the bishops, who distanced themselves from Cotegipe's state authority by making conversions to the "holy cause" of abolition. Religious orders freed their slaves, prelates issued public statements against slavery, and priests delivered antislavery sermons, organized pro-emancipation rallies (as in Goiás), and, in some cases, even harbored fugitive slaves. In May 1887, the Bishop of Pernambuco called upon the province's priests to manumit their slaves. In June, his counterpart in São Paulo received a visit from Antônio Bento, who was a member of a Catholic brotherhood, and agreed to mark the Pope's jubilee with a public declaration that the episcopate owned slaves no more. He also got the Vicar-General of the diocese to use the feast day of black Saint Benedict to call upon "the black and humble saint, yet immense before the Lord, to intercede on behalf of his brothers and sisters in Brazil that they might have their liberty." These actions had a domino effect: between May and December 1887, the bishops of Minas, Bahia, Pernambuco, Cuiabá, and São Paulo all issued letters calling for abolition. The campaign, which had previously only had the support of a handful of antislavery clerics, now had a whole "abolitionist church" behind it.

The judiciary's stance also changed during this period. Despite the failure of Gama-style activism in high-profile cases, such as those involving the murder of slave masters, Robert Brent Toplin registered an increase in favorable rulings by the courts between 1886 and 1888. In addition to prosecutors and judges turning toward the abolitionist tide, some police inspectors began to do it as well. In July 1887, the chief inspector in Recife sent out a circular ordering his officers not to hunt down runaway slaves.

Early in 1888, the mainstream press, which had always been neutral towards or against abolition, also began to address it as a fait accompli. Even the country's leading broadsheet, *Jornal do Commercio*, adopted a pro-abolition editorial line, followed by most of the medium-circulation

---

Sousa Correia took Cotegipe's complaints to the Vatican and received in turn a cardinal's promise that the encyclical's publication would be postponed, saying "that it was not the Pope's intention to interfere in any way in Brazil's internal affairs" (letter from João Artur de Sousa Correia to the Baron of Cotegipe, May 5, 1888, Oliveira Lima Library, II).

## The March to Victory

press in Court and in the provincial capitals. Those still against downsized their objections, preferring to address the issue of immigration instead.[6]

At a party conference in March 1887, the long-divided Liberal Party finally agreed to defend abolition within a timeframe of five years. Liberal MPs also put forward bills for immediate abolition, one of which provided for five years of additional service, and another, two years. In June, a bloc of fourteen senators led by Dantas put forward a simplified version of the reform his government had tried to pass in 1884. The proposal set December 31, 1889 as the date for abolition and laid the groundwork for a Rebouças-style rural democracy: "... agricultural colonies for the education of ingénus and the livelihood of freedmen, set up along navigable rivers, roadsides or the coastline. These colonies' rules will state the gradual conversion of State lease-holding tenant-farmers into landowning yeomen."[7] In February 1888, Saraiva, the most respected Liberal leader, joined the ranks of those in favor of abolition in the short term. Even Moreira de Barros, the arch-enemy of the Dantas Reform in 1884, gave up and freed his own slaves.

Among the Conservatives, desertion was discreet. On September 24, 1887, two MPs presented separate bills for immediate abolition with two and three years of additional service. The second of these added a religious note, setting abolition for Christmas Day 1889, a week earlier than Dantas' proposed date. The Hardliners, who had held ranks under Paulino and Cotegipe, began to disperse. Social unrest was troubling many Conservatives in São Paulo, where assisted collective runaways were causing such turmoil on the coffee plantations that maintaining the slavery-based social order began to look counterproductive. The assisted collective runaways weakened various regions simultaneously in São Paulo, Minas, Rio, and Pernambuco, and attempting to stem the flow

---

[6] Brito (2003, p. 106), Oliveira (1980, p. 322), AR, May 5, Jun. 9 and 23, 1887, CR, Nov. 7, Dec. 24, 1887. Pro-abolition declarations also appeared in Catholic newspapers in 1888, such as O Apóstolo. Toplin (1972, p. 197) notes the change in lawsuits, AR, Jul. 7, 1887. On changes in treatment of the issue in the press, see the Pernambuco's newspapers assembled by Leonardo Dantas Silva (1988c), and on Rio's papers, see the final chapter in Mattos (1998).

[7] AR, Mar. 27, 1887. Projects 5 and 1 were presented by Jaguaribe and Afonso Celso Jr., respectively (ACD, May 4, 1887). Dantas, unanimously endorsed by the Liberals in Bahia (Brito, 2003, p. 106), presented Project B, which lifted whole passages from his Project 48 (1884). Project B received the backing of Afonso Celso Sr., Gaspar Silveira Martins, Franco de Sá, J. R. de Lamare, Francisco Otaviano, C. de Oliveira, Henrique d'Ávila, Lafaiete Rodrigues Pereira, the Viscount of Pelotas, Castro Carreira, Silveira da Mota, Inácio Martins, and Lima Duarte (ASI, Jun. 3, 1887).

324    *The Last Abolition*

in so many far-flung locations was spreading the troops way too thin. When the president of São Paulo called for reinforcements in December 1887, Cotegipe had to admit that, with the army sitting on its hands, he was unable muster enough men to halt the exodus.[8] The monarchical state had done what it could for as long as it was able, but there was nothing more to be done for its slave owners.

*After* the coercive force of the State had been withheld by the army, the only way to maintain the status quo was for the landowners to follow the American example and to overlap their roles as producers of the economic order based on slavery with that of pro-slavery political enforcers, taking matters into their own armed hands. In 1884, when the main ingredients for the defense of slavery were social coordination and political organization, many accepted the role. However, in 1887, this defense required the extensive use of violence. Maintaining the order now required armed militias capable of keeping the slaves on the plantations and the abolitionists off them. Although the ferocious lynching in Penha do Rio do Peixe in February 1888 may have foreseen the direction they could have taken, Brazilian slaveholders did not militarize anything resembling the intensity and scale of their North-American counterparts. In fact, they considered it socially ineffectual and financially unprofitable.

From this emerged what Robert Conrad calls the "emancipationist planter" phenomenon. The landowners themselves started a wave of manumissions in the fields, with compensatory service agreements. Coffee planters in Campinas issued a manifesto in August 1887 calling for a swift resolution to the problem and, in September, freed their slaves under bonds of apprenticeship terminating in 1890. Their counterparts in Jaú announced they would end slavery by 1889, and those in Jacareí promised to free slaves who did not try to escape. Between March and April 1888, this wave of planter initiatives reached Paulino's slave-owning heartland, the Paraíba Valley, where, in Cantagalo, many plantation-owners decided to grant their slaves unconditional freedom. The Planters Congresses in these parts – Rio Preto, Campos, São Fidélis, and Santo Antônio de Padua – turned their focus elsewhere. They started discussing possible forms of controlling the free workforce.[9]

---

[8] Project O, drafted by MP Joaquim Floriano de Godoi, and Project P, by A. Taunay, Rebouças' friend and one of the few Conservatives to support Dantas (ACD, Sept. 24, 1887). Letter from the Baron of Cotegipe to Rodrigues Alves, Dec. 12, 1887, IHGB.

[9] AR, Sept. 29, 1887, Pang (1981, pp. 366–7), Mattos (1998, pp. 230 ff.).

*The March to Victory* 325

The fact that many planters were giving up on slavery of their own accord was not caused by a decline in slavery profits. Considering economic ratio alone, Robert Slenes showed that slavery was still financially viable. The decisive factor for ending slavery at that time was political: the disruption of economic production and the collapse of social order produced by abolitionist tactics. Once the assisted collective runaways fanned out, the planters decided to accept the emancipation process in the hope of controlling it. Cotegipe noted that, as in physics, a chain-reaction occurred: "A planter manumits his slaves, and these either stay or go. Now his neighbor cannot keep his own pens in line and is obliged to follow suit or risk losing his whole workforce."[10]

So the President of São Paulo proposed a federal solution to the crisis, abolish slavery gradually, province by province. Cotegipe disagreed; it would have been tantamount to sanctioning the abolitionist free soil strategy. The idea matured despite his misgivings. Antônio da Silva Prado, the author of the Black Regulation at the start of Cotegipe's government and its mainstay in the South, had a change of heart after experiencing the effects of abolition on his own lands. It was a painful blow to the government, as it was dealt from within. Prado stepped down as a minister in order to coordinate a front consisting of representatives of the three parties and twenty major coffee growers eager to find some way to protect order in their province. Their efforts to regain social control in São Paulo culminated in creating an "emancipationist" association accompanied by a free soil campaign with a deadline set for December 1890. Prado's newspaper called for immediate emancipation in November 1887, and, on December 15, the province's planters convened a meeting to discuss the prospect. Many slave owners wanted to reach an agreement with the abolitionists, so they called in the incendiary Antônio Bento in the unlikely role of fireman, and he actually succeeded in brokering an agreement to have fugitive slaves return as paid labor.[11] On February 25, 1888, the capital of São Paulo declared itself free soil, in an unexpected alliance of longstanding abolitionists and the pro-slavery actors, suddenly converted to antislavery.

Prado's defection meant political death for Cotegipe. Next to abandon ship was the "Northern lion," senator João Alfredo Coreia de Oliveira, who, in September 1887 warmed to a solution "in a matter of years."

[10] Slenes (2004). For a contrary argument, see Conrad (1972, p. 257). ASI, May 12, 1888.
[11] Letter from the Baron of Cotegipe to Rodrigues Alves, Dec. 12, 1887, IHGB; *Correio Paulistano*, Nov. 11, 1887; Andrada (1918, p. 217).

An abolitionist march, with all the usual band and suspects, rolled up outside his house, eager to turn those years into months.[12]

The loss of political support for slavery was matched by the dispersed desertion of the slave-owning social strata, creating a growing pool of what Antônio Bento called "coats-of-arms abolitionists." The members of the good society, who had never set foot in a concert-conference, started by freeing their slaves at dinners, soirées, and birthday parties. They were "prophets of the *après coup, post facto*, after the duck is dead," dedicated to wringing a little prestige out of inevitable financial loss, as Machado de Assis wrote in the May 19, 1888 issue of the *Gazeta de Notícias*. In his story, the owner of the slave Pancrácio releases the slave shortly before the abolition was approved, in accordance with the principle of these "great and true politicians" who "do not merely obey the law, but anticipate it, saying to the slave: thou art free, before declared so by the authorities, always the laggards."[13]

Abolitionists detested those antislavery newcomers, but accepted them, lauded in the abolitionist papers and by the CA, which was handing out titles left, right, and center, and hailed in a new batch of Golden Books (four in São Paulo alone), while the Black Books denounced the few pro-slavery citizens remaining. With neither naivety nor hypocrisy, longstanding abolitionists accepted new converts as a necessity. Their adherence signaled the social legitimation of abolition by the upper strata of imperial society, and that was key to having the political system finally embracing emancipation.

So did circumstantial pro-slavery countermovement disappear in 1888? No, but it shrank. Paulino in the Senate, Andrade Figueira in the House, and Cotegipe in the Prime Minister's office kept each other company in remaining solitary but true to their way of life, political creed, and own lives. In November 1887, reporting on a meeting Paulino held with planters at the Fluminense Library, the *Cidade do Rio* described him as resigned to the inevitability of abolition. The paper had to rescind that immediately: the meeting had really been about the importation of Senegalese laborers to replace the freed slaves. "Pirate" Paulino was going to be the last dark knight to dismount from his steed.[14]

---

[12] ASI, Sept. 26, 1887; CR, Dec. 13, 1887.
[13] Bento, GT, Dec. 11, 1886; Machado de Assis, GN, May 19, 1888.
[14] GT, Dec. 21, 1886; AR, Jan. 5, Aug. 11, Apr. 10, Oct. 23, 1887; CR, Nov. 18, Dec. 7, 1887.

# The March to Victory

## THE PRINCESS'S DILEMMAS

"Whether to abolish slavery in Brazil is no longer an issue; it is an open and shut case ... What is in discussion among all those desirous of emancipation, without tumult or the infringement of rights, is the practical manner of how it is to be achieved." As if the situation were not disagreeable enough, Cotegipe found himself having to hear advice from outspoken planters like this one who presented a salvage plan that proposed the conversion of slaves into serfs, subject to the strictest codes of discipline, and the use of the Emancipation Fund to compensate their masters. As a practical soul, Cotegipe was quite aware of the impossibility of pleasing the "sensible abolitionist," the slaveowner, and the nation all at once, as the planter believed his plan could.[15] His party represented the landowners, but it had lost the wherewithal to defend them. Cotegipe lost more than the repressive force to face abolitionists. The government was also short of funds to provide monetary compensation to ex-slave owners. Cotegipe's last hope was to keep in his own hands the magic wand of government, but for that he needed the support of a princess.

The abolitionists continued to prod at the regency and, in February 1888, Patrocínio went for the jugular, her fear of losing the throne: "Should a handful of men find themselves forced to campaign seriously and resolutely against the monarchy in Brazil, then all will be irretrievably lost." The Republican Party, through its spokesman Bocaiúva, declared that all they needed was for D. Pedro, still ill in Europe, to die. Rio Grande do Sul republicans brought a motion from São Borja's city hall to the Provincial Assembly, which, in turn, forwarded it to the House, demanding a referendum on the subject of dynastic succession. The abolitionist, republican, and positivist Silva Jardim, delivering radical speeches in meetings, promised the joint abolition of slavery and of the monarchy for the centenary of the French Revolution in July 1889. Abolitionists in a meeting in Santos seconded the São Borja motion, with Patrocínio adding that: "... it is important that we tell the regency just how unpopular it is; that it does not inspire the slightest confidence beyond the clergy and officialdom; that it does not have the people's support." He brought a motion of his own: "It is our understanding, like that of our friends at São Borja city hall, and of the citizens of Santos, Campinas, São Vicente, and São Simão, that the country needs a

---

[15] V.P.A.S. Feb. 17, 1888, pp. 1–2.

328 *The Last Abolition*

constituent assembly in order to discuss the constitutional clause concerning succession to the throne. Moreover: it is our heartfelt wish that the amendment results in the proclamation of a Republic."[16]

Isabel found herself at a crossroads for the Empire and for her own career. She was a lusterless Princess who enjoyed neither popularity among her subjects nor leverage on the political parties. She was cautious like her father, but had none of his schooled ability to balance conflicting forces. Worse still, the crisis she had to handle was not one of government, but of regime. Two imperial bastions were on their death beds: her father, who had already received the last rites, and the institution of slavery. As the political order crumbled, the warning lights began to flash for the Princess. With abolitionism buoyed by a wave of certification, the Crown joined Cotegipe in the firing line. The Princess was the butt of ridicule and of very serious misgivings. An abolitionist/republican pamphlet published at the start of 1888 described her as a Princess oblivious to politics, caught up in a reign of masses and soirées – "when she is among artists and priests, she hovers between the heavens and the earth."[17]

On February 14, the Princess finally asked the Prime Minister what he planned to do about abolition. His recommendation was to buy time. The Baron said that the government was examining the issue and would report on it to her in April. Since the Princess was not pleased, he "replied that there were no plans as such ... and that it was up to the Houses to address the matter." But Parliament would only convene again in May. The Count D'Eu came to his wife's rescue: the Baron should either hear the Council of State or assemble a congress of planters. Cotegipe lost his patience and told the Princess that she ought to follow the example set by her relative Queen Victoria: "Like the Queen of England, Your Highness would be better served leaving political matters to the parties." When he returned to the Cabinet, his feeling was that the Princess was "under influence" and that "the government's fate had never hung in the balance quite like it did now."[18]

That same month, February 1888, Isabel took two steps in the direction of abolition. One was domestic – her sons founded an abolitionist newsletter – and the other was the work of Rebouças, who managed to engage the Princess in the free soil campaign by picking a place where her

[16] CR, Jan. 21 and 30, Feb. 10, 1888.
[17] To complete the jeering tone, the piece was signed under the pseudonym "The Count of Cotegipe" (1888, p. 27).
[18] Conference between the Baron of Cotegipe and Her Highness, Feb. 14, 1885, IHGB.

## The March to Victory

329

prestige and security were assured, the imperial family's mountain retreat of Petrópolis. He set to work arranging a flower battle as the mise-en-scène for the Princess' pro-abolition declaration. The Regent explained the reasons for her change of stance: religion and realpolitik:

... it seems clear that we can *already* free those who will be so anyway a year and a half from now (that is my firm conviction). It is always such a powerful act of charity, and, moreover, what spurs us the most is the possibility of lending a helpful nudge to the idea of abolition within the short term, something that would seem to be the inclination of most, save for the Hardliners, who very much need awakening. Either they wake up soon, or they shall be swept away by the wave. May the Lord protect us that this revolution or evolution of ours transpire as peacefully as possible.[19]

She would apply pressure, but would stop short of calling for Cotegipe's head, because the dynastic couple liked the broader tenets of the Baron's government. The problem, as the Count D'Eu explained to his father-in-law, was that the Cabinet, "*despite its good intentions and sound doctrine*, had, mainly through its inertia on the servile question, allowed a certain spirit of agitation to kindle and spread that could become quite the danger ... Nevertheless, *my counsel is that the Cabinet be maintained* until the throne's address."[20] Isabel and her husband wanted abolition soon but not immediately, and they planned to keep Cotegipe in power until May.

The government, the second-longest of the Second Reign, would fall before then. At loggerheads with sectors of the press, public opinion, the judiciary, the church, the army, the opposition, and even part of its own ranks, on March 1 Cotegipe lost his last-remaining prop of support: the police. At Largo do Rocio, a mêlée broke out between navy seamen and patrolling policemen, and the fighting raged on through the night into the following day, when the Minister of Justice declared that he was:

alarmed by much more serious conflicts flaring between Imperials, navy soldiers, onlookers, hooligans and *capoeiras* against police posted at or patrolling the stations and squares, some of whom were disarmed violently and driven from their posts, beaten and injured by various weapons, including being shot at and cut with switchblades.

---

[19] DNAAR, Feb. 12 1888; letter from Princess Isabel to the Countess of Barral, Feb. 22, 1888, in Barman (2002, p. 246).

[20] Letter from the Count D'Eu to D. Pedro II, Apr. 14, 1888, in Rangel (1935, p. 367). My italics.

330 *The Last Abolition*

Cotegipe took the episode as a justification for stepping up repression. "We cannot," he informed the Regent, "sit idly by as such events transpire," adding that he would take "vigorous measures to repel and disperse any further gangs of troublemakers." He went on: "If the voice of authority is not heeded," he would have to consider taking an even firmer stance.[21] Was the Baron considering a state of emergency?

The dailies painted the clash as symptomatic of the tug of war going on between the armed forces and the government, the so-called military issue. Two thousand people took to the streets to protest against Cotegipe and in favor of the army. The police opened fire on the crowd, injuring many and arresting naval officers. The body of one of them had disappeared. As she read the papers in Petrópolis, Isabel was dismayed by the government's loss of moral authority at "such a time of crisis." The Minister of Justice defended the police against journalists calling for his own head and that of the chief of police (Noggin Shearer), but nonetheless stepped down from his post. For Cotegipe, this meant losing his last bastion of resistance. The Baron tried to bluff his way out of it: "we lack neither the support of true public opinion nor the physical resources to keep the peace," but he knew his government was shorn of authority. And so, on March 7, 1888, Cotegipe let his iron fist slip from the government rudder. Though he confessed his relief to a friend, he was adamant that abolition was "inevitable," but that so was its price: "I fear we are about to witness the monarchy's funeral."[22]

Afraid with that specter hanging over her head, Isabel set about assembling her first government. She decided to switch conductors but keep the orchestra. The Conservatives retained power, but the baton passed from the hardliners Cotegipe and Paulino to the moderate João Alfredo Correia de Oliveira, a minister in the government that approved the Free Womb Law. Part and parcel with Correia de Oliveira came Antônio Prado, who saw no contradiction in having been a member of both Cotegipe's pro-slavery government and the new emancipationist Cabinet.

---

[21] Letter from the minister of Justice Samuel Wallace MacDowell to the Princess Regent, Mar. 3, 1888, IHGB; letter from the Baron of Cotegipe to Princess Isabel, Mar. 5, 1888, IHGB.

[22] CR, Mar. 3, 1888. Letter from Princess Isabel to Samuel Wallace MacDowell, Mar. 4, 1888, IHGB; letter from Samuel Wallace MacDowell to Princess Isabel, Mar. 5, 1888, IHGB; letter from the Baron of Cotegipe to João Ferreira de Araújo Pinho, Mar. 19, 30, 1888, IHGB; letter from the Baron of Cotegipe to Princess Isabel, Mar. 7, 1888, IHGB; ASI, May 12, 1888.

# The March to Victory

331

Paulino learned of the dual defection on March 9. He wrote that he was "left speechless by this news," that the new government was proposing abolition with only a short term of apprenticeship, three or five years. It was a brusque switch from a government "whose policy was resistance" to one favorable to "immediate abolition," "a mortal leap over an abyss that is impossible to clear."[23]

Prado gave his riposte at a meeting also attended by Cotegipe, arguing that a Conservative failure to assemble a Cabinet would mean passing power to the Liberals, "which would do the planters no good whatsoever, as the Liberals are pursuing the same plan for immediate abolition." Circumstantial pro-slavery politics was being swapped for pragmatism. Cotegipe objected, saying that if abolition does come about, "I would rather it were done by the Liberals." Paulino resisted: "I declared that I could not accept any plan for immediate abolition, as it went against every fiber of my Conservative being and would disrupt agricultural labor in the most important provinces of the Empire."

But there was no postponing the issue any longer. A fellow party member recounted the rapid dismantling of official coercion. News of Cotegipe's fall had "resulted in such a collapse of moral authority" that roughly 1,000 fugitive slaves turned up in Campos over the course of the last two days. With the social order falling apart, the new Prime Minister decided it was time to pull the executive's head out of the sand. On March 10, Correia de Oliveira declared: "Tomorrow we present a bill of law for the immediate and unconditional abolition of slavery in Brazil."

The Princess played her part. She declared Petrópolis a free soil, with Rebouças by her side. The abolitionist ran to talk to the new ruler: "I present the Council President João Alfredo with copies of a bill of law for abolition and rural services, drafted on March 30." The ministers considered the proposals. Rural democracy was too much for the former pro-slavery politicians to swallow, but the second bill was set in motion, abolition without compensation.

### ABOLITIONIST RIFTS

With Cotegipe out of the way, the abolitionists commenced a new wave of the free soil campaign, with the restored sense of celebration seen at the

---

[23] In fact, it was a triple defection, as Rodrigo Silva remained a minister. Notes of Councilor Paulino José Soares de Sousa on the formation of the ministerial cabinet, Mar. 10, 1888, IHGB; Wanderley Pinho Archive, DL, 1593-02.

# The Last Abolition

start of the campaign. Another eighteen municipalities declared themselves free soil in Maranhão, Minas, Paraná, Rio de Janeiro, Rio Grande do Norte, and São Paulo – including Jacareí, a hotspot of conflict between the pro-slavery countermovement and abolitionists. The campaign in Court accelerated and the dominoes continued to fall reaching as far and as deep as the Paraíba Valley. In Campos, Carlos de Lacerda led the action block-by-block, street-by-street, and into the rural surroundings, freeing the whole town within a fortnight. Goiânia was also liberated in May, and Belém, São João del-Rei, and Diamantina were all on the verge of joining it. In April, Recife city hall petitioned the imperial government for immediate, uncompensated abolition.[24] The flowers, ceremonies, fêtes, and marches were back with a bang.

The big debate was now on what to do after abolition, and nobody seemed to agree. On the eve of victory, a rift tore through the movement. The first quarrel came in April, when a by-election was called to ratify the ministerial appointment of MP Ferreira Viana as part of João Alfredo's ministry. The Rebouças/Nabuco faction accepted it, as they believed it was imperative to support the new government and the soon-to-be Empress; nobody had expected D. Pedro to last long. Rebouças continued to lobby the Princess, hoping that the daughter would deliver in a matter of a few years what her father had denied for decades. Nabuco, for his part, had convinced himself that "the imperial princess had rendered an invaluable service to the cause of order and liberty by firing Cotegipe ..., I understand it our duty to give the new Cabinet all the support it need [ed] to bring our idea to bear." That was the position he brought to the table at a dinner in Recife with Dantas' family and the leader of the Termites Club.[25]

However, most of the movement felt that it was wrong to cozy up to the government and the Princess without guarantees from them. João Alfredo was no Dantas. In 1884, the movement had shored up a Prime Minister it could identify with, but here was a man who just a moment ago had been walking arms linked with Paulino and Cotegipe. As for her highness, a Third Reign was something most abolitionists were against on principle. Clapp and Vicente de Sousa, in Rio, Carneiro da Cunha, in Recife, João Cordeiro, in Ceará, the abolitionists from Rio Grande do Sul

---

[24] Sampaio (1890, p. 98); CR, Feb. 16 and 17, 1888; Pang (1981, p. 368).
[25] Letter from Joaquim Nabuco to Custódio Ferreira Martins, May 5, 1888, CIJN. In Recife, Nabuco discussed this with José Mariano, João Ramos, and the Falcão brothers (DJN, Mar. 31, Apr. 11,12, and 21, 1888).

## The March to Victory

and many of those in São Paulo, not to mention all of those in the army, interpreted the new conjuncture as an opportunity for the double whammy: the abolition of slavery and the proclamation of a republic.[26] This faction launched a candidate of its own, Quintino Bocaiúva.

As the movement split, Patrocínio, with his republican brain and abolitionist heart, suffered more than most, but decided to stay closer to Rebouças. In April, his *Cidade do Rio* recognized Bocaiúva's services to the abolitionist cause, but broke with the Republican Party. The backlash was immediate. São Paulo republicans took to *A Província de São Paulo* to accuse Patrocínio and the CA of "riding on the coattails of victory, of the Emperor, of Mr. Dantas, and now of Mr. João Alfredo too." Patrocínio replied with an attack on Bocaiúva. Nabuco then defended Bocaiúva, drawing all of the CA's ire: "fury against me at the [Abolitionist] Confederation. ... In the *Cidade do Rio*, Patrocínio is calling me absent, a diplomat, and many other things besides." Nabuco eventually caved under pressure and severed ties with Bocaiúva as well. The abolitionists were cannibalizing each other over whether or not to republicanize the movement.

And that was not all, the role of the church provoked fierce debates within the movement. The movement had formed and grown independent of the Church, indeed despite the Church. Catholic abolitionists such as Antônio Bento were the exception among a lay, scientifically-minded set that saw the Catholic Church as an archaic institution and a preserver of slavery, and Catholicism as obscurantism, hence the bitter public criticism from the movement's positivists over Nabuco's visit to the Pope.[27]

There were programmatic differences too. Like all social movements, abolitionism was a conglomerate of factions united under an umbrella cause, each with its own vague and varied notions of what to do once that had been achieved.

The factions presented a united front one last time as the bill that would fulfill their prime target went to Parliament. They pulled out all the stops, with flowers, flags, banners, fairy lights, streets strewn with petals, and embroidered quilts hanging from the windows. On May 3, 1888, the day Parliament was declared open, the movement gathered under the searing sun to symbolize its unity, when, "in the name of the

---

[26] The same can be said for the positivist abolitionists Teixeira Mendes, Miguel Lemos, Silva Jardim, the Falcão brothers, the Azevedo brothers, Coelho Neto, etc. The list is long.

[27] On the spats concerning the Republic, see CR, Apr. 23 and 30, 1888; DJN, Apr. 21 and 23, 1888, and, on the church, Lemos and Teixeira Mendes (1888).

blacks of the Leblon quilombo, the lad João Clapp Filho [Clapp's youngest son] presented the Princess Isabel with a beautiful bouquet of camellias grown by the slave runaways."[28] Final abolition was now under discussion in Parliament. It was not the abolition the movement had dreamed of, and its announcement came from the mouth of Ferreira Viana, a fierce anti-Dantista back in 1884, but it was abolition all the same. Politics truly is the art of the possible, and, occasionally, of the unlikely.

### BACK TO FLOWERS

If the debate of 1884 was a reprise of 1871, the discussion in 1888 was *sui generis*. Instead of a divided House, opposition was feeble. Nabuco, who had been under age in 1871, unelected in 1884, could finally don the mantle of abolitionist leader in Parliament. On May 7, he spoke for the movement in the House before galleries packed with abolitionists as gleeful as they were incredulous. He hailed the Prime Minister, the Princess, and Dantas, saying that it could only behove the Conservatives to pass abolition in 1888 because the Liberal dissidents had sabotaged Project 48 back in 1884. However, it was no time for bearing grudges, and he echoed the movement's campaign slogan since the days of Abílio Borges; abolition was the new national Independence. "... 1888 is a date of greater magnitude for Brazil than 1789 was for Europe. It is literally the dawn of a new patria. ... The nation, at this moment, makes no party-political distinctions. It stands as one [in] a veritable national apotheosis."

On May 8, the government sent to the floor what has to be the most laconic bill on slavery ever submitted to Parliament in Brazil: it ran to only two lines. Its simple reading was a paramount event. "The Abolitionist Confederation, behind eight standards and a marching band, led some five thousand abolitionists to House. Those that couldn't squeeze inside, huddled around outside. An delirious ovation took place in Rua do Ouvidor," wrote Rebouças, himself delirious. Nabuco, similarly thrilled, addressed the House to applause and cheering. The bill was fast-tracked. The commission issued its report, which was accepted and published the same day.[29]

[28] CR, May 3, 1888.
[29] Nabuco, ACD, May 7, 1888. DNAAR, May 8, 1888. Nabuco, ACD, May 8, 1888.

## The March to Victory

335

The veteran Conservative MP Andrade Figueira questioned the rush, which he said bordered on illegality. During the second round of debate, he urged for "good sense to prevail over the turbulence of passion." Someone interrupted him: "everything that could be said in favor [of abolition] would take eons to pronounce," while speaking against it now would be useless. A four-century wait climaxed in a single moment of impatience. During the third session of debate, another anti-Dantas MP drove the final nail into the coffin of circumstantial pro-slavery politics: "I have always opposed the idea of abolition" and "I would be as intransigent an opponent to it today were there the slightest chance of halting its progress." There was not. Andrade Figueira still opposed the lack of indemnification to slave owners, and these were seconded by the representatives for Rio de Janeiro. The well-worn schemata of threat also reared their head, with his prediction of doom: "I foresee great calamities." He proposed to postpone abolition, by adopting the Antônio Prado project instead, which set the date for December and "contained provisions on freedman labor."[30]

On compensation and worker discipline, the abolitionists and the government said nothing. To address these thorny issues would be to throw open Pandora's box and spill all the evils of the world across the floor. For Rebouças, who like Pandora held hope inside the jar, the only way to ensure the bill was passed was to keep the wording blunt and concise, with no reference to anything beyond the abolition of slavery.

Among cheers from the benches and the galleries, and with the crowd, including many women, swelling at the doors and in the press boxes, the Speaker "allowed the throng to invade the House, making it impossible to move!" In a bid to embarrass whatever pro-slavery countermovement members remained, the abolitionists called for a nominal vote. Indeed, nine MPs stood up for their convictions, with Andrade Figueira leading the way. The bill passed like a bullet through that Lower House. The same House elected by Cotegipe defeated him, with eighty-three votes for and nine against. Thirty-three MPs preferred to stay at home. Nabuco called for the session to be declared closed in honor of the day. The Minister of Internal Affairs took advantage of the moment to quash rumors of the Emperor's demise.[31]

---

[30] The pro-abolition quip was by Afonso Celso Jr., ACD, May 9, 1888. The pro-slavery retort was from Lourenço de Albuquerque, ACD, May 10, 1888.

[31] CR, May 10, 1888, ACD, May 9 and 10, 1888. "A telegram arrived in Rio saying that Pedro II was on his last breath" (DNAAR, May, 1888).

In the Senate, Dantas got his revenge on Paulino. The emancipationist Prime Minister from 1884 did in the Upper House what Nabuco had done in the Lower, speeding up protocol over the course of May 10 and 11 to accommodate the "triumphant bill." During the second round of debate, Cotegipe, aware that "there is not a man alive today more unpopular than I," took to the stand to defend his crumbling world before the packed galleries: "... such was the propaganda, such the steamrolling of events," such was Antônio Prado's betrayal, that the law was merely the "recognition of a fait accompli." However, no piece of legislation could extinguish a way of life. "There will be turbulence throughout this land for many years to come." Along with slavery, abolition was the death knell for its sister institutions of latifundia and the monarchy. Was that not precisely the spirit of Dantas' new project, drunk on Rebouças' dreams? "It is no secret: very soon there will be calls for land distribution," and by similar means, "expropriation without compensation," sending the workforce and production into turmoil. "What are the

FIGURE 9.1 Senate session that approved the Golden Law (Lei Áurea), May 13, 1888.
Unknown photographer.

*The March to Victory* 337

measures to guarantee that those abandoning the plantations will occupy their time with honest labor?" He sketched out a comparative perspective; like Peru, former slaves would become highwaymen and bandits, "perpetrating every manner of barbarity." As frank and forthright as "a dying man dictating his last will and testament," Cotegipe warned that, once all the flowers had withered, the crisis would be "grisly" indeed. To prove his point, he read in horror a speech delivered at an event in Bahia calling for abolition, a lay state, a federation, and a republic. The galleries burst into applause at the mention of these reforms, which, Dantas retorted, "will come; they cannot but come."

At the closing round of discussions before the final vote, on Sunday, May 13, Paulino, the last to embody the circumstantial pro-slavery rhetoric, uttered his signature arguments: "There never was in this whole land a single defender of slavery on principle," but it was the cornerstone of national wealth and "Brazilian civilization." Abolition was "a grave threat to the social and economic order," which was why, he said: "I have the unshakable duty" to stand against it, as he had in 1871 and 1884. In 1888, however, he had no "licit or prudent means" of keeping up the fight: "How can I resist when those who had once stood with me in resisting abolition now stand at its forefront, if the government has been overrun and absorbed by the abolitionist party?" Cotegipe had blamed Antônio Prado, but Paulino wagged his long finger at João Alfredo Correia de Oliveira, who had "picked up the torch and lit the way for the invading forces of the rival camp." He read out a lengthy attack the present Prime Minister had made against Dantas back in 1884, when he had evoked the manifold woes abolition had caused in the United States. Rather than "bask in the applause of those against large landholdings," he invited Correia to join him on the benches of the vanquished. Not even France during the Revolution had stooped to "despoiling property without compensation," nor lumped society with "seven hundred thousand people bereft of education and the habits of liberty." The law was, he said, "unconstitutional, economically adverse and inhumane." He spoke phlegmatically but succinctly, since the Princess was waiting to sanction the new law. He was a lord to the end: "I have fulfilled my senatorial duties as well as the circumstances would allow; I shall do the same with my duty as a gentleman."

Dantas – avenged for 1884 – endeavored to dispel the bad omens: "As is only right and needed, it falls to me to offer some words of hope and optimism on behalf of the abolitionist party." And he did just that.

338 *The Last Abolition*

Employing all the abolitionist rhetoric, he listed the economic, social, and political benefits that would come of abolition, first amongst which should be a raft of reforms: "Today, we have embarked on the construction of a new nation; this law is a new Constitution." He asked the House on its feet to pass the law that would be "the greatest accomplishment in our history."[32]

Correia de Oliveira was next to address the floor, and he spoke of the eradication of a "centuries-old cancer," but to only half the applause. Morally, it was the Dantas Reform of 1884 that was being passed that day, in 1888, and it was ratified by forty-six senators to six, with eight no-shows. Dantas led the special commission that took the law to Isabel's palace with a jubilant crowd in tow. The abolitionists had brought a golden quill, purchased, like everything else they had achieved on the long road to emancipation, with donations collected in the streets. The Princess received the pen from the hands of Patrocínio, who, according to those present, said, "'My soul climbs these steps upon its knees...' And we, abolitionists, have embraced and kissed each other, eyes glimmering with tears and voices hoarse from shouts of enthusiasm and joy."

The Princess had tears in her eyes too. It could be because, inadvertently, she was going down in history for a second Golden Law, a title stolen from the law of 1871. Or her tears may have been for the pro-slavery countermovement's prophecies, or even because of the telegram she had received informing her of her father's fast-deteriorating condition. "Today would be one of the most beautiful moments in my life were it not for my father's ill-health," she said, as she signed the law, countersigned by minister Rodrigo Silva, a pro-slavery MP in 1884. It was three o'clock in the afternoon.[33]

The Empire approved and signed in six days what it had resisted from the moment it was founded. On the seventh day, it celebrated. Nabuco opened the festivities by announcing the promulgation from the balcony of the House. The crowd went wild. The text of Law 3353 was the very wording Rebouças had sent to João Alfredo Correia de Oliveira:

Article 1st From this day forward, slavery is declared abolished in Brazil.
Article 2nd All provisions to the contrary are hereby repealed.

So long in coming, and so brief.

---

[32] ASI, May 12 and 13, 1888.
[33] The description of Patrocínio's actions is by João Marques, in Sena (1909, p. 705). Isabel, ASI, May 13, 1888.

FIGURE 9.2 Law 3353 promulgated on May 13, 1888 abolished slavery in Brazil, without compensation for the slave owners.

## EQUALITY PARTIES

May was the month of flowers. On the tenth, Parliament approved the bill and declared the date of its promulgation a national holiday. The abolitionists started their festivities early. On May 3, when Parliament opened, Dantas, Nabuco, and Patrocínio all addressed the crowd from the Senate House balcony and in the surrounding streets. Rio de Janeiro was celebrating with concert-conferences, theater pageants, torchlit marches, and parades. As the big day approached, the celebrations grew more euphoric. The House was packed with

> people from all social classes, with an extraordinary number of women ... and flowers rained down upon the ministers and MPs from the galleries. There was a frenetic roar of joy, cheers resounded, and all who had contributed to this great national achievement heard their names chanted by the triumphant crowd.

The board of the CA entered in solemn procession, saluting liberty with a bouquet. The abolitionist associations all turned out beneath their banners and a huge crowd followed a marching band from Primeiro de

FIGURE 9.3 Abolitionists waiting outside the Senate for the end of the vote on the abolitionist project.
**Iconographia (Iconography) Archive.**

# The March to Victory 341

Março street to Ouvidor street, stopping outside the offices of abolitionist newspapers on the way. Nabuco spoke outside *O País*, with more speeches outside the *Cidade do Rio*, and then the *Revista Illustrada*. And on they went, door to door, addressing the crowd at each stop, their voices cracking with emotion.

The movement's pioneers and latecomers celebrated together. The Princess hosted a banquet for fourteen emancipated slaves in Petrópolis early in May, but the zenith was May 13, when people crammed into Imperial Square to welcome the passage of the law with a deafening volley of cheers. Rio de Janeiro was one big open-air concert-conference. The masses arrived at ten in the morning, answering the Abolitionist Confederation's call in the morning's headlines, and they stayed there for the next three days. The CA board did another lap of honor around the premises of the abolitionist dailies, associations and faculties, with speeches, applause, and flag-waving at every stop as bands played throughout town all day long. "Sun, searing sun, that Sunday in 1888, when the Regent sanctioned the law passed by the Senate, and we flooded the streets in celebration ..., one and all breathing happiness," said Machado de Assis, who was there.

The heart of Rio de Janeiro, the capital of the Empire of Brazil, was choked with cheering crowds. When night fell, the theaters lit up for galas in honor of the movement that had begun on their very stages. "At ten o'clock that night, one could barely make it down Rua do Ouvidor, such was the throng." A torchlight parade passed beneath the fairy-lit balconies of the townhouses, with banners hanging from the parapets, "drawing behind it an enormous tail of revelers." More speeches, more flowers, more *vivas*, "a hundred score of fireworks and a twenty-one-gun salute." Among the estimated 10,000 people who took to the narrow streets of downtown Rio that day were the propagandists who had been with the cause "since when abolitionism was a leper." Rebouças, Nabuco, Patrocínio, Clapp, and Dantas were all present, with petals in their hair and their arms linked with the arms of the people.

The abolitionists lavished praise on one another in speeches, letters, interviews, and poems: for the living, pen-sketched portraits; for the pantheon (Luís Gama, Rio Branco), all the glories befitting the dead. Over the coming days, *O País* would publish reams of congratulatory telegrams coming in from all over, but it was Patrocínio's *Cidade do Rio* that led the field. The abolitionist societies marched through the streets until they could march no more, as did the railroad workers' association and even representatives of the city hall. The celebrations wore on late into the night.

Rebouças planned the triumph as thoroughly as he had the battle. If the liberation of Ceará had warranted four days of festivities, then the emancipation of the whole nation deserved twenty at the very least, three weeks of "equality parties." The largest shindigs, however, were packed into the first week. Day, night, and everything in between saw fêtes, kermises, concerts, plays, poems, parades. Abolitionism sealed its definitive peace with the church at a massive open-air Mass in São Cristovão on May 17, when lay banners flew alongside crosses. On the 19th, a huge civic procession set out, and a final parade on the 20th, closing the festivities. The campaign ended as it had begun with thousands of flowers: in the House and in the Senate, at newsrooms, associations, theaters, in the streets, in the arms of the Princess, the abolitionists, and the freedmen. Flowers were everywhere.

The abolitionists spoke themselves hoarse and hugged themselves sore over endless toasts. The city ran out of decorations, fairy lights, triumphal arches, intoxicated on theater, pomp and ceremony. There were ovations in Petrópolis, Belém, Recife, Fortaleza, São Paulo, Santos, and provincial, municipal, and village fêtes. With an eye on the throne, Prince Pedro Augusto, accompanying his grandfather in France, held a banquet in Paris. Celebrations were held in Buenos Aires and London, and congratulations flooded in from foreign cities, an expression of

FIGURE 9.4 The outdoor Mass, promoted by the Crown on May 17, 1888 to celebrate the end of slavery in Brazil.
Antônio Luís Ferreira, Instituto Moreira Salles (Moreira Salles Institute).

# The March to Victory

343

transnational abolitionism that filtered all the way back to ground zero, Africa. In Lagos, Nigeria, 300 Afro-Brazilians celebrated for six consecutive days.

Rebouças was given a lap of victory on the shoulders of his students from the Polytechnic. Nabuco was beside himself with joy. Dantas took a turn, overwhelmed by all the commotion, and Patrocínio basked in his finest hour: "A good day to die, Zé," said a friend, "in absolute apotheosis." This was a collective apotheosis. No other term could quite describe the magnitude of the celebrations. "Truly," declared Machado de Assis, "it was the only day of public delirium I can recall ever seeing."[34]

[34] The information in this section was extracted respectively from CR, May 1, 1888; DNAAR, May 3, 4, and 15, 1888; CR, May 11, 1888; GT, May 15, 1888; DNAAR, May 15, 1888; GN, May 14, 1888; DRJ, May 13, 1888; GN, May 14, 1888; O País, May 14, 1888; Carvalho (1891, p. 17); Davis (1984, p. 298); CR, May 18, 1888; O País, May 15, 1888; João Marques, in Magalhães Jr. (1969, p. 244); Machado de Assis, A Semana, May 14, 1888.

# 10

# Future of the Preterite

### THE DAY AFTER

While Rio de Janeiro celebrated, the day after abolition Rebouças worked on his next project: *Democratic Evolutionist Propaganda* (*Rural Democracy – Freedom of Conscience, Free Trade*). He drafted plans to complement the abolition because he had realized even before the festivities ended that every conquest leaves some wreckage smoldering in its wake.

The hangover came early. Two days after abolition, the Viscount of São Laurindo, a landowner in Bananal, came to the Provincial President of São Paulo, Rodrigues Alves, to complain of the "uncertainties and dangers in which we find ourselves" and to demand that steps be taken "to ensure order and the safety of our families" in the face of anarchy. "Cotegipe and Paulino's speeches [when the Golden Law was approved] spooked the already worried planters. I speak not only for myself, but for the whole class to which I unfortunately belong." This class had Cotegipe and Paulino as its spokesmen, but also many ex-slaveowers, one of whom turned an abolitionist weapon against itself, the theater. He wrote a play in which the largest slave-owning provinces – São Paulo, Rio de Janeiro, and Minas Gerais – proposed sending all the freed slaves to a new colony in Mato Grosso, with Nabuco as president, or "perhaps we could proclaim Patrocínio King or Emperor of the Blacks." The piece was as jocular as it was infuriating: "There is not a single provision in the Golden Law that is favorable to the master, despite his recognized property rights." Claims and demands like this one abounded. Abolition would bring a bevy of projected labor

344

colonies, and the nation would once again have to choose between Dantas and Paulino.[1]

The movement's parade was promptly rained on by the countermovement as Paulino rose phoenix-like from the ashes. Eleven days after abolition, his legion made a formal request for indemnification for the former slaveowners to the House, while Cotegipe sent a similar bill to the Senate. Both bills demanded a market price for the assets lost on behalf of planters, middlemen, and bankers, and government subsidies to hire labor – Chinese or southern Europeans – to replace the freedmen, whom they believed had grown lackadaisical in the absence of the whip. In a repeat of 1884, their reaction was concerted and organized. The pro-slavery side, like Rebouças, had been at work since May 14 on a new movement of their own, the "indemnizationism." Cotegipe led the charge in Parliament, backed by the legitimacy given by the eleven petitions to the House.[2] The countermovement was back.

The abolitionists, who had put their differences aside for the good of the campaign, fell asunder in its wake, "veterans of the legion which triumph demobbed," as Nabuco put it.[3] With their only shared target now achieved, abolitionists were fighting among themselves threatened by the factionalism that kills social movements.

The main bone of contention was what should become of the freed slave. On the table was the Rebouças program: free work, small properties, and European immigrant labor to help "dismantle the legacy of slavery" by bringing to the country a new work ethic. Even among the proponents of this rural democracy there was disagreement on the mechanism to create these smallholdings, whether through the redistribution of devolved public land, or through fiscal incentives that would affect the land market – nobody was contemplating the expropriation of the latifundia. There was an alternative program inside the movement, though. For many abolitionists in Court and from Pernambuco and Rio Grande do Sul, modern society concentrated capital, so dividing the land into lots would be useless, as they would just get lumped together all over again. Modernity was urban and industrial, so any rural utopia, as the Rebouças one, was outdated. They believed the State should create a

---

[1] DNAAR, May 14, 1888; letter from the Viscount of São Laurindo to Rodrigues Alves, reserved, May 15, 1888, IHGB; Dom Pascal (1888, pp. 11–12, 17, 121).
[2] Project n. 10, ACD, May 24, 1888, Project C, ASI, Jun. 19, 1888. There were three petitions from Rio de Janeiro, one from Santa Catarina, and seven from Minas Gerais (Pang, 1981, p. 372).
[3] Letter from Joaquim Nabuco to Faelante Câmara, Jan. 10, 1905, CAII.

346 *The Last Abolition*

mini-welfare state that could integrate the former slave into the national society through education, social rights, and regulations that limited the working day's hours.[4]

The fate of the freed slave was thus bifurcating into very distinct projects of society. One of these envisioned the ex-slave as a citizen in a Liberal, capitalist society, with *civil* and *political* rights, as a small landowner on equal footing with the immigrant laborers, the two building blocks of the new economy. The other future offered *social* rights and sought to meld the freed slaves into an urban proletariat of the new industrial society Brazil was expected to become. They were vague plans, and each abolitionist hashed out the details in his own way. The only real agreement was on two issues, education and tutelage. The abolitionists had never considered leaving the freedmen masters of their own fate.

There was also disagreement between abolitionist monarchists and republicans. Most saw the monarchy and slavery as heads on the same hydra that had to be lopped off together. Provincial leaders like João Cordeiro, in Ceará, were the anti-monarchy stalwarts and Liberal abolitionists from key provinces were also turning toward the republican cause, such as Rui Barbosa, in Bahia, and Carneiro da Cunha, in Pernambuco. The Rio Grande do Sul movement was almost entirely republican, as were the abolitionists in Court – Vicente de Sousa, Clapp, and Bocaiúva, who had a foot in both camps throughout the campaign. The same held for all the positivists, most of the faculty students and the young military. Even abolitionists who were not republicans suspected that the post-abolition policy of João Alfredo Correia de Oliveira would revive the spirit of the period immediately following the Free Womb Law, appeasing the reaction rather than instituting new reforms. Most of the abolitionists agreed that only a change of regime could regenerate the nation, and as soon as they lowered the abolitionist flag, they raised the republican one.

Nabuco and Rebouças had flirted with republicanism during the Cotegipe years, but their aristocratic position kept telling them that they could steer the new reign in the right direction. Nabuco tried to "pitch the dynastic ring" to the movement's heart. If the Princess was weak, she was also impressionable, Rebouças calculated. Just as readily as he had departed the palatial world in order to fight for abolition, in the 1870s, he now committed himself to the future of the dynasty. He planned to

---

[4] The positivist abolitionists were anti-immigrationists exclusively concerned with the welfare of former slaves (Lemos and Teixeira Mendes, Apr. 21, 1888, p. 21).

# Future of the Preterite

renew the Abolitionist Confederation, expanding his program beyond rural democracy, adding a rural land tax, freedom of conscience, and civil marriage, and to attract families of immigrants to settle in the countryside.[5] Nabuco and Rebouças wanted to buttress the monarchy with a new kind of social support, of abolitionists and freed slaves. They clung to the utopian vision of a reform-minded Third Reign, suddenly assured that Isabel would have the drive and power to make strides where her father had feared to tread.

Patrocínio was on the fence. He had been a republican for as long as he had been an abolitionist, but he saw the Princess' support for abolitionism in the last months of the campaign as a decisive way to ensure the peaceful denouement to the process. "So gratitude has knocked the wheels off the liberator," said one of his followers, as he left his master's side to stand with the republicans.[6] Patrocínio, however, switched camp with his customary fervor. One of his first steps was to join those creating a Black Guard to protect Isabel from the republicans, who shot back by labeling Patrocínio "the last black to sell himself in Brazil." Patrocínio would never sell out, but as a warrior with slave blood, something Rebouças never was, in backing the Third Reign he forfeited the vacant podium of Luís Gama as the symbol of abolition.

And so, before May 1888 ended, the three national abolitionist leaders, Rebouças, Nabuco, and Patrocínio, turn up in a monarchist island surrounded by a sea of abolitionist republicans.

Their hopes of unpacking new reforms under the monarchy soon ran aground on familiar shores. It became clear early on which direction Correia de Oliveira's government was taking, as a bill was sent to Parliament designed to repress idleness among freed blacks and to compensate the perpetrators of slavery rather than its victims. Rebouças branded it "the shameful 300,000-conto [de réis] bill for slavocrat landlordism." Nabuco spoke against it in the House and Rebouças expressed his dismay to the ministers João Alfredo and Ferreira Viana and wrote an article for the *Cidade do Rio* denouncing the "mendicant aristocracy," followed by a manifesto against the immigration of Asian proletarians.[7] Nabuco and Patrocínio published articles similar in tone and climbed back onto their respective pulpits, the former in Parliament and the latter at theater conferences, though neither repeated the earlier success.

---

[5] DNAAR, Mar. 31, 1889.    [6] Coelho Neto (1906).

[7] DNAAR, Jun. 26, 1888; CR, Jun. 27, 1888; DNAAR, Oct. 23, 1888. Manifesto signed also by Taunay, a Conservative friend of Rebouças.

348 *The Last Abolition*

João Alfredo Correia de Oliveira bought support by handing out titles of nobility to pro-slavery politicians, which made Nabuco refuse a viscountship and caused Patrocínio to return a medal of honor to the Brazilian Historical and Geographical Institute: "During the bitter times of the abolitionist campaign the Historical Institute sadly did not stand amongst those sacrificing their status, fortunes, and very lives for the cause. I do not, therefore, see how it could now presume to esteem the value of abolitionists."[8]

The long year – eighteen months and two days – that separated abolition from the proclamation of the Republic was far from edifying. The mood was one of dissatisfaction. On one side of the equation were the rankled slavocrats, since the imperial coffers were not deep enough to foot the compensation bill; on the other, disgruntled abolitionists bemoaned the stalled reforms. The positive agenda of social rights and rural democracy and the reaction for indemnification wrestled each other into a stalemate. Caught between a pro-slavery political coalition and abolitionists, the Princess and her cabinet were paralyzed, approving neither Cotegipe's compensation proposal nor Rebouças' reforms, dropping his bill of law on the Education, Instruction, and Moral Betterment of Freedmen. On the first anniversary of abolition, Silva Jardim rightfully accused the monarchy of consigning the former slave to a new sort of misery.[9]

### BACK TO THE THEATER

As at the opening of O *Guarani* in 1870, André cuts a dapper figure, but he is a different man, his hair gray and his shoulders stooped under the weight of his various losses – brother, father, companies, and the dream of a rural democracy. He has also lost his fellow campaigners, because the abolitionists have disbanded.

Over the course of the abolition celebrations, the lauding of the reformers transmuted into an elegy for imperial tradition. Still, in May 1888, Catholic liturgy and the aristocratic hierarchy were reaffirmed at an outdoor Mass in São Cristovão. The Church/State alliance had never been so explicit as in the choice of religious vocabulary to redefine the Princess as a "redeemer." Catholicism and the monarchy appropriated the laurels of abolition.

---

[8] Missive from José do Patrocínio to the Baron Homem de Melo, Aug. 2. 1889, IHGB.
[9] DNAAR, Jul. 17, 1888; GN, May 13, 1889.

## Future of the Preterite

Rebouças, who had been pivotal to the campaign, was similarly so in converting the achievements of a social movement into a gift from the Empire. On the first anniversary of abolition, he organized an Abolitionist Confederation Festival at the D. Pedro II Theater. It was a concert-conference shorn of its contentious bite, a celebration of the Princess, who was presented with a bouquet of white camellias by the residents of the Leblon quilombo. The following day, with Patrocínio, he led a civic procession that culminated in more plaudits for the future Empress and her old father, transformed into the "patriarch of the abolitionist family."[10]

The defining template for the national identity under the monarchy reappeared in the anthropophagy of abolitionist glory. Alencar was dead, but his Indianist romanticism, which saw the Brazilian identity as European and Amerindian, to the exclusion of all Africans, was still alive and well, as would soon become clear. During the free soil campaign in Ceará, Rebouças had commissioned a piece from Carlos Gomes to give the growing movement some extra lift.[11] O Escravo (The Slave) arrived late, in 1889, and was adopted as a commemorative composition. But what exactly was it celebrating: the decree that put an end to slavery, the abolitionist struggle, the citizenship of former slaves, the Third Reign? Not even Rebouças could say any more.

The première was held at the Teatro Lírico in Rio de Janeiro on September 27, 1889. The imperial family, in mourning, did not attend. True to the symmetries in which Rebouças took such delight, the second performance, held the following day, had the added advantage of coinciding with the 18th anniversary of the Free Womb Law. It played to a packed house. The Emperor, defying death and returned to office, had recently appointed a new Prime Minister, the Viscount of Ouro Preto, a far from reform-minded Liberal, as Nabuco and Rui Barbosa were quick to point out. However, whether the Viscount was going to get the Empire back on track is a subject for another book.

The gala performance of O Escravo received a standing ovation. Rebouças had accompanied the rehearsals and preparations, and he read

---

[10] Schwartz (2007, p. 25) drew attention to this point: "Abolition was understood and absorbed as a gift ... Isabel became the 'Redeemer' and abolition itself the work of a 'single owner' rather than the culmination of a collective process of struggle and achievement" (DNAAR, May 13, 14, 1889).

[11] Letter from Carlos Gomes to Giulio Ricordi, Jul. 16, 1884, in Vetro (1982).

350 *The Last Abolition*

the applause as a repetition of the success of *O Guarani* back in 1870, "a veritable apotheosis of abolitionist propaganda."[12] Was it?

In 1870, shortly before the Free Womb Law, the imperial elite, disagreements apart, was moving in one direction: slow modernization, controlled change, and gradual emancipation sometime in the distant future. Things looked very different in 1889. The parties were bleeding. The Liberals could not agree on which reforms to support, and the Conservatives did not know how best to block them. The Empire had lost the support of the military and was under pressure from the republican movement in the press and in the streets, as the conferences and parades continued under this new banner. Old dichotomies – abolitionist movement /pro-slavery countermovement, liberal/conservative – were lost in and replaced with new cleavages – federalist/centralist, reformist/indemnizationist, republican/monarchist. The Second Reign's slow pace, its policy of procrastination, postponement, and protraction in order to minimize conflict ended up accumulating discontent on all sides. The result was that *O Guarani* debuted before an audience ill-disposed toward applause. Rebouças himself was in no mood to rub shoulders with old enemies: "I didn't attend; I wanted to avoid the slavocrat plutocracy."[13] The pro-slavery camp also stayed at home. A man like Paulino – now president of the Senate and leader of the pro-indemnification political coalition – would not have been seen dead at an opera like that, while Cotegipe, elegant to a fault, had been kind enough to die before the Republic.

*O Escravo* met with a more tepid reception than *O Guarani,* but the two operas shared a line. The older piece honored the Emperor; the newer the heiress to his throne, to whom Gomes – forgetting the tireless efforts of his friend Rebouças – attributed abolition: "On the memorable date of May 13, in the name of countless others just like the hero of this drama, her highness, with kind and patriotic heart, had the glory of transforming captivity into eternal joy and freedom. Thus, the word 'slave' now belongs to the nation's past."[14]

As did the opera's plot. The original libretto, written by Taunay, a friend of Rebouças and a supporter of Dantas, had been set in 1801 and its protagonist, echoing many other plays, novels, and poetry of the abolitionist campaign, was a freed slave. However, the Italian librettist

[12] EDEAR, Jan. 13 and 14, Jun. 9 and 12, Jul. 11 and 13, Sept. 24, 26, 27 and 28, 1889.
[13] EDEAR, Sept. 26 and 28, 1889.
[14] Letter from Carlos Gomes to Princess Isabel, in Taunay, Paravicini, n.d., in Vetro (1982).

# Future of the Preterite

351

to whom Gomes entrusted the versification of the piece pushed the story all the way back to 1567, *before* the African slave trade had begun in earnest, and made the hero an Indian, as in *O Guarani*. The mixed-race Ricardo and Anália made way for Tamoios, Iberê, and Ilara. Taunay was furious, as indeed were all the abolitionists.[15]

Over four acts, the romance between the young slave woman Ilara and the owner's son, Américo, is broken up by the master, who marries her off to the slave Iberê. The Indian joins a Tamoio revolt against the Portuguese, during which Américo is captured and held prisoner. When Iberê finds Américo in this sorry state, he repays his debt of gratitude to the young white master for having saved him from the whips, and helps him escape with Ilara. The Indian then commits suicide so that the white man and Indian woman can ride off to a happy ending. *O Escravo* repeats the same creation myth for the national identity as *O Guarani*. Both operas end with the union of the European and Amerindian, with no mention at all of African enslavement.

The elite's celebration of abolition minimized the importance of the abolitionist movement and refashioned the Empire's old foundation myth, spun around an imagined community that erased the African. The hero of May 13 did not share the same color as Rebouças, Patrocínio, Vicente de Sousa, and Luís Gama. Pieces like *O Escravo* and other writings, including some by abolitionists, cobbled together a symbology of abolition that shunted the movement, and even more the slaves, into the background, while the Princess became the "Redeemer." The violence of slavery and of politically organized pro-slavery faded even in the prose of leading abolitionists, such as Nabuco's *Minha formação* (My Formative Years).

Even in the celebration of their freedom the ex-slaves were unwelcome. And in that symbolic elision resides the meaning of what would come after abolition: a muted denouement to a passionate movement. When Carlos Gomes' opera took to the stage a month and a half before the monarchy's final act (the proclamation of the Republic on November 15), its icon was still a mythical Indian. To the freed slaves, the Empire, once more, turned its back.

---

[15] Gomes told Taunay: "The poet [Rodolfo Paravicini], author of the verses of the libretto *O Escravo* had to make *some radical changes* to your sketch" (letter from Carlos Gomes to Alfredo Taunay, Apr. 16, 1887, Gomes' highlight, Taunay, 1910). Taunay was incensed, but answered Gomes' appeals and raised the funding for the production.

# 11

## Abolitionism as a Social Movement

Charles Tilly argues that it was during the campaign against the African slave trade that the British first invented what we now call a "social movement," a kind of politics that combines a public campaign for pressuring target authorities, the use of a common repertoire of contention (special-purpose associations, publications, and modular strategies), and repeated public demonstrations by large numbers of individuals that display commitment to the cause even in the face of adversity. A social movement is not an organic collective actor, but rather an extraparliamentary style of doing politics that is open to groups with neither access to nor influence upon institutional politics. The Brazilian antislavery mobilization ticks all these boxes. In all, counting from 1868 to 1888, institutional measures, public demonstrations in closed and open spaces, symbolic, direct action, actions of diffusion and of confrontation, there were 2,214 acts of protest. The campaign was pursued over two decades, with nationwide and coordinated civil associations and protest events, recruiting a massive number of activists in the country's towns and cities and fanning out across the hinterland. Abolitionism was Brazil's first national social movement.[1]

The movement did not choose its tactics on principle. Its choices were relational and suited to the prevailing balance of power at any political conjuncture. The action/reaction game between the movement, the government, and the countermovement delimited which strategies and arenas were *viable*. Though each faction had its own line of action, *collective*

---

[1] Tilly (2005, p. 308). Drescher (2009, p. 43).

## Abolitionism as a Social Movement 353

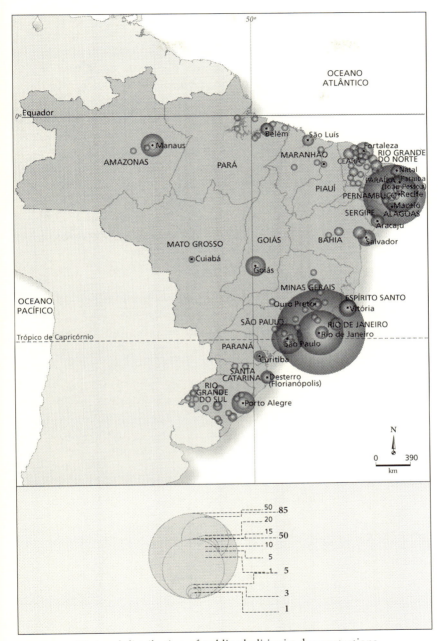

MAP 11.1 National distribution of public abolitionist demonstrations.
Designed by Sonia Vaz.

354                          *The Last Abolition*

*national* mobilization chose its *preferred* social spaces depending on the political threats and opportunities the conjuncture presented, in other words, the government's disposition toward tolerance, cooperation, or repression, the availability of resources and allies, and the level of organization of the countermovement. The changes in the balance of those elements marked the phases of the long political process of abolition.[2]

The movement's *genesis* (1868–1871) occurred when, under international pressure, the government put the abolition issue on the political agenda. It was an opportunity for social-elite based associations to emerge and for using institutional strategies: lobbying, freedom suits, and some demonstrations in the public space. The movement was formed in step with the political organization of the pro-slavery countermovement. Over the next seven years, Conservative governments steeled the political institutions against abolition. The movement nevertheless persisted in the public space, albeit small, weak, and scattered. However, it had enough strength to transmit strategies and rhetoric from its pioneers to a new generation of activists.

The movement became a national one later (1878 to May 1884). The problem was restored to the agenda towards the end of the decade for two main reasons: the Free Womb Law was about to come into effect and the Conservatives left the government. Under the more tolerant Liberal administrations, activists sought and obtained foreign support, diversified their tactics (associations, concert-conferences, free soil campaign), and created non-violent mobilization styles. These strategies resulted in public

---

[2] Some scholars, such as Toplin (1972), divide the abolitionists into "moderates" and "radicals," though without explaining the criteria for the distinction, which often seems to come down to social class. The literature on social movements criticizes this thesis and shows that movements draw their members from across the social spectrum, putting paid to the people/elite distinction and the notion of "popular" movement. Likewise, the supposition that the less privileged social strata tend to be more radical has also been contested, as those without means find it hard to get organized (for example, McCarthy and Zald, 1977). Besides, in the Brazilian case there is a counterfactual: Antônio Bento, always listed among the "radicals," was a man of considerable wealth. It was the use of this grassroots/elite distinction that divided the study of abolitionism into the discrete arenas of parliament, the public space, and the underground, as if they were autonomous movements, when in fact they were different facets of the same movement. McAdam, Tarrow, and Tilly (2001) argue that institutional politics (like parties) and the non-institutional (like social movements and revolts) belong to a continuum of forms of "contentious politics" that vary in level of violence and institutionalization, but not in nature. Nor is there any correspondence between types of agent and forms of action – pacific/violent, local/national, parliamentary/grassroots, moderate/radical. The forms of action depend less on the moral principle of the agents than on the set of circumstantial possibilities they found themselves in and the options available to their adversaries.

# Abolitionism as a Social Movement

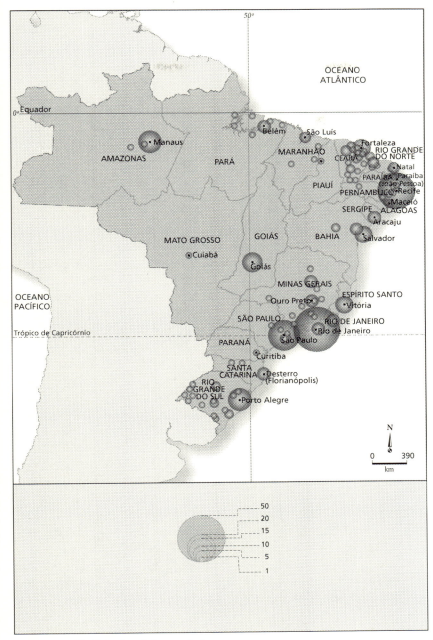

MAP 11.2 Abolitionist civil associations.
Designed by Sonia Vaz.

legitimation of abolition in major cities, a growing and socially diverse membership, and geographic expansion, all of which changed the mobilization into a national movement.

Mobilization and changes in the international conjuncture together fostered a reaction from within the political system. A facilitating government took office. Under Dantas, who committed to reform, the movement and the government aligned. The movement operated within the political system and, between May 1884 and May 1885, acted inside the institutions, collaborating with the government and launching candidates for legislative seats.

The pro-slavery counter-offensive ousted Dantas and turned the tables on the movement. The Conservatives returning to power in 1885, allied with the countermovement. Institutional doors were slammed in abolitionist faces and the authorities adopted a repressive line on their activities. Having dismantled the moral and social foundations of slavery through its propaganda campaign, the abolitionist movement then turned to *confrontation* (August 1885 to February 1888), relying on civil disobedience, direct action, and assisted collective runaways,[3] which made it impossible for slavery to continue without resorting to force.

As the prospect of civil war loomed, sectors of the social elite and state institutions who had avoided the conflict so far intervened on the side of immediate abolition. The army's alignment with the abolitionists was critical and took state repression off the table. This *certification* (October 1887 to May 1888) started during the period of confrontation as a means of containing it, and gradually encompassed the church, sectors of the social elite and imperial parties and the Crown. The conflict was defused and a compromise was achieved. The abolitionists had to give some ground: in order to have their prime objective met (abolition without compensation) they had to step back on other related reforms.

Over 1,000 in number, the abolitionists were many and diverse. The movement was a web of heterogeneous groups from different social positions, lifestyles, regions, education, professions, levels of social prestige, and access to political institutions. The activism network was cemented by personal (family, *compadrio*, friendship), professional (teacher-student, student-student, occupational) and political (affiliation and membership of associations and parties such as republicans,

---

[3] What Conrad (1975, p. 245) calls anarchic – "abolitionism's chaotic closing phase" – is explained here as a change of strategy.

## Abolitionism as a Social Movement 357

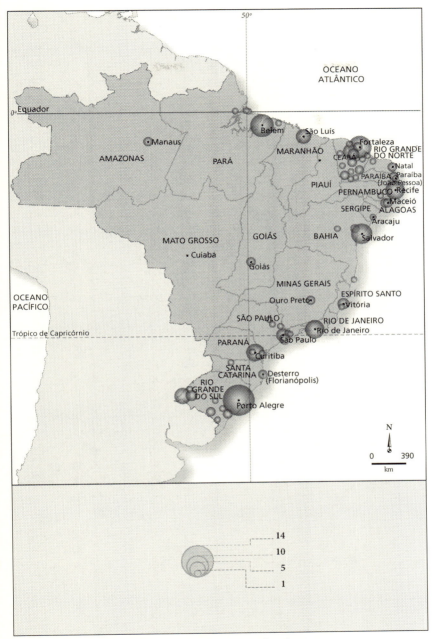

MAP 11.3 The freedom soil campaign national distribution.
Designed by Sonia Vaz.

positivists, etc.) relationships, some of them synchronic and others inter-generational.

It was also a polycentric network, and its internal variety enabled a division of labor, but also fostered centrifugal effects, with short-term goals, with its leadership and alliances being constantly renegotiated, disputed, and redefined. And yet, it was only in direct confrontation with the State and countermovement that all these players convened under the shared identity of "abolitionists."

The movement's minimal cohesion and accelerated growth were made possible by shared *portable styles of activism*, that is, stylized modular strategies that worked as scripts which each faction could adapt to suit its own local contexts, generating variations and nuances. The styles of activism of Rebouças (lobbying, brokerage between the public space and political system), Borges (associativism, civic ceremonies, the boom-erang method), Gama (freedom suits), Patrocínio (concert-conferences, freedom soil campaign), Nabuco (parliamentary action, electoral cam-paigns), and Antônio Bento (assisted collective runaways) were standard-ized and portable. This meant that strategies were easy to diffuse, since they could be unpacked and rolled out simultaneously in different parts of the country, leading to varied pockets of resistance with their own singu-larities. Thus factions were able to cluster together without needing to homogenize, which was ultimately what allowed the campaign to become national and stay the course.[4] There were many players, but one reper-toire, more like an orchestra than a choir.

Political brokers established the connections across which these modu-lar styles of activism were diffused. They wove the web among the factions that resulted in a movement that could present itself as a collect-ive political actor. Key activists included figures who moved among more than one faction or arena and could spread rhetoric and styles and build alliances.[5] There were various regional players, but only five *national leaders*. Borges connected the domestic movement with counterparts abroad, something Nabuco furthered and deepened while keeping a foot in both the public space and the institutional arena. Gama spliced together judicial activism with propaganda and clandestine activities.

---

[4] Tarrow (1995) argues that the diffusion of forms of action ripples out from the center to the periphery. However, in Brazil, while there was a general irradiation from the political center, the Court, to the rest of the country, there were other regional hubs, such as Ceará.

[5] Political brokers are activists who function as synapses between the different factions of a movement (Diani, 2003). The abolition movement's spaces for gathering and articulation included associations, theaters, the press, coffee shops, workplaces, and activists' homes.

Patrocínio coordinated the various strategies in the public space. Overseeing it all was Rebouças, the key broker of the abolitionist movement. An aristocrat and politician's son, he moved among the high-born and well-placed and the political institutions; as an entrepreneur, he had contacts in the business world and spoke its language; as a professor, he had a captive audience of students to convert to the cause; as an opera-lover, he had access to theater and arts circles; and as a black man, he had legitimacy in the movement's grassroots. Of all those devoted to the abolitionist movement, Rebouças was involved the longest, from beginning to the very end, always taking care of practical details. He was the bridge-builder who drew the various arenas of mobilization together. He worked mostly behind the scenes and was seldom seen, an unsung hero who pulled a great deal of weight. Nabuco gave him the credit he was due: "Rebouças embodied, like no one else among us, the antislavery spirit: ... his job was the most important of all. ... [I]t involved the most essential (though hidden) function of the motor force, providing inspiration to all. He almost never appeared in the foreground, but all those in the public eye looked to him, felt his influence, and were governed by his gestures. ..."[6]

Abolitionism, like slavery, had a global scale. The rhetoric, strategies, and political performances of fledgling national movements crystallized into a repertoire of antislavery contention handed down to the newcomers. Knowledge of the former experiences of others (the British, French, Spanish, and the Americans) and ties with foreign contemporaries gave the Brazilians the models they needed in terms of arenas (streets, theaters, the press), rhetoric (schemata of compassion, rights, progress), organization (special-purpose associations), expression (public ceremonies) and action (judicial, legislative, direct, and confrontational strategies). However, these methods had to be adapted to suit Brazilian political traditions. In the case of the underground railroad for example, Brazil, unlike the United States, had no "free soil" to which fugitive slaves could run, so it had to be created. That need fueled the reinvention of the emulated strategy. Brazilians invested in simultaneous free soil campaigns in non-adjacent geographic areas, producing three free soil clusters in the country: Ceará, Amazonas, and Santos. A more drastic adaptation concerned the appropriation of social spaces and mobilizing structures,

---

[6] Nabuco (1900, p. 140). Rebouças is a specific yet crucial sort of activist, activists that "do not attempt to be the main spokespersons, they defer to partners ... who ... can articulate a shared frame on the issue" (Gamson and Meyer, 1996, p. 289).

which in the Anglo-Saxon cases were built upon Quaker foundations. In Brazil, the Catholic tradition and the formal link between church and State placed the religious institutional structure on the side of slavery. Because of that, abolitionists followed the Hispanic example and used the secular space of theater. Brazilian antislavery propaganda was rooted in the theater milieu and adopted its art and language in a theatricalization of politics.

The same happened with the appropriation of the rhetoric of delegitimization from abolitionist campaigns elsewhere. The schemata of rights came bundled with the Independence trope, while the schemata of compassion, unable to draw upon Catholicism due to the association between the church and the State, drank from the secular fountain of Romanticism, which underscored the artistic flavor of abolitionist propaganda. The schemata of progress were given a scientific tinge not seen elsewhere. This secular trait lent the Brazilian movement a modern face that the religion-rooted Anglo-Saxon campaign had lacked. Appropriating aspects of the foreign repertoire (rhetoric, strategies and arenas) resulted in a reinvention, producing a very Brazilian style of activism.

The foreign repertoire also underpinned the organization and rhetoric of the Brazilian countermovement, as well as State initiatives. The Free Womb Law of 1871 and the Saraiva-Cotegipe law of 1885 were inspired by the Spanish legislation introduced in Cuba. The Cotegipe government also adapted the US Fugitive Slave Act.

All of these characteristics help to debunk three myths about nineteenth-century Brazil. One is the supposed imitation of foreign ideas and their imposition on national reality. On the contrary, the abolitionists were connected to movements in Europe and in the Americas, but reinvented schemata and strategies to adapt them to national conditions. Brazilian abolitionists were modern and creative in choosing to build a secular campaign.

Second, this reconstruction of antislavery mobilization refutes the notion that abolition was largely the handiwork of the Crown. The end of slavery resulted from a large-scale political conflict that bordered on civil war, with the governments and the Crown pressured by the abolitionist movement and the pro-slavery reaction. Far from being controlled by the Emperor or his daughter, abolition was a long and contentious political process, full of setbacks.

The third myth is that Brazilian society was politically apathetic during the Empire, that the State ran roughshod over an inert or unstructured

## Abolitionism as a Social Movement

361

civil society. The conflict surrounding abolition argues the contrary. On the one hand, there was a politically organized pro-slavery countermovement that fought tooth and nail to maintain the servile institution in Brazil. And on the other, there was a strong social movement pressuring the government to abolish bondage. Society mobilized on both sides, sometimes with and sometimes against the State, but was anything but inactive.

Beyond the Brazilian case, this interpretation of abolitionism as a social movement brings three main points of interest for scholars studying other cases of abolition of slavery. First, it shows that world history and comparative studies must take the Brazilian case seriously because it demonstrates global links among national abolitionist movements and global circulation of repertoires. The tensions between transnational repertoire and local context and political tradition led to adaptations and the creation of a portable, secular style of activism in Brazil. One can hypothesize that there was a common abolitionist repertoire of contention shared by all abolitionist movements, with local tensions and adaptation processes imposing an individuality on each of them.

Second, this study shows that civil society mobilization was not a particular feature of Anglo-American abolitionism. Brazilians built a huge and durable social movement in favor of abolition, similar to the British and American ones. The magnitude of this process has been overlooked by scholars because previous research has tended to analyze each setting (Parliament, public space, grassroots) of the Brazilian abolition process separately.

Third, studying abolitionism from a relational perspective can illuminate points that comparisons do not make visible. In comparisons, cases are assessed in isolation. A relational approach places particular cases inside the whole network of interactions and exchanges among activists on a global scale, beyond national frontiers, and investigates links between them and across generations The same can be said about the pro-slavery actors' transnational networks and those between national governments. To adopt such a relational perspective would mean going beyond comparison in favor of an actual transnational history of abolitionism.

# Annex

## TABLES

TABLE A.1 *Abolitionist civil associations founded by political conjuncture, 1868–1888*[1]

| Conjuncture | Founded associations | Association/ year |
|---|---|---|
| Liberal radicalization/Conservative rule before Free Womb Law approval (1868–1871) | 24 | 6 |
| Conservative rule after Free Womb Law approval (1872–1877) | 6 | 1 |
| Liberal rule (1878–1885) | 279 | 34.9 |
| Conservative rule (1886–1888) | 50 | 16.7 |
| Total | 359 | |

TABLE A.2 *Abolitionist public demonstrations by political conjuncture, 1878–1888*

| Political conjuncture | Indoor spaces | Outdoor spaces | Total |
|---|---|---|---|
| Liberal rule (1/1878–7/1885) | 455 | 124 | 579 |
| Conservative rule (8/1885–2/1888) | 170 | 62 | 232 |

[1] The data for the set figure comes from a databank on abolitionist protest events, based on thirty-five newspaper reports from nine provinces: Amazonas – *Commercio do Amazonas* (1/1881–12/1881), *Jornal do Amazonas* (1/1885–12/1885); Bahia – *Diário de Notícias* (3/1883–8/1884), *Gazeta da Bahia* (11/1883–12/1886), *O Abolicionista, Salvador* (1869), *O Abolicionista* (1/1874–4/1874), *O Asteroide* (9/1887–12/1888), *O Democrata*

364                                    *Annex*

TABLE A.3 *Repertoire of contention mobilized by Brazilian abolitionist movement, 1868–1888*

| Protest technique | Total |
| --- | --- |
| Institutional actions | 200 |
| Indoor public demonstrations | 646 |
| Outdoor public demonstrations | 189 |
| Diffusion actions | 442 |
| Symbolic actions | 89 |
| Direct actions | 407 |
| Confrontational actions | 71 |
| Unidentified techniques | 170 |
| Total | 2214 |

*List of abolitionist protest events and strategies*

---

**Institutional actions:** Lobbying (visits, letters, pressure on political authorities); petitions (letters or petitions to the national, provincial, or municipal executive and legislative powers); judicial actions (civil rights actions, habeas corpus, lawsuits, legal appeals and complaints to prosecutors, judges, courts, and police chiefs); parliamentary actions (speeches, national and/or provincial bills, interpellations, formation of parliamentary coalitions); political candidacies (nominations or support for electoral candidates); pressure for executive acts (promulgation of abolitionist and revocation of pro-slavery national, provincial, or municipal bill, measures, regulation or laws)

(1/1871–12/1871), *O Direito* (1/1883–12/1883), *O Guarany* (4/1884–4/1885), *O Horisonte* (1/1872–12/1872), *O Monitor* (8/1876–5/1881), *O Prenúncio* (1/1871–12/1871); Ceará – *O Libertador, Fortaleza* (1/1881–7/1885); Maranhão – *Diário do Maranhão* (1/1880–12/1887), *O Paiz* (1/1881–3/1881), *Pacotilha* (1/1881–12/1888), *Publicador Maranhense* (1/1884–12/1884), *Tribuna Liberal* (1/1889–12/1889); Minas Gerais – *17° Districto* (1/1885–12/1885), *A Actualidade* (1/1881–12/1881), *A Província de Minas* (3/1884–12/1886), *A União* (1/1887–12/1888), *Jornais de Ouro Preto* (1/1881–12/1888), *José Bonifácio* (2/1887), *Liberal Mineiro* (1/1883–12/1886), *O Arauto de Minas* (1/1884–12/1884), *O Baependyano* (1/1880–12/1885), *O Lábaro do Futuro* (1/1882–12/1882); Paraíba – *Diário da Parahyba* (1/1884–12/1885); *Gazeta da Parahyba* (1/1888–12/1888); Rio Grande do Norte – *Gazeta do Natal* (1/1888–12/1888); Rio de Janeiro – *O Abolicionista* (11/1880–12/1881), *Gazeta da Tarde* (1/1883–12/1886), *Cidade do Rio* (10/1887–5/1888); São Paulo: *A Redempção* (1/1887–5/1888). I also made use of the activity summaries of the Associação Central Emancipadora (six bulletins), Confederação Abolicionista (two bulletins, 1884) and Sociedade Brasileira Contra a Escravidão (one bulletin, 1880), found at Oliveira Lima Library, *Boletim da Sociedade Libertadora Norte Rio-Grandense* (1/1888–4/1888); and *Almanach Adm Historico Estatistico e Mercantil da Província do Amazonas* (1/1884–12/1884), of the National Library, and events registered in the diaries of André Rebouças (IHGB, Rio de Janeiro), and in the published diaries of Joaquim Nabuco.

*Annex* 365

*(continued)*

**Public demonstrations in closed spaces:** conferences (assemblies, public conferences, conference-concerts, international conferences, hall meetings, military meetings, pronouncements, demonstrations, matinées, soirées, honors, public celebrations, ceremonies, meetings, public sessions); artistic events (concerts, matinée musicale, operas, theater plays, exhibits, literary soirées, festivals); parties (literary, house parties, banquets, dances); meetings (public meetings, assemblies, receptions, visitations, congresses)

**Public demonstrations in open spaces:** meetings (in the open, in squares, embarkation meetings, landing meetings, electoral meetings, conference-concerts in the open, bazaars, kermises, fairs, outdoor parties, serenades); parades (parades, marches, torchlight processions, cortèges, solemn marches, civic processions, walks with band, caravans, regattas, political demonstrations on boats)

**Diffusion actions:** recruiting (membership organization, confederations, congresses, networks, clubs, night school for freed slaves and/or slaves, propaganda trips); proselytism (publication of newsletters, open letters, bulletins, electoral bulletins, statements, speeches, essays, serials, newspapers, manifestos, pamphlets, novels, short stories, plays, poems, translations)

**Symbolic action:** artistic actions (caricatures, anthems, paintings, allegories, ornamentations, decorations with flowers, flagging, lighting for homes, theaters, commercial buildings, gardens, streets, creation of monuments; gun salutes); attributions of prestige or stigma (creation and granting of titles and honorary or derogatory records, boycott of publication of advertisements for runaway slaves, production of symbols and abolitionist heroes, politicization of private life rituals (demonstrations at private parties, christenings, birthdays, weddings, and funerals)

**Direct action:** fundraisers (fund collections, donations, door-to-door collections or through subscriptions), free soil strategy (creation of liberating committees, closing of ports for slave embarkation, collective liberations of slaves, buying of individual freedoms, persuasion visits for granting manumission concessions in spatial sequences – home/farm, block, street, neighborhood, city, province)

**Confrontational action:** civil disobedience (disrespect for slave laws, guided slave escapes, encouragement, promotion, aid to slave escapes, transportation, and slave whippings), obstructions of slave boarding in ports and train stations, obstruction of slave arrests and abolitionist arrests, creation of an underground railroad (with escape routes, underground associations and quilombos to shelter or protect fugitives), confrontations (disturbance of institutional procedures), invasion of buildings or events; public declarations of willingness to use force; confrontations with the army, police, cavalry, civil militia, overseers, slave-owners, plantation burnings, incitement to strike, insubordination or slave insurrection in public places (ports, train stations, streets), or private spaces (houses and farms)

366 *Annex*

## *List of pro-slavery strategies against abolitionist mobilization*

**Legislative obstruction:** lobbying (visits, letters, pressure on political authorities); pro-slavery petitions (letters or petitions to the national, provincial or municipal executive and legislative powers); parliamentary actions (speeches, national and/or provincial bills, interpellations, formation of parliamentary coalitions); political candidacies (nominations or support to electoral anti-abolitionist candidates); pressure to delay or promulgate national, provincial or municipal abolitionist repression bills, measures, regulations, or laws

**Institutional obstruction and repression:** police officials' intimidation of abolitionists, criminal offenses against abolitionists, censure and dismissal of abolitionists from public jobs; electoral fraud; enforcement of repressive laws; suits against abolitionists, abolitionist arrests

**Anti-abolitionist civil associations:** plantation clubs

**Anti-abolitionist publications:** newspapers, pamphlets, manifestos and books, anonymous letters which threaten abolitionists' lives

**Anti-abolitionist private and public meetings**

**Private repression:** threats to abolitionists's lives, verbal and physical aggression, preventing or dismantling abolitionist demonstrations, destruction of pro-abolition newspaper offices, militia organization, breaking into abolitionist homes, expelling abolitionists from their cities, beating, murdering, and lynching of abolitionists

## TIMELINE

### 1823

José Bonifácio de Andrade e Silva presents a bill for the gradual emancipation of slaves to the Constitutive Assembly.
Abolition of slavery in Chile.

### 1826

On November 23, Brazil signs a treaty with Great Britain abolishing the Atlantic Slave Trade.
Abolition of slavery in Bolivia.

### 1829

Abolition of slavery in Mexico.

# Annex                                                    367

### 1831

On November 7, Brazil signs a new treaty with Great Britain, this time freeing all Africans brought into the country from that date onward.

### 1833

Abolition of slavery in British Guiana.

### 1838

Abolition of slavery in Mauritius.

### 1850

The 2nd of July Liberating Society is founded in Salvador, Bahia.

On September 4, the Conservative government approves Law 581 (Eusébio de Queirós), which prohibits the slave trade in Brazil.

The Society against the African Slave Trade and for the Promotion of Amerindian Colonization and Civilization is founded in Rio de Janeiro.

### 1851

Abolition of slavery in Colombia and Panama.

### 1852

First abolitionist demonstration in Rio de Janeiro.

The Society against the African Slave Trade and for the Promotion of Amerindian Colonization and Civilization issues its manifesto calling for the progressive emancipation of slaves, introduction of immigrant labor, and the fostering of smallholder agriculture.

### 1853

Abolition of slavery in Argentina.

### 1854

Abolition of slavery in Peru and Jamaica.

### 1855

Abolition of slavery in Moldavia.

### 1860

The Christie Affair: Great Britain severs diplomatic relations with Brazil over slavery.

Abolition of serfdom in India.

### 1861

Abolition of serfdom in Russia.

Start of the American Civil War. The Confederacy fights to preserve slavery in the southern United States.

368                                 *Annex*

### 1862

The 2nd of July Liberating Society holds the first abolitionist march in Brazil.

### 1863

Abolition of slavery in Surinam and the Antilles.

On January 1, President Lincoln issues the Emancipation Proclamation, abolishing slavery in the United States.

### 1864

The British and Foreign Antislavery Society petitions Emperor Pedro II for an end to slavery in Brazil.

In December, Brazil goes to war against Paraguay.

### 1866

The Council of State debates slavery. The Viscount of São Vicente draws up five plans for progressive abolition.

Abílio Borges starts to use the boomerang strategy, asking French abolitionists for help and, in June, a petition signed by eminent French politicians is sent to Pedro II calling for an end to slavery in Brazil.

On November 11, Decree 3725-A grants free liberty to slave conscripts in the Brazilian army.

On August 3, the Liberal Party comes to power and Zacarias de Góis e Vasconcelos becomes Prime Minister.

### 1867

The Zacarias Government puts slavery on the institutional agenda. The subject is even mentioned in the monarch's address to Parliament.

The Council of State debates slavery again.

### 1868

André Rebouças joins the abolitionist campaign.

On July 16, the Emperor replaces the Liberal Zacarias with the Conservative Viscount of Itaboraí, triggering a political crisis.

Rebouças takes his pro-emancipation plans to the government.

### 1869

Castro Alves publishes his *Navio negreiro (Slave Ship)*.

A manifesto by Liberal Party moderates calls for a Free Womb Law.

A manifesto by Liberal Party radicals calls for the gradual emancipation of slaves.

The International Abolitionist Association sends an antislavery motion to D. Pedro II.

Luís Gama starts freedom suits in the courts.

Abílio Borges founds the 7th of September Liberating Society in Salvador, which promotes pro-abolition civic ceremonies.

On September 15, Decree 1695 prohibits the sale of slaves at public or private auctions.

The Count D'Eu, commander of the Brazilian forces in Paraguay, bans slavery in Paraguayan territory.

A new petition from the British and Foreign Antislavery Society is sent to D. Pedro II demanding an end to slavery in Brazil.

1870

Abílio Borges asks the Pope to intervene in favor of abolition in Brazil.

The Liberal Manuel de Sousa Dantas succeeds Borges as the new president of the Liberating Society of Bahia.

End of the Brazil/Paraguay War.

André Rebouças starts work on the foundation of a Central Association for the Protection of Freed Slaves in Rio de Janeiro.

On July 4, Spain passes the Moret Law, which decrees the freedom of all slave-born children and slaves over the age of sixty in Cuba and Puerto Rico.

On September 29, the Conservative Government of José Pimenta Bueno (Viscount of São Vicente) is sworn in and restores the issue of slavery to the institutional agenda.

On December 4, the Republican manifesto is launched in Rio de Janeiro.

1871

The 7th of September Liberating Society in Salvador launches the newspaper O *Abolicionista* (*The Abolitionist*).

The March 7 Cabinet comes to power, under José Maria da Silva Paranhos (Viscount of Rio Branco) of the Conservative Party. His government launches a modernization program that includes the free womb bill.

André Rebouças takes his pro-emancipation projects to the Viscount of Rio Branco.

On May 12, the Rio Branco government presents its free womb bill, modeled on the São Vicente project and the Moret Law (Spain).

The Emperor departs for a year's leave in Europe. Princess Isabel assumes the throne in his absence.

The Commercial and Plantation Club is founded in Rio de Janeiro to combat the Free Womb Law. The Lower House receives thirty-three petitions against the bill, and the Senate, a further eleven.

On September 28, Law 2040 – the Free Womb Law is passed freeing all slave-born children from that date onward on the condition that they remain under their mother's master's guardianship until the age of eight, mandatorily, or until twenty-one, conditionally. The law also creates an Emancipation Fund for the purchase of manumissions.

### 1872

The first Brazilian census reveals slave holdings of 1,510,806, 15.2 percent of the overall population.

### 1875

The June 25 Cabinet comes to power under Luís Alves de Lima (Duke of Caxias) of the Conservative Party.

### 1877

José do Patrocínio writes antislavery articles in the press.

### 1878

Abolition of slavery in the Gold Coast.

On January 5, after a decade in opposition, the Liberal Party returns to power under João Lins Vieira Cansanção de Sinimbu (Viscount of Sinimbu).

Farmers organize agricultural congresses in Rio de Janeiro and Recife to discuss the labor shortfall.

Decrees 6966 and 6967 alter the deadline established in the Free Womb Law under which slave owners are to register their slaves and children born after 1871.

Parliamentary elections: the Liberal Party wins a majority, although the Conservatives obtain a robust minority, in the Lower House

### 1879

On March 5, Jerônimo Sodré Pereira, a member of the 2nd of July Liberating Society in Bahia and of the Liberal Party, speaks in Parliament in favor of abolition.

On March 22, Joaquim Nabuco, elected by the Liberal Party in Pernambuco, defends abolition in the House.

## Annex                                                    371

On September 7, João Cordeiro and José Correia do Amaral found the Perseverance and the Future Emancipation Association in Fortaleza, becoming the Liberating Society of Ceará a year later (SCL).

Nabuco forges ties with the British and Foreign Antislavery Society.

### 1880

Nabuco obtains support for abolition from the US Plenipotentiary Minister in Brazil. He travels to Europe and forms further alliances with abolitionists in Spain, France, and Great Britain.

José do Patrocínio is one of the agitators behind the Vintém (Twopence) Revolt against a rise in tram fares.

On March 28, José Antônio Saraiva, from the Liberal Party, forms a government.

In August, Rebouças, Patrocínio, and Vicente de Sousa create the Central Emancipation Association (ACE), which starts organizing pro-abolition "concert-conferences."

In August, Nabuco presents a bill to Parliament proposing gradual, indemnified abolition be to phased in by January 1, 1890. In order to back the bill, a new abolitionist caucus forms in Parliament with eighteen members from nine provinces.

On September 7, Nabuco and Rebouças found the Brazilian Antislavery Society (SBCE), which issues a manifesto and creates a newspaper, O Abolicionista.

On November 1, the Viscount of Rio Branco dies. The abolitionists try to transform his funeral into an abolitionist rally.

### 1881

Joaquim Nabuco runs for re-election for the Liberal Party and receives street-level support from abolitionists, but fails to get elected. He moves to London to strengthen his ties with European abolitionists.

The Brazilian Antislavery Society is restructured in order to accommodate the three main abolitionist factions: Nabuco's parliamentary bloc; Patrocínio's grassroots movement; and the judicial activism of Luís Gama.

In January, in Fortaleza, the SCL blocks the arrival at port of a consignment of slaves for sale in the province.

On March 17, Decree 8067 regulates declarations on the escape and capture of runaway slaves.

The SCL starts its "liberation parties" and forms connections with the ACE and SBCE.

372                                    *Annex*

In August, the SCL, with the connivance of the military troops, conducts a street march under the slogan: "Not another slave through the Port of Ceará."

### 1882

The São Paulo Abolitionist Center is formed by Luís Gama's group.

Slavery is banned throughout the Ottoman Empire.

The newspaper *Gazeta da Tarde*, with José do Patrocínio as editor-in-chief, becomes the official mouthpiece for both the ACE and SBCE.

The French abolitionist Victor Schoelcher criticizes Emperor D. Pedro II and declares his support for the Brazilian abolitionists.

SBCE-member Sancho de Barros Pimentel becomes provincial president of Ceará and introduces a hefty fine for those caught trading slaves with other provinces.

On January 21, Martinho Álvares da Silva Campos, from the Liberal Party, who declares himself "a slaver through-and-through," becomes Prime Minister.

On July 3, the Liberal Party's João Lustosa da Cunha (Marquis of Paranaguá) becomes Prime Minister. He recognizes the growing force of the abolitionist movement and puts the issue back on the government agenda.

Luís Gama dies on August 24. His funeral in São Paulo becomes a major abolitionist rally.

### 1883

On January 1, José do Patrocínio declares Acarape the first slavery-free municipality in the Empire.

On May 9, the Abolitionist Confederation (CA) is founded as an umbrella organization for the various abolitionist societies in Rio de Janeiro. To accelerate the campaign, the CA launches a free soil campaign and sends delegates to Ceará, Pará, Pernambuco, Alagoas, Bahia, and Rio Grande do Sul.

In Santos, abolitionists encourage collective slave escapes and the formation of quilombo maroon colonies.

The government sends the army's Seventh Battalion to quash abolitionist actions in Ceará.

On May 21, the abolitionists declare Fortaleza, the provincial capital, "liberated" from slavery.

On May 24, Lafaiete Rodrigues Pereira, of the Liberal Party, becomes Prime Minister.

*Annex* 373

Joaquim Nabuco publishes O *abolicionismo* (Abolitionism) in Great Britain.

On June 9, Nabuco organizes a banquet in support of Fortaleza in London, attended by international abolitionists and authorities.

On August 2, Lafaiete's government sends a bill to Parliament that boosts the Emancipation Fund but obliges slaves to have a fixed abode. Patrocínio organizes a banquet in support of Fortaleza in Paris, attended by abolitionists, such as Victor Schoelcher.

On August 11, the Abolitionist Confederation demands the immediate, indemnity-free abolition of slavery. The CA distributes 18,000 copies of its manifesto.

Mossoró is the first town in Rio Grande do Norte to be decreed slavery-free.

The journalist Apulco de Castro is murdered in Rio de Janeiro. The Luso-Brazilian Abolitionist Society, of which he was a member, transforms his seventh-day remembrance Mass into an abolitionist rally drawing nearly 1,000 protesters.

### 1884

In January, the Central Emancipation Association creates the Central Emancipation Commission (CCE) to conduct the free soil campaign in the imperial capital.

The SCL sends the abolitionist Almino Affonso to speed up the campaign in Manaus. Various abolitionist societies are formed in Amazonas.

The abolitionist Sátiro Dias takes office as president of the province of Ceará and raises taxes on slave holdings.

On March 25, abolitionists host large-scale events nationwide to declare Ceará the first slavery-free province in the Empire.

Teodureto Carlos de Faria Souto assumes the provincial presidency of Amazonas and prohibits the importation and exportation of slaves.

In April, abolitionists declare the "liberation" of Vitória, the provincial capital of Espírito Santo.

On May 11, the abolitionists declare Amazonas the second "free" province in the Empire.

On June 6, Manuel de Sousa Dantas, of the Liberal Party, takes office as Prime Minister.

On July 15, the Dantas government presents Project 48 to Parliament. The bill, which the abolitionists helped draft, calls for an end to the interprovincial trade of slaves aged sixty or over; the gradual liberation of all other slaves through the Emancipation Fund, which the bill also plans to expand; the introduction of a minimum wage; and allotments of farmable land for freed slaves.

The abolitionists defend the Dantas project in publications, the press, and at conferences.

The recently-founded Central Abolitionist Commission of Amazonas begins the free soil campaign in Manaus.

The Dantas Reform meets with stiff opposition in Parliament. Forty-nine Plantation Clubs form in a bid to block the bill.

A vote of no confidence in the Dantas government is called.

On July 29, the Emperor convenes the Council of State to discuss Dantas' fate. The majority of the council sides against Dantas, but the Emperor decides to keep him in power. Elections are called and abolitionist candidates run for parliament nationwide.

On September 7, the abolitionists declare Porto Alegre, the provincial capital of Rio Grande do Sul, a slavery-free city.

On December 3, ballot rigging and violence are rife during the parliamentary elections and various mandates are contested on the grounds of fraud. The leading abolitionists fail to get elected and the Dantas government falls.

### 1885

On May 6, José Antônio Saraiva, from the Liberal Party, becomes Prime Minister.

The Saraiva government drastically alters the Dantas Reform and pushes it through with Conservative support. Saraiva then stands down as Prime Minister.

On August 20, the Conservative João Maurício Wanderley, Baron of Cotegipe, becomes Prime Minister. He signs off on the Saraiva project at the Senate and takes a hard line against the Abolitionist movement.

José do Patrocínio's *Gazeta da Tarde* is vandalized, as well as the premises of other pro-abolition newspapers nationwide.

On June 7, Joaquim Nabuco stands as a candidate in a by-election in Pernambuco. He is elected amid a tremendous show of public support.

Joaquim Nabuco founds the fourteen-man Abolitionist Caucus in Parliament along with surviving members of the Dantas government.

On September 28, promulgation of Law 3270, the Saraiva-Cotegipe Law (or the Sexagenarian Law), which grants liberty to slaves aged

## Annex

sixty or over in return for three years' extended service by way of compensation.

On November 14, Decree 9517 calls for a new registration of the nation's slave stocks, pushing back the Sexagenarian law and introducing penalties for runaway slaves and those who abet them.

### 1886

On January 15, Cotegipe dissolves Parliament and calls new elections. The CA launches candidates in Ceará, Bahia, São Paulo, Pernambuco, and Rio de Janeiro. The government uses fraud and violence to control the outcomes. Of all the abolitionist candidates, only Patrocínio succeeds in being elected to the city council of Rio de Janeiro.

The CA marches through the streets of Rio de Janeiro with a pair of slave girls tortured by their mistress. This shock tactic is repeated in other parts of the country.

Suffering a crackdown, the abolitionists appeal for foreign support and start campaigning through art events.

Through the British and Foreign Antislavery Society, Nabuco obtains a declaration from the British Prime Minister W. E. Gladstone in favor of abolition in Brazil.

The abolitionists make nationwide systematic use of the assisted collective runaway strategy.

Dantas takes to the Senate to denounce the fact that slaves are being flogged to death. The abolitionists campaign for a ban on corporal punishment and the Liberal bloc in the Senate pressures the government on the issue.

On October 7, in Cuba, the transition to free labor reaches completion.

On October 15, promulgation of Law 3310 which repeals Article 60 of the Criminal Code and Law 4 of June 10 1835 and bans flogging in Brazilian territory.

### 1887

In February, the Emperor falls ill in February and travels to Europe for treatment. Princess Isabel becomes regent in his absence.

In March, a Liberal Party Conference proposes abolition over a five-year period. Abolitionist MPs present bills for immediate abolition.

In June, fourteen senators rally behind Dantas' proposal for an end to slavery on December 31, 1889.

The free soil campaign redoubles its efforts in São Paulo and Salvador.

376　　　　　　　　　　　　　　*Annex*

In July, the chief of police in Recife sends out a communiqué forbidding his officers to hunt down runaway slaves.

In July, Joaquim Nabuco runs for election in Pernambuco. He is elected to nationwide celebrations among abolitionists.

In August, the government issues a curfew and ban on public assembly and purges abolitionists from the civil service. Abolitionists are arrested, charged, and persecuted throughout the country.

The CA appeals to the Princess Regent to put an end to the violence and declare in favor of abolition. Isabel closes the parliamentary calendar without so much as mentioning the cause.

Relations are strained between the government and the army (the Military Crisis). The abolitionists appeal for the army to side with the movement against the government.

In October, violent clashes between abolitionists and authorities break out in Campos, Rio de Janeiro. Abolitionists are arrested. The CA tries to muster international support. In the Senate, Dantas demands that the Justice Minister guarantee the safety of the abolitionists.

In October, a mass slave break-out in Capivari marches through Itu towards Santos. The army attacks the march in the Cubatão mountains, leaving many dead. The abolitionists harbor the survivors and react with outcry in the press.

On October 25, the chairman of the Military Club, Manuel Deodoro da Fonseca, takes a petition to the Regent in which the Brazilian Armed Forces inform their refusal to capture runaway slaves.

The bishops of Minas Gerais, Bahia, Pernambuco, Cuiabá, and São Paulo issue open letters in support of abolition.

The president of São Paulo appeals to the central government for military reinforcements to help curb slave escapes and quash rebellions. With the army withholding support, the government has no way of meeting his request.

Minister Antônio da Silva Prado leaves the government in order to combat the territorial liberation process in his home province, São Paulo.

In December, to avoid disruption to production, slave owners in the provinces of São Paulo and Rio de Janeiro concede manumissions en masse.

### 1888

In January, abolitionists declare the capitals of Paraná and Rio Grande do Norte "liberated." Abolitionists in Santos and in Court back a motion from the town council of São Borja calling for a referendum

## Annex

on dynastic succession. Patrocínio argues for a Constitutive Assembly to decide upon a new form of government.

In February, Nabuco appeals to the Pope for support and the Pontiff issues an antislavery encyclical to the Brazilian bishops. Cotegipe's government manages to have the encyclical pulled.

In February, Rebouças secures Princess Isabel's support for a free soil campaign in Petropólis.

On February 21, two former Confederate soldiers incite members of the Plantation Club in Penha do Rio do Peixe (present-day Itapira) to lynch the local marshal, whom they accuse of harboring runaway slaves.

On March 1, clashes between the police and navy in Rio de Janeiro. Two thousand people protest in the streets against Cotegipe and in favor of the military. Cotegipe stands down as Prime Minister.

In March, abolitionists announce the liberation of the provincial capitals of Goiás and São Paulo.

On March 10, the Conservative João Alfredo Correia de Oliveira takes power. Rebouças sends him copies of his rural democracy and unindemnified abolition bills.

On May 8, the government sends an unindemnified abolition bill to the Lower House. The CA rallies 5,000 on a march to Parliament.

On May 10, a bill abolishing slavery is approved by the Lower House, and at the Senate three days later.

On May 13, Law 3353, the Golden Law, is promulgated. Roughly 10,000 people celebrate in Rio de Janeiro. Similar celebrations take place across the nation.

On May 24, Cotegipe presents a bill to the Senate demanding indemnification for former slave owners. A similar project is floated in the House. The "indemnification" movement begins.

### 1889

On November 15, many former abolitionists take part in a republican coup. Patrocínio proclaims the republic at the legislative assembly in Rio de Janeiro, while Rebouças and Nabuco continue to support the monarchy.

### 1890

On December 14, and with CA support, the abolitionist Rui Barbosa, the interim government's Minister of Finance, burns the slave registration records so as to prevent the indemnification drive.

378                                  *Annex*

## BRAZILIAN ABOLITIONIST ASSOCIATIONS (1850–1888)[2]

### 1850

**Bahia**
1. Philanthropic Society Established in the Capital of Bahia for the Benefit of Brazilians Unfortunate Enough to Have Been Born Slaves

**Rio de Janeiro**
2. Society against the African Slave Trade and for the Promotion of Colonization and Indian Civilization

### 1852

**Bahia**
3. The 2nd of July Liberating Society

### 1857

**Rio de Janeiro**
4. The 7th of September – Ypiranga Society

### 1859

**Pernambuco**
5. Mutual Assistance and Gradual Emancipation Association

### 1860

**Pernambuco**
6. Academic Association for the Remission of Slaves

### 1864

**São Paulo**
7. The Abolitionist Fraternity Society

---

[2] Associations and societies formed after the abolition of slavery project presentation to the House in March 1888 are not included here.

# Annex 379

## 1867

### São Paulo
8. The Hope Society

## 1869

### Bahia
9. The Abolitionist Humanitarian Society
10. The 7th of September Liberating Society

### Espírito Santo
11. The Abolitionist Society of Espírito Santo

### Maranhão
12. The 28th of July Manumission Society

### Pernambuco
13. The Humanitarian and Emancipationist Society of Nazareth
14. Emancipatory Society of Pernambuco

### Rio Grande do Sul
15. Society for the Promotion of the Emancipation of Slaves in the Province of Rio Grande do Sul

## 1870

### Amazonas
16. The Amazonian Emancipatory Society

### Bahia
17. The Commercial Abolitionist Society

### Ceará
18. The Abolitionist Society of Baturité
19. Manumission Society of Sobral

### Minas Gerais
20. The Workers for Liberty Society

## 380 Annex

**Pernambuco**
21. The Young America Society

**Piauí**
22. The Emancipatory Society of Piauí

**Rio de Janeiro**
23. The Central Association for the Protection of Emancipated Slaves
24. Campos' Emancipatory Society

**Rio Grande do Sul**
25. The Liberating Society of Cruz-Alta

**São Paulo**
26. The First Fraternity Emancipatory Society
27. The Slave Child Redemption Society

### 1871

**Bahia**
28. The 13th of March Liberating Society
29. Liberating Society of Lençois

**Minas Gerais**
30. The Liberating Society of Barbacena

**Pernambuco**
31. The People's Club
32. Liberation Society

### 1872

**Pernambuco**
33. The Angel of Liberty
34. The Liberating Society of Pernambuco

**Rio Grande do Sul**
35. The Liberating Society of the City of Porto Alegre

# Annex

## 1873

**Paraíba**

36. The Parahyba Emancipatory Society

## 1874

**Espírito Santo**

37. The 1st of January Emancipatory Association

## 1877

**Rio de Janeiro**

38. The 28th of September Emancipatory Society

## 1878

**Pará**

39. The Liberating League

## 1879

**Ceará**

40. The Perseverance and the Future Emancipation Association

**Goiás**

41. The Emancipatory Society of Goyana

**Pernambuco**

42. The Democratic Club for the Manumission of Slaves

## 1880

**Ceará**

43. The Emancipatory Society of Ceará, The Military Abolitionist Club*

**Paraná**

44. The Emancipatory Society of Campo Largo**

**Pernambuco**

45. The New Emancipatory Society

## Rio de Janeiro
46. The Central Emancipatory Association
47. Rio de Janeiro Military Academy Society for the Liberation of Slaves
48. The Brazilian Antislavery Society
49. The Polytechnic School Emancipatory Society

## Rio Grande do Sul
50. The Joyful Hope Beneficent Society

## Santa Catarina
51. The Abolitionist Society of Santa Catarina

## São Paulo
52. The Academic Abolitionist Society of São Paulo

### 1881

## Amazonas
53. The Abolitionist Club of Amazonas**

## Bahia
54. The Liberating Society of Bahia

## Ceará
55. The Liberating Society of Aracaty**
56. The Liberating Society of Quixeramboim
57. The Liberating Society of Aquiraz
58. The Liberating Society of Ceará
59. The Liberating Society of Icó
60. The Liberating Society of Maranguape

## Maranhão
61. The Abolitionist Arts Center of Maranhão
62. The Abolitionist Society of Maranhão
63. The Abolitionist Society Emancipatory Center

## Minas Gerais
64. The Abolitionist Society of Ouro Preto

# Annex 383

**Pará**
65. The Patroni Abolitionist Club
66. The Slave Emancipation Society**

**Pernambuco**
67. The Abolitionist Club of Pernambuco

**Rio de Janeiro**
68. The José do Patrocínio Emancipation Fund
69. The Abolitionist Club of Riachuelo
70. The Campos' Liberating Society
71. The Abolitionist Club of Military Academy Cadets

**Rio Grande do Sul**
72. The Jaguará Emancipatory Association

**São Paulo**
73. The Luís Gama Emancipation Fund
74. The Academic Abolitionist Society**
75. The Large Liberating Society**
76. The Dramatic Playhouse Abolitionist Society

### 1882

**Amazonas**
77. The Amazonian Branch of the Liberating Society of Ceará
78. The Liberating Society of Paranaguá

**Ceará**
79. The 25th of December Abolitionist Center
80. The Abolitionist Club of Ceará
81. The Freed Slave Club of Ceará**
82. The Liberating Society of Barbalha
83. The Redemptive Society of Acarape

**Maranhão**
84. The 28th of July Liberating Society of Vila da Barra do Corda

384                                    *Annex*

### Minas Gerais
85. The Abolitionist Society of Diamantina
86. The Abolitionist Society of Juiz de Fora
87. The Abolitionist Society of Tamanduá

### Pará
88. The Abolitionist Club of Pará**

### Pernambuco
89. The Pedro Pereira Emancipation Fund
90. The 28th of September Musical Society

### Rio Grande do Norte
91. The Liberating Society of Natal

### Rio Grande do Sul
92. The Abolitionist Center of Porto Alegre

### São Paulo
93. The Association for the Protection of Slaves
94. The São Paulo Abolitionist Center
95. The Abolitionist Club of Brás*

### Sergipe
96. The Uncle Tom's Cabin Liberating Society of Aracaju

### 1883

### Alagoas
97. The Philanthropic Association for the Emancipation of Slaves

### Bahia
98. The José Bonifácio Club*
99. The Francisco do Nascimento Club
100. The Luís Álvares Club
101. The Luís Gama Club*

### Ceará
102. The Fraternity and Labor Artistic Association
103. The Abolitionist Association of the Fifteenth Infantry in Ceará

## Annex

104. The Redemptive Association of Assaré
105. The Redemptive Dawn Society
106. The Abolitionist Club of Pacatuba
107. The Reform Club Abolitionist Fund**
108. The Abolitionist Society of Ceará**
109. The Liberating Center of Fortaleza**
110. The Abolitionist Club of the Vila de Soure Public School for Boys
111. The Commercial Abolitionist Club
112. The Abolitionist Club of Soure
113. The Emancipatory Club of Aracati
114. The Liberating Club of Morada Nova**
115. The Commercial Club of Ceará
116. 19th of October Society
117. The Russian Women Liberators Society**
118. The Liberator Women of Messejana Society*
119. The Liberating Drama Society of Sobral
120. The Liberating Society of Pereira**
121. The Liberating Society of Saboeira
122. The Liberating Society of Boa Viagem
123. The Liberating Society of Independência**
124. The Liberating Society of Sant'Anna
125. The Liberating Society of Creta**
126. The Liberating Society of Ipueiras**
127. The Pentecostes Liberating Society
128. The Liberating Women Society of São Francisco
129. The Liberating Women Society of Baturité
130. The Students Liberating Society
131. The Tutti Quanti Liberating Society
132. The Ceará Women Liberators*

### Espírito Santo
133. The Abolitionist Center of Espírito Santo
134. The Abolitionist Society of Espírito Santo
135. The Domingo Martins Liberating Society

### Maranhão
136. The Maranhão Society for the Abolition of Slavery and Organization of Labor
137. The Liberating Society of Brejo
138. The Abolitionist Club of Maranhão

386 *Annex*

**Minas Gerais**
139. The Viscount of Rio Branco Abolitionist Club of Minas Gerais
140. The Liberating Society of Minas Gerais

**Pará**
141. The Pará Abolitionist Center **
142. The Central Emancipationist Commission of Belém**
143. The Women's Liberating Society of Pará
144. The 28th of September Abolitionist Society
145. The 29th of June Abolitionist Society
146. The Liberating Society of Cametá
147. The Abolitionist Society of Mazagão**
148. The Abolitionist Artistic Society of Pará**
149. The Slave Emancipatory Society**
150. The Vila de Gurupá Abolitionist Club
151. The Viscount of Rio Branco Liberating Society*

**Paraiba**
152. The Liberating Club of Parahyba**

**Paraná**
153. The Emancipatory Society of Paraná**
154. The Liberating Society of Paraná**

**Pernambuco**
155. The Emancipatory Central of the Municipality of Recife
156. The Abolitionist Center of Pernambuco**
157. The Abolitionist Club of Escada
158. The Emancipatory Society of Pernambuco
159. The Emancipatory Society of Salgueiro
160. The Abolitionist Academics Society of Pernambuco
161. The Hail Freedom – Women's Abolitionist Society
162. The Captives Society
163. The Commercial Abolitionist Union
164. The Emancipation Savings of Piauí
165. The New Liberation Society of Pernambuco.

**Piauí**
166. The Abolitionist Society of Piauí

Annex | 387

### Rio de Janeiro

167. The Association of Abolitionist Ladies*
168. The Vasques Club Emancipatory Fund
169. The Commercial Abolitionist Center
170. The Ferreira de Menezes Abolitionist Center
171. The Forensic Abolitionist Center**
172. The 3rd of March Club
173. The Abolitionist Club of Confederated Cooks and Caterers
174. The Gutenberg Abolitionist Club
175. The Abolitionist Club of Preparatory Schools
176. The Carlos Gomes Club
177. The Lady Abolitionists' Club
178. The Abolitionist Club of Commercial Sector Workers
179. The Niterói Freedmen's Club
180. The 7th of November Club
181. The Children's Liberating Club
182. The José do Patrocínio Club
183. The Central Emancipation Commission
184. The Abolitionist Confederation
185. The Children's Abolitionist Confederation
186. The 28th of September Liberating Society
187. The Luso-Brazilian Abolitionist Society
188. The Mozart Club Ladies' Abolitionist Society
189. The Academic Liberating Society
190. The Guarany Literary Congress Donations Fund
191. The Artists' Abolitionist Association*
192. The Liberating Society of Ceará in Court*
193. The Liberating Society of Pernambuco in Court*
194. The Joaquim Nabuco Abolitionist Fund*
195. The Medical School Liberating Society*

### Rio Grande do Norte

196. The Abolitionist Society of Triunfo
197. The Liberating Abolitionist Society of Natal
198. The Assistants of Redemption Society
199. The Liberating Society of Assu
200. The Liberating Society of Mossoró
201. The Liberating Society of Rio Grande do Norte

388                                           *Annex*

202. The Sea Workers Inter-servile Society
203. The Society of Imperatriz Town

## Rio Grande do Sul
204. The 14th of July International Abolitionist Club
205. The Abolitionist Society of Uruguayana
206. The Hope and Charity Emancipation Society
207. The Literary Parthenon Abolitionist Society
208. The Sul-Rio-Grandense Abolitionist Society*

## Santa Catarina
209. The Abolitionist Society of Desterro

## São Paulo
210. The Abolitionist Club of Campinas
211. The Artistic Emancipatory Society

## Sergipe
212. The Liberating Society of Aracaju

## 1884

## Alagoas
213. The Students' Abolitionist Club of Alagoas
214. The Artistic Liberating Society of Alagoas

## Amazonas
215. The Abolitionist Club of Manacapuru
216. The Abolitionist Schools Club
217. The Emancipating Youth Club
218. The Central Abolitionist Commission of Amazonas
219. The Liberating Society of Codajás
220. The Liberation Crusade
221. The Amazonian Crusade
222. The 1st of January Abolitionist Society
223. The Abolitionist Society of the Students of the Lyceum and Normal School
224. The Ladies of the Amazon Liberating Society
225. The 25th of March Liberating Society

# Annex

### Bahia

226. The Friends of Slaves Society
227. The Abolitionist Association of Bahia
228. The 24th of May Abolitionist Club**
229. The Liberating Society of Cachoeira

### Ceará

230. The Free Ceará Club
231. The Abolitionist Confederation of Ceará
232. The 25th of March Drama Society

### Espírito Santo

233. The Abolitionist Association of Vitória**
234. The João Clímaco Abolitionist Club
235. The Viscount of Caravelas Emancipatory Society

### Maranhão

236. The Artists' Abolitionist Association**
237. The Marques Rodrigues Emancipation Fund of Maranhão
238. The Liberating Society of Parnahiba

### Mato Grosso

239. The Abolitionist Society of Mato Grosso

### Minas Gerais

240. The Abolitionist Club of Diamantina
241. The Abolitionist Drama Society of Diamantina
242. The Abolitionist Society of Minas Gerais
243. The Daughters of Calvary Abolitionist Society
244. The Viscountess of Rio Novo Freed Slaves' Society

### Pará

245. The Abolitionist Association of Marapanim*
246. The Freed Slaves' Abolitionist Club
247. The Patriots' Abolitionist Club**
248. The Abolitionist Club of Queimadas**
249. The Freed Slaves' Club of Pará
250. The Agostinho dos Reis Abolitionist Guild**

390          *Annex*

251. The Abolitionist Club of the Farmers, Merchants, and Civil Servants of Chaves
252. The Liberating Society of Benevides**

## Paraíba
253. The Liberating Society of Parayba

## Paraná
254. The Abolitionist Center of Paraná**
255. The Portuguese Slave Redemption Center**
256. The Liberating Society of Chopim
257. The Liberating Society of Palmas do Sul

## Pernambuco
258. The 25th of March Liberating Association
259. The Mixed Association for the Redemption of Slaves and Protection of Slave Children
260. The Abolitionist Club of Recife**
261. The Abolitionist Club of Goyana
262. The Martins Jr. Abolitionist Club
263. The Rodrigo Silva Emancipating Drama Club
264. The Castro Alves Emancipatory Club
265. Uncle Tom's Club
266. The Abolitionist Club of São José
267. The Tavares Bastos Abolitionist Club
268. The Termites Club
269. The Academic Emancipators
270. The Central Emancipation Commission of Recife
271. The Emancipation Guild
272. The New Liberator Society
273. The Emancipatory Society of Palmares

## Piauí
274. The Emancipation Fund of Piauyi

## Rio de Janeiro
275. The Abraham Lincoln Abolitionist Club
276. The Carlos de Lacerda Abolitionist Club
277. The 7th of November Abolitionist Club

# Annex

278. The Abolitionist Youth Club
279. The Lawyers Against Slavery Club

## Rio Grande do Norte
280. The Spartacus Club

## Rio Grande do Sul
281. The Abolitionist Association of Alegrete
282. The Ladies of Caçapava Abolitionist Association
283. The Abolitionist Club of Pelotas
284. The Abolitionist Club of Canguçu
285. The Abolitionist Club of Herval**
286. The Abolitionist Club of Laranjeiras
287. The Abolitionist Club of Rio Grande do Sul
288. The Ladies of São Sepe Abolitionist Club**
289. The Abolitionist Club of Dom Pedrito
290. The Abolitionist Club of Taquari
291. The 28th of September Liberating Club
292. The People's Commission
293. The São João de Montenegro Abolitionist Board**
294. The Civil Servants Abolitionist Society*
295. The Abolitionist Society of Quaraí
296. The Abolitionist Society of Livramento
297. The Abolitionist Society of São Borja
298. The 28th of November Abolitionist Society*
299. The Abolitionist Society of São Gabriel

## Santa Catarina
300. The Abolition and Carnival Society of the Fourfold Devil and the Good Archangels**

## São Paulo
301. The Abolitionist Association of the Typesetters of São Paulo*
302. The Joaquim Nabuco Emancipation Fund
303. The Academic Liberating Commission

## Sergipe
304. The Liberating Club of Sergipe
305. The Liberating Society of Sergipe
306. The Abolitionist Society of Aracajú**

# 392 *Annex*

## 1885

**Bahia**

307. The Cesário Mendes Liberation Fund

**Goiás**

308. The Liberating Center of Goyaz**
309. The Abolitionist Association of the Liberating Center

**Minas Gerais**

310. The Slave Redemption Association of Mariana
311. The 16th of March Liberating Club

**Paraná**

312. The Abolitionist Center of Corityba**
313. The Abolitionist Club of Paraná

**Pernambuco**

314. Abolitionist and Federal Union of Pernambuco*

**Rio de Janeiro**

315. The 6th of June Abolitionist Center**
316. The Women's Abolitionist Club

**Rio Grande do Sul**

317. The 18th of April Abolitionist Club**

## 1886

**Ceará**

318. The School of Pharmacy Abolitionist Club*

**Espírito Santo**

319. The 6th of June Abolitionist Center**
320. The Beneficent Liberating Society of Rosario

**Maranhão**

321. The José Bonifácio and Martinus Hoyer Emancipation Fund

## Mato Grosso
322. The Galdino Pimentel Emancipatory Society

## Minas Gerais
323. The 7th of September Abolitionist Society

## Pernambuco
324. The Pernambucan Society Against Slavery

## Rio de Janeiro
325. The Abolitionist Association of Rio de Janeiro*

## São Paulo
326. The 27th of February Emancipatory Society

### 1887

## Alagoas
327. The Abolitionist Society of Carrapatinho**

## Bahia
328. The Castro Alves Abolitionist Club
329. The Eduardo Carigé Abolitionist Club

## Espírito Santo
330. The Beneficent Liberating Association
331. The Liberating Society of Rosario**

## Goiás
332. The Félix de Bulhões Abolitionist Confederation
333. The Abolitionist Society of Formosa**
334. The Abolitionist Society of Privates and Cadets*
335. The Prep School Emancipatory Society

## Maranhão
336. The Liberating Association of Maranhão**
337. The Liberating Society of Caxias
338. The Club of the Dead*

## Minas Gerais
339. The Beneficent Emancipatory Society

## Pernambuco
340. The Microbes Abolitionist Society
341. The Dom José Club

## Rio de Janeiro
342. The Abolitionist Congress of Niterói

## Rio Grande do Norte
343. The Fr. Estevão Dantas Abolitionist Club

## Rio Grande do Sul
344. The Rio Branco Club**
345. The Abolitionist Commission of Rio Grande do Sul**

## Santa Catarina
346. The Abolitionist Club of Desterro

## São Paulo
347. The Ladies of São Paulo Abolitionist Association
348. The Emancipatory Society of Santos**
349. The Liberating and Labor Organizing Association
350. The Liberating Association of São Paulo
351. The Slave Redemption Assistance Fund**
352. The Abolitionist Club of Jacareí
353. The José de Alencar Club
354. The QRC Club
355. The Abolitionist Commission of Serra Negra**
356. The Academic Abolitionist Congress**
357. The Abolitionist Society of Limeira**
358. The Lady's Violet Society

## 1888

## Alagoas
359. The Liberating Society of Alagoas

## Bahia

360. The Central Emancipatory Commission of Bahia**

## Goiás

361. The João Clapp Abolitionist Society

## Minas Gerais

362. The Liberating Commission
363. The Abolitionist Board of Caldas
364. The Emancipatory Society of Sabará

## Pará

365. The Castro Alves Abolitionist Association of Curralinho

## Paraíba

366. The Rui Barbosa Liberating Center

## Paraná

367. The Abolitionist Confederation of Paraná

* The year of the association's founding could not be ascertained and so has been assumed based on when its activities are known to have commenced

** The precise name could not be identified and so has been designated in accordance with the existing information

# Bibliography

### ARCHIVES

Arquivo do Museu Imperial, Petrópolis
Arquivo Público do Estado do Ceará
Biblioteca Brasiliana Mindlin, University of São Paulo
Biblioteca do Centro Cultural Dragão do Mar, Ceará
Biblioteca do Senado Federal, Brasília
Biblioteca Nacional, Rio de Janeiro
Casa de Rui Barbosa, Rio de Janeiro
Fundação Joaquim Nabuco (Fundaj), Recife
Instituto de Estudos Brasileiros, University of São Paulo
Instituto Histórico do Ceará, Ceará
Instituto Histórico e Geográfico Brasileiro (IHGB), Rio de Janeiro
Morris Law Library, Yale University
Oliveira Lima Library, Washington D. C.
Sterling Memorial Library, University of Yale

### PRIMARY SOURCES

## National and Local Newspapers

Alagoas: *A Escola* (Jan.–Apr. 1884); *Diário da Manhã* (Jan. 1883); *Grêmio Beneficente* (Apr. 1887); *Gutenberg* (Jul. 1883–Dec. 1887); *José de Alencar* (Oct. 1883); *Lincoln* (Apr. 1888); *O Orbe* (Sept. 1881–Dec. 1887).

Amazonas: *Almanach Administrativo Historico Estatistico e Mercantil da Provincia do Amazonas* (Jan.–Dec. 1884); *Commercio do Amazonas* (Jan.–Dec. 1881); *Jornal do Amazonas* (Jan.–Dec. 1885).

Bahia: *Diário de Notícias* (Bahia) (Mar. 1883–Aug. 1884); *Gazeta da Bahia* (Nov. 1883–Dec. 1886); *O Abolicionista* (1869, 1871, Jan.–Apr. 1874); *O Asteroide* (Sept. 1887–Dec. 1888); *O Democrata* (Jan.–Dec. 1871); *O Direito* (Jan.–Dec.

398

Bibliography

1883); *O Guarany* (Apr. 1884–Apr. 1885); *O Horisonte* (Jan.–Dec. 872); *O Monitor* (Aug. 1876–May 1881); *O Prenúncio* (Jan.–Dec. 1871).

Ceará: *A Constituição* (Jun. 1882–May 1888); *Gazeta do Norte* (Feb. 1881–May 1888); *Libertador* (Jan. 1881–Apr. 1887); *Pedro II* (Jun. 1881–Jun. 1888).

Espírito Santo: *A Folha da Victoria* (Aug. 1883–Feb. 1888); *A Província do Espírito Santo* (Jan. 1882–May 1888); *O Cachoeirano* (May 1883–Dec. 1887); *O Horizonte* (Jan. 1/1883–May 1884).

Goiás: *A Tribuna Livre* (Mar. 1881–Dec. 1884); *Correio Oficial de Goyaz* (Feb. 1880–Feb. 1887); *Goyaz: Órgão Democrata* (Mar. 1887); *Goyaz: Órgão do Partido Liberal* (Nov. 1886–Mar. 1893); *O Publicador Goyano* (Jul. 1886–Jul. 1887).

Maranhão: *Brado Conservador* (Jan.–Dec. 1881); *Diário do Maranhão* (Jan. 1880–Dec. 1887); *O Paiz* (Jan.–Mar. 1881); *Pacotilha* (Jan. 1881–Dec. 1888); *Publicador Maranhense* (Jan.–Dec. 1884); *Tribuna Liberal* (Jan.–Dec. 1889).

Mato Grosso: *A Província do Mato Grosso: Órgão do Partido Liberal* (Mar. 1886); *A Situação* (Jan. 1880–Dec. 1889); *O Iniciador* (Mar. 1881–Nov. 1883); *Oasis, Órgão do Povo* (May 1888).

Minas Gerais: *17° Districto* (Jan.–Dec. 1885); *A Actualidade* (Jan.–Dec. 1881); *A Província de Minas* (Jan. 1881–Dec. 1888); *A União* (Jan. 1887–Dec. 1888); *José Bonifácio* (Feb. 1887); *Liberal Mineiro* (Jan. 1883–Dec. 1886); *O Arauto de Minas* (Jan.–Dec. 1884); *O Baependyano* (Jan. 1880–Dec. 1885); *O Lábaro do Futuro* (Jan.–Dec. 1882).

Pará: *A Constituição: Órgão do Partido Conservador* (Apr. 1883–Oct. 1884); *Diário de Belém* (Apr. 1882–May 1885); *Diário de Notícias PA* (Jul. 1881–Aug. 1888); *Gazeta de Notícias PA* (Nov. 1881); *O Liberal do Pará* (Aug. 1881–Nov. 1884).

Paraíba: *Diário da Parahyba* (Jan. 1884–Dec. 1885); *Gazeta da Parahyba* (Jan.–Dec. 1888).

Paraná: *Dezenove de Dezembro* (Jun. 1880–Dec. 1889); *Gazeta Paranaense* (Jul. 1883–Jun. 1888); *Jornal do Commercio* (Jul. 1883–Sept. 1884); *Livre Paraná* (Jan.–Dec. 1884).

Pernambuco: *Jornal do Recife* (Jun. 1880–Mar. 1886); *Libertador* (Apr.–Jun. 1883); *O Binóculo* (Mar.–Jul. 1883); *O Ensaio* (Jan.–Aug. 1883); *O Propulsor* (Jan.–Apr. 1883).

Piauí: *A Época Orgão Conservador* (Jan.–Dec. 1883).

Rio de Janeiro: *A Marmota Fluminense* (Jan.–Aug. 1857); *A Vanguarda* (Jan.–Dec. 1886); *Cidade do Rio* (Oct. 1887–May 1888); *Folha Nova* (Jan.–Dec. 1884); *Gazeta da Tarde* (Jan. 1883–Dec. 1886); *Jornal da Tarde* (Jan.–Dec. 1885); *O Abolicionista. Órgão da Sociedade Brasileira Contra a Escravidão* (Nov. 1880–Dec. 1881); *O País* (Jan. 1883–Dec. 1888); *Rio News* (Jan.–Jul. 1886; 1887–8); *A Semana* (1885–1886); *Jornal do Commercio* (Jun.1882–Apr. 1885).

Rio Grande do Norte: *Boletim da Sociedade Libertadora Norte Rio-Grandense* (Jan.–Apr. 1888); *Gazeta do Natal* (Jan.–Dec. 1888).

Rio Grande do Sul: *A Federação* (Jul. 1883–Jun. 1888); *Documentos da escravidão. Catálogo seletivo de cartas de liberdade* (2006).

# Bibliography

São Paulo: *Correio Paulistano* (Jan.–Dec. 1882); *Gazeta de Notícias* (Jan.–Dec. 1884); *A Redempção* (Jan. 1887–May 1888).
Santa Catarina: *A Regeneração* (Nov. 1880–Jun. 1888); *Conservador* (Jan.–Dec. 1885); *Gazeta de Joinville* (Jun. 1880–Dec. 1885); *O Despertador* (Feb. 1883–Aug. 1885); *República* (Jan.–Dec. 1884).
Sergipe: *A Marselheza* (Jan.–Dec. 1881); *A Reforma* (Jan.–Apr. 1887); *Gazeta do Aracaju* (Dec. 1880); *O Democrata* (Nov. 1882); *O Espião* (Dec. 1882); *O Libertador* (Mar.–Jun. 1883); *O Maroinense* (Jun. 1887); *Sergipe* (Nov. 1882).

## Foreign Newspapers

*The Antislavery Reporter*, 1865–1887
*The New York Times*, 1884–1887
*The Rio News*, 1887–1888
*The Times* (London), 1867–1888
*The Antislavery Reporter*, 1865–1887

## Official Documents

*Acta da Conferência das Secções dos Negócios da Fazenda, Justiça e Império do Conselho de Estado.* Rio de Janeiro: [s.n.], 1884.
*Anais do Senado do Império*, 1871, 1878–1888 (http://www.senado.gov.br/anais/).
*Annaes do Parlamento Brasileiro, Câmara dos Srs. Deputados.* Rio de Janeiro: Tipographia do Imperial Instituto Artístico, 1871; 1874–1889.
*Atas do Terceiro Conselho de Estado do Império do Brasil*, 1867; 1869; 1871; 1884; 1888 (www.senado.gov.br/publicacoes/anais/asp/AT_AtasDoConselhoDeEstado.asp).
Aragão, Salvador Antônio Moniz Barreto de. *Relatório apresentado ao Ilm. e Exm. Sr. Dr. Paulo Francisco de Paula Rodrigues Alves presidente da província de São Paulo pelo chefe de polícia interino o juiz de direito Salvador Antônio Moniz Barreto de Aragão*, 31 de dezembro de 1887.
Barbosa, Rui 1884. Parecer N. 48 A – Emancipação dos escravos, parecer formulado pelo Deputado Ruy Barbosa como relator das Comissões reunidas de orçamento e justiça civil, *Obras Completas de Rui Barbosa*, vol. XI, Tomo I. [Também como Parecer n. 48 Formulado em nome das Comissões Reunidas de Orçamento e Justiça Civil acerca do Projeto de Emancipação dos Escravos pelo Sr. Ruy Barbosa. In *Abolição no Parlamento: 65 anos de lutas*, Vol. II Senado Federal, 1988, vol. II.]
Calmon, P. (ed.). *Falas do Trono* – desde o ano de 1823 até o ano de 1889. São Paulo: Ed. Melhoramentos, 1977.
Câmara Municipal do Rio de Janeiro. Emancipação pelo Livro de Ouro da Ilma. Câmara Municipal no dia 29 de julho de 1885. Rio de Janeiro: J. A. F. Villas Boas, 1885.
Dias, Satyro. *Relatório com que o Exm. Sr. Satyro Dias passou a administração da província do Ceará ao segundo vice-presidente*, Fortaleza, 1884, no. 4.

400 Bibliography

Documentos da Escravidão. Catálogo Seletivo de Cartas de Liberdade. Acervo dos tabelionatos de municípios do interior do Rio Grande do Sul. Vol. 2, Porto Alegre, novembro de 2006.

DRESCDS. Discussão da Reforma do Estado Servil na Câmara dos Deputados e no Senado, 1871, Parte II, de 1º de agosto a 27 de setembro. Rio de Janeiro: Typographia Nacional, 1871.

Javary, Barão de. [1889] *Organizações e Programas Ministeriais*. Regime Parlamentar do Império, R.J., Ministério da Justiça e Negócios Interiores, 1962.

Legation of the United States. *Foreign Relations. Brazil*. No. 3, October 24, No. 64, 1861 to August 9, 1888. Legation of the United States, Rio de Janeiro, HeinOnline, Morris Law Library, Yale University (http://heinonline. org).

Phillip, George (ed.). *British Documents of Foreign Affairs. Reports and Papers from the Foreign Office Confidential Print. Part 1. Serie D Latin America, volume 3 Brazil, 1845–1914*. University Publications of America, s/d.

Projeto no.1A-1885. Extinção gradual do elemento servil. 18 de maio de 1885 *Abolição no Parlamento: 65 anos de luta, 1823–1888*. Brasília: Senado Federal, Subsecretaria de Arquivo, 1988, Vol. II.

Projeto no.1-1885. Extinção gradual do elemento servil. 12 de maio de 1885 *Abolição no Parlamento: 65 anos de luta, 1823–1888*. Brasília: Senado Federal, Subsecretaria de Arquivo, 1988, Vol. II.

Projeto no. 1B-1885. Redação para a 3ª. Discussão do projeto N. 1-A de 1885 sobre a extinção gradual do elemento servil, com as emendas aprovadas em 2ª. Discussão. *Abolição no Parlamento: 65 anos de luta, 1823–1888*. Brasília: Senado Federal, Subsecretaria de Arquivo, 1988, Vol. II.

Projeto no.1C-1885. Elemento servil. Projeto substitutivo ao de no. 1 b- 1885, apresentado na sessão de 9 de julho do corrente ano. *Abolição no Parlamento: 65 anos de luta, 1823–1888*. Brasília: Senado Federal, Subsecretaria de Arquivo, 1988, Vol. II.

Projeto no. 48-1884. Projeto apresentado por Rodolfo Dantas, em 15 de julho de 1884 à Câmara dos Deputados. In *Abolição no Parlamento: 65 anos de luta, 1823–1888*. Brasília: Senado Federal, Subsecretaria de Arquivo, 1988, Vol. II.

Rio Branco, J. M. Paranhos, Visconde do. *Discursos do sr. Conselheiro de Estado e Senador do Império J. M. da Silva Paranhos proferidos no Senado em 1870, sendo ministro dos negócios estrangeiros (Gabinete de 16 de Julho de 1868), e nas duas casas do Parlamento em 1871, sendo presidente do Conselho de Ministros (Gabinete de 7 de março de 1871)*. Rio de Janeiro: Tipographia Nacional, 1872.

Rodrigues Alves, F. P. Relatório do presidente da província de São Paulo Francisco de Paula Rodrigues Alves aos Srs Membros da Assembleia Legislativa Provincial, 1887.

Senado Federal. *Abolição no Parlamento: 65 anos de luta, 1823–1888*. Brasília: Senado Federal, Subsecretaria de Arquivo, 1988, Vols. I e II.

# Bibliography

## UNPRINTED SOURCES

### Instituto Histórico e Geográfico Brasileiro Archive, Rio de Janeiro

Amaral, José Avelino Gurgel do. Carta de José Avelino Gurgel do Amaral ao Conselheiro Paulino José Soares de Sousa, sobre sua candidatura a Deputado Geral pelo Ceará. Sem dia, sem mês, 1884. Acervo Geral, Lata 351/ Doc 68.

Clube Artístico Abolicionista Maranhense. *Requerimento de Joaquim Ferreira Reis e Avelino José da Cruz ao chefe de polícia do Maranhão solicitando licença para a criação de uma sociedade sob a denominação "Club Artístico Abolicionista Maranhense."* 28 de fevereiro de 1885. DL. 741.64.

Cotegipe, João Maurício Wanderley, Barão de. Carta do Barão de Cotegipe à Princesa Isabel, 7/3/1888. Coleção Barão de Cotegipe.

Carta do Barão de Cotegipe a Francisco de Paula Rodrigues Alves, 12/12/1887. Coleção Rodrigues Alves, lata 808, pasta 64.

Cartas do Barão de Cotegipe a João Ferreira de Araújo Pinho sobre sua retirada do Ministério e Abolição. 19/3/1888; 30/3/1888; 14/4/1888. Coleção Araújo Pinho. DL. 548. 83.

*Conferência com S.A. Paço Isabel.* 14/1/1888. Coleção Barão de Cotegipe, Lata 960, Pasta 28.

MacDowell, Samuel Wallace. Carta do ministro da Justiça, Samuel Wallace MacDowell, à Princesa Isabel sobre acontecimentos violentos ocorridos na cidade do Rio de Janeiro, na antevéspera da escrita da carta. 3/3/1888. IHGB, Coleção: Barão de Cotegipe. DL. 960.31

Carta do Ministro da Justiça, Samuel Wallace MacDowell, à Princesa Isabel. 5/3/1888. IHGB, Coleção: Barão de Cotegipe. DL. 960.31 (Carta 1).

Carta do ministro da Justiça, Samuel Wallace MacDowell, à Princesa Isabel. Data: 5/3/1888, Coleção: Barão de Cotegipe. DL. 960.31 (Carta 2).

Telegrama do Ministro da Justiça, Samuel Wallace MacDowell, à Princesa Isabel. 4/3/1888. Coleção: Barão de Cotegipe. DL. 960.31.

Orleans e Bragança, Isabel. Correspondências da Princesa Isabel sobre a exoneração do Gabinete Cotegipe. 3/3/1888; 4/2/1888; 5/3/1888; 7/3/1888. Coleção: Barão de Cotegipe. DL. 960.31.

Patrocínio, José do, Ofício ao Barão Homem de Mello, 2/8/1889, Acervo Geral, Lata 331, pasta 17.

Penido, José. *A Abolição e o Credito.* Rio de Janeiro, Typographia da Escola, 1885.

Rebouças, André. Diários de André Rebouças, inéditos (DIAR).

Romanus. *A Lavoura e o trabalho. Da emancipação ao abolicionismo. 1881 a 1884. Analise e descripção enriquecida com os documentos concernentes a formação dos clubs de lavoura, suas representações ao parlamento e attitude official.* Rio de Janeiro: Typographia Moreira, 1884.

São Laurindo, Visconde de. Carta do Visconde de São Laurindo a Rodrigues Alves, reservada, 15/5/1888. Coleção Rodrigues Alves, DL 1113.95.

Soares de Sousa, Paulino. Carta de Paulino José Soares de Sousa ao Barão de Cotegipe, sem data. Coleção Barão de Cotegipe. Lata 938, Documento 73.

# Bibliography

Carta de Paulino José Soares de Sousa ao Barão de Cotegipe, 9/12/1869. Coleção Barão de Cotegipe. Lata 938 Documento 75.

Carta de Paulino José Soares de Sousa ao Barão de Cotegipe, 25/1/1877. Coleção Barão de Cotegipe. Lata 938 Documento 83.

Carta de Paulino José Soares de Sousa ao Barão de Cotegipe, 4/1/1885. Coleção Barão de Cotegipe, Lata 938 Pasta 83.

Carta de Paulino José Soares de Sousa ao Barão de Cotegipe, 23/5/1883. Coleção Barão de Cotegipe. Lata 938 Pasta 85.

Carta de Paulino José Soares de Sousa ao Barão de Cotegipe, 22/9/1884. Coleção Barão de Cotegipe.Lata 938 Pasta 86.

Carta de Paulino José Soares de Sousa ao Barão de Cotegipe, 3/5/1887. Coleção Barão de Cotegipe. Lata 938 Pasta 87.

V.P.A.S. Resolução do Problema Servil, sem prejuízo do interesse particular, geral, moral e social, oferecido ao governo na pessoa do eminente estadista. Exmo senador Barão de Cotegipe. IHGB, Acervo Geral, Lata 960, pasta 30, 17/2/1888.

## Fundação Joaquim Nabuco Archive, Recife

Nabuco, Joaquim. Correspondência Ativa e Passiva de Joaquim Nabuco, 1871–1888.

Rebouças, André. Registro da Correspondência (RCAR), Volume 1 – junho 1873 a janeiro de 1891.

## Biblioteca Nacional Archive, Rio de Janeiro

Apocrifo. A Escravidão Examinada à Luz da Santa Bíblia, 1871.

Chamerovzow, Louis Alexis. Carta de Louis Alexis Chamerovzow a Manuel da Cunha Galvão, 08/05/1865 Manuscritos I-03,31,47[a].

## Arquivo Digital do Museu Imperial, Petrópolis

Rebouças, André. Excerptos dos Diários do Engenheiro André Rebouças. 1870; 1873; 1876; 1878; 1879; 1880; 1889.

Cartas de André Rebouças a Silio Boccanera Junior, 11/4; 24/4/1897, I-DIG-21 10_1896.

Cartas de André Rebouças a Carlos Gomes, 26/6; 11/7; 6/9; 9/10; /1896, I-DIG-09_06_1896.

Carta de André Rebouças a Joaquim Nabuco, 21/11/1896, I-DIG-21 10_1896.

## Fundação Casa de Rui Barbosa Archive, Rio de Janeiro

Carta de Rodolfo E. S. Dantas a Rui Barbosa, 12/4/1878.

Cartas de Gusmão Lobo para Rodolfo E. S. Dantas, 5; 14; 15; 22/1; 13; 14/2; 3/6; 16/7/1885; 23/8; 28/9; 22/11/1889; 29/unidentified month/ unidentified year; 25/5/ unidentified year; 2/10/unidentified year.

# Bibliography 403

Cartas de "Fr.co" para Rodolfo E. S. Dantas; unidentified date; 5/2/unidentified
year; 12/12/unidentified year.

## Oliveira Lima Library, Washington

Cotegipe, João Maurício Wanderley, Barão de. Carta do Barão de Cotegipe a
Artur de Sousa Correia, Rio de Janeiro, 9/1/1888 (II–18).
Carta do Barão de Cotegipe a Artur de Sousa Correia, Rio de Janeiro, 23/3/
1888 (II).
Sousa Correia, Artur de. Rascunho de Carta de Artur de Sousa Correia ao Barão
de Cotegipe, Roma, 5/5/1888, (II–15).

### PRINTED DOCUMENTS

A. P. de A. *A monarchia brasileira se agarrando à tabua da escravidão. Obra
cristã e philosophica por A.P. de A.* Bahia: Typografia do Bazar, 1885.
Abranches, Dunshee de. *O captiveiro* (Memórias). Rio de Janeiro: n.p., 1941.
Albuquerque, Raymundo Ulisses de. *A Egreja Catholica em face da escravidão ou
resposta as acusações do snr conselheiro Joaquim Nabuco feitas ao clero
brasileiro pelo pe. Raymundo Ulisses de Albuquerque. Ex-lente do seminário
do Pará e pároco da freguesia de Bragança e encarregado das de Vezeu e
Quatipuru.* Bragança: Edição Luiz R. Barbosa, 1885.
Alencar, José [Senio]. *O tronco do Ipê, romance brasileiro.* Tomos 1 e 2. Rio de
Janeiro: B. L. Garnier, 1871.
José Almino e Santos, Maria Pessoa dos (eds.). *Meu caro Rui, meu caro
Nabuco.* Rio de Janeiro: Casa de Rui Barbosa, 1999.
Alencar, José de (Erasmo). Ao Imperador: novas cartas políticas de Erasmo (24/6/
1867; 15/7/1867; 20/7/1867; 26/7/1867; 20/9/1867; 3/9/1867; 15/3/1868).
In Parron, Tamis (ed.), *Alencar. Cartas a Favor da Escravidão.* São Paulo:
Hedra, 2008.
*Como e porque sou romancista.* Rio de Janeiro: Typ. de G. Leuzinger &
Filhos, 1893.
*Cartas de Erasmo.* Carvalho, José Murilo (ed.). Rio de Janeiro: ABL, 2009.
*Discursos proferidos na sessão de 1871 na Câmara dos Deputados.* Rio de
Janeiro: Typographia Perseverança.
Alencar, José Martiniano de. *O Demônio Familiar* (1856). Virtual Books Online
M&M Editores Ltda., www.virtualbooks.com.br/
Alencar, Mario. Discurso de Posse do SR. Mário de Alencar. Academia Brasileira
de Letras, 14 de agosto de 1906. www.academia.edu
Alvares, Guimarães, A. *Propaganda abolicionista.* Edição *Diário da Bahia*, 1875.
Americano. *A Viagem Imperial e o Ventre Livre.* Rio de Janeiro: Typografia
J. Vianna, 1871.
Andrada, Antônio Manuel Bueno de. Depoimento de uma testemunha [a Evaristo
de Moraes]. Transcrito de *O Estado de São Paulo*, de 13 de maio de 1918.
*Revista do Instituto Histórico e Geográfico de São Paulo*, São Paulo xxvi,
[1918] 1939.

# Bibliography

Associação Central Emancipadora. *Boletim n. 1*, 28 de setembro de 1880. Rio de Janeiro: Typografia Primeiro de Janeiro.

*Boletim n. 2*, 28 de outubro de 1880. Rio de Janeiro: Typografia Primeiro de Janeiro.

*Boletim n. 3*, 28 de novembro de 1880. Rio de Janeiro: Typografia Primeiro de Janeiro.

*Boletim n. 4*, 28 de dezembro de 1880. Rio de Janeiro: Typografia Primeiro de Janeiro.

*Boletim n. 5*, 28 de janeiro de 1881. Rio de Janeiro: Typografia Primeiro de Janeiro.

*Boletim n. 8*, 20 de marco de 1881. Rio de Janeiro: Typografia Primeiro de Janeiro.

Azevedo, Aluísio. *O Mulato*, 1881 www.ebooksbrasil.org/eLibris/omulato.html

Artur e Duarte, Urbano. *O Escravocrata. Drama em 3 atos*, 1884. www.biblio.com.br/defaultz.asp?link=http://www.biblio.com.br/conteudo/arturazevedo/oescravocata.htm

Sampaio, Antônio Gomes de. *Abolicionismo. Considerações Geraes Do Movimento Anti-Esclavista e Sua Historia Limitada a Jacarehy, que foi um Centro de Acção no Norte do Estado de São Paulo.* São Paulo: Typografia a Vapor Louzada & Irmão, 1890.

Barbosa, Rui 1884. 1885. Comemoração da Lei Rio Branco (conferência no Teatro Polytheama do Rio e Janeiro a 7 de novembro). *Obras Completas*, Vol. XII. Rio de Janeiro: Min. Cultura/F.Casa de Rui Barbosa, 1988.

1884. A Situação Abolicionista. Conferência no Teatro Polytheama do Rio de Janeiro a 2 de agosto de 1885. In *Obras Completas de Rui Barbosa*, Vol. XII. 1885, tomo 1. Abolicionismo. Rio de Janeiro: Ministério da Cultura/Fundação Casa de Rui Barbosa, 1988.

1884. *Abolicionismo. Obras Completas de Rui Barbosa*, Vol. XII, tomo 1. Rio de Janeiro: Ministério da Cultura/Fundação Casa de Rui Barbosa, 1988.

1884. Emancipação dos escravos. In Moraes Filho, E. (ed.), *Rui Barbosa. Discursos Parlamentares*. Coleção Perfis Parlamentares, n. 28. Brasília: Câmara dos Deputados, 1985.

*Abolição no Brasil. Discurso pronunciado pelo Sr. Conselheiro Ruy Barbosa no meeting convocado pela Confederação Abolicionista no Theatro Polytheama a 28 de agosto de 1887 e mandado publicar pelos alumnos da Escola Militar da Corte.* Rio de Janeiro: Imprensa Mont'Alverne, 1887.

Barroso, J. Liberato. *Discurso do Conselheiro Dr. J. Liberato Barroso na Sessão Solene da Sociedade Abolicionista Cearense no dia 25 de março de 1884 para festejar a Emancipação total dos escravos na Província do Ceara.* Rio de Janeiro: Typografia Laemmert, 1884.

Bastos, Aureliano Cândido Tavares. *Cartas do Solitário: estudos sobre reforma administrativa, ensino religioso, africanos livres, tráfico de escravos, liberdade da cabotagem, abertura do Amazonas, comunicações com os Estados Unidos, etc.* Rio de Janeiro: Livr. Popular de A. A. da Cruz Coutinho, 1863.

Filitno Justiniano F. *Discurso que tinha de ser pronunciado por Filinto Justiniano F. Bastos, estudante do 5º. Anno da Faculdade de Direito do*

# Bibliography

*Recife no Festival do Club Abolicionista em a noite de 28 de setembro de 1882 no Theatro Santa Isabel*. Recife: Typographia Mercantil, 1882.

Beltrão, Pedro. *Discurso Pronunciado Na 2a. Sessão do Congresso Agrícola pelo Se. Pedro Beltrão*. Recife: Typografia de M. Figueiroa De Faria & Filhos, 1884.

Berenger, Paul. Le Brésil in 1879. *Revue des Deux Mondes*, n° 37, 1880, pp. 434–57.

Bezerra de Menezes, Adolpho. *A Escravidão no Brasil e as Medidas que convém tomar para extinguil-a sem damno para nação*. Rio de Janeiro: Progresso, 1869.

Bocaiúva, Quintino. A Questão Social. 1879. In Silva, E. (ed.), *Idéias Políticas de Quintino Bocaiúva*. Brasília: Senado Federal/Casa de Rui Barbosa, 1986.

Borges, Abílio C. *Discursos proferidos no Ginásio Bahiano por seu diretor Abilio Cezar Borges*. Paris: Livraria Aillaud, 1866.

British and Foreign Antislavery Society. *Special Report of the Antislavery Conference: Held in Paris in the Salle Herz, on the Twenty-Sixth and Twenty-Seventh August, 1867, under the Presidency of Mons. Edouard Laboulaye*. Committee of the British and Foreign Antislavery Society, 1867.

Candler, John and Burgess, Wilson. Report of the Visit of John Candler and Wilson Burgess to the Brazils. In Society of Friends. *Narrative of the presentation to the sovereigns and those in authority of the address of the yearly meeting on the slave-trade and slavery*. London: Edward Newman, 1854.

*Narrative of a recent visit to Brazil, by John Candler and Wilson Burgess; to present an address on the slave-trade and slavery, issued by the Religious Society of Friends*. London: E. Marsh, 1853.

Carvalho, Alberto. *Monarquia e República Dictatorial*. Capital Federal: Imprensa Monteverde, 1891.

Joaquim Cândido da Silveira. *José Mariano ou a Vítima Glorificada. Apotheose em 5 Quadros*. Recife: Typographia Mercantil, 1886.

Cassio. *A Escravidão. Questão da Atualidade*. Rio de Janeiro: Livraria da Casa Imperial de E. Dupont Editor, 1871.

Castilhos, Júlio de. *Propaganda abolicionista* (artigos de *A Federação* 1884–1887). In Carneiro, Paulo (ed.), *Idéias Políticas de Júlio de Castilhos*. Brasília: Senado Federal/Casa de Rui Barbosa, 1981.

Castro, Fernando de. *Conferencia Abolicionista. Theatro Sta. Isabel a 25 de março de 1885, mandada publicar pela Sociedade Aves Libertas*. Pernambuco: Typografia Apollo, 1885.

Discurso inaugural de las conferencias antiesclavistas. 5 de enero de 1872. Vila, E. and L. Vilar (eds.), *Los abolicionistas españoles. Siglo XIX*. Madrid: Ediciones de Cultura Hispánica, 1996.

Francisco. *Marquês de Paranaguá. Ensaio Biográfico*. Série Perfis Parlamentares. N. 55. Brasília: Centro de Documentação e Informação Edições Câmara dos Deputados, 2009.

Castro Alves, Antônio. *Os escravos: poesias*. Lisboa: Tavares Cardoso & Irmão, Editores, 1884.

Antônio. *A Cachoeira de Paulo Affonso – Fragmento dos Escravos – sob o titulo de Mss. de Stenio*. 2ª. Edição aumentada, Rio de Janeiro, 1882.

Celso Jr., Afonso. *Oito anos de Parlamento*. Brasília: Senado Federal, [1901] 1998.

# Bibliography

*Discurso Proferido na Sessão de 17 de julho de 1884 pelo Deputado dr. Afonso Celso Junior.* Rio de Janeiro: Typografia Nacional, 1884.

Christie, William D. *Notes on Brazilian Questions.* London: Macmillan, 1865.

Club Amazônia. *Manifesto do Club Amazônia fundado em 24 de abril de 1884.* Pará: Typografia do Diário do Pará, 1884.

Club dos Libertos Contra a Escravidão. *Homenagem a José do Patrocínio em 8 de outubro de 1883. A festa dos livres. Quarenta cidadãos restituídos à sociedade.* Rio de Janeiro: Typografia Central de Evaristo da Costa, 1883.

Clube do Cupim. *Livro de atas.* Reimpressão facsimilar. In Silva, Leonardo (ed). *A abolição em Pernambuco.* Recife: Fundaj, Editora Massangana, 1988.

Clube Vinte de Setembro. *Apelo à Província do Rio Grande do Sul pelo Clube Vinte de Setembro.* São Paulo, 20 de setembro de 1886, 51°. Aniversário da República Rio-Grandense. Redactor Bartholomeu Brazil, São Paulo: Typografia Leroy, MDCCCLXXXVI (1886).

Cochin, Augustin. Carta de Augustin a A. M. G. Faugere, 17/5/1866 in Henry Cochin, *Augustin Cochin, 1823–1872, ses lettres et sa vie: Volume 2*, Paris: Ed. Bloud & Gay, 1926.

Coelho Neto, Henrique Maximiano. Discurso de Recepção ao Acadêmico Mário de Alencar. 14 de Agosto de 1906. www.abl.br

Henrique Maximiano. *A Conquista.* Virtualbooks (1899) 2003.

Confederação Abolicionista. *Manifesto da Confederação Abolicionista do Rio de Janeiro [redigido por José do Patrocínio e André Rebouças]*, Rio de Janeiro: Typografia da Gazeta da Tarde, 1883.

*Banquete dado pela Confederação abolicionista por alguns amigos da ideia no dia 19 de agosto de 1884 em homenagem a libertação do amazonas e aos deputados que apoiaram o gabinete de 6 de Junho.* Folheto n. 7. Rio de Janeiro: Typografia Central de Evaristo da Costa, 1884a.

*Discurso pronunciado na sessão do Senado de 9 de junho de 1884 pelo exm. Sr. Senador Christiano Benedicto Ottoni, acompanhado de uma declaração da Confederação.* Rio de Janeiro: Typografia Central de Evaristo da Costa, 1884b.

*Relatório do estado e das operações da Confederação Abolicionista apresentado a assemblea geral annual de seus membros em 12 de maio de 1884 por seu presidente João F. Clapp acompanhado do Parecer da Comissão de exame de contas e balanço do movimento de capitaes* [por André Rebouças], Rio de Janeiro: Typografia Central de Evaristo da Costa, 1884c.

*Homenagem ao Patriótico Ministério Dantas. Sessão Publica Solene Realizada no dia 7 de junho de 1885 no Teatro Polytheama, Orador Oficial Conselheiro Ruy Barbosa.* Folheto no. 10. Rio de Janeiro: Typografia Central de Evaristo da Costa, 1885a.

*A situação Abolicionista. Conferencia do Conselheiro Ruy Barbosa em 2 de agosto de 1885 no Teatro Polytheama sob Presidência da Confederação Abolicionista*, Folheto no. 11. Rio de Janeiro: Typografia Central de Evaristo da Costa, 1885b.

*A segunda phase. Discurso do Sr. Quintino Bocayuva proferido em 3 de abril de 1887 no Teatro Polytheama.* Folheto no. 12. Rio de Janeiro: Typografia Central de Evaristo da Costa, 1887.

# Bibliography

407

Cotegipe, Conde de. *Os orçamentívoros ou Comedia dos Deuses pelo Conde de Cotegipe*. São Paulo: Typografia Bragancas & Orleans. S. Christovam: Typografia King, 1888.

Couty, Louis. *A escravidão no Brasil*. Rio de Janeiro: Ministério da Cultura. Fundação Casa de Rui Barbosa, 1988.

Cruz e Sousa, João. *Poesia Completa*, ed. Zahidé Muzart. Florianópolis: Fundação Catarinense de Cultura/Fundação Banco do Brasil, 1993.

D. Pedro II. Cartas ao Barão de Cotegipe. In Pinho, Wanderley (ed.), *Cartas do Imperador d.Pedro II ao Barão de Cotegipe*. Ordenadas e anotadas por Wanderley Pinho. São Paulo: Companhia Editora Nacional, 1933.

Dantas, Manuel de Souza. *Cartas*. In Lacombe, A. Jacobina (ed.), *Correspondência do Conselheiro Manuel P. de Sousa Dantas*. Rio de Janeiro: Edição Casa de Rui Barbosa, 1962.

Rodolfo. *Cartas*. In Lacombe, A. Jacobina (ed.), *Correspondência de Rodolfo E. de Sousa Dantas*. Rio de Janeiro: Edição Casa de Rui Barbosa, 1973.

Daunt, R. G. (ed.). *Diário da princesa Isabel (excursão dos Condes D'Eu à província de São Paulo em 1884)*. São Paulo: ed. Anhembi, 1957.

Dent, Hasting Charles. *A Year in Brazil, with Notes on the Abolition of Slavery, the Finances of the Empire, Meteorology, Natural History, etc.* London: Kegan Paul, Trench & Co., 1886.

Dias, Satyro. *A libertação do ceara (25 de março de 1884). Nota para a história pelo dr. Satyro de Oliveira Dias*. Bahia: Typografia do Diário da Bahia, 1911 [reproduzida em *Da Senzala para os salões* (coletânea). Fortaleza: Secretaria de cultura, turismo e desporto, 1988].

Dom Pascal (pseudônimo). *O abolicionismo perante a historia ou o diálogo das três províncias*. Rio de Janeiro: Typographia e Lithografia de Carlos Gaspar da Silva, 1888.

Dupaluoup, F. A. P. *Carta do bispo de Orleans ao clero de sua diocesa sobre a escravidão*, traduzida e offerecida ao clero Brasileiro pelo visconde de Jequitinhonha: [Orléans 6 de Abril de 1862]. Rio de Janeiro: Laemmert, 1865.

Duque-Estrada, Osório. *A Abolição: esboço histórico, 1831–1888*. Rio de Janeiro: Leite Ribeiro & Murillo, 1918.

Durocher, Marie-Josephine. *Ideias por Coordenar a respeito da emancipação por M. J. Durocher*, Rio de Janeiro: Typografia do Diário do Rio de Janeiro, 1871.

Falcão, Aníbal. *Fórmula da Civilização Brasileira (deduzida da apreciação dos seus elementos essenciais definitivamente reunidos pela luta holandesa)*. Rio de Janeiro: Ed. Guanabara, [1883] 1933.

Prefácio a Joaquim Nabuco. In Nabuco, Joaquim. *Campanha Abolicionista no Recife: Eleições de 1884*. Recife: Fundação Joaquim Nabuco/Editora Massangana, [1885] 1988.

Ferreira, Francisco Ignacio. *Projecto para Abolição do Elemento Servil por Francisco Ignacio Ferreira, ex-membro da Assemblea Provincial do Rio de Janeiro. Distribuição Gratuita*. Rio de Janeiro: Typographia Perseveranca, 1887.

408 *Bibliography*

Filho, Albano. *Resposta ao brinde.* Jantar dos Brasileiros em Londres, 9 de junho de 1883. In *A Emancipação no Ceará e os Brasileiros em Londres.* Rio de Janeiro: Typografia Central de Evaristo da Costa, 1883.

Fonseca, Luís Anselmo. *A escravidão, o clero e o abolicionismo.* Bahia: Imprensa econômica Fundaj/Massangana, 1887. Ed. fac-similar, 1988.

Manuel Deodoro da. Carta ao Ilm. Exmo. Snr. Marechal do Exercito Visconde da Gavea encaminhando petição à princesa regente. 25 de outubro de 1887. Senado Federal, *A Abolição no Parlamento. 65 anos de lutas.* Volume II, Brasília, 1988.

Franco, Tito. *Monarquia e monarquistas.* Recife: Ed. Massangana, 1990.

Freyre, Gilberto (ed.). *Perfis Parlamentares. Joaquim Nabuco.* Discursos parlamentares. Brasília: Câmara dos deputados, 1983.

Frick, João. *Abolição da Escravatura. Breve Notícia sobre a Primeira Sociedade de Emancipação no Brasil (fundada na cidade do Rio Grande do Sul em março de 1869).* Lisboa: Lallemant Frères, 1885.

Furtado, J. I. Arnizaut. *Estudos sobre a Libertação dos Escravos no Brasil.* Pelotas: Typografia da Livraria Americana de Carlos Pinto e A.C, 1883.

Gama, Luís. *Primeiras Trovas Burlescas de Getulino.* 2ª. Edição. Rio de Janeiro: Typ. de Pinheiro & C., 1861.

Gomes, Antônio Carlos. *Correspondências Italianas I,* trad. Paulo Guanaes. Rio de Janeiro: Editora Cátedra, 1982.

Gonçalves, Georgino. *Discurso de Georgino Horacio Gonçalves, orador do 1º. Anno da Faculdade de Direito na sessão magna do Club Abolicionista do Recife.* Pernambuco, 1881.

Hilliard, Henry Washington. *Politics and Pen Pictures at Home and Abroad.* London/New York: Putnam's Sons Publishers, 1892.

Homem de Melo, Barão. *Discursos pronunciados pelo Barão Homem de Melo na sessão cívica em homenagem a José Bonifácio, em 8 de dezembro de 1886, e outro, por ocasião da inauguração da estatua de José Bonifácio de Andrada e Silva no dia 7 de setembro de 1872.* São Paulo: Typografia King, 1887.

Jaguaribe, D. *Os herdeiros de Caramurú: Romance histórico.* Rio de Janeiro: Confederação Abolicionista, 1890.

Jequitinhonha, Visconde de. *Sobre a Escravidão. Carta do Bispo de Orleans ao Clero de sua diocese sobre a escravidão. Traduzida e Oferecida ao Clero Brasileiro pelo Visconde de Jequitinhonha.* Rio de Janeiro: Typografia Laemmert, 1865.

Koseritz, Carl von. *Imagens do Brasil.* São Paulo: Itatiaia/Edusp, [1883] 1980.

Lemos, Miguel (ed.). *O positivismo e a escravidão moderna; trechos extrahidos das obras de Augusto Comte, seguidos de documentos positivistas relativos à questão da escravatura no Brazil.* Rio de Janeiro: Apostolado Positivista do Brasil, 1884.

e Teixeira Mendes, Raimundo. *A Liberdade Espiritual e a Organização do Trabalho – Considerações histórico-filosóficas sobre o movimento abolicionista. Exame das idéias relativas a leis de organização do trabalho e locação de serviços. Programa das reformas mais urgentes.* 21/4/1888. Apostolado Positivista do Brasil. Rio de Janeiro, no. 54, 1902.

## Bibliography

e Teixeira Mendes, Raimundo. *Abolissionismo e Clericalismo*. Rio de Janeiro: Typographia da Igreja Positivista do Brasil, 1888.

A incorporação do proletariado escravo e as próssimas eleições. 19 de novembro de 1884. In *Boletim do Centro Positivista do Brasil*, Nº 23, Rio de Janeiro, 1936.

*Ao Ilm. Conselheiro Manuel Pinto de Souza Dantas (3/6/1886)*. Rio de Janeiro: Typografia do Centro Positivista do Brasil, 1886.

*Cartas a Teixeira Mendes (1878–1881)*. Rio de Janeiro: Igreja Positivista do Brasil, 1965.

Imigração chineza – mensagem a S. Exc. o Embaixador do Celéste Império junto aos governos de França e Inglatérra. 1881; *Boletim do Centro Positivista do Brasil*, Nº 5, Rio de Janeiro, 1927.

Livramento, Barão de. *Discurso Pronunciado na Primeira Sessão Magna da Sociedade Emancipadora de Pernambuco pelo Presidente da Assembleia Geral Barão do Livramento no dia 25 de 1870*. Recife: Typografia do Jornal do Recife, 1870.

Macedo, Joaquim Manuel. *As vítimas-algozes. Quadros da escravidão*. Recife: Fundação Casa de Rui Bargosa; Scipione [1869] 1991.

Machado de Assis, J. M. O Velho Senado. In Nabuco, Joaquim. *O estadista do Império*, Vol. II. Rio de Janeiro: Topbooks, 1997.

*Crônicas. Obras Completas*. Rio de Janeiro: W. M. Jackson, 1959.

Evolução (1884). In *Relíquias de Casa Velha*. Rio de Janeiro: Garnier, 1990.

Malheiros, Perdigão. *A Escravidão no Brasil. Ensaio histórico-jurídico-social*. Rio de Janeiro: Typografia Nacional, 1866.

Mariano, Olegário. *Discurso de Posse na Academia Brasileira de Letras*, 1927. www.abl.org.br

Mello, Evaldo Cabral de (ed.), *Joaquim Nabuco Diários*. Vols. I e II. Recife: Bem Te Vi Produções Literárias, Editora Massangana, 2005.

Monteiro, Tobias. *Pesquisas e depoimentos para a História*. Belo Horizonte: Ed. Itatiaia, [1913] 1982.

Moraes, Evaristo de. *A Campanha Abolicionista* (1879–1888). Brasília, Ed. UnB, 1986 (1ª. Ed. 1924).

Moreira de Azevedo, Duarte. Sociedades fundadas no Brasil desde os tempos coloniais até o começo do atual reinado. Memória lida nas sessões do Instituto Histórico em 1884, *Revista do Instituto Histórico e Geográfico Brasileiro*, Rio de Janeiro, 48, 2, 1885.

Nabuco, Carolina (ed.). *Cartas a Amigos*. Vol. I (1864–1898), Vol. II (1899–1909) e *Obras completas*, Vol. XIII. São Paulo: Instituto Progresso Editorial, 1949.

Nabuco, Joaquim (1870). *A Escravidão*. Rio de Janeiro: Nova Fronteira, 1999.

(1883). *O Abolicionismo*. Petrópolis: Vozes, 1988.

(1885). *Campanha Abolicionista no Recife: Eleições de 1884*: Discursos de Joaquim Nabuco. 2ª. ed. Recife: Fundação Joaquim Nabuco/Editora Massangana, 1988.

(1886b). Eleições Liberais e Eleições Conservadoras, Rio de Janeiro. In *Campanhas de Imprensa (1884–1887). Obras Completas*, Vol. XII. São Paulo: Instituto Progresso Editorial, 1949.

# Bibliography

(1897–1899). *Um Estadista do Império: Nabuco de Araújo: sua vida, suas opiniões, sua época*. Vols. I e II. Rio de Janeiro: Topbooks, 1997.

(ed.). *A Emancipação no Ceará e os Brasileiros em Londres*. Rio de Janeiro: Typografia Central de Evaristo da Costa, 1883.

Aos Eleitores do 1° distrito, 25/12/1885. In Gouvêa, Fernando da Cruz. *Joaquim Nabuco Entre a Monarquia e a República*. Recife: Fundaj, 1989.

Aos Eleitores do 5° Distrito, 18/5/1885. In Gouvêa, Fernando da Cruz. *Joaquim Nabuco Entre a Monarquia e a República*. Recife: Fundaj, 1989.

Circular eleitoral de 1888. In Gouvêa, Fernando da Cruz. *Joaquim Nabuco Entre a Monarquia e a República*. Recife: Fundaj, 1989.

Conferências de 12 e 26 de outubro de 1884, 1, 5, 9, 16, 28, 29 e 30 de novembro de 1884, 1 e 18 de janeiro de 1885. In Nabuco, Joaquim (1884b), *Campanha Abolicionista no Recife*: Eleições de 1884: Discursos de Joaquim Nabuco. 2a. ed. Recife: Fundação Joaquim Nabuco/Editora Massangana, 1988.

*Discursos parlamentares. Obras Completas de Joaquim Nabuco*. Vol XI. São Paulo: Instituto Progresso Editorial, 1988.

*Escravos! Versos franceses a Epicteto*. Rio de Janeiro: Typografia de G. Leuzinger & Filhos, 1886 c.

*Henry George. A Nacionalização do Solo. Apreciação da propaganda para abolição do monopólio territorial na Inglaterra*. Rio de Janeiro: Lamoureux, 1884.

*Minha Formação*. São Paulo: W. M. Jackson Inc. Editores, [1900] 1949.

*O Erro do Imperador*. Rio de Janeiro: Typografia de G. Leuzinger & Filho, 1886 a.

*Campanhas de imprensa (1884–1887). Obras Completas*, Vol. XII. São Paulo: Instituto Progresso Editorial, 1949.

*Conferência do Sr. Joaquim Nabuco a 22 de junho de 1884 no Teatro Polytheama*. Rio de Janeiro: Confederação Abolicionista: Typografia de G. Leuzinger & Filhos, 1884.

*Diários de Joaquim Nabuco*, Vols. 1 e 2. Mello, E. C. (ed.). Recife: Bem Te Vi Produções Literárias/Editora Massangana, 2005.

*O Eclipse do Abolicionismo*. Rio de Janeiro: Typografia. de G. Leuzinger & Filhos, 1886 d.

Nunes, Joaquim. *Corja Opulenta, drama abolicionista em 3 atos. Representado em todas as Provincias do Norte*. Rio de Janeiro: Typografia Polytechnica de Moraes e Filhos, [1884] 1887.

*O auxiliador da indústria nacional*. Periódico da Sociedade Auxiliadora da Indústria Nacional, Vol. XXIX, 1871.

Octaviano, Francisco. Cartas in Pinho, Wanderley (ed.), *Cartas de Francisco Octaviano*. Rio de Janeiro: Civilização Brasileira/Mec, 1977.

Ottoni, Christiano. *A Emancipação dos escravos. Parecer de C. B. Ottoni*. Rio de Janeiro: Typografia Perseverança, 1871.

Paes Barreto, Fernando de Castro. *Reforma Social: versos abolicionistas*. Rio de Janeiro: n.p., 1883.

Patrocínio, José do (1879).*Os Retirantes*. Col. Obras imortais da nossa literatura. São Paulo: Ed. Três, 1973.

# Bibliography

(1882). A Ponte do Catete. In Goes de Paula, S. (ed.), *Um Monarca da Fuzarca. Três Versões para um escândalo na Corte*. Rio de Janeiro: Relume-Dumará, 1993.

e Fonseca, Demerval da. *Os Ferrões*. In Nascimento, Leonardo (ed.), *Os Ferrões, 1 de junho a 15 de outubro de 1875/José do Patrocínio, Demerval da Fonseca*. São Paulo, Ed. Unesp. 2013.

Campanha Abolicionista – Coletânea de Artigos. Carvalho, José Murilo de (ed.), Rio de Janeiro: Biblioteca Nacional, 1996.

Conferência n.27. Teatro S. Luiz, domingo, 30 de janeiro de 1881. In Associação Central Emancipadora, *Boletim n. 8*, 20 de março de 1881.

*Conferencia Publica do Jornalista José do Patrocínio feita no Theatro Polytheama em sessao da Confederação Abolicionista, de 17 de maio de 1885.* Confederação Abolicionista, Folheto n. 8. Rio Janeiro: Typografia Central de Evaristo da Costa, 1885.

*L'affranchissement des esclaves de la province de Ceará au Brésil: notes par José do Patrocínio*. Paris; Rio de Janeiro: Bureaux de la Gazeta da Tarde, 1884.

Ana Flora e Inacio José Veríssimo. *Mota Coqueiro*. Col. Obras imortais da nossa literatura. São Paulo: Ed. Três, [1877] 1973.

Pereira, Baptista. *Figuras do Império e outros ensaios*. São Paulo: Companhia Editora Nacional, 1931.

Pereira Barreto, Luís. *As três filosofias: filosofia metafísica*. Jacareí: Tipografia Comercial, 1876.

*Os Abolicionistas e a situação do país*. São Paulo: Typographia A Provincia de São Paulo, 1880.

Pereira da Costa, Francisco A. *A Idea Abolicionista em Pernambuco. Conferencia por Francisco Augusto Pereira da Costa*. Recife: Typografia Boultreau, 1892.

Pereira da Silva, J. M. *Memórias do meu tempo*, 2 vols. Rio de Janeiro: Garnier, 1895–1896.

Pinto, Antônio. *Discurso proferido pelo deputado Antônio Pinto no Theatro Polytheama em 29 de junho de 1884*. Confederação Abolicionista. Rio de Janeiro: Typografia Central de Evaristo da Costa, 1884.

Pompeia, Raul. 1882. Crônicas In Coutinho, A. (ed.), *Raul Pompéia: escritos políticos*. Vol. V. Rio de Janeiro: Editora Civilização Brasileira, 1982.

*O Ateneu*. Ministério da Cultura, Fundação Biblioteca Nacional, Departamento Nacional do Livro, 1888. http://objdigital.bn.br/Acervo_Digital/livros_eletroni cos/oateneu.pdf

Porto Alegre, Manuel de Araújo. *Colombo. Poema*. Rio de Janeiro: B. L. Garnier, 1866.

Pujol, Alfredo. Discurso de posse na Academia Brasileira de Letras a 23 de julho de 1919. www.abl.com.br

Rebouças, André (1889). Depoimento de André Rebouças sobre o quilombo do Leblon e outros quilombos apoiados pelo movimento abolicionista. In Silva, Eduardo. *As Camélias do Leblon*. São Paulo: Cia das letras, 2003.

Abolição da Miséria. *Revista de Engenharia*, Vol. 10, 1888.

Charles Darwin e a Escravidão no Brasil. *Boletim da Associação Central Emancipadora*, no. 8, 1881.

# Bibliography

*Diários e Notas Autobiográficas de André Rebouças*, seleta publicada por Ana Flora e Inacio José Veríssimo Rio de Janeiro: J. Olympio, 1938.

Ephemérides de Carlos Gomes (Notas para o Taunay). *Revista do Instituto Histórico e Geográfico Brasileiro*, Tomo LXXIII, parte II, 1910.

André. *Orphelinato Gonçalves D. Araújo. Lemmas e Contribuições para Abolição da Miseria.* Rio de Janeiro: Typografia Leuzinger, 1889.

Reis, Aarão L. C. Introdução. In Condorcet. *Escravidão dos Negros (reflexões)*, de Typographia Serafim José Alves. 1881.

Maria Firmina. *Úrsula, romance original brasileiro. Por uma maranhense.* São Luís: Typographia do Progresso, 1859. [Ed fac-similar. Rio de Janeiro, 1975].

Romero, Sílvio. A Questão da Emancipação dos Escravos. *Revista Brasileira*, Rio de Janeiro, Vol. 7, 1881.

Sampaio, Antônio Gomes de Azevedo. *Abolicionismo. Considerações geraes do movimento anti-esclavista e sua historia limitada a Jacarehy, que foi um centro de acção no norte do Estado de São Paulo,* São Paulo: Typografia a Vapor Louzada & Irmão, 1890.

Santos, Luiz Alvares. *A Emancipação. Ligeiras e decisivas considerações sobre o total acabamento da escravidão.* Bahia: Typografia do Correio da Bahia, 1871.

Scalvini, C. D'Ormeville. *Il Guarany. Libretto.* 1870. www.librettidopera.it/guar any/guarany.html

Schoelcher, Victor. *Polémique Coloniale, 1871–1881.* Paris: Dentu Libraire-Editeur, 1882.

SCT (Sociedade contra o Tráfico de Africanos e Promotora de Colonização e da Civilização dos Indígenas). *Sistema de medidas adotáveis para a progressiva e total extinção do tráfico, e da escravatura no Brasil confeccionado e aprovado pela Sociedade contra o trafico de africanos, e promotora da colonisação, e da civilizarão dos indígenas.* Rio de Janeiro, 1852.

Sena, Ernesto. *Rascunhos e Perfis. notas de um repórter.* Brasília: Ed UnB, [1909] 1983.

Serra, Joaquim de Almeida. *O Abolicionista Joaquim Serra. Textos, opiniões e dados coligidos.* Rio de Janeiro: Presença, 1986.

Silva, José Cavalcanti Ribeiro da. *Cora, a filha de Agar. Drama Abolicionista em 4 atos.* Rio de Janeiro: A Fabrica Apollo, 1884.

Silva Jardim, A. *Memórias e Viagens – I. Campanha de um propagandista (1887–1890).* Lisboa: Tip. Cia. Nacional Ed, 1891.

Antônio. *Propaganda Republicana (1888–1889).* Rio de Janeiro: MEC/Casa Rui/CFCRJ, 1978.

Silva Jr. *O gabinete sete de março. O sr. Conselheiro Joao Alfredo. Perfil Historico-Biografico Publicado.* Rio de Janeiro: Typografia Carioca, 1876.

Silvado, Brazil. *Discurso Pronunciado na conferência 21 de 12 de dezembro de 1889 pelo Quarto-anista de S. Paulo Brazil Silvado, sociofundador da Sociedade Abolicionista Acadêmica de São Paulo,* 1889.

Silveira da Mota, Arthur. Discurso no banquete em homenagem à libertação do amazonas. Confederação Abolicionista. 1884. *Banquete dado pela Confederação e alguns amigos da idéia no dia 19 de agosto de 1884 em homenagem à libertação do Amazonas e aos deputados que apoiaram o*

# Bibliography

*gabinete 6 de junho.* Rio de Janeiro: Typografia Central de Evaristo da Veiga, 1884.

Sission, S. A. *Galeria dos Brasileiros Ilustres.* Coleção Brasil 500 Anos, Vol. I e Vol. II, Brasília: Senado Federal, [1861] 1999.

Soares, Caetano Alberto. *Memória para melhorar a sorte dos nossos escravos. Lida na sessão geral do Instituto dos Advogados Brasileiros no dia 7 de setembro de 1845 pelo Dr. Caetano Alberto Soares.* Rio de Janeiro: Typografia Imparcial de Francisco de Paula Brito, 1847.

Soares de Souza, Paulino José. Cartas de Paulino Soares de Souza a Maria Amelia, 5/2/1877; 2/11/1866; Carta de Paulino Soares de Souza a João Alvares Soares de Souza, 25/9/1877. Transcritas em SOARES DE SOUZA, Álvaro Paulino. *Três Brasileiros Ilustres. Dr. José Antônio de Soares de Souza, Visconde do Uruguay, Conselheiro Paulino Jose Soares de Souza. Contribuições biográficas por ocasião do centenário da independência.* Rio de Janeiro: Typo. Leuzinger, 1923.

Paulino José. *Discurso proferido na sessão de 23 de agosto de 1871 sobre a proposta do governo relativa ao elemento servil pelo conselheiro Paulino José Soares de Souza, deputado pelo 3º. Distrito da província do Rio de Janeiro.* Rio de Janeiro: Typografia Villeneuve, 1871.

Sociedade Abolicionista Bahiana. *Manifesto que vai ser apresentado ao Corpo Legislativo pela Sociedade Abolicionista Bahiana,* 1876.

Sociedade Brasileira contra a Escravidão. *Manifesto da Sociedade Brasileira contra a escravidão, 7 de setembro de 1880.* Rio de Janeiro: Typografia de G. Leuzinger & Filhos, 1880 a.

*Cartas do presidente Joaquim Nabuco e do ministro Americano H. W. Hilliard sobre a emancipação nos Estados-Unidos.* Rio de Janeiro: G. Leuzinger & Filhos, 1880 b.

*Sociedade Brasileira Contra a Escravidão oferece um banquete em honra ao ministro americano Henry Washington Hilliard, 20 de Novembro, 1880.* Rio de Janeiro: Typografia Primeiro de Janeiro, 1880 c.

Souza, Vicente de. *Conferência realizada no Theatro S. Luizs em benefício da Associação Typhografica Fluminense, em 23 de março de 1879.* Tese: o Império e a escravidão; o parlamento e a pena de morte. Rio de Janeiro, Typ. de Molarinho & Montalverne, 1879. Edição fac-símile Centro de Memória sindical/Arquivo do Estado de São Paulo, São Paulo, 1993.

Swift (Barbosa, Rui). *Uma Escaramuça Conservadora em 1883. O crime de 25 de outubro, artigos de Swift.* Rio de Janeiro: Typografia Nacional, 1884.

Taunay, Afonso (ed.). Algumas Cartas de Carlos Gomes ao Visconde de Taunay. *Revista do Instituto Histórico e Geográfico Brasileiro,* Tomo LXXIII, parte II, 1910.

*As Memórias do Visconde de Taunay.* São Paulo: IPE, 1948.

André Rebouças. *Revista do Instituto Histórico e Geográfico Brasileiro,* 1916, Tomo LXXVII.

Alfredo *Reminiscências.* Rio de Janeiro: F. Alves. 1980.

Alfredo *Memórias do Visconde de Taunay (1892–1893).* In Taunay, Afonso, e Taunay, Raul (eds.). São Paulo: Instituto Progresso Editorial, 1948.

# Bibliography

Tosta, Joaquim Ignacio. *Discurso proferido na sessão de instalação da Sociedade Emancipadora Onze de Agosto*. Recife: Typografia Industrial, 1877.

Trovão, Lopes. *Conferência Republicana*. Rio de Janeiro: Typografia Machado Costa, 1879.

Um Lavrador. *Manual do Sudito Fiel ou Cartas de um lavrador, à sua magestade o Imperador sobre a questão do elemento servil*. Rio de Janeiro: Typografia e Lith. de Moreira, Maximino & C., 1884.

Um Patriota. *O Erro do Sr. Joaquim Nabuco, O Eclipse do Patriotismo, Propaganda da Verdade*. Rio de Janeiro, 1885.

Varella, Busch. *Conferência sobre a lei 7 de novembro de 1831 realizada no dia 9 de março de 1884 a convite do Clube Abolicionista 7 de Novembro*. Rio Janeiro: Typografia Central de Evaristo da Costa, 1884.

Vindex [Alvares Augusto Guimarães]. *Cartas de Vindex ao Dr. Luiz Alvares dos Santos publicadas no Diário da Bahia*. Bahia: Typographia do Diário, 1875.

## SECONDARY SOURCES

Acebrón, M. Dolores Domingo. *Rafael María de Labra: Cuba, Puerto Rico, Las Filipinas, Europa y Marruecos, en la España del sexenio democrático y la restauración (1871–1918)*. Madrid: Consejo Superior de Investigaciones Científicas, 2006.

Affonso, Almino (ed.). *Poliantéia: Almino Affonso, tribuno da abolição*. Brasília: Senado Federal, 1998.

Albuquerque, Wlamyra R. de. *O jogo da dissimulação. Abolição e cidadania negra no Brasil*. São Paulo: Companhia das Letras, 2009.

Alencastro, Luiz Felipe de. *Trabalho escravo e trabalho compulsório no Brasil: 1870–1930*. Relatório de pesquisa. São Paulo: Cebrap, 1989.

A evangelização numa só colônia. In *O trato dos viventes. Formação do Brasil no Atlântico Sul*. São Paulo: Companhia das Letras, 2000.

Alonso, Angela. O epílogo do romantismo. A polêmica Alencar-Nabuco. *Dados. Revista de Ciências Sociais*, 39(2), 1996.

*Ideias em movimento: a geração 1870 na crise do Brasil-Império*. São Paulo: Anpocs/Paz e Terra, 2002.

*Joaquim Nabuco: os salões e as ruas*. São Paulo: Companhia das Letras, 2007.

A década monarquista de Joaquim Nabuco. *Revista USP*, 83, 53–63, 2009.

O abolicionista cosmopolita. Joaquim Nabuco e a rede abolicionista transnacional. *Novos Estudos Cebrap*, São Paulo, 88, 2010.

A teatralização da política: a propaganda abolicionista. *Tempo Social, Revista do Departamento de Sociologia da USP*, 24(2), 2012.

O abolicionismo como movimento social. *Novos Estudos Ceprab*, 100, 2015.

*Flores, votos e balas: o movimento abolicionista brasileiro (1868–1888)*. São Paulo: Companhia das Letras, 2015.

Souza e Castro, Antônio Bento de (1843–1898), White Lawyer. In Franklin Knight and Henry Louis Gates, Jr. (eds.), *Dictionary of Caribbean and*

## Bibliography

*Afro-Latin American Biography*, Oxford University Press/W. E. B. Du Bois Institute, 2016.

Alves, Isaias. *Vida e obra do barão de Macahubas*. São Paulo: Companhia Editora Nacional, 1942.

Alves, Uelinton F. *José do Patrocínio. A imorredoura cor do bronze*. Rio de Janeiro: FBN/Garamond, 2009.

Anderson, Benedict. *Under Three Flags: Anarchism and the Anti-Colonial Imagination*. Rio de Janeiro: Verso, 2007.

Azevedo, Célia. "Quem precisa de são Nabuco?" *Estudos Afro-Asiáticos*, 23(1), 2001.

*Abolicionismo. Estados Unidos e Brasil, uma história comparada (século XIX)*. São Paulo: Annablume, 2003.

*Onda negra, medo branco: o negro no imaginário das elites do século XIX*. São Paulo: Annablume, [1987] 2004.

Azevedo, Elciene. *Orfeu de carapinha. A trajetória de Luís Gama na imperial cidade de São Paulo*. Campinas: Ed. da Unicamp, 1999.

Antônio Bento, homem rude do sertão: um abolicionista nos meandros da justiça e da política. *Locus: Revista de História*, Juiz de Fora, 13(1), 2007.

*O direito dos escravos. Lutas jurídicas e abolicionismo na província de São Paulo*. Campinas: Ed. da Unicamp, 2010.

Bakos, Margaret M. *RS: escravismo e abolição*. Porto Alegre: Mercado Aberto, 1982.

Barman, Roderick J. *Citizen Emperor: Pedro II and the Making of Brazil, 1825–1891*. Stanford: Stanford University Press, 2000.

*Princess Isabel of Brazil. Gender and Power in the Nineteenth Century*. Wilmington, DE: SR Books, 2002.

Bastos, M. H. C. As conferências populares da Freguesia da Glória. In *II Congresso Brasileiro de História da Educação*, vol. 1, História e memória da educação brasileira. Natal: Núcleo de Arte e Cultura da UFRN, 2002.

Bennani-Chraïbi, Mounia and Olivier Fillieule. Pour une sociologie des situations révolutionnaires. *Revue française de science politique*, 62 (5–6): *Retour sur les situations révolutionnaires arabes*, 2012.

Bennani-Chraïbi, Mounia and Olivier Fillieule. Towards a Sociology of Revolutionary Situations. Reflections on the Arab Uprisings. *Revue française de science politique*, 62, 1–29, 2012–2015.

Bergstresser, Rebecca B. *The Movement for the Abolition of Slavery in Rio de Janeiro, Brazil. 1880–1889*, Stanford University, Doctoral dissertation, 1973.

Besouchet, Lídia. *José Maria Paranhos, visconde do Rio Branco: ensaio histórico-biográfico*. Rio de Janeiro: Nova Fronteira, 1985.

Bethell, Leslie. *The Abolition of the Brazilian Slave Trade: Britain, Brazil and the Slave Trade Question, 1807–69*. Cambridge: Cambridge University Press, 1970.

Joaquim Nabuco e os abolicionistas britânicos. Correspondência, 1880–1905. *Estudos Avançados*, São Paulo, 23(65), 2009a.

O Brasil da Independência a meados do século XIX. In (ed.). *História da América Latina*, vol. III, *Da Independência a 1870*. São Paulo: Edusp/Funag, 2009b.

# Bibliography

Bethell, Leslie and José Murilo de Carvalho (eds.). *Joaquim Nabuco e os abolicionistas britânicos (correspondência 1880–1905)*. Rio de Janeiro: Topbooks, 2008.

Blackburn, Robin. *The American Crucible: Slavery, Emancipation and Human Rights*. London: Verso Books, 2011.

Blake, Augusto Victorino Sacramento. *Dicionário bibliográfico brasileiro*, vols. II, III, V, VI, VII. Rio de Janeiro: Typographia Nacional/Conselho Federal de Cultura, 1970.

Boehrer, George. *Da monarquia à república: história do Partido Republicano do Brasil (1870–1889)*. Rio de Janeiro: MEC, 1954.

Bourdieu, Pierre. *Distinction. A social critique of the judgment of taste*. Cambridge, MA: Harvard University Press, 1984.

Braga-Pinto, César. The Honor of the Abolitionist and the Shamefulness of Slavery: Raul Pompeia, Luiz Gama, and Joaquim Nabuco. *Luso-Brazilian Review*, 51(2), 2014.

Brício Filho, Jaime. 1928. Depoimento do jornalista Brício Filho sobre o Quilombo do Leblon. In Eduardo Silva, *As camélias do Leblon*. São Paulo: Companhia das Letras, 2003.

Brito, Jailton Lima. *A abolição na Bahia, 1870–1888*. Salvador: Centro de Estudos Baianos da UFBA, 2003.

Brookshaw, David. *Raça e cor na literatura brasileira*. Porto Alegre: Mercado Aberto, 1983.

Brown, Christopher Leslie. *Moral Capital: Foundations of British Abolitionism*. Chapel Hill: University of North Carolina Press, 2006.

Buescu, Mircea. No centenário da Lei Saraiva. *Rev. do Ins. Histórico e Geográfico*, Rio de Janeiro, 330, 179–86, 1981.

Caires Silva, Ricardo Tadeu. Memórias do tráfico ilegal de escravos nas ações de liberdade: Bahia, 1885–1888. *Afro-Ásia*, 35, 37–82, 2007.

As ações das sociedades abolicionistas na Bahia (1869–1888). *4º Encontro Escravidão e Liberdade no Brasil Meridional*. Curitiba, 2009.

Câmara, Nelson. *O advogado dos escravos: Luiz Gama*. São Paulo: Lettera, 2010.

Campbell, Courtney Jeanette. *Culture, Nation and Imperialism: Iseb and U.S. Cultural Influence in Cold-War Brazil and Joaquim Nabuco, British Abolitionists and the Case of Morro Velho*. Vanderbilt University, Master's thesis, 2010.

Cardoso, Fernando Henrique. *Capitalismo e escravidão no Brasil meridional. O negro na sociedade escravocrata do Rio Grande do Sul*. São Paulo: Paz e Terra, 1977.

Carvalho, José Murilo de. *A construção da ordem. A elite política imperial*. Rio de Janeiro: Campus, 1980.

*Teatro de sombras. A política imperial*. Rio de Janeiro: Iuperj/Vértice, 1988.

*Cidadania no Brasil. O longo caminho*. Rio de Janeiro: Civilização Brasileira, 2003.

Escravidão e razão nacional. In *Pontos e bordados. Escritos de história e política*. Belo Horizonte: Ed. da UFMG, 2005.

## Bibliography

As conferências radicais do Rio de Janeiro: novo espaço de debate. In (ed.), *Nação e cidadania no Império: novos horizontes*. São Paulo: Civilização Brasileira, 2007.

*D. Pedro II. Ser ou não ser*. São Paulo: Companhia das Letras, 2007.

Apresentação. In José de Alencar, *Cartas de Erasmo*. Rio de Janeiro: ABL, 2009.

Carvalho, Maria Alice Rezende de. *O quinto século: André Rebouças e a construção do Brasil*. Rio de Janeiro: Revan: Iuperj-Ucam, 1998.

Castilho, Celso T. *Abolitionism Matters: The Politics of Antislavery in Pernambuco, Brazil. 1869–1888*. University of California, Berkeley, Doctoral dissertation, 2008.

*Slave Emancipation and Transformations in Brazilian Political Citizenship*. Pittsburgh: University of Pittsburgh Press, 2016.

Castro, Celso. *Os militares e a república: um estudo sobre cultura e ação política*. Rio de Janeiro: Zahar, 1995.

Chalhoub Sidney. *Visões da liberdade: uma história das últimas décadas da escravidão na Corte*. São Paulo: Companhia das Letras, 1990.

População e sociedade. In José Murilo de Carvalho (ed.), *História do Brasil nação: 1808–2010*, vol. 2: *A construção nacional 1830–1889*. Madrid/Rio de Janeiro: Fundación Mapfre/ Objetiva, 2012.

Childs, Matt D. A Case of "Great Unstableness": a British Slaveholder and Brazilian Abolition. *The Historian*, 60(4), 717–40, 1998.

Conniff, Michael L. Voluntary Associations in Rio, 1870–1945: A New Approach to Urban Social Dynamics. *Journal of Interamerican Studies and World Affairs*, 17(1), 64–81, 1975.

Conrad, Robert. The Contraband Slave Trade to Brazil, 1831–1845. *Hispanic American Historical Review*, XLIX(2), 1969.

*The Destruction of Brazilian Slavery. 1850–1888*. Berkeley and Los Angeles: University of California Press, 1972.

*Os últimos anos da escravatura no Brasil*. Rio de Janeiro: Civilização Brasileira, 1975.

Corwin, Arthur F. *Spain and the Abolition of Slavery in Cuba, 1817–1886*. Austin: Published for the Institute of Latin American Studies, University of Texas Press, 1968.

Costa, Emília Viotti da. *Da senzala à colônia*. São Paulo: Livraria de Ciências Humanas, [1966] 1982.

*Da monarquia à república: momentos decisivos*. São Paulo: Grijalbo, 1977.

*The Brazilian Empire*. Chicago: University of Chicago Press, 1985.

Costa e Silva, Alberto. *Castro Alves*. São Paulo: Companhia das Letras, 2006.

Cota, Luís Gustavo Santos. *Ave Libertas: abolicionismo e luta pela liberdade em Minas Gerais na última década da escravidão*. Niterói, UFF, Doctoral dissertation, 2013.

Coutinho, Afrânio (ed.). *A polêmica Alencar–Nabuco*. Rio de Janeiro: Tempo Brasileiro, 1978.

Davis, David Brion. *The Problem of Slavery in Western Culture*. New York: Oxford University Press, 1966.

*Slavery and Human Progress*. New York: Oxford University Press, 1984.

418 *Bibliography*

The Problem of Slavery in the Age of Revolution 1770–1823. In Thomas Bender (ed.), *The Antislavery Debate. Capitalism and Abolitionism as a Problem in Historical Interpretation*. Berkeley: University of California Press, 1992.

*Inhuman Bondage. The Rise and Fall of Slavery in the New World*. Oxford: Oxford University Press, 2006.

Del Priore, Mary. *Príncipe maldito – traição e loucura na família imperial*. Rio de Janeiro: Objetiva, 2007.

Diani, Mario. Networks and Social Movements: a Research Programme. In Mario Diani and Doug McAdam (eds.), *Social Movements and Networks. Relational Approaches to Collective Action*. Oxford: Oxford University Press, 2003.

Doratioto, Francisco. *Maldita guerra: nova história da Guerra do Paraguai*. São Paulo: Companhia das Letras, 2002.

O visconde do Rio Branco: soberania, diplomacia e força. In José Vicente de Sá Pimentel (ed.), *Pensamento diplomático brasileiro. Formuladores e agentes da política externa (1750–1965)*, vol. I Brasilía: Funag, 2013.

Drescher, Seymour. *Econocide: British Slavery in the Era of Abolition*. Pittsburgh: University of Pittsburgh Press, 1977.

Two Variants de Anti-Slavery: Religious Organization and Social Mobilization in Britain and France, 1780–1870. In Christine Bolt and Seymour Drescher, (eds.), *Anti-Slavery, Religion and Reform: Essays in Memory de Roger Anstey*. Folkestone: W. Dawson, 1980.

*Capitalism and Antislavery*. Oxford: Oxford University Press, 1986.

Brazilian Abolition in Comparative Perspective. In Rebecca J. Scott, et al., *The Abolition of Slavery and the Aftermath of Emancipation in Brazil*. Durham: Duke University Press, 1988.

Capitalism and Slavery after Fifty Years. *Slavery and Abolition*, v. 18, n. 3, 212–27, 1997.

*Abolition. A History of Slavery and Antislavery*. Cambridge: Cambridge University Press, 2009.

Civil Society and Paths to Abolition. *História (São Paulo)*, 34 (2), 29–57, 2015.

Durham, David I. and Pruitt Jr., Paul M. *A Journey in Brazil: Henry Washington Hilliard and the Brazilian Anti-slavery Society*. Occasional Publications of the Bounds Law Library, 6. Tuscaloosa: University of Alabama School of Law, 2008.

Elias, Norbert. *O processo civilizador*, vols. I, II. Rio de Janeiro: Zahar, 1996.

Falci, Miridan B. and Melo, Hildete Pereira de. *A sinhazinha emancipada. Eufrásia Teixeira Leite (1850–1930). A paixão e os negócios na vida de uma ousada mulher do século XIX*. Rio de Janeiro: Vieira & Lent, 2012.

Faria, João Roberto. José de Alencar: a polêmica em torno da adaptação teatral de O Guarani. *Revista Letras*, 31, 1982.

*José de Alencar e o teatro*. São Paulo: Perspectiva/Edusp, 1987.

Fernandes, Florestan. *A integração do negro na sociedade de classes*. São Paulo: Ática, 1978.

Ferreira, Ligia Fonseca. *Luiz Gama (1830–1882): étude sur la vie et l'oeuvre d'un noir citoyen, militant de la lutte anti-esclavagiste au Brésil*, Universidade de Paris 3/Sorbonne Nouvelle, Doctoral dissertation, 2001.

# Bibliography

Luiz Gama: um abolicionista leitor de Renan. *Estudos Avançados*, 21 (60), 2007.

*Com a palavra. Luiz Gama. Poemas, artigos, cartas, máximas.* São Paulo: Imprensa Oficial, 2011.

Ferreira, Luzilá Gonçalves et al. *Suaves Amazonas: mulheres e abolição da escravatura no Nordeste.* Recife: Ed. da UFPE, 1999.

Figueroa, Meirevandra Soares. *Matéria livre... espírito livre para pensar. Um estudo das práticas abolicionistas em prol da instrução e educação de ingênuos na capital da província sergipana (1881–1884).* Universidade Federal de Sergipe, Master's thesis, 2007.

Fonseca, Dante Ribeiro. O trabalho do escravo de origem africana no Amazonas. *Revista Veredas Amazônicas*, 1(1), 2011.

Fontes, Alice Aguiar de Barros. *A prática abolicionista em São Paulo: os Caifases (1882–1888).* Departamento de História da FFLCH da USP, Master's thesis, 1976.

Fradera, Josep M. and Schmidt-Nowara, Christopher (eds.). *Slavery and Antislavery in Spain's Atlantic Empire.* New York: Berghahn, 2013.

Fraga Filho, Walter. *Encruzilhadas da liberdade: histórias de escravos e libertos na Bahia (1870–1910).* Campinas: Ed. da Unicamp, 2006.

Franco, Sergio da Costa. *Júlio de Castilhos e sua época.* Porto Alegre: Globo, 1967.

Freyre, Gilberto. *Sobrados e mucambos: decadência do patriarcado rural e desenvolvimento do urbano.* São Paulo: Global, 2003.

Fundação Casa de Rui Barbosa. *Arquivo de Rui Barbosa: repertório da série Correspondência Geral.* Rio de Janeiro: Fundação Casa de Rui Barbosa, 1983.

Gamson, William. *Power and Discontent.* Homewood: Dorsey, 1968.

Gamson, William and Meyer, D. S. 1996. Framing Political Opportunity. In Doug McAdam, John D. McCarthy, and Mayer N. Zald (eds.), *Comparative Perspectives on Social Movements: Political Opportunities, Mobilizing Structures, and Cultural Framings.* Cambridge: Cambridge University Press, 1996, pp. 338–57.

Gaspar, Lúcia. *Clube do Cupim.* Recife: Fundação Joaquim Nabuco, 2009. (http://basilio.fundaj.gov.br/pesquisaescolar/index.php?option=com_con tent&view=article&id=558&Itemid=182).

Girão, Raimundo. *A abolição no Ceará* (2nd rev. ed.). Fortaleza: Secretaria de Cultura do Ceará, 1969.

A abolição no Ceará. In *Da senzala para os salões (coletânea).* Fortaleza: Secretaria de Cultura, Turismo e Desporto, 1988.

Góes, Marcus. *Carlos Gomes. Documentos comentados.* São Paulo: Algol, 2008.

Goffman, Erving. *Frame Analysis: An Essay on the Organization of Experience.* Cambridge, MA: Harvard University Press, 1974.

*Stigma: Notes on the Management of Spoiled Identity.* New Jersey: Prentice-Hall, 1963.

Gomes, Flávio dos Santos. Jogando a rede, revendo as malhas: fugas e fugitivos no Brasil escravista. *Tempo: Revista do Departamento de História da UFF*, 1, 89–90, 1996.

420                                          *Bibliography*

*Histórias de quilombolas: mocambos e comunidades de senzalas no Rio de Janeiro – século XIX.* São Paulo: Companhia das Letras, 2006.

Gondra, José Gonçalves and Sampaio, Thiago. Ciência pela força? Dr. Abílio Cesar Borges e a propaganda contra o emprego da palmatória e outros meios aviltantes no ensino da mocidade (1856–1876). *Acta Scientiarum Education,* Maringá, 32(1),75–82, 2010.

Gorender, Jacob. *A escravidão reabilitada.* São Paulo: Ática, 1990.

Gouvêa, Fernando da Cruz. *Joaquim Nabuco entre a monarquia e a república.* Recife: Fundaj, 1989.

Graden, Dale Torston. *From Slavery to Freedom in Brazil. Bahia, 1835–1900.* Albuquerque: University of New Mexico Press, 2006.

Graham, Richard. *Clientelismo e política no Brasil do século XIX.* Rio de Janeiro: UFRJ, 1997.

Graham, Sandra L. The Vintem Riot and Political Culture: Rio de Janeiro, 1880. *Hispanic American Historical Review,* 60(3), 1980.

Grinberg, Keila. *Liberata, a lei da ambiguidade.* Rio de Janeiro: Relume Dumará, 1994.

*O fiador dos Brasileiros – cidadania, escravidão e direito civil no tempo de Antônio Pereira Rebouças.* Rio de Janeiro: Civilização Brasileira, 2002.

Haberly, David T. Abolitionism in Brazil; Anti-slavery and Anti-slave. *Luso-Brazilian Review, Madison,* 2(2), 1972.

Hahner, June. *Emancipating the Female Sex. Struggle for Women's Rights in Brazil 1850–1940.* Durham: Duke University Press, 1990.

Halfmann, Drew and Young, M. P. War Pictures: The Grotesque as Moral Repertoire in the Antislavery and Antiabortion Movements. *Mobilization: An International Quarterly Issue,* 15 Jan., 1–24, 2010.

Haskell, Thomas. Capitalism and the Origins of the Humanitarian Sensibility, Part 1 and Part 2. In Thomas Bender (ed.), *The Antislavery Debate. Capitalism and Abolitionism as a Problem in Historical Interpretation.* Berkeley: University of California Press, 1992.

Hirschman, Albert. *The Rhetoric of Reaction. Perversity, Futility, Jeopardy.* Cambridge, MA: Harvard University Press, 1991.

Hochschild, Adam. *Bury the Chains: Prophets and Rebels in the Fight to Free an Empire's Slaves.* Boston: Houghton Mifflin Harcourt, 2005.

Hoffnagel, Marc J. O Partido Liberal de Pernambuco e a questão abolicionista, 1880–1888. *Cadernos de Estudos Sociais de Recife,* 4(2), 1988.

Holanda, Sérgio Buarque de. *O Brasil monárquico – do Império à República. História geral da civilização brasileira.* São Paulo: Difel, 1972.

*Capítulos de história do Império.* São Paulo: Companhia das Letras, 2010.

Holloway, Thomas H. *Imigrantes para o café: café e sociedade em São Paulo, 1886–1934.* Rio de Janeiro: Paz e Terra, 1984.

*The Defiant Life and Forgotten Death of Apulco de Castro: Race, Power, and Historical Memory. Estudios Interdisciplinarios de América Latina y el Caribe,* 2007 (www1.tau.ac.il/eial).

*Caught in the Middle: Race and Republicanism in the Writings of Apulco de Castro, Journalist and "Man of Color," 1880–1883.* Paper presented at American Historical Association, New York, 2009.

## Bibliography

Ianni, Octávio. *As metamorfoses do escravo*. São Paulo: Hucitec, 1988.
Jasper, James. *The Art of Moral Protest. Culture, Biography, and Creativity in Social Movements*. Chicago: University of Chicago Press, 1997.
Jennings, Lawrence C. *French Anti-Slavery. The Movement for the Abolition of Slavery in France, 1802–1848*. Cambridge: Cambridge University Press, 2006.
Jesus, Ronaldo Pereira de. Associativismo no Brasil do século XIX: repertório crítico dos registros de sociedades no Conselho de Estado (1860–1889). *Locus: Revista de História*, Juiz de Fora, 13(1), 2007.
Jucá, Joselice. *André Rebouças: reforma e utopia no contexto do Segundo Reinado*. Rio de Janeiro: Odebrecht, 2001.
Keck, Margaret E. and Sikkink, Kathryn. *Activists Beyond Borders*. Ithaca: Cornell University Press, 1998.
Kittleson, Roger A. *The Practice of Politics in Postcolonial Brazil: Porto Alegre, 1845–1895*. Pittsburgh: University of Pittsburgh Press, 2005.
Kodama, Kaori. Os debates pelo fim do tráfico no periódico. *O Philantropo* (1849–1852) e a formação do povo: doenças, raça e escravidão. *Revista Brasileira de História*, 28(56), 2008.
Kraay, Hendrik. Between Brazil and Bahia: Celebrating Dois de Julho in Nineteenth-Century Salvador. *Journal of Latin American Studies*, 31, 1999.
Lamounier, Maria Lúcia. *Da escravidão ao trabalho livre (a lei de locação de serviços de 1879)*. Campinas: Papirus, 1988.
Laytano, Dante de. *Manual de fontes bibliográficas para o estudo da história geral do Rio Grande do Sul*. Porto Alegre: UFRGS, 1979.
Lima, Lana L. G. *Rebeldia negra e abolicionismo*. Rio de Janeiro: Achiamé, 1981.
Lima, Raul. A abolição à luz de documentos. *Revista do Instituto Histórico e Geográfico Brasileiro*, 335, 133–4, 1982.
Lins, Ivan. *História do positivismo no Brasil*. São Paulo: Companhia Editora Nacional, 1964.
Loner, Beatriz Ana. Negros: organização e luta em Pelotas. *História em Revista*, Pelotas, 5, 7–27, 1999.
Lyra, Heitor. *História de d. Pedro II*, vol. 2, *Fastígio. 1870–1880*. Belo Horizonte: Itatiaia, 1977.
Machado, Maria Helena. *O plano e o pânico: os movimentos sociais na década da abolição*. Rio de Janeiro/São Paulo: UFRJ/Edusp, 1994.
From Slave Rebels to Strikebreakers: The Quilombo of Jabaquara and the Problem of Citizenship in Late-Nineteenth-Century Brazil. *Hispanic American Historical Review*, 86(2), 2006.
"Teremos grandes desastres, se não houver providências enérgicas e imediatas": a rebeldia dos escravos e a abolição da escravidão. In Keila Grinberg and Ricardo Salles (eds.), *O Brasil Imperial*, vol. III, *1870–1889*. Rio de Janeiro: Civilização Brasileira, 2009.
Magalhães Jr., Raymundo. *A vida turbulenta de José do Patrocínio*. Rio de Janeiro: Sabiá, 1969.
Mamigonian, Beatriz. O Estado Nacional e a instabilidade da propriedade escrava: a Lei de 1831 e a matrícula dos escravos de 1872. *Almanack*. Guarulhos, 2, 20–37, 2011.

## Bibliography

*Africanos livres. A abolição do tráfico de escravos no Brasil*. São Paulo: Companhia das Letras, 2017.

Marquese, Rafael and Salles, Ricardo. *Escravidão e capitalismo histórico: Brasil, Cuba e Estados Unidos, século XIX*. Rio de Janeiro: Civilização Brasileira, 2015.

Mattos, Hebe. *Das cores do silêncio: os significados da liberdade no Sudeste escravista, Brasil século XIX* (2nd ed.). Rio de Janeiro: Nova Fronteira, 1998.

Mattos, Ilmar R. *Tempo saquarema*. São Paulo/Brasília: Hucitec/INL, 1987.

Mattos, Marcelo Badaró. Trajetórias entre fronteiras: o fim da escravidão e o fazer-se da classe trabalhadora no Rio de Janeiro. *Revista Mundos do Trabalho*, Florianópolis, 1(1), 2009.

McAdam, Doug. Biographical Consequences of Activism. *American Sociological Review*, (54), 1986.

McAdam, Doug, Tarrow, Sidney and Tilly, Charles. *Dynamics of Contention*. New York: Cambridge University Press, 2001.

McCarthy, John D. and Zald, Mayer N. Resource Mobilization and Social Movements: a Partial Theory. *American Journal of Sociology*, 82(6), 1977.

Medeiros, Coriolano de. O movimento abolicionista no Nordeste, 1925. In Leonardo Dantas. *A abolição em Pernambuco*. Recife: Fundaj/Massangana, 1988.

Menucci, Sud. *O precursor do abolicionismo no Brasil (Luiz Gama)*. São Paulo: Companhia Editora Nacional, 1938.

Meyer, David and Staggenborg, Suzanne. Movements, Countermovements, and the Structure of Political Opportunity. *American Journal of Sociology*, 101 (6), 1996.

Monnerat, Tanize do Couto Costa. *Abolicionismo em ação: o jornal* Vinte e Cinco de Março *em Campos dos Goytacazes 1884–1888*. UniRio, Master's thesis, 2012.

Monti, Verônica. M. *O abolicionismo: sua hora decisiva no Rio Grande do Sul 1884*. Porto Alegre: Martins, 1985.

Moraes, Maria Augusta de S. *História de uma oligarquia: os Bulhões*. Goiânia: Oriente, 1974.

Morel, Edgar. *Dragão do Mar. O jangadeiro da abolição*. Rio de Janeiro: Edgar Morel, 1949.

*Vendaval da liberdade. A luta do povo pela abolição*. São Paulo: Global, 1967.

Mott, Maria Lúcia. *Submissão e resistência: a mulher na luta contra a escravidão*. São Paulo: Contexto, 1988.

Moura, Clóvis. *Dicionário da escravidão negra no Brasil*. São Paulo: Edusp, 2004.

Mulligan, William and Bric, Maurice. *A Global History of Anti-Slavery Politics in the Nineteenth Century*. New York: Palgrave Macmillan, 2013.

Nabuco, Carolina. *Vida de Joaquim Nabuco, por sua filha Carolina Nabuco*. São Paulo: Companhia Editora Nacional, 1929.

Needell, Jeffrey D. *The Party of Order: The Conservatives, the State, and Slavery in the Brazilian Monarchy, 1831–1871*. Stanford: Stanford University Press, 2006.

Brazilian Abolitionism, Its Historiography, and the Uses of Political History. *Journal of Latin American Studies*, 42(2), 231–61, 2010.

## Bibliography

Politics, Parliament, and the Penalty of the Lash: The Significance of the End of Flogging in 1886. *Almanack*, 4, 91–100, 2012.

*The Sacred Cause: The Abolitionist Movement, Afro-Brazilian Mobilization, and Imperial Politics in Rio de Janeiro*. Stanford: Stanford University Press, 2020.

Nobre, Freitas. *João Cordeiro: abolicionista e republicano*. São Paulo: Letras, 1943.

Novaes, Maria Stella de. *A escravidão e a abolição no Espírito Santo: história e folclore* (2nd ed). Vitória: Prefeitura Municipal de Vitória, Secretária de Cultura, 2010.

Novais, Fernando A. *Portugal e Brasil na crise do antigo sistema colonial (1777–1808)*. São Paulo: Hucitec, 1985.

Oliveira, Dom Oscar de. O que fez a Igreja no Brasil pelo escravo africano. *Revista do IHGB*, 326, 1980.

Paiva, Clotilde A. et al. *Publicação crítica do recenseamento geral do Império do Brasil de 1872 (Relatório Provisório)*. Núcleo de Pesquisa em História Econômica e Demográfica, Cedeplar, 2012.

Pang, Laura Jarnagin. *The State and Agricultural Clubs of Imperial Brazil, 1860–1889*. Vanderbilt University, Doctoral dissertation, 1981.

Parron, Tâmis. *A política da escravidão no Império do Brasil, 1826–1865*. Rio de Janeiro: Civilização Brasileira, 2011.

Pena, Eduardo Spiller. "Resenha de Liberata: a lei da ambiguidade." *Afro-Ásia, Revista do Centro de Estudos Afro-Orientais da Universidade Federal da Bahia*, 17, 1996.

*Pajens da casa imperial: jurisconsultos, escravidão e a Lei de 1871*. Campinas: Ed. da Unicamp, 2001.

Perussatto, Melina Kleinert. Rosa vai à justiça: agência, abolicionismo e direitos nos últimos anos do cativeiro, Rio Pardo/RS. In *Mostra de pesquisa do Arquivo Público do Estado do Rio Grande do Sul 7*. Porto Alegre: Companhia Rio-grandense de Artes Gráficas, 2009.

Pinho, Wanderley. *Cotegipe e seu tempo: primeira fase*. São Paulo: Companhia Editora Nacional, 1937.

Proença Filho, Domício. A trajetória do negro na literatura brasileira. *Estudos Avançados*, 1(50), 161–93, 2004.

Rangel, Alberto. *Gastão de Orléans (o último conde d'Eu)*. São Paulo: Companhia Editora Nacional, 1935.

Reis, João José. Quilombos e revoltas escravas no Brasil. *Revista USP*, 28, 1995–1996.

*Slave Rebellion in Brazil: The Muslim Uprising of 1835 in Bahia*. Translated by Arthur Brakel. Baltimore: Johns Hopkins University Press, 1993.

Presença negra: conflitos e encontros. In *Brasil: 500 anos de povoamento*. Rio de Janeiro: IBGE, 2000.

Rebelião escrava no Brasil: a história do levante dos malês em 1835. São Paulo: Companhia das Letras, 2003.

Reis, João José and Gomes, Flávio dos Santos (eds.). *Liberdade por um fio – História dos quilombos no Brasil*. São Paulo: Companhia das Letras, 1996.

# Bibliography

Reis, João José and Silva, Eduardo. *Negociação e conflito: a resistência negra no Brasil escravista*. São Paulo: Companhia das Letras, 2009.

Reynolds, David S. *John Brown, Abolitionist: the Man who Killed Slavery, Sparked the Civil War, and Seeded Civil Rights*. New York: Vintage Books, 2006.

Ribeiro, Maria Thereza Rosa. *Controvérsias da questão social – liberalismo e positivismo na causa abolicionista no Brasil*. Porto Alegre: Zouk, 2012.

Rizzo, Ricardo. *Sobre rochedos movediços: deliberação e hierarquia no pensamento político de José de Alencar*. São Paulo: Fapesp/Hucitec, 2012.

Rocha Penalves, Antônio. *Abolicionistas brasileiros e ingleses: a coligação entre Joaquim Nabuco e a British and Foreign*. São Paulo: Ed. Unesp, 2008.

Rolim, I. E. (ed.). *A saga da abolição mossoroense*, Livro I. Ed. especial para o Acervo Virtual Oswaldo Lamartine de Faria, 2002.

Rugemer, Edward. *The Problem of Emancipation: The Caribbean Roots of the American Civil War*. Baton Rouge: Louisiana State University Press, 2008.

Saba, Roberto. A lei dos sexagenários e a derrota política dos abolicionistas no Brasil-Império. *História Social*, 14–15, 21–33, 2008.

Salles, Ricardo. *Guerra do Paraguai: escravidão e cidadania na formação do exército*. Rio de Janeiro: Paz e Terra, 1990.

As águas do Niágara. 1871: crise da escravidão e o ocaso saquarema. In K. Grinberg and R. Salles (eds.), *O Brasil imperial*, vol. III, *1870–1889*. Rio de Janeiro: Civilização Brasileira, 2009.

Santos, Francisco Martins dos. *História de Santos*. São Vicente: Caudex, 1986.

Santos, José Maria. *Os republicanos paulistas e a abolição*. São Paulo: Martins, 1942.

Santos, Wellington Barbosa dos. *Confederações abolicionistas no Maranhão na segunda metade do séc. XIX (1870–1888)*. São Luís, Universidade Estadual do Maranhão, Undergraduate thesis, 2008.

Sayers, R. S. *The Negro in Brazilian Literature*. New York: Hispanic Institute in the United States, 1956.

Schiavon, Carmem G. Burgert. A primeira Sociedade de Emancipação de Escravos do Brasil. Paper apresentado no 4° Encontro Escravidão e Liberdade no Brasil Meridional. 13–15 maio, Curitiba, 2009.

Schmidt, Afonso. *A marcha, romance da abolição*. São Paulo: Brasiliense, 1981.

Schmidt-Nowara, Christopher. *Empire and Anti-Slavery: Spain, Cuba, and Puerto Rico, 1833–1874*. Pittsburgh: University of Pittsburgh Press, 1999.

Schulz, John. *O exército na política. Origens da intervenção militar, 1850–1894*. São Paulo: Edusp, 1994.

Schwarcz, Lilia Moritz. *Retrato em branco e preto. Jornais, escravos e cidadãos em São Paulo no final do século XIX*. São Paulo: Companhia das Letras, 1987.

*As barbas do imperador. D. Pedro II, um monarca nos trópicos*. São Paulo: Companhia das Letras, 1998.

Dos males da dádiva: sobre as ambiguidades no processo da abolição brasileira. In Olívia Maria Gomes da Cunha and Flávio dos Santos Gomes (eds.), *Quase cidadão. Histórias e antropologias da pós-emancipação no Brasil*. Rio de Janeiro: Ed. da FGV, 2007.

# Bibliography

Schwarz, Roberto. *Ao vencedor as batatas. Forma literária e processo social.* São Paulo: Duas Cidades/Ed. 34, 2000.

Scott, Rebecca J. *Emancipação escrava em Cuba: a transição para o trabalho livre, 1860–1899.* Rio de Janeiro/Campinas: Paz e Terra/Ed. da Unicamp, 1991.

Silva, Eduardo. *As camélias do Leblon e a abolição da escravatura – uma investigação de história cultural.* São Paulo: Companhia das Letras, 2003.

*Resistência negra, teatro e abolição da escravatura.* Paper apresesentado na sessão Sociedade, Cultura e Poder no Império. 26ª reunião da Sociedade Brasileira de Pesquisa Histórica, 2006.

Fugas, revoltas e quilombos: os limites da negociação. In João José Reis and Eduardo Silva, *Negociação e conflito: a resistência negra no Brasil escravista.* São Paulo: Companhia das Letras, 2009.

Silva, Leonardo Dantas (ed.). *Cinquentenário da abolição em Pernambuco.* Catálogo da Exposição realizada no Teatro Santa Isabel de 13 a 31 de maio de 1938. Recife: Imprensa Oficial, 1939. Reimpressão fac-similar. In Leonardo Dantas Silva (ed.), *A abolição em Pernambuco.* Recife: Fundaj/ Massangana, 1988a.

*A imprensa e a abolição.* Recife: Fundaj/Massangana, 1988b.

*A abolição em Pernambuco.* Recife: Fundaj/Massangana, 1988c.

Silva, Rafael Santos da. Camélias e Revista Ilustrada: o movimento abolicionista em litografias de Angelo Agostini. XIII Encontro Regional de História – Anpuh, Rio de Janeiro, 2008.

Sinha, Manisha. *The Slave's Cause: A History of Abolition.* New Haven: Yale University Press, 2017.

Slenes, Robert. The Brazilian Internal Slave Trade, 1850–1888. Regional Economies, Slave Experience, and the Politics of a Peculiar Market. In Walter Johnson (ed.), *The Chattel Principle: Internal Slave Trades in the Americas.* New Haven: Yale University Press, 2004.

Snow, David and Benford, Robert. Master Frames and Cycles of Protest. In Aldon D. Morris and Carol McClurg Mueller (eds.), *Frontiers in Social Movement Theory.* New Haven: Yale University Press, 1992.

Framing Processes and Social Movements: An Overview and Assessment. *Annual Review of Sociology*, 26, 611–39, 2000.

Sodré, Nelson Werneck. *A história da imprensa no Brasil.* Rio de Janeiro: Civilização Brasileira, 1966.

Spitzer, Leo. *Lives in Between: Assimilation and Marginality in Austria, Brazil, West Africa 1780–1945.* Cambridge: Cambridge University Press, 1989.

Stamatov, Peter. Activist Religion, Empire, and the Emergence of Modern Long-Distance Advocacy Networks. *American Sociological Review*, 75, 607–28, 2010.

*The Origins of Global Humanitarianism: Religion, Empires, and Advocacy.* Cambridge: Cambridge University Press, 2013.

Steinberg, Marc. The Roar of the Crowd: Repertoires of Discourse and Collective Action among the Spitalfields Silk Weavers in Nineteenth-Century London. In Mark Traugott (ed.), *Repertoires and Cycles of Collective Action.* Durham: Duke University Press, 1995, pp. 57–88.

# Bibliography

Studart, Barão de. *Diccionario Bio-bibliographico Cearense, de 1910, 1913, 1915*, vols. 1, 2, 3. Fortaleza: Universidade Federal Cearense, Imprensa Universitária, 1980.

Summerhill, William R. *Party and Faction in the Imperial Brazilian Parliament.* Haber: Hoover Press, 2012.

*Inglorious Revolution: Institutions, Sovereign Debt, and Financial Underdevelopment in Imperial Brazil.* New Haven: Yale University Press, 2015.

Surwillo, Lisa. Representing the Slave Trader: Haley and the Slave Ship; or, Spain's Uncle Tom's Cabin, *PMLA*, 120(3), 2005.

Sussekind, Flora. As vítimas-algozes e o imaginário do medo. In Joaquim Manuel Macedo (ed.), *As vítimas-algozes. Quadros da escravidão.* Rio de Janeiro/São Paulo: Fundação Casa de Rui Barbosa/Scipione, 1991.

Suzuki, Hideaki. *Abolitions as a Global Experience.* Singapore: National University of Singapore Press, 2016.

Swidler, Ann. Cultural Power and Social Movements. In Hank Johnston and Bert Klandermans (eds.), *Social Movements and Culture.* Minneapolis: University of Minnesota Press, 1995, pp. 25–40.

*Talk of Love. How Culture Matters.* Chicago: University of Chicago Press, 2001.

Tarrow, Sidney. *Struggling to Reform: Social Movements and Policy Change During Cycles of Protest.* Center for International Studies, Cornell University, 1983.

Modular Collective Action and the Rise of the Social Movement: Why the French Revolution was not Enough. *Politics & Society*, 69–90, 21 Jan., 1993.

Cycles of Collective Action: Between Moments of Madness and the Repertoire of Contention. In Mark Traugott (ed.), *Repertoires and Cycles of Collective Action.* Durham: Duke University Press, 1995, pp. 89–116.

*Power in Movement. Social Movements and Contentious Politics.* Cambridge: Cambridge University Press, 1998.

*The New Transnational Activism.* Cambridge: Cambridge University Press, 2005.

Dynamics of Diffusion: Mechanisms, Institutions, and Scale Shift. In Rebecca Kolins Givan, Kenneth M. Roberts, Sarah A. Soule (eds.), *The Diffusion of Social Movements: Actors, Mechanisms, and Political Effects.* Cambridge: Cambridge University Press, 2010.

Temperley, Howard. Ideology of Antislavery. In David Eltis and James Walvin (eds.), *The Abolition of the Atlantic Slave Trade. Origins and Effects in Europe, Africa and the Americas.* Madison: University of Wisconsin Press, 1981.

Tilly, Charles. *From Mobilization to Revolution.* Boston: Wesley Publishing Co., 1978.

Contentious Repertoires in Great Britain, 1758–1834. *Social Science History*, 17, 253–80, 1993.

Social Movement as Historically Specific Clusters of Political Performances. *Berkeley Journal of Sociology*, 38, 1–30, 1993–1994.

*Social Movements 1768–2004.* London: Paradigm, 2004.

# Bibliography

Introduction to Part II: Invention, Diffusion, and Transformation of the Social Movement Repertoire. *European Review of History: Revue européenne d'histoire*, 12(2), 307–20, 2005.

*Regimes and Repertoires*. Chicago: University of Chicago Press, 2006.

*Contentious Performances*. Cambridge: Cambridge University Press, 2008.

Toplin, Robert Brent. Upheaval, Violence, and the Abolition of Slavery in Brazil: The Case of São Paulo. *The Hispanic American Historical Review*, 49(4), 1969.

*The Abolition of Slavery in Brazil*. New York: Atheneum, 1972.

Treece, David. *Exilados, aliados, rebeldes – O movimento indianista, a política indigenista e o Estado-nação imperial*. São Paulo: Nankin/Edusp, 2008.

Trindade, Alexandro Dantas. *André Rebouças. Um engenheiro do Império* (Coleção Pensamento Político). São Paulo: Hucitec, 2011.

Vainfas, Ronaldo. *Ideologia e escravidão*. Petrópolis: Vozes, 1986.

Escravidão, ideologias e sociedade. In Ciro Flamarion Cardoso (ed.). *Escravidão e abolição no Brasil: novas perspectivas*. Rio de Janeiro: Jorge Zahar, 1988.

*Antônio Vieira: jesuíta do rei*. São Paulo: Companhia das Letras, 2011.

Valdez, Diane. *A representação de infância nas obras pedagógicas do dr. Abílio Cesar Borges: o barão de Macahubas (1856–1891)*. Unicamp, Doctoral dissertation, 2006.

Valle, Daniel Simões do. *Intelectuais, espíritas e abolição da escravidão: os projetos de reforma na imprensa espírita (1867–1888)*. Universidade Federal Fluminense, Master's thesis, 2010.

Vampré, Spencer. *Memórias para a história da Academia de São Paulo*, vols. I and II. São Paulo: Saraiva, 1924.

Vetro, Gaspare Nello. *Antônio Carlos Gomes: Carteggi Italiani Raccolti e Commentati*. Rio de Janeiro: Cátedra, INL, 1982.

Vianna Filho, Luís. *A vida de Joaquim Nabuco*. São Paulo: Martins/MEC, 1969.

Vila-Matas, *A Brief History of Portable Literature*. Translated by Anne Mclean and Thomas Bunstead. New Directions. 1st edition, 2015.

Vilar, Enriqueta Vila and Vilar, Luisa Vila. La abolición en España en el siglo XIX. In *Los abolicionistas españoles. Siglo XIX*. Madrid: Ediciones de Cultura Hispánica, 1996.

Williams, Eric. *Capitalism and Slavery*. Chapel Hill: University of North Carolina, 1994.

Williams, Raymond. *Culture and Society. 1780–1950*. Anchor Books. New York: Doubleday, 1960.

Wood, Marcus. Creative Confusions: Angelo Agostini, Brazilian Slavery and the Rhetoric of Freedom. *Patterns of Prejudice*, 41(3–4), 2007.

Xavier, Janaina Silva. *Saneamento de Pelotas (1871–1915): o patrimônio sob o signo de modernidade e progresso*. Universidade Federal de Pelotas, Pelotas, Master's thesis, 2010.

# Index

2nd of July Liberating Society, The (Bahia), 35, 44, 68, 149, 209

7th of September Liberating Society, The (Bahia), 17, 42, 68, 116, 133, 155, 167, 208, 229

7th of November Club, The, 195

13th of March Liberating Society (Bahia), 67

15th Battalion, 165, 187, 191, 204, 221

27th of February Emancipatory Society, The, 292

"À memória de Tiradentes" (To the memory of Tiradentes) (José do Patrocínio), 111

*Abolicionismo, O* (Abolitionism) (Nabuco), 11, 195–8, 226, 253

*Abolicionista, O* (newspaper), 41, 43–4, 68, 155, 158, 160, 162, 166, 168, 172, 176, 198, 205, 261, 363–4

*Abolicionista do Amazonas, O* (newspaper), 205

*Abolicionista Español, El* (newspaper), 155, 159

Abolition Anthem, 133

Abolition of slavery in Brazil, 6 *see also* Golden Law (Lei Áurea, 1888)

Abolitionist Anthem (Goiânia), 133

Abolitionist Center of Porto Alegre, The, 206, 213, 255

Abolitionist Club of Commercial Sector Workers, The, 195

Abolitionist Club of Confederated Cooks and Caterers, The, 140

Abolitionist Club of Military Academy Cadets, The, 195

Abolitionist Club of Recife, The, 211, 297

Abolitionist Club of Riachuelo, The, 157, 167

Abolitionist Confederation, 1 *see also* CA (Confederação Abolicionista/ Abolitionist Confederation)

Abolitionist Congress (Manaus), 205

Abolitionist Congress (Rio de Janeiro), 193

abolitionist marches, 122, 201, 220–1, 252, 256, 262, 332, 340, 365

abolitionist moral repertoire, 14, 85, 88, 91–2, 100, 106, 136, 138, 196

Abolitionist Parliamentary Group (GPA), 274

abolitionist propaganda, 2, 119, 129, 154, 173, 196–7, 204, 239, 241, 249, 253, 315, 350, 360

abolitionist proselytism, 5, 17, 194, 365

abolitionist protests, 174, 220, 289, 363

abolitionist rallies, 14, 16, 50, 90, 111, 122, 179, 201, 221, 252, 262–3, 265, 283, 300, 305, 307, 322

abolitionist rallies, 14 *see also* meetings

abolitionist rhetoric, 91, 99–100, 120, 135, 146, 168, 196, 203, 206, 288

Abolitionist Society of Espírito Santo, The, 195

Abolitionist Society of Maranhão, The, 206

Abranches, Dunshee de, 200, 300

Academia Madrileña de Legislación y Jurisprudencia, 159

# Index

Academic Liberating Commission, The, 210

*Ação, reação, transação* (Action, Reaction, Transaction) (Rocha), 254

Acarape, 187, 204, 220, 298

ACE (Associação Central Emancipadora, The Central Emancipatory Association), 39, 44, 122, 126, 129–30, 133, 139–41, 144, 155, 157, 162, 164–5, 169, 172, 176, 193, 198, 364

Affonso, Almino, 166, 204, 207

Africa, 13, 29, 57, 132, 158, 161, 273, 343

Agostini, Angelo, 14, 87, 89, 137, 171, 278, 284, 309, 317

agrarianism, 97

agriculture, 11, 29, 35, 39, 71, 92, 97, 187, 196, 233, 241, 258, 272, 323, 331

*Aida* (Verdi's opera), 2–3, 18–19, 286

Aimoré Indians, 49

*Alabama, O* (newspaper), 208

Alagoas, 77, 80, 116, 185, 200, 293, 298–9

Alaska, 47

Albuquerque, Lourenço de, 255, 335

Alencar, José de, 30, 40, 48–9, 56, 58–9, 61–2, 64, 66, 91–2, 94, 96, 111–12, 134, 137, 144, 147–8, 199, 251, 258, 349

Alencastro, Antônio Pedro de, 157

Alliance and Temperance Mission (women's abolitionist associations), 180

Almeida, F., 200, 221

Almeida, Miguel Joaquim de, 259

Alonso, Angela, 9, 90, 97–8, 120, 145, 154, 158, 172, 175, 180, 206, 210, 265

Alves, Antônio de Castro, 43, 68–9, 92, 95–6, 132, 134, 141, 156, 163, 176, 260

Alves, Rodrigues, 312, 344

Amaral, José Correia do, 159, 163, 166, 169, 186, 227, 245

Amaral, Luís, 298

Amaral, Ubaldino do, 130, 157–8, 212, 215

Amazonas, state of, 41, 67, 77, 80, 141, 167, 171, 174, 181, 186, 202, 204, 206–7, 210–12, 223, 228, 239, 248–9, 254–5, 257, 260–1, 286, 294, 297–9, 359, 363–4

Amazonian Club, The, 207

América (Masonic lodge), 104

American Civil War (1861–65), 16, 32, 62, 64, 69, 149, 316, 320

Ancient Egypt, 2

Ancient Rome, 106

Andrada e Silva, José Bonifácio de, 28, 72, 99, 177, 192, 291

Andrade, Joaquim Bento de Sousa, 259

Anglo-American abolitionism, 5, 14, 27, 30, 42, 44, 93, 120–2, 129, 143, 162, 361

Anglo-Saxon abolitionism, 97, 198, 360

anticlericalism, 131, 188

antislavery brotherhoods, 121–2; *see also* Nossa Senhora dos Remédios Brotherhood

antislavery priests, 188

*Anti-Slavery Reporter*, 47, 162, 180, 189, 274

Anti-Slavery Society, 116 *see also* British and Foreign Anti-Slavery Society

*Apóstolo, O* (newspaper), 323

Aquiraz, 188

Aracaju, 201, 206, 244

Aracati, 298

Aranha, Temístocles, 173

Araraquara, 223, 313

Araripe Jr., Tristão de Alencar, 137, 183, 212, 227

Araújo, José Ferreira de, 112, 114, 192, 330

Argentina, 12, 31–2, 36, 38, 189

aristocracy, 4, 29, 36, 49, 51, 53, 57–8, 87–8, 107–8, 117–19, 139, 145, 154, 347

Aristotle, 57, 99

Arles, 25

Armed Forces of Brazil, 20, 189, 253, 306–7, 320, 330

Army of Brazil, 165, 223, 307, 314, 320, 324, 329, 333, 356

Asia, 13, 161

Assis Brasil, Francisco de, 223, 230, 255

Associação Central Protetora dos Emancipados (The Central Association for the Protection of Freed Slaves), 46, 126 *see also* ACE (Associação Central Emancipadora, The Central Emancipatory Association)

*Asteroide, O* (newspaper), 310, 363

*Ateneu, O* (The Atheneum) (Raul Pompeia), 34

Atibaia, 209, 304

## Index

431

Austria, 27
Ave Libertas (Hail Liberty), 140, 262, 270
Azevedo, Aluísio, 112, 114, 134, 137, 141, 300
Azevedo, Artur, 114, 134, 136, 300
Azevedo, Ciro, 300
Azevedo, José da Costa, 154

Bahia, 24, 29, 35, 37, 41, 44, 50, 54, 67, 77, 85, 104, 116, 125, 133, 141, 149, 172, 174, 200, 206–7, 209, 244–5, 259, 261, 279, 281, 285–6, 296, 298, 310, 323, 337, 346
Balaiada (political revolt of 1838–41), 24
Bananal, 344
"Bandido negro" (Black Bandit) (Castro Alves), 96
Barbosa, Clímaco, 176, 292
Barbosa, Rui, 60, 104, 169, 171–2, 182, 232, 236, 246, 250–1, 253, 259, 261, 267, 269, 274, 284, 288–9, 291, 296, 306, 320, 346, 349
Barcelos, Ramiro, 206, 259
Barral, Countess of, 191, 329
Barreto, Tobias, 134
Barros, Adolfo de, 156–7, 186
Barros, Antônio Moreira de, 245
Barros, José Júlio de Albuquerque, 255
Bastos, Aurélio Cândido Tavares, 32
Bastos, João Coelho, 284
Batista, Homero, 206
Baturité, 187
Bavarian colonies, 12, 31
beatings of slaves, 111, 287, 316, 329
Belém (Pará), 191, 201, 207, 262, 299–300, 332, 342
Belém do Descalvado, 302, 304, 313
Belgium, 36
Benedict, St., 322
Bergstresser, Rebecca B., 9, 139
Besouro, O (The Beetle) (newspaper), 113
Betances, Ramón, 160, 219
Bezerra de Menezes, Adolfo, 98, 169, 171, 183, 235, 279
Bibi (Maria Henriqueta, José do Patrocínio's wife), 111, 113, 141, 186–7
Bible, 57–8, 93, 305

Bilateral treaty banning the slave trade (Brazil/Great Britain, 1826), 28, 30, 99, 101, 212
Bittencourt Sampaio Club, The, 195
Bizet, Georges, 131
Black Books, 221
Black Guard, 347
Black Regulation, 281–2, 285–6, 296, 304, 325
Boa Viagem, 313
Bocaiúva, Quintino, 140, 177, 212, 258, 267, 281, 291, 306, 308, 320, 327, 333, 346
Bolivia, 27
boomerang method (fight internal resistance by garnering support abroad), 21, 150, 157–8, 162, 170, 215, 220, 358
Borges, Abílio, 21–2, 34, 36, 39, 41, 44, 50, 67–8, 95, 99, 103, 105, 120–1, 123–4, 132, 142, 150, 155, 158, 162–3, 165, 171, 202, 206, 208, 229, 321, 334
Borges, Frederico, 163, 165–6, 229, 279, 296
Borges, Pedro, 165
Borges da Fonseca, Paulino Nogueira, 243
Bourdieu, Pierre, 86, 145
Braga, Amélio, 134
Brandão Jr., Francisco, 97
Brasil, O (newspaper), 228, 243, 283
Brazil, Tomás Pompeu de Sousa, 172, 259
Brazil Bank, 130
Brazilian Anti-Slavery Society, The, see also SBCE (Sociedade Brasileira Contra a Escravidão/Brazilian Anti-Slavery Society)
Brazilian Bar Association, 33, 74, 174
Brazilian currency, 76
Brazilian Dramatic Conservatory, 136
Brazilian episcopacy, 321
Brazilian Historical and Geographical Institute, 36, 348
Brazilian Orient Masonic Lodge, The, 195
Brazilian population, 33, 89
Brébant, Le (Paris), 219
Brest, 25
Brighton, 180
British and Foreign Anti-Slavery Society, 32–3, 35, 37, 45, 63, 116, 150, 153, 155, 160–1, 180, 199, 219, 261, 274, 311, 321

## Index

British colonies, 161, 261
British Commonwealth, 295
British Empire, 27, 237
Broglie, Albert de, Duke of, 37, 63
Brotas, 313
Brown, John, 105–6, 301, 312, 318
Buarque de Holanda, Sérgio, 40, 125, 186, 247
Buenos Aires, 342
Bulhões, Antônio Félix, 133
Bulhões, Leopoldo de, 172, 214, 255
Bulicioff, Nadina, 1–2, 4, 19
bullets, time of, 20–1, 271, 315, 318
*Burlesque Quatrains, Getulino's First* (Luís Gama), 95
Buxton, Thomas, 162, 237, 321

CA (Confederação Abolicionista/ Abolitionist Confederation), 1–2, 19, 138, 184, 188, 195–7, 199–200, 202, 207–8, 213, 217–18, 220, 222–3, 226, 239, 240, 243, 248, 252–3, 255, 255n, 259, 269, 273–4, 277, 279, 281, 283–7, 289, 291, 293, 296–7, 303, 310–11, 315, 319, 326, 333–4, 340, 347, 349, 364n
CA Manifesto, The, 195–9, 202, 213, 216, 226, 268
Cabanagem (political revolt of 1835–40), 24
*Cabrião, O* (The Gadfly) (newspaper), 87
Caçapava, 310
Cachoeira (Bahia), 188, 310
Caiaphases (abolitionist group), 288, 301–3, 314
Cain (biblical character), 57
*Ça-Ira* (newspaper), 173
camellia (symbol of the abolitionist movement), 2, 133, 221, 301, 303, 334, 349 *see also* flowers
Campinas, 29, 125, 174, 191, 304, 312, 315, 324, 327
Campos (Rio de Janeiro), 109, 288, 324, 331
Campos, Américo de, 87, 104, 258
Campos, Bernardino de, 104, 259
Campos, Martinho, 66, 151, 153, 170–1, 175, 178, 182, 213, 222, 230, 235, 241–2, 244, 251, 309
Canaan (biblical character), 57
Canada, 184, 295

Cantagalo, 53, 83, 324
capitalism and slavery, 8, 28, 93, 346
Capivari, 304, 313–14
capoeiras (black street fighters), 224, 329
Cardim, Gomes, 132
Carigé, Eduardo, 208, 285
Carlos de Lacerda Abolitionist Club, The, 257, 289
Carlos Gomes Club, The, 134, 195
*Carmen* (Bizet's opera), 131
Carneiro Monteiro, Severino Ribeiro, 171
"Carta às senhoras" (Letter addressed to the Ladies of Bahia) (Castro Alves), 163
*Cartas de Erasmo* (Erasmus' Letters) (Alencar), 59
Carvalho, Dias, 48
Carvalho, José Carlos de, 156
Cassal, Barros, 206
Castilhos, Júlio de, 206, 255, 258
Castro, Antônio Bento de Sousa e, 21, 176, 209–10, 221, 288, 291, 293, 296, 305, 322, 325, 333, 358
Castro, Apulco de, 223, 227, 244, 289
Castro, Fernando, 298
Castro, Francisca da Silva, 287, 316
Catholic Church/Catholicism, 14, 42, 93, 97–8, 121, 188, 308, 321, 333, 348, 360
"cativo, O" (The Captive) (Mendonça), 42
Caxias, Duke of, 115
CCE (Comissão Central Emancipadora/ Central Emancipation Commission), 182, 193, 262
Ceará, 11, 18, 22, 25, 29, 41, 67, 80, 113, 119, 132, 141, 163, 165–6, 168, 171, 173–4, 183, 185–90, 194, 197, 199–202, 204–6, 208, 210–12, 214–15, 217–19, 221–3, 227, 229, 245, 248–9, 254–5, 257–8, 260–1, 279, 286, 292, 294–5, 297–301, 304, 310, 320, 332, 342, 346, 349, 359, 364
Celso Jr., Afonso, 193, 222, 248, 292, 323, 335
Census of 1872 (Brazil), 33, 89, 121
Centenary of abolition (1988), 8
Central Emancipation Commission, 182 *see also* CCE (Comissão Central Emancipadora/Central Emancipation Commission)

## Index

Central Emancipation Commission of Recife, The, 256, 262
Central Emancipatory Association, The, 126 *see also* ACE (Associação Central Emancipadora)
Central Immigration Society, 224, 235, 258
Central School (Rio de Janeiro), 25–6
Chalhoub, Sidney, 8, 33, 102, 115
Chamber of Deputies, 6
change, rhetoric of, 15, 17, 91, 100–1, 138, 155
Charing Cross Hotel (London), 161, 179
Chatham, Earl of, 237
Chaves, Bruno Gonçalves, 201
Chico (slave), 26
Chico da Matilde (Francisco José do Nascimento), 166, 187
children as slaves, 105, 140, 151
children born to slave mothers, liberation of, 17 *see also* Free Womb Law (1871)
Chile, 27, 32
China, 5, 67, 117
Chinese workers, 117, 149, 158, 227, 244, 345
Christ, 288 *see also* Jesus Christ
Christianity, 65, 93
Christie, William, 30
*Cidade do Rio, A* (newspaper), 6, 281, 285, 288, 308, 311, 319, 326, 333, 341, 347, 364
civil and political rights, 346, 364
civil disobedience, 4, 19, 21, 217, 249, 286, 294, 296, 305, 307, 356, 365
civil servants, 139, 166, 184, 189, 244, 262, 305
Clapp, João, 2, 130, 138–9, 141, 143, 157–8, 183, 188, 193–5, 210, 216–17, 220, 239, 255, 257, 268–9, 280, 285, 287, 289, 291, 293, 303, 310–11, 318, 332, 334, 341, 346
Clarkson, Thomas, 162, 200, 237, 318
Clube da Reforma (Reform Club), 88
Clube do Cupim, 265 *see also* Termites Club
Clube Radical Paulistano, 87
Clube Tiradentes, 195
Coari, 204
Codajás, 204
Coelho Neto, 134, 286, 308, 333, 347

coffee plantations, 32, 40, 53, 104, 125, 170, 174, 183, 241, 243–4, 247, 258, 266, 275, 281, 286, 303, 313, 315, 323, 325
Colégio Abílio (Rio de Janeiro), 37
Colégio Pedro II (Rio de Janeiro), 146
Collectivist Socialist Party, 124
Colombia, 12, 31–2
*Colombo* (Araújo de Porto Alegre), 58
Commercial Abolitionist Center, The, 131
Commercial Euterpean Society of the Devil's Lieutenants, The (carnival block), 130, 218
Commission for the Abolition of Slavery in the French Colonies, 161
communism, 71, 250–3, 264, 283
compassion, rhetoric of, 15, 50, 91, 97, 99–100, 130, 132, 135, 138, 146, 151, 155, 164, 196, 229, 250, 263, 320, 359
Comte, Auguste, 98
Conde D'Eu R W (company), 179
Confederate States (USA), 316
Confeitaria Pascoal, 111, 114, 172
Conferências Emancipadoras (Emancipation Conferences), 126
Congress of Planters (Rio de Janeiro), 117
Conrad, Robert, 8–9, 12, 44, 67, 77, 126, 138, 174, 185, 205, 210, 232, 243, 286, 293, 297, 302, 316, 324, 356
Conservative Party, 4, 17, 19–20, 25, 27, 33, 40, 47, 49, 52, 54, 63, 65, 70, 83, 115, 147–8, 172, 176, 208–9, 247, 250 *see also* "Emperrados" (The Hardliners, anti-change Conservatives)
Constant, Benjamin, 33, 139
Constitutive Assembly (1823), 28
*Cora, a filha de Agar: drama abolicionista em 4 atos* (Cora, Daughter of Agar: An Abolitionist Drama in 4 Acts) (Ribeiro da Silva), 136
Cordeiro, João, 163–4, 172, 187, 202, 208, 215, 299, 318, 332, 346
*Corja opulenta: drama abolicionista em 3 atos* (Opulent Mob: An Abolitionist Drama in 3 Acts) (Nunes), 135–6, 141, 241
*Coroa e a emancipação do elemento servil, Estudos sobre a emancipação dos escravos no Brasil* (Silva Neto), 98
Correia, João Artur de Sousa, 322

434        *Index*

*Corsário, O* (newspaper), 223
Costa, Gaspar da, 298
Costa, Pereira da, 206
Costa Rica, 27
Cotegipe, Baron of, 12, 19, 22, 30, 40, 47,
    53, 64, 66, 115, 119, 133, 170, 176,
    208–9, 213, 235, 247, 271, 276–7,
    279–86, 290–1, 294–5, 297, 301,
    304–6, 308–9, 311–12, 317, 321, 323,
    325, 327–32, 336–7, 344–6, 348, 350,
    360
Council of State, 24, 38, 47, 54, 56, 59, 69,
    83, 191, 247, 249–50, 328
Court, The, 22 *see also* Rio de Janeiro
Cruz e Sousa (poet), 134, 286
Cuba, 13, 31, 41, 48–51, 122, 149, 158,
    160, 162, 167, 178, 233, 283, 290, 360
Cubatão, 314
Cuiabá, 262, 322
Culinary Confederation Abolitionist Club,
    140
Cunha, João Lustosa da, 178 *see also*
    Paranaguá, Marquis of
Cunha, Joaquim Firmino de Araújo, 316
Cunha, José Mariano Carneiro da, 171,
    178, 265, 279
Curitiba, 201, 294, 313
Customs Office, 26

D'Eu, Count, 45–6, 55, 179, 308, 328–9
Dantas Project, 232–3, 241, 251–2, 254,
    258, 261
Dantas Reform, 19, 234, 238, 240–1,
    250–2, 270, 273, 278, 281, 287, 323,
    338
Dantas, Manuel de Sousa, 2, 11–12, 19, 50,
    133, 149, 167, 171, 181, 203, 228,
    231, 233, 235–7, 239–43, 245, 247–9,
    251–5, 257–8, 261–2, 264–5, 267–8,
    272, 274–7, 279–80, 286, 289–91,
    294, 297, 301, 305, 309, 311, 313–14,
    321, 323, 332–3, 335–7, 340–1, 343,
    345, 350, 356
Dantas, Rodolfo, 157, 182, 186, 198, 230,
    237, 245–6, 259, 266
Davis, David Brion, 4, 57, 93
Del-Negro's (opera company), 131
*Democratic Evolutionist Propaganda*
    (Rural Democracy – Freedom of
    Conscience, Free Trade) (Rebouças),
    344

*Demônio familiar, O* (The House Devil)
    (Alencar), 59, 94, 96, 137, 147
Denmark, 29, 71
*Desenho linear ou Elementos de geometria
    prática popular* (Linear Design or
    Elements of Practical Popular
    Geometry) (Borges), 124
Desterro (Florianópolis), 134, 201, 262
*Diabo Coxo* (The Lame Devil) (newspaper),
    87, 104
Diamantina, 332
*Diário da Bahia* (newspaper),
    230, 237, 261
*Diário do Rio* (newspaper), 69
Dias, Sátiro de Oliveira, 202, 205, 210–11,
    218, 222–3, 229, 255, 260, 269
direct-vote regimen, 168–9
Diretório dos Cinco (Board of Five/The
    Club of the Dead, youthful
    organization), 300
Docks Company, 45, 118
Donizetti, Gaetano, 129
Doria, Franklin Américo de Menezes,
    172
Douglass, Frederick, 108, 120, 123,
    144, 152, 180, 184, 200, 215,
    237, 318
Drescher, Seymour, 4–5, 12, 31, 93, 120–1,
    138, 352
Duarte, Urbano, 136
Durocher, Maria Josephina Mathilde, 69
Dutch Guiana, 12

Ecuador, 32
Eduarda (slave), 287
Egydio (slave), 183
elections of 1881, 167, 179
elections of 1884, 214, 236, 258, 260–1,
    264, 305
electoral college, 168, 305
electoral reform, 55, 73, 149, 169, 228, 261,
    279
electoral system, 55, 115, 149
Emancipation Fund, 56, 83, 104, 132–3,
    142, 152, 173, 178, 193, 203, 205,
    213, 227, 233, 243, 265, 274, 327
Emancipation Proclamation (USA, 1863),
    31
Emancipation Savings of Piauí, The, 208
Emancipatory Central of the City of Recife,
    The, 208

# Index

435

Emancipatory Society of Pernambuco, The, 67
Emília (Rebouças' slave), 46
"Emperrados" (The Hardliners, anti-change
 Conservatives), 17, 40, 48, 70, 83–4,
 169, 329 *see also* Conservative Party
Empire of Brazil, 4, 7, 10–11, 19, 24, 26, 37,
 44, 49–50, 53, 56, 58, 66, 72, 76, 78,
 82, 84, 90, 111, 121, 123, 127, 133,
 141, 144, 153, 173, 187, 192, 202,
 205, 208, 219, 239, 271, 281, 283,
 285, 294–5, 301, 312, 328, 331, 338,
 341, 349, 351, 360 *see also* Pedro II,
 D. (Emperor of Brazil), Second Reign
Empyreo Theater (Rio de Janeiro), 311
engaged art, 134–6, 138
engineering faculties, 25, 89, 92, 119, 172
England, 1, 12, 27, 31, 36, 71, 75, 99, 101,
 121, 158, 160–2, 168, 170, 180, 183,
 200, 226, 328
Enlightenment, The, 15, 57, 93, 99
escapes, 295, 298–300, 302, 304, 312, 321,
 365 *see also* fugitive slaves
*escrava Isaura, A* (Isaura, The slave)
 (Guimarães), 95, 136
*Escravatura no Brasil precedida de um
 artigo sobre e a agricultura e
 colonização no Maranhão, A* (Slavery
 in Brazil Preceded by an Article on
 Agriculture and Colonization in
 Maranhão) (Brandão Jr.), 97
*Escravidão, A* (Slavery) (Nabuco), 146
*Escravidão examinada à luz da Santa Bíblia*
 (Slavery Examined in the light of the
 Holy Bible) (apocryphal representation
 to Parliament), 93
*Escravidão no Brasil e as medidas que
 convém tomar para extingui-la sem
 dano para a nação, A* (Slavery in Brazil
 and the Measures to be Taken to
 Eradicate it Without Harming the
 Nation) (Bezerra de Menezes), 98
*Escravidão no Brasil: ensaio histórico,
 jurídico, social, A* (Slavery in Brazil:
 A Historical, Juridical and Social Essay)
 (Perdigão Malheiros), 32
*escravo, O* (The Slave) (Gomes' opera), 2,
 350
*escravocrata, O* (The Slavocrat) (Duarte and
 Azevedo), 136
"Escravocratas" (Slavocrats) (Cruz e
 Sousa), 134

*escravos, Os* (The Slaves) (Castro Alves), 96,
 244
*espelho, O* (The Mirror) (Machado de
 Assis), 136
Espírito Santo, Justina do (freed slave, José
 do Patrocínio's mother), 109
Espírito Santo, state of, 41, 67, 77, 80, 174,
 185, 194, 243, 247, 256, 295, 297, 313
*estadista do império, Um* (An Imperial
 Statesman) (Nabuco), 6
Europe, 5, 13, 25, 38–9, 56, 82, 91–2, 97,
 107–8, 120, 122, 163, 168, 199,
 215–16, 226, 307, 321, 327, 334, 360
European immigrant labor, 150, 196, 233,
 345 *see also* immigration/immigrants to
 Brazil
Eusébio de Queirós Law (1850), 28, 35
Executive Power, 38, 149, 204, 210, 281,
 317, 331, 366
export-agriculture, 139, 196
ex-slaves, 20, 29, 38, 69, 86, 175, 215–16,
 234, 260, 274, 337, 346, 349, 351 *see
 also* freed slaves

Falcão, Aníbal, 158, 173, 256, 263, 299
Falcão, Júlio, 299, 301
*família Salazar, A* (The Salazars) (Duarte
 and Azevedo), 136
Farias, Antônio, 298
farmers, 29, 85, 113, 234, 303, 313, 315,
 323 *see also* landowners/
 landownership, latifundia
Farroupilha (political revolt of 1835–45), 24
*Faust* (Gounod's opera), 131
*Federação, A* (newspaper), 206, 259, 261
federalism, 193, 206, 229, 350
Fênix Theater Company, 68
Ferreira de Menezes Abolitionist Center,
 The, 195
*ferrões, Os* (The Barbs) (magazine), 112
Figueira, Andrade, 56, 63–4, 66, 73, 235,
 241, 244, 246, 251, 257, 275, 326, 335
flogging of slaves, 37 *see also* beatings of
 slaves, torture of slaves
Flotow, Friedrich von, 129
flowers, 2, 4, 18–21, 50, 80, 130–1, 133,
 141, 143–4, 165, 183, 205, 211, 217,
 220–1, 224, 239, 256, 267, 270, 287,
 291, 294, 296, 315, 320, 332–3, 337,
 339, 341–2, 365 *see also* camellia
 (symbol of the abolitionist movement)

436 *Index*

Fluminense Casino, 224
Fluminense Imperial Typographic
 Association, 126
Fluminense Library, 326
Fonseca, Antônio Henrique da, 223
Fonseca, Aquino da, 200, 221
Fonseca, Demerval da, 112
Fonseca, Manuel Deodoro da, Marshal,
 320
Fonseca, Nuno Alves da, 298
Forensic Abolitionist Center, The, 212
Fortaleza (Ceará), 164–5, 167, 186–7, 190,
 193, 198, 201, 203–4, 214, 217–18,
 220–1, 256, 262, 299–300, 306, 342,
 364
Fortaleza Trade Association, 163
Fragoso, Arlindo, 200, 221
France, 1, 4, 27, 29, 31, 36, 71, 160, 162,
 168, 180, 250, 337, 342
Franklin, Benjamin, 48
Franklin, Leocádio Gomes, 183
free Africans, 28, 212 *see also* transatlantic
 trade of Africans to Brazil, prohibition
 of (1831)
free labor, 8, 28, 34–5, 55, 69, 97–8, 100,
 117, 156, 233
Free Womb Law (1871), 7, 13, 17, 33,
 56, 64, 67, 76, 79, 81, 88, 90,
 96–7, 102–4, 114–16, 123, 127,
 135, 144–6, 149–52, 155, 163,
 165, 176, 178, 180–1, 206, 212,
 227, 232, 234, 240, 245–8, 251,
 273, 277, 281–3, 290, 330, 346,
 349, 354, 360
freed slaves, 13, 84, 98, 109, 134, 142, 146,
 164, 194, 232–3, 251, 264, 326,
 344–5, 347, 365
freedmen, 69, 77, 191, 239, 265, 272, 323,
 342, 345–6
French abolitionists, 60, 68, 105, 160
French colonies, 37, 161
French Foreign Affairs Ministry, 37
French Revolution (1789), 61, 129, 164,
 253, 327
French Society for the Abolition of Slavery,
 37
Freyre, Gilberto, 91, 125
Friburgo, 269
Frick, João Driesel, 69, 318
Fugitive Slave Act (USA), 13, 282, 296, 316,
 360

fugitive slaves, 152, 183–4, 222, 282–3,
 292, 298, 300–4, 307, 310, 314–15,
 320, 322, 325, 331, 359, 371 *see also*
 escapes

Galvão, Argemiro, 206
Gama, Chichorro da, 48
Gama, Luís Gonzaga Pinto da, 7, 21–2,
 85–8, 90, 92–3, 95, 99, 101–2, 104–7,
 110–11, 115–16, 120, 133, 135, 137,
 139, 142–3, 146, 152, 157, 164,
 172–3, 175–7, 182, 196, 207, 209,
 212–13, 215, 217, 221, 254, 256,
 259, 279, 284–5, 287–9, 292, 296,
 301, 312, 318, 322, 341, 347, 351,
 358
Garcia, José Mariano, 302
Garrison, William, 157, 162, 237, 318,
 321
*Gazeta da Tarde, A* (newspaper), 6, 34, 89,
 114, 120, 123, 126, 129, 137, 141–2,
 144, 154, 156, 160, 166, 172, 176,
 182–4, 187, 191, 194, 198, 204,
 208–9, 212, 215, 222, 236, 244, 266,
 281, 287, 295, 303, 364
*Gazeta de Notícias, A* (newspaper), 6,
 89, 98, 112–13, 140, 150, 173,
 237, 326
*Gazeta do Povo* (newspaper), 106, 175,
 311
*Gazetinha* (newspaper), 172
geopolitics of slavery, 261
George, Henry, 226, 251
Germany, 36
Ginásio Baiano (school), 36, 42–3, 163
Ginásio Theater (Rio de Janeiro), 165
*Gioconda, La* (Ponchielli's opera), 1
Gladstone, W. E., 226, 251, 311
Glicério, Francisco, 259, 292
*Globo, O* (newspaper), 119, 140, 147, 172,
 212
Glória (Rio de Janeiro neighborhood),
 123
Goffman, Erving, 13, 108, 196
Goiânia, 133, 332
Goiás, 77, 80, 133, 172–3, 185, 214, 255–6,
 260, 293, 298–9, 322
Góis e Vasconcelos, Zacarias de, 33, 39, 41,
 45, 47–8, 50, 78, 88, 115, 148, 229,
 276
Gold Coast, The, 12, 31, 370

# Index

Golden Books, 183, 188, 205, 207, 215, 221, 255, 286, 326
Golden Law (Lei Áurea, 1888), 6, 336, 338, 344
Gomes, Carlos, 2, 49–50, 107, 125–6, 134, 218, 349, 351
Gomes, Flávio, 295
Gonzaga, Chiquinha, 126, 131, 141
Gounod, Charles, 131
Grand Opera House (New York), 108
Granja (Ceará), 188
Grant, Ulysses S., 108
Great Britain, 27–9, 35
Grey, Charles, Count, 63, 237
Grinberg, Keila, 27, 101, 104
GT, 114, 177–8, 184, 203–4, 208, 210, 212
     see also Gazeta da Tarde,
     A (newspaper)
Guarani, O (Alencar), 51, 58, 199
Guarani, O (Gomes' opera), 49–50, 125, 132, 218, 348, 350
Guatemala, 27
Guimarães, Bernardo, 95
Gusmão, João Manuel Carlos de, 288
Gutenberg Abolitionist Club, The, 142, 195
Gymnasio, O (newsletter), 36

habeas corpus, systematic use of, 101, 103, 311, 364
Haiti, 13, 27, 64, 96, 98, 120, 211, 320
"Haitianism" (the fear of slave revolt), 64
Ham (biblical character), 57n
harboring fugitives, crime of, 106 see also safe houses for runaway slaves
Hardliners, 40 see also "Emperrados" (The Hardliners, anti-change Conservatives)
Hawaii, 12, 31
Henry George. Nationalization of the Land, Appreciation of Land Monopoly Abolition Propaganda in England (pamphlet), 226
Herdeiros de Caramuru, Os (Caramuru's Heirs) (Jaguaribe Filho), 137
higher-education reforms, 89
Hilliard, Henry, 156–8
Hino da Cearense (Anthem of The Liberating Society of Ceará), 132
Hispanic abolitionists, 122, 143
Historia abreviada de la literatura portátil (A Brief History of Portable Literature) (Vila-Matas), 199

Holland, 29, 71
Homem de Melo, Baron, 292, 305, 348
Honduras, British, 27
Hotel Bragança (Petrópolis), 319
Hotel do Globo (Rio de Janeiro), 254
Hotel dos Estrangeiros (Foreigners' Hotel, Rio de Janeiro), 157, 162
Hugo, Victor, 130, 217, 219
Hume, David, 57

Icó, 187
illegal enslavements, 212
illiterate people as disenfranchised voters, 168, 261
immigration/immigrants to Brazil, 32, 35, 41, 45, 67, 117, 142, 150, 196, 227, 229, 233, 247, 274, 323, 347
Imperial capital, 110 see also Rio de Janeiro
Imperial elite, 6, 17, 32, 34, 49, 64–5, 107, 123, 135, 223, 308, 350
indemnification to slave owners, 20, 71, 76, 79, 197, 207, 230, 232, 234, 243, 252, 258, 260, 268, 273, 335, 345, 348, 350
     see also slave owners
Independence of Brazil (1822), 28, 41, 44, 72, 99, 151, 155, 168, 177, 255, 334
India, 12, 31
Indianist literature, 147, 349
Indians, 49
industrialization of Brazil, 97, 253
ingénus (freed under the Free Womb Law), 273, 323 see also Free Womb Law (1871)
International Abolitionist Association (Paris), 47
interprovincial slave trade, 30, 139, 179, 186, 193, 208, 231, 234, 275, 280
Invalid Boys Asylum, 132
Ipioca, 166
Iran, 5
Ireland, 35, 226, 251
Isabel, Princess, 8, 59, 307–8, 321, 328–30, 334, 338, 347, 350
Itaboraí, Viscount of, 38, 40–1, 46, 48, 50, 52–3, 64, 74, 78, 84, 102, 148, 276
Itacoatiara, 204
Italy, 36, 218, 321
Itapira, 316
Itu, 314

Jabaquara Quilombo, 292, 302, 314
Jacareí, 223, 310, 324, 332

438 *Index*

Jaguaribe Filho, Domingos, 137, 156
Jaguaribe, Domingos, 171, 181, 188, 198, 227, 323
Jamaica, 31
Japan, 5
Jardim, Silva, 309, 320, 327, 333, 348
Jaú, 324
Jequitinhonha, Viscount of, 33, 35, 75
Jesus Christ, 93, 288, 322
Joana (slave), 287
João Carpinteiro (slave), 103
Joaquim Nabuco Abolitionist Fund, The, 195
"Joaquim Nabuco's error: the eclipse of patriotism" (pro-slavery pamphlet), 282
John Bull (codename for Sancho Pimentel), 237
*Jornal do Commercio* (newspaper), 54, 71, 77, 113, 127, 154, 170, 198, 214, 236, 254, 269, 283, 322
*Jornal do Recife* (newspaper), 299
José do Patrocínio Club, The, 141
José do Patrocínio Emancipation Fund, The, 142, 195
journalists, 17, 89, 113, 139, 155, 157, 172, 180, 184, 216, 219, 254, 262, 330 *see also* press
*Juanita* (play), 222
judicial activism, 8, 103, 120, 164, 176, 207, 212, 285, 358
Judiciary Power, 8, 38, 55, 213, 317, 322, 329
Júlia (Rebouças' slave), 46
Justina (José do Patrocínio's mother), 109 *see also* Espírito Santo, Justina do
Juvêncio (slave), 132

Kansas, 318
Kant, Immanuel, 57
Kardec, Allan, 98
Ku Klux Klan, 316
Koseritz, Carl von, 224

*Lábaro, O* (college paper), 111
labor law regulations, 34, 346
Labor Leasing Act (1879), 117, 233
Labra y Cadrana, Rafael María de, 158–9
Lacerda, Carlos de, 111, 228, 293, 318, 332

Ladies of the Amazon Liberating Society, The, 205
Lages, J., 298
Lagos (Nigeria), 343
Lamoreaux, A. J., 157
Lampedusa, Giuseppe Tomasi di, 70
Land Act (Ireland, 1881), 226
land tax, 137, 150, 152, 227, 240, 281, 347
"Land Tax applied to Slave Emancipation" (Rebouças), 154
landowners/landownership, 29, 53, 64, 116, 139, 147, 179, 196, 215, 228, 233, 241, 247, 249, 253–4, 264, 266, 309, 324, 327, 344, 346 *see also* farmers
latifundia, 113, 137, 196–7, 224, 233, 263, 336
*latifúndios, Os* (Those of the Latifundia) (Rebouças' novel), 137
Law Faculty (Recife), 134, 208, 256, 297, 306
Law Faculty (São Paulo), 43, 52, 206, 209
Law of 1831, 101 *see also* transatlantic trade of Africans to Brazil, prohibition of (1831)
Law of 1850 (ultimate prohibition to the transatlantic slave trade), 28 *see also* Eusébio de Queirós Law (1850)
Law of 1871 (liberating children born to slave mothers), 7 *see also* Free Womb Law (1871)
Law of 1885 (emancipation of elderly slaves), 13 *see also* Saraiva/Cotegipe Sexagenarian Law (1885)
Law of 1888 (abolition of slavery in Brazil), 6 *see also* Golden Law (Lei Áurea, 1888)
Lawyers Against Slavery Club, The, 212
Leblon Quilombo, 218, 334, 349
Legislative Power, 63, 69, 78–9, 82, 88, 181, 214, 258, 356, 359, 366
Leite, Eufrásia Teixeira, 146, 170
Leo XIII, Pope, 321
*Leopard, The* (Giuseppe Tomasi di Lampedusa), 70
"Letter addressed to the Ladies of Bahia" (Castro Alves), 68
Lhardy Restaurant (Madrid), 159
Liberal Center (moderate Liberals), 41 *see also* Liberal Party

## Index

Liberal Party, 2, 16, 18, 20, 25, 32, 54, 83, 86, 98, 102, 116, 150, 153, 157, 167, 172–3, 182, 191, 202, 229, 238, 260–1, 323
liberal professionals, 88, 139, 163, 168, 216
Liberating Society of Aracaju, The, 206, 244
Liberating Society of Bahia, The, 208, 218, 285
Liberating Society of Ceará, The, 163 *see also* SCL (Sociedade Cearense Libertadora/Liberating Society of Ceará)
Liberating Society of Pernambuco, The, 208
Liberation Hymn, The, 218
*Liberator, The* (American newspaper), 237
Liberator's Anthem, The, 165
Liberia, creation of, 69
*Libertador (Liberator)* (newspaper), 164, 167, 200
Lima, Alcides, 173, 206
Lima, João Antonio Ribeiro de, 302
Limeira, 313
Lincoln, Abraham, 34, 105–6, 155, 157, 237
literacy in Brazil, rate of, 121, 142
Literary Essays Society, 126
lobbying, 5, 17–18, 21, 42, 44–6, 107, 117, 120, 173, 182, 354, 358
Lobo, Aristides, 193, 195
Lobo, Gusmão, 156–7, 162, 172, 190, 237, 266
London, 18, 37, 58–9, 107, 148, 154, 161, 170–1, 179–80, 182, 189, 195, 217, 219–21, 250, 261, 266, 270, 342
Lorena, 313
Lower House, 19, 30, 39–40, 44, 47–8, 53, 56, 60–1, 65, 70–2, 74, 77–8, 82–3, 157–8, 167–8, 171, 179–80, 191, 212, 234–5, 239, 241, 247, 249–50, 252, 258, 260, 267–8, 335
Luís Gama Emancipation Savings, The, 175
lundu (Brazilian dance), 131
Luso-Brazilian Abolitionist Society, The, 223–4
Lynch Law (USA), 316
lynching, 317–18, 324, 366

Macaé, 113
Macaúbas, Baron of, 36, 142
Macedo, Joaquim Manuel de, 96

Maceió, 200–1, 221, 262
Machado, Ângelo Pinheiro, 206
Machado, Maria Helena, 295
Machado de Assis, 112, 121, 123, 136, 258, 271–2, 286, 302, 326, 341, 343
Madagascar, 12, 31
Madrid, 31, 122, 155, 158, 160
Mafra, Silva, 269
Magalhães, José de Seixas, 194, 291
Magalhães, Valentim, 134
Mahin, Luísa (African freewoman), 85
Majority of the Emperor, declaration of, 28 *see also* Pedro II, D. (Emperor of Brazil)
Malê Revolt (Bahia, 1835), 85
Mamigonian, Beatriz G., 28, 103–4
Manacapuru, 204
Manaus, 125, 167, 202, 204, 211, 239, 256, 262, 299
Manicoré, 204
manumissions, 2, 18, 32, 34, 42, 44, 46, 48, 57, 59, 69, 73, 77, 102, 104–5, 116, 124, 132–4, 142, 152, 163–4, 183–4, 187–8, 190–1, 209, 233, 240, 253, 256, 262, 265, 273, 285, 293, 302, 324, 365
Maranguape, 188
Maranhão, 24–5, 41, 67, 80, 97, 134, 172–4, 185, 200, 206, 260, 293, 295, 297–8, 300, 332, 364
Maranhão Abolitionist Arts Center, 300
*marche aux flambeaux*, 294, 365
Marinho, Saldanha, 156–7, 169, 205
*Marseillaise, La* (national anthem of France), 129
Marseille, 25
*Martha* (Flotow's opera), 129
Martins Jr., 173, 256, 299
Martins, Francisco da Rocha, 223
Martins, Silveira, 206, 323
masonry, 104, 175, 195, 205
Matias (slave), 300
Mato Grosso, 80, 133, 174, 178, 256, 295, 298, 318, 344
Matos, João Paulo Gomes de, 195
Mauá, Viscount of, 118
Mauritius, 27
maxixe (Brazilian dance), 131
McAdam, Doug, 16, 20, 41, 90, 185, 293, 320, 354
Mecejana, 188

# Index

Medical Faculty (Bahia), 35
Medical Faculty (Rio de Janeiro), 69, 110, 112, 139, 141, 149
Medical School Liberating Society, The, 195
meetings, 14, 35, 66, 72, 111, 120, 130, 133, 180, 194, 200, 220–1, 262–3, 283, 298, 309–10, 327, 365–6 *see also* abolitionist rallies
Melo, Alfredo Vieira de, 298
Mendes, Raimundo Teixeira, 98, 111, 173, 236, 333
Mendonça, Antônio Pinto de, 171, 259
Meneses, Cardoso de, 132
*Mequetrefe, O* (newspaper), 89, 112
Mexico, 27
middle class, 139, 196
middlemen, 53, 241, 243, 345
Milan, 49, 107, 180, 199
Military Abolitionist Club, The, 165
Military Academy (Rio de Janeiro), 54, 98, 139, 252, 267, 306
Military Club, 320
Mill, J. S., 26
Minas Gerais, 25, 32–3, 41, 66, 80, 171, 185, 231, 242–3, 246, 257, 260, 262, 282, 293, 295, 298, 304, 315, 344, 376
*Minha formação* (My Formative Years) (Nabuco), 6, 137, 351
minimum wage, 233–4, 251
mixed race, 87, 134, 191, 223, 313, 351
*see also* mulattos
"moderate" versus "radical" (abolitionists), 10–11, 143, 167, 354
Moderating Power, 38, 48, 63, 89, 191–2, 249, 269, 308
Moldavia, 12, 31
monarchy/monarchism, 6, 8, 40, 50, 53, 64, 69, 75, 87, 97, 115, 148, 186, 195, 258, 276, 291, 308–9, 327, 330, 336, 346, 348, 351
monoculture, 137, 196, 263
Monteiro, João Carlos, 109
Montesquieu, Baron de, 93, 99
Montevideo, 214, 299
Morais, Prudente de, 289
"moral shock" strategy, 106, 287–8
Moreira, Nicolau Joaquim, 44, 126
Moret Law (Cuba and Puerto Rico – 1870), 13, 48–9, 56, 214, 232, 283
Morocco, 261
Mossoró, 163, 207, 299–300

Mota, Silveira da, 78, 81–2, 88, 126, 159, 168–9, 173, 182, 190, 213–14, 228, 236, 247, 253, 255, 269, 277, 291, 305, 323
Mota Coqueiro, Manuel da, 114
*Mota Coqueiro ou a Pena de Morte* (Mota Coqueiro or The Death Penalty) (Patrocínio), 114
Moura, Marcolino, 154, 156–7, 160, 169, 267, 269
mulattos, 86–7, 107–8, 137, 191, 313, 351
Mulligan, W., 5
Muniz Barreto, José Alves Branco, 44, 134, 156
Muzambinho, 315

Nabuco, Joaquim, 2, 5–8, 10, 18, 21–2, 34, 37–9, 46–8, 55, 57, 82, 104, 114, 117, 137, 145–50, 152–60, 166–7, 173, 177, 179–81, 186, 189–90, 192–3, 195, 197–200, 202, 204, 207, 212–16, 218–19, 221, 223, 225, 227–8, 233, 235–7, 242, 244, 246–7, 250–1, 253, 256–7, 259–60, 262–3, 265–7, 269–70, 274–5, 279–82, 285–6, 288–9, 291, 294, 296, 299, 303, 305–6, 309, 311, 313–14, 318, 320–1, 332, 334–5, 338, 341, 343–7, 349, 351, 358–9, 364, 410, 411
Nabuco, Sizenando, 212, 279, 288
Nabuco de Araújo, José Tomás, 34, 39, 47–8, 56, 79, 117, 145, 147–8, 153, 181, 231
Napoleão, Arthur, 129
Nascimento, Francisco José do, *see also* Chico da Matilde
Natal (Rio Grande do Norte), 294
*Nation, The* (American newspaper), 321
National Anthem of Brazil, 2, 49, 217
natural right, 99, 146
"Navio negreiro", 95, 132
Navy of Brazil, 306, 329–30
Needell, Jeffrey, 8–9, 12, 39, 77
Netherlands, 31
New Emancipatory Society, The, 134, 208
New Granada, 12
New York, 107–8, 119, 137
*New York Times, The* (newspaper), 219
Nigeria, 343
Niterói, 215

# Index

441

Niterói Freedmen's Club, The, 142, 158, 189, 195, 213, 221
Noah (biblical character), 57
Noggin Shearer's boot boys, gang of, 310
Northern provinces of Brazil, 8, 67, 77, 119, 135, 163, 200, 208, 297, 325
Nossa Senhora dos Remédios Brotherhood, 175, 288, 302
*Novo Mundo* (newspaper), 119, 137
*Novos estudos sobre a emancipação dos escravos no Brasil* (Silva Neto), 98

Occident, 93
official religion of Brazil, 42 *see also* Catholic Church/Catholicism
Olegarinha, D. (Carneiro da Cunha's wife), 298
Olinda, 62, 313
Oliveira, João Alfredo Correia de, 70, 235, 247, 264, 277, 330–1, 337–8, 346–7
Oliveira, Josefa Mercedes de, 141
*On the Abolition of Slavery – A Letter to the Brazilian Bishops* (encyclical), 321
Opera Theater, *see also* Teatro Lírico (Rio de Janeiro)
*Opinião Liberal* (newspaper), 38
Otaviano, Francisco, 48, 53, 67, 168, 193, 323
Otoni, Cristiano, 213, 244, 247, 253
Ottoman Empire, 5, 12, 31
Ouro Preto, 201, 262, 293, 304, 306, 349, 364

Pacatuba, 187
Paciência, Antônio, 302
*País, O* (newspaper), 140, 243, 281, 286, 288, 290–1, 299, 306, 310, 314, 321, 338, 341
Panama, 27
Paquetá, 294
Pará, 25, 77, 80, 141, 174, 185, 191, 200–1, 206–7, 256, 260, 295
Paraguay, 25, 32, 45–6, 54, 64, 308
Paraguay War (1864–70), 30, 38, 40, 49, 54, 90, 139, 308
Paraíba, state of, 29, 77, 80, 113, 141, 185, 207, 262, 297, 299, 364
Paraíba do Sul (Rio de Janeiro), 211, 290, 314
Paraíba Valley, 32, 40, 53, 69, 242–3, 297, 301, 324, 332
Paraíso (São Paulo), 313

Paraná, 54, 77, 80, 119, 141, 174, 185, 255–6, 293, 304, 332
Paranaguá, Marquis of, 48, 54, 178–9, 181–2, 186, 191, 193, 235, 248
Paravicini, Rodolfo, 350
Paris, 18, 25, 47, 52, 71, 107, 150, 160–1, 217, 219–20, 342
Parliament of Brazil, 2, 6, 18–19, 34, 39, 42, 46–8, 53–4, 56, 63, 66–7, 69–70, 72, 76, 78, 86, 90, 93, 100, 115, 117, 120, 133, 140, 143–4, 146, 148–9, 152–4, 156, 158, 160–2, 167–9, 171–3, 175, 179, 181, 188, 193, 197, 211, 214, 219, 222–3, 227–8, 230, 234, 237, 239, 241, 244–5, 248–50, 259, 263, 266–7, 279, 281, 294, 313, 328, 333–4, 339, 345, 347 *see also* Lower House, Senate
patriarchalism, 58–9, 92, 141
patriotism, 42, 274, 282
Patrocínio Jr., José do, 1, 3, 6, 18, 21–2, 50, 109, 111–14, 116–20, 122–7, 129, 131, 133–4, 136–7, 139, 141–4, 146, 149–50, 152, 154–5, 157–8, 160, 163, 166–7, 170, 172, 174, 176–7, 181, 183, 186–9, 191, 193, 195, 198, 200, 202, 208–9, 213–16, 219, 221–3, 225, 228, 235–7, 240–1, 244–5, 247, 250, 253, 255–9, 261–3, 268–9, 272, 279, 285–7, 289, 291, 294, 296, 300, 303, 308, 310–12, 314–15, 317–18, 327, 333, 338, 341, 344, 347, 349, 351, 358–9
patronage, 118, 168
Pauper Boys Band, The, 2
Pedra Branca, 188
Pedro Augusto, Prince, 308, 342
Pedro I, D. (first Emperor of independent Brazil), 28
Pedro II, D. (Emperor of Brazil), 6, 25, 27, 29–30, 33, 35, 37, 39–40, 45, 56, 59, 65, 68, 73, 75–6, 82, 89, 118, 125, 181, 188, 191, 197, 219, 223, 227, 229, 231, 239–40, 253, 266, 276–7, 281–2, 286, 292, 307, 309, 321, 333, 335, 350, 360 *see also* Second Reign
Peking, 117
Pelotas, 69, 200, 256, 323
Pena, Eduardo, 104
Penedo, Baron of, 56, 161, 170, 193, 198, 259, 266, 270, 306

# Index

Penha do Rio do Peixe, 304, 313–14, 324
Penido, João, 246, 268
Pennsylvania, 108
Pennsylvanian Abolition Society, 48
Pentecoste (Ceará), 188
"People's Marseillaise, The" (song), 211
Perdigão Malheiros, Agostinho Marques, 32, 74
Pereira, Lafaiete Rodrigues, 192, 323
Pernambuco, 11, 29, 32, 35, 41, 67, 77, 80, 113, 136, 141, 156, 158, 169, 171, 173–4, 185, 194, 200–1, 206–7, 210, 222, 231, 235, 237, 243, 255, 259, 265, 270, 279–80, 282, 285, 295, 299, 305, 311, 313, 322–3, 341, 345–6
Perseverance and the Future Emancipation Association, The, 163, 202
Peru, 12, 27, 31–2, 337
Pessoa, Joaquim, 298
Pestana, Francisco Rangel, 292
Petrópolis, 156, 215, 319, 329–31, 341–2
Piauí, 41, 67, 80, 133, 172, 174, 185, 207–8, 256, 319
Pimentel, Adriano, 202, 255, 269
Pimentel, Sancho de Barros, 169, 171, 186, 190, 192, 198, 202, 225, 237, 259, 265, 269–70
Pinhal, 313
Pinheiro, Rafael Bordalo, 113
Pinto, Alfredo, 311
Pinto, Antônio, 131, 171, 187, 227, 235, 245, 253, 255, 259, 267, 311
Pinto, Guilherme, 311
Pio (slave), 314
Pius IX, Pope, 68
Piracicaba, 304, 315
Plantation and Commerce Club, 66
Plantation Clubs, 17, 19, 66, 91, 171, 211, 242, 244, 247, 254, 257, 283, 313
Plantation Congress of Recife, 223
plantations, 40, 53, 64–5, 96, 104, 174, 208, 210, 231, 266, 281, 294, 304, 312, 323, 337, 365
Poço da Panela (Pot Well, D. Olegarinha's farmhouse), 298
Police Department, 86, 102
political institutions, 2, 6–10, 15–16, 19–20, 22, 46, 52, 107, 116, 143, 153, 160, 172, 174, 181, 185, 188, 197, 213, 225, 230, 235, 237, 242, 286, 299, 354, 356, 359

political repertoire, 164, 180
Polytechnic School (Rio de Janeiro), 56, 97–8, 118, 139, 189, 227, 244, 252, 319, 343
Polytechnic School Emancipatory Society, The, 200–1, 244
Polytheama Theater (Rio de Janeiro), 125, 127, 131, 138, 217–18, 253, 269, 280, 310
Pompeia, Raul, 34, 36, 124, 133, 173, 175, 213, 226, 302–3
Pompílio, Numa, 298
"Popular Conferences" (Rio de Janeiro), 123
Porangabuçu, 166
Port of Fortaleza, blockade at the (1881), 164, 186, 221
portable activism, 21–2, 199, 204, 206, 284, 296, 358
Porto Alegre (Rio Grande do Sul), 9, 64, 89, 125, 134, 201, 206, 213, 255–6, 262
Porto Alegre, Manuel Araújo de, 58
Porto, Campos, 157, 215
Portugal, 4, 27, 31, 71–2, 158, 162, 219
Portuguese colonies, 12, 32, 71
Portuguese Gym Club, 175
Portuguese Literary Lyceum, 142
Positivism, 97, 123, 139, 158, 172–3, 206, 256, 263, 333, 346, 356
Positivist Center at Court, 211
Prado, Antônio, 61, 277, 290, 293, 330, 335–7
press, 17, 21, 37, 66–7, 82, 86–8, 90, 92, 97, 102, 104, 109, 112, 115, 117, 119, 134, 137, 139, 152, 154, 157–8, 168, 172, 174, 179–84, 188, 198, 215, 219–20, 222–3, 239, 248, 282, 285, 288, 291, 299, 308, 314, 322, 329, 335, 350, 359 see also journalists
priests as slave owners, 122, 285
Primeiras trovas burlescas de Getulino (Getulino's First Burlesque Quatrains) (Luís Gama), 86
Príncipe Imperial (Ceará), 188
private initiatives, 185
private property, 61, 65, 70, 190, 207, 226
Proclamation of the Republic (Brazil, 1889), 140, 306, 328, 333, 348
Progress and Poverty (George), 226
progress, rhetoric of, 15, 17, 50, 91, 100, 135, 138, 151, 155, 164, 172, 195, 229, 250, 320, 359

# Index

443

progressive abolition, 13, 28, 229, 231, 240

property rights, 75, 178, 229, 232, 251, 344

pro-slavery political coalition, 66, 152, 230, 239, 242, 258, 269, 276, 283, 294, 348

pro-slavery rhetoric, 13, 17, 57–8, 61, 66, 71, 91, 94, 97–8, 100, 131–2, 217, 240, 246, 248, 251, 337

pro-slavery's moral repertoire, 57

Protestantism, 42, 93, 121, 321

Proudhon, Pierre-Joseph, 113, 251

*Província de São Paulo, A* (newspaper), 89, 259, 261, 333

Prudhomme (Patrocínio's pseudonym), 113

public opinion, 1, 55, 67, 72, 94, 124, 138, 154, 156, 196–7, 211, 220, 250, 269, 271, 329–30

public space, 2, 5, 7, 9–10, 14–15, 17–22, 42, 44, 88–9, 91, 116, 120, 143–4, 152, 155–7, 159–60, 162, 168, 170, 172, 174, 181, 183, 195, 215–16, 220, 222, 229, 242, 254, 257, 262, 286–7, 291, 295, 309, 320, 354, 358, 361

Puerto Rico, 13, 31, 41, 48, 122, 158, 160, 162

Quakers, 14, 30, 42, 93, 121, 360

Queen Anne's Mansions (London), 189

Queirós, Eusébio de, 27, 35, 279

"Quem sou eu?" (Who am I?) (Luís Gama), 87

"Question of the day – the emancipation of slaves, The" (Romero), 144

*Quilombo dos Palmares* (Araripe Jr.), 137

quilombos (runaway slave communities), 184, 197, 215, 292, 295, 299–300, 302–4, 365

Quixadá, 188

Rabelo, Francisco Correia Ferreira, 154

Radical Club, 88

Radical Conferences, The, 115

Radical Liberals, 40, 42, 50, 67, 79, 87, 89, 101–2, 111, 115–16, 119, 123, 143 *see also* Liberal Party

*Radical Paulistano* (newspaper), 87, 101–2

rallies, 14 *see also* abolitionist rallies, meetings

Ramos, João, 223, 297–8, 300, 332

*Razón, La* (Uruguayan newspaper), 214

reaction, rhetoric of, 13, 60, 241

Rebouças, André, 1, 10, 21–2, 44, 46, 49, 56, 114, 117, 159, 180–1, 189–90, 194, 199–200, 202, 207, 215–16, 218, 227, 235, 237, 254, 281, 364

Rebouças, Antônio (brother), 24, 118

Rebouças, Dr. Antônio Pereira (father), 24

Recife, 9, 89, 92, 98, 117, 125, 134, 140, 145–6, 200–1, 208, 211, 221–2, 231, 242–3, 256, 259, 262–3, 265, 267, 269, 280, 288, 297, 299–300, 305–6, 310, 313, 322, 332, 342

*Redempção, A* (The Redemption) (newspaper), 116, 137, 281–2, 284, 293, 296, 302, 364

redemption, rhetoric of, 93, 138

Reform Club, 88

*Reforma, A* (newspaper), 111, 156, 172–3

Regadas, Luísa, 131, 134, 141

Regency, The (1831–40), 28, 32, 312, 320, 327

*rei phantasma, O* (The Ghost King) (Patrocínio), 308

Reis, João José, 295

Reis, José Agostinho dos, 217

Relâmpago Club, 297

religion, slavery and, 57, 97–8, 121, 123, 196, 224, 329

*Representação à Constituinte* (José Bonifácio), 177

*República, A* (newspaper), 89, 111, 115

Republican Manifesto (Radical Liberals), 50, 79

Republican Party, 83, 89, 104, 111, 115, 130, 157, 192, 206, 212, 261, 291, 327, 333

republicanism, 111, 135, 140, 212, 241, 289, 346

*retirantes, Os* (The Migrants) (Patrocínio), 113

*Revista Brasileira* (magazine), 144

*Revista Illustrada* (magazine), 89, 138, 140, 171, 210, 284, 341

*Revue des Deux Mondes*, 38, 150

rhetoric of change, 138, 155

Riachuelo Dramatic Theater, 207

Ribeiro, Barata, 102

Ribeiro, Severino, 198, 214, 235, 240, 245

rights, rhetoric of, 15, 17, 50, 91, 135, 138, 151, 155, 164, 195, 250, 359

# Index

Rio Branco, Viscount of, 17, 25, 47, 50, 53–4, 56–7, 60, 62–3, 65, 67, 69–71, 73, 76, 78, 81, 83, 88, 106, 115–16, 118–19, 125, 142, 148, 155, 167, 169, 176, 189, 207, 217, 225, 234, 251, 277, 289, 292, 341

Rio de Janeiro, 1, 9, 22, 26, 30, 45, 53, 66, 69, 77, 82, 85, 98, 110, 117, 125, 135, 140, 148, 158, 161, 167–8, 171, 174, 177, 189, 193, 201, 206, 216, 218, 220, 223, 235, 293, 297–9, 303, 306, 309, 345, 349, 364

Rio de Janeiro City Trade Association, 183, 243

Rio Grande do Norte, 29, 80, 141, 173, 185, 202, 207, 255–6, 260, 293, 297–9, 301, 332, 364

Rio Grande do Sul, 11, 41, 67, 69, 77, 80, 141, 171, 174, 185, 194, 200–1, 204, 206, 211, 245, 248, 255–6, 258, 260, 294–5, 298–9, 327, 332, 345

Rio Grande do Sul Society for the Promotion of the Emancipation of Slaves, The, 69

*Rio News* (newspaper), 150, 155, 157, 263, 274, 289

Rio Preto, 324

Rocha, Justiniano José da, 254

Rodrigues Jr., 272

Rodrigues, José Carlos, 119, 192, 250

Rohan, Beaurepaire, 127, 156

Romanticism, 15, 93–5, 99, 122, 349, 360

Romão, João, 299

Romero, Sílvio, 144

Roque (Rebouças' slave), 46

Royal family of Brazil, 134, 179

Rua do Ouvidor (important street in Rio de Janeiro), 53, 111, 158, 217, 223–4, 227, 334, 341

rural democracy, 127, 154, 197, 227, 234, 251–2, 323, 344–5, 347–8

rural zone, 233

Russia, 5, 12, 27, 31, 33, 47

Sabinada (political revolt of 1837–8), 24, 85, 153

safe houses for runaway slaves, 106, 166, 184, 222, 295–6, 298, 301

SAIN (Sociedade Auxiliadora da Indústria Nacional/National Association for Industrial Support), 36, 56, 67, 125–6, 174

Sales, Campos, 267, 289

Salvador (Bahia), 9, 35, 37, 41, 85, 89, 101, 124, 208, 218, 222, 229, 242, 261–2, 293, 363

Sampaio, Teodoro, 218

Santa Catarina, 25, 80, 171, 185, 206, 255–6, 260, 294, 345

Santa Isabel Theater (Recife), 125, 262, 270

Santa Maria Madalena (Rio de Janeiro), 313

Santo Antônio de Pádua (Rio de Janeiro), 324

Santo Antônio Theater (Recife), 262

Santo Domingo (Haiti), 27, 48

Santos (São Paulo), 292

Santos, José Américo dos, 156, 158

Santos, Rocha dos, 255

São Borja, 327

São Domingos (Haiti), 27

São Fidélis (Rio de Janeiro), 324

São Francisco (Ceará), 166, 187

São Francisco river, 296

São João del-Rei, 150, 332

São José Theater (São Paulo), 133, 291

São Laurindo, Viscount of, 344

São Luís (Maranhão), 201, 262, 300

São Paulo, 43, 67, 77, 85, 98, 107, 111, 116, 134, 140, 146, 171–3, 176–8, 197, 206, 209–10, 221, 227, 247, 256, 261–2, 265, 281–2, 291, 293, 296–7, 302–3, 305, 312, 316, 322–3, 325–6, 333

São Paulo Abolitionist Center, The, 173, 175, 209, 301

São Pedro Theater (Rio de Janeiro), 68, 162

São Vicente, Viscount of, 38–9, 48, 55–6, 62, 78, 148, 327

Saraiva, José Antônio, 151–2, 154, 168, 170, 181, 192, 228, 235, 247, 272–3, 275, 277, 281, 299, 323, 360

Saraiva/Cotegipe Sexagenarian Law (1885), 13, 234, 273, 277–8, 280, 282–3, 285, 290

"Saudação abolicionista" (The Abolitionist Salute) (march), 162

SBCE (Sociedade Brasileira Contra a Escravidão/Brazilian Anti-Slavery Society), 155–6, 158, 160, 162, 172, 200

## Index

445

Schoelcher, Victor, 159, 180, 219, 321
Schwarcz, Lilia Moritz, 259, 284, 308, 349
science and slavery, 98
SCL (Sociedade Cearense Libertadora/
    Liberating Society of Ceará), 132,
    163–6, 169, 173, 176, 188, 190–1,
    195n, 200, 203, 218, 300
SCT (Sociedade Contra o Tráfico de
    Africanos e Promotora da Colonização
    e da Civilização dos Índios/Society
    against the African Slave Trade and for
    the Promotion of Colonization and
    Indian Civilization), 35, 38, 42, 44, 99,
    143
*Seca nas províncias do Norte, A* (Drought in
    the Northern Provinces) (Rebouças),
    119
Second Reign, 24, 28–9, 40, 46, 49, 52, 55,
    64, 66, 83–4, 90, 94, 107, 161, 185,
    190, 193, 295, 308, 329, 350 *see also*
    Pedro II, D. (Emperor of Brazil)
secularization of the State, 89–90, 97, 140
*Século, O* (The Century) (newspaper), 267
*Semana Política* (The Political Week)
    (Parliamentary column), 113
*Semanário* (Paraguayan newspaper), 38
Sena Madureira, lieutenant-colonel, 306
Senate, 39, 53–4, 60, 62, 64, 66–7, 71,
    77–8, 80, 83, 133, 209, 213, 244, 247,
    249–50, 257, 275–7, 282, 290–1, 305,
    309, 311, 314, 326, 336, 340, 342,
    345, 350
separatist rebellions in Brazil, 24
Sergipe, 77, 80, 174, 185, 244, 260
Serpa Jr., João Ferreira, 117, 193
Serra, Joaquim, 154–5, 157, 159–60, 167,
    179, 181–2, 190, 225, 286
Sete de Setembro – Sociedade Ypiranga (The
    7th of September – Ypiranga Society),
    34–5
Sexagenarian Law, 13 *see also* Saraiva/
    Cotegipe Sexagenarian Law (1885)
sexagenarian slaves, 39, 232, 277 *see also*
    Saraiva/Cotegipe Sexagenarian Law
    (1885)
Sierra Leone, 5
Silva, Álvaro Caminha Tavares da, 259
Silva, Eduardo, 295
Silva, Pereira da, 72, 262, 264,
    268–9, 280
Silva Neto, Antônio da, 98

Simão Farm, mass manumissions at the
    (1886), 293
Sinha, 5
Sinimbu, Cansanção de, 48, 116, 149, 151,
    248
Slave Child Redemption Society, The, 140
slave families, separation of, 82, 103, 152
slave importers/exporters in world, largest,
    29
slave market, 29, 85, 167, 190, 231, 274,
    282, 309
slave overseers, 18, 20, 28, 61, 75, 78–9, 95,
    166, 169, 197, 210, 232, 240, 251–2,
    255, 273–4, 283, 291–2, 296, 301,
    325, 327, 335, 345 *see also*
    indemnification to slave owners
slave population, 62, 174, 178, 186, 206,
    210, 213, 232, 241, 301
slave registration, 57, 103, 232, 274, 280
slave trade, 7–8, 13, 16, 25, 27–9, 31,
    33–4, 38, 41, 55–6, 59, 72, 85, 92, 108,
    139, 149, 151, 153, 156, 174, 179–80,
    186, 193, 198, 203, 205,
    212, 231, 241–2, 250, 275, 279,
    321, 351–2
"Slave's Marseillaise, The" (symphonic
    march), 131, 218
slavemongers/slavemongering, 175, 183
slave-sale ads in newspapers, 152, 183
"slavocratic situation", 60
Slenes, Robert, 29, 174, 190, 231, 241, 325
small land property, 143, 224
smallholder agriculture, 11, 35, 41, 302
Smith, Adam, 93
Smith, Goldwin, 283
*Sobrados e mucambos* (Mansions and
    Shanties) (Freyre), 91
social hierarchy, 29, 87, 91
social mobilization, 5, 9–10, 42, 157
Sociedade Brasileira Contra a Escravidão,
    *see also* SBCE (Sociedade Brasileira
    Contra a Escravidão/Brazilian Anti-
    Slavery Society)
Society for Public Instruction, 123
Sodré, Francisco, 274
Sodré, Jerônimo, 44, 149, 154, 157, 169,
    209, 230
Soure, 188
Sousa Dantas, Rodolfo Epifânio de, 172
Sousa, Cacilda de, 129
Sousa, Inglês de, 103

446      *Index*

Sousa, Maria Amélia de, 53, 82–3, 148
Sousa, Paulino Soares de, 22, 40, 47–8, 50,
52–3, 55, 57, 59, 61–3, 65–6, 69–72,
74–5, 78, 82–4, 91, 97, 100, 109, 115,
143, 147–8, 151, 169–71, 175–6, 179,
187, 191, 211, 222–3, 228, 235–6,
239–40, 243–6, 248–9, 251–2, 257,
259, 264–5, 267–8, 271, 275–7, 282,
297, 309, 311, 315–16, 323–4, 326,
330–2, 336–7, 344, 350
Sousa, Vicente Ferreira de, 124, 126–7,
132–3, 139–40, 157, 162, 164, 182,
193, 200, 223–4, 332, 346, 351
Southern provinces of Brazil, 29, 67, 77,
149, 156, 174, 185, 197, 230, 301, 346
Souto, Teodureto Carlos de Faria, 205, 259
Souza, Enes de, 129
Spain, 1, 4, 13, 29, 32, 34, 38–9, 62, 72,
122, 153, 158, 160, 162, 168, 178
Spanish Abolitionist Society, 31, 122, 158
Spanish America, 27, 32, 91
Spartacus (Roman slave), 105–6
Special Emancipation Commission, 47–8
Spencerianism, 97
Spínola, Aristides, 98, 267, 269, 274
spiritism, 98
State abolitionism, 54
State Council, 53, 148
Stowe, Harriet Beecher, 95, 137
street-level abolitionism, 8, 143, 222, 237,
257
strikes, 164–5, 182, 201, 228, 297, 309, 365
students, 34–5, 43–4, 68, 88–9, 97–8, 104,
116, 124, 127, 139, 141, 146, 171–2,
194, 200, 205, 208–9, 216, 227, 256,
262, 289, 297, 300, 302, 312, 343,
346, 359
sugar in Brazil, slave-produced, 29, 183
Sumner, Charles, 150
Suzuki, 5
Sweden, 27, 71
Switzerland, 36

tango, 131
Tarrow, Sidney, 16, 20–1, 41, 143, 158,
185, 201, 293, 295, 319, 354, 358
Taunay, Alfredo Escragnolle, Viscount of,
50, 171, 235, 258, 324, 347, 350
tax on slaves, 26, 32, 35, 56, 83
Teatro Lírico (Rio de Janeiro), 1, 49–50, 68,
125, 349

Teatro Pedro II (Rio de Janeiro), 165, 222,
269, 349
Teatro Recreio Dramático (Rio de Janeiro),
188, 217
Teatro São Luís (Rio de Janeiro), 126–7,
133, 165, 188, 262
Teixeira, Alípio, 200
telegraph, 12, 72, 89, 92, 166, 206, 256, 300
Termites Club (Clube do Cupim), 265, 288,
297, 299–301, 332
Third Reign, prospect of a, 308, 332, 347, 349
Thompson, E.P., 8
Tilly, Charles, 10–11, 13, 16, 20, 31, 41, 90,
116, 183, 185, 201, 220, 262, 307,
319–20, 352
*Times, The* (British newspaper), 162, 219,
250, 261, 270, 275, 283, 286
Tocqueville, Alexis de, 63
Toplin, Robert Brent, 8, 198, 316, 322, 354
Torres Homem (pro-reform orator), 78
torture of slaves, 101, 287–8, 316, 351
*Tosca* (Puccini's opera), 1
Toscanini, Arturo, 1
"total institution", slavery in Brazil as, 196
Toussaint-Louverture, François-Dominique,
27, 211, 219
*Tragédia no lar* (Tragedy at Home) (Castro
Alves), 43
*Tragédia no mar* (Tragedy at Sea) (Castro
Alves), 96
transatlantic trade of Africans to Brazil,
prohibition of (1831), 28, 30, 85, 99,
101, 103–4, 196, 212–13, 232, 273,
285, 298 *see also* "free Africans"
Três Barras, Baron of, 78
Trial, Charles, 240
"Tribute to the Patriotic Dantas Cabinet"
(concert-conference at Polytheama
Theater, 1885), 269
*tronco do ipê, O* (The Trunk of the Trumpet
Tree) (Alencar), 58, 134
Trovão, Lopes, 144
Turkey, 151
Turkish Order of Medjidie, 52
tutelage of ingénus and ex-slaves, 56, 76,
80, 116, 233, 240, 252, 346

*Uncle Tom's Cabin* (Stowe), 94, 137, 156
underground railroad (US network of
escape routes), 19, 184, 295–6, 299,
301, 313, 359, 365

# Index

447

United States, 1, 13, 27, 31, 33–4, 36, 59, 71, 91, 98–9, 107–8, 117, 119, 121, 123, 129, 148, 150, 156, 158, 162, 168, 180, 184, 200, 220, 225, 228, 239–40, 250, 296, 337
Uorgo, Frederico Augusto, 259
urban infrastructure, investment in, 89
urbanization of Brazil, 17, 92, 97
*Úrsula, romance original brasileiro* (Maria Firmina dos Reis), 94–5, 135
Uruguay, 32, 38, 54
Uruguay, Viscount of, 52, 72, 84
US Fugitive Slave Act, 360
US slavery, 34

Vasques, Francisco Correia, 126, 131, 134
Vassouras, 147, 170–1, 191, 222, 243
Vatican, 52, 321
Vaz, José Viana, 172, 274
Venezuela, 12, 31–2
Venice, 107
Verdi, Giuseppe, 2, 19, 129
Viana, Ferreira, 61, 192, 240, 250, 252, 287, 332, 334, 347
Viana, Ulisses, 287
Victoria, Queen of Great Britain, 328
Vieira, Abdon de Morais, 285
Vieira, Antônio, padre, 58
Vieira, Damaceno, 134
Vienna, 27, 52, 107
*vientres libres* (Free Womb Law in various parts of Spanish America), 32, 48
Vila-Matas, Enrique, 199
*Vinte e Cinco de Março* (newspaper), 257, 283, 289, 294, 311, 315
Vintém (20 cent) Revolt (Rio de Janeiro, 1879–80), 144

*Vítimas e algozes: quadros da escravidão, As* (Victims and Their Tormenters: Scenes of Slavery) (Macedo), 96
Vitória (Espírito Santo), 262
Vizcarrondo, Julio, 122
Voltaire, 57
*Vozes d'África* (Voices of Africa) (Castro Alves), 132

Wales, Prince of, 261
Wanderley, João Maurício Mariani, 271 *see also* Cotegipe, Baron of
"War Cry" (Cruz e Sousa), 286
Washington Hotel (New York), 108
Washington, DC, 108, 148
Water Company (Rio de Janeiro), 68
Ways and Means and Civil Justice Joint Committees, 250–1
Western world, 4, 12, 57
wet nurses, women slaves as, 94, 96, 231
Wilberforce, William, 152–3, 157, 162, 176, 180, 225, 237, 318
women as abolitionists, 22, 41, 69, 133, 141, 163, 180, 187, 189, 205–6, 262, 298, 335, 340
women as slaves, 42, 76, 126, 135, 140, 146, 231, 298
Workers Federation, 124

Zacarias, Prime Minister, 33 *see also* Góis e Vasconcelos, Zacarias de
Zama, Aristides César Spínola, 171, 255, 269, 274, 276
Zanzibar, 12, 31
zarzuela (dance), 131
Zé do Pato (Joe Duck) (Patrocínio's pseudonym), 112, 114, 117, 187, 222
Zona da Mata, 32, 231, 243
Zumbi dos Palmares (colonial black rebel), 8

Printed in the United States
by Baker & Taylor Publisher Services